Presidential Impeachment in Latin America

Gustavo Palamone

Presidential Impeachment in Latin America

A Matter of Law or Politics?

Springer

Gustavo Palamone
Institute of General State Theory and Political Science
University of Göttingen
Göttingen, Germany

ISBN 978-3-031-44187-5 ISBN 978-3-031-44188-2 (eBook)
https://doi.org/10.1007/978-3-031-44188-2

This Springer imprint is published by the registered company Springer Nature Switzerland AG
The registered company address is: Gewerbestrasse 11, 6330 Cham, Switzerland

Paper in this product is recyclable.

Acknowledgments

Latin America is never dull, much of it thanks to the creativity and vanguardism of its statesmen. I have been able to witness first-hand many events described in this book, but its conclusions would have never reached their true potential if it were not for the prolific intellectual production the region has inspired. I am thankful to all wonderful scholars and writers who have influenced me into considering aspects of presidential impeachment critically and who revealed the devils in the details with their own accounts of these events.

The idea for this book came about and consolidated itself from conversations with Prof. Aníbal Pérez-Liñán, to whom I am thankful not only for the valuable initial insights, but as well as for the rigorous and prolific scholarly contributions on presidential impeachments from the perspective of political science. His kind words of motivation helped me push through some of the uncertainties and insecurities of the initial phases of the writing process.

The idea would, however, not have gone far if it were not for the influence of Prof. Werner Heun, who after mentoring my master's thesis invited me to the PhD program of the University of Göttingen. Despite his precocious departure in the early stages of writing, Prof. Heun has left foundational contributions to this work. His academic legacy and role model, as well as his kind and humane personality will forever live as inspiration to me.

I am, moreover, deeply grateful to Prof. Alexander Thiele, who so readily and wholeheartedly received me and my research project with open arms. The final product would not have been nearly as good if it were not for his untiring supervision, trained eye for detail, and profound insights on the workings of states and democracies.

I am greatly indebted to Prof. Ran Hirschl, who has been throughout this whole process an inspiration and a guiding light. Words cannot match the appreciation I have for his efforts in providing me with constant motivation, a supportive academic environment, and the highest class of scientific commentary. In this instance, I must extend my gratitude as well to his team in the Institute of Comparative Constitutionalism of the University of Göttingen, as well as the closely related Max Planck

Institute for the Study of Religious and Ethnic Diversity, as led by Prof. Ayelet Sachar.

Last, but far from least, I must thank my friends and family, who provided me with unwavering emotional and at times even technical support during this prolonged period of library-induced social isolation. Especially warm regards are, therefore, dedicated to Tracy Erwin-Grabner, Thiago Pécchio Gimenez, Vinícius Menezes de Sá, Mario Aguilera Bravo, Marina Musa, Lubomir Suva, Diego Pardo-Álvarez, Mariana Matos, Pedro Martins, Ellen Borges, Luiz Damy, Ann-Katrin Bohle, Paulo Puglia, Katharina Pittrich, and many others. Funding for this study was provided in part by the *Alexander-von-Humboldt Foundation* and the *Göttinger Graduiertenschule Gesellschaftswissenschaften*.

Contents

List of Figures

List of Tables

Chapter 1
Introduction

1.1 Context of the Research

In the current political climate, not a year goes by without presidential impeachments being considered at least a few times by political actors dealing with some sort of economic or constitutional crisis. Just in the past five years, for example, there have been four Presidents in the American Continent who had to face impeachment votes and/or trials more than once during a single mandate. This is a relatively new phenomenon, however. Despite impeachment being a feature present in presidentialism since its genesis, politicians have historically shied away from its use and societies looked upon it almost exclusively with scepticism and distrust. It was simply difficult to imagine a President having to face one single impeachment, much less multitudes of them. The procedure seemed just too encumbering to produce a timely response to abuses of the Executive power, too traumatic to bring upon more positive than negative change, and too stacked in favour of the President to ever result in anything other than leniency.[1]

Such reality, however, has been dramatically transformed in the past thirty or so years (see Table 1.1). With democracy consolidating itself decidedly as the only legitimate way of participating in politics, the other forms of "conflict resolution" among established and wannabe governing elites, that is, military coups, assassinations, and civil wars, fell out of fashion. In the republics of today, when political tensions build up to critical levels, alternative and institutional forms of relief are preferred, ranking among them the presidential impeachment as one of the nuclear institutional solutions.[2]

[1] *E.g.*, Rossiter (1963), p. 44: "(. . .) most observers now agree with Jefferson that [impeachment] is a 'mere scarecrow' and with Henry Jones Ford that it is 'a rusted blunderbuss, that will probably never be taken in hand again'".

[2] Pérez-Liñán (2007), pp. 11, 41 ff.

G. Palamone, *Presidential Impeachment in Latin America*,
https://doi.org/10.1007/978-3-031-44188-2_1

Table 1.1 Presidential impeachments in the Americas 1990–2022

President	Year	Country	Outcome
Fernando Collor	1992	Brazil	Conviction*
Carlos Andrés Pérez	1993	Venezuela	Conviction
Ernesto Samper	1996	Colombia	Survival
Bill Clinton	1998	United States	Survival
Raúl Cubas Grau	1999	Paraguay	Resignation
Fernando Henrique Cardoso	1999	Brazil	Survival
Alberto Fujimori	2000	Peru	Conviction*
Luis Ángel González Macchi	2002	Paraguay	Survival
Luis Ángel González Macchi	2003	Paraguay	Survival
Fernando Lugo	2012	Paraguay	Conviction
Dilma Rousseff	2016	Brazil	Conviction
Nicolás Maduro	2016	Venezuela	Survival
Michel Temer	2017†	Brazil	Survival
Sebastián Piñera	2019	Chile	Survival
Mario Abdo Benítez	2019	Paraguay	Survival
Donald Trump	2019	United States	Survival
Donald Trump	2021	United States	Survival
Martín Vizcarra	2021	Peru	Conviction*
Sebastián Piñera	2021	Chile	Survival
Mario Abdo Benítez	2021	Paraguay	Survival
Guillermo Lasso	2023	Ecuador	Survival

Source: Own elaboration based on official records and journalistic accounts. Note: Only impeachment in the strict sense is included. For more details on these and other non-impeachment oustings, see Table 4.4 in Chap. 4. Key: (†) Impeachment vote taken twice in the same year; (*) After leaving office

Some claim, however, that that is not the whole story. Some authors talk about the "flexibilization" or "parliamentarization" of presidentialism, in large part through the expansion of the impeachment's scope of use.[3] Impeachments, they claim, are no longer used in the ways they were originally planned or how they tend to be described by textbooks, in which Presidents may only be removed from office if they break the law. That would be, after all, the bread-and-butter of presidentialism: a strict separation between Legislative and Executive branches, in which the former may not interfere in the matters of the latter except in the very limited cases stablished in law.[4] A President—so the expectation goes—may be removed for

[3] *E.g.*, Pérez-Liñán (2000); Marsteintredet and Berntzen (2008); Llanos and Marsteintredet (2010), pp. 223–224.

[4] *E.g.*, Lijphart (2012), p. 106: "In a presidential system, the head of government—always called president—is elected for a constitutionally prescribed period and in normal circumstances cannot be forced to resign by a legislative vote of no confidence (although it may be possible to remove a president for criminal wrongdoing by the process of impeachment)"; Shugart and Carey (1992), pp. 28–29: "(. . .) most constitutions make provisions for impeachment, (. . .) which can be used

Table 1.2 Partisanship in Donald Trump's (Republican) first impeachment proceeding

Party/Venue	Vote					
	Article: Abuse of Power			**Article: Obstruction of Congress**		
House of Representatives	*Yea*	*Nay*	*Absent*	*Yea*	*Nay*	*Absent*
Democrats	229	2	1	228	3	1
Republicans	0	195	2	0	195	2
	Authorizing impeachment					
House of Representatives	*Yea*	*Nay*	*Absent*			
Democrats	227	1	4			
Republicans	0	192	5			
	Article: Abuse of Power			**Article: Obstruction of Congress**		
Senate	*Guilty*	*Not guilty*		*Guilty*	*Not guilty*	
Democrats	45	0		45	0	
Republican	1	52		0	53	

Source: House Resolutions 755 and 758; Congressional Record vol. 166, February 5th, 2020 (Senate, 116th Congress); Own elaboration. Procedures occurred between December 2019 and February 2020, for alleged soliciting of foreign interference in elections

actions that break the law, and not those that merely generate discontent or partisan strife. To concede the latter would be to turn the Executive into creature of the Legislature, as it would be ultimately forced to serve at its pleasure.[5]

The conclusion, therefore, is that not only has the environment changed to enable these institutional oustings, but also that impeachments have mutated to allow for more "politicized" use. So much it is so, that a compelling case has been made, for example, to classify Fernando Lugo's impeachment in 2012 as a vote of no-confidence[6]—an instrument that, on the other hand, has always been openly associated with political use. Others have argued regarding presidential impeachments in the United States that the legal standing of a case plays nearly no role whatsoever, as by merely observing the partisan alignment of Representatives one can accurately predict the outcome of an impeachment,[7] an example of which may be seen in Table 1.2.

The question is thus prompted: If law and evidence are incapable of swaying Representatives to vote in favour of the opposition's President or against their own President, then it is safe to say that party politics is what matters in impeachments and not the law, right?

---

only when there is evidence of malfeasance or disregard for constitutional procedure (. . .). In sum, presidents are elected for a fixed period (. . .) and cannot be removed for political reasons".

[5] *E.g.*, George Mason's arguments in Farrand (1911), p. 86.

[6] Llanos et al. (2012), pp. 3–4.

[7] Perkins (2003), pp. 32–40.

1.2 Object of Research

Well, maybe. The question is more complicated than it seems, especially if one seeks to understand impeachment at a deeper level or at least seeks to understand the universe of impeachments that stands beyond the United States. Among the polities existing under presidentialism, the United States is arguably unique when it comes to its economic conditions, political makeup, party system, and so on. All these peculiarities may have interfered with the political game in ways that prime impeachments to produce outcomes that align so sharply with partisan affiliation. Would parties in the US, for example, be willing to vote against their own if the country and its people were under more economic distress? Would they vote differently if the party system was more fragmented and less disciplined, in ways that Representatives could vote more according to their own consciences or less constricted by the black-and-white logic of the current bipartisan system? Would they vote differently if the internal threat to their democracy posed by an overbearing President was more palpable than it has been in the past, say perhaps with an actual militarized assault on Congress?

The cases in the United States do not offer the necessary range to answer these questions, but those in Latin America perhaps do. The region not only has an unmatched concentration of presidential systems among any other region in the world, but also amasses an incredible wealth of cases, which take place under the most varied set of conditions: there are types of crises, party systems, economic brackets, stages of democratization, and impeachable offenses for nearly all tastes and preferences. The only issue with the cases in the region is that they have remained largely unexplored in some of the perspectives, particularly the juridical one. While the region has attracted much attention from scholars looking to understand political and executive instability, thus bringing indirectly attention also to the presidents ousted under such circumstances, the accounts of the legal proceedings associated with them are limited, if existent.

The first goal of this study is, therefore, to build, as much as possible, a comprehensive repository of juridical analyses of the cases in the region, thus filling a sorely neglected gap in impeachment literature. If researchers are not sensible to the use of law in these procedures and choose instead to only focus on the juicy, arguably less ambiguous indicators of political science to make conclusions about impeachments, then it is obvious that they should conclude for the law's irrelevance. The relevant phenomena in most sciences are those that one can observe, granted the researcher puts some effort in observing all there is to be observed about the phenomena. If not, one may run the risk of confusing the lack of evidence with the evidence of absence.

So much is already well known and settled: the political environment and circumstances do influence the outcome of impeachments.[8] What lacks a proper

[8] Baumgartner and Kada (2003), Pérez-Liñán (2007), Llanos and Marsteintredet (2010), Helmke (2016), and Linz and Valenzuela (1994).

clarification is what exact role the law plays in such constellation. Merely stating that "impeachments are political" brings the question no closer to an answer, as such conclusion does not preclude impeachments from also being "legal" or a "matter of justice". Contrary to popular assumptions, this study does not endorse the understanding that law and politics, or justice and politics, are oppositional or mutually exclusive concepts. They are, in fact, complementary and inseparable, law being, as Hans Kelsen put it, a delegation of political power and discretion onto certain actors.[9]

Those who denounce in dismissive tone that "impeachments are political", be it in scholarly contexts or otherwise, may mean something else, however. They may be merely stating that the outcome of an impeachment did not meet their subjective standards of legality or justice—or, in other words, given the chance, they would have decided differently than the Assembly they criticize. Sometimes the underlying rationalizations are cynical, and the politicians are accused of having ulterior (say, legally impertinent) motives to support a certain outcome, and sometimes they acknowledge the prevalence of conservative or progressive actors in Congress, which is then said to be conducive to the enforcement of unorthodox or disagreeable legal standards.

The proper enforcement of the law is certainly an important aspect of a work that purports to discover the role played by law in impeachments. If legal provisions can be twisted and turned to fit any impeachment outcome, then saying that "impeachments are legal" is arguably as much of a platitude as saying that they are "political". The thesis must be falsifiable (*i.e.*, the violation of legal standards must be a possibility) to provide some analytical gain in its conclusion. Such an endeavour, however, raises the difficult question: Who ought to be the ultimative arbiter of legality? Who has the authority (and arrogance) to tell a People that their Representatives were mistaken in the understanding of their own legal systems?

One thing is certain: not the author of a study of comparative constitutional law. At least not in the framework most laymen traditionally understand law, in which the differences between correct and incorrect application of law are somehow sharply defined by text, precedent, or method. What an author of a comparative study can do, however, is identify the range of acceptable interpretations and practices within a legal community and, regardless of presumed ideological implications, amplify their voices and visions for the rest of the world to share. Though lawyers and politicians are no strangers to conscious obtuseness and evasiveness when it comes to defending their (or their client's) interests, they are at times also capable of remarkable clarity and articulacy. One can be surprised about how forthcoming the actors of impeachment sometimes are about their motives and actions, be them legally pertinent or not.

Assessing such range is a task that requires significant sensibility and cautiousness, however. One cannot expect a venue such as Congress to behave exactly like an ordinary court of law. Much less expect that the President be judged just like any

[9] Kelsen (1931), pp. 14–15.

other citizen would, when his or her removal can have such far-reaching consequences for the entire nation. One needs to understand, therefore, all that goes into the making of an impeachment, starting from its theory, history, constitutional contexts, design variations, structural challenges, and so on, all the way to the impeachment debates themselves, in their modern glory and infamy.

To achieve such a goal—the actual main goal of this study, in fact—the work has been divided into three parts, found in Chaps. 2, 3 and 4. In the first part, the reader will be able to observe the historical evolution of the impeachment from its monarchical origins in England into what is now known as the presidential impeachment. The theory of impeachments is built essentially during this period, both through legal practices and rational discussion among constitutional Framers, and it encapsulates a struggle towards republican and democratic ideals that is often forgotten in modern accounts on impeachments. Recovering this foundational basis, as should remain evident, will help demystify much of the skewed expectations observers of the presidential impeachment may have, which tend result from decontextualized readings of the institute. This part will also bring some more in-depth debates on legal theory, as the question posed by this study cannot be satisfactorily answered from unreflected or commonsensical understandings of law.

The second part is responsible for collecting most of empirical data used to answer the question posed. Here the reader will receive a short introduction into the political context of Latin America in the period leading to its democratization and, more importantly, into the context of each impeachment case itself. As much as the political environment of the United States can bias its impeachment procedures to produce certain outcomes, so could the environment of each country in Latin America. It is important, therefore, to be fully aware of the contexts in which impeachments take place. After such is achieved, the reader will be introduced into the debates and legal issues developed within each impeachment proceeding. These give formidable insight into the perspectives shared by impeachment actors relative to the procedure they partake in, as well as into other structural or circumstantial factors that may have taken influence on the results.

In the third part, the question is addressed on a legal-dogmatic level, going directly into legal-scholarly debates and analyses of legal provisions on impeachments. The question posed by this study has been addressed many times in legal manuals, although generally on incomplete, insular, and/or arbitrary terms. The present study will greatly expand these debates, attempting to reflect on the question considering every single perspective, and communicating with the scholarly debate across the entire American continent. It will, moreover, try to establish clearer terms in the distinction between impeachment and its surrogates, as well as explain the relation of impeachment with the rule of law.

Though each of these sections will give insight into what role law or legal accountability plays in presidential impeachments, the conclusion should present a final critical assessment of all answers that can be found throughout this work. The conclusion will discuss how impeachment ought to serve (or has served) as means of accountability, how it currently acts in observable exemplars of its use, and how, for whatever reasons, the design choices or political landscape may explain the distance between ought and is in such a question. If the conclusion ultimately fails to deliver a definitive answer to the question, in the least it will provide a solid baseline for future discussions, hopefully free from the sort of distortions and myths that pollute the current discourse surrounding presidential impeachments.

1.3 Methodological Considerations

As mentioned before, this study essentially aims to fill two scholarly gaps in the literature on impeachments and presidentialism. The first pertains to the gap in legal analyses of impeachment proceedings in the region of Latin America. A few cases have been object of extensive scrutiny (*e.g.*, Fernando Collor's or Ernesto Samper's impeachments),[10] but the rule is that analyses of Latin American presidential oustings have either remained a monopoly of journalistic accounts or of studies from the perspective of political science, where the focus typically stays on historical developments and political articulations rather than the legal proceedings of removal themselves.[11] As such, there remains a pervasive obscurity in the literature about what role the legal side of impeachments plays in practice and how rules are applied therein.

To address this first gap, multiple single-case analyses of almost every impeachment experienced in the region in the past 30 years were produced. To avoid selection bias as much as possible, all relevant cases were taken into consideration within this time frame,[12] and a few ended up being excluded due to practical limitations, especially regarding access to official documents.[13] Though the single-

---

[10] As seen in, for example, Rosenn and Downes (1999) or Comisión Ciudadana de Seguimiento (1996).

[11] *E.g.*, Conaghan (2005) on Alberto Fujimori, Coppedge (1997) on Andrés Carlos Pérez, Hinojosa and Pérez-Liñán (2003) on Ernesto Samper.

[12] Cases were thus not filtered by any principle such as "most (dis)similar" or "textbook vs. deviant cases", nor by other arbitrary features, such as outcome (*e.g.*, presidential survival vs. removal) or nature of offense (*e.g.*, constitutional vs. criminal violations). The only requirement is that the case has enough development to support a legal analysis, in practice meaning that they must have arrived *at least* to the stage of impeachment vote (or comparable stage for selected non-impeachment oustings) and detailed records are being kept. To be sure, the simple choice of region presupposes many commonalities among cases (*e.g.*, countries mostly in middle-economic bracket, mostly catholic and religious, mostly third-wave democracies, mostly sharing historical roots, mostly with an unresolved authoritarian past, etc), but there is no true homogeneity in any single feature. For considerations on case selection, see Hirschl (2014), pp. 244–267.

[13] The cases left out by this book are, therefore, the following oustings or attempted oustings: Fernando Henrique Cardoso (Brazil, 1999, impeachment), Jamil Mahuad (Ecuador, 2000, declaration of vacancy), Gonzalo Sánchez de Lozada (Bolivia, 2004, pretrial), Lucio Gutiérrez (Ecuador, 2005, declaration of vacancy), Otto Pérez Molina (Guatemala, 2015, pretrial), Nicolás Maduro (Venezuela, 2016, *sui generis* impeachment), Pedro Pablo Kuczynski (Peru, 2017–2018, declaration of vacancy), Jimmy Morales (Guatemala, 2017–2018, pretrial), Mario Abdo Benítez (Paraguay, 2019, 2021, impeachment), Martín Vizcarra (Peru, 2020–2021, declaration of vacancy and

case formula has limitations regarding the external validity of its conclusions, it allows detailed scrutiny of special factors which would otherwise go unnoticed but that may have played a significant role within a case, later possibly serving as "building-blocks" to other theories.[14] This format can be particularly interesting for legal scholars, moreover, as it allows them to see with some depth the variance in contexts, interpretations, and legal practices among different countries, which may incentivize them to reflect upon their own legal systems from new perspectives. Finally, this modality of inquiry is also capable of producing analyses that better fulfil the goal of documenting and producing well-rounded accounts of the impeachments in the region, which is one of the identified gaps in the literature.[15]

To be sure, this study draws heavily from political science analyses of impeachments, which generally aim at answering more universal and timeless questions, such as the influence of party systems, democratic consolidation, or interbranch competition on Executive stability.[16] As will be argued in Chap. 2, this book works on the premise that impeachments should not be considered as isolated events, which are either mere product of political circumstances or of the legal system. Impeachments take place at the point of inflection between law and politics, and, therefore, both analyses must be present so that the reader can make sense of what effectively motivates such procedures. All case studies also strive to bring a detailed analysis of the likely circumstances that generate such procedures, as well as of the political system and setting within they take place. The analyses will, thus, inevitably suggest conclusions about the political system commented, but with more modest ambitions than a political science work would likely seek. The focus will stay on the second, but arguably main goal of this study, which is to answer whether impeachment procedures do in fact serve as means of legal accountability or not.

---

post-hoc impeachment), Guillermo Lasso (Ecuador, 2022, mutual dissolution; 2023, impeachment), Pedro Castillo (Peru, 2021–2022, vacancy), and Dina Boluarte (Peru, 2023, vacancy). These cases were investigated and will be commented throughout the book, but by themselves they lacked substance to justify a full case study in the model proposed here. This is mostly caused by the lack of available/complete records, but at times also due to how short and lacking in content the procedures were (*e.g.*, the procedure is aborted at early stages due to the President's resignation or other reason). A few cases have not been analysed for taking place after the closure of the book (August 2022) but were included in figures as part of the revision process.

[14]George and Bennett (2005), pp. 76 ff. and 220–223.

[15]Bennett and Elman (2007), p. 171, on the example of studies in international relations: "Some of the most prominent subjects of study (. . .) often involve interaction effects among many structural and agent-based variables, path dependencies, and strategic interaction among large numbers of actors across multiple levels of analysis with private information and strong incentives to bluff or deceive other actors. (. . .) The prominence of qualitative methods in IR thus reflects these methods' advantages in studying complex and relatively unstructured and infrequent phenomena that lie at the heart of the subfield".

[16]The first part of every case study, where a historical narrative is given to situate the context of the respective procedure, is constituted of a "thick description" (*i.e.,* interpretation-laden; see Geertz 1973, pp. 312 ff.) of the context, informed foremostly by the theories of executive/political instability and party systems developed in Baumgartner and Kada (2003), pp. 7–19, Mainwaring (2018), pp. 17–101, and Pérez-Liñán (2007), pp. 176–202.

To address this second goal, multiple strategies were undertaken. One involved the already mentioned single-case study formula, where one may find indications from the involved actors relative to their leading motives or their own perceptions and attitudes relative to the proceeding. If it is not the enforcement of law that dictates the outcomes of impeachment, then there may be other observable elements that do or that at least influence them in meaningful ways. To make sure all bases are covered, a comprehensive overview of the design choices will be discussed, both from theory and practical implementation, as these other aspects may also influence whether impeachments are serviceable as means of legal accountability of Presidents. Such information is obtained through the recuperation of historical accounts, jurisprudence, and legal-scholarly discussions of the respective countries, which will then be contrasted to one another using some strategies of comparative constitutional studies.[17]

Given that this study also takes some influence from structuralism and philosophy of ordinary language,[18] not only presidential impeachments in the strict sense will be analysed. Some institutes (*e.g.*, pretrial, declaration of vacancy, recall) that are often confused or equated to impeachment need to be addressed to ascertain if the difference between them is actual and not just nominal. Structuralism posits, among other things, that meaning is ascertained not only by a unit itself (in this case, "presidential impeachment"), but also by the other units that conscribe it (the structure), which indirectly define it by putting up their own delimitations to the neighbouring concepts. Ordinary language philosophy, on its turn, denounces how meaning is constructed through the use of language, thus concluding that words have meanings that are not innate to themselves, but that result from linguistic games played by the interlocutors, changing and evolving through time. Some cases of non-impeachments are, therefore, included in the analyses contained herein, referred mostly as "atypical procedural oustings" or "impeachment surrogates". As shall become evident in the upcoming chapters, however, there are significant differences between impeachment and these other institutes, which justify the distinction among them. What that means for this book is that these other cases will not be considered in as much detail as impeachments in the strict sense, as the latter is the main object of study after all.

Finally, it is important to notice that, although this study may at many points make normative statements about impeachments, it does not aim to identify the "best" practices or arrangements for such institute.[19] In principle, the understanding put forth by this study contends the possibility of a universally uncriticizable design,

[17] See Hirschl (2014), pp. 112–150. On the historical method, see Roberts (1996), pp. 10–13 and 16 ff.

[18] Foremostly by influence of de Saussure (2016) and Wittgenstein (1968).

[19] At times, it will be mentioned that some design choices introduce vulnerabilities in the system of impeachments (*e.g.*, by allowing a single actor to dominate the course of the procedure) or may go against original understandings on theory and function of impeachments. Such are risks framers of constitutions may consciously take expecting a trade-off elsewhere, and thus do not necessarily mean that the choice for them is inherently "bad".

as any design choice made comes with its trade-offs and opportunity costs.[20] The study will, however, suggest different ways the design of impeachment can be optimized to achieve certain goals or to be consistent with certain constitutional values or contexts. The optimal choice of goals or values that ought to be pursued, however, is left to the judgement of the readers, as they are the ones to know which such normative commitments are important to them and to their own constitutional context.

References

Baumgartner JC, Kada N (eds) (2003) Checking executive power: presidential impeachment in comparative perspective. Praeger, Westport

Bennett A, Elman C (2007) Case study methods in the international relations subfield. Comp Polit Stud 40(2):170–195

Comisión Ciudadana de Seguimiento (1996) Poder, Justicia, Indignidad. Utópica Ediciones, Colombia

Conaghan CM (2005) Fujimori's Peru: deception in the public sphere. University of Pittsburgh Press, Pittsburgh

Coppedge M (1997) Strong parties and lame ducks: presidential partyarchy and factionalism in Venezuela. Stanford University Press, Stanford

de Saussure F (2016) Course in general linguistics. Bloomsbury, London [etc.]

Farrand M (1911) The records of the Federal Convention of 1787: May 14 to July 13, 1787. Yale University Press, New Haven

Geertz C (1973) The interpretation of cultures: selected essays. Basic Books, New York

George AL, Bennett A (2005) Case studies and theory development in the social sciences. MIT, Cambridge

Helmke G (2016) From power gaps to instability traps: reflections on institutional instability in Latin America. Department of Political Science, University of Rochester

Hinojosa V, Pérez-Liñán A (2003) Presidential impeachment and the politics of survival: the case of Colombia. In: Baumgartner JC, Kada N (eds) Checking executive power: presidential impeachment in comparative perspective. Praeger, Westport, pp 65–79

Hirschl R (2014) Comparative matters: the renaissance of comparative constitutional law, 1st edn. Oxford University Press, Oxford

Kelsen H (1931) Wer soll der Hüter der Verfassung sein? Walther Rotschild, Berlin

Lijphart A (2012) Patterns of democracy: government forms and performance in thirty-six countries, 2nd edn. Yale University Press, New Haven

Linz J, Valenzuela A (eds) (1994) The failure of presidential democracy, vol I. Johns Hopkins University Press, Baltimore

Llanos M, Marsteintredet L (eds) (2010) Presidential breakdowns in Latin America: causes and outcomes of executive instability in developing democracies. Palgrave Macmillan, New York

[20] As expressed by Jean Bodin: "the wise governor of a people should fully understand its humor and its nature before expecting anything from an alteration of the state or of the laws. For one of the most important and perhaps the principal foundation of the commonwealths is the adaptation of the state to the nature of the citizens, and the edicts and ordinances to the nature of the places, the persons, and the times". Julian Franklin (1963), Jean Bodin and the Sixteenth Century Revolution, p. 76, *apud* Hirschl (2014), pp. 119–120.

Llanos M, Nolte D, Tibi Weber C (2012) Paraguay: Staatsstreich oder "Misstrauensvotum"? GIGA Focus Lateinamerika, no. 8
Mainwaring S (ed) (2018) Party systems in Latin America: institutionalization, decay, and collapse. Cambridge University Press, Cambridge
Marsteintredet L, Berntzen E (2008) Reducing the perils of presidentialism in Latin America through presidential interruptions. Comp Polit 41(1):83–101
Pérez-Liñán A (2000) ¿Juício político o golpe legislativo? Sobre las crisis constitucionales en los años noventa. América Latina Hoy 26:67–74
Pérez-Liñán A (2007) Presidential impeachment and the new political instability in Latin America. Cambridge University Press, Leiden
Perkins W (2003) The political nature of presidential impeachment in the United States. In: Baumgartner JC, Kada N (eds) Checking executive power: presidential impeachment in comparative perspective. Praeger, Westport, pp 21–44
Roberts C (1996) The logic of historical explanation. Pennsylvania State University Press, University Park
Rosenn KS, Downes R (eds) (1999) Corruption and political reform in Brazil: the impact of Collor's impeachment. North-South Center Press, University of Miami, Florida
Rossiter C (1963) The American presidency, 2nd edn. Johns Hopkins University Press, Baltimore
Shugart MS, Carey JM (1992) Presidents and assemblies: constitutional design and electoral dynamics. Cambridge University Press, Cambridge
Wittgenstein L (1968) Philosophical investigations, 3rd ed. reprint of English text with index. Blackwell, Oxford

Chapter 2
Impeachment in History and Thought

Lawyers often treat their legal texts as a sort of sacred, God-given guidelines on how to deal with certain legally relevant issues. By imagining a vacuum in which laws appear, they may feel more comfortable in giving authoritative conclusions on what the 'true' or 'false' interpretation for a given case may be, as their doctrinal theory meets no constraints but that of its own presumed logic. This, however, can be a conflictive approach, as it obscures the nature of constitutions and mystifies legal practice by imposing pure and homogenous expectations on an otherwise ambiguous, multi-layered reality. Impeachments, perhaps to a higher degree than any other constitutional device, are no exception to this tension between expectation and reality. To fully grasp what drives impeachments, one needs to have a basic understanding of their genealogy and relationship with Parliament. Only by observing this organic development is that one may begin to grasp the odd and explosive mix of historical imperfections, pragmatic compromises, and heroic idealism that all impeachments entail.

In the first section of this chapter (item 2.1), the reader will be able to confront the first series of inconsistencies idealized views of impeachment and Parliament bring with themselves. As it will be shown, long before Parliaments would become known as the "legislative branch" as they are today, they have been central organs of limitation of executive power. Impeachments, which entered and reentered the parliamentary arena by an exceptional strike of luck, became one of the major instruments for setting limits to overbearing governments and, in tortuous ways, would end up contributing to the creation of what is now known as responsible government and the parliamentary system of government. Later in the chapter, it is demonstrated how the British-American colonies took admiration in the symbolism of impeachments in the struggle against monarchy and arbitrary power, and how they adapted it to their new reality. This imperfect but necessary adaptation was key to create America's novel system of government, now known as presidentialism. This section ultimately shows how many difficulties this adaptation entailed, and how much effective practice still defined what impeachment was to become.

G. Palamone, *Presidential Impeachment in Latin America*,
https://doi.org/10.1007/978-3-031-44188-2_2

The second section of this chapter (item 2.2) gives an overview of the transplant of presidentialism to the rest of the Americas, as well as its presumed consequences. As instability eventually became a common sighting of the Latin America of the twentieth century, many fingers started pointing at presidentialism with suspicion. As common as transitions of government were, impeachments were rarely ventilated. That suspicious absence ended in the early 90s, however. Military coups were abandoned in exchange for impeachments, which in turn became part of the daily political discourse. The fingers of suspicion, inferring a line of continuity from the military coups of the previous decades, started pointing at the frequent impeachments, thus prompting an important question: Were presidential impeachments really means of legal accountability as the textbooks informed? Or had they become just another tool in the arsenal of politics?

The third section (item 2.3) explains that the question can be much deeper than commonly conceptualized and that it must perhaps be reframed. Taking inspiration from legal philosophers and practitioners who have dealt with other point of inflection of law and politics before, this section explains how and why reaching any oversimplified conclusion on the topic potentially misleading and dangerous. Concluding for the impossibility of splitting law from politics in the context of impeachments, the section discusses strategies on how to discern (legitimate) political usage of law from arbitrariness.

2.1 The Historical Foundation of Parliaments and Impeachments: From England to the U.S.

2.1.1 Birth of the English Parliament

The first documented appearances of the word *parliamentum* date from early and mid-thirteenth century, in *loose* and *intermittent* references found in the writ of summons to the temporary baronial assemblies and the coming together of courts of the Kings Henry III and, later, Edward I.[1] The core of the activity of these assemblies of barons and prelates would be to aid the King in the adjudication of arduous cases and the discussions of other miscellaneous political matters. Aside from justice and administration matters, taxation and legislation were considered only in exceptional occasions, although they would slowly start requiring the consent of these

[1] Miller (1970), pp. 3 ff. These assemblies would be summoned as much as three to four times annually and last from one to four weeks (in exceptional circumstances, up to ten weeks). Brand (2012), pp. 10 ff.

assemblies to some extent to have their legitimacy recognized.[2] The commoners[3] were first brought to the King's council during Edward I's reign, around 1264–5, as part of a desperate strategy of ascribing political backing for Edward's unstable regime. Due to the increased administrative burdens that were being placed upon the shoulders of these individuals, their cooperation became fundamental to peacekeeping, as they were the ones to array troops and supplies that made military operations possible.[4]

The business and personnel of these assemblies would display a good deal of variation from one summoning to the other, always tailored by the King and his advisers in ways to guarantee that the expected agenda would be met. This underlined how much at this point the Parliament was really a "child of monarchy", as it was merely means of vesting the King's government with a pretence of consent, while neutralizing discontents aroused by its policies.[5] The barons may have learned early enough that through the Parliament the King could see limits imposed to his powers or even see himself forced to bow to the wishes of the communities—their autonomy to do so, however, still faced serious reservations. An important development to the bargaining power of the barons was introduced by the Ordinances of 1311, which determined that things such as alienation of crown lands, decisions to go to war and choice of the King's principal ministers had to undergo approval by the baronage in the Parliament. Additionally, yearly Parliaments and a panel to hear complaints against Ministers who contravened the Ordinances were instituted.[6]

During the first ten years of Edward III's reign, these assemblies would begin to settle down with the addition of commoners being nearly constant. The assemblies would become more frequent, though be temporary, and would have miscellaneous agendas, while the gross of the administrative and judicial business remained within the grip of the king's professional council.[7] In the end of this period, the so-called 'Commune petitions' became the first powerful tool of the commoners, through which the concerns of general interest would be voiced and, so, end up providing basis for legislation and other remedies.[8]

[2] Miller (1970), p. 5. Due to outrage caused by some taxes imposed in 1297, Edward I conceded that no new taxation would be imposed in the future "without the common assent of the whole kingdom".

[3] Commoners were knights and burgesses (merchants, craftsmen, landowners, officials).

[4] Miller (1970), p. 8. Edward I would repeat the strategy a few times in the following decades, tacitly recognizing the political capacity and identity of the *communities* (not class!) these commoners represented.

[5] Miller (1970), p. 6.

[6] Miller (1970), pp. 11–12. Most of this was revoked a decade thereafter by the Statute of York, leading historians to describe the latter as an attempt at "turning the clock back to a time when the parliament was indeed the child of monarchy". The Statute, however, still retained some relevant parliamentary consent requirements.

[7] Plucknett (1970), pp. 195–198. In this period, the term *parliamentum* becomes constant in writs of summons.

[8] Miller (1970), p. 16.

The moment, however, in which Parliament acquires a life of its own and becomes unmistakable with the *sui generis* great councils of the thirteenth and early fourteenth centuries was during the period of the Hundred Years' War (1337–1453).[9] The King's war-time difficulties compelled him to remedy grievances harmoniously in the hope that, by doing so, his precious military operations would not be hampered. This provided the barons, as well as the commons and their petitions with a meaningful leverage over the Monarch.[10] The establishment of early Parliament's independent authority and identity may very well have culminated in the Parliaments of 1376 and 1386–8, in which the public resentment of an inefficient, unfair, and irresponsible government led to a series of impeachments and the overhaul of the administrative bodies of the respective periods.[11]

In summary, the 'creation' of the early Parliament is perhaps to be best understood as the emancipation of one branch of the executive rather than the rise of something completely new and distinct, as someone born in a modern state might be inclined to think. It consisted of small gradual concessions from a *de jure* ruler to groups, estates, and communities, who possessed a grand but hitherto grossly unacknowledged *de facto* power.

2.1.2 Impeachment and Accountability in the Middle Ages

Such may have been the importance of parliamentary judicature, that central exponents of the classical literature claim that the dispensing of justice composed the core of the early Parliament's functions.[12] A more interesting question for the scope of this book, however, may be to analyse how much of this administration of justice could have amounted to the Parliament acting as an organ of accountability. For that, one must take into consideration what instruments were available and their peculiarities.

The first activity was the hearing of petitions and bills. Petitions and bills are terms employed interchangeably to address all imaginable kinds of supplications.

---

[9] Some historians trace the origins of the Parliament back to as early as the tenth century, such as Maddicott (2012), who focused either in the broadly defined functions or the composition of some great councils. Plucknett (1970), pp. 196–197, and Wilkinson (1937), p. 54, make a compelling argument pointing that neither aspect could be by itself a successful distinctive feature, as other organs may have similar functions and composition and yet unmistakably coexist with a Parliament. The key distinction would lie in the degree of representativity and autonomy *vis-à-vis* the Chief of Executive. In detail, see also Cam (1970), p. 277; Richardson and Sayles (1930); Richardson and Sayles (1931), *passim*.

[10] Miller (1970), pp. 18–19.

[11] Miller (1970), pp. 20–23.

[12] Maitland (2012) [1893]; Pollard (1920), pp. 35 ff.; Wilkinson (1937), p. 82. Central for this conclusion are not necessarily the impeachments, but the petitions which could also assume judicial or quasi-judicial façades. For reservations against these conclusions, see Edwards (1970), pp. 279–297.

Petitions, which predominated in the Parliaments, would generally bring complaints that could not be readily resolved in courts or requests of royal favour. Bills, on the other hand, would pertain to complaints associated with litigation and, therefore, more common in lower courts.[13] A petition may be asking for the restoration of wrongfully seized lands by the crown, asking for grants, for the payment of overdue wages, or the payment in instalments or pardon of debit; a religious house may ask for the license to acquire a reasonable quantity of land, which could generate outcry, if dismissed.[14] These petitions could be set forth by privates (individuals or small groups), by communities represented by a knight or the representative burgess, and by the commoners as a whole, in which case its presumed importance to the realm would guarantee the King's personal attention.[15]

The line between petitions and pleas, that is, the Parliaments' judicial business in the strictest sense, is also not sharp at all.[16] To some, their context of emergence may be the distinguishing feature, such as in appeals against delayed, divided, or contradictory decisions of the lower courts, and for others, their eminent criminal or administrative implications.[17] It is not hard to see, however, how the example about the wrongfully seized lands could develop into a litigious affair of both criminal and administrative nature, especially considering how the feudal thought of property was structured—the lines between private and common, favour and justice could be and often were blurred.

Even in those matters one could feel compelled to recognize as strictly legal, procedurally they left a lot to desire.[18] Trials held in these Parliaments were noisy and unseemly performances, much distant from the quite recent development of standards for judicial solemnity and decorum. Standards of proof tended to regard the ill-fame of the suspected and the statements of respected personages as conclusive (the so-called conviction by notoriety or clamour)—the unsworn word of the King most specially was enough to surpass any other recorded proof, including that acquired *flagrante delicto*. Finally, the mode of proof imposed upon a suspect could also be so difficult and dangerous as to better be regarded as punishment for being suspected rather than an opportunity for defence.[19]

[13] Dodd (2008), pp. 1–2.

[14] Maitland (1970), pp. 117–118.

[15] Businesses that were not 'so great or of so much grace' were generally left to the chancellor and others to handle without the King. Edwards (1970), p. 284; Maitland (1970), pp. 108 ff.

[16] Edwards (1970), pp. 281 ff.; Maitland (1970), p. 124.

[17] Plucknett (1970), pp. 222–224.

[18] Note that adjudication in ordinary courts during the Middle Ages did not necessarily lead to better outcomes due to the lack of proper distinctions between private and public, as well as the lack of legal specialization. Parliamentary trials could offer more accountability than their alternatives. Clarke (1968b), pp. 252–253.

[19] Plucknett (1983), pp. VI 542–559; X 146–158. The unfairness of these practices was already evident during this period, reason why, for example, the convictions of Earl Thomas of Lancaster and Earl Roger Mortimer of March ended up being reverted by Parliaments. These cases were fundamental for establishing the opportunity for defence as part of a fair trial.

The impeachment introduced to the parliamentary practices in the Good Parliament (1376)[20] offered on the other hand a relatively refreshing alternative to these archaic forms of judicature, albeit still lacking in many technical refinements. Firstly, it offered a remedy that could be activated independently of the King's authority—a "daring novelty", a true breakthrough from the child of monarchy paradigm.[21] Secondly, it granted some power over criminal proceedings to the commoners by allowing them to personally lead an accusation rather than being the provocateur of the King's or the barons' initiative.[22] This became possible due to the implied general interest of the realm in the inquests presented by the commons.[23] Finally, it also established a certain standard of "due process" that distinguished the impeachment from other criminal instruments, such as the bill of attainder or appeal of treasons. Due to the protests made by the first minister to be impeached, Lord William Latimer,[24] the right to be indicted by the Commons, to be tried by peers, and to be given the opportunity to answer the charges came to be the general rule.[25]

None of these developments were consciously planned out. The autonomous power of the Parliament was part of the increasing tendency of the Lords to exclude the King's prelates and council from their proceedings, dominating the parliamentary work. Moreover, since both the King and his eldest son, Edward the Black Prince, were incapacitated by severe illnesses, Parliament managed to get by with such novel challenges to his prerogatives without strong opposition. John of Gaunt, Edward III's second eldest son, was acting at the time as effective head of government and could have opposed the reforms and 'excesses' of the commons but had become too isolated from the Parliament due to the generalized resentment regarding England's military failures and crippling taxation.[26]

The next year, however, John of Gaunt summoned a new Parliament filled mainly with his dependents and managed to get all achievements of the Good Parliament reversed. This assured the young and newly crowned King Richard II (the Black Prince's eldest son) a decade of increasing resentment and generalized commotion,

---

[20] Before this, impeachment was purely a criminal procedure of the courts. The exact reason for this transition is controverted. In detail: Lambrick (1967).

[21] Plucknett (1983), pp. X 146 ff. There was reluctance in owning up to this kind of competence. In their first cases, the Commons still sought the King's approval and their language implied they were acting in his interest and with his authorization. Plucknett (1983); Plucknett (1942), p. 49.

[22] "The Good Parliament broke through the encirclement of statutes and achieved the transition from procedure by petition, with all its implications of grace and favour, to procedure by indictment, which is an assertion of right. Impeachment was already more than 'a criminal proceeding initiated by the House of Commons against any person'; it was a prosecution in which the Commons, as a whole, took over the functions of the jury of presentment". Clarke (1968b), p. 265.

[23] Plucknett (1983), pp. VIII 153 ff.

[24] Other three impeachments took place in this same opportunity. John Neville (Edward III's Steward), Richard Lyons (a londoner merchant), Alice Perrers (Edward III's mistress). Plucknett (1983), pp. VIII 156 ff.

[25] Clarke (1968b), pp. 262–263. The "indictment" portion of this statement is contested by Plucknett, at least as a technical term. Plucknett (1942), pp. 54 ff.

[26] Wilkinson (1937), p. 97.

as barons split into quarrelsome factions and the population suffered under crippling taxation. All of this would culminate in the Peasant's Revolt of 1381 and their violence against some of the ministers.[27]

Impeachment appeared again in full force in 1386, when under the looming threat of a French invasion King Richard was forced to summon a Parliament to collect enough resources for defence. The poor timing of the summoning, however, left Richard and his ministers in a precarious position, especially because John of Gaunt had just departed in quest of the Castilian throne.[28] The effects of the departure became visible in the opening session of the Parliament as barons and commons felt emboldened to vigorously oppose King's demands. Chancellor de la Pole, who had just made another taxation announcement, became himself target of an impeachment for malfeasance. Though Richard resented the Parliament's behaviour, he settled down after being reminded of what could happen to a King who does not respect the People's will.[29] The Parliament also appointed a commission to inquest into the King's military business, to survey the estate and conditions of the household, as well as to put in any reforms deemed necessary, for the period of twelve months.[30]

Outraged by how Parliament had been challenging his royal prerogatives, Richard consulted with judges, who confirmed his opinion that such acts encroached on royal prerogatives and that those were treasonable acts. In direct reaction, Richard plotted to destroy whom he perceived as traitors but was outmanoeuvred by the Lords. The Lords summoned a Parliament in 1388, claimed the supremacy of the Parliament, expressly revoked the legal statutes that threated their lives and heritage and, with *appeals of treason* (most converted to impeachments), effectively removed five of his favourites from his council and appointed a new administration.[31]

These, though controversial, were the crowning acts of the early Parliaments as autonomous authorities. Though impeachment remained part of parliamentary activity in the coming years, it became significantly less impactful, to the point the Commons would reject their own competence interfere in the Crown's business in the Parliament of 1397.[32] Impeachment was to be merely as part of Parliament's criminal jurisdiction, while appeals of treason and bills of attainder took the lead as the central instruments of the confrontation.[33]

---

[27] Tout (1970), pp. 304–308.

[28] Saul (2008), p. 56.

[29] A likely reference to Edward II's deposition in 1327. The Commons were going well beyond what the impeachments of 1376 were. They were not using the King's authority in his absence, but defying his wishes and, consequently, asserting their own authority as a sovereign organ. Wilkinson (1937), pp. 106–107.

[30] Saul (2008), p. 57.

[31] Saul (2008), pp. 57–58. Clarke (1968a), pp. 132–133; 141 ff.

[32] Plucknett (1983), p. X 145.

[33] Some cases after 1397 are often described as "impeachments", particularly the case of Sir John Mortimer in 1423, but are far from being clear-cut. These procedures may be seen as a middle point between attainder and impeachment, a characteristic of this transition phase perhaps. In detail: Rezneck (1927), pp. 506–508; For a timeline of medieval impeachments: Tite (1974), p. 222.

2.1.3 Rediscovery and Transformation of Impeachment into a 'Political Weapon'

Parliaments became considerably less prominent in the period after Richard II's deposition. With the royalty becoming more financially self-sufficient and having instruments of patronage and attainder at their disposal to disarm the opposition, the summoning of Parliaments could be reduced to a minimum and their freedom of questioning the government greatly suppressed. The composition of the Commons evolved to be more gentry based, entailing an improvement in the education of its members, but also a decrease in their representativeness. They also became more prone to manipulation from the Lords and government officials. Though the Commons acquired judicature to protect their own privileges and consolidated themselves as the starting chamber for legislation, certain themes remained out of bounds, such as matters of royal succession, religion, and regal administrative abuses.[34]

In 1603 James VI, King of Scotland, rose to the throne of England (1603), starting the reign of the Stuart dynasty. Much differently from the Tudors, James, as a Scotsman—a foreigner-, was much more cautious and respectful of his relationship with the English Parliaments and, as such, allowed them much space for experimentation and setting forth extravagant claims. An evolutive pattern is visible in the early Stuart era (1603–26), in which so-called "complaints" promoted by the Commons progressively reaffirmed their, as well as the Parliament's authority, by arguably encroaching on royal prerogatives.

The first complaint of notice took place in the Parliament of 1604 against John Thornborough, the bishop of Bristol. Thornborough had written a book which revealed discussions in the House of Commons on the topic of the Anglo-Scottish Union—one of James' main projects for England that had strong potential for political polarization. The Commons interpreted his book as a breach to their prerogatives, dishonouring the House and posing the risk of generating turmoil. Such complaints were usually resolved unicamerally, but as the bishop was a member of the Lords, a sort of joint action had to be arranged.[35]

In another Parliament in 1610, the Commons brought complaints against Dr. John Cowell. Cowell had written a legal dictionary known as '*The Interpreter*', in which he derived definitions of 'King', 'Parliament' and 'Prerogative' that emphasized the King's absolute power. Despite Cowell not being a member of the Lords like Thornborough was, the Commons sent a complaint to their examination, but under the argument that it involved the dignity of the Parliament as a whole. The issue gave rise to debate and was eventually settled in the sense that the Lords would hear the complaint by the Commons in another session. Before any judgement could be

[34]Fryde (1970), pp. 1–30; Lander (1961), *passim.*

[35]Tite (1974), pp. 57–59.

made, however, James intervened to reject all views supported in Cowell's book and to suppress of all its copies.[36]

At least on an abstract level, James' direct concession could be seen as an overt acknowledgement that he was bound "to the fundamental laws of his kingdom" and that he was only absolute in conjunction with his Parliaments, which he had no intent in governing without.[37] On a more concrete level, however, it was still too soon for the prosecution of the King's servants, as a complaint against Sir Stephen Proctor in the same Parliament revealed. The Commons accused Proctor of multiple abuses, racketeering among them, and were prepared to punish him swiftly. As the Commons committed Proctor to the serjeant and went on to punish him through a bill, the Chancellor complained they had been exceeding their authority and forced them to hand the case over to the King.[38]

The Commons' combativeness did get on James' nerves, however, particularly relative to negotiations on fiscal policy. The Commons refused to accept James' claims that government costs had increased, and revenues decreased, and blamed James' solvency issues on his own personal extravagance. James, despite suspecting the Commons were deliberately trying to weaken the Crown,[39] endured their recalcitrance due to his foreigner status. This is notable in the records of personal conversations of James and a Spanish ambassador:

> The House of Commons is a body without a head. The members give their opinions in a disorderly manner. At their meetings nothing is heard but cries, shouts and confusion. I am surprised that my ancestors should ever have permitted such an institution to come into existence. But I am a stranger, and I found it here when I arrived, so that I am obliged to put up with what I cannot get rid of.[40]

Presumably, the increasingly absolutist developments in the rest of Europe made the Commons particularly touchy about giving concessions to the King and made them eager to reaffirm the Parliament's authority.[41] The escalation of behaviour was eventually matched by James, who was now looking for revenue under royal prerogative (feudal dues such as wardship and purveyance) and, after 1610, impositions without parliamentary approval.[42]

The King's remedy to such reluctance would prove to be a bitter one. In the Parliament of 1614, a Committee of the Lower House concluded for the illegality of such impositions and recommended a joint conference should be requested to the Lords. In the opening debates in the Lords, Richard Neile, the bishop of Lincoln,

---

[36] Tite (1974), pp. 60–64.

[37] Smith (1999), pp. 102–103. This is not a given coming from a Scotsman since the King of Scotland could rule independently on occasion.

[38] Tite (1974), pp. 64–67.

[39] Smith (1999), pp. 106–108.

[40] Smith (1999), p. 103. The private conversation was with the Count of Gondomar, in 1614.

[41] Croft (1996), p. 168. In France, Parliaments lost control over taxation after 1583. In Spain, their power was considerably restricted by Phillip II, after the crisis of 1592.

[42] Smith (1999), p. 108.

shined with his opposition. Neile argued that the scope of such a conference was beyond the authority of Parliament, who had sworn to uphold the privileges of the Crown. The Commons, in a clearly belligerent mood, submitted a complaint to the Lords against Neile, which generated considerable friction with the Lords and the King. James, perplexed by these developments and the nature of the parliamentary discussions, dissolved the Parliament before any decision on Neile or the impositions could be met and punished some of the leaders of the Commons, coining this Parliament as the infamous "Addled Parliament".[43]

The anxieties that had been haunting the Commons were further exacerbated by the long interregnum of seven years before the next summoning, in 1621, which long postponed the resolution of many grievances.[44] The summoning itself was made necessary by the expiration of the truce treaty with Spain, which forced the Crown into new military operations and, consequently, also into the search of supporting sources of revenue that had to be conceded by Parliament.[45] Once again, similar leverages to those that made the impeachments of 1376–86 possible seemed to reappear, though the Parliament's prolonged absence made it seem more vulnerable this time around.

While the Parliament of 1621 focused on the economy, the opportunity for reconstructing the thought of impeachment emerged in surprising ways. After approving two subsidies to the Crown, the Parliament shifted its focus towards patents and monopolies, which were being widely blamed for "the decay of trade".[46] Two notorious monopolists came to the centre of the Commons' attention, namely Sir Francis Michell and Sir Giles Mompesson, who were accused abusing of their grants for personal enrichment. As the investigations evolved, the Commons were faced with insufficient tools to deliver a punishment[47] they considered appropriate. Michell could be dealt with in cooperation with the Barons through a complaint, but only because he was held in contempt against the Commons (turning into a matter of privilege, therefore). Mompesson, on the other hand, was not. No punishment greater than commitment to the Tower was available, unless a precedent

---

[43] Tite (1974), pp. 74–80.

[44] Croft (1996), pp. 168–171.

[45] Smith (1999), p. 109.

[46] Smith (1999), p. 109. Patents in this context refers to granting state functions such as licensing or, in patents of monopoly, to the protected right to pursue some method of trade or industry. They provided the Crown with alternative sources of income.

[47] In its unicameral judicature, the Commons could at best declare someone's indignity to the House, resulting in their arrest. A complaint could have harsher results if the Lords joined in jurisdiction, what was possible only in cases where privileges of the Parliament were affected. A bill of attainder was prerogative of the King and the Lords, meaning that the Commons could at best inform them about a misdeed and hope for an appropriate response. The attainder and the complaint are *ex parte regis*, whereas an impeachment would be led under authority of the Commons and, from a certain point on, of the Kingdom/Nation, standing so beyond the King's influence. By the end of the Tudor era, the Commons acquire prerogative over the initiation of all types of bills, including the attainder.

could be found, or the reach of his crime be interpreted beyond its private consequences.[48]

Both fronts were used. Investigations were broadened to reach the referees of such grants, whom, among other things, were believed to have received bribes. Mompesson's crime was declared to be against the King and the State, and Sir Edward Coke, speaker of the Commons, held an extensive speech on precedents relative to the parliamentary jurisdiction, though without mentioning impeachments. Although the investigations started casting shadows on the Lord Chancellor (Francis Bacon), the Treasurer (Henry Montagu), the Attorney General (Henry Yelverton) and the family of his favourite, George Villiers, James did not show much initiative in protecting them and restricted himself to asking the Parliament to postpone the conference, so no delay would afflict the discussion of other needed subsidies. After being assured no significant delay would come out of it, the investigations and discussions about patents went on.[49]

The trials and the investigations became dominated by the Lords and brought disappointing results to the Commons. Only Sir Francis Bacon was adequately punished, because he was very ill at the time and opted for a non-confrontative strategy, pleading guilty to part of the accusations. Bacon was sentenced to a fine, imprisonment and exclusion from Parliament, Court, and office. Sir Henry Yelverton was barely punished and would possibly be left unscathed had he not accused the King's favourite earlier that year, which led King James to intervene and demand punishment. Yelverton was sentenced to a fine, which was later partially remitted. De Villiers and Henry Montagu, the Lord Treasurer, were entirely shielded by James from prosecution.[50]

Bacon's case is often described as the case that "revived" impeachments in England,[51] but, as seen, the reality is quite underwhelming despite his ministerial rank and paradigmatic punishment. Though the Commons accused him by *informing* the Lords,[52] their role was limited and overshadowed by the Lords. It is questionable whether his case would have resulted in any such punishments had he not been in such vulnerable health or standing with the King. Moreover, the case had

[48]Tite (1974), pp. 86–90; 94–95.

[49]Tite (1974), pp. 102–103. About the precedents: There's no evidence of Coke ever using the word impeachment or much less that he recognized distinctions between impeachments and complaints. He did, however, mention some impeachment cases of 1376 in passing. Tite (1974), pp. 46–47.

[50]Tite (1974), pp. 115–122; 131.

[51]As in the respectable works of Roberts (1966), p. 28 or Smith (1999), p. 35, for example. This may come from the accounts of two members of the Commons, John Selden and Henry Elsynge, who described the case as an impeachment. It should be noted, however, that these accounts were written after the impeachment attempt of 1626 and there is no way of knowing If Bacon's case was already being thought as an impeachment in its time or whether the idea of impeachment was being applied in retrospect. The parliamentary records alone do not provide enough evidence to support such extrapolation.

[52]Paraphrasing Clarke, they had presented the man rather than the articles of accusation. Clarke (1968b), p. 268.

overtones of baronial disciplinary measures *ex parte regis* rather than genuine accountability towards the commonwealth. It did achieve more than the Parliaments of the previous decade but was still in many ways incomparable with the medieval attempts to control the King's government.

The only unambiguous appearance of impeachment came from the middle stages of the Parliament of 1621, when the tale of a lawyer, Edward Floyd, who had slandered the King and Queen of Bohemia, came to the Commons knowledge, and caused great outrage. Ordered to appear before them, Floyd denied ever making slanderous remarks. Without much care and in a poorly attended session, the Commons issued his punishment the next morning, knowing there was no precedent for their actions. James intervened, ordering the execution to be delayed until he was convinced of the legality of the acts of the Commons. He also presented an ordinance by Henry IV, in which the House was declared to have abandoned all power of judicature. Before this exchange between the Commons and James fully developed, however, James became annoyed by Floyd's utterances in his examination and himself proposed to send Floyd to the Lords. The Commons, fearing they would create a bad precedent by letting anyone else present grievances to the Lords, went out of their way to sentence Floyd. Floyd was declared "impeached before the Commons", which was the one and only entry of the word impeachment of this Parliament.[53]

The entry remains quite a puzzle. It is unknown whether the word had its own peculiar meaning by 1621, whether it was being used as a synonym to 'accusation' or whether it was some sort of acknowledgement of the conspicuously political nature of Floyd's crimes. The act was odd to the Lords as well, awarding a joint conference the next day. The Lords argued infringement of their privileges and the Commons, deeply divided but willing to conciliate, withdrew their decision. The Commons did not participate in the rest of Floyd's case, neither did the King persist with his demands of presenting the case himself or of limiting the jurisdiction of the Commons.[54]

In a more familiar complexion, impeachment procedures were used again in James' last Parliament, in 1624, with the impeachment of the Lord Treasurer, Lionel Cranfield, Earl of Middlesex, who was accused of receiving bribes, manipulating the Crown's revenues and of altering the orders of the Court of Wards, the Committee of Grievances in the Commons and the Committee of Munitions in the Lords investigated and found sufficient evidence to support the initial claims and add new ones. After investigation and discussion by committees of the Commons and the Lords on how to proceed, the Commons became responsible for charging Cranfield. Although these discussions involved bringing up emblematic cases of impeachment from 1376, such as the cases of Lord Latimer, the Chamberlain, and Richard Lyons, the

[53] Tite (1974), pp. 122–126.

[54] Tite (1974), pp. 128–131.

Londoner merchant, the right of the Commons to impeach was not wholly acknowledged, as the Lords conceded them jurisdiction solely for reasons of practicality.[55]

The Commons introduced their accusations claiming their right as the "Representative Body of the Realm" and as "the Inquisitors General of the Grievances of the Kingdom". Despite this, the Lords amended the accusations with evidence from their own Committee, extending their competence beyond that of judge and jury, acknowledging the procedure as merely another variant of a complaint against a peer. Cranfield was convicted with similar consequences as Bacon, which, while arguably insufficient to quench the appetite of the Commons, emboldened them to engage against an even more prominent public figure: Lord Admiral George Villiers, best known as the first Duke of Buckingham and for being both King James' and Prince Charles' favourite.[56]

Villiers, after successive military defeats, was openly accused in the House of Commons of incompetence—the first accusation by the Commons which did not involve illegal acts. This led King Charles to dissolve Parliament, but in pressing need for supplies, also to summon it again in the next year. It did not take too long for the attacks on Villiers to be resumed. Some had already predicted that supplies would be refused until he had been put down. Villiers was accused of mishandling the arrest of a trade ship and was put under investigations by a select committee. His defence argued he had acted under the King's express command, leaving the Commons in an uncomfortable but familiar situation. The Commons had to reformulate their case as to not challenge the maxim that "the king could do no wrong", and so redirected the investigations to be interpret Villiers as an "evil adviser".[57]

The committee picked up on many situations that could characterize as incompetent and the possibility of accusing Villiers on basis of common fame was considered, since the body of proof was relatively weak. Charles aptly considered the accusations to be unsubstantiated, claimed the attack was in fact on his and his father's government and ultimately contended that enquiries about his closest servants could not be permitted. As the House passed some subsidies, he eventually gave space for further investigations, though bitter with the situation. The committee came across many other serious suspicions and decided to keep the original claims, stating that Villiers should not have obeyed the King to the point of breaking the law. Moreover, the committee came to the conclusion that common fame could be sufficient base for their accusations since the Commons were 'not a House of

[55]Tite (1974), pp. 149–155. Due to delays and postponements in the investigation of the Committee of Munitions in the House of Lords, the Commons were invited to charge Cranfield in its place.

[56]Tite (1974), pp. 158–172.

[57]Tite (1974), pp. 178–183. In the words of Sir Robert Phelips: "(...) if anything falls out unhappily, it is not King Charles that advised himself, but King Charles misadvised by other and misled by disordered counsels." Clayton Roberts (1966), p. 69. The "evil advisers" argument respects the regal irresponsibility commanded by "the king can do no wrong" maxim, while also characterizing the same acts as unlawful and failing to provide a justification for the King's insistence in employing patently corrupt or incapable officers.

definitive Judgment, but of Information, Denunciation, or Presentment' and that only upon common fame could men safely accuse the great.[58]

Oddly enough, the Commons decided to introduce the thirteen charges by bill rather than orally like in the other cases and, although the word impeachment had not been used until then, the final document stated that '(...) the said Duke do accuse and impeach of the said Misdemeanours, Misprisions, Offenses, and Crimes', implying the word was slipped last minute. Also differently from the older cases, the accusations were delivered by and debated with multiple members of the Commons; a chance for Villiers' defence to reply was specifically asked. Keeping true to their "the king can do no wrong" belief, the Commons opted to give the King a chance to remove Villiers himself, listing the accusations and promising to give supply as soon as they received redress of Villiers' abuses. The answer of the King, who had already committed some of the members of the Commons to the Tower for the accusations against Villiers, was to immediately dissolve the Parliament.[59]

Had Villiers been judged by the Lords, it was quite likely he would have been acquitted and Charles would have received his precious supplies.[60] Instead, the rash decision of dissolving the Parliament implicitly confirmed the Commons' authority and the far-reaching implications of the impeachment, as it suggested he had no other means to shield Villiers. The Commons, thus, successfully set (or rather rediscovered) a precedent to act on their own authority for political balance, not merely pleading but *ascertaining* its redress.

2.1.4 The Failure of Impeachment in the Struggle for Parliamentary Supremacy

Though the 'impeachments' against Bacon and Cranfield are often depicted as political uses of the parliamentary judicature, the former due to his rivalry with Sir Coke and the latter due to his attempts to avoid the Spanish wars while the Commons were overtly anti-Spanish, a closer look into these narratives quickly dismounts them, even if it might have been the case that they were initially propelled by legally irrelevant criteria.[61] Not only their convictions were based unequivocally on criminal behaviour, but also the Parliament's enthusiasm in prosecuting them was anything but second-hand. Villiers' impeachment, by contrast, was almost entirely

[58]Tite (1974), pp. 183–193. The few who dared bring detailed accusations against the King's favourite were persecuted, such as the Earl of Bristol, who as charged of treason by the King in parallel to this impeachment.

[59]Tite (1974), pp. 193–202.

[60]Roberts (1966), p. 64, argues the dissolution sought the preservation of Charles' reputation. If the trial proceeded, sensible information about the Spanish journey could have been disclosed by the Earl of Bristol.

[61]For a deeper discussion into this, Colin Tite (1974), pp. 170 ff.

based on his poor performance, his monopolization of all great offices of the state with his minions and his overbearing influence on the King.

As such, Villiers' impeachment meant more than the resolution of a private spleen or of factional differences, but the rejection of a form of government, which may very well have been the most irresponsible since the Magna Charta had been confirmed. While the Tudors' government may have been largely conciliar, with Parliaments held to a minimum, the Stuarts after 1612 forcibly ignored both the Parliament *and* the Privy Council. James and Charles often held secrecy on issues until it was too late for anyone in government or Parliament to act. The King often even acted against the Council's unanimous decisions, valuing Villiers unconditionally over all others.[62]

When the Parliament of 1628 was called, Villiers was again in the spotlight. He had undertaken the siege of St Martin despite knowing England lacked the necessary resources, resulting in the death of two thousand Englishmen. Despite Villiers' clearly harmful presence in government, Charles once again determined that his removal was non-negotiable. Parliament seemed aware that insisting would only risk the introduction of an arbitrary government and, thus, sought other solutions. The Commons found that expanding the legal frameworks to restrict the acts of the Ministers could be the better solution—out of this strategy emerged the *Petition of Right*. Moreover, in their compromise was to spare Villiers, they sought to prove their points by targeting his associates, leading to a barrage of impeachments against officers somewhat involved in Villiers' decisions. As such the Commons restated the self-responsibility of officials for their acts, rejecting any 'direct command of the King' defence.[63]

The confrontation between Parliament and the King escalated even further the next year when King Charles accused the Commons of plotting to abate the power of the Crown. Charles affirmed he bore the responsibility for the government of the realm, not his servants. Despite these remarks, the Commons carried on exacting responsibility from Lord Treasurer Weston for arbitrary imprisonments and taxation. Charles reacted by once again dissolving Parliament and boycotting its re-summoning for the next eleven years.[64]

The dissonance between the idea of an infallible King and his very fallible choices had become painfully obvious at every attempt Parliament had at reforming the government. The Parliament could keep pretending not to see the incoherence of their political philosophy, but the King would not. This became particularly obvious in the Parliament of 1640–42, when Charles interrupted his period of personal rule to seek the reform the Scottish Kirk. This Parliament targeted someone who fought

---

[62]Roberts (1966), pp. 42–51. Roberts refers to this as government by courtiers; Smith, as "the Personal Rule".

[63]Roberts (1966), pp. 66–69. Villiers, the 'grievances of grievances' as he came to be known, met his fate soon thereafter. Not by impeachment or remonstrances of the Parliament, but by the dagger of John Felton.

[64]Roberts (1966), pp. 71–75.

against the abuses of government before but had now become part of it: Sir Thomas Wentworth, now Earl of Strafford and the King's Deputy in Ireland.[65]

Wentworth, like all others before him, argued to have 'acted ministerially' or, in other words, claimed he had merely administered the policies the King devised. The Commons replied as they have all others: "(. . .) The Earl of Strafford does very well know that the King's servants are to serve him according to law and not otherwise; he knows very well if an unlawful act be committed, especially to the degree of treason and murder, the King's warrant and authority is no justification at all". As Wentworth presented letters from the King to justify his acts, it became more important for the Commons to show that he had been misled by Wentworth in the first place. Wentworth tried to show the perversity such logic entailed: "If to give your opinions in political agitation shall be accounted treason, who will be willing to serve the King; or what dilemma are you in: if, being sworn counsellors, you speak not your minds freely, you are convicted of perjury, and if you do, perhaps of treason". To this the Commons partially objected: "The ground is true, (. . .) nothing corrupts counsels more than fear (. . .), but such treasons as these, the subversion of laws, violation of liberties, they can never be good or justifiable (. . .)".[66]

Wentworth would argue, moreover, that his acts had received approval of the Irish Parliament. Though the argument appealed to the sense of equity, the Commons were unconvinced that the given approval truly measured to the extent of his acts. Regardless, what became the crux of this impeachment case was the lack of evidence that Wentworth had really misadvised the King or that his supposed misdeeds did amount to treason. As Wentworth pointed out, his acts constituted multiple misdemeanours perhaps, but were not grievous enough to warrant impeachment. As the Lords acquiesced with Wentworth's remarks, the Commons became aware that the legal restraints of an impeachment would not allow for a conviction. Both Houses were, however, convinced that Wentworth was an imminent threat to the existence of Parliament, for his growing sympathy towards absolute monarchy had become very evident. Wentworth had been advocating in other opportunities a doctrine of exception government in which the King, 'deserted by the Parliament' and 'pressed by necessity', was 'loose and absolved' from the rules of government.[67] Additionally, there was a growing suspicion that the King had been raising troops to coerce the Parliament into releasing Wentworth.[68]

Frightened, the Parliament convicted Wentworth with a bill of attainder and threatened the King with the retention of supplies until their decision had been enforced. Charles, pressured by the Scottish army and the Mayor of London, who threatened not to pay the English army unless Wentworth was executed, begrudgingly signed the attainder. This was followed by the impeachment of two officials,

---

[65] Roberts (1966), pp. 77–88; David Smith (1999), pp. 120–121.

[66] Roberts (1966), pp. 87–90.

[67] Roberts (1966), pp. 90–94.

[68] This accusation has ever since been vastly confirmed. Russell (1991), p. 230, *apud* Smith (1999), p. 124.

six judges and thirteen bishops, most of which failed, because the Commons had grown too impatient to see them through. Well before proof could be produced on these cases, the Commons were demanding their removal by equating impeachment with presumption of guilt.[69]

In parallel, perhaps sensing Charles' vulnerability, Parliament mobilized to bring some of its leaders into his Privy Council. After some struggle, seven Lords were nominated to the council and one of them, the Earl of Bedford proceeded with negotiations to reach the office of Treasurer. He promised the King revenue in case he granted office to a slate of reformists in the government; Charles, in turn, asked him to save Wentworth's life, which he was unable to do. Lord Sayed, John Pym, and Edward Hyde had comparable attempts, all of which were frustrated by Charles' inflexibility and tendency to prioritize his courtiers. Charles was not going to accept any form of veto or suggestion to his choices of officials unless it came supported with the rigor of the impeachment.[70]

The years of impeachment practice had proven that the King would not expose counsellors who had given ill advice, greatly constraining the potential of legal actions, however. The following eight months made this particularly obvious as investigations were systematically frustrated by Charles' refusal to provide any assistance. This led the Commons to stop expecting any sort of cooperation and resort to general votes of condemnation, manifesting reprobation towards the action of an 'enemy of the state' or 'mischievous projector', while directing unsubstantiated impeachment and censure to merely suspected officials.[71]

The escalation of the issues in the Parliament and the rumours of a new 'popish plot' by the King led the Commons to draft an extensive remonstrance with demands and concessions to settle the spirits. The remonstrance of 1642 included many constitutional reforms, among them the requirement of parliamentary confidence of the councillors and ministers employed by the King, religious reforms, and dispositions on taxation. The Lords gave less support than expected to their cause, clinging to the model of aristocratic conciliarism. Charles, unsurprisingly, also rejected the remonstrance. He went further and attempted to arrest five members of the Commons and one of the Lords whom he deemed the troublemakers behind it all, generating great hostility inside and out of Parliament. Charles found himself forced to retreat from the capital, and the Parliament, outraged by his willingness to use violence, issued the 'Militia Ordnance', which gave it authority over the King's military. The unprecedented impetuosity of the Parliament repelled a good deal of its members away and generated a lasting schism between those who wanted to preserve the 'Crown's rightful powers' (Royalists or *Cavaliers*) and those who wanted a comprehensive reformation (Parliamentarians or *Roundheads*).[72]

---

[69] Roberts (1966), p. 102.

[70] Roberts (1966), p. 113.

[71] Roberts (1966), p. 116.

[72] Smith (1999), pp. 127–129.

On tortuous ways, the Parliament finally achieved the supremacy it so much strived for but was unable to reach through the legal and constitutional ways of impeachments and negotiation. With its greatly reduced membership and sudden radicalization, the Parliament lacked legitimacy, although it was able to make up for it for a long time with military power and Oliver Cromwell's strategic prowess. The events culminated in 1649, in which Charles I was tried and executed as a tyrant, traitor and enemy of the nation, and the monarchy as well as the House of Lords were abolished. The discrepancy between the actions and ideals of the Parliamentarians, who had on many occasions scooped law aside, imposed overbearing taxation and became themselves the tyrant, as well as the unreadiness of the English people to be ruled on completely secular terms, ended up turning the popular opinion in favour of the Royalists, who, on their turn, eventually successfully restored the parliamentary trinity (Crown, Lords, and Commons).[73]

2.1.5 Impeachment in the Construction of Responsible Government

England's republican experience may have been short-lived, but it did leave deep transformations in its constitution, despite the restauration of the state structure back to the *status quo* of 1641. The annulation of legislative acts between 1642–1660 (around 1200 acts and ordinances) and the execution of the surviving regicides did nothing to revert the change brought by the open discussions on the topics of accountability of Ministers and popular sovereignty, which were finally made available to those outside the Parliament.[74] In this context, impeachments became more than ever habitual and respectable, being carried out against 98 persons during the nearly twenty years of the Long Parliament's existence (1640–1660). The idea of a parliamentary government, on the other hand, was abandoned for the most part. The concentration of executive powers on the legislature proved to be inefficient, so much so that in 1653 these powers were transferred to the Lord Protector and his Council. The experience that followed also spoke against ministerial nominations by

[73] Smith (1999), pp. 122–146.

[74] A chief publication of this age was that of Henry Parker (1643), '*Observations upon Some of His Majesties Late Answers and Expresses*', in which, for example, he manifested something no one else had hitherto the courage: "The law says the King can do no wrong, and out of its civility it imputes all miscarriages in government to inferior agents; but policy teaches us that in nature he is strangely blameable, and deeply chargeable, when he makes an ill choice of inferior agents". Roberts (1966), p. 132. Other publications such as '*Leviathan*' (1657) by Thomas Hobbes and '*First defence of the People of England*' (1651) by John Milton would also prove remarkably influential in the following period.

Parliament, as its private ambitions and factionalism often got in the way of responsible government.[75]

As a result, the England of 1660 developed a more mature concept of balance of government through this experience that reaffirmed the importance of separation of powers. The Parliament wanted a strong, but fair executive. It stripped the King from his last few taxation prerogatives and feudal revenues, replacing them with permanent revenue, thus acknowledging the core of his autonomy, but reserving its right to be the harshest critic of the regal administration. Mature constitutional concepts were not the only remains left by the civil war which divided the country, however. Like in any polarizing or traumatic experience, some conflicts remained unresolved and, consequently, some spirits remained inflamed and reactive when the circumstances were so favoured. The impeachments of the following era reflected this as they were more clearly turned into instruments of partisan and factional confrontation. Principles of responsible government, while still part of parliamentary objectives, mattered when the target was seen as inimical or collateral to greater interests.

The impeachment of the Lord Chancellor Edward Hyde, Earl of Clarendon, and his colleagues in 1667 is said to illustrate this well. Hyde became a target of the Commons after the disastrous English military campaign of 1665–67 (Anglo-Dutch War) even though he advised the King against it. He was impeached for corrupting the laws of England despite being one of its steadiest defenders. This was only possible due to the political articulation of his strongest enemy, the second Duke of Buckingham. Buckingham had opposed King Charles II vigorously in the Commons, seeking popularity as the champion of the people, and, as a result, Hyde had advised the King to imprison Buckingham. This strategy backfired as Buckingham became more popular than ever and Charles opted to release him. Emerged as a martyr of the nation and Hyde's declared enemy, Buckingham was reinstated to the Court as Gentleman of the Bedchamber and used his favour to demand Hyde's impeachment. Though the King consented, the Lord Keeper drew up articles of impeachment composed of misdemeanours only, dooming the impeachment to failure.[76]

Buckingham, who could not afford to have Hyde in office after an unsuccessful impeachment, sought support from other talented and ambitious members of the Commons who felt their royalist efforts had gone unrecognized by the Crown. These men would introduce more grievous articles of impeachment, covering the holes left by the Lord Keeper. To approve these articles, however, Buckingham and his lieutenants had to win over factions in the Commons who were mostly loyal to Hyde. In face of that difficulty, Buckingham sought the King's active participation, who, through his prestige, influence, and knowledge of the situation, could be persuasive in his conviction. Convinced of Buckingham's command over the

[75] Smith (1999), pp. 147–148; Roberts (1966), pp. 120–133; 142–149; For details on the 98 impeachments p. 133, fn. 3. A good deal of these persons were not officials, but citizens who plotted against the new regime.

[76] Roberts (1966), pp. 155–160.

Parliament and pressured by the unpopularity of his government's military achievements and the extravagance of his Court, Charles II accepted a deal with Buckingham, agreeing to play the role of chief prosecutor and to entrust the Duke and his allies with office, in case he could also undertake to secure supplies.[77]

Despite the King's appeal to loyalty, few of the Commons were really convinced that Hyde had committed high treason on the articles brought by the Lord Keeper. Buckingham's lieutenants claimed that Hyde had betrayed counsels to the enemy during the war, a matter that was indubitably treasonous. For the lack of evidence, the Commons would have to accept the accusation without articles of impeachment, much like in the infamous impeachment attempt against Wentworth, Earl of Strafford. Fearing a similar fate, Hyde fled to France and three weeks later the King signed a bill banishing him. Buckingham failed to secure supplies to Charles, but he and his supporters nonetheless manage to secure office by persisting on the relentless opposition of Hyde's colleagues, forming what would be known as the Cabal Ministry (an acronym of the main ministers: Clifford, Ashley, Buckingham, Arlington, and Lauderdale). During this period three minor officials ended up fleeing or being dismissed by the King under the threat of impeachment; Clarendonians (Hyde's associates) of higher reputation also became targets, but proved impervious to attacks, despite the extents to which their antagonists went, spreading rumours and offering patronage in exchange of support. In reprisal to one of these attacks, the Earl of Orrery (an anti-Clarendonian) became himself target of an impeachment.[78]

The comedy of impeachments failed to amount to anything more than the King's disillusion with the Cabal Ministry, as it promised more than it could achieve. As a result, Charles opted for a strategy of parliamentary management rather than parliamentary undertaking.[79] He would, like his father, ignore the Privy Council in favour of a single minister or favourite and, consequently, lead the Cabal Ministry to execute many unpopular policies that would set them in the aim of more angered accusations by the Parliament.[80]

By 1674, however, the Commons had dealt with enough embarrassment with the abuse of impeachment and so preferred to draft a petition to the King asking for the dismissal of Buckingham and the Secretary of State Lauderdale.[81] Their behaviour

---

[77] Roberts (1966), pp. 156–164. Charles had reasons to resent Hyde, despite him being a respectable Chancellor. Roberts suggests that personifying the loss of the Anglo-Dutch War on Hyde eased the spirits.

[78] Roberts (1966), pp. 164–183.

[79] The distinction of parliamentary management and undertaking is one Clayton Roberts (and other English historians) recurs to in his writings. Though never expressly defined, undertaking can be understood as the government seeking support of the parliament for its policies, while management, as the government working on the mere taming of the opposition in Parliament. The former relies more on power sharing and the use of influential politicians, while the latter, on authoritative use of prerogative and patronage.

[80] Roberts (1966), p. 183.

[81] The other three cabal Ministers escaped this remonstrance. Clifford died short before 1674; Arlington became Buckingham's scapegoat and target of impeachment by his adherents, but the

often involved morally and legally reprovable acts, but the leading force behind these was their influence on foreign affairs. Resolving the issues through a petition to the King had the benefit of removing the Lords from the equation, but the fatal drawback of depending on the King's favour. Though the Commons threatened to refuse supply until their petition was redressed, at this time they were short of leverages, as Charles had just made peace with the Dutch and supplies were no longer a pressing matter. Charles preferred to restate his prerogative for dictating the course of state affairs and the employment of Ministers at own his pleasure, rather than acquiesce the demands of the Commons.[82] Only Buckingham was dismissed on the Parliaments request, but mostly because the King was already waiting for an excuse to get rid of his insubordinate behaviour. Lauderdale, on the other hand, was kept in office, even after the Commons recommended his removal other three times.[83]

The Cabal Ministry was eventually succeeded by one led by the Earl of Danby, who was more eager to give in to the prevailing parliamentary mood of the political elite regarding foreign policy and make extensive use of patronage to build reliable and consistent support within the Parliament. Despite the seductive appeal of this strategy, the fate of Danby's Ministry was not more peaceful. Former Cabal ministers Ashley and Arlington attempted to impeach Danby in 1675 and 1677 but failed under the same limitations Buckingham's impeachment had failed. Danby's Ministry was disintegrated by the sheer violence of this opposition, who instilled suspicion upon Danby's and Charles' every move. In December 1678, Ashley and Arlington finally achieved Danby's impeachment for high treason. Before he went on trial by the Lords, Charles attempted to protect him by negotiating and prorogating Parliament. The best he could achieve, however, was an agreement to dismiss Danby and dissolve Parliament, ensuing new elections and supplies.[84]

The promise of peace in a newly elected Parliament also quickly evaporated. The new composition wiped out the support built by Danby and filled it with extreme opponents of the Court. As a result, Danby's impeachment seemed nonetheless unavoidable. Charles knew Danby had done nothing but ensured the best interests of the Crown as he had conceived them and so dismissed and pardoned him. This pardon reopened an important question into the authority behind impeachment, however. To accept the legality of the pardon meant that the injured party was not

---

lack of evidence buried frustrated his attempt. Ashley, known as the Earl of Shaftesbury, was too popular to be opposed.

[82] Roberts (1966), pp. 183–195.

[83] Regarding the rest of Cabal, Lord Chancellor Ashley was dismissed without parliamentary provocation, due to his suggestion that the King should remarry to secure a Protestant heir. Arlington retired in office despite Buckingham's attempts of shifting the blame onto him. David Smith (1999), p. 153; Clayton Roberts (1966), p. 211.

[84] This Parliament (The Cavalier Parliament) was sustained under successive prorogations since the Restauration, being England's longest Parliament. By maintaining its composition, the King managed to prevent the escalation of anti-France and anti-popery policies wanted by the public at the time. Roberts (1966), pp. 221–222.

the nation or the laws of the realm, but the King's person and authority. The Commons immediately saw what the act communicated and urged the Lords to reject the legality of the pardon. The Commons may even have gone too far in their attempts to preserve the power of impeachment, usurping prerogatives of the Lords and impeaching five of its members, all of them Bishops, who would indubitably support the King. Such high-handedness may have been misplaced, as the Lords, a proud body, long jealous of the privileges achieved by the Commons, voted for the legality of the pardon.[85]

Charles resorted to pardons against impeachments seven times before Danby's case,[86] but only this once had it truly outraged the Commons, in part because the new Parliament was no longer on the King's payroll, but also because they were slowly becoming aware of how supine to the Crown's designs they had become, despite of having managed to dismantle a government that acted against their interests. The dismissal of Danby generated a new Ministry formed with the oppositionists who brought him down, which nonetheless remained incapable of responding to the new Parliaments' demands. Addresses for removal and impeachments proved futile, as leverages over supplies began to wane. In 1685, Charles's brother, James II, ascended to the throne only to annihilate any remaining hope of re-establishing such leverages, for he was able to achieve sufficient permanent revenue to rule autonomously from Parliament.[87]

James II's three years of reign marked a great downfall in balance of power, but at the same time served to put its relevance back into perspective. As a result, the same urge responsible for the Petition of Right of 1628, would come this time around for the Bill of Rights and a few other statutes of 1689, in a new attempt to consolidate principles of law that promoted healthy governmental practices. The overhaul of the financial system to re-establish the Crown's dependence on the Parliament, the restatement of the Parliament's freedom of speech and other prerogatives, as well as prohibition of some potentially arbitrary or tyrannical mechanisms of coercion, all contributed to re-establishing balance and the leverage needed for impeachments and other parliamentary remedies to be effective.[88]

Both King William III (1689–1702) and Queen Anne (1702–1714) were the exact antithesis of their predecessors in the way they exercised executive power. They made sure their policies were sympathized with by the nation, they named men of talent to high office, gave them no unlawful orders, met with Parliament often and protected no man from its censure. Yet, the Parliament's behaviour was as belligerent as before, frequently attacking Ministers. The Monarchy's collaborative mood

---

[85] In 1701, the Act of Settlement prohibited such use of pardon. See Roberts (1966), pp. 252–253 and 299.

[86] Roberts (1956), p. 219.

[87] Roberts (1966), pp. 224–244; Smith (1999), pp. 160–162. Peace with the Dutch, a surge of ordinary revenue and financial grants from France provided for Charles' relative autonomy against the Parliament's 'power of the purse'. James became even more independent in 1685 when the Parliament provided extra revenues meant to deal with rebellions in the Highlands and in the west.

[88] Roberts (1966), pp. 245–248; David Smith (1999), pp. 161–166.

was obfuscated by the troubled times, which were riddled with permanent wars and military upsets. The revitalized leverages of the Parliament and the mostly non-confrontative attitude of the Monarchs, however, facilitated that these frustrations would be dealt with, not only with dismissals and resignations upon impeachment or remonstrance, but also by the Monarch inviting the Commons to name substitutes to those whom they opposed.[89]

The Commons rejected participating in the formation of government, perhaps now more convinced of the value of separation of powers. Their powers as critics of the government, which on the other hand they much enjoyed and did not shy away from, met again many limitations; the most crippling of them was the need to attend the standard of proof set by the Lords regarding impeachments or by the Monarch regarding remonstrances, not because the standard was particularly high, but because pin-pointing the author of an ill-advice seemed unachievable in most situations. The right of inquiry into the records of the Court did not provide enough clues and requiring publicity of advice was unsustainable, since many state affairs and specially war efforts require a certain secrecy to be effective (most criticized advice was related to war miscarriages and foreign policy).[90]

This *cul-de-sac* of irresponsibility produced only more frustration with the incipient culture of party politics that was being built at the time, which gazed into the idea of coalitions and cohabitation in government with striking suspicion. Neither Whigs nor Tories were willing to share power and, as a result, impeachments and remonstrances were the common place for removing the opposition from high offices, so one party could rule undisturbed. There was a lot of demand for penalizing officials for their political decisions but little output. Most of these attempts failed for the lack of legal support to such intrinsically political motives, and would deeply annoy both Monarchs, who had sought to rule with mixed compositions in hope to achieve moderation of government.[91]

English politicians knew well that this culture of rejection to power-sharing was their ruin, as the words of Lord Wharton to Lord Dartmouth indicate: "If you have the majority we are undone, if we have the majority, you are broke".[92] Yet, the parties persisted in this exercise in futility for nearly two decades, until it finally

[89]Roberts (1966), pp. 249–255. Some important impeachments and impeachment threats of this period were against Lord Chancellor Nottingham (1693), President of the Council Leeds (1695), Lord Treasurer Godolphin (1697), Lord Chamberlain Sunderland (1697), Lord Treasurer Halifax (1698), Lord Chancellor Somers (1699), Lord Treasurer Oxford (1715), and Secretary of State Bolingbroke (1715).

[90]Roberts (1966), pp. 255–256; 257; 262.

[91]Roberts (1966), pp. 353–355. The Commons' negligence regarding these impeachments epitomized the flimsiness of their accusations. Roberts claims the Commons often knew they would not manage to sustain the accusations and just hoped the impeachment itself to be enough pressure to cause a dismissal or a resignation (Charles II, for example, lost 11 officers under such circumstances). Not rarely such accusations were abandoned. Only 5 of 57 impeachments involving Ministers, clergymen, judges, and high officers were taken to trial in the period between 1626 and 1715. See also Roberts (1975), pp. 1433 ff. and Roberts (1956), pp. 226–227.

[92]Roberts (1966), p. 353.

came to them that, if sharing the fruits of office was impossible, perhaps sharing the risks of office would finally bring them to an acceptable middle ground. If individualizing responsibility was impossible, collectivizing it ensured that, for better or worse, those behind misconduct or those that could have prevented them are ultimately called to account. Since collective responsibility is not exactly possible in a proceeding that claims criminal nature such as impeachment, the first solution found was to embody collective responsibility in one single person, namely the one whose influence on the Monarch was so great, that he quasi monopolized the counsels of the Monarch and closely superintended his/her administration.[93]

An opportunity for such a development surfaced in 1715, in an impeachment against the Lord High Treasurer Robert Harley, Earl of Oxford. In the previous years, Harley, an incredibly able and influential Minister, worked on the conclusion of the War of Spanish Succession (1701–1714), resulting in the signature of the Treaty of Utrecht by the belligerents. The treaty established many compromises that infuriated the Whigs, as they favoured France in many ways. Knowing how polarizing the treaty would be, Harley sought Parliament's approval for the treaty before accepting its terms. The approval was given in two consecutive Parliaments, whose composition was predominantly Tory. Harley is known to have asked the King to create extra twelve peers of Tory inclination in Parliament to ensure the treaty would be passed; Harley was further suspected in having actively engaged James the Pretender to give him sensible information leading to military defeats, which would consequently work to establish the treaty in such favourable terms towards the French, possibly restoring the succession of the throne towards him.[94]

Once the Whigs recovered majority in Parliament, Harley was targeted with an impeachment and identified as 'notoriously the first minister and chief director' behind the treaty. The main accusation brought by the Commons was of High Treason for his involvement with the French, but the charge was dropped by the Lords upon the lack of evidence; the Commons left the remaining misdemeanours unprosecuted out of spite against the decision by the Lords.[95] The event marked another humiliating defeat in the history of impeachment proceedings and produced enough criticism to herald the end of its era. It obviated how obsolete and unjustifiable impeachments had become in political warfare.

Impeachments seemed unjustifiable because they were serving only to throw innocent men into disrepute and remove from them power that had been in legal and constitutional wisdom invested into them. A proceeding that should be as exceptional as any criminal proceeding, became almost as habitual as any divergence of opinion. Impeachments also seemed obsolete because the main reason for why they

[93] Roberts (1966), pp. 263; 401 ff.

[94] Roberts (1966), pp. 414–416. The twelve peers were created but were not necessary for the approval of the treaty, which passed with a majority of thirteen votes. Regarding the suspicion, it is nowadays known to be true by correspondence recovered by historians, but at the time it was only an unsubstantiated rumour.

[95] Roberts (1966), pp. 416 ff.

were so common in the English parliamentary praxis was already achieved. No Monarch or Minister dared to ignore the counsels of the Parliaments or their prerogatives anymore. The fact that Harley sought parliamentary approval for the Treaty of Utrecht was by itself a concrete proof of the consolidation of the paradigm. Ministries were composed of men that could effectively manage and communicate with the Parliament. When their actions could lead to impeachment, they would exercise self-restraint or resign, thus conforming to the wishes of the Parliament.

The last nail in the coffin of the English parliamentary impeachment came when it became unnecessary to deal with treason. Remonstrances asking for a dismissal required much less investment in effort and time to produce evidence and conduct trial. For this reason, they had become much more common and, since Anne and William III had been so respectful of Parliament, also effective. However, since the decision did not lie completely within the Parliament's grasp, impeachments did not become completely negligible, as the King maintained leeway to shield his favourites otherwise. Only with George I's ascension, in 1718, and his decision of withdrawing from the Cabinet and leaving his Ministers entirely answerable to the nation, is that impeachments became neglectable.[96] Impeachments then were reserved for criminal cases of high officers and, in less than one century hereafter, impeachments disappeared completely, the last one being in 1806.[97]

Though the impeachment ultimately failed in building a responsible government by itself, its unique contribution should not be understated or overlooked. Its use was fundamental alongside the parliamentary 'power of the purse' to condition the King and his Ministry to accommodate the interests of the nation represented through the Parliament. The impeachment ultimately came to be too inadequate to reach the designs the Commons had set for it, as the general standards for its success were being progressively set higher by the Lords or undermined by limited information. The inflexibility and ruthlessness of the instrument and its practical difficulties were simply too much to serve the balance of power. As new and more appropriate means of warranting such balance came into place (addresses and remonstrances), much more natural to a political landscape ruled by parties and national interests, impeachments aptly fell into desuetude, but not without leaving behind a strong Parliament whose opinion any government had to remain mindful of.

[96] Roberts (1966), p. 426.

[97] Caird (2016), p. 7. Multiple Select Committees on Parliamentary Privilege have since 1967 recommended that impeachments be formally abandoned via legislation as they considered the procedure incompatible with modern standards of due process and fairness. This is mainly due to criminal nature of English impeachments and the lack of democratic legitimation of the Lords, as is noted in the parliamentary briefing of 2016 (pp. 7–8).

2.1.6 Excursus*: Deposition of Monarchs*

Before tackling the American impeachment, one last question should be addressed: What about the deposition of Kings? How comparable are they to impeachments? One might perhaps feel inclined into seeing similarities between the modern impeachment and these other often bloody practices, at least in the sense that they both may target the chief of executive and that they were sometimes associated with the summoning of Parliaments.

A closer look will reveal, however, why historians resist portraying such procedures as any sort of parliamentary activity at all. Edward Miller, for example, would rather describe the attempt to summon a Parliament in such arbitrary contexts as "a nervous desire to spread responsibility as widely as possible for an act which had no justification in any past precedent".[98] Edward II's deposition in 1326 is emblematic in this sense, for these 'procedures' were largely military operations orchestrated by Barons and which a 'Parliament', also ordered by them, would then give some sort of authorization to declare Edward unfit to rule, without an opportunity for a formal judgment. The lack of records of these procedures suggests that the very assemblies conducting the procedures doubted their own parliamentary nature. The same can be said of the leaders of the rebellion, who refused to concede any responsibility for these acts upon the Parliament.[99] The same conclusions may be extended with minor reservations to the deposition of Richard II in 1399[100] or Charles I in 1649.

Elsewhere in Europe where depositions were not based on sheer, ruthless violence, as was the case of the Holy Roman Empire, for example, deposals could be led by a council of Prince-Electors. This was the case in the deposals of the Monarchs Adolf of Nassau (1298), Louis IV (1346), Wenceslaus IV (1400) and the attempt against Frederick III (1456).[101] So the deposition would be considered legitimate, the council of Prince-Electors had to divest the Monarch of his kingship either through a litigious procedure, in case of bribery during the election procedures, appropriation of imperial fief and other limited legal infractions; or through an unilateral declaration, in case of a papal excommunication, in which case the referred Monarch lost one of requirements of eligibility, the blessing of the Catholic Church. This kind of accountability was recognized by the Golden Bull of 1356 (Chap. 5, § 2), but was practically ineffective due to its redaction, which required the King to be present at the trial for it to be valid. As such, the King's mere default could render himself unaccountable.[102] These cases come closer to the idea of an impeachment as a litigious, procedural instrument for change in the government, but still seem insufficient in terms of content to be considered comparable. An incredibly broad

---

[98] Miller (1970), pp. 11–12.

[99] Wilkinson (1970), pp. 337 ff.

[100] Wilkinson (1970), pp. 346–349.

[101] Steinbarth (2011), pp. 33–35; Weizsäcker (1886), pp. 61 ff.; 43 ff.; 76 ff.

[102] Steinbarth (2011), pp. 28–31.

array of criminally and politically irresponsible conducts are still unaccounted for, and the underlying legitimation of the deposition procedure is essentially unrelated to the idea of popular sovereignty, both in terms of the composition of the Council of Prince-Electors, as well as the ideals protected under the few 'deposable' conducts, which basically entailed only electoral integrity and feudal property rights.

2.1.7 Impeachment in American Colonial History

Stories about the highest-ranking officers of the realm being brought to justice by the vote of knights and burgesses[103] carried a special significance to colonial Parliaments and other men who were so far from the source of royal power. Eager to provide safety for their communities and advance their own political projects, many of these men applied and incorporated the power of impeachment into their provisions, such as in the Pennsylvania Charter of 1682 or in the Massachusetts judicial code of 1684. Both were deemed unjustifiable by British authorities. From their perspective, American states were no better than an English borough and had, therefore, the same right to impeach a royal officer as the Council of London had to impeach the Lord Chancellor: *none*. Most legal documents regarding impeachment were dismissed by Crown officials and attempts at interfering in government were only met with growing recalcitrance. The single best weapon left in the armoury of the colonial lower houses was an address, appeal or petition to the Governor and his Council, who, with the King's consent and under the authority of the Crown, could dismiss the accused official. Such an alternative was obviously underwhelming, given that the interests of the local populaces and the Crown were often at odds.[104]

The English Parliaments dedicated a good deal of time and effort into perfecting their leverages and establishing a parliamentary culture to turn impeachments and the Parliament's opinion into something the government and the Crown would reckon with. It would be naïve to expect something different under colonial settings. It took the American impeachment circa 138 years to fully mature, from its first case, the impeachment against Royal Governor John Harvey of Virginia, to the last, against Chief Justice Peter Oliver of Massachusetts. This period could be divided in three phases: a phase of weak and blunt *criminal impeachments* (1635–1699), a phase of even weaker, but considerably more pretentious *provincial impeachments* (1701–1755), in which a theory of impeachment would slowly appear claiming its own sovereignty by challenging the imperial shackles of English precedent; and,

[103] Colonial knowledge of impeachments was limited. Only the word of mouth and a few books/pamphlets with brief mentions on impeachments were available, such as John Rushworth's (1659, 8 volumes) *Historical Collections* (a selection of parliamentary and royal documents), John Selden's (1681) *Of the Judicature in Parliaments* and Sir Matthew Hale's (1713) *History of the Common Laws*. Hoffer and Hull (1984), p. 10.

[104] Hoffer and Hull (1984), pp. 9–11.

finally, a phase of *revolutionary impeachments* (1756–1776), in which such sovereignty was authoritatively ascertained, in parallel to the rise of the American republican thought.[105]

Much like its Stuart era counterpart, the American impeachment was initially a sort of complaint. In the case against Governor Harvey (1635), for example, he was accused of series of crimes against public interest in the General Assembly of Virginia (a unicameral legislature until 1643), the burgesses sitting for the counties framed the charges and these were then trialled by the council of Virginia in James City. In fear of displeasing the Crown, no punishment other than loss of office was applied and Harvey was sent to England with the articles of accusation to Charles I's Privy Council. The Council, on its turn, refused to recognize the self-proclaimed powers of the General Assembly of Virginia and returned Harvey to his office in Virginia. The Virginians still lacked a sense of popular sovereignty and the leverages to ascertain the right of self-determination entailed by it, unlike the English, who on their turn had the 'ancient law of the land' and the power of the purse to challenge the Crown's *de jure* and *de facto* powers. Discouragingly, the Virginians laid precariously in the 'ancient domain' of the Crown, with a government by the King's grant and lands in his gift.[106]

Colonial assemblies often tried to circumvent their lack of authority over the enforcement of impeachment convictions by either delegating the final decision to England, by ascribing the jurisdiction for such cases to the provincial courts or a higher executive authority, or by asking the lower house to pass a bill of attainder.[107] The savagery of attainder was systematically refused by the lower houses and no criminal punishment was forced upon the defendants, despite the charges being eminently of criminal nature. In Pennsylvania, where impeachment happened to be legally established, there was a slight shift in this pattern. In the impeachment of Chief Justice Nicholas More (1684), in the context of ten criminal abuses of office, the assembly's prosecutor accused him of a general disregard for his duties. The assembly ultimately failed to enforce any form of punishment, but a tendency to reprehend more 'politicized' crimes and official irresponsibility began to develop.[108]

With the Glorious Revolution and William III's ascension (1689), the reorganization of the colonial offices became a priority. Colonial laws were revised over and over until they met the Crown's approval, providing them with a more provincial aspect. As impeachments were known to be a sworn enemy of autocratic and imperial designs, the few existing legal provisions were inevitably suppressed and its praxis harshly reprehended. In 1691 the legislature from Massachusetts (the General Court) lost its right to impeach and completely surrendered its criminal

[105] Hoffer and Hull (1984), p. 14.

[106] Hoffer and Hull (1984), pp. 15–16.

[107] Examples of these cases being, respectively, William Harris' impeachment in Rhode Island (1657); John Morecroft (1669) of Maryland; and Thomas Trueman (1676) and Jacob Young (1681), both from Maryland.

[108] Hoffer and Hull (1984), pp. 17–26.

jurisdiction to a separate court system. In 1707 the Governor of Pennsylvania John Evans and his Council refused to play to role of the House of Lords and requested the Assembly to stop its impeachment proceedings in respect to English precedent and proceed through complaints. In the Carolinas, overbearing officials came close to being ousted, if were not for the last-minute influence of England or the proprietors.[109]

Most impeachments ended up frustrated in reverence or submission to the imperial power, but they also inadvertently introduced a bit of substance to a theory and idea of a colonial constitution, resulting from an odd mix of circumstances, much like in the first introduction of impeachments during Edward III's reign. The lower house of Massachusetts, for example, was able to hold impeachment trials against four traders in 1706, despite having formally surrendered its jurisdiction. This was possible because the Governor was involved in illegal trading with France and wished that the case stayed away from the Superior Court, where the traders would be pressured to reveal his involvement under the much harsher trial for treason. Only after the Governor himself came to be under the threat of impeachment, did he challenge the lower house's power of impeachment. Though Massachusetts eventually lost this battle, it influenced the Assembly of Pennsylvania. The Assembly claimed that if one colony was able to impeach, so should others also be able, as an inherent right of colonial lower houses.[110]

In the revolutionary era, on the other hand, such confrontations made no pretence of concealing intentions. The Assembly of Pennsylvania, for example, had no problem in stating to its Lieutenant Governor William Denny that its right to impeach a county judge was "incontestably in the Assembly, by the Charter of Privileges, and an established Law of the Province" and that if any attempt to circumvent such right would be "an innovation in the Constitution, as it would be erecting a new Court of Judicature, unknown in the Government before". When Denny, like his predecessor, adopted the idea that his council could not act in the role of the House of Lords, the Assembly lashed on the recurrent behaviour of the proprietors which kept 'the Rights of the People in perpetual jeopardy' by 'arbitrary and unjust invasion', which remained enabled by the lack of a check such as that of the impeachment. In Massachusetts, impeachment became the sword hanging over the necks of officials caught in the power struggle between rebellious assemblies and the proprietors, in which those involved were expected to pledge allegiance to either side, the 'Inhabitants of the American Colonies' or the imperial power. The Governor of Massachusetts was pressured by his own Council to recognize the parliamentary power of impeachment, for such denial had "an unhappy tendency to encourage

[109] Hoffer and Hull (1984), pp. 27–38. There are only four cases of impeachment in this era. Trader Samuel Vetch and his cohorts (1706, Massachusetts; these proceedings were indirectly aimed at uncovering Governor Joseph Dudley's participation at the illegal trade scheme with France), Counsellor James Logan (1707, Pennsylvania), Chief Justice Nicholas Trott (1707, South Carolina) and Chief Justice William Smith (1739, North Carolina).

[110] Hoffer and Hull (1984), pp. 28–40.

the executive officers of the government to deviations from their duty" and were "incompatible with the safety and happiness of the people".[111]

These impeachments may have been frustrated or reverted, but in the court of public opinion they were effective in putting the royal government into question. Particularly in Massachusetts, the impeachment crisis escalated to a deadlock that had to be resolved by proroguing the General Court, leaving the government weakened and incapable of effectively dealing with riots, among them most notably the Boston Tea Party. The Crown overreacted to this crisis of governability reinstating nearly dictatorial powers to the local government, which, in its turn, also generated severe responses from Parliament and set off protest in the other colonies. Local conditions and several other long-standing controversies would be the leading causes behind the American Revolution, but the experiences and the ideas underlying impeachments remained fresh much after its end.[112]

2.1.8 Impeachment in the First Decade of Independence

On the 4th of July of 1776 the American states finally claimed their independence from the British Empire, rejecting the royal rule and constituting autonomous republican governments. While the framing of a federal constitution would still take another ten years, the states could risk experimenting with their legal and political theories. Impeachment provisions were inserted in the constitutions of Pennsylvania, Massachusetts, New Jersey, Delaware, New York, North Carolina, Virginia, and Vermont; some of them, in much different terms than their English predecessor. Pennsylvania and Vermont, for example, considered "every officer of the state" impeachable, in case he or she incurred in the broad concept of "maladministration"; "punishments" were indicated as consequence, but not individually specified; trial rested upon the president and an executive council advised by the state supreme court. Both constitutions created a "Council of Censors" to inquire into the administrative activity, with power to order impeachment. Most other states also had broad definitions of impeachable offenses, targeting corruption and maladministration. New York and New Jersey, for example, adopted even broader definitions, impeaching for "misbehaviour" (NJ) and for "mal and corrupt conduct" (NY). Delaware, on the other hand, was much more specific, defining them as "offending against the state by maladministration, corruption or other means, by which the safety of the commonwealth may be endangered".[113] Virginia introduce a middle-

[111] The main cases of this period are the impeachments against County Judge William Moore (1757, Pennsylvania) and Chief Justice Peter Oliver (1773, Massachusetts); the near impeachments of Chief Justice Charles Shinner (1767, South Carolina) and Treasurer Stephen Skinner (1770–4, New Jersey) also displayed some of these characteristics. Hoffer and Hull (1984), pp. 41–55.

[112] Hoffer and Hull (1984), p. 56.

[113] An interesting aspect about Delaware is that its Constitution considered officials impeachable even up to eighteen months after leaving office (penalty of disqualification).

term between both, requiring that such offenses be against the state, the public trust or the office, and also not just be any common-law crime, but in form of corruption, maladministration or 'other means'. Regarding trials, New York, North Carolina, and Virginia had unique arrangements: the first established a special court for hearing impeachments, composed of the president of the Senate, the Senators, the Chancellor, and the Supreme Court bench; the last two delegated the function to the Supreme Court.[114]

All this goes to say that by the time the Framers would start their discussions on the federal constitution, they had developed their own understanding of impeachments working on the drafts of the state constitutions and exchanging of letters on the topic over a decade. While it is true that they were influenced by English experience, they might not have been as 'steeped in English history' as some classical manuscripts on impeachments make them out to be, at least to what pertains the history and practice of English impeachments.[115] The republican adaption of impeachments shared many of the underlying principles of English impeachments, but it was also a genuinely American invention on its own merit. As it will be stressed in the following section, the opinions, and propositions of many Framers on impeachment often reflected their previous experiences and their original thought on what a well-balanced separation of powers looked like.

2.1.9 Excursus: *Impeachment in Colonial Latin America?*

Viceroys (comparable to the English Proprietors), Governors, Mayors and other government authorities also had their offices threatened in Latin America during its colonial period (approx. 1490s to early 1800s), likewise by means of a legalistic procedure known as *juício de residencia* (lit. trans., trial of residence). Because of this, it is not rare to find in Latin American literature references to these procedures as a sort of precursor to modern day presidential impeachments of the region.[116] While there are some similitudes between these procedures, there are some major differences between the instrument of impeachment and of *juício de residencia* that arguably set them decisively apart. It is hard to give a definitive answer on behalf of all Latin America on the topic, however, as there are strong differences between

[114] Hoffer and Hull (1984), pp. 68–70.

[115] Berger (1974), pp. 4 ff., 56–107; Rodino (1974) and many others, usually in the attempt of restoring the meaning of "high crimes and misdemeanors", tend to overstate the Framers' knowledge of English impeachments. Neither the actual references mentioned in the discussions, nor the literary sources of the time, books, collection of documents and pamphlets, which were relatively scarce and limited in scope, seem to truly allow for such a conclusion. It seems more sensible to assume that the framework adopted for actual impeachments was based on the closely lived experiences of colonial and post-independence times. For more insight into this matter: Roberts (1975), pp. 1427 ff.; Bowman and Sepinuck (1999), pp. 1525 ff.; Hoffer and Hull (1984), p. 10.

[116] *E.g.*, Eguiguren Praeli (2008), Smietniansky (2007), Gutiérrez Mendoza (2014), to name a few.

some of the countries, some having assumed sharper anti-Spanish or pro-American attitudes in their constitutionalization processes than others.[117] So, what is the trial of residence exactly, and why is it fundamentally different than the kind of impeachment this study is dealing with?

The trial of residence was a procedure applied to public officials and their family members at the end of their mandate, obliging them to reside in the place of their jurisdiction while being questioned and investigated on the practice of their duties. If evidence of misconduct was found, this would be taken to trial in an *ad hoc* court of law and a conviction could lead to the consequences of removal, disqualification, damages, forfeiture and, in extreme cases, criminal punishments. These trials were practiced for over three centuries, starting in June of 1500, extending itself to the entirety of Crown of Castile's (and from 1715 on, Spain's) territory and its colonies. Its rationalization was like that of impeachments, as jurists of the time affirmed in its defence that, for example, "nobody is entirely fair, nor perfect; those who have ample powers, will presumably commit excesses due to ambition and greed", acknowledging the inherent dangers of power and the need for accountability.[118]

Differently from impeachment, however, responsible government, balance of powers and subjection of the powerful to the law were only by-products of an arguably more pressing concern, that is, safeguarding of the Crown's economic interests, which were truly made vulnerable to corruption and abuse by virtue of the vast extension of the regal territories. Surely citizens could feel heard when the Crown acted upon their complaints and held pernicious officers accountable, but for all intents and purposes this form of control was exercised by courts subordinate to the Crown and its wishes, likely being yet another historical 'Child of Monarchy'. As the legal historian José Garcia Marín notices, the trial of residence was to

> consolidate a regime of civil servants as an instrument of regal strengthening and political and administrative centralization. On the other hand, and more theoretically than effectively, it served as means through which citizens could voice their complaints and grievances against the acts of authorities which harmed their interests.[119]

Because of this difference, the trial of residence did not put as emphasis in exemplary punishment as the English impeachment and, instead, focused on recovering damages, making even the families of a *residenciado* (person undergoing a trial of residence) simultaneously accountable in case he or she could not repay for the damages or fines (possibly in attempts to hide property), which tended to be the main form of punishment. Additionally, the judges of residence were not elected or thought to be representative in any way but were handpicked by the Monarch or

[117] Eguiguren Praeli (2008), p. 114. It should be added, moreover, that *caudillos* (see next Chapter) had low tolerance for accountability mechanisms and may have contributed to its extinction in the post-colonial era.

[118] Author's translation of Collantes (1998), pp. 151–152. Pecuniary compensations were usually preferred in lieu of criminal punishments. Prison was considered only in case of capital crimes or lack of finances.

[119] Collantes (1998), p. 153 (Author's translation); Smietniansky (2007), p. 73.

the Council of Indies to serve their interests. In fact, a requisite of being a judge of this kind was to be neither natural nor neighbour of the jurisdiction in question, effectively excluding any potential claim to representativity in favour of an ideal of impartiality. In the exceptional occasion that conviction entailed a harsher punishment, such as dismemberment or death, or in case the *residenciado* appealed the sentence, the judge of residence had to leave the final decision to the Monarch and his Council. A lot of documental evidence was expected from the *residenciados*, usually tax, accounting and privilege related, so at least in this sense authorities were placed under exhaustive oversight. The determinants for conviction sounded very familiar to those of impeachment, as according to Garcia Marín, they would succeed if they detected "professional immorality, economic immorality, negligence of office and abandonment of functions, disobedience and offense of the King, falsity or treason, and breach of the duty to professional secrecy".[120]

The number of cases of these sorts of trials is impressive,[121] as nearly every Viceroy and Governor answered to them at some point, either in person during their lives or represented by their successors, after their death. The impressiveness of their numbers and reach, however, was not matched by the trials' effectiveness, as the literature seems to unanimously point out that only few and far between were truly made accountable and, when done so, only to paid small amounts of money back to the Crown. It did nonetheless promote responsible government to a limited extent, as the trial of residence was expected by any incumbent and having a trial that led to local commotion was frowned upon. Moreover, the 'rituals' stablished by these trials in some of its phases ensured the public felt heard and part of the political life of their governments, thus contributing to the Monarch's legitimacy and to the instilling of a sense of official preoccupation with responsible government.[122]

As decades passed without yielding significant results, the obsolescence of this control mechanism became inevitable. As it turned out, these trials became a purpose in themselves, often turning into long, drawn out *pro forma* solemnities whose only reason of existence was seemingly to provide the judge of residence with a source of revenue.[123]

A more proper form of control was instituted by the Constitution of Cádiz in 1812, as it truly instituted constitutional government, subjecting even the King's will to the letter of the law. This Constitution was modelled after the British experience and brought with it the *juicio politico* (lit. trans., political trial; currently one of the official names given to impeachment in many Spanish speaking countries), a more suitable candidate for the title of Latin America's prototypical presidential

[120] Collantes (1998), pp. 154–179.

[121] For a comprehensive overview, see Mariluz Urquijo (1952).

[122] Herzog (2005), pp. 30–31; Mariluz Urquijo (1952), pp. 283–296; Smietniansky (2007), pp. 75, 92–96; Collantes (1998), pp. 182–184. The trial had two phases, one secret and one public. In the secret phase, evidence was gathered and analyzed. On the public phase, charges were announced and an opportunity for raising further complaints and grievances against the administration of the *residenciado* was given.

[123] Collantes (1998).

impeachment. It should be noted, however, that the Constitution of Cádiz was removed shortly thereafter, in 1814, being ineffective as the rule in colonial Latin America. By 1820, moreover, most colonies would have claimed their independence and given start to their own constitutional history, one that was inspired both in the Constitution of Cádiz, but also in the American Revolution.[124]

2.1.10 *Framing of the Presidential Impeachment in the Constitution of the United States*

The Constitution of the United States was discussed and drafted between May 25th and September 17th of 1787, when it was signed and then sent to the thirteen states for ratification. To ensure the ratification by most states and to answer objections raised by those who opposed the final draft (later known as the '*Anti-Federalists*'), Alexander Hamilton, James Madison and John Jay collaborated to publish a series of newspaper articles in its defence. The 85 articles came to be known as *The Federalist Papers* and were fundamental to the ratification of the Constitution in some states believed hotbeds for Anti-Federalist thought, such as New York. In both opportunities impeachment was framed as a centrepiece to the establishment of a republican government and to the justification of the concentration of power in the executive, which would otherwise consist, as the opposition argued, in a wholesale departure from the revolutionary ideals.[125] But which were these ideals and why would impeachment be so significant in this new context? Was impeachment still needed?

In various senses republicanism was thought of as the negation of aspects of the monarchy despised by American revolutionaries.[126] It was the rejection of a state grounded on blood, family, kinship, patronage, and fear; the rejection of a system of dependency and subservience that often-tolerated degrees of self-interestedness, private gratification, and corruption. If anything, American republicanism idealized a system sustained by the citizens' voluntary patriotism and willingness to abide to public authority; it bred the virtues of prudence, frugality, industry, and devotion to the commonweal.[127]

As much as possible nonetheless, the founding fathers sought to find a balance between the optimism of revolutionary idealism and the harsh realities of new republics and human nature. Benjamin Franklin, for example, reminded that the

---

[124] Gutiérrez Mendoza (2014), pp. 279 ff; Mirow (2015), pp. 40–41.

[125] Sunstein (2017), pp. 54–55.

[126] The new Constitution would not focus only on revolutionary values, however. It was also meant to fill the voids left unaddressed by the Confederation. Governor Randolph summarized these as follows: "1st. It [The Confederation] does not provide against foreign invasions. 2nd. It does not secure harmony to the States. 3rd. It is incapable of producing certain blessings to the States. 4th. It cannot defend itself against encroachments. 5th. It is not superior to State constitutions". Max Farrand (1911b), p. 24.

[127] Wood (1992), pp. 104–105.

frugality and grandiose aspirations presupposed by republican thought did not exactly go hand in hand, for "ambition and avarice are springs of action so utterly opposite, that they never did or ever will unite in the same person";[128] Thomas Jefferson was also sceptic towards what could be achieved solely on mutual trust and argued that "free government is founded in jealousy and not in confidence; it is jealousy and not confidence which prescribes limited constitutions, to bind down those whom we are obliged to trust with power (. . .)".[129]

A robust system of checks and balances were to be, therefore, a fundamental part of the new constitution. The answer as to why *impeachment* specifically and not, for example, votes of censure, votes of no confidence or ordinary judicature, however, comes from a series of compromises between federalist and anti-federalist currents, and, again, between idealism and pragmatism. Balancing an independent, diligent, and responsible executive with the principle of separation of powers was an enormous challenge. The new government had to be energic and effective and yet always remain mindful and reasonable; had to be made accountable and yet not become a creature of its controller; needed to be given autonomy and yet not be permitted to do whatever it pleased. More than just means to accountability of high officers, the Framers found in the impeachment a mechanism that enabled strong government while keeping the maladies of monarchy in check. To better understand this, it is important to notice how the debate on impeachments in the Constitutional Convention were always linked with plans on the structure of the executive power and its balance in face of the judicature and the legislature.

The base framework for the new Constitution was drafted by James Madison; Madison was the first delegate to arrive for the Constitutional Convention in Philadelphia and had around ten days to draft his ideas on state and government before enough delegates arrived and the quorum to assemble was achieved, on May 25th, 1787. His plan came to be known as the Virginia Plan and, on May 29th, was formally proposed by Virginia's Governor, Edmund Randolph. Along its fifteen propositions, it established the national executive would be chosen by the legislature on a fixed term without possibility of re-election and that the judiciary would have jurisdiction over impeachments of 'any national officers', among other things.[130]

The first concerns regarding impeachments appeared three days later, on June 1st, when the committee agreed on a fixed term of seven years for the executive government. Gunning Bedford opposed the seven-year term believing it to be too long and uncapable of addressing situations such as the case of supervening incapacity or a mistake in judgement about the Chief(s) of Government's qualifications to assume the role of first magistrate. Such situations could not be properly addressed by impeachments, nor by fixed terms, especially when so lengthy. Roger Sherman's proposition of displacement left to the pleasure of the national legislature was

[128] Wood (1992), p. 108.

[129] Thomas Jefferson's "*Draft of the Kentucky Resolutions*" (1788) *apud* Hoffer and Hull (1984), p. 111.

[130] Farrand (1911b), pp. 16, 20–22 (Virginia resolutions).

dismissed by George Mason, who believed it would turn the executive into "the mere creature of the Legislature" and would be a "violation of the fundamental principle of good government", although he recognized that "some mode of displacing an unfit magistrate is rendered indispensable by the fallibility of those who choose, as well as by the corruptibility of the man chosen". Madison and James Wilson concurred, imagining ease of displacement could turn to intrigue in states where the administration was unpopular, which could then lead to the temptation of engaging in factional collusion as to topple a majority government. The proposition was convincingly rejected, but no alternative was put in its place. Without further debate, the dispositions were altered to consider the chief magistrate "be removable on impeachment and conviction of mal-practice or neglect of duty", as proposed by Hugh Williamson.[131]

With these initial amendments, the Virginia Plan was ready to be taken to deliberation; the section on impeachment, however, would only be rediscussed a month and a half later, between July 17th and 20th. Gouverneur Morris of Pennsylvania started by questioning the indirect elections as foreseen in the Virginia Plan. Morris claimed the legislature should not both be responsible for the executive's appointment and impeachment, as this would, again, reduce the executive to 'the mere creature' of the Legislature. Morris had a very high opinion of those who would be directly elected by the people: "If the people should elect, they will never fail to prefer some man of distinguished character, or of services; some man (...) of continental reputation. If the Legislature elects, it will be the work of intrigue, of cabal, and of faction: (...) real merit will rarely be the title to the appointment". Despite these remarks, the indirect election and the seven-year-term were retained. Thanks to Morris, the possibility of re-election was inserted, as he argued that ineligibility "tended to destroy the great motive to good behaviour, the hope of being reward by a re-appointment".[132]

The argument of good behaviour proved seductive and was further enhanced by other delegates. James McClurg moved to strike out the seven-year-term, exchanging it for a term "during good behaviour", which was approved by many as measure of 'good government'. Madison strongly contended that such solution could turn the Executive connivant to tyrannical laws made by the Legislature, as observed by Montesquieu. Madison was equally sceptical of the practicability of impeachments in courts of law. Sherman argued that good behaviour would already be rewarded with re-elections as far as necessary, and that such tenure would be pointless. To

[131] Farrand (1911b), pp. 63–74 (Bedford, Sherman, Mason), 85–86 (Madison, Wilson, Mason), 88 (impeachment).

[132] Farrand (1911a), pp. 29–31 (elections); 33 (re-election). Morris was entirely alone in defence of direct elections. Roger Sherman summarized the general feeling of the Framers at this point: "the Nation would be better expressed by the Legislature, than by the people at large. The latter will never be sufficiently informed of characters, and besides will never give a majority of votes to any one man. They will generally vote for some man in their own State, and the largest State will have the best chance for the appointment"; George Mason, in his characteristic bluntness, equated direct elections to "a trial of colors to a blind man".

effectively put this matter to rest, Mason considered "an Executive during good behaviour as a softer name only for an Executive for life" and "the next would be an easy step to hereditary Monarchy". Most Framers could not bear the thought of being associated in any form with the shadows of monarchy and the motion was negated.[133]

In the following days, Morris kept being the impeachment's greatest opponent: "This [the impeachable Executive] is a dangerous part of the plan. It will hold him in such dependence that he will be no check on the Legislature, will not be a firm guardian of the people and of the public interest. He will be the tool of a faction, of some leading demagogue in the Legislature". Morris clearly saw in limited terms an elegant solution, a key to a truly unlock a clear-cut separation of powers. He proposed terms be reduced to only two years, without the possibility of impeachment. Such arrangements could ensure good government was kept in place for as long as it could prove itself, while at the same time shielding it from a mischievous Legislature. Additionally, irresponsible government would not prosper for too long, for it would not be re-elected. The other delegates were sceptical, however. They believed the Legislature could still influence elections with momentary lies to which incipient administrations could be particularly vulnerable, equally defeating good governments and generating a subservient Executive.[134]

Morris saw no such risks and, with Charles Pinkney's support, moved to strike out impeachment from the draft; Pinkney suggested impeachment should at least not be possible *whilst* in office.[135] William Davie added a new twist to the Framer's high opinion of re-elections and considered that an overbearing chief magistrate would "spare no efforts or means whatever to get himself re-elected". In other words, impeachments were not really made obsolete by frequent elections and still were "an essential security for the good behaviour of the Executive". Morris could not foresee how much clientelism and patronage would become transforming elements of republicanism as they had been for the English monarchy and duly believed that "in case he [the Chief Magistrate] be re-elected, that will be sufficient proof of his innocence" and that the accountability of his coadjutors would suffice to cripple his criminal behaviour. Mason may have provided the strongest pro-impeachment arguments simply by reminding the other delegates of the core set of republican values. Mason stated that "no point is of more importance than that the right of impeachment should be continued. Shall any man be above Justice? Above all that man be above it, who can commit the most extensive injustice? When great crimes were committed, he was for punishing the principal as well as the Coadjutors"; Benjamin Franklin, on the other hand, was strikingly pragmatic: "What was the

---

[133] Farrand (1911a), pp. 33–36.

[134] Farrand (1911a), pp. 52–57.

[135] The Constitution of Delaware of 1776 had such provisions: "Art. 23: The president, when he is out of office, and within eighteen months after (...) shall be impeachable by the house of assembly before the legislative council". The same goes for the Constitution of Virginia of 1776 with slightly different language and no prescription period.

practice before this in cases where the chief Magistrate rendered himself obnoxious? Why recourse was had to assassination in which he was not only deprived of his life but of the opportunity of vindicating his character".[136]

Madison summarized all the dangerous scenarios left uncovered by checks based solely on fixed terms (already mentioned June 2nd, *i.e.,* electoral fraud, supervening incapacity, abusiveness, and corruption) and argued the risks of personal corruption of the chief magistrate greatly outweighed the risks of collective corruption of the Legislature:

> It could not be presumed that all or even a majority of the members of an Assembly would either lose their capacity for discharging, or be bribed to betray, their trust. Besides the restraints of their personal integrity and honor, the difficulty of acting in concert for purposes of corruption was a security to the public. And if one or few members only should be seduced, the soundness of the remaining members, would maintain the integrity and fidelity of the body. In the case of the Executive Magistracy which was to be administered by a single man, loss of capacity or corruption was more within the compass of probable events, and either of them might be fatal to the Republic.[137]

Morris finally capitulated: "This Magistrate is not the King but the prime-Minister. The people are the King. When we make him amenable to Justice however we should take care to provide some mode that will not make him dependent on the Legislature". He admitted some acts, as long as well-defined and enumerated, ought to be impeachable.[138]

The delegates had agreed on the necessity of the chief magistrate being impeachable. The true challenge, however, came the next few days, after the Committee on Detail vested the general framework agreed until then with a properly legal, precise language; the language necessary to truly define to what measure and by whose hand should such impeachability be sought.[139] Madison later confessed to Jefferson that these were "among the most puzzling articles of a republican Constitution", proof of which was the 'embarrassing' diversification of "expedients adopted in the

[136] Farrand (1911a), pp. 64–65. Edmund Randolph concurred: "Should no regular punishment be provided, it will be irregularly inflicted by tumults and insurrections" (p. 67). Franklin reminded the other delegates of some treacherous acts of William III and the instability caused his unaccountability. Franklin is referring to the power struggle between Tories and Whigs between 1693 and 1715, which resulted in the rise and fall of the Godolphin-Marlborough and later the Oxford-Bolingbroke Ministries. In detail: Clayton Roberts (1966), pp. 249 ff.

[137] Farrand (1911a), pp. 65–66.

[138] Farrand (1911a), pp. 68–69. Pinkney remained critical of impeachments, as he believed the presidential powers could be so limited as to never truly warrant impeachments against deviations of its use. His state, South Carolina, and Massachusetts were the only to vote in favor of striking out the resolutions.

[139] The Committee was composed of Edmund Randolph, Oliver Ellsworth, James Wilson and Nathaniel Gorham and met between July 26th and August 6th, 1787. Farrand (1911a), p. 106. There is no record of the debates of the Committee, but it clearly took liberties when transposing the main ideas into a legal text. As it may be of notice, much was altered and added before any consideration of the whole Convention.

Constitutions of the several States".[140] The Committee stablished the House of Representatives to have 'the sole power of impeachment', by which the President shall be 'removed from his office on impeachment' and later convicted 'in the supreme Court, of treason, bribery, or corruption'. It also stated that "in cases of Impeachment, [judgement] shall not extend further than to removal from Office, and disqualification to hold and enjoy any office of honour, trust or profit, under the United States", being nevertheless liable to 'indictment, trial, judgment and punishment according to law'.[141]

On August 24th and 27th some of these articles were brought to debate, but little was accomplished as the delegates could not agree on a method of selecting the Executive and, later, on the impropriety of the Supreme Court as a forum for trying the president, for, at this point, the Chief Justice was being considered as a member of the presidential Privy Council. To this and other unresolved matters, as occurred many times before in these proceedings, the Conference elected a committee composed of eleven delegates to address the controversial portions of the draft and so avoid persistent deadlocks.[142]

On September 4th, the Committee presented its partial report, recommending considerable changes. It recommended a four-year term for the President, created the office of the Vice President, and stablished an electoral system carried out by electors appointed by the representation of the states in the federal Legislature. Regarding impeachments, the competence for trial was dislocated from the Supreme Court to the Senate, with a two-thirds vote required for conviction on charges of treason or bribery (corruption was dropped). In addition, the trial should be presided by the Chief Justice in case of presidential impeachments, or by the Vice President otherwise.[143]

Morris justified the choices of the Committee very pragmatically. Differently from its English counterpart, no historical tradition or refined theory of representation was introduced to justify why the lower house should impeach, whereas the higher should trial, and not the other way around or some other alternative; this version of the American impeachment solely sought to achieve an accountable, but independent Executive, hence why impeachment could not be thought of without

---

[140] James Madison (1952), commenting Jefferson's draft of the Constitution of Virginia.

[141] Farrand (1911a), pp. 176–187. Art. IV, §6 (power of impeachment), Art. X, §2 (House of Representatives and Supreme Court) and Art. XI, §5 (consequences), respectively. Art. X, §2 denies presidential pardons against impeachment convictions, much like England's Act of Settlement of 1701 (Section III). While the records of the Federal Convention provide no discussion on the topic, Mason clarified in the ratifying convention of Virginia the need of such provision: "[The President] may frequently pardon crimes which were advised by himself. It may happen (...) that he will establish a monarchy and destroy the republic. If he has the power of granting pardons before indictment, or conviction, may he not stop inquiry and prevent detection?". Elliot (1836c), p. 497.

[142] Farrand (1911a), pp. 401–404 (elections), 427–431 (Supreme Court and postponement), 473 (appointment of the Committee). In this opportunity, the Committee of Eleven was composed of Madison, Morris, Sherman, Gilman, King, Brearley, Dickinson, Carrol, Butler, Williamson, and Baldwin.

[143] Farrand (1911a), pp. 496–499. The Vice President was to preside the Senate *ex officio*.

electoral considerations, for example. He listed the compromises and cautions as the Committee perceived them:

> The 1st. was the danger of intrigue and faction if the appointment should be made by the Legislature. 2nd the inconveniency of an ineligibility required by that mode in order to lessen its evils. 3rd the difficulty of establishing a Court of Impeachments, other than the Senate which would not be so proper for the trial nor the other branch for the impeachment of the President, if appointed by the Legislature. 4th no body had appeared to be satisfied with an appointment by the Legislature. 5th many were anxious even for an immediate choice by the people. 6th the indispensable necessity of making the Executive independent of the Legislature.[144]

With this electoral plan, the same organ to appoint the President would not be the same organ to try him in case of impeachment. The President would not depend on the Senate for re-appointment and would thus be less like to become co-dependent. Morris also considered the plan able to significantly reduce the dangers of 'cabal and corruption'. The form of choosing the Executive and the concentration of power in the Senate, however, remained divisive factors, accused of having an aristocratic complexion; some argued they should first define the extent of the presidential powers before deciding on the impeachment clause. As a result, details on impeachment were only brought back to discussion a few days later, on September 8th.[145]

The scope of impeachable conduct was considered only very briefly. Mason opposed the current state which restricted impeachments to treason and bribery, arguing it would not reach many serious and dangerous offenses, and exemplified the situation with the impeachment of Warren Hastings.[146] He proposed to add 'maladministration' to the list of impeachable offenses and was met with resistance from Morris and Madison; the former believed the addition had already been made obsolete by fixed terms, the latter believed the terminology equated to a tenure to the pleasure of the Senate. Mason withdrew his proposal and substituted it for "other high crimes and misdemeanours against the State", a terminology that had become usual in England after Sir Edward Hebert's impeachment in 1642 but was also far from being unambiguous. Without any further (recorded) debate, the motion was approved with 8 against 3 votes.[147]

---

[144] Farrand (1911a), p. 500.

[145] Farrand (1911a), pp. 500–550.

[146] Hastings was impeached as Governor-General of India, for a series of charges related to abuse of power, which Edmund Burke, the case's manager, introduced under the general title of 'high crimes and misdemeanours'. Madison's notes of the Convention indicate that Mason mentioned the Hastings' case, but do not reveal how extensively it was discussed. In retrospect, it seems possible that the case was indeed largely discussed, hence the choice for the phraseology 'high crimes and misdemeanours' being later accepted without (recorded) opposition. The Hastings case in detail: Carnall and Nicholson (1989).

[147] Farrand (1911a), p. 550. Most sources on impeachment history attribute the terminology to Earl of Suffolk's or Duke of Suffolk's impeachment in 1386 and in 1450, respectively, being misled by John Hatsell's and T.B. Howell's classical accounts on the cases. The case is, however, that the phraseology used strongly varied until 1642. It is also worth noticing that very few impeachments based on 'high crimes and misdemeanours' led to convictions by the House of Lords, who strongly

Regarding the Senate as the Court of Impeachments, the delegates considered it the lesser of evils. While they considered that the President could end up impeached for whatever the Senate believed a misdemeanour and so rendering him improperly dependent, the Supreme Court were too few in numbers and appointed by the defendant himself, facilitating both corruption and collusion. Pinkney saw in the Senate the risk of turning impeachments into a weapon of faction, in case he opposed a favourite law; Hugh Williamson, on the other hand, considered the Senate's leniency towards presidential misconduct more likely than any form of overbearing rigor. With 9 votes against 2, the Senate was kept as the Court of Impeachments, effectively concluding the topic.[148]

2.1.11 Reception and Quarrels of the American Impeachment

After the conclusion of the Constitutional Conference, impeachments attracted a lot of attention in different opportunities. The first were during the ratifying conventions in the states (1787–88), where the delegates exchanged a good deal of letters, published articles (*The Federalist Papers*, among them) and debated profusely in the Assemblies themselves. Another six opportunities were the high-profile impeachments of Chief Justice Samuel Chase (1804), President Andrew Johnson (1867–68), President Richard Nixon (1974), President Bill Clinton (1998–99), and President Donald Trump (2017–18 and 2021).[149] In the first of these, the relations between Parliament and Executive are the main object of criticism; in the remaining opportunities, the problems of legality and proportionality of impeachment charges, which also were no strangers to English lawyers.

---

opposed the broad interpretation the House of Commons gave to the impeachable offenses. Most of these convictions happened either in the exceptionalism of the transition phase initiated in the 1640s or were carried out against crimes that could have been punished in ordinary courts. The terminology still became known in practice of English impeachments for its threatening power; it could lead to many resignations and dismissals, even when it was known that the accused would end up acquitted by the Lords. Roberts (1975), pp. 1430 ff. and Roberts (1956), *passim*. For a more modern discussion on the topic see: Gerhardt (1999), pp. 609–610.

[148] Farrand (1911a), p. 551. After this, only the portion "against the State" was altered, being changed to "against the United States" and later removed by the Committee on Style on September 12th (pp. 551–552, 612–613).

[149] These are the most outstanding examples, Johnson, Clinton, and Trump for reaching trials and Nixon for the shocking nature of the Watergate affairs. There are many other cases that did not get as much attention from the Press and, consequently, did not kindle nearly as much interest or discussion on impeachments. John Tyler (1843), James Buchanan (1860), Grover Cleveland (1896), Herbert Hoover (1932 and 1933), Ronal Reagan (1983 and 1987) and George Bush (1991) were all targets of impeachment votes; Harry Truman (1952) and George W. Bush (2008) were target of resolutions to establish investigation Committees for the purpose of impeachment. As for impeachment intrigues, not even George Washington was spared. William Perkins (2003), pp. 21–22; H. Res. 1258 and 1345, 110th (George W. Bush); H. Res. 438, 115th and H. Res. 24, 117th (Donald Trump).

Alexander Hamilton was left with the challenge of advocating the impeachment clause to the people of New York, people who were believed to be unconvinced of the whole proposition of the Federalists. Hamilton's defence of the clause goes well beyond the debates of the Convention. He justifies, for example, why the House of Representatives should hold the power of impeaching the President and other civil officers—a matter that had been apparently completely ignored by the delegates and just accepted, arguably as something self-evident. Hamilton justifies the choice as the English once did: "What, it may be asked, is the true spirit of the institution itself? Is it not designed as a method of NATIONAL INQUEST into the conduct of public men? If this be the design of it, who can so properly be the inquisitors for the nation as the representatives of the nation themselves?".[150] The choice for the Senate as the Court of Impeachments is justified, on the other hand, by exclusion:

> Where else, than in the Senate, could have been found a tribunal sufficiently dignified, or sufficiently independent? What other body would be likely to feel confidence enough in its own situation, to preserve, unawed and uninfluenced, the necessary impartiality between individual accused, and the representatives of the people, his accusers?[151]

He proceeds in his exclusion logic by indicating the limitations of the Supreme Court as an alternative:

> (...) it is still more to be doubted, whether they [the Supreme Court] would possess the degree of credit and authority, which might, on certain occasions, be indispensable towards reconciling the people to a decision that should happen to clash with an accusation brought by their immediate representatives. A deficiency in the first, would be fatal to the accused; in the last, dangerous to the public tranquility. (...) The awful discretion which a court of impeachments must necessarily have, to doom to honor or to infamy the most confidential and the most distinguished characters of the community, forbids the commitment of the trust to a small number of persons.[152]

To the nature of the proceedings and its substantiating grounds, Hamilton states: "The subjects of its jurisdiction are those offences which proceed from the misconduct of public men, or, in other words, from the abuse or violation of public trust. They are of a nature which may with peculiar propriety be denominated POLITICAL, as they relate chiefly to injuries done to society itself". Corroborating such ideas, he mentions the impeachment's punishment consists in "a perpetual ostracism from the esteem and confidence, and the honours and emoluments of his country",

---

[150] Hamilton et al. (2001), p. 338. The terminology "Grand Inquest of the Nation" is not discussed in the Convention but is suggested by the Committee of Detail. It comes close to what was used, for example, on Middlesex's (Lionel Cranfield) impeachment, "the Inquisitors General of the Grievances of the Kingdom". Hoffer suggests the terminology comes from one of the few pamphlets available in America, Sir Matthew Hale's (1713) *History of the Common Laws*. Farrand (1911a), p. 154; Tite (1974), pp. 158 ff.; Hoffer and Hull (1984), p. 10.

[151] Hamilton et al. (2001), p. 339.

[152] Hamilton et al. (2001), p. 339. He also excludes possibility of mixing the Senate with the Supreme Court for a series of logistic limitations which come into play specially when one considers the impeachment as foreseen in the Constitution is not limited solely to the President, but potentially all other civil officers (p. 341).

while the criminal consequences should be left to the "ordinary course of law". The environment in which impeachments are carried out and the consequences they entail "can never be tied down by such strict rules [of ordinary courts], either in the delineation of the offense by the prosecutors, or in the construction of it by the judges, as in common cases serve to limit courts in favour of personal security".[153]

Hamilton conceded these arrangements were only 'perhaps the prudent mean' between the myriad of considerations linked with the power of impeachment. Hamilton did not deny impeachment could generate deep divisions in the community, as well as agitate factional struggles in the parties, leading to decisions regulated by comparative partisan strength, rather than real demonstrations of innocence or guilt. He did, however, also believe it was a risk worth taking. Naïve perhaps, but he considered the presidency would be filled exclusively by men with "talents for low intrigue, and the little arts of popularity" and, most importantly, men of ability and virtue, *established in the esteem and confidence of the whole union* and, so, unlikely to put themselves situations warranting of an impeachment.[154]

Many of the delegates in the ratification conventions in the states were convinced by Hamilton's ideas and advocated them; others were strongly critical. James Monroe, in the Virginia Convention, argued the Senate would be too much in conflict of interest to trial a President: "To whom is he responsible? To the Senate, his own council. If he makes a treaty, bartering the interest of the county, by whom is he to be tried? By the very persons who advised him to perpetrate the act. Is this any security?".[155] Luther Martin, speaking to the Maryland House of Delegates, made a similar argument:

> (...) there is little reason to believe that a majority will ever concur in impeaching the President, let his conduct be ever so reprehensible; especially, too, as the final event of that impeachment will depend upon a different body, and the members of the House of Delegates will be certain, should the decision be ultimately in favor of the President, to become thereby the objects of his displeasure, and to bar to themselves every avenue to the emoluments of government.[156]

Luther Martin made, moreover, a visionary argument considering how patronage would affect politics in the coming decades and centuries, not only in the United States:

> (...) will any person conceive it to be difficult for the President always to secure himself more than one third of that body? Or can it reasonably be believed that a criminal will be convicted, who is constitutionally empowered to bribe his judges, at the head of whom is to

[153] Hamilton et al. (2001), pp. 338–340. Some of these arguments were part of Hamilton's exclusion of the Supreme Court as a Court of Impeachments but were gathered in this paragraph for pertaining more objectively to the nature of impeachable offenses.

[154] Hamilton et al. (2001), pp. 338, 354. The confidence of the union, argues Hamilton later in The Federalist n. 70, is subjected to the restraints of public opinion. To this, the public censure, and the possibility of inquiry into the public conduct may be of greater use and significance than the possibility of punishment introduced by the impeachment itself (p. 366).

[155] Elliot (1836c), p. 489.

[156] Elliot (1836b), p. 379.

> preside, on those occasions, the chief justice – which officer, in his original appointment, must be nominated by the President, and will, therefore, probably, be appointed, not so much for his eminence in legal knowledge, and for his integrity, as from favoritism and influence; since the President, knowing that, in case of impeachment, the chief justice is to preside at his trial, will naturally wish to fill that office with a person of whose voice and influence he shall consider himself secure.[157]

Fisher Ames brought attention to other hitherto unconsidered, but fundamental matters. Firstly, in the Massachusetts convention, he criticized the duration of the mandates of those supposed to judge, as the convention was considering reducing from biannual to annual elections. He stated: "One year will not suffice to detect guilt and to pursue conviction; therefore they will escape, and the balance of the two branches will be destroyed, and the people oppressed with impunity. (. . .) Will the people, then, blind the eyes of their own watchmen? Will they bind the hands which are to hold the sword for their defense?".[158] One year and a half later, at the first congressional session in June 1789, he criticized the duration impeachment proceedings could reach, arguing on top of the Hastings' impeachment case that the mechanism was too slow and formal to effectively prevent or, in more extreme cases, even punish mischiefs. At this point the Hastings' affairs in Britain had been dragging for years and was used by many as perhaps the ultimate proof of the impeachment's impropriety to reach its goals. As John Vinning of Delaware referred to this case in the same opportunity, it was "a transatlantic instance of incompetency" that portrayed how much impeachment could be "a tedious and uncertain at best" way of removing officers.[159]

When the first impeachment trials began being carried out, however, the potential corruptibility and slowness of the procedure was overshadowed by more intrinsic problems. The suspicion was now that impeachments were generally incapable of providing basic conditions for a fair trial, even in the most immaculate of set-ups. The first suspicion can be referred as a problem of legality, as it related to the possibility of knowing in advance that certain activity is deemed reprehensible and not only retrospectively. The second, as a problem of proportionality, that is, the possibility of stipulating a punishment that matches the seriousness of the impeachable offenses and, thus, does not come off as neither lenient nor excessive. A third and final issue was the problem of partisanship or factionalism, that is, the suspicion

---

[157] Elliot (1836b), p. 380.

[158] Elliot (1836a), p. 11. Ames described an appropriate term as: "The term of election must be so long, that the representative may understand the interest of the people, and yet so limited, that his fidelity may be secured by a dependence upon their approbation" (p. 8).

[159] Labovitz (1978), pp. 23–24. One year and a half of Hastings' impeachment had elapsed by this point. The trial ended seven years later in 1795 with Hastings' acquittal. It must be noted, however, that these proceedings were not held continually and posed much deeper and polarizing questions than just the removal of an official. On one side, it represented a slanderous attack on 'the great men' that pioneered the colonization efforts and promoted the 'greatness' of the British Empire, and, on the other, it represented a daring step towards the defence of the ideals of racial equality, colonial agency, and international justice. Its swift and equitable resolution was arguably nowhere among the metropole's interests.

that reaching verdicts that genuinely reflect proof of guilt and innocence under a politically charged atmosphere was not feasible.

In Chief Justice Samuel Chase's impeachment (1804–5),[160] the defence expertly questioned these points, setting the tone for many impeachments to come. To argue legality, the defence imbued the argument with other two elements, namely arguing the necessity of criminal nature to Chase's acts so that they are minimally reprehensible and impeachment-worthy; and the impossibility of an external organ holding him responsible for something that lies within the bound of his functional autonomy. Chase himself claimed:

> (...) a judge cannot be indicted or punished according to law, for any act whatever, done by him in his judicial capacity, and in a matter of which he has jurisdiction, through error of judgement merely, without corrupt, motives, however manifest his error may be, is a principle resting on the plainest maxims of reason and justice, supported by the highest legal authority (...).[161]

His defence attorney further added: "They [the House of Representatives] are not to create the offense, and make any act criminal and impeachable at their will and pleasure. What is an offense is a question to be decided by the constitution and the law, not by the opinion of a single branch of the legislature". Moreover, he suggested that the Senate does not sit "to scan and punish paltry errors and indiscretions too insignificant to have a name in the penal code, too paltry for the notice of a court of Quarter sessions". Appealing to a common sense of justice, the defence conceded that Chase's acts may have been "ill-judged, indiscreet or ill-timed", but that did not equate to criminal intent and accepting less ultimately was an attack to the separation of powers and to judicial independence.[162]

Although the impeachment managers attempted to point out the *reductio ad absurdum* of the defence, claiming that "the doctrine [of judicial independence] has been carried to such an extravagant length, that the judiciary may justly be considered like a spoiled child", as well as attempted to argue that impeachments are much "more in the nature of a civil investigation, than of a criminal prosecution. (...) [it] may fairly be considered a kind of inquest into the conduct of an officer, merely as it regards his office; the manner in which he performs the duties thereof; and the effects that his conduct therein may have on society". They further qualified that removal and disqualification "cannot be considered a criminal punishment; it is merely a deprivation of rights; a declaration that the person is not properly qualified to serve his country (...) We are not bound to make out such a case as would be punishable by indictment in a court of law (...)". In conclusion, Chase had "transgressed the line of his official duty, in violation of the laws of his country;

[160] Eight charges were presented against Chase, accusing him of using the office as means to persecute and oppress James Callender, the author of a book allegedly libellous of President Adams.

[161] Labovitz (1978), p. 38.

[162] Labovitz (1978), pp. 39–41. The argument goes even further, claiming the need of *indictable* offenses (*i.e.,* as opposed to summary offenses, which have smaller penalties).

and that this conduct can only be accounted for on the ground of impure and corrupt motives".[163]

The defence still contested the managers had to prove pure motive and unintentional error by satisfactory and incontestable evidence, otherwise "why the solemn mockery of articles alleging high crimes and misdemeanours, of a court regularly formed, of a judicial oath administered to the members, of the public examination of witnesses and of a trial conducted in all usual forms" if in the end "no offense against any law of the land could be proved" and the conviction would not depend on his culpability, but rather other expediency that the Legislature believed to be demanding of removal. The managers argued the intent was entailed in Chase's very agency: "How could any judge with upright intentions commit so many errors, or hit upon so many mistakes in the course of one trial (. . .)? They must have been the result of design and predetermination to bear down all opposition, in order to convict and punish the defendant".[164]

The second problem, the problem of proportionality, is intimately connected with the problem of legality. Chase had committed many petty misconducts, which individually considered would never warrant such radical step as removal and disqualification, but, when collectively considered, could denounce a deeper, more abrasive corrupt design, which, on its turn, seemed justifying of a radical measure. The defence, in another hyperbolic turn, contested: "although no single act alleged in the articles should be considered as an impeachable offense, and a sufficient ground of conviction, yet all the acts taken together may constitute such an offence. That is, in other words, that many nothings may make something; that many noughts may make a unit; that many innocent acts may make a crime". Having to consider each charge individually as potentially impeachable had impactful consequences on the perception of adequacy of the procedures. Moreover, this argument became particularly convincing after the managers undercut their own strategy and conceded that the proceedings were of criminal nature after all, raising even more the suspicions of *ex post facto* criminalization by the Senate.[165]

Chase was acquitted from all charges, what may be partially attributed to the skill and prestige of the defence, as well as some clumsy improvisations of the managers; nevertheless, both these two general lines of critic became the go-to arguments of those who oppose impeachments or defend themselves from them, despite being incongruent with the opinions uttered by the Framers. It is interesting to notice, however, that these practices are comparable to a limited extent to that of the English House of Lords; much like the Senate in this opportunity rejected the idea of non-criminal "high crimes and misdemeanours" (supposing Chase's acquittal was

---

[163] Labovitz (1978), p. 42.

[164] Labovitz (1978), pp. 42–44.

[165] Labovitz (1978), p. 45. The question of proportionality will become clearer in the case study of Latin American impeachments, where we will meet cases that possess many 'lesser', but legally clear-cut impeachable offenses, which are in later stages of the proceedings partially removed, generating a situation in which someone is clearly guilty, but arguably punished in excess with removal from office.

motivated by the arguments of defence), so did the House of Lords consistently reject minor criminal trespasses or the purely 'political' charges brought by the Commons; much like the Senate opted for considering the charges individually, the House of Lords had consistently rejected the so-called thesis of 'cumulative treason' brought up by the Commons, for example, in the case against the Earl of Strafford (Thomas Wentworth). The Lords had much more reason for acting so, however, considering how the instrument was much more eminently of criminal nature. The English impeachment could potentially go well beyond removal and disqualification, and include imprisonment, forfeiture and, in convictions of treason, a sentence to be hanged, drawn, and quartered, which arguably explains the need for special precautions.[166]

Andrew Johnson's defence followed the same path. It argued impeachable conducts had to fit some "high criminal offences against the United States, made by some law of the United States existing when the acts complained of were done", that is, even more restrictive than Chase's defence proposed.[167] As a consequence of criminal culpability, not only had the managers the burden to prove that Johnson's conduct was led by his spontaneous designs, but it also had to prove that such designs were directed at achieving noxious consequences. Finally, once that subjective chain was established, it had to prove the consequences of Johnson's acts were still evil enough to warrant such a strong remedy. By itself, this was a considerably high standard for a conviction, which could pose a significant challenge even for the strongest of cases; as for Johnson, his impeachment charges had major weaknesses in regards to all of these points, much more than Chase's.[168] What one would expect to be a clear case of acquittal, ended up being a very close call, with an acquittal by a margin of one vote on three of the eleven charges, strengthening the suspicion of the partisan nature of the proceedings, as Democrats (Johnson's party) voted entirely for his acquittal and Republicans voted entirely for his conviction, with exception of seven defectors. The thesis of the proceedings being a pretext for confrontation of unpopular policies (the continuation of Lincoln's lenient reconstruction policies) under a divided Parliament, seemed suddenly more plausible than that of an effort to remove a mischievous agent from office.[169]

By the time the Nixon inquiry came along, some of these perspectives had changed. A few judges had been convicted for non-criminal petty misconducts, but perhaps most importantly a strong consensus was formed around the nature of impeachment as a constitutional remedy, rather than a substitute for criminal

---

[166] Roberts (1975), p. 1438 (political charges); Roberts (1966), pp. 90–94 (cumulative treason); 436.

[167] Labovitz (1978), p. 67.

[168] Johnson was charged with eleven articles of impeachment, all of which were founded on the Tenure of Office Act, which stablished limitations and requirements to the nominations of civil officers. Johnson would have breached it by removing the Secretary of War, nominating a substitute for him without consulting the Senate and refusing to comply with Senate's orders to repair the situation. Problematic was, however, that the Act was in historical perspective arguably not applicable to the case and its constitutionality was under challenge. Labovitz (1978), pp. 58–89.

[169] Perkins (2003), p. 43.

indictment of the President. Though Nixon's attorneys argued for restricted criminal offenses, accusing its broadening of being "destructive of our system of government, and to the fundamental principle of separation of powers (...)", this new understanding could nonetheless be seen as being in his favour.[170] Since Nixon eventually conceded that he engaged in obstruction of justice, the dumbing-down of the proceedings to the mechanical application of law could be by prejudicial to him, as it obscured other narratives that appealed to a sense of equity: the narrative he had been breaking the law in benefit of the Nation.[171]

Regarding the problem of partisanship, the situation does not change in the slightest from Johnson all the way to Trump. The following numbers breaking down party alignment in impeachment voting may indicate the overarching trend beyond doubt (see Table 2.1).

As seen in these tables, there are only five opportunities in which the votes were not strongly partisan, defined as cases in which 80% of one party is opposing 80% of the other. The first was on Johnson's acquittal, in which ten republicans voted with the democrats. Three votes were expected from the Senators' previous voting behaviour, but the other seven were a surprise. Suspicion regarding their true motivation was raised and investigated, proving to some extent justified.[172] The second was on the vote for investigating the Nixon's affairs. Due to the sensationalistic nature of the revelations of the 'smoking gun tape', the House passed the resolution for a Judiciary Committee almost unanimously. Despite the robustness of the proof, nearly two-thirds of the Republicans in the Committee still opposed the first two articles of impeachment (third and fourth mentioned opportunities), which is still palpably partisan. Representative William Hungate, perplexed by the situation, commented: "there are some Democrats on the committee who would vote to

[170]Labovitz (1978), p. 94.

[171]Labovitz (1978), pp. 91–98. A report from the Inquiry Committee summarizes this point: "Richard M. Nixon, in violation of his constitutional duty to take care that the laws be faithfully executed and his oath of office as President, seriously abused powers that a President possesses. (...) This conduct, undertaken for his own personal political advantage and not in furtherance of any valid national policy objective, is seriously incompatible with our system of constitutional government". Though ten republicans of the Committee voted against some of the charges, they unanimously recognized indictable crimes as *not a* necessity for impeachment, despite partially insisting in proof of criminal intent defined as 'an intent to do wrong' (pp. 99–100).

[172]On the first day of decision, before vote was taken, one of the defecting voters was threatened with investigations for bribery in case he voted for acquittal. As the first charge failed by one vote, the Senate adjourned for ten days and a resolution to investigate "improper or corrupt means used to influence the determination of the Senate" was passed, arguably in hopes of persuading one of the defectors to change their vote. Despite the pressure, the situation repeated in the next day of vote. Later more inquiries on potential bribes were made and more evidence was collected pointing in the direction that some acquittal votes were indeed acquired by promises of patronage, though no actual charge was moved. Two of the seven became democrats thereafter, other four retired or died, and one took a pause to come back years later. Stewart (2009), pp. 240–249, 284–299; Perkins (2003), p. 37; van Tassel and Finkelman (1999), p. 226; Labovitz (1978), pp. 68–69.

Table 2.1 Johnson, Nixon, Clinton, and Trump breakdown of partisanship

President—Vote	For	Against	President—Vote	For	Against
Johnson (Dem.)—House					
Democrats	0	44	Clinton (Dem.)—House (Article IV)		
Republicans	125	0	Democrats	1	204
Third Parties	1	3	Republicans	147	81
Total	*126*	*47*	*Total*	*148*	*285*
Johnson (Dem.)—Senate			Clinton (Dem.)—Senate (Article I)		
Democrats	0	9	Democrats	0	45
Republicans	35	10	Republicans	45	10
Total	*35*	*19*	*Total*	*45*	*55*
Nixon (Rep.)—House			Clinton (Dem.)—Senate (Article III)		
Democrats	231	0	Democrats	0	45
Republicans	179	4	Republicans	50	5
Total	*410*	*4*	*Total*	*50*	*50*
Nixon (Rep.)—Committee (Article I)			Trump 1 (Rep.)—Committee (Article I)		
Democrats	21	0	Democrats	23	0
Republicans	6	11	Republicans	0	17
Total	*27*	*11*	*Total*	*23*	*17*
Nixon (Rep.)—Committee (Article II)			Trump 1 (Rep.)—Committee (Article II)		
Democrats	21	0	Democrats	23	0
Republicans	7	10	Republicans	0	17
Total	*28*	*10*	*Total*	*23*	*17*
Nixon (Rep.)—Committee (Article III)			Trump 1 (Rep.)—House (Article I)		
Democrats	19	2	Democrats	229	2
Republicans	2	15	Republicans	0	195
Total	*21*	*17*	*Total*	*229*	*197*
Nixon (Rep.)—Committee (Article IV and V)			Trump 1 (Rep.)—House (Article II)		
Democrats	12	9	Democrats	228	3
Republicans	0	17	Republicans	0	195
Total	*12*	*26*	*Total*	*228*	*198*
Clinton (Dem.)—Committee			Trump 1 (Rep.)—House (Appointment)		
Democrats	0	16	Democrats	227	1
Republicans	21	0	Republicans	0	192
Total	*21*	*16*	*Total*	*227*	*193*
Clinton (Dem.)—House			Trump 1 (Rep.)—Senate (Article I)		
Democrats	31	176	Democrats	45	0
Republicans	227	0	Republicans	1	52
Total	*258*	*176*	*Total*	*46*	*52*
Clinton (Dem.)—Committee (Articles I, III and IV)			Trump 1 (Rep.)—Senate (Article II)		
Democrats	0	16	Democrats	45	0
Republicans	21	0	Republicans	0	53
Total	*21*	*16*	*Total*	*45*	*53*
Clinton (Dem.)—Committee (Article II)					

(continued)

Table 2.1 (continued)

President—Vote	For	Against	President—Vote	For	Against
			Trump 2 (Rep.)—Committee of Rule (Article I)		
Democrats	0	16	Democrats	7	0
Republicans	20	1	Republicans	0	4
Total	*20*	*17*	*Total*	*7*	*4*
Clinton (Dem.)—House (Article I)			Trump 2 (Rep.)—House (Article I)		
Democrats	5	201	Democrats	222	0
Republicans	223	5	Republicans	10	197
Total	*228*	*206*	*Total*	*232*	*197*
Clinton (Dem.)—House (Article II)			Trump 2 (Rep.)—Senate (Article I)		
Democrats	5	201	Democrats	48	0
Republicans	200	28	Republicans	7	43
Total	*205*	*229*	*Total*	*57*	*43*
Clinton (Dem.)—House (Article III)					
Democrats	5	200			
Republicans	216	12			
Total	*221*	*212*			

Source: Own elaboration with data from Perkins, pp. 34–36 (The table is part of Perkins 2003 analysis (pp. 34–36), which also includes data on Jackson, Tyler, Buchanan and Hoover. Perkins concludes for strong partisanship (at least 80% of one party opposing 80% of the other) in most of impeachment related votes (18 of 28), six of them being perfectly partisan.), and congressional records

impeach Nixon today. And there are a few Republicans who wouldn't vote to impeach Nixon if he were caught in a bank vault at midnight".[173]

Finally, the last opportunity of least partisanship was on Clinton's impeachment vote in the House on article n. 4 (accused Clinton's legalistic answers to the Committee of configuring abuse of power), which seemed like a clear stretch of the power of impeachment and insufficient to warrant removal and disqualification from office. One would perhaps expect the remaining articles of impeachment to face a similar rejection by the Senators and Representatives, since they also dealt with arguably paltry infractions. As symptomatic as lying under oath and attempting to cover one's tracks about an adulterous relationship can be about a man's character and its incongruity with the dignity of office expected from the presidency, the impeachable offenses were said to be too private and flimsy to be elevated to the concept of a "high crime".[174]

Although the Framers most definitely did not want to see impeachments turn out to be partisan strength measuring contests, there was little they could do about the culture of party politics that was under development in America or worldwide. The two-thirds threshold assured no President would be convicted unjustly or for petty

[173] Perkins (2003), p. 21.

[174] van Tassel and Finkelman (1999), pp. 280 ff.

infractions, as Johnson's or Clinton's impeachment showed, but, on the other hand, its use as a check on irresponsible government may also have been compromised. Nixon was pressured out of government in a context of overwhelming proof of his guilt, but perhaps only because his irresponsibility would be secured by a pardon from the Vice-President the month after his resignation and because it could spare his party of the true and definitive display of partisanship that would probably come out of the votes to be taken in the House and in the Senate. The value of impeachment as an instrument in this case is that it existed as possibility, rather than its quality as mechanism of accountability.

2.2 The Aftermath of Presidentialism

> (. . .) in one hundred years of presidentialism, we have spent over 60% of the period in dictatorships. (. . .) The evil is to not advance but to persist in the mistake. And the presidential system has been repetitively a mistake (. . .). The governments do not generally support crisis: they either renounce, die or get killed.[175] Deputy Fernando Santana in the Brazilian Constitutional Convention of 1988

The constitutional arrangements produced by the Framers of the US Constitution proved to be very influential, with nearly every country in the American continent adopting its general, character-defining outlines. While the United States became a world power and stablished what may very well be the most stable democratic regime in the world, the same cannot be said about all other countries who followed its footsteps. In fact, most of them went through a troubled nineteenth and twentieth century with constant democratic breakdowns and, because of that, presidentialism became the first suspect cause of this instability.[176] Scholars and professional politicians alike pointed the rigidity entailed in the presidential system with scepticism, which, they argued, impaired necessary political transformations and incentivize relief only through extraconstitutional means, such as *coups*, assassinations, military interventions and civil wars. Impeachment seemed unreliable and too legalistic to be democratic. They recognized, moreover, the presidential system had inherent, difficult to manage sources of tension. The difficulties and impracticalities of the branches' mechanisms for holding each other accountable for their actions, as well as their capacity of ruling autonomously and in antagonism to each other, would be unescapably at odds with stable democratic government.

In the past 30 years, however, the ever so unstable presidencies, particularly those in Latin America, have no longer experienced widespread democratic breakdowns. While the presidencies themselves may have remained unstable to a degree, Latin American nations seem to have decidedly chosen for sustaining democracy and its

[175] Author's translation of *Diário do Congresso Nacional* n. 13/1988, p. 573.

[176] Linz (1990) and Hiroi and Omori (2009).

games.[177] Presidents—quite a few of them, in fact—have been brought down, but not a drop of blood needed to be shed in the process. Countries with working impeachment provisions have found solutions to political tensions before thought solvable only through violent means. Although Latin America has not yet fully cleansed itself of the shadows of its authoritarian past, the path of institutionalized conflict resolution seems to be consolidating itself.

This section is an attempt at explaining this phenomenon in deeper detail, which is foundational to this study. It is important, however, to remain vigilant. These are not *the only explanations* to why these other presidencies have been unstable, although some of these explanations might sound particularly compelling. Instability and extraconstitutional interventionism have not been exclusive to presidential systems, and, therefore, one should also consider the bigger picture, that is, the historical, social, and economic contexts in which these systems of government are embedded in, as well as the impact of individual actors in these transformations. Stability, moreover, is arguably not the end-all-be-all feature of a good government. As Deputy Brandão Monteiro answered back to the citation in epigraph, the Brazilian experience with parliamentarism was one that connived with slavery and abuses for hundreds of years—history, he claimed, is sometimes overly mystified and, thus, nuance is necessary.[178] These nuances, which are indebted not only to Brazil, but the whole Latin America, will be discussed in the next chapter.

2.2.1 Unstable Presidencies

Latin America has experienced several regime breakdowns and interrupted presidencies in the last century. Just between 1945 and 2003, some authors indicate over 80 transitions between democracy, semi-democracy, and authoritarianism in the region.[179] Multiple reasons have often been argue for such intense variation,[180] such as continuity of post-colonial conflicts,[181] a vicious cycle of low legitimation

[177] Alcántara Sáez et al. (2018), p. 6.

[178] *Diário do Congresso Nacional* n. 13/1988, p. 573.

[179] See *Hagopian and Mainwaring (2005), p. 3, for a detailed breakdown.*

[180] Not confined to Latin America, Leo Hurwitz (1972), discusses the main eight causes of instability usually described in the literature, namely: (i.) economic underdevelopment; (ii.) high economic growth; (iii.) dominance of catholic religious belief; (iv.) party system fragmentation; (v.) religious heterogeneity; (vi.) linguistic heterogeneity; (vii.) ethnic/racial heterogeneity; (viii.) lower levels of democratization. He concludes that none of them have much actual explanatory power and that stability may be more influenced by self-inflicted decisions independent of deterministic environmental factors or societal attitudes. See also Huntington (1993), pp. 37 ff.

[181] Piketty and Goldhammer (2014), pp. 155 ff. The argument is that the perceived excessive quantity of foreign capital (generally by-product of colonial or neo-colonial interference) may spark conflict for its nationalization.

and low performance,[182] political-ideological attitudes that had not quite yet settled in favour of liberal democracy,[183] lack of a culture of institutional forbearance,[184] and US political interventionism as part of the Cold War.[185] On a more systematic note, however, Juan Linz presented the thesis that implied that such instability was founded on institutional choices made by Latin Americans, namely, the choice for presidentialism over parliamentarism. Of the many issues Linz argued for presidentialism's incapacity to dissolve pre-existing tensions or perhaps intensifying them, five seem to be of major importance.

The first issue would be that of (i.) dual democratic legitimacy of the branches responsible for policy making. In a presidential system, Executive and Legislature are elected separately from each other and, as such, both may lay claim to be the foremost representative of popular interest. In other words, Presidents may lay claim to be the better legitimated to speak in the name of the people over the parliamentary majority and choose not to harmonize their interests with Parliament. While the inverse may also be true, the President may emphasize his majoritarian legitimacy over that of the Parliament, which is proportional. Moreover, in contrast to parliamentary systems, since the Chief of Government does not derive from the Parliament, the popular expectations and perceptions of the President differ from those of the Parliament, what may very well be yet another source of conflict.[186]

The second issue is that of (ii.) rigidity. If it is the case that such a conflict as described above arises, presidentialism may be in an uncomfortable situation. Impeachment is a complex, encumbering, and legalistic solution for interbranch tensions, and, as a result, can be perceived to lack democratic legitimacy. In a parliamentary system, such conflict could be easily and transparently dissolved via a no-confidence vote. Moreover, and this is Linz's main critique on presidentialism's rigidity, the fixed time mandates do not allow for a fluent adaptation of policy making to the current needs.[187] The political processes often cannot be prolonged nor shortened in response to readjustments the diverse political, social, and economic events may require. Unpredictable events, such as the death of the incumbent

[182] Diamond et al. (1989), pp. 13 ff. New democracies are said to be often unable to act efficiently due to their shallow rooting (low legitimacy), leading to a display of low performance. Low performance, on its turn, leads to the questioning of government legitimacy, damaging it and starting a vicious, self-reinforcing cycle.

[183] As famously argued by Fukuyama (1989) who saw in the end of the Cold War the crowning act of liberal democracy and its games above all other alternatives.

[184] An explanation for the stability of the US governments is that its institutions avoid legal hardball strategies and the escalation of political conflict. See Linz (1994), p. 7 and Levitsky and Ziblatt (2018), p. 106.

[185] In favour of this thesis: Grandin (2010), and against it: Schenoni and Mainwaring (2018).

[186] Linz (1994), pp. 6–8. See also Suarez (1982).

[187] George Tsebelis (1995), pp. 321–322, explained these democratic breakdowns specifically with this aspect of presidentialism: "In regimes where government change is impossible (except for fixed intervals like in presidential regimes), policy immobilism may lead to the replacement of the leadership through extra-constitutional means (regime instability)".

or his/her serious errors in judgment, cannot be swiftly addressed, and have effectively intensified constitutional crises.[188]

A third issue is that of (iii.) identifiability and accountability. Linz argues it is more difficult to identify the policy to be undertook by a presidential candidate and, later, to hold whoever is responsible for an eventual crisis accountable. He claims the voter casting his ballot, although he may be able to clearly identify the person for whom he is voting for, may not know how the executive policy is going to turn out, as the candidates often have no prior record as political leaders and may not be particularly identified with a party ideology or program (*e.g.,* mavericks and outsiders),[189] meaning that, ultimately, the vote will be informed by the opinion on the individual, the projected (often artificially created by advisers) persona and unbinding promises. Candidates seldom have a known shadow cabinet and nominations start only after election. Moreover, if it is the case that a constitutional crisis arises, the sharp separation of Executive from Legislature may result in the shifting of blame from one branch to the other, in the exchange of accusations of mismanagement, inefficiency, and corruption. The same is less likely to happen in parliamentary systems, where unified legitimacy also means unified responsibility.[190]

A fourth issue, (iv.) the zero-sum (winner-take-all) character of the political game in presidential regimes, Linz considered particularly polarizing. Since only one candidate gets to be elected and obtains control of the entire executive branch, the defeated party is likely to be ostracized from government and from the patronage entailed in it. Moreover, the defeated candidate is likely to lose prestige and leadership positions in the party or even in the coalition for opposition. Stakes are raised remarkably high, inciting tensions, uncompromising attitudes, and polarization.[191]

Finally, Linz also argued presidentialism had a (v.) tendency to specific political styles. Since the presidential election tendentially promotes a sort of "winner-take-all" game and because of the president's personal claim to democratic legitimacy, his/hers the political style of the will likely tend to a style without much power sharing. The president will have a sense of power and purpose potentially in contradiction with the plurality that elected the Legislature, and, consequently, is likely to get frustrated when proposed policies are met with resistance therein. If extensive powers for rule-by-decree are available, he/she may feel tempted to solve

---

[188] Linz (1994), pp. 7–10.

[189] Mavericks and outsiders can be dangerous to democracy because parties cannot filter or keep a tight leash over them in case they happen to be or turn to would-be authoritarians. See Levitsky and Ziblatt (2018), pp. 24–25. Presidentialism is said to provide better conditions for the electoral success of such antisystem candidates and, thus, to favor the emergence of authoritarianism.

[190] Linz (1994), pp. 10–13. Parliamentary systems may run into in the same issue if there are many unstable governments or shifting coalitions, with no party assuming a central role.

[191] Linz (1994), pp. 14–16, 19. This is a disputed aspect of presidentialism as proposed by Linz, as parliamentary systems may share these characteristics at a lower degree. See Mainwaring and Shugart (1997).

differences without negotiation and compromise, stirring friction between branches. The same would not be as likely to happen in parliamentary systems, where the prime minister clearly comes from a parliamentary plurality and may be easily swapped out once there is a shift on the support of his/her own party or other parties.[192]

Linz presented empirical evidence to support his thesis that presidential systems offered, in fact, less stable democratic regimes and executive branches than those offered by parliamentary regimes,[193] which, however, ended up being contested. Scott Mainwaring and Matthew Shugart pointed out in a later study that much of Linz's conclusions were compromised by a selection bias and that presidential democracies, when compared with parliamentary democracies of similar socioeconomic level, display no conclusive variation in stability performance.[194] In other words, as presidentialism was more likely to be adopted by Latin American and African states, which had to deal with formidable obstacles to democracy regardless of the form or system of government, and as parliamentarism was the regime of choice by most of Europe and the former British colonies, many of which are microstates, where democracy generally met favourable conditions, it is sensible to assume that the correlation between regime and democratic success is partially predicated on where they have been implemented.[195]

The case study in the next chapter will show that, although these tensions are awfully present in the periods that precede presidential impeachments, Latin American democracies have adapted to accommodate them—something that seems consistent with Mainwaring's and Shugart's conclusions. Presidentialism has grown towards more consociational attitudes, in that the governments are being formed and reshuffled to accommodate parliamentary demands and ensure governability; overwhelming presidential powers were reduced or became dependent of parliamentary ratification to discourage personalistic rule, and so on. Nonetheless, blame shifting between the branches or presidents challenging parliamentary legitimacy for impeachment due to their own independent claim to democratic legitimation, among a few other things, remain present when conflict seems insoluble.

---

[192] Linz (1994), pp. 14–19. Mainwaring (1999), p. 272, adds, moreover, that presidents have little incentive to be loyal to their parties and to work in cooperation with them. Since they are elected independently, they do not need to aspire to be a party leader to the reach the highest office, as it would be the case of a prime minister; they lack the congressional experience that would ensue from such practice, and, lastly, they can more easily resort to popular appeal, particularly in the age of digital media.

[193] Linz (1994), pp. 62 ff, but also in the already referenced pages and in Linz (1990).

[194] Mainwaring and Shugart (1997), pp. 451–460. Hiroi and Omori (2009) argues that previous history of democratic breakdown correlates more strongly with regime instability. Parliamentary systems may be more unstable than presidential systems when such history is present, depending on the degree of party system fragmentation.

[195] Mainwaring and Shugart (1997), p. 460.

2.2.2 *Surge of Impeachments, New Suspicions and New Concerns*

Whatever the reasons behind regime and presidential instability may be, the fact is that in the four decades that preceding the 1990s only one of these transitions truly happened via impeachment, the trial of José Guizado of Panama in 1955, and even so, under unclear circumstances.[196] It is no wonder that in the early 90s political scientists were declaring impeachments to be unfeasible in context of institutional crises.[197] Fortunately, they were not alone in this misjudgement, as legal scholars and politicians have similarly immortalized their opinions on impeachments as "rusted blunderbusses" never to be used,[198] only to be subsequently disproved. Regarding Latin America, most notable is perhaps Supreme Court Justice Paulo Brossard (Brazil), who presided over Fernando Collor's impeachment and stated in his legal handbook about the topic repeated opinions about impeachment accusing it of being a "useless precaution", or an "empty threat", whose purpose was to serve a "purely fictitious" or "illusory" sense of accountability.[199] Such sentiment was shared by many other jurists, such as Carlos Alberto Gallo, who corroborated that impeachment rules "remain in our legislation as decorative figures, destined only to make foreigners believe that our Chief of State really is accountable for his acts and answers for the abuses he commits, when in reality his persona is, like that of the emperor, holy and unchallengeable, standing beyond any sort of accountability whatsoever."[200]

Historical irony aside, many of these scholars may have overlooked or could not predict that in their latest transition to democracy, Latin American nations conceded more control of state revenue, security forces, and popular legitimacy to the Parliaments, making the task of challenging a powerful president a lot less dauting and, consequently, more likely.[201] Aníbal Pérez-Liñán attributes this change, moreover, to the transformations in the international context, political learning among Latin

[196] Pérez-Liñán (2007), p. 6. Keywords here are *truly* and *transition*. There were impeachment-like removals such as Café Filho and Carlos Luz (both in 1955, Brazil), and impeachments after one has already left office, as Carlos Ibáñes del Campo (1931, Chile). Most of these, however, occurred in clear states of exception. See Beçak (2003) and Loveman and Lira (2000), pp. 29–41.

[197] Linz (1994), p. 10; Shugart and Carey (1992), p. 29.

[198] This specific wording is from Henry Jones Ford as cited by Rossiter (1963), p. 44. Rossiter later states he did not think that "we are likely to ever witness such a trial again" (p. 232), ten years prior to the Nixon inquiry.

[199] Author's translation of Brossard de Souza Pinto (1965), p. 196.

[200] Author's translation of Carlos Alberto Gallo (1992), pp. 45–46.

[201] Pierson and Gil (1957), p. 240, argued that it was the case that Latin American Parliaments failed to control the Executive precisely because of this monopolization of resources. Inversely, noticing the constitutional changes brought by the latest transition, which assured a better division of resources, we could speculate this to be a possible explanation for the rise of impeachments. This was also the case as we observed in England. The more the Parliament controlled revenue sources and the less it was pressured by external wars that required the troops to be loyal to the King as well

American elites and the rise of legitimacy of democratic institutions in the end of the twentieth century.[202]

The "(re)discovery" of the power of impeachment, however, probably depended on a very unlikely set of circumstances, much like it was the case in England with Edward III or, later, with James I. Arguably, even if the conditions of the previous decades had extended themselves into the 90s, keeping someone like Fernando Collor in power would have been an incredible challenge. Collor inherited a country in the brink of hyperinflation, failed colossally to curb the crisis, and punished severely all social classes with his economic response plan. So severe were his mistakes, that corruption had to be institutionalized to allow for basic everyday operations, such as allowing companies to pay their employees' wages. Not only did he make things palpably worse, but he soon was also targeted by corruption accusations founded on incredibly damning evidence: spreadsheets, pay checks, confessions from his closest friends and family, and so on. In his public appearances, he made things difficult for himself as he contradicted his previous statements, was caught openly lying and was often behaving in opulent ways that seemed to mock the hardships society endured at the time.[203] With so much out in the open, his impeachment became nearly a moral necessity.

The removal of President Collor may not have required the boldest confrontation by the Legislature, but it served nonetheless as inspiration for the rest of the continent to tackle even consolidated and experienced politicians such as Carlos Andres Pérez of Venezuela or Ernesto Samper of Colombia, who also happened to become implicated in scandals. The following table shows in more detail how many presidential crises the region had since 1992, demonstrating the prominence impeachments have attained:

As the table shows, more than half of recent presidential crises in the region have since been tackled through impeachments, indicating its consolidation as a crisis resolution mechanism—and as being a far cry from the 'useless empty threats' they were accused of being. Coups are still timidly present, but they seem to have given significantly more space to democratic and institutional solutions.

This direct and somewhat abrupt substitution of coups for institutional ousting mechanisms, however, has not yet convinced every observer of presenting a qualitative shift in the dispute or control of Executive power. Some have remained sceptical and even suggested these new solutions would be coups with extra steps, or coups but with a liberal-democracy-friendly guise. Those who do not reject institutional oustings out of principle (*e.g.*, because they violate the sacredness of the elective mandate and the people's sovereign choice for ruler), generally point out to the ambivalence or flaws of these methods.

---

as the Parliament to give supply for reasons of self-preservation, the more impeachments became effective.

[202] Pérez-Liñán (2007), pp. 11, 41 ff. Policy change became less connected with the idea of regime change, and the military perceived less incentives.

[203] See Collor's case study in the next chapter for details.

Indeed, one thing not shown by Table 2.2 is that there were many times in which these mechanisms were employed in ways far from 'kosher' (*e.g.*, Samper, Bucaram, Mahuad, Gutierrez, Lugo) or/and for behaviour many may deem of little relevance (e.g., Pérez, Rousseff) or for behaviour that is only politically but not legally disavowed (*e.g.*, Zelaya, Lugo). In other words, this table does not show that many of these impeachments (and its surrogates) arguably applied law in contested ways, in ways arguably incompatible with an *idealized* perspective of the American presidential impeachment and that only very suspiciously may have served the purpose of holding presidents legally accountable for their actions. This was a hypothesis that Pérez-Liñán, for example, was already putting into question in the first decade of impeachments, when he stated that

> If the Latin American political leaders accept the possibility of invoking impeachment procedures in a flexible fashion, as if they were a parliamentary vote of no-confidence, then a form of 'constitutional' legislative coup will be created; legally derived, but politically distant from the North American model of impeachment.[204]

Some see this as a positive thing: Latin America would be learning to deal with the shortcomings of presidentialism, as they have been described in the last section. By making removals easier, presidentialism's alleged problematic rigidity (*i.e.*, the difficult and encumbering substitution of incapable leaderships or failed policies) would be eased, and presidentialism would become more predictable and efficient.[205] It would be a sort of improvised "parliamentarization" of presidentialism.

Needless to say, most seem to be much less beholden of these developments and, in fact, see it only with more concern.[206] Pérez-Liñán has, nearly two decades later, basically still repeated the aforementioned statement, indicating how persistent this problem has been and how it may be among the reasons for democratic backsliding in the region.[207] He does, however, change one part of his statement regarding '*legislative coups*' fundamentally, acknowledging something that is often overlooked in impeachment discussions:

> (...) stretching the concept of *coup d'État* to label controversial impeachments is problematic for analytic and for political reasons. Analytically, we cannot conduct empirical research to identify similarities and differences unless we have a clear conceptual distinction between the two categories. Politically, the identification of impeachments and coups creates unexpected challenges: it implies – in revisionist fashion – that social movements that advocated for impeachments in the 1990s were antidemocratic, it naturalizes the role of military intervention in anti-corruption narratives, and it obscures the fact that powerful presidents – not powerful legislators – are the main peril for democratic stability.[208]

In the same vein, one could argue, moreover, that holding impeachments to an untenable ideal of legality and legal formalism, or to ideals of clear-cut separation of

[204] Author's translation of Pérez-Liñán (2000), p. 74.

[205] Marsteintredet and Berntzen (2008), Hochstetler and Samuels (2011), to name a few.

[206] *E.g.*, Carey et al., Santos and Guarnieri (2016).

[207] See Pérez-Liñán (2018).

[208] Pérez-Liñán (2018), pp. 10–11.

Table 2.2 Presidential crises in Latin America after 1990

Name	Year	Country	Instrument	Outcome
Fernando Collor	1992	Brazil	Impeachment	Conviction
Jorge Serrano	1993	Guatemala	Resignation	–
Carlos Andrés Pérez	1993	Venezuela	Impeachment and Vacancy (absence)	Conviction
Joaquín Balaguer	1996	Dominican Republic	Resignation	–
Ernesto Samper	1996	Colombia	Impeachment	Acquittal
Abdalá Bucaram	1997	Ecuador	Vacancy (mental)	Conviction
Rosalia Arteaga	1997	Ecuador	Resignation	–
Raúl Cubas Grau	1999	Paraguay	Impeachment and Resignation	–
Alberto Fujimori	2000	Peru	Impeachment* and Vacancy (moral)	Conviction
Fernando de la Rúa	2001	Argentina	Resignation	–
Adolfo Rodríguez Saá	2001	Argentina	Resignation	–
Jamil Mahuad	2002	Ecuador	Military Coup and Vacancy (absence)	Conviction
Luis Ángel González Macchi	2002, 2003	Paraguay	Impeachment	Acquittal
Gonzalo Sánchez de Lozada	2004	Bolivia	Impeachment and Resignation	
Hugo Chávez	2004	Venezuela	Recall	Acquittal
Carlos Mesa	2005	Bolivia	Resignation	–
Lucio Gutiérrez	2005	Ecuador	Vacancy (absence)	Conviction
Manuel Zelaya	2009	Honduras	Military Coup and Anomalous Criminal Suit	–
Fernando Lugo	2012	Paraguay	Impeachment	Conviction
Otto Pérez Molina	2015	Guatemala	Pretrial and Resignation	–
Dilma Rousseff	2016	Brazil	Impeachment	Conviction
Nicolás Maduro	2016	Venezuela	Impeachment	–
Michel Temer	2017	Brazil	Impeachment	Acquittal
Jimmy Morales	2017, 2018	Guatemala	Pretrial	Acquittal
Pedro P. Kuczynski	2017, 2018	Peru	Vacancy (moral) and Resignation	Acquittal
Mario Abdo Benítez	2019	Paraguay	Impeachment	Acquittal
Evo Morales	2019	Bolivia	Military Coup	–
Sebastián Piñera	2019	Chile	Impeachment	Acquittal
Martín Vizcarra	2020	Peru	Vacancy (moral)	Conviction
Manuel Merino	2020	Peru	Resignation	–
Mario Abdo Benítez	2021	Paraguay	Impeachment	Acquittal
Martín Vizcarra	2021	Peru	Impeachment*	Conviction
Sebastián Piñera	2021	Chile	Impeachment	Acquittal
Pedro Castillo	2022	Peru	Vacancy (moral)	Acquittal

(continued)

Table 2.2 (continued)

Name	Year	Country	Instrument	Outcome
Guillermo Lasso	2022	Ecuador	Mutual dissolution	Acquittal
Pedro Castillo	2022	Peru	Vacancy (moral)	Conviction
Dina Boluarte	2023	Peru	Vacancy (moral)	Acquittal
Guillermo Lasso	2023	Ecuador	Impeachment	–

Source: Own elaboration based on official documents and newspaper articles. Presidential crises were here understood as intensified inter-branch conflict that led to attempts at removal. Impeachments marked with an asterisk were initiated after the President left office. "Acquittal" and "conviction" are used in a loose sense

law and politics, are equally troublesome. Analytically, it neglects an incredible amount of work of genealogical reconstruction of impeachments and creates models of understanding and expectations about impeachments that may be in disconnect with reality. It denies a serious intermingling of theory and practice of law, of the reciprocal influence its substance and its processes may have on one another. It purports to create a system of purity where ambiguity is the rule. Politically, it characterizes Latin America—in colonialist fashion—as the region that is always lagging behind "the West" and is unable to solve its own institutional problems; it gives Latin Americans reasons for feeling inadequate, inferior or illegitimate, while failing to acknowledge how inappropriate the actual frames of reference may be and how the region may have its own path to follow and develop. It legitimizes cynical, often unverifiable narratives over cautious, well-grounded analyses, and with that, reinforces latent polarizations and dependencies.

A lot of this has already been addressed in the previous sections through the discussion of the history and thought behind impeachments. By now there should be a clear understanding that impeachments are vastly more complex than the average criminal court case and simply cannot be understood in the same way. Impeachments are a synthesis of political and legal theory with many practical compromises that are entailed in the making of a President (and by transference, a government) accountable for his or her actions. If impeachments were to be graphically represented, they would be represented as a function of law and politics, and not just as a quantity of one or the other. There is an ambiguity, an impurity that must be digested instead of being used as an excuse to delegitimize impeachments at every opportunity.

2.3 Impeachment: A Matter of Justice or Politics?

"Impeachment is not a political tool. It has to be based on just the law and the facts", claimed Nancy Pelosi, democratic leader in the House of Representatives, as she justified her rejection of an impeachment attempt against President George Bush for leading the war in Iraq.[209] In a more recent opportunity, Steve Bannon, a former White House strategist for President Donald Trump made a similar accusation regarding criminal investigations targeting the President. "This is political", he claimed, "(...) It's not going to be just pure legal process. The legal process is going to attune itself to the political process".[210] Also the constitutional law professor Lawrence Solum describes similar accusations between legal scholars when he says: "Originalists argue that living constitutionalism is a thin disguise for Supreme Court decisions that are based on naked politics".[211]

Although accusations like these are common, what they mean to portray can be quite elusive. What do these sentences communicate exactly? What do these sentences tell us about the understanding of law and justice of their interlocutors? Could we infer from Pelosi's use that what is political does not base itself on "the law and the facts" or, if it does, it still is more fundamentally based on a third element (*e.g.,* ideology, interest)? Could we infer from Bannon's use that the political and legal processes should be entirely separated? Could we infer from Prof. Solum's description that the Courts are not a place for politics?

These uses of the words "political" and "politics" can be representative of how the general populace and perhaps also traditional jurists understand the relation of law and politics. A compilation of the intended meanings of sentences like these, could arguably be look this way: (i.) Law is to be strictly separated from politics; there is a meaningful distinction between the work jurists and politicians do, for law application is not the same as law making; the former is subordinated and rigorously bound to the latter by method, reason, and authority; (ii.) Law must be impartial; it shall not favour or disfavour anyone based on legally irrelevant features of those judging or of those being judged; (iii.) Law requires a different kind of legitimacy than politics; politics can only be done by those who are elected, directly or indirectly, to do so.

In general outlines, in a legal context, someone will claim a certain act, decision or idea is political if they feel it attempts to reach ends which are not within the scope of its accepted authority. For the cases mentioned above, it would be to say, respectively: It is not in impeachment's authority to judge anything beyond the impeachable offense. It is not in a criminal investigation's authority to bring forth political transformation. It is not within the judge's authority to decide over certain things or in certain ways.

Given that many of these lines can be blurred, these are all valid objections and the extra effort into justification of a doubtful act is arguably salutary. In constitutional contexts, however, particularly involving impeachments where they *invariably* pop up as opposition talking points, these challenges need further qualification.

---

[209] Toobin (2018).

[210] Samuelsohn (2018).

[211] Bennett and Solum (2011), p. 1. Originalism posits legal interpretation should be guided by the originally intended and ostensive meanings law or the constitution had when created. Living constitutionalism argues for the continuous recontextualization of legal text.

Constitutional law is the highest and likely most abstract set of positive rules within a state, which informs many of the limits of politics itself—any effort in clarifying these lines will necessarily entail political consequences. In impeachments, these consequences are especially evident.

It is important, therefore, to know what can be realistically expected from impeachments. How legitimate can an impeachment possibly be? What gives a Court of Impeachment the legitimacy to make such a decision removing and disqualifying a President? How bound is such a court to the legal rules? What factors may or may not influence the interpretation of rules? May the Court of Impeachments understand law differently than a court of law?

Most of these points of contention have been mystified by legal discourses, superficial understandings of language, and an incomprehension of certain ambiguities and tensions of systems of rules. The following sections will show that (i.) political courts receive their legitimation via nomination and ratification of their members by the political branches; (ii.) since this legitimation is fairly limited, their power is also limited; they are dependent on other more legitimated actors to offer them a matter for judgment and their decisions should not go beyond the claiming that something is against the constitution (they would not be allowed, for example, to say something is more appropriate and prescribe a course of action); and (iii.), although this may be a fairly reasonable response, the denial of a course of action may logically coerce an authority into another course; in other words, denial can also in many regards be equivalent with affirmation, the rejection of an action leads to an omission and the rejection of an omission leads to an action. After this, a few challenges to the very idea of legality will be presented, claiming that (iv.) law is not neutral and impartial, and its application entails the application of underlying commitments; this is the case regardless of what is understood to be the ultimate source of law's authority; (v.) the line between core and contingent aspects of law is a discretionary one, for both lie within a continuum of determinacy; (vi.) law application and law making are also part of one and the same continuum of individuation of normative meaning; (vii.) law and its meaning are a synthesis of many constitutive tensions, linguistic and evaluative differentiation processes, as well as of human imperfections and limitations. Vis-à-vis all these difficulties, expecting perfectly unambiguous interpretations can be an unrealistic goal. These limitations of the idea of legality are particularly present in impeachments, where decisions are made by large collegiate organs, in a politically charged environment, and potentially carry enormous consequences, regardless of outcome. It will ultimately be argued that one should be particularly cautious with arguments over legality and that, if the idealization of legality is to be kept, it should be understood with significant reservations in the context of impeachment procedures.

2.3.1 *Classical Debates on Courts and Their Involvement in Politics*

One of the most interesting discussions on the topic happened in 1928, in Vienna,[212] when some of the greatest legal scholars of the German speaking realm met to discuss the installation of the *Staatsgerichtshöfe* of the Republic of Weimar, following the trend of Constitutional Courts that started that decade in Austria. A particular avant-garde aspect of Constitutional Courts is that they are conscious efforts of turning something eminently political, such as the Constitution, into something also subjectable to the dispensing of justice, contradicting the common understanding of justice as something apolitical and universal that pre-exists the state. One could perhaps argue that modern courts do not dispense justice exactly, but legality, and that the Constitution, as a kind of law, would be well within its reach, without invading the realm of politics; after all, the Constitution would have already been established, so courts would not be making up constitutional values, but objectively applying them over the conduct of political actors and the issuing of laws.

As intuitive as such this logic may sound, the legal scholars involved in this debate seemed unanimous in establishing that constitutional interpretation inevitably constituted a political activity. Heinrich Triepel stated quite bluntly that the opposition between politics and legality is, to start with, arbitrary and artificial. The *Rechtsstaat* (Rule of Law) would already be itself a commitment of a specific political nature. He did give in that, however, there were things which could be considered highly political, such as policy decisions which aim at specific goals the State had set for itself (*Staatszwecke*), and others which were more managerial in nature, thus less political, but never entirely apolitical.[213] To depoliticize the law would be to deprive it of its core. Within such understanding, the rule of law create an awkward arrangement requiring "the political" to work within the framework of "the legal" while, at the same time, requiring "the legal" not to entrench the activity of that which is "political". There would never be a point in which both do not intersect, although arguably there is a lot of which is "political" but is not, nor could possibly be fixated in legal terms.[214]

How should this tension be dealt with? Should political actors stand beyond any judicial control to preserve the rule of law and its implied clear distinctive line between what is legal and what is political? Should this control reach only that which

---

[212]Documented in *Veröffentlichungen der Vereinigung der Deutschen Staatsrechtslehrer* (1929), vol. 5. Verhandlung der Tagung der Deutschen Staatsrechtslehrer zu Wien am 23. und 24. April 1928.

[213]The distinction between government (*Regierung*) and administration (*Verwaltung*), respectively, would reflect this. Although the control of "managerial" activity of the administrations was already well established in administrative courts, extending such control to reach political actors or acts of policy was still seen with suspicion. This same critique to Constitutional Courts was present at the introduction of Administrative Courts in 1863, claims Triepel.

[214]von Hippel et al. (2013), pp. 1–12.

is mildly political as to reach a balance between rule of law and checks-and-balances, or should this control reach even the highly political disputes, tipping the balance even further in direction of the checks-and-balances? If one decides for the latter, would that mean a fatal blow to the political processes entailed in the republican principle or perhaps also to the relative independence the principle of separation of powers seeks to construe?

As already implied, Triepel saw no great dilemma in these questions, he argued that the judge as well as the legislator are both delegates of the Constitution and of the People, and that neither of them is given the right to go against this delegated power, be it by creating unconstitutional laws as legislators, be it by applying unconstitutional laws as judges. If anything, the oversight of a Constitutional Court would only further strengthen these cardinal values which are supposedly under tension. Truly *highly* political, in his opinion, was only the Court's competence of ministerial suits (*Ministeranklagen*), which, he aptly notices, was modelled after the English Impeachment and, though equally claiming being instrument of criminal accountability, would likewise be (and had already proved to be by the Republics of Baden, Hessen and Mecklenburg-Schwerin at this point) medium for political dispute. The principal use of such suits would be to defeat a Minister, not punish him or her; a clear political goal, he argued. He then pointed out that the use of apparently harmless legal questions to further political goals in other civil and criminal spheres, often secretly backed and financed by political parties, is a general, unavoidable phenomenon. The best one can hope for as to reduce the risk of judges subrogating themselves in the place of the Government would be to establish clear and objective procedures, for undue influence of the controller over the controlled is an immanent risk of any control function.[215]

Hans Kelsen, the founding father of the Austrian Constitutional Court, unsurprisingly concurs in the defence of a constitutional jurisdiction, though on different arguments and with some critical distantiation from metaphysical and irrational aspects he identifies in the idea of "state goals".[216] The first myth Kelsen attempts to dispel is that there is a fundamental distinction between rulemaking and rule-applying.[217] There is no opposition between these concepts, he argues, but a mere relation of subordination. Both are, contradicting classical, formalistic legal understanding, only different stages of the same process, the process of rulemaking. The stage of rulemaking is not concluded with the issuing of a law, for its content will

[215] von Hippel et al. (2013), pp. 15–19, 27.

[216] His point is arguably proven in the next few years, as many dubious pamphlets were published to support racial hygiene as a state goal, such as Hitler's (1925, became popular in the 1930s) *Mein Kampf* or Verschuer's (1936) *Rassenhygiene als Wissenschaft und Staatsaufgabe*.

[217] Kelsen refers to this as *Rechtsschöpfung* and *Rechtsanwendung*, respectively. *Recht* (*jus*) is broader concept than *Gesetz* (*lex*), usually connotating ethical or other non-written commitments, in a similar aspect as, in English, the concept of lawful contrasts with that of legal. For the lack of a better alternative, *Recht* was translated as rule/norm in this section to portray the broader sense of the word Kelsen is trying to convey here, although admittedly *Recht* and rule are incomparable on many other senses.

only be defined once regulations, sentences, administrative acts, and enforcement contribute to establishing its limits. Enforcement is the application of a sentence, which is the application of a regulation, which is the application of a law, which is the application of the Constitution. Whether one specific phase is interpreted as rulemaking instead of rule-applying will depend ultimately on the frame of reference for analysis. Qualitatively, what can be said is that Constitution, law, and regulations are abstract-general rules, while administrative acts and sentences are concrete-individual rules. After each step in this process the proportions between freedom of structuration and bindingness to the superior rule may change, but instances of production and reproduction of rules are always present.[218]

With this initial consideration Kelsen strongly pointed out, though arguably not conclusively, that neither political and nor legal "shaping" of the state reality would be radically opposed processes classical legal understanding may make them out to be, and that the material Constitution is not essentially different from other legal norms. As a result, at least the instances of ministerial suits and constitutional complaints (*Verfassungsbeschwerde*) would be unproblematic under this framework, as they seem concrete and individual enough to not present a threat to the other two Powers. Arguably, however, this argument only postponed the true dilemma a bit further down the line of rulemaking/rule-applying. What about the Court's abstract control over laws? Should courts restrain themselves to just making concrete-individual rules or are they also entitled to make abstract general rules?

The answer to this, Kelsen believes, lies in a theory of a constitutional and democratic state rather than in the theory of law. On one hand, he argues that the Constitution implies a series of commitments to limitation of powers (often referred by him as the "rationalistic ideal of security"), seeing in the Constitution many binding rules concretely applicable to the procedure and content of laws in abstract. On the other, he also recognizes the need of reinforcing the Court's political legitimacy to make this new layer of abstract control palatable, ideally in a selection method of its members that involves the collaboration between the two other powers and that seeks jurists of general esteem and talent. Moreover, he argues the acts of a Court cannot be equated to that of the other Powers, for it only represses (he rejects the possibility of reformation) unconstitutional acts and rules, and only functions on request of democratically legitimate actors (parties and authorities).[219] There would be no blemish on the political consequences of such a Court both from a legal-theoretical as from an institutional standpoint, except when, and here he agrees with Triepel, *partisan* influence (conscious or not) over the Court's work takes place.

The rest of the discussion does not centre itself in the distinction between law and politics[220] anymore, for all seem to agree that the question is not actually if a Court

---

[218] von Hippel et al. (2013), pp. 30–31.

[219] von Hippel et al. (2013), p. 56.

[220] Some still attempt to define politics or its use in this context, worth mentioning are: "[Politics] as the struggle for power" (Laun; Max Weber 1919's *Politik als Beruf* is directly and indirectly cited throughout this discussion); Walter Jellinek argues for not using the word "political" at all in this

can "make" politics, but rather to what extent. The controversial points seemed more a matter of worldview, in the sense it was reduced to one's inclinations either to argue against or in favour of the classical idea of separation and balance of powers as in the work of Locke or Montesquieu, which concentrates political decision-making in the Executive and Legislative power, relegating the Judicative to smaller questions, and to argue about what extent constitutional law was formalizable, in the then heated positivist *versus* anti-positivist debate.[221]

Since then, debates with the same underlying thematic have been repeated numerous times by the same circle of professors and their academic successors.[222] With economic and social crises mostly overcome, as well as with an already well consolidated Constitutional Court, more common ground could be found in the new debates and the new challenge became rather to find areas where most could concur the Court was doing the job of a Court rather than that of a politician. In the encounter of 2001, Robert Alexy offered a retrospective evaluation on the work of the *Bundesverfassungsgericht*, where he concluded that while the Court may have overstepped its competences a few times, it had more pronouncedly adjudicated constitutional disputes in ways not to undermine the democratic processes. Alexy, based on many decisions where the word *Spielraum* (discretion or leeway) comes up, develops a framework of analysis one could use to properly identify regions of acceptable encroachment of the political realm by the Court. The problem of discerning between law and politics becomes masked under the problem of "over- and underconstitutionalization" of the realm of politics, hinting into the idea that, although constitutional law is essentially political, Courts are limited by strictly legal methods in its treatment. He identified two main situations where a court may have

context and that there is a misunderstanding between applying exiting values and creating new ones; "every act that builds the unity of the state" (Hermann Heller). von Hippel et al. (2013), pp. 89, 96 and 113, respectively.

[221] Both sides saw, *grosso modo* (for there are schisms inside these groups), a necessity in constitutional review. The anti-positivists were critical of how law could be self-sufficient in dealing with the constant state of crisis Germany had been thrown in since the end of the First World War. Legislation was passed quickly, often fallible, and often subsequently repealed; promises of moralization and idealization of law through courts were seen as the guiding light needed to regaining trust in the State. The positivists, on the other hand, saw in this methodical "impurity" of mixing legal dispositions with unscrupulous speculation on the nature of "good government" and "correct state goals" the risk of naturalizing antisemitism and clericalism in state action. By formalizing a concept of constitution and granting it enforceable supremacy through Constitutional Courts, such risks could be minimized. Michael Stolleis (2003), p. 278; Stolleis (2014), pp. 90–95. During the debates, Richard Thoma (moderate positivist) metaphorically argues that Kelsen (neokantian positivist) and Triepel (anti-positivist) entered the same forest from different sides but managed to meet each other at the end point; it is no accident, however, that Kelsen denies that as vehemently as he does when given a chance to reply. The consequences of what Triepel defended (constitution as continuity of morality) went directly against what Kelsen sought (constitution as limitation to legality). von Hippel et al. (2013), pp. 88–122.

[222] See, for example, volumes 7 (Gerhard Leibholz), 9 (Erich Kaufmann), 20 (Peter Schneider), 39 (Karl Korinek), 61 (Robert Alexy) and 62 (Matthias Herdergen) of the *Veröffentlichungen der Vereinigung der deutschen Staatsrechtslehrer*.

an unusual degree discretion in dealing with constitutional violations, namely in (i.) discretion caused by structural lack of clarity, that is, situations in which the Constitution neither prohibits nor demands *one* specific action or medium, possibly requiring the weighing of multiple solutions, and (ii.) discretion caused by epistemological ambiguity, that is, situations in which the interpretation of the facts or of the competencies is controversial.[223]

Across the Atlantic, the famous *Political Question Doctrine* sought to produce a similar framework to separate a judge's work from that of a politician's, though in considerably more concrete fashion. Instead of defining a grey zone of jurisdictional discretion as Alexy does, American Courts attempt to define their no-go zones, that is, situations in which they unequivocally identify to be the realm of politics and, thus, are not authorized to make decisions. Justice Brennan, in *Baker v. Carr* (368 U.S. 186, 217; 1962), purportedly gave a definitive face to the doctrine in question as he defined judicial decisions should be precluded when there is: "(1) a textually demonstrable constitutional commitment to a coordinate political department; or (2) a lack of judicially discoverable and manageable standards for resolving it; or (3) the impossibility of deciding without an initial policy determination of a kind clearly for nonjudicial discretion; or (4) the impossibility of a court's undertaking independent resolution without expressing lack of the respect due coordinate branches of government; or (5) an unusual need for unquestioning adherence to a political decision already made; or (6) the potentiality of embarrassment from multifarious pronouncements by various departments on one question".[224]

The resulting framework is considerably more restricted than that of Alexy's,[225] for it focuses on competence invasions and excludes much of the Court's discretion on weighing of multiple standards. Consequently, Courts should have little say on whether authorities have carried out their obligations wisely or well. In reality, however, it has ever since become more common for legal scholars and practitioners to argue law from a perspective of fundamental rights, and Courts have been quite elusive in their avoidance of political questions,[226] to the point some have even declared the doctrine inexistent. Louis Henkin suggests that the Court's abstention, translated into words, would be in fact communicating:

> We have reviewed your claims and we find that the action complained of involves a political question, and is within the powers granted by the Constitution to the political branches. The

[223] Alexy et al. (2013), pp. 12–30. The specific language Alexy uses is: 1. Structural discretion: a. Goal setting discretion, b. Medium-choice discretion, c. Weighing discretion; 2. Epistemological discretion: a. Empirical-epistemological discretion, b. Normative-epistemological discretion.

[224] Laurence Tribe (2000), p. 366.

[225] Some authors attribute the difference in "constitutionalization" of political disputes between both legal systems to their contrasting handling of the federative commitment (stricter control of constitutional standards in the US would mean reducing State discretion *vis-à-vis* the Union), as well as to the fact that the German State, as a Social State, has many commitments in its Basic Law that require active engagement in basic rights and individual well-being. Alexy et al. (2013), pp. 212 ff.

[226] For a short overview: Tribe (2000), pp. 375–384.

> act complained of violates no constitutional limitation on that power, either because the Constitution imposes no relevant limitations, or because the action is amply within the limits prescribed. We give effect to what the political branches have done because they had political authority under the Constitution to do it.[227]

In effect, to be able to avoid a "political question", a Court will necessarily verify that the accused authority is in fact the competent authority and that the complained fact did not exceed its legal scope of action. Formally, the Court will recognize its lack of jurisdiction; materially, however, the Court will indirectly recognize the legitimacy of the authority in question and the legality of its course of action. Perhaps more superficially and with less sensibility to reasonableness and effectiveness than what would be expected from a German Court in a similar position, but would offer recognition, nonetheless. Based on observations like these, but more importantly on the fact that the American Constitution does not expressly limit what can be subject of a Court's decision at any point, Henkin argues there is no real justification for the Courts' omission when called to remedy legal disputes.[228]

The point of this section is not to give a comprehensive view of how jurists have come to terms with the classical separation between law and politics, but rather to demonstrate how many different interpretations may be given to the same problem. It also means to point out that this is a matter that will not, nor could ever achieve some sort of unanimous understanding of where to draw the line. This happens basically because of dissent on two different levels, one of them, epistemological, the other, one of worldview, as will be argued in more detail in the next sections.

On the epistemological level, there is what an individual may value as *reliable sources of information*; it is to ask for what kind of evidence a person considers necessary to inform their acts and beliefs. This varies greatly among populations and is often discussed, for example, in the debates between science and religion, where some are sceptical to the point no religious belief is possible, some are more permissible and can see an unproblematic compatibility between both, and some may see in science a threat of subverting religion. Conversely, when it comes to law, there are those who see law as "neutral grounds", for whatever ontological or methodological reasons, allowing for a clear-cut separation from politics, and there are those who see law irreparably mixed with politics, whatever the context may be. The more a political matter gets legally or constitutionally entrenched, the more likely it is the case that a Court acting upon its predicaments may be perceived as compliant with its legal obligations rather than the usurper of political faculties. How much definition is enough definition or how much positive law is enough positive law, however, is up for debate. On the second level, the one of worldview, it comes

[227] Henkin (1976), p. 601. In other words, inversely as Hegel/Spinoza have put it a few centuries before: '*omnis determinatio est negatio*' (every determination is [also] negation). From Roman Law, a similar form is also found in Justinian's digest as '*expressio unius est exclusio alterus*' (the expression of one excludes others).

[228] Henkin (1976), p. 625; Scharpf (1966), p. 597, equally rejects that such a doctrine could result from the interpretation of the Constitution, criticizing how many times the "political question" label has been ascribed on grounds far from compelling.

down to *what one (and the society in which one is inserted) wishes for democracy and balance of powers*. Some may value more the rationality of the Courts and choose to entrust them with a bigger slice of the power, others may value more the legitimacy and communicative deliberation of the Parliament and opt to shift their bias towards it, and, finally, there are those who may favour the energy and diligence of the Executive. Still on the same level, there are those who favour substantial elements of democracy (equity, inclusiveness, individual freedom) over procedural ones (elections, deliberation, textuality), and vice-versa. Depending how one weighs these elements, one will value differently the role of Courts as political protagonists, as well as the "acceptable" ranges of interpretation.[229]

2.3.2 General Problems of Legal Interpretation

There are many ways one could answer the question confronted by this section, the question of whether there is a distinction between law and politics and whether this distinction is meaningful in the context of impeachment. It will all ultimately depend on what set of beliefs are predicated within the reasoning of who is answering.

A legal naturalist may argue, for example, that the correct *legal* answer for an impeachment question is that which was answered with respect to the inherent virtues of human nature, which, to the naturalist, tend to be objective, eternal, and immutable. Consider Clinton's case, for instance. An jus-naturalist could argue his adultery was grievous enough to justify its classification as 'high crimes and misdemeanours' for it undermined trust in the family unity; an attack against the institution 'family', especially if committed by the highest magistrate of the nation, would constitute a crime against the nation by extrapolation, since families are ultimately the units that compose community, which on its turn compose society and state. Assuming the 'eternality, objectivity and immutability' of such reasoning, the *jus*-naturalist would see any other interpretation of Clinton's infractions as an abnormality that exceeded the limits of legality and would be more akin to a political resolution. At the time, one of the defence's argument was that his infractions were committed in the private sphere and thus were not impeachable, for impeachments

[229] This separation of epistemology and worldview stems from post-kantian epistemology. Unlike some other epistemologies, post-kantians do not think of knowledge and belief as two fundamentally different things, but rather as different degrees of a same attitude. Philosophically speaking, what is known is never conflated with what there is ("the thing in itself"), as would be the case of those who adopt that knowledge is the depiction of truth, rather than one possible, perhaps unstable belief of what truth could be. Consequently, any kind of moral realism is strongly hampered. A moral realist could argue against this separation that certain things such as democracy or freedom are "objectively good" and that they can be ascertained from reality just as any fact of physics. If that is accepted, then worldview may coalesce into epistemology. I do not subscribe to this, but I also do not have the space to go in detail about these matters. In the next sections, I can only hope to give small hints into the critiques that undermine this view and that support the separation argued here.

ought to be a remedy only against public wrongdoing; in case the Senate confirmed (and it largely did) such thesis, the result would not be legally legitimate, but only politically.[230]

Another possible basic set of beliefs is that of the legal doctrinalism. A legal 'doctrinalist' believes there are many cases in which the legal understanding (doctrine) over a particular question can reach a high level of certainty, incorporating itself as part of the law. Even something as tendentially broad as constitutional law could achieve clear-cut meanings to its content. To illustrate this, let us consider Dilma Rousseff's impeachment, who was convicted of issuing supplementary credit without parliamentary approval, effectively usurping part of the Parliament's power of the purse. Let us assume that multiple similar cases involving Governors and Mayors were taken to court, and all resulted in acquittal and the hegemonic doctrinal understanding that such misconducts were not sufficiently grievous to warrant any sort of punishment (in reality, this matter has been deeply controversial). A legal doctrinalist who faced this case would probably interpret Rousseff's conviction as a deviation from standard legality, thus being some sort of politicized use of law.

A school of thought that is often deemed oppositional to doctrinalism is that of originalism. Originalists conceive the 'original intent' behind the interpreted norm as the true source of its interpretation. Whatever goal the Framers intended for that specific norm will be the ultimate defining factor on its understanding. The already mentioned Clinton's defence claimed exactly this; it recovered historical moments in which the Framers declared impeachment to be directed exclusively to public wrongdoing, such as James Wilson's quote: "our President (...) is amenable to [the laws] in his private character as a citizen, and in his public character by *impeachment*".[231] To an originalist, any other result than acquittal to Clinton's impeachment would be a deviation of the Framer's original intent and most likely to be interpreted as the result of political deliberation rather than legal subsumption. Originalists may reject doctrinal interpretative constructions if they believe it contradicts the original intent (doctrinalism may also resort to historical interpretations though).[232]

There are many other approaches one could exemplify here to illustrate the variability of conclusions jurists come to in relation to this theme. Instead, we shall consider the approach adopted for this book, that of legal realism,[233] as it

---

230 van Tassel and Finkelman (1999), pp. 296–299 (Clinton's private wrongdoing defence); See Brendan Brown (1955) for the specific understanding of marriage related matters under natural law. Natural law is usually given supremacy over the law and politics. For naturalists, law and politics need to fulfil their natural purposes, Sellin (1978), p. 822.

231 van Tassel and Finkelman (1999), p. 296.

232 For the debate between "living Constitution" and originalism, see Bennett and Solum (2011).

233 We are referring to the American and not the Scandinavian Legal Realism here. Although both have much in common, the former may be seen as a ramification of political progressivism and the latter of positivism. The Scandinavians demystify what the 'Old Orders' used to call 'legal science', to produce more grounded, empirically driven legal understandings; The Americans undertake a similar project with common starting points, but yet embrace the unavoidable political and ethical

arguably offers a more unifying, grounded, and thorough understanding of law and its consequential tension with politics than the ones cited above. Legal realism rejects many of the predicated epistemological assumptions that tend to confer a degree of certainty to legal interpretation, undermining much of their appeal. Regarding naturalism, realism rejects the possibility of deducing values from any sort of 'inherent' nature or of eternal reason. Bridging the gap of 'what is' and 'what ought to be' is, at best, an ambiguous endeavour, if not at all misdirecting.[234] Moreover, the kind of naturalism based on analytic *a priori* deductions tend to be self-reflexive tautologies and offer no substantial direction to agency.[235] Realism rejects the objectivity doctrinalism claims to achieve, for the multiplicity of doctrinal materials potentially applicable at a given case tend to render legal doctrine hopelessly indeterminate. Doctrines tend to form patchworks of contradictory premises, partly inconsistent with one another, often suggesting two or more opposing tendencies at every point.[236] As to originalism, realism would reject the existence of singular, coherent objectives in legal norms, as well as their historical stagnation. As seen in previous sections exemplified through the framing of impeachment in the Constitutional and Ratifying Conventions, legal norms are usually result not of a singular legislator, but a synthesis of compromises of multiple concurrent opinions and interests, possibly imperfectly executed, being meant for one or more objectives, which will not necessarily be mutually inclusive. Moreover, as also seen before exemplified in the rise of political partisanship transforming impeachments, the content and objective of a legal norm is constantly transformed by the environment and the circumstances in which it is inserted.

In other words, the 'idealism' to which legal realists express their rejection is that of immutable truths, of argumentative safe harbours one may feel tempted to seek refuge in when baffled by the multitude of opposing interpretations offered to a specific legal problem; the end-all and be-all sources of legal substance promised by these idealists offer nothing but a false sense of security that is quickly dissolved by the scrutiny of legal practice or of its grounding principles; of the many faces legal formalism may assume. Realists advance the view that no set of institutions that compose the law can be so static. Law is a *going* (dynamic) set of institutions

aspects of law. In detail: Alexander (2002), *passim*; Llewellyn (1962), pp. 53–57; Leiter (1998, 2012).

[234] Nature's ambiguity and its impropriety to serve as standard-setter of conduct is perhaps best epitomized by John Stuart Mill (1875), p. 29: "Nature impales men, breaks them as if on the wheel, casts them to be devoured by wild beasts, burns them to death, crushes them with stones like the first Christian martyr, starves them with hunger, freezes them with cold, poisons them by the quick or slow venom of her exhalations, and has hundreds of other hideous deaths in reserve, such as the ingenious cruelty of a Nabis or a Domitian never surpassed. All this Nature does with the most supercilious disregard both of mercy and of justice, emptying her shafts upon the best and noblest indifferently with the meanest and worst; upon those who are engaged in the highest and worthiest enterprises, and often as the direct consequence of the noblest acts; and it might almost be imagined as a punishment for them."

[235] See Bieri et al. (1979) and Wenzel (1992).

[236] Dagan (2015), pp. 1891 ff.; Llewellyn (1988), pp. 998 ff.

distinguished by the difficult task of accommodating three constitutive yet irresolvable tensions: the tensions between (i) power and reason, (ii) science and craft, and (iii) tradition and progress.[237]

The first tension (i) is the realization that law, albeit also a portrayal of power, interests, and politics, can never be reduced to purely that. Law is also a forum of reason which imposes real constraints on the choices of legal decisionmakers. It is not a forum of pure reason, nor of pure interest; neither too romantic, nor too cynical—it is rather a complex interaction that needs to be accounted "to accentuate the distinct responsibility incumbent on the reasoning of and about power, minimizing the corrupting potential of the self-interested pursuit of power, and the perpetuation of what could result as merely group preferences and interests". Not only being reductionist on either side (legal reasoning or reasoning about power and interest) would be intellectually negligent (or worse, dishonest), but would be morally irresponsible for undermining the possibility of criticizing state power and the option of taking affirmative action regarding morally necessary social changes.[238]

The second constitutive tension (ii) identifies the need of conjugating both empirical data and normative judgements. On one side are social facts that reveal the practical consequences of law to guide its evolution and protect its legitimacy, and on the other, ethical standards that guide the evaluation and realization of such empirical research. One without the other would be either a quest without objective or an objective without a quest; neither could possibly be solely by itself a valid test of law's merits.[239]

The final constitutive tension (iii) is between progress and tradition. As mentioned, a common starting point to all legal realists is the dynamism of law. Law is an ever-evolving enterprise, constantly being tested and retested, and in search of improvement. The law's past serves as a valuable "anchor of intelligibility and predictability", but its execution may have been or may have become imperfect, given the circumstances it was or ought to be applied, and so it cannot be final. As described by Llewellyn, law is "a functioning harmonization of vision with tradition, of continuity with growth, of machinery with purpose, of measure with need", mediating between "the seeming commands of the authorities and the felt demands of justice".[240]

Facing so many tensions, one may be inclined to ask: how much guidance can such a method offer? When so many decisions are plausible, does not the realist

[237] Dagan (2015), p. 1893.

[238] Dagan (2015), pp. 1894–1895.

[239] Dagan (2015), p. 1896.

[240] Dagan (2015), pp. 1897–1898. Moreover, the judicial system is a system within other systems, which carry with themselves their own restraints. The restraints imposed by language, culture and ideology predetermine to some extent the realm of possible outcomes. Hirsch (1982), p. 237.

approach equate with open-ended discretionary decision making?[241] May this not be an excuse to justify adjudication based on personal predilections and beliefs? To some extent this is true, if a minority of the realist movement known as the "idiosyncratic wing" is considered; most realists would deny such extreme understanding, however. They would claim law is not a mass of unrelated 'hunches', but a product of a specific group of individuals, inserted in a system full of regular and consistent revisions, tending to wash away eccentric decisions and so promote some regularity and predictability.[242] Moreover, realism does not abolish the methodology of its precursors (*i.e.*, the naturalist's search for systemic congruency and overarching *telos* of legal institutions,[243] the doctrinalist's strive for the construction of precise categories or the originalist's search for genealogy), but builds upon them,[244] recognizing their merits and their limitations in face of the inevitable gaps between norms, language, interpretative methodologies and judicial outcomes. It does not follow that "because there is no such thing as traditional formal realizability, [that] everything is indeterminate or up for grabs".[245]

Some positivists acknowledge part of these critics, but accuse realists of overstating their claims. Herbert Hart would claim that, yes, there are some gaps between concepts and their application, but ultimately concepts have a core of certainty in them, which allows for a considerable degree of objectivity in adjudication. There is also a part of their meaning, the penumbra, which requires the effective use of discretion, but these situations would be exceptional and restricted to "hard cases". It is the very restricted hypothesis in which judges legislate and the model of rules is swept aside. Ronald Dworkin, on the other hand, says such an attitude is politically inacceptable. Judges should never be allowed that kind of

[241] Margaret Radin eloquently summarizes this traditional view: "(. . .) the Rule of law demands that judges 'apply' rather than 'make' the law. If rules do not tie judges' hands with their logical or analytic application, the traditional view is that judges will have personal discretion in how to apply the law. This will undermine congruence and confuse those who are supposed to follow the rules. It will diminish the efficacy of the system (in the instrumental view) and the liberty of the rule-followers (in the substantive view). It will also confer on judges a realm of 'arbitrary power' and undermine democracy". Radin (1989), p. 796.

[242] Dagan (2015), pp. 1899–1900.

[243] Legal Realism, both Scandinavian as well as American, are fierce opposition of Naturalism, but only to what pertains their ontological or metaphysical claims (natural entities whose properties define all properties). Regarding methodological naturalism, the idea that "acceptable methods of justification and explanation are continuous, in some sense, with science", realism may be compatible and sometimes particularly strong, if sociological strands of legal realism are considered. Spaak (2009), p. 36.

[244] Cohen (1935), p. 829.

[245] Margaret Radin (1989), p. 803. The criticism realism faces is comparable to that which Wittgenstein's ordinary language philosophy had to face in his time. Answering the suspicion of 'emptying' philosophy, he stated: "Where does our investigation get its importance from, since it seems only to destroy everything interesting, that is, all that is great and important? (. . .) What we are destroying is nothing but houses of cards and we are clearing up the ground of language on which they stand" Ludwig Wittgenstein (1968), §118. See Leiter (1997), pp. 267–268, for a collection of misreadings of Realism.

discretion. He posits the "penumbra" is insignificant in comparison to the core and that even in situations where the law seems relatively indeterminate, such as in principles (as opposed to rules), objectivity is achievable. The objective answer would be that which is entailed in the entire body of past legal authoritative acts, where interpretation rests on the best political theory available.[246] Realists would see this strive for objectivity commendable, but much more complex than the binary solutions proposed. Rules and concepts vary within a spectrum of continuity, with differing degrees of certainty, and more often than one may care to admit with no clear-cut transition between situations of penumbra/core or rule/principle.[247]

Legal realism makes a radical claim by acknowledging the wide range of *potential* judicial choices, but this claim does not entail that judges should recur to this wide array of options in every case. It recognizes stability and predictability are fundamental elements in granting the law its ability of providing effective guidance and allowing for planning.[248] This stability and predictability, however, do not inhere from the sources of interpretation, but from the broader social practice of law. It is to say that the seemly natural agreement legal practitioners have over 'the correct use of legal norms' is not a result of an analytical realization of the said rules (or concepts) in the particular, but of an acknowledgement of the prevalent understandings of the legal community, which may in a point in time value a single interpretation more than others[249] and which will evolve and transform over time.[250]

Where does this leave the interpret when it comes to impeachments, however? Courts of Impeachment are arguably the most exceptional example of judicature available. Not only the proceedings are incredibly rare with only the United States, Brazil, and Paraguay having multiple occurrences in the Americas,[251] but are also directed to an incredibly peculiar array of conducts, circumstances, and subjects. How is the interpret to infer stability in understanding in such small samples? Moreover, how is he/she to assess the set of possible sources of interpretation in such ambiguous and incompletely regulated proceedings?

---

[246] Hart (1958), pp. 606–615; Dworkin (1977), pp. 44–45, 81–130; Radin (1989), pp. 793–806.

[247] As a demonstration of this, see Kennedy (1982).

[248] Raz (2002), pp. 214 ff.; Radin (1989), p. 796.

[249] We come once again *close* to Wittgenstein and his understanding of what constitutes 'rule-following' (§198-242), as, for example, in: "Following a rule is analogous to obeying an order. We are trained to do so; we react to an order in a particular way. But what if one person reacts in one way and another in another to the order and the training? Which one is right? (. . .) The common behaviour of mankind is the system of reference by means of which we interpret an unknown language [set of rules]" and "If language is to be means of communication there must be agreement not only in definitions but also in judgments. This seems to abolish logic, but does not do so. It is one thing to describe methods of measurement, and another to obtain and state results of measurement. But what we call 'measuring' is partly determined by a certain constancy in results of measurement". Wittgenstein (1968), §§ 206 and 242.

[250] Arguably in predictable patterns alternating between periods of fixity and innovation, as Pound (1908), pp. 606–608 suggests.

[251] If one also considers impeachment surrogates (*e.g.*, declaration of vacancy), then also Peru and Ecuador.

Being this the case, a realist will not directly assume any decision is necessarily *entirely* arbitrary, for, despite being exceptional proceedings, impeachments have many *material* points of convergence with other disciplinary, criminal, and civil proceedings. There are consolidated, though not necessarily unproblematic, understandings of things such as treason, bribery, abuse of power or criminal negligence/malfeasance, that may, by extrapolation, suggest an adjudicative standard also in the realm of impeachments. The grey zones are then the offenses specific to Presidents, which have most of the time little to no practical incidence and, consequently, do not allow for an observation of standards in legal practices; the legal community may offer multiple solutions based on the approaches already cited here, but as will be commented in more detail in the next section, none of them can be authoritatively deemed "the correct solution", and much will effectively be left within the discretion of the adjudicator (usually the Senate, but also possibly the Supreme Court). From the *procedural* perspective of presidential impeachments, the question becomes more obscure. There is hardly any point of procedural convergence between presidential impeachments and other types of proceedings. The proceedings themselves tend to be not thoroughly regulated and require by default already considerable constructive efforts from the adjudicator in order to merely make the impeachment charges at all triable. Additionally, the subjective circumstances of the President tend to undermine any hope of an impartial, "due process" trial as would be guaranteed to a common citizen or a lower officer. The best one may hope for, from the perspective of a realist, is to tell what kind of practices fall outside the realm of what could be legally expected.

This solution may seem underwhelming in comparison to what formalists/idealists promise with their peremptory methods, but it seems by far a more honest and achievable program by simply admitting there is no such thing as "application without interpretation, or interpretation without politics and value, or politics and value without commitment".[252]

2.3.3 Specific Problems of Legal Interpretation and Impeachment

The problems of interpretation are naturally not restricted to the question of what valid sources of legal agency are. Even if there was such a thing as an *ultimative* source, that source would still suffer with the immanent and intertwining shortcomings of language, logic and human agency.[253] Whatever the source may be, it will use different concepts and categories to guide human action; these concepts and

[252] Radin (1989), p. 814.

[253] Specifically on human agency, Llewellyn points out: "(. . .) one of the more obvious and obstinate facts about human beings is that they operate in and respond to traditions (. . .) Traditions grips them, shapes them, limits them, guides them". Such circumstances may often prime one into

categories may, *intentionally or not*, have multiple meanings (polysemy), be indeterminate ('diffuse' or demanding of 'constructive' meaning), be incomplete (loopholes or imperfect execution), be or become inadequate for a specific case (anachronic, anatopic and other inconsistencies), may significantly overlap each other or even be contradictory among themselves, all of which burden the adjudicator with a greater or lesser degree of discretion. As a result, even in ideal circumstances, adjudication is *never a cognitive act*, but *an act of will*, for there is never one possible 'right decision', but multiple instances of potential 'right decisions', among which the adjudicator will attempt to select within the constraints of his reasoning power and of the social pressures of legal practice. Legal outcomes are not 'discovered' but ascribed.[254]

Restraining the scope of acceptable interpretations is one of the greatest challenges of legal theory, however. Any person, jurist or otherwise, may strive to find justification for the feeling of 'injustice' in the most rational way possible, but will eventually be driven down by the shortcomings encountered as he or she becomes more critical of their own ways. Deep down many of us believe that we share the same *qualia*, that the feeling of injustice we once felt is alike that which was described previously to us by others, much like we tend to represent objects like the sun, the moon and nature in general in similar ways. Naturalists and rationalists sought 'moral truths' in the divine creation, attempted to read between the lines of what nature and universal logic was communicating through its being; doctrinalists and classical positivists attempted to create concepts and categories so precise one could deal with legal issues like a mathematician deals with Newtonian algebra;[255] neokantian positivists attempted to create systems so logically hermetic a jurist could find in it, particularly in the Constitution, all tools needed to face any legal problem. All this falls short, as will be argued, for taking a fundamental piece of the puzzle too lightly, the medium through which all law incarnates within and is communicated through: language.[256]

---

certain pitfalls of unreflected and irrational decision-making. Karl Llewellyn, *The Common Law Tradition* (1960), *apud* Brian Leiter (1997), p. 284; In deeper detail, Karl Llewellyn (1988), p. 995.

[254] Hans Kelsen (2009), pp. 348–355; Margaret Radin (1989), pp. 793 ff. This makes Kelsen fundamentally different from many of the classical positivists of his time (or more precisely, representatives of the *Begriffsjurisprudenz*), such as Paul Laband or Carl Friedrich von Gerber, who believed in the certainty of legal meanings to allow for something such as "pure calculation with concepts", that is, the idea that certain legal situations have one definite solution discoverable through logical-formal methods. Werner Heun (1989), p. 381.

[255] See, for example, Rudolf von Jhering's humorous essay *Im juristischen Begriffshimmel* ("In the legal-conceptual heaven") for an account of how this idea is in itself already absurd. von Jhering (2009), pp. 245 ff.

[256] "There is no reason why the fundamental operations in law, *i.e.*, its creation and its application, should be perceived as something else than linguistic operations. But, surprisingly, they are even today approached from all but linguistic points of view." Marcus Galdia (2017), p. 59. The last statement is, of course, a hyperbole. Many have critically denoted the importance and pitfalls of language in law in the last 70 years, such as Charles Perelman, Michel Foucault, Alf Ross, Karl Olivekrona, Felix Cohen, and David Mellinkoff, to name a few. It is surprising, however, how

To explain this more didactically, consider the following thought experiment. Imagine you were first teaching a child its first words. You point at an object and say its name, hoping the child will catch on the connection between the word uttered and the object it designates. Let us suppose for the sake of argument that this object indicated is a tree. How can the child conclude that the object pointed to is the general concept of tree or perhaps just that specific kind of tree? She will likely for a while confuse the idea, maybe thinking that the word "tree" designates only the specific tree you pointed out; maybe she will associate the word "tree" with an unexpected aspect or feature of a tree, such as its trunk or its colour. Given enough time, practice, and immersion, however, she will notice that the use of the word "tree" designates a general idea of tree and not only the specific tree that was pointed out the first time or that its trunk or its colour are referred to by different words.

This is a fundamental concept of what came to be known in linguistics as structuralism, that is, the idea that language is constructed not by individual units, but by a complete structure. Each unit must be understood by their relation to the other units, occurring through a process of differentiation, which was re-enacted above. To truly grasp a unit, one must understand the other units that circumscribe it.[257] Post-structuralists would go further and claim that this process of differentiation is never truly complete because the context in which it happens is never completely stable. The meaning of words is never truly perfected and contained, depending strongly on use and context.[258]

Like linguists, jurists share a strong connection with language and tend to obsess with precision of what is being communicated, seeking to devise unambiguous concepts. Jurists often work with affirmative processes, however. In other words, they impose meanings to words and claim to have reached definitive understanding of their limits. As much as clarity is salutary, their contribution cannot go beyond being more than just one step in the grand scheme of the differentiation process.

---

generally law has stubbornly resisted critique of its foundations. As Alf Ross (2004), p. 18, puts it "Who would ever think of tracing the valid norms of chess back to an a priori validity, a pure idea of chess, bestowed upon man by God or deduced by man's eternal reason? The thought is ridiculous, because we do not take chess as seriously as law - because stronger emotions are bound up with the concepts of law".

[257] de Saussure (2016), pp. 132[156] ff. "(...) in a language there are only differences, and no positive terms. (...) In a sign, what matters more than any idea or sound associated with it is what other signs surround it. The proof of this lies in the fact that the value of a sign may change without affecting either meaning or sound, simply because some neighbouring sign has undergone a change" (pp. 140–141[166]).

[258] Barthes (2007), pp. 260 ff; Derrida (1998), pp. 33–70. Post-structuralists are often accused of nihilism and "relativism" (as in, 'any claim is as good as any other') because of this idea. This is mostly not the case. Post-structuralism is a suspicion of concise meanings and, as a result, often leads to scepticism towards the apparently harmless or intuitive ideas of essentialism, absolutes, universals, and common metanarratives, such as justice, science, and so on. Similarly to scientific scepticism, but generally with more self-criticism (*e.g.*, Thomas Kuhn, Paul Feyerabend), post-structuralist scepticism takes nothing for granted. It tends towards pragmatism and contextualism which are not "relativistic".

Their concepts will acquire and lose meaning through recurrent use and change of contexts, possibly transforming themselves completely in unforeseeable ways. Meanwhile language shall remain the means through which orders are given, this will unavoidably be the case. It is fundamental to notice that, if language is undergoing constant change, so is the letter of the law. *Language is form, not substance.*[259]

The creation of axioms to consolidate meaning, as often found in law and legal textbooks, gives a false sense of security. The units which compose these axioms are themselves subjected to uncertainty and instability, rendering legal systems unavoidably open to subtle and not-so-subtle transformations. If one thinks, for example, of how the concept of *persona* was transformed throughout legal history so that different legal consequences could have been drawn to different people, this may be reasonably clear. In Roman law, for example, the concept of *persona* was long inconsequential. Both free men and slaves were seen as persona, though the latter was treated more like an object in most circumstances.[260] To the Roman, *persona* was any human being, anyone who played a role in society. As the legal concept of *persona* advanced to encompass the capacity of being a subject of rights and duties, the persistence of slavery compelled the understanding that slaves no longer belonged to that category, at least in some cases. In some of the cases, the contradiction of being a human being but at the same not a person was embraced by legal systems under different justifications,[261] but there were also those who redrew the lines of humanity to push slaves to the outer border. Thomas Jefferson and lawyers of the Southern States, for example, justified slavery on the inferiority of "reasoning", "cultivation", and other "real distinctions nature has made" upon Black peoples; in other words, they did not possess the faculties of being a subject of law and could, therefore, be reduced to objects.[262]

The United Nations Universal Declaration of Human Rights marks an important milestone in recognizing basic rights to every human being, and attempting to close all gaps that could be explored to decategorize someone from the concept. Legal

[259] de Saussure (2016), p. 143[169]. This not to say that language (form) has no effect on substance, it does, but not in the sense argued by platonism (as in transcendent perfect archetypes to which objects and concepts of the everyday world only imperfectly reproduce) or logocentrism (as in the regarding of words and language as fundamental expression of an external reality). Wittgenstein (1968), §41, and Austin (1979), pp. 55 ff., would come to the same consequences by stressing that the meaning of words are more related to their use than their imposed distinctions; that is to say, recognizing meaning is more akin to recognizing the "rules of the game" than certain "facts about the world".

[260] Buckland (1908), pp. 2–5.

[261] Wilson (1957), points out a few these justifications: i. Religion ("slavery is a reward for our missionary efforts"); ii. Legal consequence ("slavery as redress of obligations or infractions"); iii. Utilitarianism ("slavery is necessary for progress; slavery is good for the slaves"); iv. Race ("inferior races shall serve superior races"). Military domination usually fits ii. or iii. ("being a slave is better than being slain in war").

[262] Finkelman (1999), pp. 83 ff. Immanuel Kant and David Hume make similar arguments, although it is unclear whether they would draw consequences so far as to deny personhood or basic dignity.

theoreticians must remain aware of the fact that this is no safeguard to the redrawing of linguistic lines. If the current economic consensus shifts towards, say, a sort of neo-feudalism, this redrawing would be likely. It may be something as blatant as Jefferson's justification, but it may also be much subtler, perhaps redrawing the lines of reason or of legal consent—the latter being already something one may observe in the justification of forced labour in prisons or other forms of economic exploitation of the very poor (sometimes described as *labour analogous to slavery*). As Hans Kelsen teaches us, a gap in a legal definition can always be argued and, consequently, an exception can always be justified.[263]

As a final remark, it is important to notice that the processes of differentiation are not limited to language and are applicable to any system of values, be it culture, morality, or law. The value of one piece of the structure changes once another piece is added, removed, or transformed. If one considers the right to free speech, for example, it is visible how free speech means one thing in one system where it is not confronted by certain values, and means another completely different thing, when it is confronted. If a system has at the same time the right to free speech and the right to honour, name, and dignity, each of them will have to be made compatible to the other. That is to say, for example, one may exercise his right to speech as long as it does not cripple the honour of the other, and vice versa. New limits are drawn every time a new value is added or removed, and every time their actual meanings are transformed. Values may even conflict with themselves, as in the free speech of one harming the free speech of another. This is, for example, the case that justifies Germany's or France's ban on speech that supports Nazism or historical revisionism, for, in the last instance, these forms of speech, when led without the proper critical distance, may result in the suppression of other speeches and basic rights.[264]

These are blatant examples to get the point across, but one should not be mistaken: transformations in meaning are common and even reach legal dispositions imagined as being of crystalline clarity. The consensus of the legal community presents meaningful standards, but they are not final, absolute, or transposable to every context. Again, the position argued in this book does not advocate for radical instability and uncertainty. The legal community and the judicial processes have a tendency of creating stabler concepts than ordinary language and washing away eccentric understandings due to their characteristic composition and their use of judicial revision and reasoned, methodical discussion. What this section attempted to portray is that limits may be elusive and that language works in ways that may not be commonsensical to most who are born into societies of written language.[265] It is

---

[263] von Hippel et al. (2013), p. 121.

[264] Stein (1986).

[265] "The written form of a word strikes us as a permanent, solid object and hence more fitting than its sound to act as a linguistic unit persisting through time", de Saussure (2016), p. 29[46]. Saussure suggests that mankind's insistence in clinging to a purported stable and absolute (logocentric) use of words stems from a confusion with the stability of their graphical appearance. The phonetic "making sense of meaning" of language (distinguishing sounds chained together from each other) would exacerbate its ephemeral and context dependent nature.

fundamental to reckon that impeachments take place in the intersection with the legal community (not every legislator is a jurist and, when even they are, they are more than just jurists), that they are not subjected to recurrent revision, that they tend to be few and far between, and that their circumstances are exceptional. Expecting stability of meaning in the same sense one would from a court of law is not only unrealistic, but also arguably unfeasible for the lack of enabling circumstances for such stability.

2.3.4 Coup, Constitutional Hardball or (Political) Justice?

It is certainly more difficult to assess the commitment to legality in an impeachment than in a regular court case. What works for the latter can only incompletely address the problems that typically appear in the former. Once one has acquired the fundamentals of legal theory and understands the kinds of tensions that underpin the relationship of law and politics, however, reaching a satisfying answer becomes more feasible.

This section purports to demonstrate how one may find such answers, firstly by pointing out how strict separations of law and politics, even the most promising of them, fatally fail, and then by arguing how one may be able to think and operate within the inflection of both elements. An interdisciplinary method will be suggested, requiring both an analysis of executive instability and of the respect to the rule of law, albeit with some reservations imposed by the practical reality of impeachments to the latter. A tripartite form of classification will be suggested, and the risks of mischaracterization will be discussed, particularly in the confusion of flawed impeachments with *coups d'état* or other *coup* related neologisms.

2.3.4.1 Strict Legal vs. Political Separation of Impeachment

One way of digesting and sustaining the legal/political dichotomy in impeachments is to split it in phases. In one phase, there would be a prevalence of considerations regarding the legal soundness of an impeachment and, in another, the prevalence of considerations of political opportunity. In the American-style presidential impeachments, this would function in the following fashion: the lower House in Parliament would find evidence of the President's unfitness for office and, as the closer representant of the people, would voice an accusation against him or her before the higher House. This first phase, since it is more focused on the likelihood of a misdeed and the opportunity of an impeachment, would be said as being of a political nature. The second phase, when the higher House joins in to try the evidence collected and the articles of impeachment presented, is the one that is to be considered properly legal. Here, the Court focuses on legality rather than opportunity, certainty rather than likelihood. This dynamic is said to have been the case of the late Stuart England as commented before, where the House of Commons fiercely attacked their political antagonists, but then had their efforts frustrated by the House of Lords, who acted effectively as the guardian of legality and only endorsed legally robust causes.

This same type of division is possible even in impeachment procedures that involve more phases, such as was the case in Venezuela in the 1993 impeachment of Carlos Andrés Pérez. Venezuela, a unicameral system, has the Supreme Court acting as part of the Court of Impeachments. There, in the first phase, the Supreme Court verifies any impeachment accusation against the President to check if it holds any water in a strictly legal perspective. Only then the accusation reaches the Parliament, where the considerations of opportunity are brought up and the President is impeached. The case then returns to the Supreme Court to be taken to trial. In this situation, there would be two properly legal phases and one political phase in between them, to procedurally separate the work of jurists and politicians as much as possible, while still acknowledging their integral and legitimatizing roles.

As straight-forward as these divisions look and as well intentioned as they may be, they end up being more programmatic than factual. Many factors have been pointed out the that invariably conduce to a 'mixed' and ambiguous nature, such as the extraordinary nature of impeachment cases, the eclectic composition of the adjudication organ, the highly loaded political atmosphere (*e.g.,* the expectation of quick and efficient resolution of economic, humanitarian or constitutional crises), the subjective features of the President (*i.e.,* status, power, political affiliations, democratic claim to legitimacy), among other things, which all lead to a confluence of legal and political considerations where ideally only one or the other should be present. All points out to the fact that a strict division between law and politics is inappropriate and perhaps even counterproductive in the context of impeachments.

Indeed, even if one is generally sceptical of the legal realist stance about the three constitutive tensions within law, one is likely to acknowledge them at least in the context of impeachments, particularly the first tension, the one between reason and power. Or would it be outlandish to say that somehow the stakes of an impeachment also play a fundamental role in determining its outcomes? Would a group of representatives choose to interpret law more strictly if they saw in it an opportunity to avert democratic backsliding caused by increasing rumours of an outbreak of civil war or of a military coup? Would they interpret it more laxly if they saw in the procedures a disproportionate burden on the economy, one much heavier than the offenses allegedly attributed to the President? How big is big enough for a concerning impeachable offense, and under which circumstances?

This book is advocating for the embracement of ambiguity, though it is an uncomfortable endeavour for most jurists and scientists. Unfortunately, if the political actors in impeachments are not given at least a bit of the benefit of the doubt, impeachments are doomed to be forever perceived as legal shams due to their invariably 'impure' quality—and this would arguably be an injustice to a feature of presidentialism that allows it to become truly republican in nature and which has arguably averted many larger conflicts in the countries they took place. Naturally, impeachments may also happen by virtue of less noble considerations than those presented above, such as self-interest, revenge, and sheer animosity. It is important, therefore, to discuss where impeachments could possibly be misused and where genuine ambiguity is present, as will be done next.

2.3.4.2 Sifting Wheat from Chaff: A Standard for Legitimate Impeachments?

When people claim an impeachment was decided politically, they are voicing an important disagreement with its outcome or conduction. It may be the case that they have an idealist conception of legality that is commonly entailed in the use of ordinary language, or it may be the case that they indeed see something very fishy in the procedures.

The first hypothesis should have already been sufficiently addressed in this chapter, as we have argued impeachments are essentially imperfect procedures and, thus, elevating them to the highest standards of legality is bound to make them look like a sham, regardless of context and merit. It is inevitable and it is no blemish for impeachments to have a political dimension—affirming impeachments are political is tautological and brings no analytical gain.

The second hypothesis is a more serious one and the one that will be dealt with in this section. Questioning the legitimacy of an impeachment is serious because it may mean that impeachment, an instrument meant to make republicanism in the presidential system feasible, is being used precisely against its original intent. It is to say that an impeachment was instrumentalized to attack an innocent president or to safeguard a guilty one. Over time, persistent suspicion about how the democratic game is being played will lead to mistrust in the political system, arguably contributing to political apathy, erosion of institutions, emergence antisystem parties/political leaders, among other potential maladies for democracy.

It is important, therefore, to correctly identify these situations. Sometimes passable impeachments are accused of being illegitimate, thus unnecessarily contributing to the demoralization of the political system and distorting the diagnosis of what may be working or dysfunctional within that system. This is an important remark, as all Presidents from the upcoming case studies claimed being victims of a corrupt plot at some point and so attempted to escape accountability for crises endured during their administrations. Reproducing those narratives uncritically may be irresponsible as it has the potential of legitimizing and reproducing disruptive behaviour in the Executive branch, which, as noticed before, has been historically more reprehensible than abusive behaviour of the Legislature.

To properly assess the legitimacy of these impeachment narratives, something other than the standards of legality applied to courts of law is needed—something tailored specially towards the ambiguous and extraordinary nature of impeachments.[266] There will be a baseline of legality to be observed within the procedures,

[266] Pérez-Liñán (2020), pp. 215–223, suggests the legitimacy of asymmetric control procedures (impeachments among them) ought to be asserted from 3 criteria: legality, fairness, and due process.

but also a series of extra-procedural considerations that will be more "political" or circumstantial in nature. There will be an analysis at two levels, therefore, one (i.) intrinsic to the impeachment procedures or intra-procedural, and another, (ii.) extrinsic to the impeachment procedures or extra-procedural.

At the (i.) procedure intrinsic level, one shall consider elements proper of the rule of law, such as the observation of a degree of (a.) legal certainty, (b.) proportionality, (c.) anteriority and (d.) fundamental rights on one hand, and, on the other, a degree of (e.) 'judicial' autonomy of the ruling court of impeachments, as well as their (f.) legal legitimation to act as such. All this must be considered with some sensibility to the reality of impeachments in order to be make the institute legally feasible and to avoid falling in the pitfalls of the unfalsifiable conclusion that impeachments are inherently illegitimate because they do not take place in the 'ideological vacuums' expected from typical courts of law.

Translated into more tangible terms, this would mean that: (a.) the articles of impeachment offered will be concrete enough to allow for a defence and a degree of predictability on the part of the presidential conduct (no trial by ambush or unfalsifiable accusation charges); (b.) the impeachable offense is serious enough or has brought with itself serious enough consequences to make the removal of a president justifiable (match between punishment and offense); (c.) the rules for the procedure were stablished and discussed with sufficient time to allow for a reasonable defence; (d.) part of those rules include effective opportunities for defence and effectively give the accused the chance to make their case; (e.) the ruling body is not *irresistibly* compromised by outside influence; and finally, (f.) the ruling body has been recognized as such before the commitment of the offense.

At the (ii.) procedure extrinsic level, one shall consider elements of presidential instability, since those are the ones that correlate the strongest with impeachment as an outcome. Political scientists have extensively studied the phenomenon of presidential instability and have listed literally dozens of potential indicators.[267] For the sake of simplicity and intelligibility, these multiple factors can be aggregated in three overarching categories, which would be: (a.) generalized public outrage and dissatisfaction, (b.) government's political isolation and loss of support from key stakeholders, and (c.) circumstantial urgency for removal of the President, such as a patent incapacity of averting an ongoing crisis.

For the reasons discussed in this section, these criteria are not enforceable in practice, at least not in the sense argued in that article. The model argued here is less strict and adopts other non-legal criteria that are meant to also inform the political legitimacy of impeachments. As such, this framework may better accommodate impeachment's "impure" and extraordinary character.

[267] See, for example, Llanos and Marsteintredet (2010), pp. 33 ff; Baumgartner and Kada (2003), pp. 7 ff; Pérez-Liñán and Polga-Hecimovich (2013), pp. 6 ff; Helmke (2016); Negretto (2006); Morgenstern et al. (2008); Kim and Bahry (2008). Beyond what is mentioned here, these scholars list media influence, poor institutional design, parliamentary deadlock, presidential defiance of democratic rules, interbranch competition, and access to pork-barrel as other significant aspects of presidential instability. The proposed framework attempts to synthesize these elements in ways to make them representative of the leading forces behind impeachment.

There are ways of measuring these elements with some objectivity, which may allow competing narratives to find common ground for debate. (a.) Outrage and dissatisfaction may be noticed by measuring the degrees of approval or rejection of the ruling administration/President, loss in trust on certain institutions, support of impeachment among the population, as well as by the frequency and intensity of popular demonstrations. (b.) Isolation may be inferred from the incapacity of forming functional coalitions and cabinets, the animosity/apathy of certain stakeholders and the persistence of gridlocks between Executive and Legislature. (c.) Urgency comes into play when all this happens during times in which it most certainly should not, as quick and effective measures are needed to avoid greater damage. For this element, many indicators of an economic, humanitarian, or constitutional crisis may be considered, such as recession, rampant unemployment, high mortality or homelessness rates, high perception of political normlessness, very low degrees of political participation/turnout, and so on, all depending on the kind of crisis the country is facing.

These elements do seem, in retrospect, integral to any impeachment, but most narratives often overlook them, intentionally or not. They can also be framed in awkward ways to justify or demonize an impeachment, so caution and nuance are necessary. A fully fleshed-out version of the framework above can be found in Sect. 5.7.

2.3.4.3 Considerations on Nomenclature: Coup and Hardball

Equating a disagreeable impeachment to a *coup d'état*[268] may be tempting, especially when strong emotions are involved. As will be seen in the case studies, many Presidents reach such high office precisely for being able to evoke such strong connections with their electorate. As a result, odious labels such as *coup* are understandably thrown around as knee-jerk reactions of dismissal and denial. Using value-laden labels, however, can be dangerous, as they have the tendency of overlooking or downplaying important constitutive aspects of an impeachment or the importance of horizontal control mechanisms altogether.

If one takes these coup narratives and their consequences to the letter, one will sooner or later come to the inevitable conclusion that no impeachment is ever legitimately possible, except perhaps in the unrealistic contrafactual examples given by impeachment manuals on Presidents personally committing murders or other crimes that do not in the slightest capture the complex reality of the presidential office or the politically charged environment of impeachments. There is little, if any, analytical gain to be made by utilizing such terminology so indiscriminately.

[268] *Coup d'état* is typically defined as the "illegal overthrow by actors within the state", but are also typically associated with the secondary qualities of "secrecy, speediness, and small group size". Marsteintredet and Malamud (2019), pp. 12 and 16.

That is just the tip of the iceberg, however. There are many other pernicious consequences to the misuse of the term coup in this context. The misuse may be (i.) stigmatizing in that it places coups at level with institutional solutions for political tensions, while there are clear qualitative advantages to the latter. Even if the outcome of an impeachment is far from optimal, it will more likely be supported by a significant part of the institutions, political elites, and population, and thus end up being less conducive to breakdowns and other frictions of readjustment.

The misuse is (ii.) misdirecting. By pinpointing the impeachment as the weapon used by crooks to take power or the reason for political instability, those who scream coup lose sight of the bigger picture, one of which the impeachment is likely to be merely a symptom. It is important to notice, moreover, that the association with the term coup may generate grave consequences from the international community, such as the withholding of aid, suspension from international organizations and triggering of international sanctions.[269]

The most grievous of the potential consequences, however, is that it can be (iii.) delegitimizing and revisionist of popular movements. The stigma of coup not only disavows the procedures and idea of impeachment, but also everything that has set it in motion. If the only legitimate movements are those that comply entirely with one's political alignments, then one might be claiming to have monopoly of the truth or of the political 'good', which can easily turn into an undemocratic and historical revisionist attitude.

Finally, the use of the term coup is also damaging from some more theoretical perspectives.[270] It (iv.) obscures the role of impeachments in enabling presidentialism as a truly republican form of government, as well as its current role in Latin America, as an effective mechanism for resolution of political conflicts, without resorting to violence and widespread conflict. It may contribute to (v.) blindside analysts to the fact that illegitimate impeachments are not only those that lead to undue change of government, but also to the undue permanence in government, since term coup is only applicable to the overthrow of someone in power. In some cases, it can also be argued that the term coup (vi.) can be somewhat mystifying of impeachments, in that they tendentially transfigure the pure ideals of justice found in courts to the politically charged environment of impeachments, which, as has been argued over and over, is inadequate.

There are other terminologies which seem to be more appropriate for cases of abuse of the power of impeachment, as well as its flawed or ambiguous exercise. Hardball impeachments, as to describe the uncompromising and ruthless employment of the institute, likely motivated by immediate partisan goals and conducted with disregard to the democratic spirit of cooperation, could be, for example, a better

[269] Marsteintredet and Malamud (2019), p. 18.

[270] Marsteintredet and Malamud (2019), pp. 16–18, argue, moreover, that the use in this family-resemblance form may be prejudicial to the concept of *coup* itself, since it may suggest shared causal relations among things such as 'self-coup' (incumbent takeover), 'parliamentary coup' (illegal removal by the Parliament) and 'civil-society coup' (revolution), when in fact these refer to radically different phenomena.

terminology for controversial impeachments. Equally, the terms flawed, or illegitimate impeachments can also serve as better descriptors of impeachments that failed to meet societal expectations, though not necessarily implying malicious intent from its actors. This terminology, albeit negatively charged, recognizes certain institutional means as a natural part of the democratic game, even though it may, at the same time, express some scepticism or moral reprobation towards their use in a particular case. By adopting the terminology, the critics of an impeachment may use it to describe its shortcomings, while avoiding all stigmatizing pitfalls listed above.[271]

Some coup theorists argue that this stance would be in denial of the "new generations of coups in Latin America" and would be pushed either "out of bad faith, political interest or theoretical conservatism" by their proponents,[272] but clearly there is much more to this than cynical interests or dogmatism. In this context, the term coup can effectively be used to plough through legitimate democratic claims and necessary political reforms, while not providing any significant analytical gain, thus being more harmful than good.

References

Alcántara Sáez M, Blondel J, Thiébault J-L (eds) (2018) Presidents and democracy in Latin America. Routledge, New York

Alexander GS (2002) Comparing the two legal realisms-American and Scandinavian. Am J Comp Law 50(1):131–174

Alexy R, Epiney A, Hermes G, Kunig P, Streinz R, Heun W, Höfling W, Erbguth W (2013) Verfassungsrecht und einfaches Recht - Verfassungsgerichtsbarkeit und Fachgerichtsbarkeit. Primär- und Sekundärrechtsschutz im Öffentlichen Recht. Berichte und Diskussionen auf der Tagung der Vereinigung der Deutschen Staatsrechtslehrer in Würzburg vom 3. bis 6. Oktober 2001. s.l. De Gruyter

Austin J (1979) Philosophical papers, 3rd edn. Oxford University Press, Oxford

Barthes R (2007) Introduction to the structural analysis. In: Sontag S, Barthes R (eds) A Roland Barthes reader. Vintage, London, pp 251–295

Baumgartner JC, Kada N (eds) (2003) Checking executive power: presidential impeachment in comparative perspective. Praeger, Westport

Beçak R (2003) Sucessão presidencial de 1955: Aspectos políticos e jurídicos. Editora Juarez de Oliveira, São Paulo

Bennett RW, Solum L (2011) Constitutional originalism: a debate. Cornell University Press, Ithaca

Berger R (1974) Impeachment: the constitutional problems, 2nd edn. Harvard University Press

Bieri P, Horstmann R-P, Krüger L (1979) Transcendental arguments and science: essays in epistemology. D. Reidel Pub. Co., Dordrecht

Bowman F, Sepinuck S (1999) High crimes and misdemeanors: defining the constitutional limits on presidential impeachment. South Calif Law Rev:1517–1600

[271] For more considerations on this topic, see Pérez-Liñán (2020). The term constitutional hardball as proposed by Tushnet (2004) is also fitting for the situation.

[272] de Freixo and Rodrigues (2016).

Brand P (2012) The development of parliament, 1215-1307. In: Jones C (ed) A short history of parliament: England, Great Britain, the United Kingdom, Ireland & Scotland. Boydell Press, Woodbridge

Brossard de Souza Pinto P (1965) O impeachment: Aspectos da responsabilidade política do Presidente da República. Saraiva, Sao Paulo

Brown B (1955) The natural law, the marriage bond, and divorce. Fordham Law Rev 24(1):83–101

Buckland W (1908) The Roman law of slavery: the condition of the slave in private law from Augustus to Justinian. Cambridge University Press

Caird JS (2016) Briefing Paper n. CBP7612 of the House of Commons. Impeachment

Cam H (1970) Representation in Medieval England. In: Miller E, Fryde EB (eds) Historical studies of the English Parliament: origins to 1399. Cambridge University Press, Cambridge

Carey JM, Corrales J, Llanos M, Marsteintredet L, Pérez-Liñán A. The threat of impeachment can push presidents out the door. But there's a catch. The Washington Post

Carnall G, Nicholson C (eds) (1989) The impeachment of Warren Hastings: papers from a bicentenary commemorations. Edinburgh University Press, Edinburgh

Clarke M (1968a) Forfeitures and Treason in 1388. In: Clarke M, Sutherland L, McKisack M (eds) Fourteenth century studies, (Reprint). Oxford, pp 115–145

Clarke M (1968b) The origin of impeachment. In: Clarke M, Sutherland L, McKisack M (eds) Fourteenth century studies, (Reprint). Oxford, pp 242–271

Cohen FS (1935) Transcendental nonsense and the functional approach. Columbia Law Rev 35(6): 809

Collantes MJ (1998) El Juício de Residencia en Castila a través de la Doctrina Jurídica de la Edad Moderna. Historia Instituciones Documentos 25:151–184

Croft P (1996) The debate on annual parliaments in the early seventeenth century. Parliam Estates Represent 16(1):163 174

Dagan H (2015) Doctrinal categories, legal realism and the rule of law. Univ Pa Law Rev 163: 1889–1917

de Freixo A, Rodrigues T (eds) (2016) 2016, o ano do golpe. Oficina Raquel, Rio de Janeiro

de Saussure F (2016) Course in general linguistics. Bloomsbury, London [etc.]

Derrida J (1998) Of grammatology, Corrected ed. Johns Hopkins University Press, Baltimore

Diamond LJ, Linz JJ, Lipset SM (1989) Democracy in developing countries. Rienner; Adamantine, Boulder

Dodd G (2008) Justice and grace: private petitioning and the English Parliament in the late Middle Ages. Oxford University Press, Oxford

Dworkin RM (1977) Taking rights seriously. Harvard University Press, Cambridge

Edwards G (1970) 'Justice' in early English Parliaments. In: Miller E, Fryde EB (eds) Historical studies of the English Parliament: origins to 1399. Cambridge University Press, Cambridge

Eguiguren Praeli FJ (2008) Antejuicio y Juicio Político en el Perú. Pensamiento Constitucional 13: 111–162

Elliot J (1836a) The debates in the several state conventions on the adoption of the Federal Constitution as recommend by the General Convention at Philadelphia: volume 1, 2nd edn. Washington

Elliot J (1836b) The debates in the several state conventions on the adoption of the Federal Constitution as recommend by the General Convention at Philadelphia: volume 2, 2nd edn. Washington

Elliot J (1836c) The debates in the several state conventions on the adoption of the Federal Constitution as recommend by the General Convention at Philadelphia: volume 3, 2nd edn. Washington

Farrand M (1911a) The records of the Federal Convention of 1787: July 14 to September 17, 1787. Yale University Press, New Haven

Farrand M (1911b) The records of the Federal Convention of 1787: May 14 to July 13, 1787. Yale University Press, New Haven

Finkelman P (1999) Thomas R.R. Cobb and the Law of Negro Slavery. Roger Williams Univ Law Rev 5(1)
Fryde EB (1970) Introduction. In: Miller E, Fryde EB (eds) Historical studies of the English Parliament, Repr. Cambridge University Press, Cambridge, pp 1–31
Fukuyama F (1989) The end of history? Natl Interest 16:3–18
Galdia M (2017) Lectures on legal linguistics. Peter Lang Edition, Frankfurt am Main
Gallo CA (1992) Crimes de responsabilidade no impeachment. Freitas Bastos, Rio de Janeiro/Sao Paulo
Gerhardt M (1999) The lessons of impeachment history. William Mary Law School Scholarship Repository, pp 603–625
Grandin G (2010) Empire's workshop: Latin America, the United States, and the rise of the new imperialism. Metropolitan Books; Holt Paperback, New York
Gutiérrez Mendoza O (2014) El Juicio de Residencia Espanol, Antecedente del Juicio de Responsabilidad y no del Juicio de Amparo Mexicano. Revista de Derecho UNED 14:271–294
Hagopian F, Mainwaring S (eds) (2005) The third wave of democratization in Latin America: advances and setbacks. Cambridge University Press, Cambridge
Hamilton A, Jay J, Madison J, Carey GW, McClellan J (2001) The federalist: a collection. Liberty Fund, Indianapolis
Hart H (1958) Positivism and the separation of law and morals. Harv Law Rev 71(4):593
Helmke G (2016) From power gaps to instability traps: reflections on institutional instability in Latin America. Department of Political Science, University of Rochester
Henkin L (1976) Is there a "political question" doctrine? Yale Law J 85(5):597
Herzog T (2005) Ritos de Control, Prácticas de Negociación: Pesquisas, Visitas y Residencias en las relaciones entre Quito y Madrid (1650-1750). In: Andrés-Gallego J (ed) Tres grandes cuestiones de la historia de iberoamérica. Fundación Ignacio Larramendi; Fundación Mapfre Tavera, Madrid
Heun W (1989) Der staatsrechtliche Positivismus in der Weimarer Republik: Eine Konzeption in Widerstreit. Der Staat 28:377–403
Hiroi T, Omori S (2009) Perils of parliamentarism? Political systems and the stability of democracy revisited. Democratization 16(3):485–507
Hirsch ED (1982) The politics of theories of interpretation. Crit Inq 9(1):235–247
Hochstetler K, Samuels D (2011) Crisis and rapid reequilibration: the consequences of presidential challenge and failure in Latin America. Comp Polit 43(2):127–145
Hoffer PC, Hull N (1984) Impeachment in America, 1635-1805. Yale University Press, New Haven
Huntington SP (1993) The third wave: democratization in the late twentieth century. University of Oklahoma Press, Norman
Hurwitz L (1972) Democratic political stability. Comp Polit Stud 4(4):476–490
Kelsen H (2009) Pure theory of law. Lawbook Exchange, Clark
Kennedy D (1982) Stages of the decline of the public/private distinction. Univ Pa Law Rev 130(6): 1349
Kim YH, Bahry D (2008) Interrupted presidencies in third wave democracies. J Polit 70(3): 807–822
Labovitz JR (1978) Presidential impeachment. Yale University Press, New Haven
Lambrick G (1967) The impeachment of the Abbot of Abingdon in 1368. English Hist Rev LXXXII (CCCXXIII):250–276
Lander JR (1961) I. Attainder and Forfeiture, 1453 To 1509. Hist J 4(02):119–151
Leiter B (1997) Rethinking legal realism: toward a naturalized jurisprudence. Tex Law Rev 76(2): 267–315
Leiter B (1998) Realism, hard positivism, and conceptual analysis. Leg Theory 4(4):533–547
Leiter B (2012) Legal realisms, old and new. SSRN Electron J
Levitsky S, Ziblatt D (2018) How democracies die, First edition. Crown Publishing, New York
Linz J (1990) The perils of presidentialism. J Democr 1(1):51–69

Linz J (1994) Presidential or parliamentary democracy: does it make a difference? In: Linz J, Valenzuela A (eds) The failure of presidential democracy, vol I. Johns Hopkins University Press, Baltimore, pp 3–90

Llanos M, Marsteintredet L (eds) (2010) Presidential breakdowns in Latin America: causes and outcomes of executive instability in developing democracies. Palgrave Macmillan, New York

Llewellyn KN (1962) Jurisprudence: realism in theory and practice. University of Chicago Press, Chicago

Llewellyn KN (1988) The case law system in America. Columbia Law Rev 88(5):989

Loveman B, Lira E (2000) Las acusaciones constitucionales en Chile: Una perspectiva histórica. LOM Ediciones; FLACSO Chile, Santiago de Chile

Maddicott J (2012) Origins and beginnings to 1215. In: Jones C (ed) A short history of parliament: England, Great Britain, the United Kingdom, Ireland & Scotland. Boydell Press, Woodbridge

Madison J (1952) IV. Madison's Observations on Jefferson's Draft of a Constitution for Virginia [October 1788]. In: Boyd J (ed) The Papers of Thomas Jefferson: 21 May 1781 - 1 March 1784. Princeton University Press, Princeton, pp 308–317

Mainwaring S (1999) Rethinking party systems in the third wave of democratization: the case of Brazil. Stanford University Press, Stanford

Mainwaring S, Shugart MS (1997) Juan Linz, presidentialism, and democracy: a critical appraisal. Comp Polit 29(4):449

Maitland FW (1970) Introduction to Memoranda de Parliamento, 1305. In: Miller E, Fryde EB (eds) Historical studies of the English Parliament: origins to 1399. Cambridge University Press, Cambridge, pp 91–135

Maitland FW (2012 [1893]) Records of the Parliament holden at Westminster: on the twenty-eighth day of February, in the thirty-third year of the reign of King Edward the First (A.D. 1305). Cambridge University Press, New York

Mariluz Urquijo JM (1952) Ensayo sobre los Juicios de Residencia Indianos. Consejo Superior de Investigaciones Científicas, Sevilla

Marsteintredet L, Berntzen E (2008) Reducing the perils of presidentialism in Latin America through presidential interruptions. Comp Polit 41(1):83–101

Marsteintredet L, Malamud A (2019) Coup with adjectives: conceptual stretching or innovation in comparative research? Polit Stud

Mill JS (1875) Nature, the utility of religion and theism, 2nd edn. Longmans, Green and CO., London

Miller E (1970) Introduction. In: Miller E, Fryde EB (eds) Historical studies of the English Parliament: origins to 1399. Cambridge University Press, Cambridge, pp 1–30

Mirow MC (2015) Latin American constitutionalism: the constitution of Cádiz and its legacy in Spanish America. Cambridge University Press, New York

Morgenstern SJ, Pérez Liñán A, Negri J (2008) Parliamentary opposition in non-parliamentary regimes: Latin America

Negretto GL (2006) Minority presidents and democratic performance in Latin America. Latin Am Polit Soc 48(3):63–92

Pérez-Liñán A (2000) ¿Juício político o golpe legislativo? Sobre las crisis constitucionales en los años noventa. América Latina Hoy 26:67–74

Pérez-Liñán A (2007) Presidential impeachment and the new political instability in Latin America. Cambridge University Press, Leiden

Pérez-Liñán A (2018) Impeachment or backsliding? Threats to democracy in the twenty-first century. Revista Brasileira de Ciências Sociais 33(98):33

Pérez-Liñán A (2020) Narratives of executive downfall: recall, impeachment, or coup? In: Welp Y, Whitehead L (eds) The politics of recall elections. Springer International Publishing, Cham, pp 201–228

Pérez-Liñán A, Polga-Hecimovich J (2013) Political elites, democratic breakdown, and presidential instability in Latin America. Instituto de Iberoamérica

Perkins W (2003) The political nature of presidential impeachment in the United States. In: Baumgartner JC, Kada N (eds) Checking executive power: presidential impeachment in comparative perspective. Praeger, Westport, pp 21–44
Pierson W, Gil F (1957) Governments of Latin America. McGraw-Hill, New York
Piketty T, Goldhammer A (2014) Capital in the twenty-first century. The Belknap Press of Harvard University Press, London
Plucknett T (1942) The origin of impeachment. Trans R Hist Soc 24:47–71
Plucknett T (1970) Parliament. In: Miller E, Fryde EB (eds) Historical studies of the English Parliament: origins to 1399. Cambridge University Press, Cambridge
Plucknett T (1983) Studies in English legal history. Hambledon Press, London
Pollard A (1920) The evolution of the parliament. Longmans, Green and CO, London
Pound R (1908) Mechanical jurisprudence. Columbia Law Rev 8(8):605–623
Radin MJ (1989) Reconsidering the rule of law. Boston Univ Law Rev 69(4):781–819
Raz J (2002) The authority of law: essays on law and morality, Reprinted. Oxford University Press, Oxford
Rezneck S (1927) The early history of the parliamentary declaration of Treason. English Hist Rev XLII(CLXVIII):497–513
Richardson H, Sayles G (1930) The parliaments of Edward III. Hist Res 8(23):65–82
Richardson H, Sayles G (1931) The parliaments of Edward III (concluded). Hist Res 9(25):1–18
Roberts C (1956) The growth of ministerial responsibility to parliament in later Stuart England. J Mod Hist 28(3):215–233
Roberts C (1966) The growth of responsible government in Stuart England. Cambridge University Press, Cambridge
Roberts C (1975) The law of impeachment in Stuart England: a reply to Raoul Berger. Yale Law J 84(7):1419–1439
Rodino P (1974) Grounds for presidential impeachment: report by the staff of the impeachment inquiry. U.S. Government Printing Office, Washington
Ross A (2004) On law and justice. The Law Book Exchange, Clark
Rossiter C (1963) The American presidency, 2nd edn. Johns Hopkins University Press, Baltimore
Russell C (1991) The fall of the British monarchies, 1637-1642. Clarendon Press; Oxford University Press, Oxford
Samuelsohn D (2018) Trump's Russia strategy: Bash Mueller to beat impeachment. Politico, May 4
Santos F, Guarnieri F (2016) From protest to parliamentary coup: an overview of Brazil's recent history. J Latin Am Cult Stud 25(4):485–494
Saul N (2008) The three Richards: Richard I, Richard II, and Richard III, Repr. Hambledon Continuum [u.a.], London [u.a.]
Scharpf FW (1966) Judicial review and the political question: a functional analysis. Yale Law J 75(4):517
Schenoni LL, Mainwaring S (2018) US hegemony and regime change in Latin America. Democratization 49:1–19
Sellin V (1978) Politik. In: Brunner O, Conze W, Koselleck R (eds) Geschichtliche Grundbegriffe: Historisches Lexikon zur politisch-sozialen Sprache in Deutschland. Klett-Cotta, Stuttgart, pp 789–874
Shugart MS, Carey JM (1992) Presidents and assemblies: constitutional design and electoral dynamics. Cambridge University Press, Cambridge
Smietniansky S (2007) El Juicio de REsidencia Como Ritual Político en la Colonia. Memoria Americana 15:71–101
Smith DL (1999) The Stuart parliaments, 1603-1689. Arnold; Co-published in the U.S.A. by Oxford University Press, London
Spaak T (2009) Naturalism in Scandinavian and American realism: similarities and differences. In: Dahlberg M (ed) Uppsala-Minnesota Colloquium: law, culture and values. Iustus förlag, Uppsala, pp 33–83

Stein E (1986) History against free speech: the new German law against the “Auschwitz”: and other: “Lies”. Mich Law Rev 85(2):277
Steinbarth S (2011) Das Institut der Präsidenten- und Ministeranklage in rechtshistorischer und rechtsvergleichender Perspektive: Ursprünge, Erscheinungsformen und bleibende Sinnhaftigkeit von Gerichts- und Impeachmentverfahren zur Durchsetzung gubernativer Verantwortlichkeit. Nomos, Baden-Baden
Stewart DO (2009) Impeached: the trial of President Andrew Johnson and the fight for Lincoln’s legacy. Simon & Schuster, New York
Stolleis M (2003) Judicial review, administrative review, and constitutional review in the Weimar Republic. Ratio Juris 16(2):266–280
Stolleis M (2014) Öffentliches recht in Deutschland: Eine Einführung in seine Geschichte (16.-21. Jahrhundert). Beck, München
Suarez WC (1982) El Poder Ejecutivo en America Latina: Su Capacidade Operativa Bajo Regimenes Presidencialistas de Gobierno. Revista de Estudios Políticos 29:109–144
Sunstein CR (2017) Impeachment: a citizen’s guide. Harvard University Press, Cambridge
Tite C (1974) Impeachment and parliamentary judicature in early Stuart England. Athlone Press, London
Toobin J (2018) Will the Fervor to Impeach Donald Trump Start a Democratic Civil War? The New Yorker, May 25
Tout TF (1970) Parliament and Public Opinion, 1376-1388. In: Miller E, Fryde EB (eds) Historical studies of the English Parliament: origins to 1399. Cambridge University Press, Cambridge, pp 298–315
Tribe LH (2000) American constitutional law, 3rd edn. Foundation Press, New York
Tsebelis G (1995) Decision making in political systems: veto players in presidentialism, parliamentarism, multicameralism and multipartyism. Br J Polit Sci 25(3):289–325
Tushnet MV (2004) Constitutional hardball. John Marshall Law Rev, pp 523–553
van Tassel E, Finkelman P (1999) Impeachable offenses: a documentary history from 1787 to the present. Congressional Quarterly, Washington, D.C
von Hippel E, Triepel H, Kelsen H, Layer M (2013) Wesen und Entwicklung der Staatsgerichtsbarkeit. Überprüfung von Verwaltungsakten durch die ordentlichen Gerichte. Verhandlungen der Tagung der Deutschen Staatsrechtslehrer zu Wien am 23. und 24. April 1928. Mit einem Auszug aus der Aussprache. S.l. De Gruyter
von Jhering R (2009) Scherz und Ernst in der Jurisprudenz, Leipzig, Breitkopf und Härtel, 1884. Linde, Wien
Weizsäcker J (1886) Der Pfalzgraf als Richter über den König. Dieterichsche Verlags-Buchhandlung, Göttingen
Wenzel UJ (1992) Anthroponomie: Kants Archäologie der Autonomie. Akademie-Verlag, Berlin
Wilkinson B (1937) Studies in the constitutional history of the thirteenth and fourteenth centuries. Manchester University Press, Manchester
Wilkinson B (1970) The deposition of Richard II and the ascension of Henry IV. In: Miller E, Fryde EB (eds) Historical studies of the English Parliament: origins to 1399. Cambridge University Press, Cambridge, pp 329–353
Wilson RD (1957) Justifications of slavery, past and present. Phylon Q 18(4):407
Wittgenstein L (1968) Philosophical investigations, 3rd ed. reprint of English text with index. Blackwell, Oxford
Wood GS (1992) The radicalism of the American revolution. Knopf A.A., New York

Chapter 3
Impeachment in Latin America

3.1 Latin America as a Region: The Context of Impeachments

The idea of Latin America is quite a disputed one. Why or how should America be 'split' into regions? Is there a meaningful distinction to be made between Latin America and Anglo-Saxon America (United States, Canada, Belize, and Guyana)? Is a division between north, centre and south more meaningful? To what sort of *Latinness* does the Latin of Latin America refer to? Is it historical, linguistic, or ethnical? Should the concept include the Caribbean islands or the very few continental countries that do not have an official Iberian language (Belize, Guyana, French Guyana, Suriname)?

While there is much to be said and criticized about the scientific and discursive adequacy of the concept, particularly about it serving to erase African and Native presence and history,[1] as well as it serving as means to exclude the region from select few that compose the 'West',[2] this study chooses to use it out of two preoccupations: (i) intelligibility, that is, Latin America, despite the need for a few conceptual tweaks here and there, communicates a sufficiently clear message about the geographic scope dealt by this study; (ii) a peculiar observational overlap or, in other words, the phenomena under study seem to be quite common in this limited territory known as Latin America, suggesting the existence of unifying or shared local factors when it comes to presidential impeachments.

This study, therefore, does not purport to offer a definitive concept of Latin America, but will instead use one that is specific enough to sift through excess

[1]Mignolo (2012), pp. 89 ff.

[2]It is often argued that Latin America was created after the Spanish-American War (1898), as the US defeated a powerful European empire, thus, earning its seat on the table with the 'West'.

G. Palamone, *Presidential Impeachment in Latin America*,
https://doi.org/10.1007/978-3-031-44188-2_3

data and noise, but also general enough avoid the pitfalls of selection bias.[3] This is achieved by concentrating the study only to the 17 countries in the American Continent that have Iberian colonization history, thus, being countries that have either Spanish or Portuguese as official languages. As will be pointed out in the following sections, this division will be enough to encompass practically all presidential systems of the whole western hemisphere, with the notable exception of the United States, which, nonetheless, must be considered at least indirectly at every point for being highly influential to the region. A case could be made to include Cuba and the former island of Saint-Domingue (now Haiti and Dominican Republic) for their deep historical ties with Latin America, but generally speaking, the Caribbean has so many particularities, it should better be spoken of as a region in its own merit.

The next few sections will serve both as a short introduction to the shared history of Latin America, as well as a more detailed justification for the scope of this study. Many issues that are brought up in impeachments are often connected with this history and understanding them is key to the comprehension of the political context of the upcoming analyses.

3.1.1 Colonization and Its Shackles

Colonization and colonialism leave enduring consequences on the regions affected by them. They may destroy or reshape existing societies, or they may even create new ones entirely. Regardless of how one chooses to value these historical processes, the legacies left by them arguably display discernible patterns, depending on (i) when the colonization process was started, (ii) how or with what goals in mind it was executed, and (iii) when and how the process was terminated.

The first characteristic informs how deeply rooted in society colonialism is, or in other words, how naturalized the relation of powers between colonized and colonizer have become. This serves as an indicator of how latent tensions and resentments may be in society and may be contributing factors to internal instability. The second characteristic complements the first, by determining how much of the original society was left by the colonizer and what kind of society was built on top or beside it. Colonies treated as a mere source of extractable wealth have different outcomes than those that were seem as attractive settling destinies, such as displaying varying degrees of racial and cultural mixing, retention and reinvestment of locally produced wealth, societal development, among other things. Finally, the last item informs for how long and under what circumstances a society has been free to follow its own path unencumbered by imperial powers. The intensity of conflict during the

[3] In other words, a concept that, for the goals of this study (understanding presidential impeachments in the region), is composed of only the necessary and sufficient parts, thus excluding the superfluous but including enough features to allow the observation of potential common underlying patterns.

independence process is of obvious consequence to the new forming nation, as impoverished, broken, and contested societies will likely take longer to turn into functioning states.[4]

Regarding the first aspect, the whole American Continent and Caribbean have a long relationship with colonialism, starting around the years following 1492. The region of current Latin America was divided between by the two strongest maritime powers of the time, the Spanish and Portuguese empires, who, by means of the Treaty of Tordesillas, sought to keep peace among themselves, while at the same time close out rivals. As Spain's power in Europe began to wane, however, France and Britain could successfully challenge Spain's military dominance in the seas and capture islands in the Caribbean between 1628 and 1763.[5]

At the time, Spain had become dependent on the exploitation of its own colonies to finance its supremacy. It had imposed a system by which the colonies would be used to fulfil its needs for commodities, while at the same time serving as a captive market for the Empire's industrial goods. The close presence of the British, however, would come to mean more economic deterioration for Spain, as it could now smuggle its own goods into the Spanish colonies, bypassing the heavy colonial taxation. British pirates could, moreover, intercept much of the wealth transported back to Spain, as well as ransack some of its colonial capitals, thus further aggravating Spain's economic situation.[6]

This brought a chain reaction to the region. With less resources, Spain had even less leeway to reinforce its military and was more likely to suffer upsets in the battlefield. Its military defeats and economic backwardness undermined its authority, its attempts at training local militias to cover for the professional armies' deficiencies blurred the lines between governor and governed,[7] and its crackdown on smuggling to recreate a source of revenue instilled resentment in the population. Adding to the mix the fact that the French and American revolutions offered blueprints and inspiration for Latin America's own uprising and that the writings of Voltaire, Rousseau, Locke, and other enlightenment thinkers were circulating freely, despite censorship, it would become certain that the region would be yearning for change by the end of the eighteenth century.[8]

---

[4]Most of these conclusions are suggested by Acemoglu et al. (2001). Regarding specifically Latin America, other conclusions are implied in Furtado and Macedo (1976) and Huntington (1993). More generally, to other regions of the world, Rodney (1981); Fukuyama (2012); and Acemoglu and Robinson (2019).

[5]Calvert and Calvert (1993), pp. 3 ff.

[6]Lewis (2006), pp. 12–13.

[7]Regarding this specific feature, it is important to notice that Spain had hitherto devoted much attention into creating a clear distinctive line between both. The governing class, for example, was exclusively composed of *peninsulares* (Spaniards born in Spain), who were forbidden from permanently settling in the colonies and were subjected to a number of measures that ensured they would not build emotional connection with the governed. Lewis (2006), p. 10.

[8]Lewis (2006), pp. 12–13.

With the breakout of the Napoleonic Wars (1803), both Spain and Portugal were forced into uncomfortable positions. Spain had its King replaced by a Frenchman, which gave the colonies an eagerly awaited reason to reject the crown's authority, leading to a power vacuum and civil wars in the Hispanic America. Portugal, on the other hand, had its monarchy flee to Brazil before the French invasion, and recognized the country's independence, albeit remaining in power as rulers of the Brazilian Empire. By 1825, all continental Latin American countries had become independent. Comparatively, the rest of the countries, namely Belize, Suriname, Guyana, French Guyana, and the Caribbean (exception of Cuba, Haiti, and Dominican Republic), became independent later, between 1960 and 1980, if at all.[9]

The end of colonial rule, with its heavy tax burdens and its lopsided trade restrictions, did not necessarily mean the beginning of an era of prosperity, as much of these advantages were offset by other hardships of the newly found political strife (*e.g.*, doubled costs with defence, law enforcement, provision of public goods; regional and monetary disintegration), but it did mean, *on average*, a better start compared to countries that remained under it.[10]

Finally, it is important to notice that the societies built in this time were steeply hierarchical and left little space for social mobility. Through a series of ingenious practices (*e.g., encomiendas, repartimiento*) these societies consolidated a social pyramid with "pure" Spaniards on top (the governing class), followed by "creoles" (colony-born Spaniards; likely landowners, large merchants, upper clergy, militia officers), "mestizos" (mix of Spanish and Indian), "mulattos" (Spanish and African), and "zambos" (African and Indian), respectively. Moreover, since very few Spanish women immigrated to the New World, there was considerable racial mixing of populations. As will be seen next, all these elements were consequential in forming the Latin American identity and its state building struggles.[11]

3.1.2 Emancipation and Revolutionary Ideals

Achieving full emancipation was not an easy task for most Latin American countries. Those who managed to defeat the European powers that oppressed them, soon had to face new domestic challenges. The vacuum of power left by the Spanish

---

[9]Calvert and Calvert (1993), pp. 6–7. The 1960s–80s was also the period in which most of colonial Africa and Asia achieved independence.

[10]Prados de Escosura (2009), pp. 282–283. Keyword is "on average", since there are large regional disparities, which are too complex (*e.g.,* landlocked vs. coastal economies, Pacific rim vs. Atlantic Ocean; climate, demographic density, political instability) to be explained in the scope of this book. Mexico and Brazil seem to have had the poorest performance in the years following independence, and Chile and Uruguay, the best. Notice, however, that generalist literature, such as Calvert and Calvert (1993), pp. 10ff, tends to have a more negative outlook on this matter, claiming Latin America ended worse off than it was during colonial times.

[11]Lewis (2006), pp. 8–12.

meant that any oligarch commanding a powerful militia could *de facto* claim the rule of the nation for themselves. These contenders for local power were known as *caudillos*, and the period of intense conflict between them is known as *caudillismo*; a period so traumatic and character defining for these nations, that some authors root Latin America's recurring taste for dictatorships, authoritarianism and messianic personalism in it.[12] Only three countries achieved independence without prolonged fragmentation and conflict, namely Paraguay, Chile, and Brazil. Paraguay managed to swiftly eliminate old colonial elites and implant a sort of socialist regime; Chile had its criollo elites gather around one single uniting figure, Diego Portales; and Brazil avoided the power vacuum altogether, as the Portuguese monarchy was succeeded by a creole monarchy, who was perceived as legitimate, albeit being tightly connected with its Portuguese predecessors.[13]

All other fourteen Latin American nations were war torn by the *caudillos* in the period of, approximately, 1820–1870. After decades of endemic violence, compromises and back-and-forth between loosely organized political coalitions, a tendency to centralization could be observed, which abided to two foundational principles: the right of collective self-government and the guarantee of individual autonomy. Conservative, liberal, and republican factions interpreted the balance between these two principles differently, but the experiences with colonialism and emancipation had nonetheless consolidated a consensus around their nuclear importance to good government. Even conservatives who were favourable of unitarian government and the strong presence of the Church as the backbone of society were to some degree suspicious of the Churches' historical role in monarchical legitimation and its implications on autonomy and self-determination, and were, thus, liberal/republican in this regard.[14]

It is precisely in this context that the US constitutional model becomes so attractive to Latin Americans. *Caudillo* led anarchy had left an experience that corroborated the value of a powerful Executive branch. The scars left by colonialism and some of the early dictators, on the other hand, reminded them of the risks of such a powerful Executive. Fortunately for these revolutionaries, however, the US presented more than just a blueprint to revolution, but also a blueprint to a constitutional order that enabled a division of powers so strict, it could safely harness a powerful Executive. Despite understandable pushback from anti-presidentialists and anti-authoritarians of the time, presidentialism was widely embraced by Latin

---

[12]This sort of 'historical heritage' argument is grounded on the interplay of a certain kind of nationalism and leftover deficiencies in the existing political structures, as seem, for example, in: Beezley (1969), pp. 348–351. For a discussion of this hypothesis: Waldmann (1978).

[13]Lewis (2006), pp. 31 ff.

[14]Lewis (2006), pp. 27–30; Gargarella (2013), pp. 4–33; Calvert and Calvert (1993), p. 9. This characteristic is part of what Gargarella aptly calls "conservative-liberal fusion". Notice, moreover, that theocrats and monarchists were by no means entirely extinct, as seen, for example, in García Moreno's administration of Ecuador, but their beliefs were largely perceived as backwards by then.

Americans, often with comparatively more reserved powers to the President than those listed by their role model.[15]

These constitutions aspired to be democratic and republican, but their framers, like those in the US, were still sceptical of the political aptitude of the people:

> If we closely examine the origins of our disgraces we will find that all of them derived from bad administrations, and also that these bad administrations resulted from lethal elections... in which political rights were distributed to notoriously incapable people, who should have never taken part of those electoral processes. (...) To put it simply, we need national Congress to define who has the capacities necessary for exercising citizens' rights, and to exclude all those who cannot inspire any confidence at all, namely the non-proprietors [the dispossessed].[16]

Proper political participation was to be achieved only after emancipation, between the 1870s and 1920s. It is in this period that Latin American economies begin to catch up and produce an urban middle class eager to participate in politics. Materially speaking, however, longstanding popular agendas such as land redistribution, indigenous rights or labour demands would still take more time to achieve a political voice, as the middle classes still reproduced some of the elitist perspectives on politics common to the traditional elites.[17]

3.1.3 Hardships of Postcolonial State Building and New Dependencies

In the celebrated romance *One Hundred Years of Solitude,* García Márquez tells an ever-repeating story of a family who is both cut off from the external world and whose identity is hard to distinguish among themselves, as generations come and go sharing the same name, personalities, and fates. More importantly, this family endures all kinds of hardships which from time to time recycle themselves, fuelled by the collective amnesia and nostalgia of its characters. This peculiar story is one that reverberates with many Latin Americans, as its fiction is strongly grounded on reality of the region. As aptly identified by Daniel Erickson, the romance showed how:

> Ideological transfiguration ensured that Macondo and the Buendías always were ghosts to some extent, alienated and estranged from their own history, not only victims of the harsh reality of dependence and underdevelopment but also of the ideological illusions that haunt and reinforce such social conditions.[18]

---

[15] Gargarella (2013), pp. 38–80. Chile was the only nation to adopt parliamentarism

[16] Words of Luis Mora (1794–1850), a Mexican jurist and politician of the time. Gargarella (2013), p. 29.

[17] Lewis (2006), pp. 101 ff; Gargarella (2013), pp. 105 ff.

[18] Erickson (2009), p. 193. See also pp. 163 ff.

Allegories aside, the story of the average Latin American country tends to go this way: a people, highly oppressed but dependent of a highly unequal power structure, rebels against it; to have success in its rebellion, it sought external aid that, in of itself, came conditioned to a new chain of dependencies and another oppressing power structure, that, somehow, strongly resembled the ones rebelled against.[19] Impoverished by these outcomes, the people lacked the conditions of achieving a certain degree of self-reflexivity and material conditions that would allow them to find their own path and, instead, they modelled themselves to fit the expectations of those whom they were dependent upon.[20] When, unsurprisingly, "development" or "progress" were not achieved and unsatisfaction reached unsustainable levels, the history repeated itself, and the dictatorial shackle was substituted by the revolutionary ball and chain (or vice-versa). This conclusion may be ascertained by observing the following three generally repeating cycles:

(i) In the transition of colonial to emancipated regimes (1808–1870), the colonial captive markets were substituted by open markets entirely pointed at exportation of cash crops, meaning less focus on internal development or supply of food crops, while producing wealth concentration at the hands of the landowning creole elites. 'Development' of the commodities exporting nations remained highly linked to the 'development' of industrial nations. Moreover, so that some of the elites could finance and actualize their military edge over their contenders, large debits and political commitments with foreign nations had to be assumed, which ensured new dependency links, although this time around more pronouncedly with England than Spain or Portugal.[21]

(ii) In the transition of emancipated regimes to the consolidation of proper nation states (1870–1930),[22] the urban populations rose significantly, creating a mass of citizens coming from literate middle classes that demanded participation in politics. Surprisingly, however, the inclusion of the masses in politics did not implicate in an impactful change in power structure or distribution, as they still

[19] As Bodenheimer (1970), pp. 113–114, points out, the *need of external capital for development* has been long an unchallenged assumption by those who proposed plans of development for Latin America. As it turns out, however, the correlation between foreign capital imports and Latin American growth tended to be inverse rather than positive.

[20] This vision is somewhat compatible to what Hector Murena suggests in *El pecado original de América*: "Through misinterpreting their past, Latin Americans construct false projects for the future, and every step they take in the present in accordance with those projects, vitiated by that initial falseness, only serves to sink them deeper in their sickness, as in a circle from which there is no way out", as quoted by Erickson (2009), p. 192. The vison presented in this book, however, puts emphasis on the interplay of a more complex set of factors.

[21] Lewis (2006), pp. 17–29; Bodenheimer (1971), p. 332.

[22] The greatest challenge to the consolidation of Latin American polities as national or modern states was the *caudillismo*, which posed far from trivial challenges to their claims to monopoly of power, territoriality, impersonal administration, etc. For the definitions of and relationship between modern and national state, see Pierson (2011), pp. 4–51; Thiele (2019), pp. 47–108; Mann (2012), pp. 44 ff.

strongly supported the traditional agrarian elites.[23] In other words, while societies became more liberal, they remained largely oligarchical and mass participation in politics, a *façade*.[24] At the same time, the United States emerged as a world power, once it defeated Spain in 1898, increasing its influence on Latin America. Particularly after the breakout of the Great War in Europe and the ensuing weakening of those economies, the US had more leeway to infiltrate its economic interests into Latin America and to intervene more often in the local governments.[25]

(iii) Finally, in the period of national developmentalism (1930–1990), Latin Americans began a decided strive towards economic arrangements that were more capable of producing more equalitarian and thriving societies.[26] Incapable of achieving such goals democratically, authoritarianism was used to dislodge recalcitrant agrarian elites and to swiftly restructure economic policy and favour industrialization. Financing infrastructural reforms and acquiring technology to do so, as well as the celerity in which it was done, however, caused a greater presence of foreign ownership, capital outflow, and a period of serious social friction (*e.g.*, unemployment caused by the disregard to the composition of local labour markets, structural inflation).[27]

The post-World War II period saw a rehash of the same national developmentalism, except under different economic paradigms, which this time around mirrored trickle-down approaches employed in the economic recovery of Europe. Despite the objections of vanguard dependency theorists of the time such as Raúl Prebisch, the pressure to adequate oneself to these paradigms only grew stronger in the attempts of integrating the continent in a sort of Inter-American system. Moreover, particularly with the Cold War and its struggle for stablishing the supremacy of capitalism over communism, those who deviated from the norm could be quickly labelled as communists and suffer reprisal in different forms, including direct intervention, whereas those who decidedly supported the mainstream understanding of capitalism gained access to perks and compensations (*e.g.*, the *Alliance for Progress* program).[28]

---

[23] Calvert and Calvert (1993), offers (part of) a possible explanation: "Under the influence of what had come to be known as Social Darwinism, the ruling classes regarded the position of their social inferiors as a sign of their unfitness to rule, and this view had consciously or unconsciously come to be accepted quite widely by those they ruled".

[24] Lewis (2006), pp. 75–105.

[25] Calvert and Calvert (1993), pp. 16–22, 38 ff.

[26] World War I and the Great Depression of 1929 disrupted traditional trading arrangements, causing hardships in the dependent economies, and urging for economic restructuration. More details in the next section.

[27] Bodenheimer (1971), pp. 336–337; Furtado and Macedo (1976), pp. 100–130.

[28] Calvert and Calvert (1993), pp. 84–118. For a comprehensive analysis of programs such as *Alliance for Progress* or the general workings of dependency mechanisms through foreign aid, see Bodenheimer (1971), in particular pp. 352 ff. for the latter.

This situation brought to a halt or even reversed meaningful successes in the efforts of land redistribution and other social agendas, and, consequently, destabilized several legitimate governments. One of the most emblematic and well-documented cases of the kind certainly was the conflict between the Guatemalan President Jacobo Árbenz (1951–1954) and the United Fruit Company, in which over 150,000 acres of unused land were redistributed after compensation, but had to be largely returned after a CIA orchestrated *coup* replaced Arbenz with a puppet government.[29] With the Cuban Revolution, the consequent approximation of the Soviet Union to the region and the outbreak of urban violence against US diplomats and transnational corporations, US interventionism escalated into more violent and more covert interactions in order to secure an iron grip at the region. No corners were cut when it came to rooting out the basis of any left-wing power: massacres of union workers and social movements, financing of death squads, direct aid of authoritarian governments, bombings, etc.[30]

It is important, one more time, to acknowledge that these issues, as presented here, are broad generalizations about highly complex historical events (peculiarities will be underscored in the case studies when necessary), but also, at the same time, acknowledge that these are nonetheless generalizations that reverberate profoundly with Latin Americans who saw and perhaps still see themselves as caught up in these vicious cycles. Perhaps the success of works such as *One Hundred Years of Solitude* goes beyond the mere literary craftsmanship of its author, and is also to be attributed to its capacity of speaking truth to power, especially one that seems to be often so suppressed or bastardized as Latin American history.[31] It is no wonder that Latin Americans—and this can be observed in every upcoming impeachment cases—are often suspicious of foreign (albeit mostly US, due to its historical proximity) and corporative involvement in their national interests and that these suspicions are not likely to be readily dismissed as some ungrounded conspiracy thinking.

The reason why this part of Latin American history goes so unacknowledged outside of its borders, is perhaps best explained by Greg Grandin, a historian who worked closely with the Cold War and US foreign policy:

> To be sure, there is no shortage of critiques of US Cold War foreign policy (...). Latin America in particular has long been the Achilles' heel in the hard armor of US virtue, and even the most triumphal of Cold War scholars have been forced into moral contortions to explain away US actions that contributed to torture and murder of hundreds and thousands of individuals. Aside from making visibly disastrous and deadly interventions in Guatemala in 1954, the Dominican Republic in 1965, Chile in 1973, and El Salvador and Nicaragua

[29] Calvert and Calvert (1993), pp. 89–91.

[30] Calvert and Calvert (1993), pp. 92–151.

[31] Case in point being the section in which García Márquez relives the Banana Massacre of 1928, in Magdalena, Colombia. At the time, the government opened fire against striking United Fruit plantation workers, killing up to what is estimated to be 2000 people. Later, the government took responsibility for only 47 deaths, justifying it on grounds that these people were subversives. The abyss between official and popular perception of the facts is one that remained unbridged. Posada-Carbó (1998), pp. 395 ff.

during the 1980s, the United States has lent quiet and steady financial, material and moral support for murderous counterinsurgent terror states (...). But the enormity of Stalin's crimes ensures that such sordid histories, no matter how compelling, thorough, or damning, do not disturb the foundation of a worldview committed to the exemplary role of the United States in defending what we now know as democracy.[32]

3.1.4 The Military as an Autonomous Political Force

Salus publica suprema lex [public safety, supreme law]
Cicero, in De Legibus

The military is a topic that deserve special attention when it comes to this part of the globe. Its intervention in politics is not by any stretch exclusiveness of Latin America, but nowhere else in the world has the military been comparatively as active as it has in the region.[33] Under such circumstances, entrenchment of military privilege and influence is up to this day noticeable in Latin American constitutional orders,[34] and special caution is assured regarding the military in public discourse, as these themes hold potential to spark both unrest and nostalgia in the civil society; neither being a good option for a democracies looking to consolidate themselves. Impeachments, however unfortunately, offer the ideal opportunity for reopening wounds left by military authoritarian regimes, as due to the usual circumstances of impeachment, that is, a state of crisis and failure of civilian government, the old narratives of professional and technocratic military government recover their populistic appeal.

Indeed, the main characteristic of the military that act independently is its contempt for civilian politicians, which, according to them, lack the elevated *ethos* of the military, its patriotism and devotion to the absolute welfare of the nation.[35] Politicians would be self-interested and inept, blocking necessary reforms and modernization of the state apparatus. This is clear, for example, in the following discourse of Peruvian army officers:

---

[32] Grandin (2011), p. xx.

[33] Loveman (1993), p. 30.

[34] One of the most obvious places to find such influence is in *National Security Councils* which still are dominated by the military and provides it voice in highest levels of government, as well as to the so-called *fueros* (immunities and corporativist jurisdiction). Loveman (1993), p. 6 and Dix (1994), p. 452.

[35] Loveman and Davies (1978), p. 7. It's beyond the scope of this work to discuss every single characteristic of these regimes, but it is interesting to notice that these regimes worked under the principles of (i) centralization of authority; (ii) hierarchical rule through administrative (nonparliamentary) agencies at the provincial and local levels; (iii) flexible constitutions that offered little to no constraint to exercise of power; (iv) official recognition of governance through a state of siege. Moreover, their practices usually entailed (i) systematic persecution of opposition; (ii) pragmatic repression of those who resisted their policies or programs; and (iii) nonrecognition of the legitimacy of political bargaining. Loveman and Davies (1978), p. 5.

> For some time now, since politics infiltrated the army, we military officers have been serving as steppingstones for unscrupulous politicians. They use our services, and then they promote us. This must stop. Promotions must be based upon professional competence and not on political activity (...) We [must] assume the reins of government of the country in order to root out political influence, the worst of all plagues, and we shall shape Peru's destiny with our own hands and our own initiative (...) Our fatherland suffers daily from the partisan struggles of politicians who care nothing for the development and progress of the nation. It is our task to normalize the institutional life of the country (...) The army, drawn from all social classes of the nation, must intervene directly in the management of the affairs of the state.[36]

This line of discourse has been sometimes described as "(new) professionalism"[37] in the specific context of the military, but also sometimes more generally as "anti-politics".[38] As Samuel Huntington aptly describes it, the military mind presupposes a sort of "conservative realism",[39] that is, the idea that core military conservative values are a factual "part of reality", therefore being objectively ascertainable, and the act of disagreeing with them, regardless of one's social, political or religious affiliations, would be akin to lying, being unscientific or in denial of reality. The military mind, in these contexts, would project its professionalized expectations onto the world, integrating them into reality: The military "opinion must never be coloured by wishful thinking (...) The military man will be dealing with military fact, hard figures, grim realities of time and space and resources".[40] Akin to its behaviour in the battlefield, the military are conservative in taking risks, but progressive in employing the newest strategies and technology.

In Latin America, the periods that called most for military intervention were approximately the post-World War years, the 1920s–1945 and then the 1950s–1980s, also the periods in which the urge for industrial and national development was most obvious. The decades that led to the first phase were dominated by David Ricardo's Comparative Advantage doctrine, which stated that countries should specialize in whatever was their economic strengths and then trade their goods with those of other countries, who would likely be working under the same dogma. Resulting from this compromise would be something advantageous for both sides since their commodities/industrialized goods would be produced by less than otherwise and both sides would comparatively profit the most from it. This made Latin American countries wish to specialize in the exportation of commodities, since they were lowly industrialized, and import the needed industrialized goods from Europe and North America. When the stock market crash of 1929 came about, however, the weaknesses of the Ricardian approach became clear. Latin American countries had produced much, but the recession in the industrialized countries did

[36]Loveman and Davies (1978), p. 4. For other discourses by the military of other Latin American countries corroborating this view, see Loveman and Davies (1978), pp. 173–222.

[37]Huntington (1957).

[38]Loveman and Davies (1978).

[39]Huntington (1957), pp. 59–79.

[40]Huntington (1957), p. 67.

not provide a matching demand for commodities. As a result, Latin American countries had their own recessions and, on top of that, also suffered with the lack of industrialized goods since they lacked means of manufacturing their own. Economic nationalism, or import-substituting industrialization, therefore, became the obvious ideology to substitute liberalism as the dominant ideology.[41]

These were, however, transformations in society that the established agrarian elites were inept or unwilling to implement, leading to military unrest towards what they saw as the objective source of national progress. Moreover, the precarious economic conditions generated disorder as workers revolted and communism spread, due to critiques of capitalism only seeming more and more accurate over time.[42] Under such unseemly deterioration of circumstances, the military, also by virtue of its professional logic, felt compelled to takeover many governments in the region (*i.e.,* Brazil 1937, Argentina 1944). The same pattern repeated along the 50s until late 70s (*i.e.,* Brazil 1964, Chile 1973, Uruguay 1973, Argentina 1976),[43] but with more overtly political features, as this time around the military had stablished centralized education for their higher officers (and some civilian politicians) in so-called war schools (*i.e., Escola Superior de Guerra*, in Brazil; *Centro de Altos Estudios Militares*, in Peru; *Escuela de Altos Estudios*, in Argentina; or *Instituto de Altos Estudios de la Defensa Nacional*, in Venezuela),[44] and a few different perspectives on economy announced themselves as the future of development.[45]

The military, as expected from its high degree of organization, proved efficient in dealing with some problems it had identified, particularly that of the spread of subversives. By using "dirty war" tactics, many of the revolutionary movements were quickly rooted out. Similarly, for some time the economy of some Latin American countries thrived, further bolstering the belief in the military's superiority of leadership, upon which most of the military's legitimacy was predicated.[46]

For some other problems, particularly those of more complexly organized societies, however, the military structure and education did not provide any special qualification and the legitimacy of the military suffered drawbacks.[47] In mid to late 70s, the OPEC oil crises fatally undermined the military's legitimacy, as pretty much

[41] Lewis (2006), p. 132.

[42] Lewis (2006), pp. 209–224.

[43] Loveman and Davies (1978), pp. 4–5.

[44] Loveman and Davies (1978), pp. 11, 16–2; Lewis (2006), pp. 214–215. These were openly supported by the US government.

[45] Augusto Pinochet's Chile became known for its involvement with Chicago School's chief neoliberal mind, Milton Friedman, while the Brazilian military still insisted in mainstream Keynesian approaches.

[46] Lewis (2006), p. 219. Dirty war tactics (*Guerra sucia*) involved the indiscriminate use of torture (both of suspects or anyone associated with them, including children), prison camps, death squads, and the infamous helicopter rides that disposed of political opposition (in Argentina, estimated over 30,000 victims by the ex-dictator himself, Jorge Rafael Videla) in the high seas. For a discussion on the economic performance of military regimes, see Remmer (1978) and Dix (1994).

[47] Finer (1976), pp. 12–14.

the only string of legitimacy that attached it to power, that of economic performance, was cut. The military proved unable to react to crises of such an enormous breadth and gradually were forced to negotiate the return of the government to civilian authorities.[48] Additionally, as more information about institutional abuses and forged intrigue to justify the military's clinging to power were discovered, the decaying moral prestige the military also put its suitability for governing the nation in check.[49]

The military's return to the barracks in the 80s seemed to be a lasting one this last time around. The business community learned that the military may serve only inadequately as a partner, being often deaf to the interests outside of the military corporation. Moreover, the left-wing political movements that once seemed so threatening have become harder to find and many of the following civil governments have in some degree given continued pursuit to policies of fiscal restraint, trade liberalization, and privatization that many late military governments started.[50] Arguably, it became clear in terms of policy preferences and outcomes, that democratic processes offered better, more predictable alternatives to military intervention, impeachment also ranking among them. Nevertheless, the spectre of the military as a fourth, potential "moderating power" still lingers in Latin America and regional crises often offer an opportunity for its comeback, as people seem more open to relativize, forget, or even revise the shortcomings of the military in favour of the promise of easy, short-term solution for their misfortunes.[51]

3.1.5 *Late Democratization and Its Consequences*

By 1977 all Latin American countries apart from Colombia, Venezuela, and Costa Rica, were under authoritarian regimes. By 1995, the whole region had reversed back to democracy.[52] This did not exactly mean a fresh start or a clean slate, neither did it mean the continuation of older democratic traditions. The authoritarian past

---

[48] Dix (1994), p. 447. Huntington (1993), pp. 51 ff., adds that the policies adopted by the regimes mostly led to a sharp deterioration of the national economies.

[49] Dix (1994), p. 449. On the military's general claim to legitimacy, see Finer (1976), pp. 5–19.

[50] Dix (1994), pp. 449–452.

[51] Besides what has been already discussed in this section (failure of military projects and economic shocks), Huntington also speculates that the end of military regimes could be founded on (i) unprecedented economic growth in the 1960s, fitting the expectations of modernization theory regarding democratization; (ii) change in the activity of Catholic Churches by the Second Vatican Council of 1963–65 (shift from pro-*status quo* to pro-social reform); (iii) shifting in European and US policies towards the promotion of human rights and democracy; (iv) "snowballing" of democratization by the enhancement of international communication. Huntington (1993), pp. 45–46.

[52] Pérez-Liñán (2007), pp. 41–43. Whether Mexico has been authoritarian in the 1945–1987 period is debatable, but the tendency in scholarly literature is in that direction. See Booth and Seligson (1984). Some authors consider Colombia semi-democratic between 1958 and 1992. See Mainwaring and Pérez-Liñán (2005). Moreover, as a reminder, we are not considering the

had fatally uprooted a political culture and substituted much of it with its own. Old traditional political parties by whom many felt represented were brutally repressed and disbanded. After such a long period of inexistence, they could not just be re-established as if nothing had ever happened. The politicians were different, the electorate was different, the consensus on politics had yet again been transformed. Liberal democracy had won, but not on its own merits. There was no widespread *popular* belief on the inherent value of democracy, but rather only that the military could not really deliver what it had promised and that elites should be rearranged. Democracy had not been conquered but given back through compromises and agreements marked in a bitter note of shame.

This top-down concession of democracy has been one of the distinguishing features of Latin American democracies (partial exception of Nicaragua) and also the reason why many expected them to quickly ebb away once again, as soon as the inherited institutional dysfunctions and illiberal practices undercut the legitimacy of the new systems.[53] It turned out, however, that these new democracies were much more resilient than predicted, with many of them not only managing to preserve their condition of democracy, but also making substantial advances since their transition in terms of quality.[54]

Other predictions relative to these democracies have been more accurate and thus deserve mention so a better understanding of the context of our case studies is achieved. Samuel Huntington argues third wave democracies carry two fundamental dilemmas, the so-called (i) "torturer problem" and (ii) the "praetorian problem". The first (i) pertains the question of how these new democracies deal with the abuses of their authoritarian predecessors, choosing either to 'prosecute and punish' or to 'forgive and forget', whereas the second problem (ii) pertains to how former powerful and rebellious militaries were tamed by the democratizers. Both issues are intertwined and hide beneath themselves foundational questions of national identity and political legitimacy.[55]

Whatever path is chosen to answer these problems, the result is always a trade-off which will appease one side more than the other and leave latent tensions between former antagonistic forces, as well as between old and new goals of government. In other words, "punishing torturers", for example, may denote the strength of the commitment to rule of law, a centrepiece to democracy, but will at the same time be seen as defiance of the old elites and perhaps even as taunting of their wrath,[56] which

Caribbean as part of Latin America for this study, but if we were, only Cuba would be a fully authoritarian regime by 1995.

[53] Mainwaring and Hagopian (2005), pp. 1–2; Mainwaring and Bizzarro (2019), p. 99; Huntington (1993), pp. 174, 255.

[54] See Mainwaring and Bizzarro (2019) for a full description of advances and setbacks. Power centralization, learning processes and ideological moderation are often cited as the reasons for enduring new democracies.

[55] Huntington (1993), pp. 208–270.

[56] "The day they touch any of my men will be the end of the state law", threatened Gen. Pinochet in the 1989 transition of Chile. Huntington (1993), p. 216.

may, consequently, undermine the stability of the new government. Not punishing, on the other hand, will avoid a clash with powerful actors, but will leave unmended wounds in society that may lead to future polarization and vest the democratic commitment with an unhealthy veil of cynicism.[57]

One would perhaps expect a "middle of the road" solution to this problem, entailing a patchwork of punishments and concessions, maximizing a net positive between democratization, keeping of peace, and the discovery of historical truth, but the reality is that most third wave democracies failed egregiously in punishing and prosecuting authoritarian criminals, Argentina being the only exception. Since in most cases the military led the transition back to democracy, they have also given themselves amnesty either unilaterally or as a condition for peaceful transition. Moreover, many managed to stay entrenched in power, alongside with a series of prerogatives that ensured impunity and leniency, even despite the erosion of many of these amnesty pacts as a by-product of application of international law.[58]

Make no mistake that these issues, although dubbed 'transitional' in nature by Huntington, can be very enduring and encompassing consequences, many of which, as the case studies will show, reappear during impeachments, if are not themselves among their indirect causes. Broadly speaking, the following issues are recurring in these new democracies: (i) multiple coup attempts or persistent coup intrigues/threats, usually by military factions that resent the loss of power, institutional capacity, or status; (ii) persistent power and influence of military leaders over democratic processes resulting in unsatisfactory, incomplete, or illegitimate political reforms, as well as in the sustenance of economically encumbering prerogatives of public authorities; (iii) persistence of authoritarian mentality and practices, which held authorities above law and critique.[59]

Resulting of this are weak, inefficient, and vulnerable democracies, which, by virtue of these same characteristics, may suffer from self-reinforcing legitimacy deficits—the thrill initiated with the dawn of freedom and democracy was soon matched by swift frustration and disillusionment brought by its shortcomings, which then led to an era of apathy that produced further shortcomings. Severe contextual circumstances (*i.e.*, extreme poverty and social inequality, encumbering external debt, chronic inflation, insurgency, and widespread violence) were often left

[57] An Uruguayan judge described these tensions when deciding on amnesty laws: "Democracy isn't just about freedom of opinion, the right to hold elections, and so forth. It's the rule of law. Without equal application of the law, democracy is dead. The government is acting like a husband whose wife is cheating on him. He knows it, everybody knows it, but he goes on insisting that everything is fine and praying every day that he isn't going to be forced to confront the truth, because then he'd have to do something about it". Huntington (1993), p. 213.

[58] Huntington (1993), pp. 215 ff. Huntington also speculates that most transitions would have failed, had the democratic successors not accepted the terms of the authoritarians. Roht-Arriaza (1998), pp. 313–316, moreover, argues that reformers have generally given precedence of peace and truth-seeking over justice and democracy.

[59] Huntington (1993), pp. 231–279.

unresolved by virtue of the incapacity of reforming structural and cultural issues of the former regimes.[60]

For the context of this book, these matters usually reveal themselves in the form of democratically dysfunctional party systems, overly corporatist behaviour and prerogatives for public authorities (and its ensuing corruption/impunity), lacking representation and deliberation devices for the people or rank-and-file politicians, as well as costly and overbearing bureaucracies. Impeached Presidents seem to be often caught in the crossfire between those attempting to change and those attempting to maintain the *status quo* on these kinds of subjects. Carefully analysing a case of impeachment will, therefore, give significant insight into much more than just the occurrence of "presidential misdeed"—such issues seem to pale in comparison with all else an impeachment case has to offer, even. It will, in fact, provide insight into the whole functioning of a democracy, denounce its weaknesses to those who willing to see them and to accept their truths (denialism and conspiracy-thinking are, however unfortunately, often prevalent), and finally serve as harbinger of its future success or failure as a political system.

3.2 Case Study

This section will explore how impeachments take place, what motivates them and how jurists in different Latin American countries tackle problems with so many political aspects and pragmatic limitations. Each case has been divided into two parts. The first part will propose an encompassing narrative that seeks to appropriately analyse all elements that gave rise to an impeachment controversy, while the second will describe the proper legal issues that the Parliament, Courts, and other officials dealt with. The first, due to its empirical nature, will be analysed inspired by works of political science with a methodology already described in the first, introductory chapter. Not all elements will always be thoroughly analysed due to restrictions of reliable sources of information, but as far as possible, this study will strive to provide enough information to form cohesive narratives and give a comprehensive overview of the relevant aspects of each legal system. The second part of the analysis will compare legal arguments brought by those involved in impeachments. It is always in good measure to remind the readers that the author may have, directly or indirectly, built biases through the sources used in these analyses, and that, therefore, they should take in the information with a degree of scepticism. One's perceptions of political events can be easily tinted by first and second-hand beliefs and biases. Reason, as David Hume famously put it, is slave of passion.

[60]Huntington (1993), pp. 253–270. Mishler and Rose (2001), pp. 32 ff, also offers interesting insights into the vulnerability of new democracies.

3.2.1 *Typical Procedural Oustings*

This section will describe concrete cases of *impeachment in the strict sense*, that is, cases in which a House of Parliament brings forth accusations against a President, potentially leading to a trial and conviction before a Court of Impeachments. These procedures have been dubbed 'typical' for being legal mechanisms originally designed to make Presidents accountable for their misbehaviour, even though they may display some distinctions from the role model developed by the United States. These procedures, for example, may go by other names (*e.g.*, political trial, constitutional accusation), and may have more influence of the Judiciary, which may act as a gatekeeper or investigator of presidential misconduct, or even as a Court, where the impeachment case is taken to trial. These variations, however, are often merely nominal, or not too character defining to justify their own categories.

This separation is relevant because in the next section these mechanisms will be contrasted with proceedings that sought achieve similar goals, though they had not been originally designed for such. Such 'atypical' proceedings are generally adaptations of other mechanisms to make them act as a surrogate to impeachment, where impeachment itself is unavailable or unfeasible (see Sect. 4.5.1 for detailed taxonomy and explanations).

3.2.1.1 The Example for Latin America: Fernando Collor (1992), Brazil

A Historical Narrative

The first impeachment case of the newly democratized Latin America of the 1990's would be that of Fernando Collor de Melo, Brazil's first directly elected president to take office since the military *coup* of 1964. The Brazil inherited by Collor had been left in critical conditions by the abuses, mismanagement, and corruption of both the military (1964–1984) and the transitional government (1985–1990). At the brink of hyperinflation and possessing the world's largest foreign debt and levels of inequality at the time, Brazilians were politically apathetic and longing for a strong leader to single-handedly set the country back on track.[61] These conditions, and the fact that for most citizens this would be their first experience with direct elections,[62] made them especially vulnerable to demagoguery. Collor, despite being challenged by more experienced and prominent politicians, such as Ulysses Guimarães, Lionel Brizola or Luís Inácio Lula da Silva, was able to capitalize on this vulnerability.[63]

[61] Mainwaring (1999), pp. 127–128; Skidmore (1999), pp. 4 ff. 92.1% of respondents of a July 1989 survey agreed that Brazil needed a "great leader" (IBOPE 1989).

[62] Flynn (1993), p. 355. The electorate grew from 15 million voters in the last election held (1960) to 82 million by 1989. From these, ten million were illiterate and 68% never finished primary school.

[63] Guimarães was a much-respected politician for his resistance against the military rule. Brizola represented a long tradition coming from the Vargas era (1930–45, 1951–54) known for introducing

Perhaps Collor's lack of prominence was what gave him an edge: being an unknown politician, he could market himself as an outsider and present himself as the antidote to the corrupt and inept who had installed themselves in power in the last decades.[64] Self-entitled the "maharajah hunter",[65] Collor promised to moralize and "modernize" the country's administration, heralding economic development and job creation. Well received, this rhetoric led him to the first round against other 21 candidates with a total of 30.5% of the votes.[66] In the run-offs, Collor faced Lula, who ran a similar anti-establishment rhetoric, but from the left. Exploiting Lula's unionist background, Collor stressed his own neoliberal leanings while accusing his adversary of having intentions of seizing people's bank accounts and installing a socialist-totalitarian regime. With 53% of vote, Collor won the elections and assumed the presidential sash on March 15th, 1990, with substantial popular and mediatic support.[67]

This initial support, however, did not translate into parliamentary seats. Member of the small and newly created *Partido da Renovação Nacional* (PRN), Collor had only a small minority in Congress (8% of Deputies, 4% of Senators), even after forming a coalition with two offshoot parties of the former military party ARENA, namely PDS (*Partido Democrático Social*) and PFL (*Partido da Frente Liberal*). Still unexperienced with the federal executive and too idealistic regarding the possibilities created by the Constitution of 1988, Collor made several political choices that undercut his support even further. Accustomed to giving orders rather than negotiating, Collor chose not to share power but rather to pack his cabinet with close acquaintances, who were neither experienced politicians nor renowned experts in their fields.[68]

Unchecked by system insiders or experts, Collor caught the country by surprise with one of his most controversial actions already in the first day of his administration, as he introduced a series of radical interventive measures in the economy via a provisional decree (Collor Plan I).[69] Besides initiating processes of privatization, slashing public spending, and introducing a new currency, the decree temporarily

important labour reforms. Lula was then a less experienced politician, but was influential among workers. Flynn (1993), p. 356.

[64] Skidmore (1999), pp. 2 ff; Flynn (1993), pp. 361 ff.

[65] "Maharajah" (*marajá*) is used as a pejorative term used to designate fat-cat bureaucrats, that is, a sort of "high caste of public officials", who got into wealth by leeching on emoluments and privileges of office.

[66] Figueiredo (2010), p. 113.

[67] Figueiredo (2010), p. 114.

[68] Figueiredo (2010), pp. 116 ff. The choice for personally close personnel should have enabled Collor to assert a dominant position in his cabinet, but even this failed, for in practice he exercised little control over them.

[69] Provisional decrees (*medidas provisórias*) are executive decrees for urgent issues that stay in effect for 30 days after enactment. If confirmed by Congress within such period, they are converted into law. If not, they lose validity and may be reissued. Consecutive reissuance of decrees was deemed illegal by the Supreme Court the next year (ADI 365 AGr, 15.03.1991).

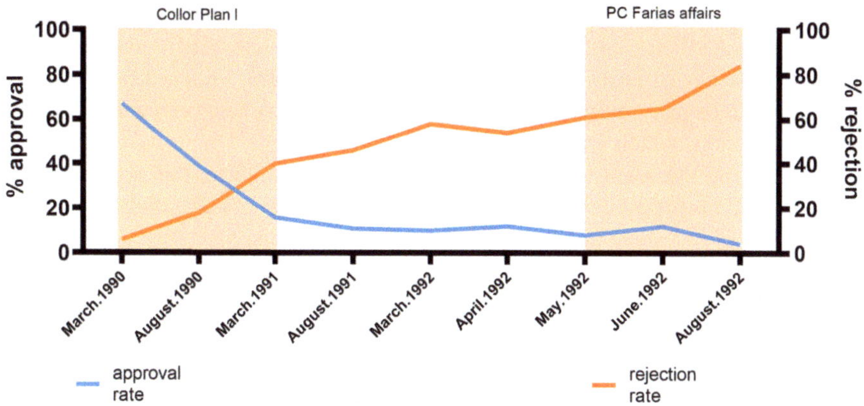

Fig. 3.1 Collor administration's approval and rejection rates, 1990–1992. Source: Own elaboration with data from DataFolha (1992) "Avaliação governo Collor" apud Souza (1999), p. 104

froze most of the savings and checking accounts above a certain limit to deal with issues of internal liquidity. This last measure was, ironically, nicknamed the "seizure of savings accounts", something Collor had so much projected onto his opponent during the presidential debates.[70] This measure, beyond being indiscriminately punishing to most citizens, later also proved ineffective to achieve the goals it had been conceived for, as the private sector found ways of circumventing the restrictions it imposed and soon mobilized to pressure Congress to open up more exceptions and further compromise Collor's plan. Moreover, those who still could not find ways to legally sidestep the limitations had to resort to illegal strategies make ends meet, pay employees, and so on, quasi-institutionalizing corruption as part of daily life.[71] This event alone sunk the Collor administration's approval rate within its first 3 months of administration by 30 points (Fig. 3.1).[72]

Collor's remarkable unpopularity and an isolative political style would be contributing factors to the apparent surge of corruption which was about to be discovered within his administration. Since Collor could barely rely on any genuine support from Congress, more obscure channels of parliamentary management were sought, among them many forms of patronage that extrapolated the typical shadowy use of influence and departed into more direct and unequivocally corrupt transactions. The first scandals on these issues were discovered still in the first year, in October 1990, when Collor's right-arm, the campaign manager Paulo César Farias, as well as his brother-in-law, Marcos Coimbra, were accused of pressuring a state oil

[70]This unpopular measure, in due fairness, was consensus among scholars of the time. Collor's economic advisors are said to have adopted the concept in December 1989, thus after the election. Carvalho (2006).

[71]Weyland (1993), p. 364; Mainwaring (1999), p. 301.

[72]Pérez-Liñán (2007), p. 96.

company (Petrobrás) into borrowing US$ 40 million to one of the recently privatized company (VASP) at odd conditions (*i.e.,* US$ ten million in cash) and with intermediation of one of Farias' companies (BR Distribuidora). This accusation would later prove to be just the tip of the iceberg of a much greater network meant to siphon public resources, which are still being unveiled to this day.[73]

Though the President managed to disentangle himself from this scandal, more soon reached his inner circle. In April of 1991, the Minister of Labour resigned under accusations of accepting kickbacks from public contractors. Just a few months later, in August, it was the first lady's turn to resign as multiple irregularities were found in the philanthropic organization under her direction. In January of 1992, the Minister of Health's was also forced to resign under accusations of approving shady government contracts.[74] The *coup de grâce* to Collor's administration would come from his brother, Pedro, who near the end of May 1992 gave an interview exposing more of the Farias' affairs and implied presidential involvement. Though Pedro backed away from his original version in the following days to exempt Fernando from personal involvement, the momentaneous uproar was sufficient to justify the installation of a Parliamentary Commission of Inquiry (RQN 52/92-CN) into the issues. Congress was visibly unwilling to confront Collor, believing his participation was minor, his crimes (if any) were not too serious, and his ousting was dangerous, as Itamar Franco, the Vice-President, was thought to be a statist and a nationalist, and therefore a threat to the modernization of the Brazilian economy.[75]

Despite the institutional resistance against Collor's impeachment, the clumsiness of the Farias' affairs would make overlooking such accusations incredibly hard. Not long after Pedro, the driver of Collor's personal assistant would denounce that she had been receiving checks to pay for Collor's personal expenses (c.a. US$ 2.5 million). These checks would come from twelve fraudulent accounts, likely the product of kickbacks from the Farias' schemes. As the investigations unfolded, the Commission found that expenses of Collor's mansion and the first lady's car, among other things, had been paid with such checks.[76] At each new discovery, Collor appealed to his charisma and denied every accusation on TV, sometimes offering an alternative interpretation that was quickly debunked the following days. For instance, Collor claimed to have received a loan of US$ five million from Uruguay to pay for reforms on his mansion, which was later found to have been forged *post-facto* to give the transaction a guise of legality.[77] The investigation also found

---

[73] iG São Paulo, February 28th, 2015: *"Denúncia de propina a Collor faz da Petrobrás elo entre impeachment e Lava Jato"*.

[74] Souza (1999), p. 94.

[75] Souza (1999), pp. 94–96. When Pedro came out with the accusations, Collor had just overhauled his cabinet to form a more functional and stable coalition (reaching 41% support in the Chamber of Deputies), as well as had changed his attitude towards the Congress radically, frequently expressing his intent of cooperating in every step of the economic recovery.

[76] Final report of the Mixed Parliamentary Commission of Inquiry (CRN n. 52/92-CN), pp. 397–398.

[77] Geddes and Ribeiro Neto (1999), pp. 26 ff; Skidmore (1999), p. 12.

computer files containing spreadsheets with fraudulent transactions, accurately described with value and beneficiary. This much detailed information of corruption schemes was partially self-inflicted by the Collor administration, as it had outlawed checks to the bearer as part of an early anticorruption package of laws, thus forcing every check in the country to be signed and be, consequently, traceable. Thereafter, linking the culprits with the illegal transactions became a remarkably uncomplicated task.[78]

In August 1992, the Workers' Party put efforts into rallying support for Collor's impeachment and, with assistance of a unionist organization (*Central Única dos Trabalhores*, CUT), started mobilizing protestors against the President. President Collor, in a visibly tense public announcement, appealed to his charisma once again, asking people to protest in his favour, wearing the colours of the national flag, as to send a message to those he called a minority of *coup*-makers that the majority still supported him. Two days later, over 250,000 protestors flooded the streets, wearing overwhelmingly black in what had turned into a day of mourning for Collor's administration. In the next days, tensions escalated further, as the Brazilian Bar Association (OAB) announced it would ask for impeachment as soon as the Commission's report was done. Moreover, protests spread through the country for the next 2 weeks, the largest reaching up to 750,000 protestors in the eve of the impeachment.[79]

As soon as the report was published, impeachment procedures were formally initiated. Drawing on evidence produced by the Mixed Commission, the Impeachment Commission of Inquiry was able to produce its own quickly and, in just 1 month, the plenum of the Chamber of Deputies impeached Collor with 441 votes to 38. It took another 3 months until the case was trial ready, and December 30th of 1992, the Senate chose to convict President Collor by 76 votes to 3, removing and disqualifying him from office for 8 years. Hoping to escape conviction, Collor sent a resignation letter before the end of the trials, but the act was interpreted as a confession of guilt by the Senators and his resignation, denied.[80]

Just as in the first English impeachment during Edward III's reign, the "first" Latin American impeachment would depend on a collection of highly unlikely events to prosper. To name a few: (i) corruption scandals stretching from the inner political circle to the extended and nuclear family; (ii) accusations coming from allies and enemies alike, most notably from the own family; (iii) blatant failure to cover up crimes; constant self-contradiction in public appearances; (iv) persistent difficulty in cooperating with other branches of power; (v) heavy popular mobilization despite mistrust of institutions and widespread political apathy; (vi) no noticeable attempt to embarrass the work of the media in the coverage of the scandals; (vii)

[78] Skidmore (1999), pp. 11 ff.

[79] Folha Online, April 30th, 2008: *"Saiba mais sobre os cara-pintadas"*.

[80] President Collor had publicly stated before that he would not resign, as that would be a confession of guilt. A few of his opponents aptly remembered the incident: *Diário do Congresso Nacional* n. 32/92, p. 2920.

unexpected lifting of multiple corporatist prerogatives to favour investigation and public accountability (*i.e.,* massive lifting of bank secrecy by the Commission of Inquiry and public broadcasting of the impeachment proceedings; more details in the next section); (viii) economic reforms created dissatisfaction on all levels of society; (ix) the media followed closely patronage proposals made by Collor, frustrating any last attempt at building a parliamentary shield.[81] From a more personal perspective, Collor's personality was also conflictive as he: (i) was often too arrogant to negotiate and share power, leading to unnecessary conflict (and perhaps an unnecessary impeachment, as a more realistic President would arguably have resigned earlier); (ii) lived a lavish lifestyle in times of enormous economic distress, seemly mocking the hardships endured by his countrymen; (iii) was a bit too sure of his impunity, not dispensing the proper cautiousness to his public relations.[82]

Just like the first impeachments, however, the legal aspects of the procedures were not completely flawless from the outset and so have given space for some interesting debates that will be discussed next.

Impeachment in the Chamber of Deputies

The paradigm shift brought by the third wave of democratization did not stay only in the streets in the form of massive protests urging for the ousting of a President by the rules of the democratic game but was also to be observed in the parliamentary discourses and in decisions of the Supreme Court. The intent of breaking with the tradition apathy and cynicism that reinforced *de facto* unchecked powers manifested itself in many ways. Ironically, one of them came from Collor's first legal defensive reactions to impeachment.

As soon as the impeachment accusation piece was formally accepted by Ibsen Pinheiro, the President of the Chamber of Deputies, Collor's lawyers rushed to the Supreme Court with writs of security (MS 21,564/DF) arguing the illegality of many rules stablished by Pinheiro for the procedure, possibly looking to bury the procedures in legal quarrels. So that these defence arguments could be considered by the Supreme Court, however, it would have to change its stance on interfering in the "core functions", "political activities" or "*interna corporis* matters" of other branches of power. Historically, until then, the Supreme Court had refused to intervene in the Legislative branch, even in cases of blatant illegality or unfairness, arguing that any intervention of the Court would amount to usurpation of competences, a violation of the principle of separation of powers. Regarding impeachments, the Supreme Court had consistently refused to reform procedural rules stablished by state legislatures for impeaching Governors, under the argument that anything impeachment-related was political question of the legislature and,

[81] On this last issue see, Skidmore (1999), pp. 12 ff.

[82] See Souza (1999), pp. 95–97.

therefore, a realm for which a court of law had no adequate toolset or legitimacy to contemplate.[83]

Naturally, what is or is not "core", "political", or "internal to the corporation" in this context is up to debate. Justice Paulo Brossard, who incidentally authored perhaps the most well-known manual on impeachment in the country, voted for the wholesale rejection of the writ, in a declaration of total incompetence of the Supreme Court to interfere in the decisions of the Legislature. This opinion, although consistent with previous decisions on the topic, was defeated by the newer Justices, who considered "core" entailed solely the merit, opportunity, convenience, or grounding of the parliamentary decisions. The formal aspects which condition the validity of such decisions, therefore, were not immune to revision of the Supreme Court.[84] By deciding this, the Supreme Court broke away from its stance of isolating itself from the power clashes and assumed a more universalizing commitment to legality and the rules of the democratic game—a stance that had hitherto connived with the abuses of the Executive and Legislature alike, and had insidiously given legitimacy to whoever came out the strongest.[85]

Conforming to its new competence, the Court moved on to consider the actual defence arguments, namely that: (1) the law of impeachment, a law from 1950, had been tacitly revoked by Brazil's short-lived experimentation with parliamentarism in 1961–62, thus rendering the opening of the procedures void; (2) if the law was still valid, then the Senate was the one legitimized to start the procedures, rendering the acts of the Chamber completely invalid; (3) the Chamber's bylaws required 10 sessions for defence, and not 5, as stablished by Pinheiro; (4) the Chamber's bylaws required vote to be taken secretly, and not openly and nominally, as stipulated by Deputy Pinheiro.

These arguments, with exception of (3), were promptly rejected. The transition to parliamentarism was said to not have turned the President irresponsible—the office may have less power to abuse and thus be less likely to fuel an impeachment, but the responsibility had to remain and was not to be completely transferred to the Prime

[83] Brossard de Souza Pinto (1965), pp. 155–160. This, as will be noticed, is still not a rare stance in Latin America.

[84] *Acórdão* MS 21,564/DF, pp. 9–10. To some extent self-contracting, the Justice-*Rapporteur* claims that interpreting the parliamentary by-laws, which happen to be laws with the same rigor and formality as any other ordinary law, is a core activity of the Parliament and, thus, immune from his considerations.

[85] As an example, consider the ousting of President Carlos Luz in 1955. Carlos Luz had his permanent absence from office declared by the Parliament, while being held for a day at gun point in a vessel by a faction of the country's military. Neither was a declaration of absence a constitutional possibility of the Constitution of 1946, nor was such situation of absence a justification for it, if it did exist. Regardless of its blatant illegality, the Supreme Court refrained from intervening, and the situation was only made right by another faction of the military still committed to democracy. Beçak (2003), pp. 26 ff.

Minister.[86] The only parts of the impeachment law that lost validity were those that were in conflict with the new Constitution, thus defeating argument (2) and confirming the Chamber's competence to impeach. The Court recognized, however, the need of extending Collor's due for defence by five sessions, overturning Pinheiro's decision, which he had justified on the urgency bylaws of the Chamber. Finally, the Court also rejected the plea to change voting to secret, clarifying that secret votes were only possible if expressly demanded by law. In any other case, the general rule of open and nominal votes was the case. The Justices further argued that impeachments required an extra commitment to democratic legitimacy, hence why the whole event had to be as transparent as possible to the population.

The interpretation for more transparency, however, may have put Collor in a predicament. September, the month in which impeachment votes were to be taken, was also the month in which a significant part of the parliamentary body started campaigning for municipal offices.[87] Citizens were paying special attention to anything that happened in Congress to inform their votes. The short space of time between impeachment and elections would ensure that whatever decision made would directly impact the electoral results. Candidate-Deputies had special motivation, therefore, to conform to popular wishes since the ballot box would make them immediately accountable for their actions and, so, were less likely to remain true to their consciences and perceptions of justice. Indeed, the act of impeachment was perhaps more televised than a World Cup final—and this is a powerful statement considering the country in question-, with mega screens all over major cities and Congress entirely open to observers. Each of the 336 "yes" votes necessary for impeachment was cheered as a goal for the national team, and each "no" booed as foul play. The well-known Collor loyalists were booed even before getting a chance to declare their votes on the microphone.[88] As enough votes for impeachment were achieved, the session was brought to an unscheduled pause, as many cheered, cried and sung the hymn of independence (not the national anthem!).[89]

Now, more properly to the legal discussions in the Chamber:

---

[86] For context, the transition to parliamentarism was articulated to neutralize President João Goulart, who was considered a communist threat by the military. Parliamentarism was the compromise offered by Congress to the military to avert a direct *coup*; it was only a delay, however, as the *coup* still occurred in 1964.

[87] The Legislature offered then unappealing offices, with little access to resources or prominence. Deputies and Senators were, therefore, tempted to run for any Executive office they could get their hands on and so move up the political ladder. See Samuels (2002) and Mainwaring (1999), p. 265.

[88] Allegedly, some of the anti-impeachment Deputies even had their personal information leaked by the Workers' Party (PT), to physically pit the population against them and so coerce them into voting for the impeachment. *Diário do Congresso Nacional* n. 161/1992, p. 22130. Deputy Paulo Pretto (PT) stated the implications loud and clear: "I want to state publicly, Mr. President, that I won't attend the burial of Deputies who will be lynched by the people, if we can't bring this corrupt down". *Ibid.*, p. 22091.

[89] This was arguably a revealing choice, as the lyrics of the former are centred around the overcoming of tyranny and servitude, whereas the latter emphasizes predominantly nationalistic self-exultation.

The central point of conflict came from the objective element of the impeachable offenses suggested by the accusation. Brazil has one of the broadest ranging laws of impeachment in Latin America, containing 7 general categories of impeachable offenses (*i.e.*, acts against the existence of the Union, acts against the free functioning of the political branches, etc.) in the Constitution of 1988 (art. 85), which are subdivided into 60 specific impeachable offenses described in the impeachment law (Law n. 1079/50). Yet, of all possible articles the accusers could have picked from—and in the words of one of Supreme Court Justices of the time, the President's behaviour had been enough to fill any of the legally available impeachable offenses-,[90] the accusation chose perhaps the broadest available and demanded Collor be declared unfit for office for "behaving inadequately with the dignity, honour and decorum of the office [of President]" (art. 9, 7, Law n. 1079/50).

The difficulty of pinning down what exactly dignity, honour, and decorum may objectively mean was obvious in the accusation, as it had to reach back to definitions given by Cicero and those used in Roman Law.[91] Later, however, it left the true meaning of such concepts implied in the boiled down acts of the president the accusation considered "undignified acts" for the presidency, namely: (1) receiving undue benefits; (2) influence-peddling; (3) lies; (4) breach of decorum; (5) omission. However more tangible these charges made the accusation, they were hardly ever systematically analysed by the Deputies in their argumentation, as most still clung to their personal understandings of indignity, dishonour or breach of decorum, and more importantly, to their own standards of proof—the more feverous supporters of Collor requiring incontrovertible proof, while his antagonists felt his mere unpopularity was already enough evidence of indignity.

It is interesting to notice, however, that Deputies were arguing that the impeachment phase of impeachment procedures was to be understood analogously to the presentment a criminal procedure. It was, in other words, a sort of preliminary analysis of the alleged offensive conduct, meant to verify whether the accusation was robust enough to justify more invasive and time-consuming inquiry, and thus arguably avoid ungrounded and speculative diligences, harassment, and persecution. This was relevant because much of the charges against the President were underpinned by the final report of the inquiry into Farias' affairs, which were not directed at Collor specifically but implied his participation or some degree of criminal negligence. Although an Impeachment Commission was formed to allow independent production of evidence with participation of the defence, the investigation against Farias was still said to bear most weight. To some Deputies such was not even to be considered an irregularity given how notorious and factually undeniable the affairs had been in the public eye. Deputy Sandra Starling's (PT), for example,

---

[90] Acórdão MS 21,564, p. 32, Justice Paulo Brossard.

[91] *Diário do Congresso Nacional* n. 1/1992 (*Diversos* n. 12), pp. 7–27. As an example of the intangibility of the definitions offered, it is argued that dignity is gained "by bringing upon the facts of life certain order and measure (. . .)"; and is associated with modesty, honesty, temperance, and domain over one's passions.

despite her legalistic language, put these evidentiary objections as secondary to the notoriety of offenses:

> All conditions of admissibility of the accusation are verified. The listed facts (. . .) are of notorious public knowledge; they fit in the constitutional and infra-constitutional types of impeachable offenses [crimes de responsabilidade]; There are strong reasons to believe that the President was involved in the practices described in the opening piece, that would make the accused a citizen deprived of the dignity and decorum required for the office of President.[92]

Others, however, did not buy into the imagined legalistic division of presentment and trial argued by most Deputies, and claimed the impeachment phase amounted to the trial itself. More concerningly, because of this, some argued Collor's defence was being curtailed. In their argument, by the time the opportunity was to be given to Collor to produce evidence of his innocence in the Senate trials, the President's reputation would have been broken beyond repair. The impeachment was to become self-fulfilling prophecy by time the matters were taken to trial, as argued by Deputy Ricardo Fiuza:

> There [in the report from the Commission] is nothing categorical, only one statement about Mr. President's involvement. (. . .) None of our trials [to remove Deputies] has ever lasted less than six months (. . .) Now it's intended to remove in record time the Supreme Magistrate of the Nation. I'm astonished (. . .) that the Nation is being told that this is only an authorization to indict the President. (. . .) That's an absolute untruth (. . .), as, if the Senate is authorized to trial the President, his Excellence will be automatically ousted[93] (. . .). I think it is absolutely unfair and haphazard that the Chamber of Deputies won't allow defence, as it indeed hasn't. My dear friend Nelson Jobim, the Commission's Rapporteur, had his report ready even before receiving the President's defence piece. What we are doing here (. . .) is the lynching of the Mr. President.[94]

As mentioned, a great deal of evidence against Collor had been borrowed from the Farias' affairs investigations, which, under the pretext of not targeting the President, did not give him opportunity to contradict the evidence found. As a result, much of the evidence was later declared illegal for being obtained without the necessary legal formalities (*i.e.,* the disk containing spreadsheets linking Collor to Farias' racket and many intercepted phone calls had been obtained without warrant). Had this step been taken before, the conducts that supported the claim of "indignity for office" would surely have been more fragile.

It is unclear whether clinging to evidentiary rules would have been of consequence to Collor's fate. Legally stablished truths and historical truths surely operate at different levels. This is seen, for example, at the palpable frustration in part of Justice Sepúlveda Pertence's sentence regarding Collor's criminal offenses, which would be trialled 2 years later:

---

[92] Author's translation of *Diário do Congresso Nacional* n. 161/92, pp. 22,130–22,131.

[93] Impeachment causes suspension from office for the duration of the trial (Art. 86, §1, of the 1988 Const.).

[94] Author's translation of *Diário do Congresso Nacional* n. 160/92, pp. 22032.

> (. . .) seldom do I hope to have the opportunity, or better yet, the need to hold back [ficar na contingência de] on voting due to missing proof of a single fact, whilst intimately being convinced that the fact occurred. (. . .) when one sees that big companies, like some of the referred – "suddenly, and no more than suddenly" – since 1990 or the election of Fernando Collor, convinced themselves that the destiny of their entrepreneurial planning depended on the 'services' of an obscure company in Maceió of property of PC Farias, it is evident that a lot had to be discovered about the true cause of those payments. We cannot, however, escape the documental evidence brought to these procedures, the declaration of businessmen and the proof of tax collection, which could not completely destroy this montage of apparent service provision.[95]

When in doubt, the legal method urges us to suppose innocence, even if it may mean being overly naïve for the sake of fairness. The same is not true in politics, on the streets, or in history books.[96] To the Deputies, the mere state of disrepair and outrage created by Collor's administration were enough to prove the President's unfitness for office—and with just one article of impeachment on "indignity" rather than multiple articles on racketeering, corruption, graft, influence peddling or perjury, they could do just that. Out of the 101 Deputies that took the opportunity to publicly debate the accusations, 68 discussed the accusations in the terms the accusation piece had proposed; the other 33, focused on matters of political opportunity (*i.e.*, popular commotion, economic distress) and, a minority of this last group, on unrelated matters, such as presidential succession or upcoming municipal elections.

To this last group belonged a faction of the Workers' Party, who seemed beholden with of the idea of creating an "exclusive constitutional amendment" to anticipate presidential elections as soon as Collor was ousted and so circumvent the legal succession of the feared Itamar Franco administration. It would admittedly be another opportunity for Lula to revert his latest electoral upset. In Deputy Ernesto Gradella's (PT) words:

> (. . .) 49% [of the Brazilians] want new elections immediately and only 14.6% want Itamar Franco to take office. (. . .) Itamar taking office is a coup against the 'Fora Collor' [Out with Collor] movement (. . .), it's the continuity of the plan of misery. (. . .) We need a government of workers, a Lula administration (. . .).[97]

Even with the "Itamar-threat" looming on the horizon, however, most of the other deputies were categorical about respecting the rules of legal succession. It is worth noticing that the Workers' Party was still perceived as a radical-leftist party at this point and the prospect of having Lula as the next President was also unenticing.[98]

---

[95] Author's translation of AP 307-3/DF, pp. 2785–2786 *(voto sobre Art. 299, CP—Paulo César Farias)*.

[96] To this day, Collor displays his acquittal letter as the ultimate evidence of his innocence. In his return to politics as Senator for Alagoas in 2007, he claimed to be victim of a coup orchestrated by the Establishment, who felt threatened by his policies. This discourse and his account of the facts can be read in Collor (2007).

[97] Author's translation of *Diário do Congresso Nacional* n. 161/92, pp. 22075.

[98] The Workers' Party would have to go through many reforms and restructurings to achieve the electoral success it did in 2002. See Samuels (2004) for details.

Either way, the Deputies insisted there was more to the impeachment than just law and justice. It was about "restoring governability",[99] "creating jobs and giving people their dignity back",[100] "condemning the neoliberal model of economics",[101] "providing the youth with pedagogic action",[102] and so on. The most popular of the political reasons, however, was the renewed commitment to the republican form of government, well epitomized in Deputy Starling's closing remark: "Here, today, the Republic starts. Here, now, we start to reformulate Brazil, so that, from now on, the actions of every public man, regardless of how powerful, always be subjected to the law!".[103]

Conviction in the Senate

> It is true that this is not a 'cold' trial, based solely on legal arguments and confirmed evidence. The fact that it has the heat and unction of the streets, the fact that it is made sacred by popular demonstrations and especially by the youth does not belittle it but legitimates it even further.
>
> Senator Nelson Wedekin (PDT)[104]

One of the central legal questions raised by the time the procedures moved to the stage of trial pertained to the impartiality of the Senators. In the months between the Senate's admission of impeachment (October 2nd), the completion of the Special Commission of Impeachment's final report and final preparations for trial (December 29th), many Senators were asked by media outlets on their opinions about Collor's fate. Many were categorical about convicting him. Senator Ronan Tito (PMDB), for example, stated to São Paulo's biggest newspaper that: "The people have already convicted Collor, and the Senate will not go against the people's will"; Senator José Paulo Bisol (PSDB) claimed, in another opportunity, that "the contradictions in the depositions of Collor's defence witnesses were already enough to convict him".[105]

Collor's defence caught on these open declarations of vote and argued in another writ of security (MS 21,623/DF) that Senators who made remarks of such nature had to be considered suspect and removed from trial, as would be the case for judges found in the same circumstances, according to the code of criminal procedure. He argued, moreover, against a few of his historical enemies, from whom one could expect nothing short of sheer animosity and lack of judiciousness, and against those

---

[99] *Diário do Congresso Nacional* n. 161/92, pp. 22082–83.

[100] *Ibid.*, p. 22089.

[101] *Ibid.*, p. 22090.

[102] *Ibid.*, p. 22115.

[103] *Ibid.*, p. 22131 (Author's translation).

[104] Author's translation of *Diário do Congresso Nacional* n. 32/92, p. 2900.

[105] Author's translation of *Folha de São Paulo*, October 27th, 1992; and *Correio Braziliense*, September 9th, 1992, respectively.

Senators who participated in the investigations. The latter, he claimed, were already in the mindset of prosecution and could detach themselves to properly form a neutral judgment, as historical evidence on inquisitorial trials would suggest. In total, Collor's defence accused 28 Senators of incurring in one of these three hypotheses and, thus, of being fatally biased: this would be enough to make conviction impossible, as 28 Senators comprise more than veto threshold of 1/3 potential votes. But was Collor justified? Was a fair trial still possible? Was there still a point in being trialled by one's own prosecutors, mortal enemies, and those who had already made their mind about the outcome before even considering what the defence had to say?

Though the Supreme Court did, in fact, generally recognize the subsidiary applicability of the rules of criminal procedure to impeachment, it rejected Collor's plea under the argument that its applicability, as well as the applicability of any other rules stemming from the rule of law, had to be understood with many reservations imposed by the nature of the procedures and the organ of adjudication. It openly recognized that Brazil's model of presidential removal had followed the US's model, equally being an eminently political procedure and a place where political considerations unavoidably take over. Justice Paulo Brossard argued "(. . .) the impeachment has political features, has no other causes than political ones, aims for political objectives, is initiated [*instaurado*] under considerations of political nature and trialled with political criteria", and so, it would be unfeasible to ask from Senators to be unbiased towards the political stances they were elected to represent, especially in matters so divisive and far-reaching as impeachments.[106] Moreover, it was argued that simply because the Senate has quasi-judicial functions [*funções judicialiformes*], it does not turn itself entirely into a court of law. It still is and ought to act as the political organ it was elected to be. The impartiality in impeachment would not consummate itself in the individual relations between Senators, procedures, and defendant, but rather in the high threshold of approval, which should guarantee a supra-partisan consensus on the topic.[107]

The 'inquisitorial-judge' argument was weakly analysed by the Justices, apart from those whose defeated opinion identified in it a truly fatal bias. Conveniently for the majority, the impeachment law has a *numerus clausus* rule for bias suspicion, removing only those Senators who are relatives of the President or have acted as witnesses in the procedures (art. 36 and 63, L.n. 1079/50). This being the case, Collor's attorney's argument could be comfortably put away simply by claiming "it is political and that is how the constitution wanted it after all". This is unfortunate, as it ended up being a missed chance of discussing one awkward feature of the Brazilian impeachment law: the redundancy of its phases. Unlike the American impeachment, the Brazilian impeachment has two phases in which investigations take place and impeachment articles are offered. Once the President of the Chamber decides to accept an accusation piece, a Commission of Inquiry is initiated to verify

[106] Acórdão MS 21,623/DF, pp. 15–16.

[107] Brossard is implicitly citing conclusions brought by Hamilton in *The Federalist* n. 65 and 66, as well as by Senator Charles Sumner in Andrew Johnson's trial.

if the accusation piece truly holds water; later, the Commission produces a report with articles of impeachment, which is then approved by the plenum of the Chamber. This report is sent to the Senate, where it needs to be confirmed to validate the impeachment, and yet another Commission of Inquiry is formed to produce another report. This report will be significantly deeper, as it means to fill gaps from the previous report, hearing witnesses and experts, as well as confronting the evidence found. This report is then sent to the plenum of the Senate, who then votes for the "indictment and trial" of the President. After this, the actual trial starts, and witnesses and experts are once again heard, questioned, and discussed.

The same level of redundancy does not happen in the American model, as the Lower House does the complete job of prosecution and investigation, leaving little wiggle room for new evidence to be presented before the Senate; the creation of biased "inquisitorial-judges" is, thus, much less likely. It seems the Brazilian legislators had criminal procedures in mind, when framing their own version of the presidential impeachment: a sort of preliminary investigation by the police (Chamber of Deputies, 'presentment' phase), which at some point becomes robust enough to justify judicial warrants for more invasive proof and is thus lead with the help of the prosecution (Senate, 'indictment' phase), and only then is taken for trial for proper confrontation (Senate, trial phase).[108]

All things considered, it is nonetheless hard to speculate whether the faithful adaptation of the Brazilian model to the American would be of consequence, since, as discussed before, members of the Parliament are tendentially strongly partisan either way. It seems that recognizing the unconstitutionality of a system that breeds "inquisitorial-judges" would be, at least in this specific moment, more problematic than helpful. The Supreme Court would be single-handedly voiding a decision made by smashing majorities in the Senate and Chamber of Deputies, with massive popular backing. It would, moreover, cause quite some friction with the abrupt interruption of the interim government. Naturally, none of this was mentioned in the decisions, though it has likely been considered. Either way, this topic was never reopened again, and the impeachment procedures remain strongly redundant and somewhat questionable in their framework.

As for the discussions in the Senate there is not much that can be added, as there was significant repetition of arguments from the writs of security and the previous session in the Chamber of Deputies. Moreover, the trial was cut short by the resignation letter of the President, a final desperate attempt of salvaging his political rights by avoiding an impeachment conviction. The strategy did not work, however. The Senators voted about whether they should continue the trial session (approved on 71 to 8 votes, simple majority necessary)[109] and so still decide on Collor's culpability for impeachable offenses. Senators were convinced that, legally or not,

[108] Perhaps in a silent acknowledgement of this, many of the Justices use criminal-procedural vocabulary when referring to the phases of impeachment, even though the law of impeachment does not employ such terms.

[109] *Diário do Congresso Nacional* n. 32/92, p. 2782.

they had the moral duty of seeing the procedures through and state on which side of history they stood:

> Everything happened, we struggled, we worked, and we discussed so much not to go beyond the mere limits of the impeachment of Mr. Collor? In the end, aren't we beginning a new era, aren't we building a new conscience? (. . .) Is that our moral misery? No. We are convinced (. . .) that this is about radical transformations in Brazil's culture.[110]

Others claimed it was no more than what equality before the law demanded: "A man of the people, a simple man, who commits a crime will be punished. A President, on the other hand, (. . .) may commit an impeachable offense and be left unpunished just because he, by his individual decision, renounced his mandate?".[111] Once this plea was approved, even those who defended Collor voted in favour of his disqualification for office, consolidating his most smashing defeat, with 76 to 3 votes.[112] The 3 votes against were cast by Senators widely known as Collor's "Shock Troops" (also referred to mockingly by their colleagues as Collor's "Check Troupe", for their patronage-hungry behaviour), who were the ones to irreducibly defend Collor's interests in the Senate. It is safe to assume that, if there ever was an impeachment whose success was representative of generalized social consensus, this was it.

3.2.1.2 Quest for Legitimacy: Carlos Andrés Pérez (1993), Venezuela

A Historical Narrative

By today's standards, ousting someone like Collor would be a non-issue, as far as impeachments go. Everything about Collor's administration was conducive to the interruption of his presidency: he was unexperienced, stubborn, confrontative, isolated; democracy was fragile, inefficient, and unconsolidated; parties extremely fragmented and volatile; economy was in disrepair; corruption was widespread and vulgarly exposed for the popular gaze. In his favour stood only the centuries of institutionalized complacency, democratic irresponsiveness, cronyism, and self-serving corporatism that made presidential accountability unthinkable until then. His impeachment was perhaps the first evidence for Latin Americans that this was a bridge that could be crossed, although surely the region still had a long way to prove it had undergone a civilizational shift towards true republicanism.

The impeachment of Carlos Andrés Pérez (CAP) is one of the cases that truly put this hypothesis to the test. Like Collor, CAP inherited an economy in shambles and

[110] Author's translation of *Diário do Congresso Nacional* n. 32/92, pp. 2757–2758.

[111] Author's translation of *Ibid.*, p. 2763.

[112] The consensus around Collor's conviction can arguably indicate a lack of partisanship in the decision. Collor's last coalition was formed April 15th of 1992, with the PRN, PFL, PDS, PTB and PL, summing up to a theoretical support of 43.54% (6.2% of the PRN) in the Chamber and 41.75% (3.7% of the PRN) in the Senate. In Senate, the government was supported by 3 out of its theoretical 34 Senators (8.8%), therefore.

had to make truly risky and unpopular choices to turn it around. Unlike everything else about Collor's Brazil, however, Venezuela had everything conducive to political stability. It was one of the few countries spared from the recent military authoritarian experiences, being a democracy since 1958, being a more consolidated, second wave democracy, therefore. The party system was bipartisan and weakly polarized, with two large parties alternating in power (but always sharing cabinets!), AD (*Acción Democrática*, centre-left) and COPEI (*Comité de Organización Política Electoral Independiente*, centre-right).[113] Venezuela's economy had boomed since the 1920s, when oil exploration brought the country into a world of wealth and development, being often regarded by observers as Latin America's favourite to join the club of developed nations. CAP's personality, moreover, opposed that of Collor. He was an experienced and highly regarded politician, having one highly successful mandate as a President in 1974–1979. As such, a repetition of Brazil's 1992 seemed, on the surface, unlikely. CAP himself was presumably sure of that as well, as in his own words: "*I am not a President like Collor de Mello, who rose to power overnight by a media miracle. I am a man in a [political] trajectory ever since I was a boy, with many years of struggle and not a single tarnish in my life (...)*".[114] If anything, however, Venezuela was about to teach the world about the elusiveness of stability indicators, especially when artificially inflated or weakly rooted.

Venezuela's easy and abundant oil wealth, from which up to 70% of the government's income derived, had long created illusions of progress and forestalled necessary but unpopular reforms. The functioning of democracy, party and electoral systems, and the economy all became dependent on one single commodity, even though there were multiple efforts at diversification.[115] When the oil shocks of the 70s and 80s came about, these systemic distortions erupted: at first, "positively", as government revenues skyrocketed, enabling it to invest massively (but unwisely, given the unforeseeable and unprecedented influx of income); and, at a second moment, negatively, when it no longer could keep up with the investment commitments made in the period of bonanza. The bulk of investments could not be simply interrupted, forcing the government to run budget deficits and to borrow foreign money aggressively. This worked fine until 1982, when Mexico defaulted on its

[113] Michael Coppedge (1999), pp. 3 ff, points out that the COPEI, although often merely described as center-right, is best understood as a Social Christian party, with different factions, some more socially reformist (some of which, such as the 1960s *astronautas*, could be considered progressive even today) and others more reactionary. Polarization may be, therefore, even more moderate than the cardinal positions in the political spectrum may suggest. Moreover, the transition from authoritarianism and subsequent consolidation of democracy required both parties to make concessions to the former ruling elite, pulling their political agendas even closer.

[114] Author's translation of Pérez and Blanco Muñoz (2010), p. 335.

[115] Diversification and industrialization are harder when one sector of the economy becomes too strong and single-handedly inflates the value of the country's currency. This, in turn, makes other exports more expensive and less competitive, atrophying unrelated industries (*Dutch disease*). See Terry Karl (1997), pp. 71 ff.

creditors and startled those who invested in Latin America, halting the flux of foreign funds into the region. As such, one of the few surrogates Venezuela found for oil revenue cut short. When CAP took the presidency in 1989, Venezuela's money reserves were already depleted, and its foreign debt, unrepayable.[116]

CAP was aware of the 'distortions' that held Venezuela back and was determined to end them. What his electorate may have overlooked or underestimated, however, was how much he changed in the ten years between his first and second mandates. 1989s CAP was no longer the one who defended and strengthened an interventionist state, the one who was responsible for the nationalization of Venezuela's oil and iron companies, and who denounced multinational corporations and international financial institutions.[117] CAP had updated himself to the new mainstream of economics and did what most of the other Latin American also did in the 1990s, as part of their stabilization plans: composed a cabinet of young, foreign trained technocrats recruited from thinktanks, universities and professional organizations, who made up for their lack of political skills and capital with technical knowledge. What came from this was a neoliberal economic plan called "*El Gran Viraje*" (The Great Turnaround), whose foremost focus was lifting price and interest rate controls.[118]

It is unclear whether CAP originally intended to introduce the plan incrementally or in one fell swoop, but the latter ended up being the case. Moisés Naim, CAP's Minister of Industry, suggests the mere possible end of state intervention instilled fear and greed, causing controls on the economy to just fall apart entirely by themselves. The administrative system that sustained price controls simply failed to keep up with the high levels of repressed inflation, hoarding of goods and black-market speculation. As a result, scarcity and inflation went immediately to dangerous levels, leaving society in a state of shock.[119]

In less than a month of CAP's administration and the introduction of the Great Turnaround, demonstrations spread throughout the country, protesting initially against high transportation fares and scarcity of food stuffs. As the situation deteriorated into weeklong indomitable riots, with several reports of looting and vandalism, the military were brought to the streets as reinforcement. Due to perhaps a lack of planning and preparedness for such situations, many clashes turned violent and at least 270 people died and another 1800 were injured, with an estimated four million rounds being shot in confrontation.[120] This event, known as *El Caracazo,* marked a waking moment in Venezuelan democratic history.

The reason why so many citizens felt compelled to rebel for such a long time, despite violent repression, went beyond the mere circumstantial hardships caused by

---

[116] For a more nuanced overview, see Maingón and Sonntag (1990), pp. 129 ff; and Naím (1993), pp. 19–28.

[117] Pérez-Liñán (2007), p. 18.

[118] Naím (1993), pp. 47 ff.

[119] Naím (1993), pp. 54 ff.

[120] Rey (1993), pp. 5–7.

CAP's economic stabilization plan. It was a rebellion against a larger political system that had been failing Venezuelans for decades, it was a system that demanded too much sacrifice from them, while denying a political voice.[121]

As it would become clear in the next months of debate (and was already under the suspicion of the academia),[122] Venezuelan democracy was long withering away under a deficit of legitimate channels for voicing popular political demands, as well as under the irresponsiveness of the ruling elites to the last few available channels. The two hegemonic political parties had become so pervasive that all relevant political decisions were made within the parties themselves and not in the general democratic arena. This was made emblematic through CAP's economic plan, which promised the continuity of popular economic agendas, but delivered something contradictory without proper consultation or communication.[123]

This, however, had to a larger extent become the *modus operandi* of Venezuelan politics, a phenomenon which had been described by its critics as *partidocracia* or, in its English adaptation, *partyarchy*, that is, a system in which democracy plays a formal role in legitimizing elected officials, but, in the end of the day, political elites define entirely on their own the outcomes of politics by means of an all-encompassing, overbearing party system. In concrete terms, it meant that the hegemonic parties had thoroughly infiltrated all channels of representation, had stacked every relevant political organization with their loyalists, owned and operated media outlets and enforced such strict party discipline, that manifestation of interests unaligned with the party's leadership was unlikely. As a result, the political system suffered from serious issues of accountability, transparency, responsiveness, and representativity, ultimately eroding regime legitimacy, as the typical democratic arenas were perceived as puppet theatres with parties pulling the strings from outside.[124]

The exhaustion of the political model would become more evident in the course of the following year, when (1) general strikes made a comeback in May 1989, after having effectively disappeared since 1958, the start of Venezuela's democratic era; (2) governmental and mayoral elections in the end of 1989 were met with a 55% voter abstention rate, which is specially telling for Venezuela, who had single digit

[121] Coppedge (1997), pp. 160.

[122] For the intellectual trajectory of this discussion, see Coppedge (1997), pp. 5–7.

[123] Maingón and Sonntag (1990), pp. 137–142, describes CAP's campaign as self-contradicting. It talked often about neoliberal change but also of securing past popular agendas. Without a timely clarification of such fundamental ambiguities, the electorate could not help but to feel betrayed. CAP himself admitted he would not have been elected had he been forthcoming about his plans. Pérez and Blanco Muñoz (2010), p. 350. Naím (1993), p. 47, confirms Perez's ideological shift caught most by surprise.

[124] Coppedge (1997), pp. 19, 39, 129 and 163; Levine (2002) offers a good discussion of likely hypotheses.

abstention until the early 1970s;[125] (3) all ensuing elections showed a significant increase in the share of votes by antisystem parties;[126] (4) a group of celebrities (nicknamed *the Notables*) pressed for substantial reforms in the political system (*Pact for Reform*), with massive popular support.[127]

Even though CAP's administration proved effective in dealing with inflation and stagnant growth, especially in 1991, when Venezuela's GDP grew over 10%, the President's rejection remained high. The severe hardships Venezuelans had to endure in the first years of stabilization made them particularly sensitive to the few corruption scandals, much more than the government could foresee.[128] For CAP's misfortune, moreover, his faction lost internal elections in the AD in September 1991, eroding his parliamentary support, despite the AD's near majority in both houses. As mentioned before, party leaders exerting strict party discipline could have more influence over the government in certain instances than the President himself. One of the first steps taken by the AD's new leader, for example, was to publicly demand the resignation of all cabinet members in charge of economy, since they were perceived to have betrayed the expectations of many both inside and out of the party.[129]

With a political landscape so critically charged, even the most uneventful corruption case, which in other times would be overlooked or quickly forgotten, could be blown out of proportion to further impair CAP's administration. A few significant cases were present, however, namely a scandal in which the Minister of Transportation was found to be demanding kickbacks from state Governors (April 1990), another in which the Ministers of Health and Agriculture were found to be conniving with corruption in a public corporation (June 1990), and yet another involving CAP's mistress, Cecília Matos, who was accused of influence peddling and participation in phony military contracts. As a result, in conjunction with the increasingly dire prospects for constitutional reform, about 1500 violent protests took place within the first 3 years of CAP's administration.[130]

The snowball of ever-increasing dissatisfaction and inappropriate government responses reached its climax on February 2nd of 1992, when an insurgent faction of the Venezuelan military took on itself to make change by force. Despite the insurgents' diligence, the coup failed, as CAP narrowly avoided being captured and the loyal sections of the military frustrated the takeover of media outlets and other strategic goals. The leader of the movement, Hugo Chávez, was arrested and ordered to call off the coup on national television. As he did so, however, Chávez

[125] *Consejo Supremo Electoral, Estadísticas Electorales, Cuadro Comparativo 1958–2000.*

[126] 6% for presidential elections in 1988 raising to 39% for regional elections in 1989, 32% for regional elections in 1992; and 54% for presidential elections in 1993. Dietz and Myers (2007), p. 66.

[127] Pérez-Liñán (2007), pp. 19–20.

[128] Naím (1993), pp. 11, 14–16.

[129] Pérez-Liñán (2007), pp. 19–20. Coppedge (1997), p. 129.

[130] Suárez (1997), p. 144.

openly admitted his failure and stated his only goal to be the welfare of Venezuela, displaying a kind of honesty and nationalism that seemed to many as long foregone from politics. Inadvertently, much sympathy for his movement was fostered in this opportunity, causing the spectre of another imminent coup to continue to overshadow public sentiment. CAP's political opponents, moreover, managed to leverage the event against him, claiming at every opportunity that, as long as he stood in power, another coup or civil war could erupt.[131]

No modification to the economic plan was proposed after this event, but a cabinet reshuffle was undertaken to incorporate members of COPEI and, so, minimize further polarization between the political elites (Pact of Guanábana). Tensions within the AD, however, frustrated the stability of the cabinet and led to a rupture within 3 months. The volatile circumstances were further exacerbated by the economy, which seemed to be slowing down again after another fall in petrol prices, the public polls that showed that CAP's administration was now mistrusted by 75% of the population, and pressures from multiple sides asking for CAP's resignation (among them also the MRB-200, Chávez's rebellious military group). The Senate, listening to the widespread dissatisfaction, approved a recall referendum to take place, but was met with CAP's intransigence, who refused to subject himself. The General Prosecutor, who was already by default unsympathetic towards CAP, claimed he would be held accountable if another coup attempt took place.[132]

On November 8th of 1992, José Vicente Rangel, one of the notables, a former presidential candidate and journalist, denounced Pérez for what seemed to be a case of embezzlement and mismanagement of public funds. 250 million bolivars had been secretly converted into 17.2 million dollars for use in undisclosed national security affairs by the Ministries of Interior and of the President's Secretariat, amidst what seemed a serious economic crisis. Just 20 days after this revelation, Chávez ordered another military coup from confinement. The coup failed but demonstrated the momentum the rebellious factions had gained nonetheless, as they indicated how much its adherence had expanded since February.[133]

An impeachment resolution on the alleged embezzlement was passed in the Supreme Court a few days after the coup attempt, and a Committee in the Chamber of Deputies started investigations into the scandal brought by Rangel. The Ministers involved revealed that the money had been entirely used to provide security to the

[131] Suárez (1997), pp. 145–147; Pérez-Liñán (2007), p. 20; Coppedge (2002), p. 14.

[132] Suárez (1997), pp. 145–150; Pérez and Blanco Muñoz (2010), pp. 20–21.

[133] Pérez and Blanco Muñoz (2010), p. 21. It may be relevant to notice that Rangel was later made Minister of defence and Foreign Relations (1999–2002) and Vice-President (2002–2007) in Chavez' administrations, putting suspicions of *quid pro quo* on the revelations, a collusion of interests in generating instability or a sort of unplanned, opportunistic approximation between both. Though we may never know the truth, Pérez always adamantly decried Rangel, Chávez, and Caldera, as well as Uslar Pietri, the leader of the Notables.

new democratic president of Nicaragua, Violeta Chamorro,[134] but admitted that the money should have been handled differently between the Ministries and the Central Bank. As a result of the investigation, the Supreme Court rejected the embezzlement charges on lack of evidence. The next month, however, the General Prosecutor passed yet another resolution in the Supreme Court on the grounds of generic mismanagement of funds (*malversación genérica*). On a 9 to 6 vote, the Supreme Court approved a report recommending the subjection of the President to criminal procedures. The following day, May 21st of 1993, the report was then approved by Congress in a joint session and Pérez was suspended from office.[135]

Three months after Pérez' suspension and 5 months before the end of his mandate, on August 21st of 1993, still before much of preliminary legal issues could be resolved, Congress, in an unprecedented interpretation of the hypotheses of absolute absence in the 1961 Constitution, met once again to declare the temporary leave permanent. A criminal conviction would only come in May 1996, though meanwhile the Minister of Interior, who had been accused with Pérez, and Hugo Chávez, the author of two *coup d'états*, received pardon from Rafael Caldera, the then acting President, independent from AD or COPEI.[136]

Procedure in the Supreme Court and Declaration of Absence

The first notable aspect of the procedure against CAP pertains to the (i) form of impeachment used. Unlike our previous case, impeachments in Venezuela happen through the judiciary and are divested of much of the traditional impeachment aesthetic, that is, with the Lower House as the closest representative of the people investigating and charging the President, and the Higher House, as a council of elders choosing the wisest decision for the case. Instead, in this case, the Supreme Court received a charge, on which it then prepared a sort of preliminary report attesting to its soundness and recommended criminal prosecution to the Senate, which then analysed its opportunity/convenience and, by corroborating the report, lent it with democratic legitimacy. The President was then suspended during the time ordinary criminal trials would take place, as to as much as possible secure the trial from his potential undue influence. Under this framework, the Supreme Court acted as a gatekeeper against purely political attacks by limiting the breadth of "impeachment cases" that reach the Senate, who then, on its turn, acted as a filter for inopportune, ill-intentioned, and merely disruptive legal attacks. There was,

---

[134]The election of Chamorro crowned the end of the Somoza dynasty in Nicaragua, fruit of a longstanding conflict. She was suspected, however, of being another US puppet ruler like the Somoza had been, as well as product of electoral fraud. The uncertainty led to worries about her security and Nicaragua's success in transitioning to democracy. Leiken (2003), pp. 213 ff.

[135]Pérez and Blanco Muñoz (2010), pp. 22–25.

[136]Pérez and Blanco Muñoz (2010), pp. 25–29. Alejandro Izaguirre, the Minister of Interior, was pivotal in linking Pérez to the criminal charges, as he testified to have been following Pérez' orders. Martin (1996), pp. 21–23.

therefore, less emphasis on democratic legitimacy and more emphasis on stability, legality, and institutional forbearance.[137] Unfortunately, however, as we have seen, Congress still found ways to abuse its faculties by declaring the President permanently absent before a conviction.

A second, inter-related issue pertains to the (ii) undue influence on the Judiciary in a politically charged environment. Despite the arrangements meant to prevent abuse from one organ over the other, the Judiciary was still reportedly intimidated to approve a positive report on CAP's "impeachment". At least one of the fifteen Supreme Court Justices, Hildegard Rondón de Sansó, is said to have visited CAP and apologized for voting in favour of the report out of fear.[138] The small size of the Supreme Court made it easier to manipulate results via intimidation, since its members could be easily singled-out. Congress, by contrast, would not be better equipped to deal with such pressures, since navigating public opinion is their bread and butter, but also and foremostly because it spreads the responsibility of decision in its hundreds of members and its projected electorate. One could argue that even Congress would struggle to decide with genuine autonomy in these circumstances (and this will be shown to be also true in many of the other upcoming cases), since there was a looming threat of further military coups and civil wars on the horizon, and safeguarding democracy seemed as a more urgent and noble need. Would things have been different if Congress had to decide the impeachment entirely on its own?

A possible answer to this riddle leads us to the third issue, (iii) the conversion of temporary absence into permanent or absolute absence by the Congress. This decision was formally unforeseeable at the time: legally unprecedented, linguistically dubious (equating *falta* with *suspención*; absence with suspension),[139] dogmatically unsupported and teleologically conflictive (suspension is preventive measure, not an end itself). By all typical parameters of legal certainty, it seemed like Congress was overreaching its competencies to settle a political goal. Not only that, but its own justification for that resolution made the fact glaringly obvious, as it stated that their decision was meant to "strengthen legitimate government, construct stability and social peace in democracy, as well as create better conditions for the economic development and overcoming of the fiscal situation of the Republic", because the current "situation may introduce (. . .) elements of doubt or uncertainty, having an undesirable effect over the national life and, therefore, calls Congress to take action and overcome them". Moreover, there is a suggested sense of harmlessness in that decision when the resolution states that there are "only 5 months left of the constitutional period",[140] thus probably not enough for a criminal conviction to

[137] It should be noted, however, that the Lower House, or at least a part of it (a special commission), completely by chance in this case still acted as the "Grand Inquest of the Nation" by going after the first accusations made by Rangel in November 1992, and, as such, also produced the bulk of evidence later used to convict CAP and his Ministers.

[138] Pérez and Blanco Muñoz (2010), p. 51.

[139] The Art. 188 of the 1961 Constitution states that the Congress may meet to declare temporary absence (*falta,* not *suspención*) longer than 90 days permanent.

[140] Arteaga Sánchez (1994), pp. 31–32.

take place. In other words, if the 'temporary' had by virtue of the context been permanent since the beginning, why keep encumbering the country with unresolved tensions? For the sake of formalism? It may be easy to look down upon such a decision as an unaffected outside observer, but the constant protests (1993 and 1994, were among the most violent years in the 90s), the recent coup attempts, and the deepening of the recession (1993 displayed the worst economic indicators of CAP's administration) may have pushed the representatives to decide pragmatically rather than principledly.[141]

Another issue brought by this may pertain (iv) the likely impropriety of criminal procedures for the purposes of impeachment. The American style, parliamentary impeachment on itself is already criticized for its slowness, possibly taking months to reach closure, and being overly punishing to the economy and political development for its long period legal uncertainty, whereas a no-confidence vote would perhaps swiftly come about within a few days of its proposal. This kind of judicial impeachment, as the example of CAP demonstrates, seems to be even more justifying of such critique. The procedures started in May 1993 and ended only in May 1996, that is, nearly 2.5 years after the end of the presidential mandate. Had the Constitution imposed no temporary suspension, the impeachment would have been ineffective for the purposes of safeguarding democracy. Had, moreover, the Constitution imposed no re-election limitations for such a case, there would still be a risk of re-election, potentially raising another myriad of legal quarrels with which to drown a final decision.[142] The great issue with the Supreme Court acting as a criminal court is that it likely has a high case load per Justice due to its small size, that it is burdened by its other, more typical responsibilities (*i.e.*, judicial review, control of constitutionality), and that it concentrates many high profile cases which by default may bring with themselves more time consuming legal manoeuvres (*i.e.*, voluminous discovery requests, interlocutory applications, etc.) than usual. Moreover, the cautiousness demanded by the adjudication of a criminal case is on itself conducive to longer, drawn out procedures even in the most efficient of Courts.[143]

Another side of this impropriety pertains to (v) the "impeachable" offenses available. CAP, despite the hardships directly created by his administration, was seemingly a law-abiding citizen. An impeachment in Venezuela, however, arguably

[141] For information on protests, see Lopez-Maya (2001), p. 6; for economy, see Suárez (1997), p. 152.

[142] This is all counterfactual, naturally. CAP's stay in politics was highly unlikely as the situation stood, being mistrusted by the population, and ostracized by political parties. The same situation transposed to 2016, in a potential impeachment of Nicolás Maduro, however, could give rise to such a dilemma. Despite the economic, humanitarian, and constitutional crises, Maduro remained popular and likely to win re-elections.

[143] Due to the scope of this study, this argument is proposed only in speculative fashion. Notice, however, that many features typically found in the specific caseload of these courts correlate with longer trials, as one may conclude by the framework provided by Economides et al. (2015). This does not necessarily mean that these courts are "slow" *per se*, but just perhaps that these cases are more procedurally time consuming.

required that a crime be committed. This made CAP nearly impervious to being held politically accountable, despite much agreement by the political elites, the rebellious military, and the population that his administration was being objectively harmful. As a result, his enemies tried to pin him down on an arguably underwhelming crime, that of mismanagement of funds. Charges of embezzlement, which were much more significant, were quickly discarded. From what could be gathered on the judges' opinions, there was nothing wrong with a secret mission of national security in Nicaragua, nor there was anything wrong with the quantities employed in it, but it was the administrative mistake of accounting the issue as "for internal use" in *lieu* of "for international use" that was considered 'fatal'.[144] As such, one may speculate that charging CAP with "aggravated generic mismanagement of funds" as a proxy chosen to make him accountable for political offenses and tensions Venezuela lacked means to address.

As a summary, one could say that CAP's impeachment bears much similitude to the event that hallmarked the beginning of his downfall, the *Caracazo*. On February 27th, 1989, Venezuelans took the streets and responded with unprecedented violence, because all legitimate channels of democratic participation had been closed to them. The few available proved illusionary and futile, as however they expressed their political choices, they would be met with irresponsiveness or perhaps with answers that directly conflicted with their demands. On August 31st of 1993, Congress assembled in an extraordinary joint session to remove CAP in arguably extraconstitutional fashion, because all else had failed. CAP refused to realign his policies with his party or the popular demand, refused to step down when all sectors of society demanded it and refused to subject himself to a recall referendum. Moreover, his judicial impeachment offered only an incomplete solution, as it opened space for readjustment, but sustained frightening tensions and uncertainties. In both cases those who acted against the government were not completely free of blame, as they wilfully lived under their own illusions of not bearing any responsibility in the circumstances they rebelled against, the first its reluctance in accepting that the bonanza era had ended a decade before and that a readjustment was long overdue, and the second for their refusal to accept their role in the alienation of their own people from the political system. Nonetheless, both had legitimate demands and managed them as they could in the face of their own limitations and the imperfections of their political system.

[144] Martin (1996), p. 223. It may be the case that sources used left out the reprehensible aspects of this crime, such as potential fiscal consequences. As it stands, however, nothing suggests more than a clerical error.

3.2.1.3 *Pecunia non olet*: Ernesto Samper (1996), Colombia

A Historical Narrative

Colombian constitutional history bears remarkable similitude to that of Venezuela's, making it a fortunate follow-up for our case studies. Both countries transitioned to democracy in the same period (1958), having similarly longer periods of time to consolidate their democratic culture and institutions than the rest of Latin America. Both countries had as a product of such transition a pact which attempted to damp from top-down the emergence of polarization by stablishing a bipartisan political system: in Venezuela, it was the Pact of Punto Fijo and, in Colombia, it was the National Front (*Frente Nacional Colombiano*), which forced sharing and alternation of power between the Liberal and Conservative parties. In both cases, this imposed bipartisanship created deficits of democratic representativity, which needed to be then supplanted by the establishment of wide clientelistic networks.[145]

Venezuela sustained its networks and patronage-hungry politicians for a long time with petrodollars pouring in steadily and abundantly, especially during the 1970s oil boom. Colombia did not have the same 'luck' and, thus, had to face its issues with democratic representativity sooner than Venezuela. While the National Front ended already in 1974, the Punto Fijo survived well into the late 1990s. This does not mean, however, that Colombia arrived in the 1990s, without significant artifacts from that time. Many leftist movements who felt excluded from the political system formed guerrilla groups and posed significant threats to the new democracy, among them the FARC (Revolutionary Armed Forces of Colombia), the ELN (National Liberation Army) and the M-19 (19th of April Movement). Moreover, like in Venezuela, Colombian political elites competed inside the two hegemonic parties for power, sometimes as Liberals, sometimes as Conservatives, and sometimes even as both. As a result, parties became highly factionalized and weakly cohesive, often depending on patronage-hungry *ad hoc* coalitions for agenda setting. This proved particularly concerning in the 1970s, when the urban populations began expanding and their demands, though highly legitimate by their numbers, clashed with those of the hegemonic rural political elite and its clientele. As a result, despite nominally having strong legislative powers or majority in Congress, Colombian Presidents struggled severely, for example, to open markets and restructure public administration.[146]

Another important factor unparalleled in Venezuela, was the intense spread of organized crime and violence in Colombia. In the 1970s, drug trafficking boomed, especially under the Medellín Cartel and its ruthless leader, Pablo Escobar. In the

[145] Hinojosa and Pérez-Liñán (2003), pp. 65–66; Conaghan (1996); Archer and Shugart (1997), pp. 132 ff.

[146] Archer and Shugart (1997), pp. 110 ff.

1980s, multiple paramilitary groups were formed as a reaction to the constant extorsion practices of the guerrilla groups. These groups were often financed and operated in an unholy alliance of drug cartels, large landowners and corporations that sought the extermination of the guerrillas. These organizations did, however, end up developing their own designs, and through that also committing political genocides such as the MAS (Death to Kidnappers, a death squad under Escobar's command) did against the UP (Patriotic Union, a political branch of the FARC founded in 1985), as well as other numerous assassinations and terrorist acts. By the mid-80s, Colombian democracy could no longer be taken for granted.[147] The situation did improve a bit in 1993, however, when Escobar was killed and the Medellín Cartel lost its preponderance to the Cali Cartel, who had much more of a "bribes rather than bullets" ethos.[148]

It is within this new constellation that the scandals involving President Samper unfold. Like in Pérez's case, scandals broke out early on, threatening his administration with a short honeymoon period and, consequently, more difficulty in setting campaign promises in motion. Only 3 days after Samper's election, a narrow win (50.57%) against Andrés Pastrana of the Conservative Party,[149] a recording was leaked, containing a conversation in which one of the leaders of the Cali Cartel, Miguel Rodríguez Orejuela, talked about donating 3000 million pesos (then approx. US$ 3.5 million) to Samper's campaign. The conversation implied Samper's campaign had liquidity issues after the first round of elections and that Santiago Medina, Samper's campaign treasurer, reached out to the Cartel.[150]

The revelations were so spectacular and unlikely, however, that they were received with scepticism from the public and unwillingness from the institutions to confront his government. As Samper argued it was nothing but an ill-attempt to topple his administration, the General Prosecutor Gustavo de Greiff shelved the case 3 months later arguing lack of evidence that indicated any donation at all. Coincidently, however, de Greiff was forcibly retired in the same month by the Supreme Court in a reinterpretation of the rules on the retirement of public prosecutors, causing a new General Prosecutor, Alfonso Valdivieso, to be elected.[151]

It did not take long for Samper's peace to be at odds again, as in December 1994 Valdivieso announced the reopening of investigations after documents linking politicians to the Cartel were found during a raid at one of Miguel Rodríguez's houses. After some of these documents were leaked by the magazine *Cambio 16* in January 1995, pressure for clarification grew immensely, both internally and from

[147] Watson (1991), pp. 25–29, 32–35.

[148] Hinojosa and Pérez-Liñán (2003), p. 68; Crandall (2002), p. 82.

[149] *El Tiempo*, July 8th, 1994: "*Ernesto Samper ganó por 156,555 votos*". It may be worth noticing that the first and second rounds of the presidential elections had only 33% and 43% voter turnout, respectively.

[150] For reference, the campaign spending ceiling was set at 4000 million pesos by the National Electoral Council for that year. Hinojosa and Pérez-Liñán (2003), p. 68; Betancourt (1997), p. 248.

[151] Betancourt (1997), pp. 23–25. De Greiff's daughter, Mónica, is said to have been involved in the Liberal's campaign administration, what may explain his unwillingness to further investigate.

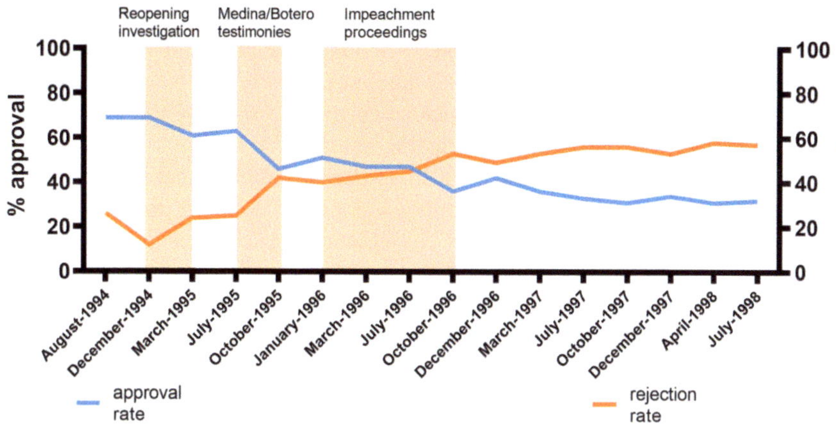

Fig. 3.2 Samper administration's approval and rejection rates, 1994–1998. Source: Own elaboration with data from Gallop Poll, C 137 04 09

the United States, who was now questioning Colombia's efforts in the war against drugs and threatened to decertify the country, potentially bringing sanctions to its economy (*i.e.*, loss of foreign aid, vetoes in lending forums).[152]

In April 1995, Valdivieso officially reopened investigations on the Liberal's campaign finances, kicking off a procedure that would be known as the *Proceso 8000* and would reach multiple members of Congress and government. In the next months a few spectacular discoveries were made, only to be soon overshadowed by even more spectacular captures and surrenders of six of the seven top officials of the Cali Cartel. Most impactful were perhaps the capture of Miguel Rodríguez Orejuela, which just a few days after the newspaper *Semana* announced it had tapes of Samper having a friendly conversation with a well-known drug dealer, and the capture of José Santacruz Londoño, the third chief of the Cartel, a few days after the same newspaper announced the risk of an imminent military *coup d'état*.[153]

As a result, Samper remained popular during the larger part of the scandals (see Fig. 3.2). Samper would only be truly affected by the investigations after Santiago Medina was arrested, as he testified that Samper and his campaign manager, Fernando Botero (at this point Minister of defence), deliberately sought the Cartel's aid. Only with a testimony as impactful as Medina's is that the General Prosecutor Valdivieso could finally charge Samper before the Chamber of Representatives with (i) accepting campaign money of illegal precedence ('illicit enrichment'),

[152] "Drug certification" is a procedure enacted by the US Congress in 1986 to demand tough counternarcotic measures from other governments. It has particularly affected Latin America, as the region produces most narcotics ending up in the US. Betancourt (1997), p. 25.

[153] This known drug dealer, Elizabeth Montoya, was murdered before testifying. This was the third of four murders of potential witnesses and antagonists during these investigations. Betancourt (1997), pp. 28, 203 ff.

(ii) exceeding the legal campaign spending limits, and (iii) attempting to cover up these irregularities by tampering with evidence. On September 10th of 1995, about 2 months after Valdivieso's request, the Committee of Investigation and Accusations (*Comisión de Investigación y Acusaciones,* henceforth CdIA) of the Chamber of Representatives officially started investigating Samper.[154]

In parallel to these developments, the Liberals made it clear that their efforts in protecting the President would go much beyond simply debating impeachment on the issues presented by the accusation. Systematic legal changes were sought to legalize the presidential infractions, to prematurely bury the procedures, and to remove/hinder opposition. Last minute articles were introduced in new laws or reforms to (i) end Valdivieso's mandate already in early 1996, (ii) to hinder any future investigations (*auto inhibitorio*) on a shelved topic, regardless of discovery of new evidence, (iii) to free all implicated in the *Proceso 8000* by changing the definition of the crime of 'illicit enrichment'—the clause became known as a "*narcomico*" (approx. translation 'narco-plot/conspiracy').[155] The first two were blocked by the Supreme Court and the last, after some media backlash, suffered a surprising upset once the Minister of Justice and Samper himself began opposing the initiative.

Though these attempts were insidious, they could still be detected and neutralized by the people, the investigative media, and counter-majoritarian organs like the Supreme Court. What proved to be uncontrollable by these actors, however, were the more complex aspects of the discussions and investigations led by the CdIA, the permanent organ of inquiries of the Colombian Congress. The CdIA, ignoring all appeals by society and doing everything within its reach to circumvent even the Oversight Commission (*Comisión Ciudadana de Seguimiento*) created specifically to hold it accountable, managed to release a final report exculpating Samper and to voted it before the public and the Representatives themselves could fully grasp the extent of the President's involvement or the evidence gathered.[156] This may have been, as it will be argued next, the leading force being the survival of the presidency, even more so than the typically named factors, such as the broad control of Samper's party over parliamentary seats, his relative popularity or the use of pork-barrel to gather support in a context of relatively weak parties.[157]

---

[154] Comisión Ciudadana de Seguimiento (1996), p. 26.

[155] The expression *narcomico* is used repeatedly in Colombian politics to describe potential legal innovations that favor drug lords or their associates. Such was also the case, for example, for the drug decriminalization proposal of 1989, which was introduced to deescalate Pablo Escobar's terrorist attacks that year.

[156] This will be described in detail in the next section.

[157] As in Hinojosa and Pérez-Liñán (2003), for example.

Acquittal in the Chamber of Representatives

As mentioned in Chap. 2, successful impeachments are usually correlated with a series of other factors not necessarily linked with the robustness of the impeachment charges. It has been mentioned that successful impeachments are (i) demanded by the people (*i.e.*, high rejection rates of the government, intense protests), (ii) find themselves in urgent circumstances (*i.e.*, serious economic or constitutional crises), in a moment of (iii) political vulnerability (*i.e.*, President is politically isolated, and no key stakeholders are willing to shield him/her from prosecution). Arguably, during Samper's impeachment none of these elements were present. The campaign financing scandal shook public opinion and Congress, but not to the point of generating mobilizations, political ruptures, or gridlock. Samper's popularity stayed out of the 'danger zone' in the first years of rule (rejection only rose to 45% until the acquittal), the economy continued in undisrupted growth (8–9% unemployment, 1.7% inflation and over 5% GDP growth in 1994 and 1995) and Congress remained appeased by the steady flow of resources from the Executive branch (no meaningful intraparty breakdown, control over 58% of seats in Lower House, passive opposition).[158] By all means, an external observer could legitimately come to the conclusion that Samper's impeachment boiled down to *just* a legal dispute between a President and a General Prosecutor.

While this assessment bears much truth—indeed, political conditions for instability and, consequently, for impeachment were not present-, it might obscure how much conscious effort was put into keeping things that way. If the procedures had not been led the way they were, history could have been much different. As the Nixon case might serve as an example, all these correlating factors are only indicators and are not by any means determinants of impeachment or factors that are unchangeable, fixed in time. An impeachment query may well impact the political landscape to such an extent that the conditions for its own success may in turn be created, perhaps as a sort of self-fulfilling prophecy.[159] Just like Samper, Nixon was a relatively popular President and held control over veto threshold in Parliament. Strategically speaking, his defence had everything to succeed and yet resignation became imperative as the impeachment query took off in increasingly more impactful discoveries. Unlike Samper, however, the institutional configuration of the US did not allow Nixon as much slack to end investigations on his suspicious activities.[160] On the Samper case, on the other hand, there was plenty of room within the

[158] Hinojosa and Pérez-Liñán (2003), pp. 72 ff.

[159] In 1996 Colombia's situation deteriorated, as unemployment rose to 12%, GDP growth deaccelerated to 2%, inflation rose to 2.4% average, Colombia was decertified by the US, among other things. By 1998, the situation was even more concerning, but reopening the case was no longer possible. Hinojosa and Pérez-Liñán (2003), pp. 72ff; Betancourt (1997), pp. 41 ff.

[160] This is not to say that US Presidents have not tried similar strategies, they were just limited in options and horizontal control mechanisms were stronger. When Nixon fired his own prosecutor (Archibald Cox) or Donald Trump fired his own investigator (James Comey), constitutional organs promptly decried the attempts.

organization and composition of Congress to secure such results, despite mounting pressure from the media, Supreme Court, and the Citizen's Oversight Commission.

The main vulnerabilities of the Colombian system of accountability seem to be that (i) its work is led by a permanent committee, (ii) whose composition is disproportionally dominated by the largest party in Congress, (iii) whose chairman has too much directive power but little accountability, (iv) whose work is not made public, and (v) who does not give much space for dissenting votes. The sum of these factors, it will be argued, enabled the Liberals to control the flow of the investigation and of the information made available to the public, allowing them to frame the facts in the least negative light, thus salvaging Samper's reputation and crippling the proper development of a case against him, both in the sense of creating a libel and a political environment conducive to the impeachment's success.[161]

The issue of permanent committees (i) is not necessarily detrimental by itself, but in certain circumstances such as those presented by Samper's impeachment it can turn out to be.[162] A permanent committee is useful for persistent and recurrent issues of parliamentary work such as budget and constitutionality oversight, infrastructure planning, and so on, where incremental learning and systematic understanding of cases play a significant role. The downside, however, is that it entrenches certain actors in those roles, enabling them to put long-term commitments ahead of more urgent short-term goals. That may mean, for example, that parties are likely to nominate loyal members to secure party interests in the long-term, perhaps in detriment of the immediate goals of the committee. It may also mean that its composition may undergo more lax scrutiny during its election, because there is no tangible frame of reference to consider. In an *ad hoc* Committee, on the other hand, the pertinence of a candidate can be assessed immediately in reference to the goal of the Committee, allowing opposition members of the Parliament to pose strong objections against them and thus effectively control the quality of the Committee. Moreover, it is important to notice that opposing a candidacy and removing an elected member are two different activities, with different standards of confirmation, arguably making the former the easier and more effective path.

In Samper's case, the element of permanence meant that the members of the Commission of Accusation and Investigation (CdIA) were elected and entrenched in their roles before an accusation against the President even existed. As it turned out, however, most of its members had direct interest in the outcome of the investigations, because it could threaten their offices as well. After all, Samper was charged with electoral financing crimes from which all the Liberals inside the Commission (10 out of the 15 total members) had also likely profited.[163] One could hardly expect

[161] See for Kada (2003) a similar analysis comparing Collor and Samper impeachments.

[162] The US Congress also works with a permanent Committee for justice related issues (House Judiciary Committee), among which impeaching stands out as a central function. One may argue this to be among the potential reasons behind the lack of successful impeachments in its history.

[163] Betancourt (1997), pp. 38–39; Comisión Ciudadana de Seguimiento (1996), p. 33.

that they would dedicate their dearest efforts into investigations that had potential to destroy their careers and reputation.

A balanced composition, fully transparency, and a democratic structure to the Commission could have minimized these issues, but none of these were present. Instead, (ii) the Liberals secured more seats in the Commission than they were proportionally allotted, excluding representation of small parties. The remaining seats were given to five Conservatives considered closely aligned with the Liberals, ensuring cooperation but undermining horizontal accountability. Only one of the Conservatives, Francisco Canosa, displayed some opposition, but apparently by chance or oversight, as he entered the Commission as a designated substitute. Only because of his intervention, for example, is that Samper was at all invited to depose before being acquitted by the Commission.[164] If a member of an independent small party had entered the Commission, perhaps many other meaningful interventions would have taken place, considering that they were introduced by the 1991 Constitution to make up for effective opposition that the two largest parties did not enforce against each other.[165]

Even with active opposition in the Commission, (iii) Chairman Heyne Mogollón monopolized enough power to singlehandedly disrupt any of the Commissions outcomes. Still in relation to Samper's deposition, for example, he gave the President ample time to answer in written form, thus arguably frustrating any chance of spontaneous responses or questioning that challenged his lawyer's version of the facts. Even more impactful, however, was his influence over the investigation, both in terms of its direction and of its publicity. Mogollón assured the investigation was as rushed and superficial as possible by nominating a loyal principal investigator and by denying the hearing of objections or the production of evidence. As a glaring example, the two key authorities behind the electoral investigation, namely the General Prosecutor and National Electoral Council, could not present their chief documents to the Commission in time. A liberal representative who conducted her own independent investigations denounced that many of the documents sent by these two authorities were left in unopened briefs, not to mention those that disappeared from the National Archives or even the Prosecution's office, which were indicative of the lack of serious effort in conducting, or possibly even the conscious effort of undermining, a reliable inquiry.[166]

The media or the Supreme Court could have acted to curb these abuses as they when they prevented General Prosecutor Valdivieso's premature dismissal or the legalization of crimes Samper had been accused of, but for that they would need to

[164] Betancourt (1997), pp. 38–39; Comisión Ciudadana de Seguimiento (1996), p. 38.

[165] Regarding Colombian constitutional history, see Moreno (2005), pp. 497 ff. and Archer (1996), pp. 191 ff. On a more general note on Committees, see Krehbiel (1991) and Cox and McCubbins (1993). The former analyses the strategic use of information by Committee members (*e.g.*, leaking or withholding information), the latter discusses how majority parties may further their private goals by instrumentalizing Committee structures.

[166] Betancourt (1997), p. 59; Comisión Ciudadana de Seguimiento (1996), pp. 34–38.

have knowledge of the full extent of what happened within the Commission. Because (iv) the flow of information to the public and even to representatives outside of the Commission was strongly curtailed, however, Mogollón reigned supreme. A Citizen's Oversight Commission created to ensure publicity of these acts did not possess the means to impose cooperation from the CdIA and thus failed to bring transparency. It did, however, pressure Congress into passing a bill to make some documents public. This led the CdIA to haphazardly publish incomplete, highly redacted, unordered documents, that generated confusion and primed representatives outside of the Commission to take the Rapporteur's word for its face value in the final report.[167]

Mogollón's final report was emblematic of the interests of the CdIA. Among its many issues, the evaluation of the evidence stood out. Although there were five witnesses confirming Samper's involvement, Mogollón dismissed their testimonials by pointing out minor inconsistencies between the versions presented by them. Because, for example, Santiago Medina and Fernando Botero disagreed on certain details with no impact on the investigation, their accounts of the facts were discarded. He argued, moreover, that Botero's version, in which he shifted blame towards the President, could not be trusted because he considered them a clear tactic of evading punishment. Naturally, he did not feel the same way about Samper's excuses that sought to do the exact same with Botero, the US government, or the drug cartels, which had become motive of ridicule in the public opinion.[168] Rejecting all witnesses, key expert witnesses, and not allowing enough time or opportunity for the production of evidence by leading authorities, any result other than acquittal would have been surprising. The report even omitted the analysis of the charge of indignity for office as if it had corroborated enough the irreproachable behaviour of the President.[169]

Mogollón's double standards did not end there, however. He reintroduced the concept of illegal enrichment that had been rejected by Congress and the media, the *narcomico*, exclusively to acquit the President. Under this concept, enrichment had to be immediate and personal, and as the funds were sent to his campaign and not his person, he would not be punishable, even though his access to office was likely predicated on those resources.[170]

The approval of this report by the Commission on December 15th, 1995, was given on a 14 to 1 vote, without (iv) an opportunity being given for the defecting vote or reservations against the procedures to be presented—Mogollón rejected the

---

[167] Betancourt (1997), pp. 42–45; Comisión Ciudadana de Seguimiento (1996), pp. 31–32; Law n. 273 of 1996.

[168] Betancourt (1997), p. 11; Comisión Ciudadana de Seguimiento (1996), pp. 28–29.

[169] Betancourt (1997), pp. 49–52, 223–225; Comisión Ciudadana de Seguimiento (1996), p. 40.

[170] Betancourt (1997), pp. 48–49; Comisión Ciudadana de Seguimiento (1996), pp. 46–60. The involved often mentioned that Samper's campaign had run out of resources after the first round and that it would not be able to compete in the run-offs without the Cartel's aid. See Comisión Ciudadana de Seguimiento (1996), pp. 64–91.

Table 3.1 Partisanship in Samper's impeachment vote, Chamber of Representatives

Party	Acquittal	Impeachment	Total
Liberal	80	10	90
Conservative	21	27	48
Others	10	6	16
Total	111	43	154

Source: Own elaboration with data from Hinojosa and Pérez-Liñán (2003), p. 75. Vote taken on June 12th, 1996. Impeachment threshold of ½ + 1 (78 votes)

authority of anyone who attempted it, thus further disabling horizontal checks.[171] With knowledge of this and other issues, a group of Conservatives considered entering a hunger-strike to fight for due process. For unclear reasons, however, they did not see through to their plan after Congress returned from its end-of-the-year recess. One of the possible explanations for the passivity of the opposition may be the intensified distribution of resources of the Executive branch to the pet projects of the Representatives by means of the so-called *Fondos de Cofinanciación,* as it is known that those favourable to Samper's acquittal did receive substantially more resources than their counterparts, particularly those in the Commission itself.[172] Other explanations may lie on intimidation (Alvaro Gómez Hurtado, one of the most vocal opposition leaders was assassinated during the procedures), apathy, ignorance, generalized confusion, or/and pragmatic acquiescence. The latter may be one of the strongest factors since many other Representatives outside the Commission too had interest in Samper's acquittal. This was arguably most obvious in the text of the resolution that gave form to the impeachment's conclusion, as it stablished not only the acquittal of the President but the wholesale amnesty of all involved. The *auto inhibitorio* attributed to the decision foreclosed any future investigation on the finance scandal, effectively shielding all other politicians that my have in some way owned their mandates to illicit funding sources (Table 3.1).[173]

The Commission's popular nickname, "Commission of Absolutions and Investigations",[174] is arguably indicative of the chronic issues of impunity its institutional configuration has generated and this case is a prime example of why. Rules that allow one single person, in this case the Chairman, to monopolize an entire procedure can be formidably risky, especially in a context of weak parties (proneness to *ad hoc* collusions and cronyism), weak opposition (lack of horizontal checks), systematic favouring of the majority party in Parliament (dominance of key positions; leniency towards the Executive abuses, in case of alignment of interests), and

[171] Comisión Ciudadana de Seguimiento (1996), p. 39. See Strøm (1990) for a deeper debate on opportunities for opposition within investigative Committees.

[172] Hinojosa and Pérez-Liñán (2003), pp. 75–78; Pizarro (2002).

[173] Comisión Ciudadana de Seguimiento (1996), pp. 100–106. A bill attempting to legalize the mechanism of the *auto inhibitorio* had been passed before but was declared unconstitutional by the Supreme Court still in 1995. The legality of this resolution is also questionable in face of this. Betancourt (1997), p. 27.

[174] Hinojosa and Pérez-Liñán (2003), p. 67.

widespread political apathy (lack of electoral consequences for misconduct). Engineering away the problems in the Commission would come a long way into achieving fairer results, though it would likely not be a definitive solution. Without a fully functional democratic culture and environment, the millenarian question of *quis custodiet ipsos custodes* (who watches the watchmen?) will remain unsatisfactorily addressed so long the last *custodes* in line are not willing to watch over themselves.

3.2.1.4 Horseman's Maze: Cubas Grau (1999) and Gonzaléz Macchi (2003), Paraguay

A Historical Narrative

The impeachments against Presidents Raúl Cubas Grau (1999) and Luís Angel González Macchi (2002–2003) took place within a single presidential mandate and are both developments of a chain of interconnected political crises. Like in the case of CAP's Venezuela (1989–1993), Paraguay's political system is also characterized by its "partyarchy" (*partidocracia*), that is, it possesses a system in which traditional parties have become so influential and entrenched that they can effectively get away with being unresponsive and unrepresentative of popular demands, as any electoral backlash is incapable of shaking off their grip over the country's rule.[175] In Paraguay's case, the partyarchy was, at this point in time, constituted of two very long-lived parties, as both traditional parties are over 100 years old. These parties are namely the Radical Liberal Authentic Party (PRLA or "Liberals"; centre) and the National Republican Association (ARN or "Colorados"; right-wing), the latter being the undisputed hegemonic party since 1947 and the party to which both Cubas and Macchi belong.[176]

Unlike the Venezuela of the 1990s, however, the main source of political instability in the country was not generated by the partyarchy's chronic unwillingness to resonate popular demands—all indicates that, on the contrary, Paraguayans did generally feel reasonably represented by the Colorados.[177] Instead, the stability expected from well-institutionalized parties[178] has been undermined by harsh competition between powerful and highly militarized factions of the parties

[175] For a rigorous definition of partyarchy and a discussion of its consequences, see Coppedge (1997), pp. 28 ff.

[176] López (2018), pp. 26–66. The Colorados did not lose grip on power despite regime change during 1947–1954 (semi-democracy), 1954–1989 (Alfredo Stroessner's dictatorship), and the post-1989 period (democracy).

[177] For a careful analysis, see López (2018), pp. 146–166.

[178] On how party institutionalization influences political stability see: Schenoni and Mainwaring (2018), pp. 15–132.

themselves.[179] Backstabbing, dirty tricks, and backroom-deals are commonplace to get ahead, cost whatever they may cost. Such ease to resort to uncompromising tactics seems to be directly linked with volatility in alliances and a proneness to the escalation of conflict, which are frequent in Paraguayan politics and make a mix ripe for coups or impeachment intrigues. In fact, intrigues became so prevalent that electoral processes are difficult to be dissociated from them.

The election of Raúl Cubas Grau, an unlikely character given his limited visibility, is a good example of that. Originally chosen in internal elections of the Colorado party as the Vice-President to the popular but controverse general Lino Oviedo, Cubas ended up being "promoted" to the position of President in his electoral ticket after, in an expected turn of events, Oviedo was convicted to 10 years in prison over a mutiny he was said to have organized against the previous President, Juan Carlos Wasmosy (1993–1998; ANR).[180] Despite Cubas being relatively unexperienced,[181] the Colorados did not alter the presidential ticket in its entirety, but instead chose to place one of their most influential veterans, Juan María Argaña, as his running-mate.[182] Electorally, the decision paid off, as the Cubas-Argaña ticket was elected with a substantial lead (53.7% against 42.6% of the Domingo Laino and Carlos Filizzola ticket by the Liberals), and was supported by a comfortable parliamentary majority earned in the same elections (approx. 56% in the Chamber of Deputies and in the Senate).[183]

Though the union succeeded initially, the schisms inside the Colorado party immediately became apparent once Cubas started showing that he was still strictly loyal to Oviedo, despite owing Argaña and his faction for their electoral support. Just 3 days into his mandate, Cubas conceded Oviedo a presidential pardon, an act which strongly boosted his popularity, but also caused outrage among powerful actors and

[179] On the factions of the Colorados, see Soler (2002) and López (2010), pp. 93–97. These factions, though adaptable to their periods, generally align themselves along two poles, one being more given to traditional politics, as conducted by professional politicians with clear representation of ideological lines and societal interests (the traditionist wing), while the other is more adept to technocratic ("apolitical" or "antipolitical") conceptions of rule (the militant wing), thus valuing of the democratic game less. Cubas and Oviedo are closer to the traditionalist wing, while Macchi, Argaña, and Wasmosy are closer to the militant wing, in what was then known as the Movement for the Colorado Reconciliation. Though the latter is decidedly closer to Stroessner's dictatorship, both sides are deeply intertwined with the country's military and displayed authoritarian features.

[180] Amaral and Paredes (2005), pp. 117–119. For details on the Wasmosy-Oviedo intrigue, see Soler (2002), p. 22.

[181] Cubas initiated a military career but had to leave due to physical disabilities. Though he went on to become an engineer, he never lost contact to the military. This was his gateway into the Colorados, which has always been militarized. He administered organizations until being nominated by Wasmosy to the Ministry of Economy, position he eventually left when Wasmosy entered in conflict with Oviedo. Amaral and Paredes (2005), p. 117.

[182] Amaral and Paredes (2005), p. 119.

[183] Amaral and Paredes (2005), pp. 119–122.

political sectors due to its defiance of a previous decision of the Judiciary.[184] It is said that Oviedo's release not only the frustrated of a rumoured plan by Argaña and Wasmosy for succeeding Cubas in power, but also generated panic among these groups under the suspicion that Oviedo would seek revenge for his legal persecution.[185] *Ipso facto*, just 2 days after his release, on August 19th of 1998, Congress issued an official complaint against Cubas in a joint session, initiating investigations into the matter and threatening impeachment were the country to fall into further unrest due to Cubas' conduct.[186] A few months later the Supreme Court declared the presidential pardon to be unconstitutional, decision which, however, was not accepted by Cubas or Oviedo.[187]

While the Oviedo-question still pended an institutional resolution, in yet another unexpected turn of events, on March 23rd of 1999, Vice-President Argaña was ambushed and killed by a group of armed men just outside of his home in Asunción. Media outlets and Cubas' opposition, despite lacking any evidence, immediately ventilated the idea that the assassination had been masterminded by Oviedo and was part of an on-going coup.[188] As a result, pro-Argaña crowds marched to Congress and demanded Cubas' impeachment, as well as Oviedo's arrest. As the procedures against Cubas started being discussed Congress, pro-Oviedo crowds also marched to the proximity of the building, coming into confrontation with the *Argañistas.* As in the few following days of protest the local police forces seemed to be unable to separate the confrontations, Cubas ordered national security forces to intervene. In its intervention, the national forces were harsh in their repression of anti-Oviedo protestors. By the end of it, 8 protestors were killed and other were 100 injured, motivating Congress to pursue Cubas' impeachment even more vigorously. As Cubas realized his conviction was imminent and unavoidable, he issued his resignation and fled the country. Before a hostile President took Cubas' place, so did Oviedo go into exile in Argentina.[189]

With both Argaña and Cubas out, it was up to the President of the Senate Luis Ángel González Macchi to assume the *interim* presidency. This was no small task, given the precarious conditions under which he was about to assume office. Cubas

---

[184] Decree n. 117 of 1998. Cubas argued the decision of the military court had been unconstitutional, for it had no jurisdiction over retired officers, nor had it been impartial in its conduction of the proceedings.

[185] Amaral and Paredes (2005), pp. 123–124.

[186] *Diario de Sesión* n. 301568, pp. 2–3 (Joint Session of Deputies and Senators, on August 19th, 1998).

[187] Folha de São Paulo, December 3rd, 1998: *"Justiça anula libertação de Oviedo"*.

[188] The Argaña murder has never been solved. The suspicion has always been that Oviedo had predicted Cubas' impeachment and wanted thus to prevent Argaña's succession. One of three gunmen arrested claimed to have been paid US$300,000 by Oviedo and Cubas for the hit. Amaral and Paredes (2005), pp. 128 ff.

[189] Amaral and Paredes (2005), pp. 124 ff. In 2002 Cubas returned to Paraguay to face trial regarding the killings. The defence shifted blame onto Oviedo, who was described as the *de facto* leader of the security forces.

had grown to be very popular (he had 74% of approval rate by the time of his resignation), while Macchi as an unelected President and a Cubas-antagonist, was seen with suspicion. Even the legitimacy of succession was uncertain, as some argued the Constitution implied the need of anticipating presidential elections in such cases. The traumatic series of events of March (later known as *Marzo Paraguayo*), moreover, left society profoundly divided and unwilling to cooperate around many pressing issues, such as Paraguay's much awaited economic recovery.[190]

The fear of a near-future presidency with Oviedo hindered the thesis for new elections from gaining any traction, and, instead, the political elites formed a broad coalition with the Macchi administration to secure a smoother transition. The coalition involved the explosive mix of the opposing faction in the Colorados, the National Encounter Party (PEN; centre-left), as well as its historical antagonists in the Liberal party. Like the partisan support for Cubas before it, the new "government for national unity" disintegrated almost instantly as soon as policies, goals, and distribution of offices were disclosed. Macchi, a politician created in Alfredo Stroessner's inner circle, chose to favour *Stronista* politicians in his ministerial nominations, quickly earning the generalized repudiation from the public and coalition mates. In less than a year in power, rejection rates rose to 70%. On May 18th of 2000, this widespread rejection turned into a real coup attempt by retired military and policemen. On one side, tanks shot their cannons at Congress and sought to take control of TV stations, while, on the other, the navy and air forces restated their loyalty to the government and threatened bombing rebel forces.[191]

The coup attempt was eventually defused, but it became evident that an institutional exit for Macchi had to be created. A resignation was not an option initially, as his legal successor, Juan Carlos Gavalerna (ANR), was perceived as an even more unpopular and unpredictable alternative. Instead, vice-presidential elections were carried out to handpick a safe alternative. The Colorados proposed an *Argañista* candidate but ended up losing the elections to the Liberals by a very narrow margin. Unwilling to concede the presidency to their opposition, the Colorados decided to push through with Macchi's unpopular presidency.[192]

What followed was a period of extreme instability, which only became more aggravated as time passed. With little popularity to lose, Macchi pushed austere economic reforms that led to the economy to convulsion and generated deep popular discontent.[193] Public relations further eroded as evidence of rampant corruption in

---

[190] Amaral and Paredes (2005), p. 140. For an overview of Paraguay's economy, see Soto (2001).

[191] Amaral and Paredes (2005), pp. 141–143. Macchi also refused to meet many demands of the PLRA. Pérez-Liñán (2007), p. 33.

[192] Amaral and Paredes (2005), pp. 141–143. Both the PEN and Oviedo, who was jailed in Brazil during this time, campaigned in favour of the Liberal candidate, giving him an edge. Pérez-Liñán (2007), p. 34.

[193] LMTonline, February 10th, 2003: *"Senado paraguayo cierra juicio político contra González Macchi"*. In the year leading to Macchi's impeachment, the GDP retracted 4%, the local currency devaluated by 51%, foreign reserves were nearly depleted, and inflation reached 14.5%.

the presidential circle came to light, suggesting that the President had been engaging in embezzlement of public funds and currency flight. Adding insult to injury, a stolen armoured BMW was said to have been acquired by the Ministry of Finance to be used as the presidential state car.[194] Macchi faced multiple protests accusing him of being an illegitimate President and demanding his resignation. He also faced multiple impeachment procedures for poor performance in office ("*mal desempeño de sus funciones*"), though only one ever got to trial level. Macchi survived the removal attempts, despite having the worst approval rates among all democratic Presidents and having delivered the worst economic indicators the country encountered since the 1980s (the "lost decade").[195] Despite being politically isolated, Macchi was able to maintain control of the veto threshold of the impeachment conviction, although that is arguably more to the demerit of his legal successors than his own merit in articulating a legislative shield.

The Impeachment Procedures

Both Raúl Cubas Grau and Luis Ángel González Macchi were charged with all impeachable offenses made available by the 1992 Constitution of Paraguay, namely poor performance in office, and perpetration of common and proper crimes.[196] The narratives that underpinned these charges, however, varied considerably. Cubas was said to have (a) threatened the separation of powers with his abuse of the presidential power of pardon, (b) failed his presidential duties by not complying with a resolution of the Supreme Court, (c) disrespected the supremacy of the Constitution, (d) obstructed justice by refusing to cooperate with the Judiciary, and (e) publicly denied subjecting himself to any form of accountability.[197] Macchi, on his turn, was accused of (a) severely mismanaging the economy; (b) embezzling (or at least enabling the embezzlement of) 16 million dollars in public funds; (c) violating, among other things, anti-monopoly laws by privatizing state communication companies without obligatory auditing; (d) having fictitious soldiers (*soldados fantasmas*) on the army's payroll, and refusing to clarify the situation; (e) conniving with human rights abuses, particularly the kidnapping and torture of two leftist opposition leaders of the party *Patria Libre*; (f) being in possession of a stolen vehicle.[198]

---

[194] Macchi was initially convicted on these charges but was later acquitted by the Supreme Court due to statute of limitations. BBC News, December 10th, 2009: *"Absuelven a ex presidente paraguayo"*; Los Angeles Times, December 14th, 2002: *"As corrupt as it gets"*.

[195] Amaral and Paredes (2005), pp. 142–143.

[196] See Resolution n. 162 of 1999 (Cubas Grau), and Resolution n. 993 of 2002 (González Macchi).

[197] *Diario de Sesiones* n. 326SE-25 (Senate, extraordinary session n. 47 of March 25th, 1999), pp. 6–7.

[198] *Diario de Sesiones* n. 100512 (Senate, extraordinary session n. 36 of January 23rd, 2003), pp. 3–28; According to Pérez-Liñán (2007), p. 34, Mácchi is said to have faced impeachment votes another two times, once in March 2001, for economic mismanagement, and once around April

The Impeachable Offense of "Common and Proper Crimes" One of the key contributions of this case study is its insight into the workings of impeachments that deal with misconduct codified in criminal codes. It is easy to presume that, if the President is being accused of a crime in impeachment procedures, then necessarily the accusation needs to meet all standards imposed by criminal law. This presumption may overlook or downplay the fact that, despite being sometimes based on criminal activity, impeachments have no commitment to or even the means to address the sphere of criminal accountability. A President convicted in impeachment proceedings does not face a prison sentence, but only removal from office and, in some jurisdictions, disqualification. Be it for constitutional violations or for criminal offenses, the sanctioning of an overbearing President has the sole purpose of preventing actual or imminent misuse of office and so safeguard democracy. Whether the conduct is deserving of criminal punishment is a separate question, one that modern Parliaments generally have no competence to deliberate upon or enforce in anyway.

This case is one of the few met in the case studies where clarity on this issue is abundant. Even the President's supporters, presumably in an implicit acknowledgement of the overwhelming evidence against the President, acknowledged that the constraints applicable to criminal courts were not applicable. As one argued in favour of Macchi, it was not because they were convinced of the President's culpability that they should convict him—what really mattered was whether the decision brought most benefit to Paraguay's political future. He further added that, since the next general elections were only 2 months away anyways, it would be preferable to avoid the insecurity and instability generated by the constant change in the country's direction. It would, moreover, spare the country from achieving the infamous milestone of having three different Presidents within only 3 months.[199]

The accusation was less direct about the aspect of political convenience, but still argued in ways that clearly stated the prevalence of political considerations over legal accountability in impeachments. Despite the long lists of crimes imputed to Macchi, for example, the case made was not set up as a criminal case would be, that is, with the subsumption of each element of the criminal category from the concrete behaviour of the President. Instead, the list of trespasses and shady associations was used as indicative of the extent to which the President had fallen into suspicion and how he should be stopped from performing his duties as soon as possible. Indeed, criminal categories were mentioned in passing and seemed only to build up the

2002, for violence against journalists (described then as "state terrorism"). The records of the Chamber of Deputies for these periods are incomplete, making it impossible to recover the exact content or scope of those charges. Moreover, since they were failed attempts, their contents were never submitted to the Senate, who keeps better records of its activities.

[199] *Diario de Sesiones* n. 100519 (Senate, extraordinary session n. 42 of February 11th, 2003), p. 17.

actual impeachment offense that mattered, namely, that the President performed his duties poorly.[200]

A Gap Between Formal and Real Reasons for Impeachment? This is perhaps more blatantly clear in Cubas' impeachment than in Macchi's, although both cases display this aspect well. In the procedures against Cubas, it was obvious how much more Vice-President Argaña's murder contributed to the mistrust of the President over any other consideration. To be clear, the main impeachment issue, that is, Cubas' pardon of Oviedo, had indeed led to a constitutional crisis and in no way was the Representatives' contempt for it second handed. The riots and killings taking place just outside the walls of Congress did indubitably add to the sense of urgency for Cubas' removal. What seemed to be the prevalent concern of those involved, however, was that Cubas' *could* and *in their judgment likely had* some degree of involvement in the murder of Argaña,[201] regardless of the lack of evidence or even thematic pertinence of such suspicions to the charges that had been formally offered.

Legally speaking, any lawyer would be perplexed by a procedure that succeeded without any grounding on evidence, or for a charge that the defendant was not even supposed to formally defend himself from. The unverifiability of claims[202] and the impossibility of a reasoned and informed defence against 'shifting goal posts' arguably make for direct violations of the rule of law by most standards. The standard by which the Representatives were judging, however, was clearly not a legal one. While most did genuinely care about the reality of Cubas' personal involvement in the events leading to the crisis, their first order concern was that he, regardless of any merit in the situation, was putting the country through dangerous amounts of stress that could, indeed, harm the newly founded democracy. That is not to say that, at any rate, such outcome was not also convenient to those who so staunchly opposed Cubas. Partisan interests may and often do attune themselves to other larger overarching goals of politics, such as the preservation of democracy.

[200] *Diario de Sesiones* n. 100512 (Senate, extraordinary session n. 36 of January 23rd, 2003), pp. 3–28.

[201] See, for example, the many comments that start by prefacing *Diario de Sesiones* n. 4968217 (Chamber of Deputies, extraordinary session n. 4 of March 24th, 1999).

[202] At least on short notice. One other characteristic of the procedure against Cubas' was its expeditiousness, picking up speed as soon as the impeachment vote was passed, and the riots took the streets. Cubas resigned about 4 days into the procedures, though the whole procedure could be estimated to last about 9 days in the tempo imposed by the Senators. That is much quicker than Macchi's procedure, which lasted about 3 months, though sessions dedicated to the analysis of the case only took place in the last month.

3.2.1.5 *Post-hoc*-Impeachment: Alberto Fujimori (2001), Peru

A Historical Narrative

Peru became a democracy in 1980, after a failed military dictatorship (Juan Velasco's and Francisco Morales' Revolutionary Junta, 1968–1980) was toppled by the grim economic conditions of its time. Though all Latin America struggled to stabilize their economies in the 1980s, Peru's situation was perhaps one of the direst, as it had to deal with the added stressor of a public security crisis caused by insurgent groups such as the *Sendero Luminoso* (transl. Shining Path) or the *Movimiento Revolucionario Tupac Amaru* (MRTA), which terrorized local communities.[203] The concomitant and persistent failure of the new democratic governments (1980–1985, *Acción Popular* or AP; and 1985–1990, *Alianza Popular Revolucionaria Americana* or APRA) in both of these fronts was particularly effective in generating discontent and suspicion towards the political class.[204]

By 1989, year of the presidential elections, all Peruvian traditional parties had become heavily discredited, while outsiders became increasingly more seductive in the eyes of the disgruntled electorate.[205] As such, the favourite presidential candidates ended up being both political outsiders: the award-winning novelist Mário Vargas Llosa of the AP, on one side, and the agricultural engineer and mathematics professor Alberto Fujimori of the newly formed party Cambio 90, on the other. Vargas Llosa, despite having the strongest results in the first round, alienated much of the Peruvian electorate due to his proximity with far-right movements and proposed radical neoliberal answers to the economic problem. Fujimori, on the other hand, held generally more moderate views outside perhaps on the topic of domestic terrorism, and thus had more success with left-wing voters in the second round. This led to a landslide victory with 62.4% of the votes in the run-offs.[206]

For the surprise of many, President Fujimori used his political honeymoon period to immediately betray his electoral promises and enact economic reforms more radical even than that proposed by Vargas Llosa, leading to an economic convulsion later nicknamed the 'Fujishock'. The effects were comparable to what had been observed in the previous case of CAP's 1989 Venezuela, evoking strong social reactions that led to riots, looting, confrontation with security forces, scarcity of goods, hoarding, black markets and so on. Differently than Venezuela, however, Peru was able to manage a more adequate response and avoided creating a trauma

[203] For details on these groups, see Seawright (2012), pp. 60 ff. and McClintock (1998), pp. 73–81.

[204] Seawright (2012), pp. 38–41.

[205] Seawright (2012), pp. 2 ff. 88% revealed not trusting political parties (earliest available data from 1993) and only 20% trusted Congress (March 1992). By contrast, the Executive and the armed forces enjoyed approval ratings above 50% in the same period. See Conaghan (1996), p. 36, and Conaghan (2005), pp. 31–32.

[206] Seawright (2012), pp. 23 ff. In the first round, Fujimori (29.1%) was behind Vargas Llosa (32.6%). Vargas Llosa's failure to draw left-leaning voters achieved him meager 37.6% in the second round. Nohlen (2005), p. 473.

comparable to that of the *Caracazo*.[207] By 1991 the reform had already succeeded in controlling the inflation and reducing further decline of per capita GDP, thus reinforcing the idea that the outsider could indeed outperform the professional politician.[208]

With the crisis under control in 1991, Fujimori shifted his efforts towards the terrorist activity and attempted to pass progressively more invasive and incisive policing and national security laws, arguably ensuring the formation of, in practice, unaccountable death squads. Given that the Shining Path was an insidious organization, with hidden identities and secretive activities, it did not take long for the innocent population to be caught in the middle of a vicious cycle of violence.[209] Congress, which was still dominated by the opposition of traditional parties,[210] however, sought to limit Fujimori's advances towards an unconstitutional police state, though still willing to find moderate compromises to his plans. Fujimori stubbornly rejected negotiation attempts and antagonized Congress, leading to deadlocks and casting Congress into a negative light, given the rising popularity of the Presidency, as well as the sense of urgency the terrorist threats had taken.[211]

On April 5th of 1992, about 6 months into the quarrels on the new anti-terrorism bill, Fujimori, fed up with the slowness of democracy and with support of the army, dissolved Congress, dismissed the judiciary, suspended the 1979 Constitution, took hold of media outlets, imprisoned political opponents, and began ruling by decree.[212] This event brought the terminology "self-coup" (*autogolpe*) into common parlance[213] and marked the precocious end of Peru's infant democratic experience. Despite the chilling scenes of military takeover, few came to the streets to protest the end of democracy. Quite the contrary: Fujimori seemingly became more popular with his iron-fisted style of rule and his make-it-happen delivery,[214] or at least so the

[207] *New York Times*, August 12th, 1990: *"Peru's Poor Feel Hardship of 'Fuji Shock' Austerity"*.

[208] Weyland (2006), p. 21.

[209] According to the truth commission formed to investigate these crimes, around 69,200 people fell victim to this confrontation between 1980 and 2000, 46% of the cases accounted to the Shining Path, 30% to state forces, and 24% to other causes (*e.g.*, MRTA, vigilante groups, self-defense, unidentified offenders). See *Informe Final de la Comisión de la Verdad y Reconciliación*, *Anexo* n. 2 (https://www.cverdad.org.pe/ifinal/).

[210] Fujimori's Party, *Cambio 90* (transl. Change 90), achieved only 32 out of 180 seats in the Chamber of Deputies (16.5%) and 14 out of 62 in the Senate (21.7%) in 1990. Nohlen (2005), pp. 465 and 467.

[211] Weyland (2006), pp. 22 ff.

[212] Conaghan (2005), pp. 28 ff.

[213] Marsteintredet and Malamud (2019), p. 13.

[214] Conaghan (1996), pp. 32–35, mentions the approval ratings for the coup remained in the 70–80% range in the following weeks. 54% still regarded Peru as a democracy after the coup, as respondents pointed out the continued presence of civil liberties and of an elected president. This suggests Congress was perceived as an elitist body that served as an arena to unsavory political practices rather than as a space for creating links between citizens and the democratic state, thus making its absence inconsequential or even salutary to democracy.

polls said.[215] The arrest of Abimael Guzmán, the head of the Shining Path, just a few months later, consolidated his popular support even further.[216]

External pressure, however, particularly from the OAS,[217] Japan, and the United States, led Fujimori to loosen his authoritarian grip in its most brazen aspects. Their eagerness in having Peru as a democracy again may nevertheless have compromised the quality of the compromises the Fujimori regime made for its transition. On April 21st Fujimori announced a referendum for July 5th, in which a Constituent Assembly was to be elected. Given the state of public opinion in the short term, it was evident that the government would end up overrepresented, a fact acknowledged by the OAS and the political opposition, who still rather had returned to the 1979 Constitution. Fujimori's stubbornness in combination with the Bush administration's precocious recognition of the post-coup regime and the OAS's omission ensured the defeat of the traditional parties' wishes. After some effort by the Fujimori administration to muddy public discourse around the new constitution, as well as to mute, resource-starve, and disenfranchise political opposition, government achieved the expected majority, alongside with OAS's blessing.[218]

In the interregnum between the coup and the conclusion of the Constituent Assembly's work, Fujimori captured most of the Executive and Judicative branches by resorting to mass firings and selective rehiring. Evidence of misdeeds and official documents were 'disappeared', the state finances made secret (so large sums could be syphoned for sustaining informal clientelistic networks), the intelligence agencies majorly expanded, and rules were passed expanding the concept of terrorism, reducing defence rights and assigning life sentences and capital penalty to offenders.[219] Fujimori's power was not *de jure* unchecked, but *de facto* the institutional environment was rigged to make his administration unaccountable.

When the time finally came to vote for the referendum on the new Constitution, near the end of 1993, it was becoming increasingly clear that Peruvians had turned sceptical of the federal government. Despite the absolute disparity of conditions favouring the government's victory, the new Constitution was approved on a near fifty-fifty split, in which only one-third of eligible voters were accounted for and an enormous number of legal challenges to ballots cast in Lima were lodged. The

[215] At the time there was intense discussion around the validity of the polls, as they were intensely used by Fujimori to derive legitimacy to his actions. Little effort was put into debunking them, however, and eventually other sources, even those who opposed the coup, confirmed the results. Conaghan (2005), pp. 32–36.

[216] Fujimori's popularity peaked at 75%. Weyland (2006), p. 22.

[217] Art. 1 and 2 of the Inter-American Democratic Charter requires from OAS member states the commitment to the democratic form of government.

[218] Fujimori's party, now C90-NM (Cambio 90-Nueva Mayoría), achieved 44 out of 80 seats. The opposition shared the rest with "independent" representatives, which were expected to be co-opted by the government. Conaghan (2005), pp. 36–56.

[219] Conaghan (2005), pp. 41–43.

electoral oversight organs, which had also been captured, however, dismissed the claims and confirmed the result.[220]

Despite consolidating concentration of power in the Executive, the Constitution of 1993, was by itself in no way prototypically authoritarian, endorsing most traits of modern constitutions.[221] It did, however, make the Legislature more amenable to external influence by drastically reducing the number of seats and, arguably, also by turning it unicameral. The Constitution, moreover, remained embedded in a context that had all institutions loyal to the Executive and, thus, skewed the balance of power, despite formally restoring the autonomy of many such organs.[222] From this point on, impeachment (known in Peru as *acusación constitucional* or *juício politico*) and its potential surrogates (*e.g.,* declaration of vacancy/moral unfitness) became a legal possibility, but one which stood nonetheless behind the iron curtain of fear, loyalty, and clientelistic networks of implicit authoritarianism.

Some initial evidence of this veiled authoritarianism could be observed in the legal imbroglios around one of Fujimori administration's first scandals, the so-called '*La Cantuta* Massacre'. The case started on July 18th of 1992, when a group of nine students and one professor, all suspected of being involved with the Shining Path, were kidnapped, and executed. The military came under suspicion due to records of it being in the location on the same date, but its officers were shielded from investigation by the Minister of Defence for 'security reasons'. After the Supreme Court predictably dismissed the case, it was picked up by the opposition in Congress, which had received a memorandum from whistle-blowers, arguing that the operation was authorized by high officers of the Fujimori administration. A committee of inquiry was formed, instigating an immediate reaction from the military, who made an unusual 'tank parade' in downtown Lima the following day, while spouting accusations against Congress. Not much later, however, a general brought more details on the case, confirming the existence of a death squad called *Grupo Colina*, identifying its members, and giving details about the operation.[223]

The committee of inquiry received several death threats, but nonetheless published a report calling for the indictment of members of the military. Fujimori's party nonetheless succeeded in blocking the report on a 39–19 vote in the plenum of the Congress. More damning evidence was brought up once the graves of the victims were found, and the Prosecution's Office had no choice but to reopen the case. Not long thereafter, as yet another captured institution, the General Prosecutor order the case be shelved, arguing that the Military Supreme Court was already conducting an

[220] Conaghan (2005), pp. 64–65. A post-referendum survey revealed that 78.9% of the interviewed agreed that the Constitution still needed work before enactment.

[221] Conaghan (2005), pp. 66 ff. The more critical modifications were: (i) extension of death penalty to terrorism; (ii) allowing presidential reelection; (iii) reforming of the structure of the Judiciary/ Prosecution's Office; (iv) allowing constitutional change via referendum; (v) extending some of the presidential powers, especially urgency decrees; (vi) single chamber Congress.

[222] Conaghan (2005), pp. 66–81.

[223] Conaghan (2005), pp. 66–69.

investigation and thus a civil investigation would be redundant.[224] International criticism eventually made Fujimori 'spontaneously' offer some minor arrests as a token of his commitment to the discovery of truth and democracy, in hopes it would lay the case to rest before it reached higher echelons.[225]

This case proved hard to bury, however. Despite the Prosecutor General's orders, the original civil prosecutor assigned to the *La Cantuta* case continued the investigations and eventually dug up new evidence and more arguments to bring the case back to the ordinary criminal jurisdiction. Fujimori's party, knowing this would be a close decision by the Supreme Court, moved to change ruling guidelines overnight, ensuring the military jurisdiction.[226] Ten days after, the military courts convicted 9 out of the 10 charged individuals with paradigmatic sentences. Just 1 year after, however, Fujimori conceded amnesty to the convicted.[227]

Around this time Fujimori's popularity and populistic appeal started showing signs of strain. Not only were the people's desires shifting as the Fujimori administration successfully dealt with some of them,[228] but also the development of the whole *La Cantuta* ordeal was exposing the darker sides of authoritarianism in ways hard to ignore. Coming to the 1995 presidential elections, Fujimori could no longer take his re-election for granted, even in the context of a highly advantageous playing field and optimistic attitudes towards the government, as experienced in the elections for the Constituent Assembly in November 1992. In short, a few of the questionable expedients used by Fujimori to assure re-election were: (i) using the state machinery and resources for self-promotion (*e.g.,* distributing calendars with his image to schools, having the secret service campaign for him); (ii) using the prominence of the Presidency as opportunity for campaign (*e.g.,* using the inauguration of public school and hospitals as opportunities for attacking the opposition); (iii) disenfranchising and silencing opposition (*e.g.,* preventing his wife, Susana Higuchi, of competing for the Presidency and blocking investigations into scandals revealed by her); (iv) staying 'one step ahead' of the opposition by having the secret services

[224] Presumably, this would entail trial by the corporatist justice system of the Military, which was expected to have lenient sentencing, if any.

[225] Conaghan (2005), pp. 69–72

[226] Keeping military jurisdiction required a 4/5 majority decision by the Supreme Court. Knowing the vote would narrowly fail, one of the unsympathetic justices was removed before the decision and the Legislature changed the rule to allow a decision by simple majority. Conaghan (2005), p. 74.

[227] Conaghan (2005), p. 75.

[228] Weyland (2000), p. 236, notices that in 1990, 55% of interviewed Peruvians perceived terrorism as the biggest challenge the country had to face, whereas in 1994 only 24.7% believed that. As commented before, administrations whose legitimacy strongly depends on the delivery of certain projects or of certain performance are likely to struggle both in case of success or of failure. If they fail to deliver, they betray the promises that lent them legitimacy; if they deliver, on the other hand, they have nothing left to legitimate their continued stay in power, unless a new agenda emerges. Moreover, in the specific case of outsiders, their legitimacy may be time-limited, as the longer they stay in power, the more likely they are to be perceived as the new Establishment or the new 'old'. See Casullo and Freidenberg (2017), pp. 275 ff.

monitor their communication and disrupting their campaign, at times with fabricated evidence of illicit activities; (v) engaging in basic clientelism, such as distributing consumer goods to voters; among other things. With the Congressional majority approving every tweak in favour of Fujimori, as well as blocking any threat; with the Prosecutor's Office and the National Jury of Elections (JNE) burying every investigation into criminal and electoral misconduct, as well as with the OAS's unwillingness to confront the government, Fujimori could get away with all those 'mere irregularities' and 'isolated cases', to use the language employed by these organs.[229]

The result was a 64% victory in the presidential election, as well as a congressional victory of 52% (67 seats) to Fujimori's party, the C90-NM, something well above the 1/3 predicted by the polls. The congressional results were filled with questionable features, with 41.5% of the votes being invalidated for technical reasons and over 835 thousand votes simply 'missing'. These occurrences were dubbed as by the JNE as two unforeseen 'anomalies' and 'confusions' caused by the local authorities, which also could not be double-checked, as the tallies were destroyed after the first counting.[230] This outcome, legitimate or not, solved one of Fujimori's greatest pre-coup weaknesses, namely his weak congressional support, which limited how the Executive could expand its power and shield itself from accountability—two extremely valuable assets, especially with the agendas that generated the bulk of his support (anti-terrorism and economic recovery) losing protagonism.

Fujimori's newly found congressional support enabled more brazen attempts at controlling public opinion during his second mandate (1995–2000). Another case of death squad massacre came up, the *Barrios Altos* Massacre, which prompted the same sort of official cover-up strategies discussed before, except this time around Congress went as far as giving a blanket amnesty to all crimes committed in the counterinsurgent struggle since the 1980s (Law n. 26479), reaching even the convictions of the *La Cantuta case* itself. Other bills were passed to prohibit such amnesty from ever undergoing judicial review (Law n. 26492), as well as to give Congress veto power over referenda by means of a 3/5 majority (Law n. 26592), as those could be used to bypass congressional legislative prerogatives in certain ways.[231]

Despite the pervasiveness of the Fujimori administration, the only way it could assure lasting impunity would be by perpetuating itself in power and, thus, re-election quickly became one of its top objectives. It was already clear by the end of 1996, however, that there were no electorally viable successors to Fujimori. By the same token, his re-election for a third term also seemed difficult, though

[229] Conaghan (2005), pp. 78–99.

[230] Fujimori's 64% vote was calculated only with basis on the 'valid votes', thus excluding null and blank votes cast. 64% of valid vote, however, meant only 39% of the electorate in total. Conversely, the congressional vote of 52% corresponded only to 18.5% of the total electorate. Conaghan (2005), pp. 98–104.

[231] Conaghan (2005), pp. 105–124. 69% thought the amnesty law should be reversed. 87% rejected its effects being extended to those convicted for *La Cantuta*.

Congress went a long way to ensure the possibility. Congress passed a bill (law of authentic interpretation; Law n. 26657) which denied retroactive effects to the re-election rules of the 1993 Constitution (art. 112), meaning that Fujimori's third election had to be counted as his second term under the new Constitution. As the Constitutional Court moved to declare the law inapplicable, Congress impeached 3 of its 7 judges, effectively blocking it from ever taking decisions on the constitutionality of laws, since that required a quorum of 6/7. For the first time since 1992, outrage was great enough break the political apathy and, so, motivate mass protests.[232]

As Fujimori's legitimacy came increasingly into question, it seemed that government agents became more willing to leak information to the media. As a response, the Fujimori administration also became more violent and audacious, creating a self-reinforcing vicious cycle. The acts of the government in its last years can only be described as acts of state terrorism. A short and incomplete catalogue should include: bombings of TV stations, (moral and legal) harassment, robbery, mugging, kidnapping, arresting, torturing, mutilating and beheading of journalists, opposition politicians and whistle blowers, particularly the ones resistant to bribery and favour exchanges.[233] While these methods served their function of achieving 'closure' in unpleasant hot topics for the Fujimori administration, they also had the fallout of generating more loose ends and more unpopularity (Fig 3.3). These cycles repeated and intensified up to the point of reaching the man who made the artificial cohesion of the Fujimori administration possible: Vladimiro Montesinos.

Vladimiro Montesinos played the role of Fujimori's chief political advisor while being the *de facto* head of the Peruvian intelligence agency (SIN, *Servicio de Inteligencia Nacional del Perú*). Making use of SIN's infrastructure and illegally diverted resources, Montesinos made sure every major institution (judiciary, Congress, military, and media) ticked in favour of his designs. By tampering with evidence, bribing, and intimidating the right people, Montesinos managed to always get away with his abuses and claim a certain degree of 'plausible deniability'. Covering-up for the abuses of leading to the 2000's general elections, however, was too much. Too many became involved, and his acts became too brazen to be realistically denied. On September 14th of 2000, a few months after the elections, a 'smoking gun' emerged: A video with Montesinos negotiating bribes with Representatives and executives of TV conglomerates that would ensure their loyalty to the government. The leaked video, recorded by Montesinos himself, unambiguously revealed everyone's intentions in those meetings and confirmed every suspicion and

[232] The Constitutional Court (*Tribunal Constitucional*) is a separate organ from the Supreme Court, which was not captured and was considered a wild card to the government's plans. 74% of the public opposed the impeachments, 76% believed they were part of the government's plan to weaken institutions and 80% believed they were direct consequence of the votes against reelection. Conaghan (2005), pp. 118–131.

[233] The campaign of intimidation did have some effect. Journalists admitted off the record that they practiced self-censorship and sometimes avoided pursuing sensitive stories. Also finding sources willing to tell on the government became rarer to find. Conaghan (2005), pp. 140–162.

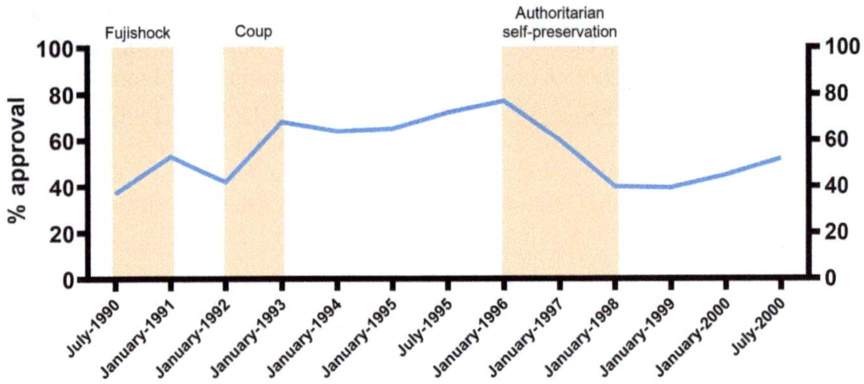

Fig. 3.3 Fujimori administration's approval rates, 1990–2000. Source: Own elaboration with data from Carrión 2006, p. 129. Note: "Authoritarian self-preservation" indicates the series of actions taken by Fujimori to cover-up crimes of his subordinates (amnesties to perpetrators of Barrios Altos and La Cantuta massacres), as well as other acts of persecution of political opponents

accusation the opposition had leveraged in the past years. Cornered, Fujimori had to let Montesinos go and do so with much care, not to implicate himself or become a victim of a *coup*.[234]

Despite his attempts, Fujimori was unable to convince Montesinos to resign. An arrest was unfeasible, given Montesinos' grasp on the military high officers. Other actors were also unwilling to cooperate. The Prosecutor General, Blanca Nélida Colán, a protégé of Montesinos, shelved all charges. The congressional majority, who was also beneficiary of his services, quashed any hope of parliamentary inquiries into the theme. Fujimori saw no exit but to fire himself to take down Montesinos. On a public announcement, Fujimori stated that, despite being democratically elected, he did not want to disrupt Peru's future and, thus, would be calling early elections in which he would not participate. This, alongside with some financial compensation and extensive lobbying, led Montesinos to accept political asylum in Panama. The years of exposure to the Fujimori administration's doubletalk, however, made Peruvians impervious to its promises and outlooks. Rumours of imminent *coups* and scepticism about a veritable transition remained in place.[235]

Despite some initial foot-dragging, the news of Montesinos having returned to Peru on October 23rd led external pressure to become too great for Fujimori or Congress to resist. A few key actors were fired from the SIN and presidential cabinet, the General Prosecutor's office was replaced, and proper investigations discovered Montesinos' slush funds, weakening his clientelistic network. In a matter of time, Fujimori's party fell apart and the opposition managed to take control of the

[234] Conaghan (2005), pp. 222–230; Berntzen and Holvik Skinlo (2010), p. 199.

[235] Conaghan (2005), pp. 227–235; Berntzen and Holvik Skinlo (2010), p. 199.

parliamentary majority and the presidency of Congress. Finally, conditions for impeachment had materialized. Fujimori, who was attending the Asia-Pacific Summit in Brunei at the time, did not return to Peru and, instead, fled to Japan. A few days after, on November 19th, Fujimori sent his resignation letter from Tokyo. His Vice-Presidents followed suit and Valentin Paniagua, the new President of Congress, assumed the *interim* presidency of Peru.[236]

Declaration of Vacancy

> (...) I have to call him morally incapable, he who has lied to the country, has refused to make himself accountable [dar la cara] and renounce [the Presidency] by his own hand; he who leaves the country to send us a letter from Tokio, to take care of whatever treasure; for sure not the treasure of appreciation for citizenry or for the dignity of office, since he has left Peruvians humiliated in the face of the whole world.
>
> Henry Pease García (Acción Popular)[237]

Fujimori's resignation letter was interpreted as a grand act of cowardice and national humiliation by the opposition in Congress. When the time came for the members of Congress to accept the letter, they thought it would be more suiting to declare Alberto Fujimori permanently unfit for public office, on grounds of moral incapacity.[238] The act was more than a defence of national honour, but also a demonstration to the rest of the world that Peru was about to enter a new era of democracy, this time around with genuine commitment and no hidden political calculations. The representative Ana Elena Townsend (*Somos Perú*) summarized the general mood of Congress perfectly:

> Enough with authoritarianism, enough with corruption, and enough with lies! In name of all those who want this Congress to recover its moral and efficacy, as well as of those who believe that democracy is a system worth respecting, and all of those who reaffirm that in no circumstance a coup d'État can be the solution for national development; In name of them all, we need to show that vacancy of the Presidency on grounds of permanent moral unfitness is absolutely justified and that it [the vacancy] will come from serenity, firmness and justice,

[236] Conaghan (2005), pp. 235–242.

[237] Author's translation of *Segunda Legislatura Ordinaria de 2000, 4a. Sesión*, November 21st, 2000, p. 18. The use of word treasure is likely a reference to Fujimori's resignation letter, where he justified his self-exile as necessary for stability and consequence of his treasuring of Peru's economy.

[238] *Resolución Legislativa* n. 009-2000-CR: "Art. 1: It is declared the permanent moral unfitness of the President of the Republic Alberto Fujimori, according to the paragraph 2 of the art. 113 of the Peruvian Constitution". The phrasing of this statement is tricky. 'Permanent' in the sense of art. 113 does not mean 'everlasting' as in ordinary language, but something more in the sense of 'more than merely temporary', or, in practical terms, longer than what is left of the presidential mandate. It sounds like the penalty of permanent disqualification for office (which is adopted by many Constitutions in case of impeachment conviction), but in reality it is not.

> and not as mere 'forget and pretend it never happened' [borrón y cuenta nueva], or as revenge, as some claim.[239]

At the time, the 'declaration of vacancy' (*declaración de vacancia*), the instrument used to achieve this goal, however, was not sufficiently set in law. The art. 113, §2 of the 1993 Constitution recognized the powers of Congress to declare the Presidency vacant on physical or moral grounds, but offered no procedure, quorum, or any further explanations on what constituted the said physical or moral grounds. Fujimori's party at the time, Peru 2000, raised this objection, claiming the need for proper rules before moving forward, but most representatives were positive that the case was clear-cut and the vacancy could be voted just as any other generic plea and their respective procedural rules, thus, were already sufficiently determined by the congressional bylaws.[240]

In retrospect, this overconfidence of the Peruvian Congress or its eagerness in proving a point seem a bit problematic. The first issue was its interpretation of what constitutes 'moral unfitness' (*incapacidad moral*), which, in comparative perspective (and arguably also in historical perspective),[241] sounded unorthodox. Most Latin American Constitutions have a provision which allows for the presidency to be declared vacant,[242] but in none of them they are used as a form of dispensing judgement on acts of the President and they rather only acknowledge a fact of life, namely that the President is no longer physically (died, is bed ridden, disappeared, etc.) or mentally (illnesses or other impairing conditions) able to perform his or her duties. Such provisions were arguably imagined serving the necessary formalities that allow presidential succession or new elections to take place, and not as a way to impose sanctions.[243] In a way, therefore, the Peruvian Congress created a new instrument which conflated the purpose of impeachment with that of the declaration of vacancy, keeping some of the functions of the former but with the ease of use of the latter. In effect, unless one subscribes to a form of moral realism, judging the morality of a person or his acts is not a mere empirical judgment, but a normative

---

[239] Author's translation of *Segunda Legislatura Ordinaria de 2000, 4a. Sesión*, November 21st, 2000, p. 17 (Townsend Diez-Canseco).

[240] *Ibid.*, p. 5 (Lozada de Gamboa).

[241] The 1834 Constitution of Peru is the first to expressly mention the declaration of vacancy. García Chávarri (2013), p. 386. Its art. 80 stated: "The [office of] President of the Republic becomes vacant in case of death, admission of his resignation, permanent physical impossibility, legal destitution, or the end of his mandate" (author's translation). There were, however, two practical cases in which Presidents (1823 and 1914) were ousted with vacancy on moral grounds for trying to dissolve Congress (nowadays classified as a ground for impeachment on art. 117 of the 1993 Constitution). García Chávarri (2013), p. 390.

[242] *E.g.*, Art. 233 of the 1999 Venezuelan Const.; Art. 145 of the 2008 Ecuadorian Const.; Art. 170 of the 2009 Bolivian Const.; Art. 194 of the 1991 Colombian Const., etc.

[243] In multiple instances, members of Congress made the confusion between (i) permanently vacating an office on grounds of moral unfitness and (ii) vacating an office and declaring the President permanently unfit (*e.g., Segunda Legislatura Ordinaria de 2000, 4a. Sesión*, November 21st, 2000, p. 20).

one, requiring the subsumption of moral principles/virtues over contextualized acts and personality traits.[244]

This created a confusing precedent. It created an instrument that resembled to some degree the dreaded bill of attainder, which combined the traumatic power of an impeachment with the ease of use of common bill or congressional plead. With just a simple majority for approval and the undefined objective element of 'moral incapacity', which could theoretically be leveraged against any objectionable act or subjective characteristic of a President.[245] This would be even more concerning, when compounded by the fact that the Peruvian party system became more fragmented and polarized after Fujimori. In such context of volatility and many unprincipled actors, executive instability could intensify. Though Fujimori left, the *fujimorismo* and its uncompromising style of politics would indeed continue to be a plentiful source of conflict.[246] By a recommendation of the Supreme Court in 2003, the threshold of approval was raised to qualified supermajority (2/3), which restricted to some degree the ease of abuse, but did nothing to prevent the declaration of vacancy from being used as means of intrigue, as the threshold for bringing this matter to appraisal by Congress was nonetheless reduced to 4/10.[247]

The most likely explanation for the choice of using the declaration of vacancy against Fujimori seems to be the eagerness in engaging in a symbolic act of rejecting his resignation and expressing contempt against everything he represented. Another possible explanation, however, may come from a peculiar characteristic of impeachable offenses in the 1993 Constitution. Although 'abandoning office' did constitute an impeachable offense, it did not constitute an impeachable offense applicable to *sitting* Presidents. A Peruvian President may be held accountable for any legal or constitutional transgression committed whilst in office for up to 5 years after the end of his or her mandate (art. 99), but, as a sitting President, that rule is only applicable

---

[244]Very few recognized this issue. Marique Pacheco (*Acción Popular*) was one of the few to point out that what was being discussed there actually needed proper evidence, clarification, and debate to be voted. *Ibid.*, p. 51.

[245]The problem of such broad definitions is that they allow the 'goal posts' of a discussion to be shifted freely, making defense nearly impossible. Most representatives concurred that (i) not presenting the resignation personally to Congress was a sign of 'moral unfitness', but there were also those who mentioned: (ii) deceit and the lack of trustworthiness of the Fujimori administration; (iii) the damage caused to Peru's image in the international realm; (iv) the desertion from the country in times of crisis; (v) non-compliance with duties and obligations of office; (vi) connivance with corruption, abuse of power and genocide; (vii) corruption and abuse of power; (viii) causing economic and/or constitutional crises; (ix) obstruction of justice; (x) gross mismanagement; (xi) illicit enrichment; among other things. *Segunda Legislatura Ordinaria de 2000, 4a. Sesión*, November 21st, 2000.

[246]The attempt against Fujimori's successor, Alejandro Toledo (2001–2006) may be symptomatic. The declaration of his moral unfitness was debated due to extramarital affairs. García Chávarri (2013), pp. 397–398.

[247]As recommended by STC n. 006-2003-AI-TC, pp. 11–12, and introduced by the *Resolución Legislativa del Congresso* n. 030-2003-CR in the *Reglamento del Congreso de la República*, art. 89-A, b and d.

for "committing high treason; preventing presidential, congressional, regional or municipal elections; dissolving Congress (...), and preventing the meeting or operation of Congress, the National Election Board, or other Bodies of the election system" (art. 117).[248] As such, Congress may have used the "moral unfitness" ground for vacancy (art. 113, § 2) as a proxy for its goals, as the vacancy on the grounds of impeachment (art. 113, § 5) was effectively unavailable.[249] The vacancy was approved on a 62 to 9 vote, with 9 abstentions and 40 absences, in one 12-h long session.[250]

Impeachment

One could speculate whether Peruvian impeachments will end up following the same fate as England's: the same way the 'great remonstrance' made English impeachments obsolete, unnecessary, and redundant, so may it also turn out to be the case for Peru, by virtue of the declaration of vacancy. The key difference here would be one of historical context, that is, England's impeachments being part of a larger struggle towards balance of power and parliamentary supremacy over the Monarchy that, once achieved, no longer had use for impeachments, despite their theoretical applicability for serious abuses that needed exemplary punishment. In Peru, as well as in other modern presidential systems, this overarching struggle to which impeachment belongs to is not as clearly defined or may not even exist.[251] The main suspects are, of course, the never-ending struggle against tyranny and authoritarianism, as well as the enabling of republican government within a system of concentrated powers in the Executive branch. If these suspicions are right, the Peruvian impeachment may be well on its way to desuetude and extinction, as the declaration of vacancy is largely sufficient and efficient means of achieving such goals.

Whatever the future may hold, at least for now impeachment is not thought of as entirely obsolete. The key element here is not just the ousting of overbearing Executives, but also the prevention of their reconduction to power through disqualification, something that the declaration of vacancy cannot guarantee. In an ideal

[248] As translated by the Constitute Project.

[249] For disclosure, this was not some crafty form of unaccountability introduced by the Fujimori dominated Constituent Assembly of 1993, but was, in fact, an inherited trait from the 1979 Constitution (art. 210).

[250] 62 votes are barely over absolute majority (51.6%), but the vote was taken on simple majority, meaning an overwhelming defeat for Fujimori (77.5%). *Segunda Legislatura Ordinaria de 2000, 4a. Sesión*, November 21st, 2000, p. 156.

[251] Taking the Hegelian hypothesis of "end of history" as true, that is, assuming liberal democracy to be the end point of human institutional evolution, then impeachments may be said to have just a regulatory role, instead of a broader change, as the somewhat revolutionary English impeachment.

political system,[252] citizens would not re-elect someone who has been ousted for mismanagement and abuse and would instead pick an untainted alternative. Powerful, messianic figures like Fujimori, however, can make anyone have second thoughts about such expectations. Because of considerations like this, the Peruvian Congress thought it was necessary to go further and impeach Fujimori even after his resignation was rejected to allow a removal to be granted. Fujimori himself was sure of the reach of his persona and it is known that he was preparing himself for another presidential bid in the years following his self-exile. It is important to notice, moreover, that the Peruvian criminal code does, in fact, allow for the penalty of disqualification for many of the crimes against the public administration committed by Fujimori, but presumably a criminal trial would not conclude quickly enough to prevent his presidential bid in 2005, as it effectively did not. Fujimori would be first criminally sentenced in 2007.[253]

Presumably with such calculations in mind, twelve members of Congress presented a *Denuncia Constitucional* (Constitutional Accusation) against Fujimori on November 30th of 2000 targeting the conduct that had already been object of the declaration of vacancy, namely his 'desertion' from the country. Constitutional Accusation is the name given to the traditional impeachment in Peru, except it can have any legal or constitutional infraction as object and the procedures occur in only one House, thanks to the 1993 Constitution which made Congress unicameral. In this procedure, the Permanent Commission of Congress accepts the *Denuncia* and then chooses a Sub-Commission of Investigation, which takes over all other phases of the procedure, namely investigating, modifying impeachment charges, trialling and then proposing a sentence that must be voted by the plenum of Congress.[254] Originally, the *Denuncia* accused Fujimori of violating arts. 38 and 118 of the 1993 Constitution, both articles which stipulate the obligation of complying with and defending the Constitution and the laws. Despite sounding very broad, the *Denuncia* restricted its claim to two specific normative acts, Law n. 25656 and the Legislative Resolution n. 27355, both which stipulated rules for presidential travel. The charges were greatly expanded later during the investigation to encompass some of the most critical abuses of the Fujimori administration, but the analysis of these issues was postponed in favour of a streamlined impeachment procedure. Indeed, instead of expanding the scope of accusation to encompass all of Fujimori's dubious acts, the

[252] The whole idea of limited mandates as means of prevention of overbearing Executives was grounded on the expectation that people would become critical of their behavior and would avoid their re-election. In that context, the penalty of disqualification from impeachments was at times thought of as redundant and mere product of English institutional legacy. See Sect. 2.1.10.

[253] Ambos (2009), p. 558.

[254] If the accusation contains criminal accusations, they must be further taken to trial before the Supreme Court (art. 100 of the 1993 Constitution). A criminal acquittal may revert the outcome of impeachment, however.

Commission chose to charge him with only those first two, since their case was clear-cut and already sufficient to satisfy the goals of impeachment.[255]

Fujimori did not present a defence piece or make use of his personal time for defence before the Investigation Sub-Commission or the plenum of Congress,[256] making for an uneventful procedure. It became a repetition of the declaration of vacancy, except under more defined legal terms. The events were so similar, in fact, that a few staunch *fujimoristas* accused the procedures of inflicting double jeopardy.[257] This claim, much like most presented by the *fujimoristas* in this session, were readily dismissed by other representatives, since they were disconnected from the legal reality in question (*e.g.*, claiming Fujimori could not be impeached after leaving office while the Constitution expressly says otherwise; claiming that an officer cannot be held accountable for crimes committed in office after leaving office; etc.) and ended up not offering any further insights into the Peruvian impeachment.[258]

This is unfortunate because the Fujimori case could have shed light upon one of the more thorny and obscure subjects of impeachment theory, namely the concrete limits of presidential political accountability and imputability. In none of the more conspicuous crimes of the Fujimori administration was Fujimori personally implicated,[259] at least not until the capture of Vladimiro Montesinos, who then claimed Fujimori knew about the wrong doings of the Intelligence Agency (SIN), if was not supportive of them or had directly given orders.[260] Even so, those revelations would still only mean an easily challengeable indirect authorship and omission, due to the difficulty of verifying the claims and the direct interest of Montesinos in implicating the President to reduce the burden upon himself. Either way, it should come off as

[255] *Informe Final de La Subcomisión Investigadora Designada por la Comisión Permanente Para investigar las Denuncias Constitucionales n. 57, n. 58 and n. 87.*

[256] *Ibid.*, p. 3. Defense is warranted in both instances by art. 100 of the 1993 Constitution.

[257] *Segunda Legislatura Ordinaria de 2000, 17a. Sesión*, February 22nd, 2001, pp. 77 ff. The declaration of vacancy and impeachment have different objects, scopes, and outcomes, making the double jeopardy claim unfounded. The confusion was warranted, however, since some representatives (wrongly) implied permanent moral incapacity was the same as a sanction of permanent disqualification for office. See Sect. 4.5.1.3 for clarification.

[258] Impeachment passed on a 37 to 24 vote, with 4 abstentions, giving rise to the Legislative Resolution n. 018-2000-CR, which disqualified Fujimori for office for 10 years. Members of the Investigative Commission (24 Representatives) were not allowed to vote (art. 100 of the 1993 Constitution and art. 87-J, Parliamentary Bylaws). The simple majority vote was possible for this question at the time, but since June 2004, the quorum has been raised to 2/3 (Legislative Resolution n. 030-2003-CR).

[259] By 2001, the illegal dissolution of Congress in 1992 had already prescribed. The 1993 Constitution stablishes a 5-year period after the end of the mandate for impeaching an officer, though it is not clear whether prescription is suspended upon reconduction. If it did and all the self-amnesties given by the Fujimori administration were declared illegal, then Fujimori could perhaps be held accountable for an act he uncontrovertibly was directly involved. The Inter-American Court of Human Rights did roll back most self-amnesties in 2001 and 2006, opening this theoretical possibility. Ambos (2009), p. 556.

[260] Conaghan (2005), pp. 244–245.

perplexing to see that the acts of enabling people and institutions like Montesinos and the SIN, as well as the undeniable profiting from their obnoxious behaviour, were to remain entirely unaccounted for due to practical limitations largely imposed by the accused themselves.

Despite the underwhelming impeachment, it should be noted that in November 2005, in the hopes of running for the Presidency once more in April 2006, Fujimori made the mistake of travelling to Chile, where he was arrested and extradited back to Peru to be trialled on 3 cases of human rights violations (*La Cantuta, Barrios Altos, Sótanos*) and 5 other cases of corruption (*Allanamiento, 15 Millones, Congresistas Tránsfugas, Medios de Comunicación, Interceptación Telefónica* cases), all which ended in conviction.[261] These decisions made exemplary use of concepts such as co-perpetration, indirect perpetration, and joint criminal enterprise in order give an appropriate response to such systemic, macro-criminal sort of injustices,[262] which could be used perhaps as inspiration also for understanding political accountability within large frameworks. The potential merits and limitations of these frameworks for the context of impeachments are discussed in Chap. 4.

3.2.1.6 Conviction by Notoriety: Fernando Lugo (2012), Paraguay

A Historical Narrative

The former bishop Fernando Armindo Lugo de Méndez was elected President of Paraguay on April 20th of 2008, marking a significant shift in Paraguayan politics. For the first time in 61 years a member of an opposition party reached the presidency of the country, putting an end to the hegemony of the National Republican Association (ANR; right-wing), better known as the Colorado Party. It was, moreover, the first time in Paraguay's history that a transference of power between political opponents happened without violent conflict.[263]

Lugo's surprising victory was merited in part to the growing influence of one party of his coalition, the Authentic Radical Liberal Party (PLRA, or the Liberal Party; centre), who had taken larger shares of municipal and departmental elections and had greatly expanded its activist networks in the previous years.[264] His victory was also, however, partly attributable to the miscoordination and fragmentation of his opponents. The Colorado's previous presidential administration under Nicanor Duarte had become plagued with corruption and attempts at opposition suppression,

---

[261] Ambos (2009), pp. 556–558. In short, Fujimori was convicted of multiple counts of murder, kidnapping, severe assault, bribery, illegal wiretapping, among other things. His punishment was capped at the maximum allowed by Peruvian law, 25 years.

[262] Ambos (2009), p. 564.

[263] Ultima Hora, April 20th, 2008: "*Nicanor reconoce la derrota del Partido Colorado*".

[264] Abente-Brun (2008), pp. 148–149. The PLRA was the only party with the infrastructure to challenge the ARN but had until then never backed presidential candidates from other parties. Abente-Brun (2008), p. 149.

making Paraguayans crave for change.[265] Sensing the likely erosion of the Colorado electorate, Duarte pressured the Supreme Court to release the controversial General Lino Oviedo from prison, and so appease Colorado dissidents, possibly having him in the vice-presidency.[266] The plan, however, backfired with Oviedo running independently for President and drawing more votes from the Colorado constituency than from the Liberals.[267] As a result, Lugo (PDC, Christian-Democratic Party; centre-left) was elected with 40.9% of the vote, against Blanca Ovelar's (Colorado) 30.63%, and Lino Oviedo's (UNACE; National Union of Ethical Citizens) 21.93%.[268] In the legislature, Lugo's coalition (APC, Patriotic Alliance for Change; mix of left and centre parties) achieved 17 out of 45 seats (37.7%) in the Senate, and 31 out 80 seats (38.75%) in the Chamber of Deputies.[269]

Despite all odds, Lugo's administration had a popular start, with visible achievements in the anticorruption front and a praised 5-year economic plan, which promised sustainable growth and social justice.[270] It did also, moreover, achieve an important review of contractual terms with the Brazilian government regarding the binational Itaipú Powerplant, which nearly tripled the revenue on the sales of surplus energy.[271] On the political-partisan front, however, the Lugo administration stumbled in its efforts of appeasing supporters and building consensus around its policies. Lugo chose to not proportionately share power with the Liberals, who composed nearly 90% of his representation in Congress.[272] The communication and

[265] Abente-Brun (2008), p. 150. Some authors describe Lugo's triumph as consequence of the Colorados' collapse. For explanations in those lines, see Pérez Talia (2019), pp. 496 ff.

[266] Abente-Brun (2008), pp. 147–148. Oviedo (Colorado's traditionalist wing) was responsible for the coup against the dictator Alfredo Stroessner (Colorado's militant wing) and Paraguay's transition to democracy. Battalions associated with Oviedo attempted another coup in April 1996, which failed and resulted in Oviedo's 10-year conviction for mutiny. The Supreme Court, which had been stacked by Duarte in 2003, overturned the conviction, allowing Oviedo to run for office. See also Ultima Hora, November 2nd, 2007: *"Duarte Frutos habla de cogobierno con Lino Oviedo"*; Ultima Hora, October 31st, 2007: *"Lugo habla de manejo político de la Justicia"*; Ultima Hora, March 2nd, 2021: *"Exministro dice a la Corte IDH que juicio político fue para la reelección"*.

[267] Abente-Brun (2008), p. 151; Lachi (2010), p. 37. In comparison to previous elections, the Colorados lost about 10% in support, which seems to have been incorporated by the UNACE in the presidential ticket. In the Legislature, the variations were less notable.

[268] Justicia Electoral de Paraguay (2008), pp. 229–230. The election had 65.48% of turnout. The President is elected on a relative majority, meaning no run-offs take place (art. 230, 1992 Constitution).

[269] Justicia Electoral de Paraguay (2008), pp. 277, 339–341. Senate: 14 seats to the PLRA, 1 seat to the PPS (Popular Solidary Party), 1 seat to the MPT (Tekojoja Popular Movement), and 1 seat to the PDP (Progressive Democratic Party). Chamber of Deputies: 27 to the PLRA, 1 to the MPT, 1 to the PDP, and 2 to the APC.

[270] Abente-Brun (2008), p. 152.

[271] Turner (2010), p. 448. Paraguay was contractually obliged to sell Itaipú's surplus energy to Brazil at production cost. The new terms brought in US$ 360 million a year, which, although insufficient to the eyes of hard-line nationalists, was widely considered a victory and honouring of one of Lugo's central campaign promises.

[272] Abente-Brun (2008), p. 152. Only 4 out of 10 Ministries were handed to the Liberals.

coordination between him and the Vice-President Frederico Franco (PLRA) was also lacklustre, resulting in conflict with and the isolation of Franco's faction within the Liberals, as well as in rumours about an imminent hostile takeover of the presidency.[273]

Among all occurrences that could be pointed out as part of Lugo's undoing,[274] however, the largest contributors were probably his administration's approximation to left-leaning governments in Latin America and the disastrous unfolding of land redistribution policies. Regarding the first, besides associating himself with socialist Presidents such as Evo Morales or Daniel Ortega, Lugo stroke significant deals with Hugo Chaves' Venezuela, which sought to solve the country's issues with petroleum supplies.[275] Such proximity raised suspicions and alienated Lugo's popular and partisan support, particularly from the Liberals. Compounded by Lugo's aversion to old, well-stablished political practices such as the "*cuoteo*" (*i.e.,* the distribution of offices according to shares decided in backroom deals among political parties, particularly relevant regarding Supreme Court nominations), Lugo's presidency frequently saw itself vulnerable and politically isolated, with the Liberals leaving its stable position in the coalition within the first months of government.[276] Not partaking in *cuoteo* or other pork-barrel related practices meant Lugo was sacrificing crucial means for building *ad hoc* majorities or securing support for his policies.[277]

The Liberals' withdrawal from the coalition, however, did not mean their automatic shift into the role of opposition. Indeed, after the coalition break Lugo was still subjected to 23 other impeachment attempts, calls for resignation, or impeachment threats before being finally removed in 2012.[278] Only the last attempt was successful because of a final attitudinal shift by the Liberals, most likely caused by the disastrous unfolding of the land redistribution policies and its aftermath. The policies not only stirred rifts within the coalition but also drew animosity from the Paraguayan establishment. As disclosed in a 2008 by the Truth Commission on the

[273] Abente-Brun (2008), pp. 152–153; América Economía, October 22nd, 2010: *"Diputados de Paraguay amenazan con un juicio político al presidente Lugo"*.

[274] Due to space constraints, not every relevant event or aspect of the Paraguayan political system can be described here. Some important occurrences were nonetheless: (i) Constant presence of scandals in Lugo's intimate life, such as four paternity claims from extramarital affairs, two of which were confirmed; (ii) Lugo's frequent change of command of the Armed Forces. BBC News, February 3rd, 2010: *"Lugo se livra de última ação de reconhecimento de paternidade"*; ABC, September 20th, 2010: *"Lugo ordenó nuevos cambios en la cúpula de las Fuerzas Armadas"*. Both occurrences were object of failed impeachment attempts in 2009 and 2010, respectively. The paternity scandals are said to have had a heavy negative impact on Lugo's popularity due to Paraguay's strongly religious and conservative society.

[275] Abente-Brun (2008), p. 154. Only 12% of Paraguay's population identifies itself as left leaning.

[276] ABC, August 29th, 2009: *"Lugo rechaza designación de Lovera Cañete en la Corte"*; Cooperativa.cl, June 30th, 2009: *"Principal partido aliado de Lugo se retiró de coalición de gobierno"*; América Economía, January 12th, 2010: *"Lugo descarta romper con liberales"*.

[277] Lachi (2010), pp. 37–41. Pérez Talia (2019), p. 493, adds, moreover, that the lack of institutionalization of the APC further undermined Lugo's capacity of rebuilding trust and support.

[278] Paraguay.com, June 21st, 2015: *"Las 23 amenazas de juicio a Lugo"*.

abuses committed by the Stroessner regime (1954–1989), the laws on equitable land distribution had been misapplied to favour Alfredo Stroessner himself, his generals and associates, as well as other members of the Colorado Party.[279] Advocating for the faithful application of land redistribution statutes meant challenging powerful factions long entrenched in positions of power, as well as a sector of the economy responsible for close to a fifth of the country's GDP and 70% of its export revenue.[280] The landless worker unions and peasants who benefited from the redistribution, by contrast, offered comparatively little political capital to counterbalance the inevitable backlash Lugo would face.

The first phase of the land conflict mentioned took place between April 18th of 2011 and February 25th of 2012, in the region of Ñacunday. The conflict was set off when authorities detected large soy producers to be in possession of excess landmass to which they lacked the proper legal titles. Such land became subsequently occupied by peasants of the landless movement (*sin tierras*), bringing them to clash with the soy farmers who nonetheless still sought to care for their plantations or rejected the peasants' claims. Seeking some legal security, both sides pursued judicial and political protection to their interests. At a certain point, the peasants were simultaneously given injunction by civil court to stay in the occupied land, and a note eviction, given by a criminal court. Both national and local governments (the latter led by José Ledesma, an ally of Lugo and the landless movement) were strongly pressured to enforce the evictions, but consistently rejected or purposefully delayed the use of security forces for such goal. Though the peasants would eventually agree to leave before further escalation of the conflict, the government's handling of the situation generated animosity among its opponents and frustration among its supporters.[281]

The second phase of the conflict overlapped partially with the first, starting January 12th and ending June 15th of 2012, in the district of Curuguaty. The events essentially repeated the patterns described above but after so much build-up of frustration and mistrust in government that the involved were much more willing to brazenly act out their dissatisfaction.[282] Moreover, these conflicts met much less

---

[279] Data from the Comisión de Verdad y Justicia, Paraguay (2008), pp. 25–37. Over 60% of Paraguay's farmable lands was distributed irregularly with abuse of these statutes (the Agrarian Statutes of 1940, 1963 and 2002).

[280] See Harvard's atlas of economic complexity entry on Paraguay (2013).

[281] Vallejos (2014), pp. 16–62. Two events were critical. The first was the stand-off between Governor José Ledesma (PLRA) and the Minister of Public Works and Communication, Efraín Alegre (PLRA), which revealed or started a rift in the Liberal Party. The second was the break-up of leaders of the landless movement with Lugo, whom they perceived to neglect their interests. For details see also: ABC, July 7th, 2011: *"Ledesma presionó en MOPC"*, and *"Peritaje técnico confirma que no existe excedente de tierras en Ñacunday";* Ultima Hora, February 20th, 2012: *"Dirigente de carperos rechaza propuesta oficial y anuncia enfrentamientos si son desalojados"*.

[282] Vallejos (2014), pp. 71–81. Peasant groups who protested the authorities' partiality, for example, came to siege the Prosecutor's Office (*Ministerio Público*) of Curuguaty, requiring interference of the national police. One of the peasant leaders, Rubén Villalba, sought support of paramilitary forces to resist the enforcement of eviction.

favourable conditions for their peaceful resolution, given that the affected parties were even more powerful than the soy farmers of the previous conflict. Among the affected this time around was none less than Blas Riquelme, an influential Paraguayan business mogul, who had also been a Senator and a party leader for the Colorado Party.[283] With open manifestations of political influence in the land disputes and the increasing incapacity of the national government in moderating resolutions, the peasant groups decided it made more sense to resist power than to continue negotiations, given that such option never seemed to yield any positive outcome. Long story short, after a long streak of failed resolution attempts, confrontation escalated during the enforcement of an eviction notice, resulting in 17 dead, 80 injured, and numerous arrests.[284]

The shocking violence brought fingers pointing at the national government, who though arguably no longer much influential in the direction of the involved peasant movements, was still seem as associated with them or at least at fault for losing its directive input. President Lugo embarked into a damage control campaign, in hopes of salvaging whatever was left of his time in the presidency. As it turned out, however, the damage control produced more damage than control. Lugo's all-out strategy at securing governability by incorporating Colorado representation into government and by bending to its whims did not produce any reliable support, nor did it manage to divide the Colorados from unanimous opposition. Lugo nominated the Colorado Rubén Candía Amarrilla as the new Ministry of Interior and had a conservative turn on to several of his own policies, but the Colorados rejected the idea that these movements were in any way representative of an approximation with Lugo. It did, on the other hand, achieve the unambiguous reprisal of his historical allies, most critically by the *Luguistas* within the Liberal Party, who felt betrayed by Lugo's lack of consideration in consulting with them about these decisions.[285] Lugo made multiple offers to appease these sectors of the Liberals, but ultimately failed to grant their core wishes. This resulted in a resolution declaring the Liberals' definitive distancing from Lugo, abandoning their last few Ministries, and announcing their support for his impeachment.[286]

The day following the resolution, June 21st of 2012, the Colorados offered impeachment charges against Lugo, claiming the need to assess his degree of responsibility in the crisis. The charges were approved in the Chamber of Deputies on a 76 to 1 vote (2 absences), which were then considered and approved by the Senate the next day, on a 39 to 4 vote.[287] Lugo was thus convicted and ousted in the quickest and perhaps most unanimous impeachment procedure of Latin America's

[283] Vallejos (2014), p. 65.

[284] Vallejos (2014), p. 86.

[285] Candía Amarilla was known for his hardliner stance in repression of peasant movements as General Prosecutor of the previous administration. He was also accused of unduly favouring landowners involved in Curuguaty's conflict. Vallejos (2014), pp. 91–95.

[286] Vallejos (2014), pp. 98–100.

[287] Vallejos (2014), pp. 102–107.

history. The same degree of unanimity over Lugo's unfitness for office could not be found in the general population, who neither protested much his impeachment, nor mobilized for his removal.[288] The international community, on the other hand, seemed more unambiguous in condemning Lugo's impeachment procedures for its procedural flaws, resulting in the non-recognition of the succeeding government as legitimate rulers of Paraguay and the subsequent suspension of the country from the Unasur and Mercosur, for violations against the democratic clause.[289]

The Impeachment Procedures

> Obviously, as someone said, this is a political trial, but it is unsettling [how] overnight it has been decided (...). I shook their hands, I greeted them beside the President just two days ago, and now they are the most fervorous supporters of this impeachment. This is no minor change that they ask, it is no more and no less than cutting the presidential mandate short.
>
> Senator Carlos Filizzola in the first day of Impeachment[290]

The accusation piece presented on June 21st of 2012 brought forth a single charge against Fernando Lugo, namely poor performance of the presidential functions (*mal desempeño de sus funciones*), which, however, was argued upon eight categories of occurrences during his administration, ranging from policy failures to other more suspicious activity.[291] The largest part of the accusation, however, was modified by the "Commission on Constitutional Affairs, National Defence, and Public Forces",[292] who was entrusted with the accusation management. The final document of the Commission pointed as indicative of poor performance the facts that Lugo

---

[288] ABC, June 22nd, 2012: *"Policía repele a luguistas*"; BBC News, June 23rd, 2012: *"¿Por qué pocos protestaron por la salida de Lugo?"*. Latinobarometro's historical datasets for Paraguay (2011 and 2013; 2012 is not available) indicate that (i) rejection for President Lugo was considerably lower (42% in 2011) than for his successor (66% in 2013), (ii) Congress, an already mistrusted institution, became even more mistrusted (from 68% in 2011 to 77% in 2013 of low or no trust in Congress). Though inconclusive, these measurements may suggest the public did not perceive Lugo's ousting as being as legitimate as presented by its Representatives. An opinion poll carried out by Ati Snead Consulting concluded, nonetheless, that 56% of the population agreed with the ousting. See Voz de America, July 16th, 2012: *"Paraguay: Lugo es más popular que Franco"*.

[289] BBC News, 30th of June 2012: "*Unasur suspende temporalmente la membresía de Paraguay"*, and *"Paraguay suspended from Mercosur"*. The OAS expressed concerns regarding the procedure, but ultimately acknowledged it had "followed constitutional procedure". OAS, July 10th, 2012: *"OAS Permanent Council Receives Report of the Secretary General and Delegation to Paraguay"*.

[290] Author's translation of *Diario de Sesiones* n. 1509, p. 10 (*Cámara de Senadores, sesión extraordinaria* n. 196).

[291] Nota n. 035/12 *Honorable Cámara de Diputados*. Among the narratives that were excluded by the accusation management were (i) the failed acquisition of lands to be distributed to peasants; (ii) numerous cases of misuse of presidential nomination powers (*e.g.*, Caso Lacognata, nepotism, favouring of underqualified officers).

[292] This is a fusion of two permanent commissions of the Chamber of Deputies one on Constitutional Affairs, and other on National Security (art. 137 and 147 of the bylaws of the Chamber of Deputies).

(i) misused buildings of the armed forces for the furthering of his political agenda;[293] (ii) instigated and facilitated the invasion of lands in the region of Ñacunday; (iii) failed to develop or implement policies that tackled the rise of insecurity;[294] (iv) subscribed the Protocol of Ushuaia II, undermining the country's energetic sovereignty;[295] and (v) mismanaged the crisis that originated the Massacre of Curuguaty. This last item was only briefly mentioned in the original accusation but was indicated as the true motivating reason for impeachment, presumably in acknowledgment that the other narrated occurrences had been object of previous impeachment attempts, which failed to gather the necessary support to fuel a parliamentary inquiry by themselves.[296] The avoidance of the truly suspicious activity mentioned in the original accusation piece was presumably a strategic decision of the Commission, arguably seeking to sidestep the need for time demanding investigations.

Lack of Real Scrutiny of Presidential Misbehaviour The mentioned avoidance of complex investigations did not quite stop there and may have been excessive by most legal standards, including those stablished by Paraguayan officials during this trial. According to art. 189 of the bylaws of the Chamber of Deputies, the Commission could have used up to 30 days for investigation and deliberation on the matter at hand but, instead, chose to simply declare in its accusation piece that all facts were "of public notoriety" and thus "[did] not need to be proven, according to our legal order".[297] Though the rules stablished by the Senate for Lugo's impeachment did mention multiple opportunities and steps for producing evidence,[298] the conspicuous lack thereof went on to be passively tolerated and later ratified by the majority of Senators, despite direct and non-trivial challenges posed by the defence.[299]

[293] The piece narrated that Lugo permitted the use of the buildings of the Armed Forces for a meeting of the socialist youth. *Libelo acusatorio contra el Presidente de La República Fernando Lugo Méndez*, pp. 1–2.

[294] The piece does not cite information or evidence on this supposed growth in insecurity, but merely states that Lugo had been complacent with the assassinations carried by the *Ejercito del Pueblo Paraguayo*, a paramilitary organization said to have been involved in the escalation of the Curuguaty massacre. *Ibid.*, pp. 3–4.

[295] The protocol of Ushuaia II stablishes the democratic clause for participation in the Mercosur. The piece argues that it gave neighbouring countries the ability to influence Paraguay's Ministry of Energy. It claimed, moreover, that the protocol could be used by Lugo to shield himself from accountability, as it subjected the country to economic sanctions in case of ousting. This last part indicated perhaps a degree of foresight and self-awareness relative how the impeachment procedures were about to be carried out. *Ibid.*, pp. 5–6.

[296] Paraguay.com, June 21st, 2015: *"Las 23 amenazas de juicio a Lugo"*.

[297] *Libelo acusatorio contra el Presidente de La República Fernando Lugo Méndez*, p. 8.

[298] Art. 4, 5, 6, 7 and 8 of the Legislative Resolution n. 878 of 2012.

[299] *Diário de sesiones* n. 12511, pp. 5–9, 13–29 (*Cámara de Senadores, sesión extraordinaria* n. 198). The ratification was discussed in *Diário de sesiones* n. 12512 (*Cámara de Senadores, sesión extraordinaria* n. 199), without the presence of the defence.

Such oversight was justified by, among other things, the fact that the narrated misconduct in the accusation did indeed take place.[300] Such consideration, however, seemed to misunderstand what it really means to legally prove something for purposes of conviction. Legal standards of proof stablish not only the minimum requirements for the recognition of facts for them to have legal validity, but also how those legal facts to amount to a valid legal argument. It is to say, in other words, that it does not suffice to prove that multiple individuals indeed died in conflict, but it is also necessary to link the perpetrator with such deaths, evidencing the wrongfulness and blameworthiness of the accused misconduct. To legally prove something means not only to engage in an empirical activity of fact discovery, but also in a normative one, that requires an effort in hermeneutics and legal subsumption. The Senate, therefore, seemed to obtusely conflate both things in its declaration of notoriety, when it failed to further create a real opportunity for the normative portion of the proof to take place.[301] In a sense, it created a situation alike the infamous "conviction by notoriety" of the Middle Ages, in which justice, while still lacking much of its modern refinement and impersonality, enabled such conflation. At any rate, for many external observers, this characteristic of the procedure tainted it with an irreparable degree of illegitimacy and made it, thus, worthy of the epithet of "parliamentary coup".[302]

Fast-Track Conviction, Rush to Judgment, and Uneven Playing Field Such conclusion would be reinforced even more by the time frame in which all of this took place, that is, less than 2 days between the presentation of the accusation piece, its vote by the Chamber of deputies (Thursday, 12:00), its referral to and the meeting of the Commission of Constitutional Affairs, the creation of impeachment rules, the trial and conviction by the Senate (Friday, 17:32). It is arguably unreasonable to expect a lawyer, regardless of skill, to muster an informed defence for such a complex case in such short notice. The accusation, by contrast, had been compiling its dossier against Lugo for the past years, thus arguably consolidating, moreover, an uneven playing field simply by virtue of having proper time for preparation.

One important thing to notice about such rush to judgment and curtailment of defence is that they are not consequences of any "inherent" viciousness or hastiness of the rules of impeachment created by the Senate. Indeed, the rules against Lugo

[300] There were other even less charitable arguments, namely the argument that the defence did not need extra time for production of evidence, because it did not use its full time for opening arguments. *Ibid.*, p. 4. The accusation did bring some evidence, however, in the sense that it annexed two newspaper articles about the facts and some correspondence sent from Congress to the presidency.

[301] The defence questioned, for example, what kind of contribution Lugo gave to the chain of events, as the accusation did not clarify if he was among the perpetrators, accomplices, or instigators, nor how exactly the conducts amounted to poor performance. *Diário de sesiones* n. 12511, pp. 20–21 (*Cámara de Senadores, sesión extraordinaria* n. 198). A proper answer to those questions was only given in the accusation's closing remarks.

[302] Mohallem (2012), pp. 30–31.

were largely the same as those used in previous (and posterior) impeachments,[303] but the way they were applied and interpreted by the Senate was arguably uncharitable in comparison. As had always been the case before, space between each procedural step was stipulated in "sessions", which, under normal circumstances, happen weekly or daily, setting a somewhat predictable pace. In Lugo's case, by contrast,[304] the interval between sessions was cut down to 15 min, and the sessions themselves were often motioned to end prematurely. Session 201, for example, in which Senators were expected to discuss the case at hand, had one single manifestation of an opposition Senator before a motion was passed to kick off the voting phase.[305] The hastiness was justified by a few Senators as needed due to rumours of imminent violence planned by Lugo and backed by other socialist leaders, as well as by a comparison with the impeachment of Collor, which was accused of putting Brazil's economy under strain for taking 3 months to conclude.[306]

If 'Poor Performance' Is What the Senate Says It Is, Does Procedure Matter? One could perhaps argue that such strict adhesion to rules or respect to defence rights did not matter that much anyways. Congress is the one to precise what poor performance is and, therefore, if it decided Lugo's guilt to be notorious, it would be because it was so for all intents purposes. In some senses, this was a stance assumed by the Supreme Court, when it dismissed Lugo's unconstitutionality suit that questioned, among other things, the absence of due process mentioned.[307] According to that decision, since the category of poor performance lacked justiciable standards, it would be immaterial for it to even stablish basic ground rules for the Senate, as it had free reign to decide matters of impeachment.[308]

---

[303] See, for example, Resolution n. 825 of 2015 or the rules created for the impeachment of President Raúl Cubas Grau, in *Diário de Sesiones* n. 332S-24, (*Cámara de Senadores, sesión ordinaria* n. 45—March 24th, 1999).

[304] By any measure, Paraguayan impeachments are quick. Those against the Colorado Presidents Cubas Grau (4 days—interrupted by his resignation) and Gonzales Mácchi (approximately 3 months) at least leveraged charges with evidence and coherent legal arguments, conceded the defendants with at least 3 days for defence, and had trial sessions with full duration and at least a day of spacing between them.

[305] *Diario de Sesiones* n. 12514, pp. 1–7 (*Cámara de Senadores, sesión extraordinaria* n. 201).

[306] Rumours: *Diario de Sesiones* n. 12509, pp. 17–18, 22–23 (*Cámara de Senadores, sesión extraordinaria* n. 196); Collor comparison: *Diario de Sesiones* n. 12514, p. 7 (*Cámara de Senadores, sesión extraordinaria* n. 201).

[307] *Acción de Inconstitucionalidad* n. 1533 and 1323.

[308] This stance differs a lot from the rest of Latin America, who generally accepts review of rules of impeachment and interlocutory decisions. There are reasons to believe, however, that the Supreme Court's decisions were more based on circumstances than a commitment to an actual doctrine of political self-restraint. Unlike judicial review of impeachments in neighbouring countries, the Paraguayan Supreme Court after the ousting. This put the Court in a vulnerable position of confronting an uncompromising Congress, who, as history tells, could oust Justices to get its way, if they were not already tightly controlled by other means.

While there is some truth to this assertion, this an understanding that is disputed by this book from a historical and theoretical perspective. As mentioned before, impeachment is not only about "ousting the President" but also about providing the nation with a grand inquest into presidential conduct. Impeachment releases political tensions not only by removing an officer perceived as a pernicious influence on the political system, but also by giving clarity into public misconduct and stimulating the open discussion on its wrongfulness. The lack of justiciable standards is no blemish to political decisions such as these, so long they are representative of the consensus of the political community, a consensus which, however, can only be formed in informed fashion if enough time and energy is invested in its construction. Presidential impeachments become too haphazard as tools of accountability if they do not serve as well as building blocks that help constitute historical materiality and the concept of responsible government for a particular society. While impeachment is generally circumscribed to the parliamentary realm, its functioning is not exhausted therein, and should necessarily communicate with society at large. Flawed impeachments such as Lugo's seem to conspicuously neglect this dimension of impeachments, acting as if the institute is no more than a mere lawyerly solution to a political problem rather than an integral part of politics itself under presidentialism.

Exploitation of Brief Moments of Unpopularity or Vulnerability Finally, it is also worth noticing the value of impeachment's slowness, which, as argued before, is not a defect, but a feature. The Lugo impeachment offers a prime example as to why impeachment's much criticized cumbersomeness has a place in avoiding that momentary swings in popularity or in partisan support be opportunistically instrumentalized to subvert the general will or to cause more harm than good to democracy. Again, though it is impossible to predict how things would have playout otherwise, it is imaginable that, given more time, perhaps the Lugo would have had more leeway to negotiate with the Liberals and regain their trust. By avoiding taking a decision "in the heat of the moment" so to say, Paraguay could have avoided its international backlash and the Liberals would have avoided the attrition of a deadlocked and unpopular interim presidency, which arguably hurt their results in the following elections.

3.2.1.7 No Half-Impeachments: Dilma Rousseff (2016), Brazil

A Historical Narrative

After Collor's impeachment in 1992 much changed in Brazil's political landscape, making the country less prone to the types of conflict witnessed during his administration. The presidential powers for ruling-by-decree (*medidas provisórias*) had their scope greatly reduced and became easier for the Parliament to control.[309] Some

[309] Constitutional Amendment n. 32 of 2001.

steps were taken to tame the volatility and fragmentation of the party system, though many of them were frustrated or eventually reversed, producing elites that, although still extremely fragmented, at least were more likely to display partisan loyalty and solidarity.[310] Most significant perhaps was the realization made by these elites that, for good or bad, Brazil was a country that could not be ruled without compromise, and that democracy had necessarily to be conducted in consociational fashion.[311] The country's economy also started to thrive in the following terms, as Collor's legal successors were finally able to stabilize the economy, and a few years later, the economy boomed alongside the so-called commodity super-cycle of the 2000s.[312]

The impeachment of President Dilma Rousseff, however, comes at the end of this cycle of prosperity. Just a few years after Rousseff took power in January 2011, commodities start lost their prominence as China, Brazil's biggest trade partner, started restructuring its economy towards greater independence from commodity imports.[313] This imposed on the Rousseff administration the hard task of either taking the unpopular road of slashing public spending or the more elusive road of finding complementary sources of state revenue. Arguably, the first path was unfeasible given Rousseff's electoral promises of maintaining and expanding investment in social programs and infra-structure of her predecessor and mentor, President Luis Inácio Lula da Silva (2003–2010).[314]

In pursuance of this latter goal is that Rousseff went to commit her first impeachable offenses. September 6th of 2012, Rousseff presented her plan for the economy, named the New Economic Matrix (*Nova Matriz Econômica*). The plan had among its key components the intervention in the energy sector, reducing petrol and electricity prices in hopes of reducing the cost of goods and services, which, on their turn, would increase consumption and propel the economy.[315] In an unforeseen turn of events, however, this strategy became more costly than planned. Brazil, a country highly dependent on hydrothermal powerplants, went through several enduring draughts.[316] Costly coal-fired powerplants had, thus, to be activated to keep the country supplied with energy, undermining Rousseff's plans.

The Rousseff administration, however, was obstinate in honouring her electoral promises and continued seeking ways to finance the new energetic policy. Just in 2013, for example, the energy sector had a 14 billion reais (approx. six billion dollars at the time) of budgetary deficit, out of which 7.85 billion would be financed by the

---

310 Clève (2010), Mainwaring et al. (2018).

311 The unavoidability of consociational rule imposed to Brazil's presidency has led national scholars to label it "coalition presidentialism". See Abranches (2018).

312 Almeida (2004), pp. 25–28, and Barbosa (2020).

313 Villaverde (2016), pp. 54–59.

314 O Globo, June 26th, 2010, *"Dilma diz que dará continuidade ao governo Lula, sem repeti-lo"*.

315 Estadão, July 5th, 2012: *"Mantega indica novo modelo econômico"*.

316 G1, January 29th, 2013: *"Dilma volta a rechaçar racionamento e diz que 2013 terá recorde de energia"*; Uol, March 19th, 2017: *"Conta de luz caiu 16% em 2013, mas subiu 58% desde então; o que deu errado?"*.

standard means stablished by financial law, that is, by the issuing of treasury securities (*títulos da dívida pública*), while the rest would be "creatively" financed. Part of the resources came from a fund that, although related to the energy sector (RGR, *Reserva Global de Reversão*), was bound to other goals, and other part would be loaned from national banks, in violation of other rules of financial law.[317] The more serious practices of creative accounting remained concealed for a long time, as the Central Bank overlooked or omitted much information in its reports. Eventually, however, such practices were brought to light by whistle-blowers and a mutiny of analysts of the National Treasure. As it turned out, the government had been masking its accounts by delaying part of its obligatory spending,[318] underreporting costs, and mislabelling spending to avoid immediate negative impact on the budget.[319]

The true state of the national budget would only become known after Rousseff's tight re-election in October 2014,[320] when the national government decided to come clean and pay many of its debts.[321] A report presented by audits of the Court of Accounts in December further denounced practices coordinated by the Ministry of Finance and the National Treasury, culminating in the rejection of the government's accounts in mid-2015.[322]

The revelation confirmed that Brazil's economy was indeed going through a recession,[323] despite the government's attempts at dismissing such claims in the past

---

[317] Silva 2015, p. 22, fn. 60; and 35. Also, Villaverde (2016), p. 73. Complementary Law n. 101 of 2000 (financial responsibility law) stablish most rules on financial law.

[318] National banks must by law pay the government's 'obligatory spending' (*i.e.*, social welfare, pensions, salaries) on time even if they do not receive the resources to do so. In accounting practice, this makes the National Treasure seem to have more resources than it should have at the end of the month, inflating the budget.

[319] Villaverde (2016), pp. 83–87; Valor Econômico, January 24th, 2014: *"O ano com 13 meses";* Valor Econômico, June 9th, 2014: *"União adia repasse de royalties para atingir meta";* Estado de São Paulo, March 12th, 2014: *"Governo atrasa pagamento do Minha Casa, Minha Vida para melhorar situação fiscal"*.

[320] Dilma won with 51% against Aécio Neves (Brazilian Social-Democratic Party, PSDB; center-right). Jornal Nacional G1, October 27th, 2014: *"Dilma vence eleição mais acirrada da história da democracia brasileira"*.

[321] The timing of the payments avoided negative impacts on Rousseff's re-election and precluded any sort of political accountability for the irregularities that they imply. Presidents are only accountable for acts committed in the current mandate, which would leave less than 3 months for investigation and trial of any misdeed committed between 2011 and 2014 (art. 86, §4 of the 1988 Constitution).

[322] For the audit report, see TC 021.643/2014-8*: Relatório de Fiscalização, Fiscalis* 621/2014. For the decision of the Court of Accounts, see TC 021.643/2014-8: *Acórdão* n. 825/2015, pp. 1 ff. For Rousseff's initial responses to these revelations, see Estado de São Paulo, July 24th, 2015: *"Se for para revisar o passado, é preciso condenar todos"*. For the opposition's reactions, see Estado de São Paulo, April 16th, 2015: *"Líderes de oposição dizem que decisão do TCU abre caminho para pedido de impeachment"*.

[323] A study conducted by the Inter-American Development Bank (Ames et al. 2016, p. 6) indicated that 80% of participants perceived their economic situation as regular or good. Less than 40%

years.[324] The backlash was immediate, and Rousseff was pressured to take drastic measures to bring the budget back into balance. Demoralized for the failures of her heterodox economic policies, Rousseff picked a libertarian Minister of Economy, who enacted such a severe package of austerity measures that it was later nicknamed "the austericide" by its critics.[325] Compounded by pessimistic prospects and widespread suspicion of the government, Brazil's economy plunged to the worst recession of its history and Rousseff's popularity reached the lowest of known to any Brazilian President until then.[326]

In parallel to these events, the Rousseff administration went through several other crises. In June 2013, it took a massive hit to its popularity after public outrage grew unforeseeably out of control.[327] Essentially, what initiated as a small demonstration against a raise in public fares in the city of São Paulo turned into a country-wide revolt due to the violence of with which it was initially repressed by state security forces. The shocking images of repression moved populations from other cities to protest in solidarity, making São Paulo lose its centrality and expanding the scope of popular demands into others of national importance. The protests criticized foremostly the prices of public services, the faltering investment in infra-structure, police violence, as well as the government's priorities, particularly in hosting the Olympics and the World Cup in face of so many other necessities.[328] The Rousseff administration was initially only tangentially related to the June protests' origins, in perhaps its weak results regarding infra-structure investments[329] or for its role in enacting anti-terrorism legislation that enabled arbitrary repression and persecution of protestors,[330] but once the cat was out of the bag, so-to-say, all eyes were on the President. Rousseff's proposal of response plan (*agenda positiva*) calmed the spirits for so time, but they soon got heated again once the World Cup of 2014 approached as an unescapable reminder of the national government's irresponsiveness.[331]

Rousseff's party, the Worker's Party (*Partido dos Trabalhadores,* PT; centre-left) also lost a significant part of its political capital in events leading up to

---

noticed deterioration in the economy in the past year (p. 33). Participants also classified problems of public healthcare and security as the most important themes for the 2014 elections (pp. 31–32).

[324] Estado de São Paulo, December 4th, 2013: *"Tesouro paga mais para vender títulos e técnicos pressionam Arno Augustin"*; G1,

[325] Folha de São Paulo, February 21st, 2016: *"Austericídio de Levy?"*.

[326] Época, April 4th, 2016: *"Como o Brasil entrou, sozinho, na pior crise da história"*; BBC, March 18th, 2015: "De campeã de popularidade a 62% de rejeição".

[327] Folha de São Paulo, June 29th, 2013: *"Popularidade de Dilma cai 27 pontos após protestos"*.

[328] For a detailed analysis of the "journeys of June", see Avelar (2017).

[329] For an overview of Rousseff's infra-structure policy, see Zuanazzi et al. (2015).

[330] Publica, January 29th, 2013: "Com leis próprias, megaeventos criam estado de exceção"; EBC, June 5th, 2014: *"Anistia Internacional aponta abuso policial em protestos de junho de 2013"*.

[331] BBC News, June 13th, 2014: *"Brazil World Cup: Clashes at Sao Paulo and Rio protests"*.

Rousseff's second mandate (2015–2016). Though the party leader Luis Inácio Lula da Silva achieved messianic status through his presidency,[332] the party itself suffered significant losses due to its shift in attitudes and behaviour while in power. The party became implicated in many corruption schemes which damaged its reputation as a grass-roots party genuinely interested in the best interests of the working classes. Also, despite its at times incendiary leftist rhetoric, the party was perceived to be behaving too often as a centrist catch-all party, who did the bidding of the powerful and resisted implementing structural change.[333] As a result, many of its members migrated to other parties or formed their own splinter parties.[334] Many of these politicians remained supportive of the Worker's Party, but even they were eventually alienated by the party's uncompromising electoral campaigning style, which sought to exclude similarly aligned contenders from presidential run-offs and so secure polarized (centrifugal) competition that generally favoured the party's electoral strategy.[335]

General rejection for the party itself expanded during Rousseff's mandates, as anti-corruption operations took off. Actualizing its commitment to the Convention of Palermo against transnational organized crime in its national laws, Brazil introduced in its legislation multiple new instruments of criminal procedural law that sought to enhance the leverages of investigators and prosecutors of complex crimes.[336] As a result, an unprecedented flow of information on age-old corruption schemes poured through media channels that followed closely its developments, unveiling the perplexing scope and reach of corruption in the country. Though the Worker's Party was not the most implicated party in the grand scheme of things,[337] the surfacing of the scandals during its rule generated a sense that the party was

[332] Lula is foremostly known for his social program's impact in lifting millions of citizens from extreme poverty. Bloomberg, December 19th, 2010: *"Brazil's Lula leaves office with 83% approval rating"*.

[333] This is made abundantly clear by many Rousseff's disgruntled former allies during her impeachment, as they denounce the party's betrayal of its programs. For quantitative data on the subject, as well as a general discussion on negative partisanship regarding the Worker's Party, see Samuels and Zucco (2018), pp. 28 ff.

[334] Folha de São Paulo, September 26th, 2005: *"Petistas históricos anunciam saída do partido e filiação ao PSOL";* October 5th, 2018: *"Marina Silva encolhe, não supera trauma de 2014 e chega miúda à reta final"*.

[335] Rousseff was sharply criticized for her electoral disinformation campaign against the left-centre contender Marina Silva (Brazilian Socialist Party, PSB). R7 Notícias, October 23rd, 2014: *"Jornal britânico destaca acusações de Marina Silva sobre mentiras do PT";* Folha de São Paulo, October 5th, 2018: *"Marina Silva encolhe, não supera trauma de 2014 e chega miúda à reta final"*.

[336] Laws dealing with cartels and joint criminal enterprises (12,529/11 and 12,850/13, respectively) implemented or expanded the inquisitorial system equivalents of plea bargain, which incentivize suspects to offer information on criminal activity in exchange for lighter punishments or protection from prosecution.

[337] El País, March 31st, 2016: "*Campeão da Lava Jato, PP cresce e vira trunfo na barganha do impeachment*"; Publica, September 26th, 2018: "*Lava Jato atingiu membros de 33 partidos*".

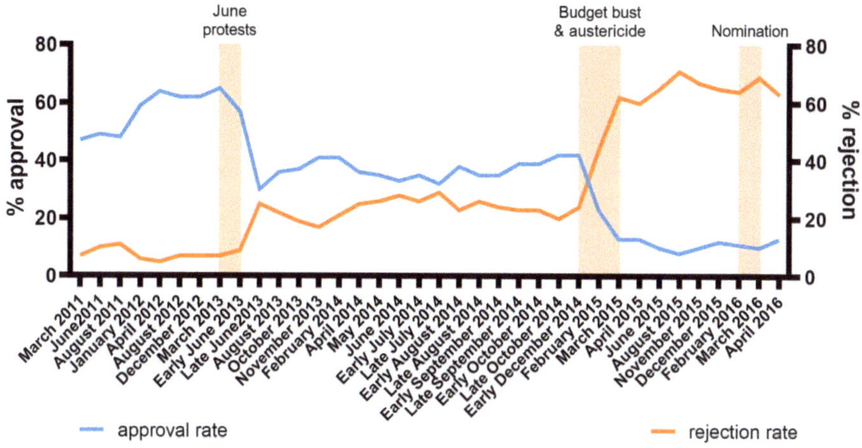

Fig. 3.4 Rousseff administration's approval and rejection rates, 2011–2016. Source: Own elaboration with data from Instituto de Pesquisas DataFolha (2016), pp. 13–14

somehow enabling corruption. Rousseff attracted in a sense a certain 'guilt by association' in the judgment of the public opinion (Fig. 3.4).[338]

Many of Rousseff's allies or associates were investigated and/or prosecuted for corruption during her mandate, making it difficult for her to keep stable coalitions, as the costs of remaining associated with the Worker's Party were becoming greater and greater as the negative feelings against the party grew.[339] This became more obvious in 2015 when Brazilians started mobilizing regularly to protest corruption and ask for Rousseff's resignation/removal,[340] and when details on the potential involvement in corruption of the Worker's Party frontman himself, former President Lula, started pouring into the media.[341]

In face of these issues piling up beside the mismanagement of the national budget, Rousseff's impeachment finally started being seriously ventilated by Congress[342] and, after some direct conflict between the Worker's Party and the President of the

[338] Exame, June 30th, 2017: *"PT é o partido mais associado à Lava Jato, mostra pesquisa"*.

[339] El Pais, February 5th, 2015: *"O tesoureiro discreto que expõe o PT no escândalo da Petrobras"*; G1, August 3rd, 2015: *"José Dirceu é preso na 17ª fase da Operação Lava Jato"*, and November 25th, 2015: *"Líder do governo no Senado, Delcídio do Amaral é preso pela Polícia Federal"*; O Globo, December 19th, 2015: *"Sigilo bancário e fiscal de Renan Calheiros é quebrado"*; Uol Notícias, January 17th, 2016: *"PP desviou R$ 358 milhões dos cofres da Petrobras, diz procurador-geral"*; G1, August 26th, 2016: *"Polícia Federal prende Antonio Palocci na 35ª fase da Operação Lava Jato"*.

[340] Folha de São Paulo, March 15th, 2015: *"Protestos contra governo reúnem quase 1 milhão pelo país"*; CartaCapital, April 12th, 2015: *"Manifestações contra o governo encolhem em todo Brasil"*; El País, August 19th, 2015: *"Manifestações anti-Dilma votam às ruas do Brasil"*.

[341] El País, April 8th, 2018: *"A cronologia da investigação que levou Lula à prisão"*.

[342] Estado de São Paulo, April 16th, 2015: *"Líderes de oposição dizem que decisão do TCU abre caminho para pedido de impeachment"*.

Chamber of Deputies (see next section), impeachment accusations were accepted by the latter in December 2015.[343] Rousseff's political isolation expanded towards the very core of her administration, with even the Vice-President Michel Temer (PMDB, Brazilian Democratic Movement Party; centre/centre-right) publicly announcing his break up with government.[344]

Though Rousseff attempted, among other things, cabinet reshuffles and offering patronage to secure governability and a legislative shield, in 2016 her support became too volatile and unreliable.[345] Further developments in corruption investigations generated outrage against the President and motivated millions of Brazilians to take the streets, producing the biggest manifestations in the country history, reaching up to over three million participants asking for Rousseff's removal.[346] Particularly dramatic was an episode in which wiretappings of conversations between Lula and Rousseff were leaked to the media right after Lula had been nominated to the position of Chief of Staff (*Ministro da Casa Civil*) in an expedited process. The leaked conversations suggested that the nomination was motivated by an intent of obstructing justice, and the decision was reversed by the Supreme Court the following day.[347]

In acute political isolation and unprecedented popular rejection, when it came to the impeachment vote in April 2016, Rousseff was impeached and suspended from office with little resistance in Congress, including from those expected to be historical allies.[348] Though Temer's interim government became more contested and unpopular than Rousseff's by the time her impeachment trial came to an end on August 31st of the same year, her conviction was nonetheless convincingly approved by the Senate with 61 votes against 20.[349]

---

[343] Until her party's conflict with the President of the Chamber of Deputies, Rousseff was shielded by him from forty-eight other impeachment accusations. Uol Notícias, December 3rd, 2015: *"De 132 pedidos de impeachment desde Collor, ação contra Dilma é a segunda aceita"*; Estado de São Paulo, December 2nd, 2015: *"Eduardo Cunha aceita pedido de impeachment contra Dilma Rousseff"*.

[344] G1, December 7th, 2015: *"Leia íntegra da carta envida pelo vice Michel Temer a Dilma"*.

[345] O Globo, April 13th, 2016: *"Debandada de partidos amplia o isolamento de Dilma";* Folha de São Paulo, April 7th, 2016: *"Governo libera emendas em troca de voto contra impeachment, diz senador"*.

[346] Época, March 13th, 2016: *"As manifestações de 13 de março em todo o Brasil"*.

[347] The nomination would vest Lula with ministerial immunities. G1, March 16th, 2016: *"Planalto anuncia Lula como novo ministro da Casa Civil";* March 16th, 2016: *"Moro derruba sigilo e divulga grampo de ligação entre Lula e Dilma";* and March 18th, 2016: *"Gilmar Mendes suspende nomeação de Lula como ministro da Casa Civil"*.

[348] G1, May 12th, 2016: *"Processo de impeachment é aberto, e Dilma é afastada por até 180 dias"*.

[349] BBC, July 26th, 2016: *"Nem Dilma, nem Temer: maioria da população quer eleição antecipada, aponta nova pesquisa";* G1, August 31st, 2016: *"Senado aprova impeachment, Dilma perde mandato e Temer assume"*.

Impeachment in the Chamber of Deputies

The accusation piece against Rousseff charged her with a total of seven impeachable offenses listed in Brazil's impeachment law (Law n. 1079 of 1950), namely: (i) not holding her subordinates accountable for crimes or unconstitutional acts, (ii) acting in manner incompatible with the dignity of the office of President, (iii) authorizing issuing of credit in disagreement with limits established by Senate, (iv) not cancelling the issuing of credit or not creating reserves to accommodate the effects of credit operations executed in violation of legal limits, (v) not promoting the full liquidation of anticipated credit operations before the end of the accounting period (*encerramento do exercício financeiro*), (vi) authorizing credit operations in disagreement with the law, be it through new contracts, refinancing, or payment delays.[350] The narratives that supported these charges were partially explained in the previous section, and involved multiple irregular and/or illegal operations in the management of the national budget, such as delaying payment of obligatory spending, and thus forcing public banks to pay out of pocket debts of the national government, and enacting decrees that, uncompliant with proper legal requirements, issue credit without parliamentary approval.[351]

As one of the most eventful and polemic impeachments in history, the Rousseff case gives valuable insights into the workings of such procedures, starting out from even before its official introduction in the Chamber of Deputies (Lower House). As it turned out, the President of the Chamber of Deputies, Eduardo Cunha, played a much greater role in Rousseff's impeachment than one would imagine possible for the office he occupied.

The Role of the President of the Lower House in Impeachment Officially, the President of the Chamber acts as the gatekeeper of impeachments: he or she is responsible for selecting which accusations offered against the President are to be investigated by a Commission of Impeachment, based on criteria of admissibility (*i.e.*, accusation relates to the President, describes valid impeachable offenses, etc).[352] Deputy Cunha, however, was accused of actively contributing to Rousseff's impeachability by using his office to damage her reputation and political capital, thus facilitating her removal. By using his prerogative of setting the Chamber's agenda, Cunha was said to have prioritized selecting bills with direct impact on the Rousseff administration, either by being highly unpopular (*e.g.*, bills reducing worker rights) or by encumbering the national economy to an extent that would make recovery from the crisis in the short-run difficult or unlikely (*e.g.*, increasing wages of federal

---

[350] *Denúncia por crime de responsabilidade (DCR) n. 1 de 2015*, p. 62. In the Constitution, items i. and ii. are categorized as violations against probe administration, and the remaining, as against the budgeting law.

[351] *Ibid.*, pp. 13–39. In simpler words: the national government took money that did not belong to it, from institutions it is supposed to oversee, to hide its negative economic results; it also usurped the Legislature's power of the purse by taking money without permission.

[352] Art. 14–16 of the Law of Impeachment (Law n. 1079 of 1950).

officers).[353] Given the political isolation of the Worker's Party in 2015 and 2016, these were offensives that Rousseff had little means of outmanoeuvring. The only leverage the party had in face of Cunha was that of shielding him against upcoming cassation procedures before the Ethics Committee, something that, however, the Worker's Party was unwilling to concede.[354]

Arguing on the supposed ulterior motives of Cunha's actions, many who supported Rousseff put the impeachment procedures in its totality in question, claiming that the perverse nature of its origin poisoned any potential outcome the procedures could produce. Though many Representatives were willing to concede that Cunha's conduct was suspicious and perhaps even deserving of its own removal procedures, the decision of accepting impeachment charges itself was not to be tainted by his bad reputation, because it not only answered a real demand from society, but also because it dealt with facts that were deserving of investigation and, if endorsed by the supermajority in Congress, of impeachment.[355]

Judiciousness of the Parliament as a Court Another issue that affected the perceived legitimacy of the procedures against Rousseff occurred during the roll-call vote for her impeachment by the plenum of the Chamber of Deputies. The event, which was enormously awaited and televised,[356] should have consisted in merely collecting yeas and nays from the 513 Deputies regarding their endorsement of the Impeachment Commission's report, which recommended impeachment. Quickly, however, the event became heated, as the involved Deputies used their 15 s of spotlight to promote themselves or send other signals to their constituencies that had little thematic pertinence with the impeachment vote. Beside the somewhat harmless but criticized conduct of the Deputies who dedicated their votes to their constituency, their grandchildren, God, or whoever else may be, there were those who took the opportunity to take victory laps on their opponents, instigating animosity. More dramatically, there were those who consciously misrepresented the content of the impeachment accusation, claiming the vote represented the expurgation of

[353] In detail: Deputy Silvio da Costa (PTdoB), *Diário da Câmara dos Deputados*, n. 55/2016, pp. 157 ff. See also Folha de São Paulo, October 18th, 2015: *"Cunha sequestrou o governo e a oposição"*.

[354] G1, December 2nd, 2015: *"Deputado do PT diz que vive dilema sobre Cunha no Conselho de Ética"*. Cunha was suspended from office by a decision of the Supreme Court in the next month and was later removed by the Chamber of Deputies. G1, May 5th, 2016: *"Liminar de Teori Zavascki suspende mandato de Cunha como deputado"*; G1, September 13th, 2016: *"Câmara cassa mandato de Eduardo Cunha por 450 votos a 10"*.

[355] *E.g., Diário da Câmara dos Deputados*, n. 54/2016, pp. 37–39, or *Diário do Senado Federal*, n. 140, pp. 69–70.

[356] The impeachment debate took place in three sessions preceding the vote and were also televised, but not in equal extent, leading many spectators to think that the superficial exchanges in the rollcall was the actual impeachment discussion. This misunderstanding was used by Rousseff supporters to question the procedures, charactering the impeachment decision as arbitrary and unfounded. For the debates, see *Diário da Câmara dos Deputados* n. 054, 055, and 056 of 2016 (April 16, 17, and 18th, respectively).

corruption from the country, or the victory of capitalism over communism, so on and so forth.[357]

This collection of unwarranted remarks, magnified by the vulgar exchange of physical and verbal abuse between some of the actors, led many of the spectators to question whether the Chamber of Deputies was indeed apt to decide the future of the country. Rousseff ended up being impeached by an overwhelming majority, but a bitter aftertaste was nonetheless left at the mouths of even those who supported the decision, generating some erosion of the popular support for Rousseff's removal in the next months.[358]

Trial and Conviction Before the Senate

Once the impeachment vote was approved in Chamber of Deputies, the decision was sent to the Senate to be ratified and so that impeachment could take effect (*i.e.,* cause impeachment and suspension from office) and the next steps of the trial could be planned more concretely (*i.e.,* establishing the trial's schedule and rules). Most importantly, this also meant electing another Special Commission of Impeachment composed by Senators, which would be responsible for examining the impeachment charges, producing further evidence, and drafting a final report that would be discussed during the trial itself.

Commission Composition and Even Playing Field One of the first issues raised in this phase pertained the partiality of those composing the Special Commission. Though extra-care was dedicated to giving representation to small parties in the Commission, the Worker's Party still felt its composition was stacked against Rousseff. In its view, the *elected* rapporteur for the Commission, Antonio Anastasia (PSDB), was not guaranteed to act impartially because he belonged to the same party as the lawyers who drafted the impeachment charges. In their argument, Senators from the Worker's Party claimed Anastasia was bound to rubberstamp the accusation's case in the final report purely out of partisan fidelity. Such arguments were further enhanced by the dispositions in the Parliamentary Code of Ethics (Art. 15, III) and Senate Bylaws (Art. 127) which prohibited accuser or accused to preside over Commissions on disciplinary issues or to be nominated to author its report.[359]

[357] *Diário da Câmara dos Deputados* n. 056/2016, pp. 56–120.

[358] From April to July, the popular support for Rousseff's impeachment would drop from 68% to 48%. BBC, July 26th, 2016: *"Nem Dilma, nem Temer: maioria da população quer eleição antecipada, aponta nova pesquisa"*.

[359] Part of the coup narratives claimed the impeachment was a vessel for the reversal of the results of the presidential election of 2014. Anastasia would be doing Aécio Neves' (Rousseff's opponent) bidding by recommending Rousseff's conviction to the plenum. Anastasia was, however, elected by the members of the Commission, who saw his background as professor of constitutional law as desirable for the position. *Comissão Especial de Impeachment no Senado Federal, Ata Circunstanciada*, first meeting, April 26th, 2016: pp. 5–15.

As troubling as they sound, such claims were quickly dismissed on technical grounds—essentially, argued the President of the Commission, Senator Anastasia could not be confused with the lawyers of his party or his party itself, nor could impeachment be confused with disciplinary hearings. Only those who authored the accusation piece could formally be considered accusers and thus also legally proscribed from presiding or reporting.[360] In line with impeachment theory, one could add that the standard of impartiality presupposed by this objection was arguably unfeasible in a parliamentary setting, particularly in highly polarized events such as impeachments. Every Representative can be said to have allegiance to one side of such matters, and no one can convincingly pose as a neutral, uninterested party in the same way a judge in a court of law would. The ulterior motives of Representatives can always be presumed from their previous statements and partisan affiliations, be it for or against the accused. As argued before, partiality in impeachments is an issue that is neutralized by high thresholds and decision-making by large, representative organs, where ample opportunity for defence and dissenting opinions are generated.[361] Particularly the latter was found in these procedures, with dissident voices being given opportunity to present their own dissenting report to the Senate—unlike was seen in Samper's case, for example.

Criminality Argument: Redux A second issue brought in this phase was a new take on the criminality argument, which is so typical of impeachments. In its original version, the criminality argument proposes that Presidents are not impeachable for constitutional violations or abuses of power, because, if such acts are *not* enshrined in a criminal code, then it must be because they are not serious enough to warrant the title of "crime" and, consequently, are not serious enough to justify a presidential removal.[362] The version presented by Rousseff's defence argued something similar, but on much less solid footing, given that Brazil's does indeed enshrine Rousseff's conduct both as crimes in the criminal code, as well as impeachable offenses, in the law of impeachment. The defence had to argue, therefore, from a sociological perspective of law, in which effectiveness of legal dispositions determines whether laws do really "exist" or, as dead letter, do not. In other words, the defence argued that, since previous Presidents committed similar violations but went unpunished, so should Rousseff also go unpunished, as her conduct was not really "criminal" either.[363]

[360] *Ibid.*, pp. 12–16.

[361] The Supreme Court answered this issue on these terms before. See ADPF 387 and MS n. 21,623.

[362] For a detailed account on this argument, see Labovitz 1978, pp. 38–45.

[363] *Comissão Especial de Impeachment no Senado Federal, Ata Circunstanciada,* fourth meeting, pp. 16689 ff. The defence did also challenge the existence of objective elements of the crime to claim that Rousseff's conduct was not criminal, arguing that the questioned activity did not constitute "credit operations". The authorities on the question (*i.e.,* audits, prosecutors, and the Court of Accounts), on the other hand, agreed on the illegality of the accounting activity but were ambiguous on who should be held responsible for the acts or to what extent. In the criminal sphere, two Ministers were convicted.

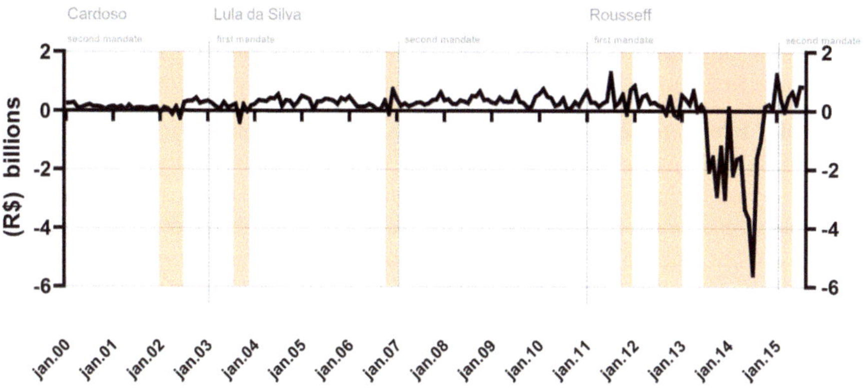

Fig. 3.5 Delays in obligatory spending, 2000–2016. Source: Own elaboration with data from Caixa Econômica Federal. Line indicates payment sum of obligatory spending, including salaries, pensions, and other social benefits. Deficits are highlighted

This argument, though bearing some truth, was not very convincing to the Senators, who saw qualitative differences between the conduct of Rousseff's predecessors and her own. While payment delays and the irregular enactment of credit are relatively common occurrences, never had they been committed with such frequency, intensity, and intent. Rousseff's predecessors had violated the budget in similar ways in about four opportunities, but which were excused by the Court of Accounts for their small dimension and for being caused by unforeseen events. The Rousseff administration, on the other hand, though also motivated by an event originally outside its control (droughts and economic shifts), integrated the dubious practices in its budgetary modus operandi, and kept pressing on despite the cautionary notes from its team of analysts and Congress. It systematically cheated on the national accounts between 2013 and 2015 to a degree that had no precedence in the history of the country, which thus justified the difference in treatment in the eyes of the Senators.[364]

The Problem of Proportionality The controversy of Rousseff's impeachment, however, was not whether she did or did not commit offenses, but if the offenses committed were sufficient to warrant an impeachment conviction. As the Brazilian Constitution happened to be interpreted by Deputy Cunha in the admission of the accusation piece,[365] Presidents could not be held accountable for actions that took place before their current mandate. This meant, in other words, that Rousseff was not to be held accountable for the mismanagement of the budget before 2015 (Fig. 3.5), when her second mandate started, and thus most infractions could not technically integrate the object of impeachment. By 2015, the imminent budget bust was already public, and the Rousseff administration was working on damage control—a few slip-

[364] As argued, for example, in *Diário do Senado Federal* n. 139/2016, pp. 26–27.

[365] *Diário da Câmara dos Deputados* n. 210/2015, pp. 42–47.

ups were still committed, but they paled in comparison to anything that came before. In a strictly legal sense, therefore, Senators were hard-pressed to find justifications that made Rousseff's 2015 violations fit the impeachment sanctions.

Informal Broadening of the Scope of Accusation The initial solution found by some Senators was to informally broaden the scope of accusation. Despite the constitutional limitations stablishing that impeachment could only reach the current mandate, some Senators chose to nonetheless consider the original charges. Others chose a more questionable approach and argued one should consider "the big picture" (*conjunto da obra*), that is, one should take in consideration the whole context of Rousseff's impeachment, with the economic crisis, the widespread public discontent, and the ever more present corruption in the national public administration, all of which were somehow being aggravated by Rousseff's stay in power and her incapacity to bring forth any policy shift. The argument, in other words, put the aspects of political opportunity in the front line of impeachment justifications, positing that the charges, while by themselves not massively reprehensible, warranted nonetheless punishment when all other aggravating circumstances were taken in consideration.[366]

A Half-Impeachment? Fitting Punishment to the Crime Such broadening of scope was still insufficient for many Senators to justify conviction, however. Many considered that, while removal from office was salutary to the country's immediate future, personally punishing Rousseff with disqualification would be excessive. As far as anyone could tell by the time, conviction entailed both sanctions (removal and disqualification) and the 1988 Constitution did not create any form of adjusting the severity of the consequences.[367] In a creative interpretation of the Collor precedent, however, the Justice presiding over Rousseff's trial suggested the consequences be voted separately, as when Collor resigned during his trial in 1992, Senators still insisted on voting for his disqualification, arguing that the object of impeachment was not exhausted by the President's ousting. In Rousseff's trial, he argued therefore, it would be within the scope of past practices to split the decision in two different votes, what did in fact happen: one vote succeeded and removed Rousseff from office, and another that failed and did not disqualify Rousseff for future public offices.[368]

Impeached Presidents Meet: Collor vs. Rousseff Finally, it is interesting to point out that Fernando Collor, the man whose ousting inspired many Latin American Parliaments to confront their leaders by means of impeachment, was back in politics

[366] *E.g., Diário do Senado Federal* n. 140/2016, pp. 104–105.

[367] As had been previously decided by the Supreme Court (MS 21,689/DF): "(. . .) the application of only removal from office or only of disqualification is not possible (. . .)"; "(. . .) article 52, §, of the Constitution does not stablish autonomous penalties (. . .)".

[368] *Diário do Senado Federal* n. 141/2016, pp. 12 ff. Conviction vote: 61 to 20; Disqualification vote: 42 to 36. Only 60% of those who voted for Rousseff's conviction also voted for her disqualification.

as a Senator in this time. During Rousseff's trial, Collor shared his thoughts on the conditions given to his impeachment versus those given to her, and indirectly pointed out to the dissonance between the coup narrative now argued by the Worker's Party and their previous uncritical support of the impeachment against himself. In short, he remembered how much quicker his procedure was, how much less cautious Parliament had been in its conduction, and how much more questionable was the evidence laid out against him. In his view, if the Worker's Party wanted to claim the impeachment against Rousseff was a sham, so should they do the same in relation to the one against himself. Naturally, neither the Worker's Party nor Collor was ready to recognize the merits of each other's arguments, and both parties continued seeing only their impeachments as shams, while that of their opponent, as entirely legitimate.[369]

3.2.1.8 Rethinking and Doublethinking Impeachment: Michel Temer (2017), Brazil

A Historical Narrative

Michel Temer's (PMDB, *Brazilian Democratic Movement Party*) case is in many regards a continuation of Rousseff's. Many elements that were conducive to Rousseff's impeachment and conviction remained present for the *interim* (May 12th to August 2016) and, later, permanent (September 2016 to December 2018) presidency of Temer. The judiciary and its anticorruption task force gave no quarter to the political establishment. As a result, executive instability kept looming around, leading to parliamentary deadlocks, and curtailing the approval of reforms deemed urgent by the government. In effect, within the first 6 months of the Temer administration, six of its Ministers were fired or forced to resign due to their involvement in corruption.[370]

Temer himself was under attack in many fronts as well. One of the attacks had been initiated even before Rousseff's impeachment and targeted the validity of the outcomes of the 2014 presidential election. The Rousseff-Temer slate was accused of abusing economic power and of committing campaign financing fraud—an accusation that became increasingly stronger with developments of the anticorruption operations.[371] Though Temer ultimately narrowly survived this threat, the leaked testimonies and wiretappings from the investigations, some of them involving Temer passively hearing suggestions from implicated businessmen

[369] *Diário do Senado Federal* n. 64/2016, pp. 98, and n. 140/2016, pp. 55.

[370] G1, May 12th, 2018: *"Aos 2 anos, governo Temer festeja economia, mas enfrenta impopularidade, denúncias e crise política"*; Exame, November 25th, 2016: *"6 baixas em 6 meses: por que estes ministros de Temer caíram"*.

[371] G1, June 9th, 2016: *"Relator no TSE vê abuso em repasses da Odebrecht para campanha de 2014"*.

about bribing of federal judges and prosecutors,[372] made for one of the most tense trials in Brazilian history.[373]

Still during Rousseff's trial, some members of Congress were already seeking to impeach Temer on similar grounds, as he was said to have allowed such conduct as a Vice-President while Rousseff was traveling on official missions.[374] The managers of accusation in the Rousseff case were, moreover, tricked by some Deputies into admitting that Temer's actions were indeed impeachable offenses. Some of these Deputies even motioned for Rousseff and Temer to undergo the impeachment trial together—a motion that was denied by the President of the Chamber, Eduardo Cunha.[375] Fortunately for Temer, both Cunha and his successor in the Chamber's presidency, Rodrigo Maia (DEM, *Democrats*), remained faithful allies and shielded him from attacks until the end of his mandate.[376]

What no President of the Chamber could stop, however, were motions of impeachment presented by the General Prosecutor, Rodrigo Janot.[377] Since these motions bypassed the scrutiny of the President of the Chamber, whoever was in charge, ally or not, could not act as a gatekeeper. The scope of action available to the Prosecutor General was much more limited than what was available to Congress, however. Janot could present only impeachment accusations that involved common crimes, which limited the kinds of abuses available and raised legal standards to be observed during the procedures significantly. Moreover, by involving common crimes, the Supreme Court became the official Court of Impeachments, in case the Chamber of Deputies did in fact impeach President Temer.[378]

As robust as Janot could build his impeachment cases, reaching Temer was a much more difficult task than Rousseff. Temer was the party leader of the country's largest party at the time; he had spent decades inside Congress leading and building ties with the political establishment; he was an influential academic of constitutional law, meaning he was not only politically influential, but also arguably possessed the technical knowledge and experience to face all kinds of challenges that surfaced. Even on the slight off-chance impeachment was approved, Temer had close ties with

---

[372] Consultor Jurídico, December 24th, 2017: "*Retrospectiva: Gravação de conversa entre Temer e Joesley batista foi destaque em maio*"; UOL Notícias, May 18th, 2017: *"OAB vê crime de responsabilidade em diálogo e vai pedir impeachment de Temer"*.

[373] El País, June 9th, 2017: "*Herman Benjamin: o voto do Ministro do TSE pela cassação de Temer*".

[374] G1, December 8th, 2015: *"Temer assinou abertura de créditos suplementares"*.

[375] The Supreme Court was issued to review the decision (MS 34,099/DF) but dismissed the case. G1, April 6th 2016: *"Celso de Mello nega incluir Temer em processo de impeachment de Dilma"*.

[376] Maia's refusal to consider impeachment accusations was eventually judicialized (MS 34,970 AgR/DF), but the Supreme Court dismissed the case in its understanding of a political question (*interna corporis acta*).

[377] Agência Câmara de Notícias, June 29th, 2017: *"Câmara recebe denúncia de Janot contra Temer*"; and September 21st, 2017: *"Chega à Câmara segunda denúncia contra Michel Temer"*.

[378] Art. 86 of the 1988 Constitution, and art. 217 of the Chamber's bylaws (Resolution n. 17/1989). See Inq 4483/DF (decision of Justice Edson Fachin).

some of the Justices of the Supreme Court, arguably tipping the scales in his favour. Conversely, none of these assets could really be claimed by Rousseff, who, until achieving the presidency, spent most of her political career on the side-lines of the Executive branch and was known for being inflexible.

Indeed, Temer's intent and prowess in surviving in the presidency were made evident, as he arguably dedicated most of his efforts into managing Congress. Two of his most impactful measures were the refinancing of tax debit (*Refis,* or Fiscal Recovery Program) to the business community and the financing of parliamentary pet projects (*emendas parlamentares*, or parliamentary amendments to the budget plan). With the first, nearly half trillion reais in credit owned to the state was 'refinanced' to ensure short term liquidity and granted up to 99% of debt pardon to companies, sacrificing about 63 billion of state revenue for the next 3 years. With the second, Temer redirected about 4 billion reais from the executive federal budget to feed the pet projects of Deputies at the eve of impeachment votes—those who openly defended his stay were promised one million extra in relation to the rest.[379]

Temer was also shielded by some legal innovations. One of them was set in motion still by the Rousseff administration itself, as part of a plan of avoiding repetition of the impeachable offenses in 2016. Rousseff had submitted a bill that increased the threshold of acceptable issuance of credit without parliamentary approval, making budgeting more flexible and thus less likely to turn on red flags from the Court of Accounts, as it had happened in 2013, 2014, and to a lesser extent, 2015.[380] The budget projection was also much more realistic than the previous years, making it harder for Temer to repeat Rousseff's behaviour.

The only factors speaking against Temer's presidency were his rampant unpopularity and weak claim to legitimacy. Temer inherited Rousseff's low levels of approval and plummeted them even further, remaining between 13 and 3% throughout his mandate. With the economy in shambles (stagnant GDP growth, rising unemployment and inequality, among other things),[381] close proximity corrupt actors, and a policy plan that strived to austerity to a much larger degree than Rousseff's, the Temer administration was frequently met with hostility in public appearances, such as in the 2018 Olympic Games.[382] Perhaps for the first time in history, Brazilians were truly questioning the place of the office of Vice-President in

---

[379] Debit relief by itself is no indicator of parliamentary management, especially in times of crisis. What makes these pardons look suspicious are their beneficiaries, which have significant influence on Congress. El País, August 15th, 2017: *"O plano da Câmara para perdoar 543 bilhões que empresários devem à União"*; Deutsche Welle, August 1st, 2017: *"Quanto a tentativa de salvar Temer de denúncia custa ao Brasil"*.

[380] Minutia of budgeting rules are redefined yearly by law. The threshold's calculation basis is defined by the budget projection. An inflated projection makes rules harder to satisfy, as was the case with Rousseff. Jornal Nexo, September 8th, 2016: *"O que diz a lei sancionada pelo governo Temer sobre créditos suplementares"*.

[381] G1, May 12th, 2018: *"Aos 2 anos, governo Temer festeja economia, mas enfrenta impopularidade, denúncias e crise política"*.

[382] Veja, September 7th, 2016: *"Temer é vaiado no início, meio e fim dos Jogos Olímpicos"*.

the Constitution, as well as realizing how little attention had been given to past Vice-Presidents, many of them unknown by the electorate at large. Despite all this and the support for impeachment soaring at 81%, not much momentum was built in support of Temer's ousting.[383] A few protests took place, but none of them in the intensity observed during the Rousseff administration,[384] which, as it should be noted, needed years and a lot of organization to develop the momentum observed in 2016.

In summary, though President Michel Temer found himself deep in scandals, popular rejection, and unfavourable economic circumstances, he was able to manage Congress to shield himself from his political opponents. The fact that popular movements started to dwindle after Rousseff's removal, may have enabled him to achieve such an outcome, as the low visibility of his impeachment procedures allowed Deputies to dismiss even the most damning evidence and accusations without fear of political or electoral repercussions.

Impeachment Attempts

> Brazil bleeds, it is true. But I've never seen someone use ticks to stanch a bleeding.
> Deputy André Figueiredo on the dissonances of impeachment rejection[385]

Michel Temer faced two impeachment attempts in close succession. The first dealt with an accusation of bribery, in which Temer would have received at least 500,000 reais (approx. US$ 160,000 at the time) from a major Brazilian holding (*Grupo J&F*) to sort out issues it had with federal regulatory agencies, among other things.[386] The second dealt with criminal acts discovered in the same investigation, in which Temer would have asked members of the mentioned holding to silence potential witnesses and whistle-blowers to a racket he allegedly had with other members of Congress. He would be answering for two crimes, therefore, obstruction of justice and

[383] The poll was conducted 1 week before Temer's impeachment vote at the Chamber of Deputies. Uol Notícias, July 31st, 2017: *"81% dos eleitores defendem processo contra Temer, diz pesquisa IBOPE"*.

[384] Protests did not exceed one to two hundred thousand participants, in the most favourable measurements. Some general strikes occurred when passing harsher policies such as decade-long budget cuts or social security reforms, but they did not achieve broad popular adhesion. El País, May 25th, 2017: *"Em dias de protesto em Brasília, 'Diretas já' começa a caminhar no Congresso"*; G1, August 7th, 2016: "*25 estados e DF têm protestos contra Michel Temer*"; Carta Capital, March 16th, 2017: "*Protestos contra a reforma da Previdência*".

[385] *Diário da Câmara dos Deputados* n. 130, August 3rd, 2017, p. 224. Figueiredo referred to the blame shifting towards the left-leaning portion of Rousseff's administration for the authorship of the crisis, whereas the parties in the succeeding presidential cabinet remained mostly the same and had obvious contributions towards that outcome (*e.g.*, pushing for 2015's '*austericide*').

[386] *Solicitação para instauração de processo* n. 1/2017 (Inq 4517/DF, or originally Inq 4483/DF). The accusation was offered by the General Prosecutor on June 29th, 2017. It was rejected by the Chamber of Deputies on August 2nd, 2017. 227 votes were in favour of impeachment (44.2%), 263 against (2/3 threshold, or 342 votes needed). Two deputies abstained and 19 were absent.

racketeering (*formação de quadrilha*).[387] With charges that constituted common crimes rather than constitutional violations, Michel Temer became the first Brazilian President in history to potentially face impeachment in its judicial form, as the 1988 Constitution stablishes a whole different procedure for such cases.

Differences from the Rousseff Impeachment: The Unbalanced Nature of Brazil's Predominantly Judicial Impeachments The differences in procedure on impeachment accusations that involve common crimes and those that involve constitutional violations go well beyond just having a judicial organ responsible for the final decision. While that is certainly a feature which may greatly favour leniency towards the President, as discussed in other parts of this book (see Sect. 4.5), other issues have shown to have great impact. Indeed, neither of these two impeachment attempts went so far as to the trial stage. Instead, they were quashed at an early stage through other practices that reveal this modality's particular tendency towards leniency also in the small portions that take place in Congress.

Intermediated Accusation and Its Limited Opportunities for Arguing a Case The first thing that comes to attention is the odd relation the General Prosecutor has with the Lower House. The General Prosecutor, when asking for a presidential impeachment, does not address the Lower House directly, but instead requests it the Supreme Court, who directs the investigation's discovery to the Lower House. If the House considers the investigation to be appropriate, it will produce a report recommending or not the impeachment. What ends up being voted in the impeachment vote is not the accusation's case *per se*, but the Commission's report. The Commission and the defence get to present their case to the plenum before the vote. However, if both recommend the rejection of the impeachment, there is effectively no case being made for the accusation and only defence arguments get exposition. No accusation management team, no author of the accusation piece, nor the General Prosecutor gets a voice to ensure a balanced debate takes place.[388] The only opportunity the General Prosecutor or those supporting the impeachment got to *fully* make their case was in the scope of the Commission that precedes the impeachment vote, which does not come with a comparable level of publicity to anything done by the plenum.

Grand Rubber-Stamp of the Nation In a sense, therefore, the procedure failed to serve as a "grand inquest of the nation", given how little importance and visibility

[387] *Solicitação para instauração de processo* n. 2/2017 (Inq 4483/DF and Inq 4327/DF). The accusation was offered by the General Prosecutor on September 22nd, 2017. It was rejected by the Chamber of Deputies on October 25th, 2017. 233 votes were in favour of impeachment (45.4%), 251 against (2/3 threshold, or 342 votes needed). Two deputies abstained and 25 were absent.

[388] See the discussion in *Diário da Câmara dos Deputados* n. 129, August 2nd, 2017, pp. 127 ff. Commission members who wrote dissenting opinions asked for an opportunity to make their case, but their demands were dismissed for lacking statutory support. They could only speak for 15 s to state their vote or, under agreement, use the statutory 5–10 min guaranteed to their party leaders in such procedures. By contrast, the defence and the commission rapporteur had 50 min combined to argue in favour of Temer.

was given to the alleged misconduct of the President.[389] Although the official investigation and the Commission produced sufficient and compelling material, it stayed mostly limited to the written form, leaving out an opportunity for most of the population and, realistically, even for most representatives to meaningfully engage with the supposed presidential misconduct.

The Presidency of the Chamber intervenes: strict adherence to the bylaws This whole situation could have been avoided, however. As mentioned in previous chapters, the rules of impeachment often come with gaps and vices, since they are rarely ever used, and their true consequences come to light only when put to practice. Congress has competence to fix said gaps and vices before they get to undermine the procedures, and, indeed, such competence was generally employed at the start of every impeachment commented in this book. In this particular instance, however, the President of the Chamber Rodrigo Maia was adamant about keeping close loyalty to the text of the Chamber's bylaws, after attempts of finding common ground had failed.[390] Such was arguably a rationalization to a different fact perhaps, namely that Maia was closely aligned with Temer and that adherence or deviation from the text was, in reality, only permissible inasmuch it could be instrumentalized in the favour of the latter. Eduardo Cunha's behaviour (see the Rousseff case), by contrast, was much more permissible. Such fact became particularly clear in the impeachment vote under Maia's presidency, in which most Deputies had no more than exact 15 s to state their vote before having their microphones cut out, whereas under Cunha's, they would a much longer chance to state their reasons and values, on top of a longer period for debate and a flexible grace period so that deputies could conclude their remarks. Cunha was also much more permissive to personal attacks against the presidency, which may also have played a role creating an environment more conducive to a successful ousting.

Accusation of Double Standards The mentioned difference in procedure brought up accusations of unequal treatment being applied to both Presidents. This discussion was even more pronounced in relation to the impeachable offenses in question, however. In the eyes of Rousseff supporters, there was a clear dissonance between the Rousseff and the Temer impeachment, given that the accusations against the latter were much more serious, reprehensible, and clear in implicating the exclusive and personal agency of the President. Additionally, Temer had also been accused

[389] Additionally, close to half of the debate time was spent on the discussion of whether the impeachment vote should be ended precociously, as requested by Temer's party. Such act forced the vote to take place with fewer deputies, increasing the likelihood of acquittal. *Diário da Câmara dos Deputados* n. 130, August 3rd, 2017, pp. 63–99. Further, unlike in Rousseff's impeachment, access to Congress was restricted to the public and the vote was televised at a time most were at work. *Ibid.*, pp. 193–194.

[390] *Diário da Câmara dos Deputados* n. 129, August 2nd, 2017, p. 130.

before of committing the same impeachable offenses as Rousseff, but the charges were shelved by the President of the Chamber of Deputies.[391]

Political Opportunity: Context and Alternative Resolutions The main justification to such apparent disparity resided in the political dimension of impeachments. There were naturally legally driven arguments for rejecting Temer's impeachment as well, but the Deputies were generally in a consensus the that the accusations were serious and needed investigation. The main point of divergence was whether the charges were to be investigated and trialled immediately or after the presidential mandate. In that regard, a minority of Deputies (but still in a number sufficient to frustrate impeachment) considered that submitting the country to a prolonged period of uncertainty would yield negative results that outweighed the positive brought by impeachment. As the Commission Rapporteur set the tone of the discussion:

> The reason for the constitutional norm [on impeachment procedures for common crimes] is to allow the competent power the examination of whether there may be prevalence of national interest over the initiation of the [criminal] procedures. There is no harm to justice in (. . .) the Chamber's decision of selecting a more appropriate opportunity for the criminal suit. (. . .) Once the presidential mandate is concluded, he will answer to the Supreme Court for his indictment (. . .). Allowing the criminal suit means suspending the President from office in a crucial moment of the country's restauration (. . .) which currently shows signs of recovery.[392]

Counterpoint: Risks of a Compromised Presidency As the opposition noticed, however, these were very abstract, perhaps speculative considerations that were meaning to outweigh other real and imminent dangers. There was no guarantee that justice would find its way otherwise or that the modest improvement of the circumstances of the crisis were to the merit of the Temer administration. There were, however, very real risks in leaving a highly suspected officer with access to so many powers, including some to frustrate his own accountability. And the intention to frustrate accountability was palpable in the evidence and the accusations related to obstruction of justice. As one Deputy put it:

> These are not conjectures. They are recordings, depositions, images. It is shown in images: Rocha Loures [Temer's former aide] running with a suitcase stuffed with half a million in cash. It is not acceptable to sweep this under the rug (. . .). The President hosted criminals in the presidential palace in the dead of night, for conversations not in the least republican. It was taped, they engaged in shady dealings. (. . .) It is unacceptable that the President may use

[391] Folha de São Paulo, May 1st, 2016: *"Cunha arquiva pedido de abertura de impeachment contra Temer"*.

[392] Paulo Abi-Ackel (PSDB, Brazilian Social-Democratic Party) in *Diário da Câmara dos Deputados* n. 130, August 3rd, 2017, pp. 26–27. Abi-Ackel did consider some of the legal arguments superficially, though mostly dismissing the evidence as unreliable (*e.g.*, suspected tampering of audio recordings of Temer discussing bribes or obstruction of justice). Contrary to expectations, the PSDB leadership instructed the party to vote against the Commission's report, despite integrating the government, instigating conflict during the procedures and calls for the renunciation of their cabinet positions. *Ibid.*, pp. 213–216.

> the pen to embarrass Parliament (. . .) especially so because the pen that endorses peace is the same that orders war: [the pen] condemns, kills, and buries humanity's dreams depending on whose hands hold it.[393]

Though conflicting among themselves, both arguments are consistent with concerns found in the study of impeachment theory and history. Impeachments are not only ambiguous in their confluence of legal and political dimensions, but bring within themselves ambiguities of second order, namely in the multiplicity of goals sought through the introduction of the mechanism, such as in its attempt of generating responsible and diligent, though nonetheless balanced and stable governments. In Rousseff's impeachment, the push for responsible government was able to overwhelm concerns of balance and stability, resulting in her removal from office. In Temer's, by contrast, the Chamber of Deputies remained practically divided, resulting in a victory of stability by default—an outcome to which impeachment is biased towards given its high approval thresholds.

3.2.1.9 Bridging Normalcy and Revolution: Sebastián Piñera (2019), Chile

A Historical Narrative

Latin America's latest impeachment case to reach closure was that of the Chilean President Sebastián Piñera. Piñera was throughout his long involvement in politics (Senator 1990–1998, president of the centre-right-wing party *Renovación Nacional* 2001–2004, presidential candidate 2005, 2009 and 2017, and President in 2010–2014 and 2018–2021)[394] also a prolific businessman and investor, a fact that boosted his political career as it served as proof of his managerial competences and acumen, while also at times putting his intentions under suspicion. Indeed, Piñera was so successful as a businessman that he became one of Chile's top ten richest citizens,[395] and rose to be one of Chile's most respected and prominent voices regarding the economy, having his expertise much sought by the Media.[396] Piñera did, however, also attract a significant amount of controversy towards his economic activity due to his proximity to power, which often seemed too favourable to his

[393] Pompeo de Mattos (PDT, Democratic Worker's Party) in *Ibid.*, pp. 44–45.

[394] Chilean Government's website, access January 18th, 2022: https://www.gob.cl/instituciones/presidencia/.

[395] According to Forbes, Piñera ranked n. 1064 as the World's richest persons in 2022 (US$ 2.7 billion net worth). He is said to have made fortune primarily through credit card and airline companies. After his 2010 election, he unloaded his stakes at the Chilean airline LAN for US$ 1.5 billion. *Forbes* website, "*Sebastián Piñera and Family*", accessed January 18th of 2022: https://www.forbes.com/profile/sebastian-pinera/?sh=10191227a75d.

[396] Piñera being, furthermore, a Harvard-taught economist, who also lectured economics in three different Chilean universities, also contributed to his expert status.

interests.[397] The two impeachment attempts commented in this section are intimately connected with this background, which were arguably symptomatic of larger, deep-seated issues of the Chilean political system, namely one that created economic inequalities while safeguarding the irresponsibility and irresponsiveness of those in power.[398] To understand how this is the case, a closer look at Piñera's promises and achievements in the presidency is needed.

Piñera became President for the first time in 2010, as part of the so-called 'Coalition for Change' (*Coalición por el Cambio*), which consisted in a partnership of right and centre-right political parties that grew apart or never joined the hegemonic grand coalition that ruled Chile since its re-democratization in 1990, known as 'the *Concertación*' (*Concertación por la Democracia, i.e.,* Coalition for Democracy).[399] Part of the electoral success he achieved that year was predicated on his recognition of the main appeal of his opponents, namely their preoccupation with social inequalities and the rooting of democracy, while offering an alternative to their shortcomings, such as their recurrent failure in curbing corruption or in breeding a

---

[397] Piñera's family had close ties with Augusto Pinochet's dictatorial administration (1973–1990), which was suspected of having influenced a lenient outcome regarding criminal accusations of fraud Sebastián Piñera faced in 1982. *La Nacional*, June 28th, 2009: "*Nunca inocente*". More direct influence of power was argued, for example, in the *Caso Chispas* (1997), which involved the alleged acquisition of stocks by Piñera at (overly) advantageous prices, and a case of insider trading (2009). See *El Mercurio*, April 12th, 2009 (updated): "*Sebastián Piñera paga hoy la multa y Cueto decide apelar*"; *Radio Cooperativa*, January 12th, 2006: "*El Caso Chispas*".

[398] Due to space constraints, these issues will not be described in detail. A few facts about Chile must be known nonetheless: i. The end of the dictatorship did not result in the unequivocal condemnation of its abuses; ii. Democracy, instead, inherited many highly conservative institutions tailored to uphold the unaccountability and unresponsiveness of those in power (*e.g.*, the '*leyes de amarre*', a set of laws that entrenched Pinochet's personnel in positions of power and heavily favoured their interests over competing groups); iii. Society, moreover, changed in a much faster pace than institutions (*e.g.*, homosexual relations were only decriminalized in 1999, divorce was only legally introduced in 2004); iv. Participation in and regard for politics suffered steady and significant erosion (*e.g.*, turnout in elections fell from over 80% in the 1980s to less than 50% in the 2010s); v. Although the country became richer, entering the World Bank's high-income bracket in 2012, and a significant part of the population was lifted from poverty, inequality fell at much slower rate; vi. Such uneven growth meant a compression of the middle and lower classes' purchasing power, resulting in one of the highest perceptions of unfair income distribution in Latin America; vii. Compounded with the permanence of market liberalization policies that greatly reduced social safety nets, citizens became prone to indebtedness, particularly affecting young adults (18–39 years old, 54.5% in debt, in 2017), situation which became even more widespread after the COVID pandemic. For details, see Morales Quiroga (2020); Cornejo-Saavedra et al. (2017); Heiss (2017); Sanhueza and Mayer (2011); Diario UChile, February 18th, 2021: "*Estudio señala que 65% de los chilenos se endeudan para enfrentar gastos de marzo*"; Nación, April 13th, 2003: "*Pepito paga doble*".

[399] For an account of the *Concertación's* achievements and shortcomings, see Oppenheim (2007), pp. 169 ff.; Avendaño Pavez (2013), pp. 183 ff. The main *pathos* the *Concertación* developed over the years was that of not living up to its promises, *i.e.*, of running a centre-left political platform, but never fully implementing it due to concerns of governability. So many concessions were made to the conservative wings of the coalition or the opposition, that the electoral program found itself constantly debased, slowly alienating the constituency.

sense of economic security. Piñera, therefore, rebranded his political persona as a centrist, moralizing alternative to the increasingly worn-out centre-left of the *status quo,* distancing himself, thus, from his right-wing and somewhat *Pinochetismo*-aligned history.[400]

This election was part of a rearrangement phase within Chile's political elites. Part of the *Concertación* fragmented into smaller unions with clearer identities, and the core parties shifted further and more decidedly leftward, incorporating the Communist Party and popular leaders who became prominent in student protests that took place in 2011.[401] Moving away from grand coalitions proved an effective electoral strategy, as Piñera's opposition won the next elections in a landslide by marketing itself more unambiguously as the solution to Chile's mounting social tensions. Rather than being subtly apologetic for the interests of corporations, the new administration (Michelle Bachelet, 2014–2017) accepted that the richer would have to make some sacrifices in name of curbing inequality and other social grievances, particularly those related to affordable education. In practice, however, the administration delivered outcomes that still resembled those of the *Concertación*: the central promises were delivered, but without the expected 'oomph'. Other promises were met with stalemates by Chile's highly conservative political elites, and achievements eventually became overshadowed by accusations of being responsible for the slowing down of the country's economic growth, as well as by a few corruption scandals close to the presidency.[402]

Sebastián Piñera's second presidency (2018–2021), therefore, was one that inherited a people who had grown particularly wary of politics, but more importantly perhaps, a people who had become more conscious that the unchanging ways of Chilean politics was not only rooted in its political elites but was also something that had been a system feature from the start. Indeed, from the 2010s onwards the talks of political reform became more recurrent, albeit still somewhat timid. The 2011 student protests and the underwhelming education and tax reforms of the Bachelet administration had been strong indicators that meaningful change was essentially precluded under the 1980 Constitution.[403]

---

[400] El Mostrador, January 3rd, 2010: *"Piñera da a conocer principales propuestas de su futuro Gobierno".*

[401] Diario UChile, August 19th, 2013: "*Voces fuera del pacto Nueva Mayoría*".

[402] France24, March 11th, 2018: *"Chile: ¿cómo recordará la historia a Michelle Bachelet? Un análisis de su legado".* See also Madariaga 2019, for details on the stalemates, and Diario UChile, March 20th, 2018: *"Legado Bachelet en Educación: ¿cambio de paradigma o maquillaje?",* for the limitations of the education reform.

[403] Heiss (2017), pp. 472–473. As Heiss, pp. 474–475, summarizes it: "The 1980 constitution in contrast [to the liberal-constitutional principle of limited government] restrains people by 'turning its back' and 'neutralizing' the democratic principle (. . .). It is rather the result of a radicalism that forcefully imposes a status quo that could never have been achieved except by the force of a military dictatorship. It is not moderate, centrist politics, but a polarizing right-wing veto against democratic decision-making".

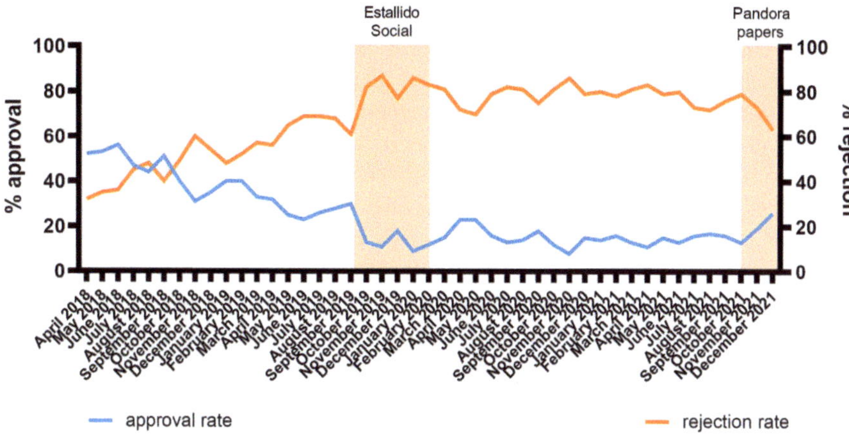

Fig. 3.6 Piñera administration's approval and rejection rates, 2018–2021. Source: Own elaboration with data from Agenda Criteria's report of December 2021, p. 9

Despite being 'more of the same' in many senses, Piñera managed to achieve electoral success foremostly by promising to set the country back on its path to robust economic growth, one that would be unimpaired by the 'opportunistic' and 'unrealistic' ideas of socialist utopia of his opposition.[404] Piñera's greatest legacy had undeniably been the robust GDP growth experienced in his first administration, an yearly average of 5.3%, much greater than the opposition's 1.7% average.[405]

Indeed, Piñera's first year in power delivered the regain of GDP growth reaching up to 4%, which could be explained in the renewed trust of foreign investors.[406] The said economic growth, however, followed the old pattern of being disproportionately concentrated on the richest. In other words, inequality, unemployment, costs of living, and social insecurity kept on the rise, eroding Piñera's popularity at a much faster rate than his achievements managed to improve.[407] As may be ascertained in Fig. 3.6, Piñera's administration suffered the loss of over 30 points of approval between June 2018 and June 2019, which, despite being in of itself a worrisome finding, still paled in face of what was about to come.

Starting on October 18th of 2019 in Santiago, following the announcement of a raise in public transport fares,[408] Chile witnessed its largest and longest popular uproar since its redemocratization. In a similar fashion to the protests observed against Dilma Rousseff in 2013 (the Journeys of June), peaceful protests escalated into riots and confrontation between protestors and state security forces, particularly

[404] See Piñera (2017), pp. 23–27, available at: https://www.sebastianpinera.cl/images/programa-SP.pdf.

[405] El Mostrador, October 20th, 2017: *"¿Adónde se fue el crecimiento de Piñera?"*.

[406] La Tercera, March 18th, 2019: "PIB *de Chile creció 4% en 2018 gracias a la inversión*".

[407] 24Horas, October 31st, 2018: *"Desempleo en Chile vuelve a subir y llega al 7.3%"*.

[408] Biobio Chile, October 4th, 2019: *"Cambio en tarifa de pasajes"*.

the *Carabineros* (national law enforcement/military forces).[409] The shocking scenes of state sanctioned violence, followed by the government's immediate response of invoking the national security law (Law n. 12,917) and decreeing state of emergency,[410] ensured that the protests gained support from larger groups within society and spread throughout the country. In matter of days, on the 25th of the same month, over one million protestors were in Santiago alone, with the confrontation taking 19 lives, and leaving 600 injured, as well as other 6000 detained.[411] The demands for reduction of fare prices were quickly overshadowed by new and more deeply rooted demands evidenced by the government's response. The whole situation was seen as symptomatic of the government's insensibility and unwillingness to resolve the plights of the lower and middle classes, while also resembling Pinochet's dictatorship too much for comfort in its disproportionate use of repression.

The *Estallido Social* (social outburst), as the event would become known, lasted until March of 2019, a total of 166 days, and resulted in a massive loss of support for Piñera's government. Piñera's approval fell around another 20 points and his rejection soared to 84%. While such numbers are quantitatively smaller than the losses of the previous year, qualitatively they were possibly much more meaningful, as they indicated that even the more principled supporters were becoming sceptical and were too partaking on a transformative process.[412] Arguably, the abuses had become difficult to justify in face of the many damning accusations brought forward by many institutions regarding the conducting of the crisis:

> The intention of the Chilean security forces is clear: injure those who protest to discourage demonstrations, including going to the extremes of using torture and sexual violence against protestors. Instead of taking steps to stop the serious crisis of human rights, the authorities have, under the command of Sebastián Piñera, sustained their politics of punishment for more than a month, causing more people to sum themselves to the shocking number of victims that grows to this day.[413]

The public outcry was so intense that the Piñera administration eventually gave in. As *mea culpa*, 8 ministers were jettisoned from the presidential cabinet, most

[409] The protests started as mass evasion from payment of the transport fares. As a response, the national government put the *Carabineros* up to the task of enforcing payment, resulting in brutal confrontation between both groups. See Deutsche Welle, November 25th, 2019: *"La cronología del estallido social de Chile"*.

[410] Biobio Chile, October 18th, 2019: "*Gobierno invocará Ley de Seguridad del Estado por manifestaciones en el Metro*"; La Tercera, October 19th, 2019: *"¿Qué significa el Estado de Emergencia decretado por el Presidente?"*.

[411] El País, October 25th, 2019: "*Al menos un millón de personas protestan en Santiago contra Piñera*".

[412] As evidenced, for example, by an audio leaked of the First Lady's stating: "It is like an alien, a foreign invasion and we don't have the tools to deal with. (. . .) We will have to reduce our privileges and share with the others". La Tercera, October 22nd, 2019: *"Cecilia Morel acapara la atención de medios internacionales"*.

[413] As stated by Erika Guevara Rosa, Director of Amnesty International for the Americas. See Amnesty International, November 21st, 2019: *"Chile: Política deliberada para dañar a manifestantes apunta a responsabilidad"*.

notably Andrés Chadwick, the Minister of Interior responsible for invoking the law of national security and also a former outspoken supporter of the Pinochet dictatorship.[414] An agenda of concessions was also negotiated, offering a referendum on a new constitution and an abstract commitment to social justice.[415] Despite these concessions, the opposition still came forward with impeachment charges against Piñera a few days after, on November 19th, 2019. The attempt failed, however, as Piñera still held substantial and unwavering support in Congress.[416]

Though Piñera survived the toughest phase of his term, the period of turbulence was far from over. The next year the global SARS-CoV-2 pandemic put Chile under serious humanitarian and economic strains, once again breeding popular discontent and confirming the limited capacity of the country's social safety nets. Foremostly the prospects of the private pension system, which under normal circumstances already led over 80% of its beneficiaries to live with considerably less than minimum wage, were looking particularly grim.[417] Congress approved early withdrawals of pension funds so that citizens could endure the economic retraction caused by the pandemic, an act that was fiercely opposed and judicialized by the Piñera administration. The negative consequences such withdrawals could have on the long run led Piñera to dub the measures as short-sighted and populistic, earning him more public discontent. Piñera's approval reached its all-time lowest in November of 2020 (7%), when masses took the streets to protest his conduct and ask for his resignation.[418]

As revolting as the situation was for many Chileans, the outrage did not produce mobilization comparable to that of the *Estallido Social*, and Piñera's presidency did not have to face any real threat. A real threat only emerged in October 2021, when the release of the Pandora Papers brought new accusations, as it suggested the President had engaged in illicit transactions with mining companies during his first mandate and had hidden assets in tax havens.[419] Though the accusations had little effect on the President's already devasted reputation, the opposition was quick to seek accountability. Given the slight shifts in balance of power between government and opposition, this attempt was more successful than the last, reaching trial phase before the Senate, but failed, nonetheless.[420]

---

414 The Guardian, October 29th, 2019: *"Chile: protesters light bonfires and clash with police despite cabinet reshuffle"*.

415 Senado de Chile, November 15th, 2019: *"Logran histórico acuerdo para Nueva Constitución"*.

416 El Mostrador, December 12th, 2019: *"Resultado predecible: por falta de votos, Piñera se salva de acusación tras aprobarse la 'cuestión previa'"*.

417 Financial Times, November 15th, 2020: *"Chile's famed pensions system faces an existential crisis"*. For a general outlook on the pandemic confrontation policies in Chile, see Heiss (2020).

418 Euronews, November 28th, 2020: *"Disturbios en Chile durante las protestas contra Sebastián Piñera"*.

419 France24, October 8th, 2021: *"Chile's President Pinera under the lens over Pandora Papers leak"*.

420 Senado de Chile, November 16th, 2021: *"Acusación contra Presidente Piñera: Senado no reúne el quórum"*.

Impeachment Attempts

> To them, Chadwick is not responsible, nor is Minister Blumel or President Piñera. Nobody is responsible. In reality, they are only updating a sadly known playbook like it happened a couple of decades ago, when they defended the impunity of their epaulette-wearing leaders, trying to restrict accountability [only] to those who pulled the trigger.
>
> Deputy Boris Barrera responding to the defence arguments[421]

Piñera faced two distinct impeachment procedures, one during November–December 2019, and another during October–November 2021.

In the first case, Piñera was charged with violating the Constitution and the laws, as well as the national honour, by consenting with the Armed Forces perpetration of multiple, grievous, and systematic violations of human rights, despite knowing and having the means to stop such violations.[422] In the second case, Piñera was again charged with violating the Constitution, the laws and the national honour (thus also covering all potential impeachable offenses allowed by art. 52, n. 2 of the Constitution), but through the favouring of a mining company and the hiding of personal assets during his presidential mandates, both of which could constitute multiple legal and constitutional violations.[423] A few things are worth commenting about these attempts and the particular configuration of impeachments in Chile.

No Gatekeepers One of the most notorious features of the Chilean impeachment provisions is that they do not stablish gatekeepers for the initiation of procedures, meaning, in other words, that once charges are offered by representatives, they are necessarily investigated by an impeachment commission and lead to an impeachment vote.[424] This is arguably a risky feature from the perspective of systemic stability and Executive-Legislative relations, as impeachment accusations could theoretically be constantly offered against a controversial President, muddying the

[421] Records of the 123rd Session of the Chilean Chamber of Deputies (367 Legislature), December 12th, 2019, p. 84. Barrera refers to the Ministers of Interior and Public Security during the *Estallido Social*, Andrés Chadwick and Gonzalo Blumel, respectively. Chadwick had been effectively impeached and convicted in the previous day for his management of the crisis, despite his defence presenting similar arguments to Piñera's. See Senado de Chile, December 11th, 2019: "*Respaldan acusación constitucional contra exministro Chadwick*".

[422] *Acusación constitucional en contra del Presidente de la República Miguel Juan Sebastián Piñera Echenique* (November 19th, 2019), p. 104. The piece listed numerous homicides, injuries, sexual harassment, and other evidence of human rights abuses (pp. 10–45), which were then linked with the decreeing of state of emergency and poor management of state forces (pp. 45–69).

[423] *Acusación constitucional en contra del Presidente de la República Miguel Juan Sebastián Piñera Echenique* (October 13th, 2021), pp. 49–95. Presidents are, for example, required fully disclose their assets to prevent the co-optation of office for furthering their private interests. The undue favouring of mining companies, on its turn, was argued to have had several illicit or reprehensible environmental, economic, and diplomatic consequences. The link between violations of the first and second presidential mandate were argued based on the President's rejection of the Escazú Agreement, which would impose (arguably self-incriminating) duties of transparency on certain projects with environmental impact.

[424] Art. 37 of the Parliamentary Bylaws (Law n. 18,918 of 1990).

communication between branches of power and overloading the Legislature with impeachment commissions and votes. Despite such potential 'ease of use', however, presidential impeachment procedures have remained remarkably side-lined from the political landscape, something that is arguably to the merit of Chile's political elites in exercising forbearance and the relative economic stability of the past decades. It is questionable, on the other hand, whether that is a feature that should remain in Chile's future Constitution, as the presumed 'stable' political landscape has been changing since the *Estallido Social*, arguably towards more uncompromising competition between elites.

Preliminary Vote (*questión prévia*) Gatekeepers are generally responsible for verifying whether the accusation presented before them fills the basic requirements of an impeachment accusation (*e.g.*, the charges implicate the President, they describe an impeachable offense, they are offered by the legitimated actors, they are not precluded by limitations, etc), which is a function that also exists in the Chilean system, but one that is postponed to a vote by the plenum of the Chamber of Deputies, taking place immediately before the impeachment vote.[425] From what could be observed on the two impeachment attempts against Piñera, however, it was not clear whether this step plays a role that is meaningfully different from that of the impeachment vote. The debates rarely restrain themselves to such preliminary requirements and, instead, result in just another debate on the merits of impeachment. In the second impeachment, moreover, the defence abstained from arguing preliminary issues, despite originally presenting them in the defence piece.[426] On one hand, this was a surprising move, since the first impeachment attempt had been rejected at the preliminary vote. Theoretically, if the arguments presented the last time worked, they would be acknowledged again, despite some changes in context. On the other hand, however, the abstention was arguably the recognition of an unspoken understanding in the Chamber of Deputies, namely that the preliminary arguments of the last session played a secondary role to the outcome of acquittal, if they played a role at all. What really mattered to the outcome was arguably not the ingenuity and persuasiveness of those arguments, but really the partisan support that they could gather regardless of content.[427]

---

[425] Art. 42 of the Parliamentary Bylaws (Law n. 18,918 of 1990). The preliminary vote needs to be argued by the defence to take place.

[426] The accusation suggested that the defence's abstention from the preliminary vote was motivated by the wish of ending the session as soon as possible. The defence arguably knew that prolonging the session would allow for more deputies to arrive and meet the 2/3 threshold. Special Session 97, p. 27.

[427] Partisanship in the first impeachment was high but not perfect (<92%; 6 opposition deputies defected the expected partisan alignment), while it was perfect in the second attempt (100%; no defections). For specifics, see Emol, December 12th, 2019: *"Cómo votaron los diputados la cuestión previa de la acusación constitucional contra el Presidente Piñera";* Emol, November 9th, 2021: *"Cómo votaron los diputados al aprobar la acusación constitucional en contra del Presidente Sebastián Piñera".*

Conflation of Preliminary Conditions and Merit Not to be too cynical, it must be noted that the mixing of merit and preliminary issues was warranted to some degree, due to how the defence presented some of its arguments. In the first impeachment attempt, for example, the defence attempted to infiltrate the preliminary issue debate with questions of merit. It presented a strict textualist interpretation of art. 52, n. 2, which defines impeachable offenses as "*acts of the presidential administration that may have gravely compromised the honour or safety of the Nation or [which] may have openly violated the Constitution or the laws*" (free translation). In the defence's interpretation, 'acts' could only refer to 'actions' that had been personally and directly been executed by the President. Omissions, for example, would be excluded and so would be also the case of indirect perpetration, although such portion was not outwardly argued. The defence then argued that 'to consent' is not an 'act' or 'action', but an omission. By such virtue, the accusation piece had to be dismissed as inadmissible, for lacking the basic requirements (*i.e.,* no valid impeachable offense).[428]

A Successful Defence? The King Can Neglect No Wrong Such thesis was *theoretically* accepted by most deputies (79 voted for the rejection of the impeachment accusations for lacking admissibility conditions, 73 voted for the approval, and one abstained). If one reads the transcripts, however, one will find that even those who voted for the rejection were hesitant to accept the idea that impeachable offenses could not be committed by an omissive President. In fact, those who supported the defence thesis modified it significantly, overlooking its understanding of the word 'act'. They recognized that omissions could be impeachable offenses, but they needed to fill certain requirements. Such requirements were naturally unrealizable once transplanted into the constitutional context, at least under the current rules of impeachment. One argued, for example, that omissive categories had to be expressly stablished in the catalogue of offenses, as is the case with omissive crimes in the criminal code, otherwise it had to be considered as a violation of the principle of legality.[429] As Chile lacks such catalogue of limited impeachable offenses, the deputy in question was effectively arguing for unaccountability for presidential omission, but only indirectly and arguably leaving some room for 'plausible deniability' when it is their turn to impeach the opposition's President. Given the nature of impeachment sentencing, which offers little opportunity for debating the details and nuances of a case in question, the idea that the President cannot be held accountable for omissions seems to have nonetheless prevailed and has since been argued quasi as a legal fact in the media.[430]

[428] Session 123, pp. 29–39.

[429] *Nullum criminen, nulla poena sine legem scripta/certa*. Session 123, pp. 71 ff. (Gastón von Mühlenbrock), 84–94 (Sofia Cid). It was also argued that interpreting otherwise would be an expansive interpretation *in malam partem*. The same was said of interpreting the word 'administration' in anything else than its technical-legal use, thus leaving the President unaccountable for acts of 'government' (p. 34).

[430] Cooperativa, December 12th, 2019: *"Cámara de Diputados desechó acusación constitucional contra Piñera"*.

The Actual Debate and the Necessity Justification The preliminary questions, however, were but window dressing to a debate centred on whether the President had or not violated the Constitution, the laws, and the national honour. The defence, which was conducted by a criminal lawyer, chose the well-known argument structure of a necessity justification (*estado de necessidade*, *Notstand*). Essentially, the moral argument that underlies this defence is that, while there may have been violations by one of the agents, such violations were justified by the circumstances. A successful necessity defence needs to, *grosso modo*, demonstrate that: (i) The agent's violation sought to prevent a greater unjust violation; (ii) there were no other reasonable alternatives available; (iii) the great unjust was unprovoked by the agent; and that, (iv) once the greater violation was deterred, the agent did not commit further violations.[431]

The framework mentioned was not presented under the title of a necessity justification, presumably because it would entail the implicit acknowledgement of personal contributions to the violations that took place, but such was essentially what was argued by the defence and supporting deputies. The defence argued that the circumstances of the *Estallido Social* were exceptional and unforeseeable, and thus did not have a clear-cut resolution that could be demanded of it. The use of the state of emergency and the armed forces to contain the riots would have been the appropriate, if not the only choice in face of the damages and risks imposed by them.[432] Piñera would have done everything reasonable within his grasp to avoid human rights violations (in practice, he promised to investigate the accusations and hold the perpetrators accountable; he removed objected ministers and accepted negotiations on a new Constitution). He would also not have had any culpability in motivating the riots or the human rights violations, as his administration had taken multiple steps to address the demands before the riots even took place.[433] Impeachment supporters objected such statements, as to them there was more that the President could have done having command over the *Carabineros* and the state of emergency. His contribution to the outburst of the crisis, as had been made evident by the protestors' demands for resignation, was also argued to be more deeply rooted than what he was willing to concede.[434]

[431] A typical example would be that of the medic who performs a tracheotomy without consent to save a life. For details on this justification, see Roxin (2006), pp. 720 ff.

[432] A considerable effort was made in characterizing the rioters as vicious and harmful to the public wellbeing, by, for example, citing numbers of casualties, arsons, private business and public institutions affected, and so on. Despite being reverential of the democratic heroism of the protestors, this defence often conflated rioters and peaceful protestors, as the accusation had handpicked violations against the latter group.

[433] Session 123, pp. 22–29.

[434] Session 123, pp. 40–54 (Gastón Saavedra). Some deputies argued that liability could not be transferred to the President, if he consented with investigating and prosecuting human rights violations (p. 69, Gastón von Mühlenbrock; p. 93, Sofia Cid). Such was argued to be a standard held by international courts of human rights.

Nature of Impeachments: Political for Acquittal, Legal for Conviction A final defence thesis presented in the first impeachment attempt pertained the nature of impeachments, which was said to impose a 'dynamic' standard of proof. Acknowledging that the domestic legal community understands the impeachment as a procedure of juridical-political nature, the defence argued that the political dimension of the procedure would be constituted in the representatives' discretion in rejecting impeachment accusations, while the legal dimension was one that had to be applied strictly throughout. In practical terms, it meant that the judges of impeachment had discretion to acquit the President, if political convenience said so, but they could not convict the President if the case was also not legally uncontroversial.

In this logic, given the broad scope of consequences a presidential impeachment may have on society, such as its potential of violating the principles of popular sovereignty (*i.e.*, by cancelling out the democratic choice of President), of separation of powers, of fixed presidential terms, and so on, the Parliament would be enabled to avoid seeking accountability for legal or constitutional violations that affect juridical goods of lesser importance than such cornerstone principles. The defence argued, moreover, that given the extraordinary and exceptional nature of impeachment proceedings, they should be used sparingly under the principle of *ultima ratio* (last resort). It is to say, in other words, that if a crisis may be averted or resolved through alternative pathways, those must be preferred, and impeachments must be dismissed until all other paths were fully explored.[435] The resulting formula sets an incredibly high bar for impeachments, requiring them to only address codified violations which single-handedly and unequivocally throw an entire country into crisis.

Desperate Times and Desperate Means: Impeachment During the Pandemic A final particularity of these impeachment attempts worth commenting pertains to how the pandemic circumstances affected the procedures. On the streets, the social isolation measures had a direct suppressive effect on public mobilization.[436] Simply put, occupying public spaces to protest the presidency became an illegal affair, regardless of how legitimate or urgent the demands could be. Such situation thus imposed less visibility of popular dissatisfaction, which, on its turn, affected the procedures by reducing the sense of impeachment being opportune and urgent. The political dimension of impeachment, therefore, arguably became 'undernourished' for a successful ousting.

[435] Session 123, pp. 30, 35–36. For a contrasting view, see Chap. 4. From a comparative perspective, the political dimension is generally applied as a 'two-way-street', meaning that it may be exacerbated both for acquittal, as well as for conviction. The main goal is that neither the President nor that the impeachment procedures serve as grounds for destabilizing democracy. It is to say that, if a President is understood to have a destabilizing presence, conviction could be motivated also by minor violations, unlike argued by Piñera's defence above.

[436] Heiss (2020), p. 6.

The pandemic, moreover, also affected the procedures in much more concrete ways. The second procedure against Piñera nearly failed in early stages due to pandemic restrictions. While the opposition had just enough votes to approve the impeachment in the Chamber of Deputies, two of its Deputies were prohibited from entering the building for voting. One of them was in his last day of quarantine and could not leave his home, while the other had felt sick in the afternoon, and was thus preventively mandated to stay out of the building and get himself a PCR test. To meet the impeachment threshold, the opposition had to engage in a filibuster, arguing the accusation case for over 15 h. It was just enough time for the quarantined Deputy to regularly participate in the session, and for the sick deputy to get tested and, with the aid of distractive manoeuvres from other deputies, to sneak through security (which had been made particularly tight for this specific event).[437]

3.2.2 Atypical Procedural Oustings

Up until this point the case studies have focused on presidential oustings realized in their traditional form, that is, through impeachment in a strict sense. Some had the participation of the judicial branch, which can be considered an innovation in relation to the prototypical presidential impeachment as devised by the Framers of the US Constitution. Those were, nonetheless, procedures which also were conceived as means of presidential accountability and were, therefore, considered 'typical' for the purposes of this study. In this section, however, more radical deviations are considered. These are classified as atypical or impeachment surrogates, because the procedures used to achieve presidential accountability were not originally conceived for such goals. They are creative improvisations used to circumvent legal or factual constraints that block access to typical impeachments. They are tendentially unforeseeable, simpler, and quicker ousting mechanisms, which, by virtue of such features, are likely to be called into question by legal communities and the public itself.

The analyses on this section will be shorter,[438] but no less valuable than those that preceded it. These cases serve as contrasting examples and, arguably, may pose existential questions regarding the future of presidentialism and the institution of impeachments. On one hand, they challenge the very cornerstones of impeachment theory, such as the assumption that: (i) procedural presidential oustings must be slow and encumbering; (ii) their legitimacy is strongly tied to the legality and due process of the procedures; (iii) democracy may be harmed by anything less;

[437] The filibuster consisted mostly of a single deputy, Jaime Naranjo, reading the accusation piece in its entirety and the strategic manipulation of quorum to pause the session. See Special Session 97, pp. 40–205. La Tercera, November 9th, 2021: *"Cámara aprueba acusación constitucional contra Piñera tras extensa jornada de debate"*.

[438] Due to space constraints, many cases could not be included, but they are commented and described whenever relevant throughout Chap. 4.

(iv) presidentialism is impossible with easily and readily accessible means of parliamentary control; among other things, to name a few. On the other, however, they may arguably confirm many of the fears the Framers had such as that: (i) procedural oustings that are too quick can be used in momentaneous downswings of popularity against an otherwise legitimate, law-abiding President; (ii) their ease of access turns Presidents into creatures of the Parliament; (iii) their weak legal rationality may have erosive effects on democracy; and so on. As such, atypical proceedings may provide fruitful insights about the object of this study.[439]

Finally, it is important to notice that two cases of the previous section were presented as 'typical cases of impeachment', despite also making use of surrogates. Those were the cases of Carlos Andrés Pérez (Venezuela, 1993) and Albert Fujimori (Peru, 2000). The first was impeached and then ousted by a declaration of vacancy before the impeachment trial could be concluded; in the second, the president was ousted by a declaration of vacancy and then impeached. The cases were dealt as typical, but in reality they are more of syncretic nature.

3.2.2.1 In One Fell Swoop: Abdalá Bucaram (1997), Ecuador

A Historical Narrative

Abdalá Bucaram had his entry in the world of politics in 1979, when his brother-in-law and then President of Ecuador Jaime Roldós offered him a management position at the Police of Guayas (Ecuador's largest province).[440] Despite being a relatively menial position for the realm of politics, Bucaram made name for himself, becoming known for his hardliner stance.[441] After Jaime Roldós' death in airplane crash in 1981, Bucaram founded his own political party evoking Roldós' figure and achievements, the *Roldosista* Party of Ecuador (*Partido Roldosista Ecuatoriano*, PRE; self-declared centre-left). The linkage with Roldós' legacy was a political powerful tool in Bucaram's rhetorical arsenal, as it provided him with a popular image of someone who truly cared about the Ecuadorian people (before his death, Roldós doubled the minimum wage and limited weekly work hours to 40) and an antagonistic edge against the traditional oligarchies that ran deep in Roldós' tradition and now was strengthened by the rumours of Roldós' death being a commissioned assassination.[442]

---

[439] As pointed out in the theoretical discussions, this study applies certain assumptions of structuralism, namely that to make sense of a unit, one needs to understand the structure in which it is inserted, as well as its neighbouring units. Something is defined not only by that which it is, but also by that which it is not.

[440] Ecuador's administrative subdivisions are as follows, from larger to smaller: Union, Province, Canton, Parish.

[441] Pachano (1997), pp. 230–231.

[442] Pachano (1997), pp. 231–232. On Roldós and *Roldosismo*, see Freidenberg (2003), pp. 94–115. On the rumors, see Perkins (2016), pp. 164–168, 173–177. The official investigation attributed the crash to human error. On Bucaram's rhetoric, see La Torre (1996).

Not long thereafter, in 1984, Bucaram achieved his first position of visibility and power as the mayor (*alcade*) Ecuador's second largest city: Guayaquil, capital of Guayas. In this position he expanded the presence of his party in national politics, eventually becoming the second largest in the country. The office enabled the party to build clientelistic networks (*e.g.*, concession of jobs, land, and other sources of revenue) with which it secured the loyal militancy of regional leaders and consolidated Bucaram as the sort of political leader that delivered the demands of the people unhampered by the 'formalities' of old politics.[443] The coastal elites, which were usually relegated to the periphery of national politics, saw in Bucaram potential for getting power from the traditional aristocrats of Quito (Ecuador's capital city, in the mountains) and thus were inclined to finance his political project.[444] Bucaram's wayward ways, however, led him to self-exile in Panama between 1985 to 1987, once he criticized the country's armed forces. Despite this, his party's success allowed Bucaram to run for the presidency and sponsor those close to him to prominent positions of power, including his sister Elsa to the mayoralty of Guayaquil in 1988.[445]

Electoral success in presidential races, however, came only in Bucaram's third attempt, in 1996. Bucaram ran against Jaime Nebot of the conservative Social Christian Party (*Partido Social Cristiano*, PSC; Ecuador's oldest and largest party), being defeated in the first round (27–25%), but winning the run-offs (54.5–45.4%).[446] The repeated poor performance of previous administrations[447] made Bucaram's antisystem rhetoric and personality relatable, as his fierce attacks to the oligarchies, his promises of ending austerity, his nods to marginalized communities and his charismatic informality presented as him as an alternative to the same old PSC candidate.[448] To be sure, Bucaram's style was certainly not everyone's cup of tea. Negative partisanship, however, gave him an edge in the

[443] Pachano (1997), pp. 232–238; Freidenberg (2003), pp. 195–214.

[444] One of the key cleavages of Ecuadorian politics rests in the coast vs. mountain dichotomy (*costeños vs. serranos*). The coastal elites are more recent and thus are said to lack the blood lineage, 'glorious past' or 'refined culture' of the mountain elites. Pachano (1997), pp. 238–239; Freidenberg (2003), pp. 118 ff.

[445] Pachano (1997), p. 231.

[446] Pérez-Liñán (2007), p. 25.

[447] Like in the other cases of the 90's, this outcome was also linked to the Latin American debt crisis and massive foreign debt accrued by the military dictatorships (in Ecuador, 1972–1979). Other local factors, such as the presence of terrorist groups and drug cartels, contributed to the difficulties of recovering the economy and governing peacefully. For details on this era, see Stornaiolo (1999), pp. 191–231.

[448] Pachano (1997), pp. 246–248. Freidenberg (2003), p. 267, points out this was one of the few elections in which the coast/mountain cleavage did not play a significant role, since both candidates were from the coast. Stornaiolo (1999), p. 224, on the other hand, suggests the tipping point was the choice for Rosalía Arteaga for the Vice-Presidency. Arteaga offered balance and moderation to Bucaram's platform.

second round, as rural and small-town voters had strong reservations against Jaime Nebot.[449]

Once in power, Bucaram's ruling style was as controversial as his campaigning style. In fact, one could even argue the difference between the candidate and the President Bucaram was neglectable. The publicity stunts were as flamboyant as before: Bucaram danced and sang in appearances, he organized a televised charity spectacle ('*Teleton*') for shaving off his moustache, he recorded a full-length album as a singer ("*Un Loco que ama*"), and he continued relentlessly attacking his opponents and oligarchies. His critics accused him of not working and others claimed his conduct ashamed Ecuador before the international community and was incompatible with the dignity of office.[450] Particularly the traditional elites of Quito took issue with his flamboyance, as it reflected that of the new-rich of the coastal region.[451] More concerningly, his behaviour alienated potential coalition partners, who were reluctant to associate themselves with someone so controversial and unpredictable.[452]

Ultimately, Bucaram's behaviour undermined his political project, and his administration had to seek costly solutions to compensate for his isolation. This became particularly clear when members of the opposition began having to publicly explain their alignment with the PRE on hotly debated bills, which were often explained as mere favourable coincidences. Due to continued pressure, however, after other attempts of co-opting the traditional parties failed or were publicly denounced, parties organized to form stronger and more coherent opposition through a coalition named '*Frente Patriotico*' (Patriotic Front), which further consolidated Bucaram's political isolation and struggle against legislative stonewalling.[453]

The main drive towards Bucaram's ouster, however, came from popular movements. Very early on the Bucaram administration alienated many marginalized communities, despite its constant use of pro-minority rhetoric. The indigenous population (approx. 40% of Ecuador's population has indigenous roots to some degree),[454] for example, took issue in his creation of a Ministry of Ethnical Minorities, which neutralized other previously consolidated, working institutions with related goals. Workers of the energy sector, moreover, also went on violent protests against Bucaram's reforms which allowed the private sector to acquire significant

[449] Pachano (1997), p. 247; Freidenberg (2003), p. 269. The PSC's electorate had, for unclear reasons, reservations against Nebot. Whatever the case, the result was a highly heterogeneous, volatile popular support.

[450] Stornaiolo (1999), pp. 225, 227.

[451] Pachano (1997), pp. 257–258.

[452] Pachano (1997), p. 255.

[453] Mejía Acosta and Polga-Hecimovich (2010), p. 82.

[454] Inter Press Service, October 11th, 1996: *"Ecuador: Indígenas rechazan Ministerio de Minorías Étnicas"*.

shares in their economic activity.[455] These two groups were the ones to spearhead protests against Bucaram, particularly after more momentum was achieved.

Adhesion from other sectors of society depended on more grievous mishaps and scandals, which did not take long to emerge. Bucaram's inner circle bombarded the news with scandals,[456] denouncing his administration's propensity to patrimonialism, nepotism, authoritarianism, and corruption. Bucaram's family members and close friends were often given ministries or other managerial positions in the public administration and were soon discovered to have misbehaved in one way or another.[457] On the economy, Bucaram subverted expectations, betraying his electoral promises and delving deeper into neoliberal reforms he so much criticized in campaign. The austerity measures rose the price of utilities and services to levels untenable to most of the population, causing massive protests between January and February 1997, vocally demanding Bucaram's resignation and the rollback of the economic policy.[458] So great was the commotion, the Vice-President Rosalía Arteaga (*Movimiento MIRA*) broke up with government and requested Bucaram to step down. February 5th, 1997, the protests reached an unprecedented historical peak, generating concerns about the country's democratic future and urging the National Congress to act.[459]

Procedures in Congress

> The problem with members of Parliament is that there is no good faith; treaties are [mere] paper, constitutions are books, freedom is anarchy and people's lives, torment.
>
> Deputy Marco Proaño Maya (PRE) quoting Simón Bolívar[460]

Upon searching the congressional registers, the first thing that catches the eye is the improvisational nature of the procedures for ousting President Bucaram, which makes itself visible already on the lengthy, relatively open-ended title given to the session/goal of the day: "Analyse and resolve the crisis that Ecuador and the

---

[455] Inter Press Service, September 23rd, 1996: *"Ecuador: Petroleros se unen a huelga de trabajadores eléctricos"*.

[456] Pérez-Liñán (2007), p. 26, calculates about one *new* scandal every 2 weeks.

[457] Stornaiolo (1999), p. 225. For a detailed list of accusations, see El Universo, June 4th, 2017: *"Abdalá Bucaram a la presidencia: A la tercera fue la vencida"*. Freidenberg (2003), pp. 200 ff., points out the extensive tradition in these kinds of practices within the Bucaram Ortiz family. Bucaram himself often stubbornly defended the accused in his administration instead of avoiding his association with the scandals. Pérez-Liñán (2007), p. 26.

[458] See Pachano (1997), pp. 249 ff., for an overview of economic measures and popular reactions. The increases ranged between 150 and 600% on costs of electricity, communication, gas and transports. Stornaiolo (1999), p. 225.

[459] Stornaiolo (1999), p. 226. Polls that week indicated 92% of popular support towards the protests; 57% wanted Bucaram's removal, whereas 41% conditioned his stay on the rollback of economic policies.

[460] Author's translation of CE-008-96-97 (February 6th, 1997), p. 36.

National Government are undergoing".[461] It seemed almost as if the members of Congress were caught off-guard by the immense protests, and saw no other option to but give it an immediate response, whatever it could turn out to be. To be sure, it was no secret that Bucaram had become unpopular and that many resented the betrayal of his electoral platform, but it was nonetheless shocking that within only 7 months of administration an estimated two million protestors would already be personally knocking on Congress' door asking for change so assertively.[462]

Indeed, the first manifestations of the session denounce how politically charged the environment was that day. Many participants expressed concern for their and their peers' safety and pleaded for restricted public access to the congressional chambers, as they described threats and aggressions to representatives entering the building.[463] Despite the palpable indications of intimidation, all parties recognized the value and the legitimacy of the demands of the protests, albeit at times for radically different reasons. For those critical to the presidency, it was clear as day that what people really wanted was Bucaram's ouster and the end of the neoliberal takeover of government; for the government's allies, on the other hand, the protests were proof of the government's impact in people's lives, empowering them and giving them the strength to fight the problems of the country, which, they underscored, were mostly inherited from previous administrations. The latter attempted, moreover, to deescalate the fatalist tone of the opposition, pointing out that Bucaram had just recently made a public announcement reverting unpopular policies and that, thus, his ouster could be avoided without further harm to democracy or the rule of law.[464]

At any rate, the opposition made clear that legal issues had secondary importance. Some deputies, such as Salem Mendonza (PSC), saw an act of bravery in Congress' cutting through 'the red tape' to address the urgent realities of the country.[465] Though the government, in particular Bucaram's brothers Santiago and Jacobo, did a good job of pointing out the legal deficiencies of what was being proposed, their complaints fell on deaf ears. With the President of Congress, Fabián Alarcón (FRA, *Frente Radical Alfarista*), apparently eager to close this late-night extraordinary session, no votes or further debates were called to address what seemed like limitations of congressional competence. Indeed, the two main outcomes of that session, that is, (i) the removal of Bucaram, by declaring the presidency permanently vacant on grounds of mental incapacity, and (ii) the election of the Fabián Alarcón to

---

[461] *Ibid.*, p. 2: "*Orden del Día. Analizar y resolver la crisis que vive el Ecuador y el Gobierno Nacional*".

[462] Pérez-Liñán (2007), p. 27, acknowledges the massive protests did take place, but notes that the paradigmatic number of two million does not seem to have been verified.

[463] CE-008-96-97 (February 6th, 1997), pp. 2 ff.

[464] *Ibid.*, pp. 5–41. There were, moreover, claims of double standards. The presidency of Leon Febres-Cordero (PSC, 1984–1988) lived through similar circumstances but was given more leeway.

[465] *Ibid.*, pp. 30 ff.

the presidency, were at least intuitively beyond Congress' constitutional mandate.[466]

Regarding the ouster (i), it was clear that Bucaram was not really 'mentally unfit' for the presidency, despite his playful nickname of '*El Loco*', which served as an acknowledgement of his flamboyance. The subject was, in fact, not seriously discussed at any point of that session and arguably no deputy in that session ever really believed Bucaram had become any less mentally fit than he had been by the event of his swearing in, 186 days prior. The legislative resolution ousting the President on such grounds was presented at the first minutes of the session, but the subtext of its purpose had always been part of an unspoken consensus. The final text of the said resolution corroborates such conclusion, as it names three justifications for its existence, none of them alluding to Bucaram's mental fitness:

> In face of the events that paralyze and cause commotion in the Ecuadorian nation provoked by the embarrassing and illegal conduct of the President of the Republic (...) who in repeated and constant manner violates the Constitution and the Laws (...), runs over civil society, threatens and assaults the press (...), uses the Armed Forces in acts foreign to its functions, harming its image, stars in artistic, musical and sport activities clashing frontally with the majesty of the Presidency of our Republic, (...)
>
> [Considering] That the President (...) has attempted to intimidate the deputies blocking the traffic to the Legislative Palace and threatened the President of the Parliament and its main leaders (...)
>
> [Considering] That the virtually unanimous demand of the population is that this state of chaos and disorder orchestrated by the Executive be put to an end, [the National Congress] resolves (...)[467]

These justifications would serve well as an impeachment sentence but are beside the point on the judgment of someone's mental faculties, thus making it clear what the procedures really were about. Even in the event of Congress suggesting pertinent arguments to the evaluation of one's mental fitness, it would have been questionable whether Congress itself could carry out such evaluation.[468] The legal means for destitution, however, like mentioned before, was the less controversial part of the legislative resolution. Proper outrage was more focused on the (ii) legally unprecedented election of the President of Congress to the *interim* presidency. An official referendum carried out 3 months later seems to imply this, albeit inconclusively: 75.7% voted in favour of ratifying the ouster of Bucaram, whereas 68% voted in favour of ratifying Alarcón's election, though this latter result arguably was still high due to the tricky wording of the question, which could give the idea that the question was about people's agreement on the legal means used in the ouster of Bucaram instead.[469]

---

[466] Legislative resolution I-97-065-R.

[467] Legislative resolution I-97-065-R, p. 1 (author's translation).

[468] Since then, Ecuador has stablished objective criteria for mental incapacity, which must be assessed by a group of certified medical professionals (art. 167, IV, 1998 Const.; art. 145, IV, 2008 Const.).

[469] *Informe del Presidente del Tribunal Supremo Electoral sobre la Organización de la Consulta Popular del 25 de Mayo de 1997* (June 1997), p. 97. The question about presidential succession read as: "*Are you in agreement with the resolution of the National Congress that, as it ceased the*

While most of PRE's deputies and allies were ready to acknowledge their administration's shortcomings, they were much less enthusiastic about Alarcón's self-proclamation as to the presidency. In fact, although the official records do not register these events, footage of the session shows that, after debates on presidential succession, deputies engaged in the symbolic action of ripping their constitutions apart and marched towards the floor of Congress, pointing at Alarcón and the secretaries, while calling them traitors of the nation. To them, Alarcón's act of simply glossing over the fact that Vice-President Rosalía Arteaga was still in the game was inexcusable.

Although art. 77 of the 1978 Constitution arguably left some interpretative leeway in its redaction of the rules for presidential succession,[470] Ecuadorians still had in relatively recent memory the experience of a Vice-President succeeding a permanently incapacitated President, that is, on the event of Jaime Roldós death in 1981. This made this portion of the legislative resolution sound particularly arbitrary (and arguably self-interested) and led to the awkward outcome of 3 high level authorities claiming the presidency simultaneously—an event later infamously known as "the night of the three Presidents".[471]

Finally, regarding this legislative resolution, it is important to point out it may have carried at least one crucial flaw of legislative technique, which can be observed in its excessive thematic breadth. Not only the resolution disposed about the vacancy and succession of the presidency, but it removed of various other officers, such as the Prosecutor General, and stablished a wide array of policies and commitments to reform, including a Constituent Assembly. Although this outcome is arguably consistent with the purpose of the congressional session of 'resolving the crisis' which did demand taking a varied set of actions, it insidiously mixed in the Deputies' decision-making many other criteria that would be impertinent to the decision of on presidential removal. When voting, therefore, the deputies would be not only considering the 'net-positive' of criteria for presidential removal, but also whether they considered a Constituent Assembly timely or the proposed economic policy proper. A deputy's decision of 'acquitting' the President could have been offset by these other considerations.

As such, by itself, it is hard to say what the vote on the legislative resolution really was representative of. Was it a consensus on Bucaram's removal? Was it a consensus on the need for a new Constitution? Was it a consensus on the need to reverse

functions of (...) Abdalá Bucaram, elected Dr. Fabián Alarcón (...) as the interim Constitutional President of the Republic?" (author's translation).

[470] The rules of succession did not stablish a hierarchy between Vice-President, President of Congress, or President of the Supreme Court. Reforms were discussed in 1995, but the prospect of having the Vice-President Alberto Dahik succeed Sixto Duran-Balén dissuaded Congress from improving the text. Stornaiolo (1999), p. 228.

[471] Arteaga advocated for a constitutional amendment to resolve the succession conundrum and polls showed her as the favorite candidate for the interim presidency, with 55% of the interviewees' approval. She remained in power for 48 h, but eventually conceded to the pressure of military to step down. She was Ecuador's first and last female President. Stornaiolo (1999), p. 228.

fiscal austerity policies and reduce the prices of gas and public services? Or was it all the above? The vote numbers do not denounce a smashing consensus, as the resolution was approved with only a surplus of 3 votes on an absolute majority vote (44 in favour, 34 against, 2 abstentions and 2 absent),[472] and thus there remains much space for subjective interpretation.

3.2.2.2 Institutional Vacuum: Manuel Zelaya (2009), Honduras

The ousting of President Manuel Zelaya, despite being often lumped together with the impeachments of Fernando Lugo and Dilma Rousseff,[473] does not fit the scope of this book. For it to be included among these or other cases discussed prior, his ousting would have to have been operationalized through impeachment or other similar enough means, one could argue that its distinction *vis-à-vis* the impeachment would be merely nominal and not essential. This is not the case, as will be argued next.[474]

Though the proceedings against Zelaya were sprinkled with acts of state authorities that carry a semblance of constitutionality, the ousting itself was so riddled with incongruencies and usurpation of competencies that it would be better characterized as a military operation rather than an institutional solution for unresolved political tensions. In fact, some decisions taken by the actors involved do denounce that they were well-aware of the precarious legal status of their actions and that, therefore, they could not apply the logic of their improvised legalism to its final consequences without making themselves immediate targets of popular and legal backlash.[475] This is seen, for example, in the Judiciary's use of the army instead of the police to enforce its decision against the President;[476] or the army's decision of sending the President to exile in Costa Rica instead of arresting him for treason, as was the objective of his arrest order (*orden de captura*);[477] or also the secret criminal proceedings that justified the legal action against the President, indicating the

[472] CE-008-96-97 (February 6th, 1997), pp. 65–66. The data provided is not detailed enough to allow for a detailed breakdown of partisanship in this vote. Anecdotally, it is noticeable that the PSC voted entirely in favor and the PRE entirely against the resolution. The other parties who share the remaining 36 seats were more divided about their support, independently of their ideological alignment.

[473] *E.g.*, Marsteintredet and Malamud (2019), p. 1021.

[474] The case was kept for its contrastive value and to address mainstream scholarship on the topic.

[475] For a perspective on domestic law, see Comisión de la Verdad y la Reconciliación (2011), pp. 167–201.

[476] Comisión de la Verdad y la Reconciliación (2011), pp. 170–171.

[477] *Orden de Captura en contra de José Manuel Zelaya Rosales, 26 de junio de 2009, Corte Suprema de Justicia.* The newspaper El Faro suggested that both the arrest order and its solicitation by the Prosecutor's Office were fabricated after the fact. El Faro, May 31st, 2011: *"Militares capturaron a Zelaya sin tener una orden judicial"*.

unwillingness of their leading actors in being scrutinized or confronted for their actions.[478]

The fact that Congress connived with and ultimately ratified the trespasses committed by the Judiciary and the Armed Forces does not revert this conclusion, especially when one considers the questionable circumstances in which the ratification was voted.[479] The aftermath of these events, moreover, indicated that there was ample societal recognition around the illegitimacy of Zelaya's removal and that Congress' connivance was not representative of society's wishes.[480] Civil resistance movements took form after this period and have persisted to this day, despite the violence and censorship exercised by state security forces in its suppression.[481] From these movements, new political parties emerged and transformed Honduras' political landscape significantly, occupying the national government under the Xiomara Castro's administration (Liberty and Refoundation Party, left-wing), and becoming the largest party in Congress.[482] If it were not for Honduras' severe congressional malapportionment, the traditional party system (composed by the Liberal and the National parties, both who enabled Zelaya's removal) would arguably have already collapsed,[483] indicating the citizen's marked disagreement with the behaviour of its longstanding elites.

At any rate, it must be recognized that Zelaya's presidency did display many symptoms of instability once his administration switched from his original campaign promises to a political platform that was radically opposed by the parties in Congress, including his own.[484] Zelaya's antagonism of Congress and the Supreme

---

[478] Comisión de la Verdad y la Reconciliación (2011), pp. 169–170.

[479] Congress voted a resignation letter attributed to Zelaya, which lacked any sign of authenticity, such as his signature or official seals. The records show that the resignation was accepted with no discussion and was followed by the nomination of Roberto Michelleti (President of Congress) as acting President. No resolution/decree was enacted to formalize the act. Comisión de la Verdad y la Reconciliación (2011), pp. 391, 171–173.

[480] 58% disapproved the ousting. BBC Mundo, December 11th, 2009: *"Encuesta muestra rechazo al golpe"*.

[481] Multiple protestors, opposition activists, and journalists were assassinated. Media channels were occupied by the military to limit diffusion of independent information on the events. El País, June 30th, 2009: *"La policía carga contra los partidarios de Zelaya"*; BBC Mundo, June 30th, 2009: *"El "apagón" de los medios";* Human Rights Watch, July 29th, 2010: *"Honduras: Ongoing Attacks Foster Climate of Intimidation"*.

[482] Cespad, February 8th, 2022: *"Análisis de los resultados de las elecciones generales 2021 en Honduras"*.

[483] The Liberal and National parties experienced constant erosion in the past elections. Both parties concentrate together 41.3% of the vote for the current legislature (2021–2025), but 51.6% of the seats. Particularly paradigmatic of malapportionment are the results of the second most voted non-traditional party, the Savior Party of Honduras, who received 14% more votes than the Liberal party, but gained less than half of its seats.

[484] Zelaya was elected on a centre-right, "law-and-order" platform of the Liberal Party, but later sought alliances with Venezuela and Nicaragua, introduced massive raises in the minimum wage, among other things. BBC News, June 29th, 2009: *"Zelaya, un liberal enemistado con los suyos"*.

Court by insisting on holding a public consultation sharply opposed by both predictably led to his political isolation and to direct institutional confrontation.[485] Though Zelaya remained relatively popular and Honduras' economy was not particularly affected by his conduct, impeachment or a comparable surrogate would not have been unthinkable solutions for the constitutional crisis observed in 2009.[486] Such mechanisms were not introduced in the Honduran Constitution until 2013, however, so it is not surprising that the improvised solution fared as poorly as it did.[487]

In conclusion, it can be said that Zelaya's case is a better fit to the standard discussed in Chap. 2 relative to the deposition of monarchs: a procedure of dubious legality, perceived even by its perpetrators as poorly legitimated and hence often lacking in formalities that vest the rituals of deposition with official attire. It is better described as a military operation with no interest in scrutinizing the misconduct of high officers, nor any regard to the representativeness of the popular will. It should not, therefore, be put at level with impeachment or even its more flawed surrogates.

References

Abente-Brun D (2008) Paraguay: the unraveling of one-party rule. J Democr 20(1):143–156

Abranches S (2018) Presidencialismo de coalizão: Raízes e evolução do modelo político brasileiro. Companhia das Letras, São Paulo

Acemoglu D, Johnson S, Robinson J (2001) The colonial origins of comparative development: an empirical investigation. Am Econ Rev 91(5):1369–1401

Acemoglu D, Robinson JA (2019) The narrow corridor: states, societies, and the fate of liberty. Penguin Books, London

Almeida PR (2004) A experiência brasileira em planejamento econômico: uma síntese histórica. Planejamento e Orçamento governamental, en portugués, Coletânea

Amaral R, Paredes R (2005) Los presidentes del Paraguay, 2nd edn, (corr. y aum). Servilibro, Asunción

Ambos K (2009) Politische und rechtliche Hintergründe des Urteils gegen den ehem. peruanischen Präsidenten Alberto Fujimori. Zeitschrift für Internationale Strafrechtsdogmatik 11

[485] *Ibid.* Congress passed a law specifically forbidding Zelaya's wishes of conducting a popular consultation on a new constitution during the general elections. The Supreme Court declared his consultation illegal, and the Armed Forces refused to carry it out.

[486] Even after his removal, Zelaya still maintained 44% of approval rate. BBC Mundo, December 11th, 2009: *"Encuesta regional muestra rechazo al golpe"*.

[487] The pretrial (*desafuero, antejuicio*) existed in art. 313, 2 of the Honduran 1982 Constitution until 2004, when the article was modified to allow prosecution of high officers without need of parliamentary approval. In such cases, a criminal procedure subjected to special rules (arts. 414 ff. of the Code of Criminal Procedure) is carried before the Supreme Court and conviction may cause removal and disqualification from office. In 2013, art. 324 of the Constitution was modified to introduce a form of impeachment, which does not require a court-like trial, but which has the supermajority threshold of ¾ for approval (see Decree n. 231 of 2012, and n. 51 of 2013).

Ames B, Machado F, Renno L, Samuels D, Smith AE, Zucco C, Huberts A (2016) Brazillian Electoral Panel Study: 2014 results. Technical Note IDB-TN-915 of the Inter-American Development Bank

Archer RP (1996) Strengths and weaknesses of Colombia's besieged democracy. In: Mainwaring S (ed) Building democratic institutions: party systems in Latin America. Stanford University Press, Stanford

Archer RP, Shugart MS (1997) The unrealized potential of presidential dominance in Colombia. In: Mainwaring S, Shugart MS (eds) Presidentialism and democracy in Latin America. Cambridge University Press, Cambridge, pp 110–159

Arteaga Sánchez A (1994) El juicio político al Presidente Carlos Andrés Pérez: Escritos y alegatos jurídicos en el sumario. Centauro, Caracas

Avelar I (2017) A response to Fabiano Santos and Fernando Guarnieri. J Lat Am Cult Stud 26(2): 341–350

Avendaño Pavez OA (2013) Las reformas políticas en el gobierno de Sebastián Piñera Chile, 2010-2013. Revista Mexicana de Ciencias Politicas y Sociales 218:167–191

Barbosa IP (2020) A alta das commodities agrícolas e o estabelecimento do milagrinho na economia brasileira do governo Lula. Conjuntura Global 9(2)

Beçak R (2003) Sucessão presidencial de 1955: Aspectos políticos e jurídicos. Editora Juarez de Oliveira, São Paulo

Beezley WH (1969) Caudillismo: an interpretive note. J Inter-Am Stud 11(3):345–352

Berntzen E, Holvik Skinlo T-E (2010) Peru and the Fujimori Presidential Breakdown in 2000: Continuismo Gone Bad. In: Llanos M, Marsteintredet L (eds) Presidential breakdowns in Latin America: causes and outcomes of executive instability in developing democracies. Palgrave Macmillan, New York, pp 197–212

Betancourt I (1997) Sí Sabía: Viaje a través del expediente de Ernesto Samper, 2nd edn. Ediciones Temas de Hoy, Bogotá

Bodenheimer S (1970) The ideology of developmentalism: American Political Science's Paradigm Surrate for Latin American Studies. Berkeley J Sociol 15:95–137

Bodenheimer S (1971) Dependency and imperialism: the roots of Latin American underdevelopment. Polit Soc 1(3):327–357

Booth J, Seligson M (1984) The political culture of authoritarianism in Mexico: a reexamination. Lat Am Res Rev 19(1):106–124

de Souza B, Pinto P (1965) O impeachment: Aspectos da responsabilidade política do Presidente da República. Saraiva, Sao Paulo

Calvert P, Calvert S (1993) Latin America in the twentieth century, 2nd edn. Macmillan, Basingstoke

Carrión J (ed) (2006) The Fujimori legacy: the rise of electoral authoritarianism in Peru. Pennsylvania State University Press, University Park

Carvalho CE (2006) As origens e a gênese do Plano Collor. Nova Econ 16(1):101–134

Casullo ME, Freidenberg F (2017) Populist and programmatic parties in Latin American party systems. In: Holtz-Bach M, Heinisch R (eds) Handbook on populism: a handbook. Nomos, Baden-Baden, pp 275–292

Clève CM (2010) Expulsão do partido por ato de infidelidade e perda de mandato. Paraná Eleitoral 1(1):161–169

Collor F (2007) Um Relato para a História: A verdade sobre o processo de impeachment. Brasília

Comisión Ciudadana de Seguimiento (1996) Poder, Justicia, Indignidad. Utópica Ediciones, Colombia

Comisión de la Verdad y la Reconciliación (2011) Para que los hechos no se repitan: Informe de la Comisión de la Verdad y la Reconciliación Julio 2011. Comisión de la Verdad y la Reconciliación, Honduras

Comisión de Verdad y Justicia, Paraguay (2008) Informe final: Anive haguã oiko: Tierras Mal Habidas. Asunción

Conaghan CM (1996) A deficit of democratic authenticity: political linkage and the public in Andean polities. Stud Comp Int Dev 31(3):32–55

Conaghan CM (2005) Fujimori's Peru: deception in the public sphere. University of Pittsburgh Press, Pittsburgh

Coppedge M (1997) Strong parties and lame ducks: Presidential partyarchy and factionalism in Venezuela. Stanford University Press, Stanford

Coppedge M (1999) Venezuela: Conservative Representation without Conservative Parties. The Helen Kellog Institute for International Studies, no. 268

Coppedge M (2002) Explaining democratic deterioration in Venezuela through nested inference. Congreso Latinoamericano de Ciencia Politica

Cornejo-Saavedra E, Umaña-Hermosilla B, Guiñez-Cabrera N, Muñoz-Silva D, Mardones-Lagos C (2017) Endeudamiento y educación financiera del adulto joven en Chile. Revista Academia & Negocios 3(2):33–44

Cox GW, McCubbins MD (1993) Legislative leviathan: party government in the house. University of California Press, Berkeley

Crandall R (2002) Driven by drugs: US policy toward Colombia. Lynne Rienner Publishers, Boulder Colorado

Dietz HA, Myers DJ (2007) From Thaw to Deluge: party system collapse in Venezuela and Peru. Lat Am Polit Soc 49(2):59–86

Dix RH (1994) Military coups and military rule in Latin America. Armed Forces Soc 20(3): 439–456

Economides K, Haug A, McIntyre J (2015) Toward timeliness in civil justice. Monash Univ Law Rev 41(2):414–444

Erickson D (2009) Ghosts, metaphor, and history in Toni Morrison's beloved and Gabriel García Márquez's one hundred years of solitude. Palgrave Macmillan, Basingstoke

Figueiredo AC (2010) The Collor impeachment and Presidential Government in Brazil. In: Llanos M, Marsteintredet L (eds) Presidential breakdowns in Latin America: causes and outcomes of executive instability in developing democracies. Palgrave Macmillan, New York, pp 111–127

Finer SE (1976) The man on horseback: the role of the military in politics, 2nd edn. Penguin Books, London

Flynn P (1993) Collor, corruption and crisis: time for reflection. J Lat Am Stud 25(02):351

Freidenberg F (2003) Jama, caleta y camello: Las estrategias de Abdalá Bucaram y el PRE para ganar las elecciones. Corporacion Editora Nacional, Quito

Fukuyama F (2012) The origins of political order: from prehuman times to the French revolution. Farrar, Straus and Giroux, New York

Furtado C, Macedo S (1976) Economic development of Latin America: historical background and contemporary problems, 2nd edn. Cambridge University Press, Cambridge

García Chávarri A (2013) La incapacidad moral como causal de vacancia presidencial en el sistema constitucional peruano. Pensamiento Constituticional 18:383–402

Gargarella R (2013) Latin American constitutionalism, 1810–2010: the engine room of the constitution. Oxford University Press, Oxford

Geddes B, Ribeiro Neto A (1999) Institutional sources of corruption in Brazil. In: Rosenn KS, Downes R (eds) Corruption and political reform in Brazil: the impact of Collor's impeachment. North-South Center Press, University of Miami, Florida, pp 21–48

Grandin G (2011) The last colonial massacre: Latin America in the cold war, Updated edn. University of Chicago Press, Chicago

Heiss C (2017) Legitimacy crisis and the constitutional problem in Chile: a legacy of authoritarianism. Constellations 24(3):470–479

Heiss C (2020) Chile: Entre el estallido social y la pandemia. Análisis Carolina 18:1–13

Hinojosa V, Pérez-Liñán A (2003) Presidential impeachment and the politics of survival: the case of Colombia. In: Baumgartner JC, Kada N (eds) Checking executive power: presidential impeachment in comparative perspective. Praeger, Westport, pp 65–79

Huntington SP (1957) The soldier and the state: the theory and politics civil-military relations. Belknap Press of Harvard University Press, Cambridge
Huntington SP (1993) The third wave: democratization in the late twentieth century. University of Oklahoma Press, Norman
Instituto de Pesquisas DataFolha (2016) Avaliação da presidente Dilma Rousseff (PO813859): 07 e 08/04/2016
Justicia Electoral de Paraguay (2008) Elecciones Generales y Departamentales 2008: Memoriy y Estadisticas Electorales. Asunción
Kada N (2003) The role of investigative committees in the presidential impeachment processes in Brazil and Colombia. Legis Stud Q 28(1):29–54
Karl TL (1997) The paradox of plenty: oil booms and petro-states. University of California Press, Berkeley
Krehbiel K (1991) Information and legislative organization. University of Michigan Press, Ann Arbor, MI
La Torre C d (1996) Un solo toque: populismo y cultura política en Ecuador. Centro Andino de Acción Popular
Labovitz JR (1978) Presidential impeachment. Yale University Press, New Haven
Lachi M (2010) La construcción de la gobernabilidad en Paraguay. Centro de Estudios y Educación Popular Germinal 7
Leiken RS (2003) Why Nicaragua vanished: a story of reporters and revolutionaries. Rowman & Littlefield Publishers, Lanham
Levine DH (2002) The decline and fall of democracy in Venezuela: ten theses. Bull Lat Am Res 21(2):248–269
Lewis PH (2006) Authoritarian regimes in Latin America: dictators, despots, and tyrants. Rowman & Littlefield, Lanham
López M (2010) La democracia en Paraguay: un breve repaso sobre los partidos políticos tradicionales, el sistema electoral y el triunfo de Fernando Lugo Méndez. Revista Enfoques 8(13):89–106
López M (2018) Transición y democracia en Paraguay (1989–2017): "el cambio no es una cuestión electoral". Sb Editorial, Ciudad Autónoma de Buenos Aires Argentina
Lopez-Maya M (2001) Venezuela después del Caracazo: Formas de la protesta en un contexto desinstitutionalizado. Kellog Institute Working Paper, 287 July
Loveman B (1993) The constitution of tyranny: regimes of exception in Spanish America. University of Pittsburgh Press, Pittsburgh
Loveman B, Davies TM (1978) The politics of antipolitics: the military in Latin America. University of Nebraska Press, Lincoln
Madariaga A (2019) La Continuidad del Neoliberalismo en Chile. Revista de Estudos e Pesquisas sobre as Américas 13(2):81–113
Maingón T, Sonntag HR (1990) Las elecciones en Venezuela en 1988 y 1989: del ejercicio del rito democrático a la protesta silenciosa. Rev Mex Sociol 52(4):127
Mainwaring S (1999) Rethinking party systems in the third wave of democratization: the case of Brazil. Stanford University Press, Stanford
Mainwaring S, Bizzarro F (2019) The fates of third-wave democracies. J Democr 30(1):99–113
Mainwaring S, Hagopian F (2005) Introduction: the third wave of democratization in Latin America. In: Hagopian F, Mainwaring S (eds) The third wave of democratization in Latin America: advances and setbacks. Cambridge University Press, Cambridge, pp 1–13
Mainwaring S, Pérez-Liñán A (2005) Latin American democratization since 1978: democratic transitions, breakdowns, and erosions. In: Hagopian F, Mainwaring S (eds) The third wave of democratization in Latin America: advances and setbacks. Cambridge University Press, Cambridge, pp 14–59
Mainwaring S, Power TJ, Bizzarro F (2018) The uneven institutionalization of a party system: Brazil*. In: Mainwaring S (ed) Party systems in Latin America: institutionalization, decay, and collapse. Cambridge University Press, Cambridge, pp 164–200

Mann M (2012) The sources of social power, New edn. Cambridge University Press, Cambridge
Marsteintredet L, Malamud A (2019) Coup with adjectives: conceptual stretching or innovation in comparative research? Polit Stud 68(4):1014–1035
Martin C (1996) El juicio a CAP: Culpable o Inocente? Arte Fotolitográfico, Caracas
McClintock C (1998) Revolutionary movements in Latin America: El Salvador's FMLN and Peru's Shining Path. United States Institute of Peace, Washington, DC
Mejía Acosta A, Polga-Hecimovich J (2010) Parliamentary solutions to presidential crises in Ecuador. In: Llanos M, Marsteintredet L (eds) Presidential breakdowns in Latin America: causes and outcomes of executive instability in developing democracies. Palgrave Macmillan, New York, pp 73–90
Mignolo W (2012) The idea of Latin America. Blackwell Pub, Malden
Mishler W, Rose R (2001) What are the origins of political trust? Comp Pol Stud 34(1):30–62
Mohallem MF (2012) Paraguay: 'there is no coup here, no institutional breakdown'. Socialist Lawyer 62
Morales Quiroga M (2020) Estallido social en Chile 2019: Participación, Representación, Confianza Institucional y Escándalos Públicos. Anal Polit 98:3–25
Moreno E (2005) Whither the Colombian two-party system? An assessment of political reforms and their limits. Elect Stud 24(3):485–509
Naím M (1993) Paper Tigers and Minotaurs: the politics of Venezuela's economic reforms. Carnegie Endowment for International Peace; Distributed by the Brookings Institution, Dept, Washington, D.C, p 029
Nohlen D (2005) Elections in the Americas: a data handbook. Oxford University Press
Oppenheim LH (2007) Politics in Chile: socialism, authoritarianism and market democracy, 3rd edn. Westview, Boulder
Pachano S (1997) Fuera Bucaram! Fuera Bucaram? In: Báez R (ed) Y ahora qué?--: Una contribución al análisis histórico-político del país. Eskeletra Editorial, Quito, pp 229–264
Pérez CA, Blanco Muñoz A (2010) ¡Yo sigo acusando! Habla Carlos Andrés Pérez el defenestrado. Cátedra Pio Tamayo, Universidad Central de Venezuela, Caracas
Pérez Talia M (2019) Lugo y el Partido Liberal: una alianza (poco) exitosaen Paraguay. In: Sevilla AEG, Prado JH (eds) Música, sociedad y cultura: Rutas para el análisis socioantropológico de la música, Primera edn. Universidad Autónoma Metropolitana Unidad Azcapotzalco, Ciudad de México, pp 487–528
Pérez-Liñán A (2007) Presidential impeachment and the new political instability in Latin America. Cambridge University Press, Leiden
Perkins J (2016) The new confessions of an economic hit man, 2nd edn. Berrett-Koehler Publishers; O'Reilly Media Inc., Sebastopol
Pierson C (2011) The modern state, 3rd edn. Routledge, London
Piñera S (2017) Construyamos Tiempos Mejores para Chile: Programa de Gobierno 2018–2022
Pizarro E (2002) La Atomización Partidista en Colombia: El Fenómeno de las Micro-empresas Electorales. Working Paper, no. 292
Posada-Carbó E (1998) Fiction as history: the bananeras and Gabriel García Márquez's one hundred years of solitude. J Lat Am Stud 30(2):395–414
Prados de Escosura L (2009) Lost decades? Economic performance in post-independence Latin America. J Lat Am Stud 41(2):279–307
Remmer K (1978) Evaluating the policy impact of military regimes in Latin America. Lat Am Res Rev 13(2):39–54
Rey JC (1993) Crisis de la responsabilidade política en Venezuela: La remoción de Carlos Andrés Pérez de la Presidencia
Rodney W (1981) How Europe underdeveloped Africa, Rev pbk edn. Howard University Press, Washington, DC
Roht-Arriaza N (1998) Truth commissions and amnesties in Latin America: the second generation. Am Soc Int Law 92(1–4):313–316

Roxin C (2006) Strafrecht Allgemeiner Teil: Grundlagen. Der Aufbau der Verbrechenslehre, 4. vollständig neu bearbeitete Auflage. Beck, Munchen
Samuels D (2004) From socialism to social democracy: party organization and the transformation of the workers' party in Brazil. Comp Pol Stud 37(9):999–1024
Samuels D, Zucco C (2018) Partisans, anti-partisans and non-partisans: voting behavior in Brazil. Cambridge University Press, Cambridge
Samuels DJ (2002) Pork barreling is not credit claiming or advertising: campaign finance and the sources of the personal vote in Brazil. J Polit 64(3):845–863
Sanhueza C, Mayer R (2011) Top incomes in Chile using 50 years of household surveys 1957-2007. Estudios de Economía 38(1):169–193
Schenoni LL, Mainwaring S (2018) US hegemony and regime change in Latin America. Democratization 49:1–19
Seawright J (2012) Party-system collapse: the roots of crisis in Peru and Venezuela. Stanford University Press, Stanford
Silva R (2015) Impactos dos Subsídios Custeados pela Conta de Desenvolvimento Energético. Núcleo de Estudos e Pesquisas/CONLEG/Senado
Skidmore T (1999) Collor's downfall in historical perspective. In: Rosenn KS, Downes R (eds) Corruption and political reform in Brazil: the impact of Collor's impeachment. North-South Center Press, University of Miami, Florida, pp 1–20
Soler L (2002) La transición perenne: Partidos políticos y coyuntura electoral en Paraguay (1989-2000). E-Latina 1(1):15–25
Soto C (2001) Paraguay bajo el signo del estancamiento. Nueva Soc 176:11–16
Souza A d (1999) Collor's impeachment and institutional reform in Brazil. In: Rosenn KS, Downes R (eds) Corruption and political reform in Brazil: the impact of Collor's impeachment. North-South Center Press, University of Miami, Florida, pp 87–118
Stornaiolo U (1999) Ecuador: Anatomía de un país en transición. AbyaYala, Quito
Strøm K (1990) Minority government and majority rule. Cambridge University Press, Cambridge
Suárez D (1997) La segunda transición democrática en Venezuela. In: Anderle Á, Girón J, Horváth G (eds) Estudios sobre transiciones democráticas en América Latina. Universidad de Oviedo, Vice-Rectorado de Extensión Universitaria, Servicio de Publicaciones, Oviedo, pp 133–162
Thiele A (2019) Der gefräßige Leviathan: Entstehung, Ausbreitung und Zukunft des modernen Staates. Mohr Siebeck, Tübingen
Turner B (2010) Paraguay: Muchas novedades y poco cambio. Revista de Ciencia Politica 30(2): 439–450
Vallejos ND (2014) Juicio político y destitución de Fernando Lugo. Dissertation, Argentina. http://www.memoria.fahce.unlp.edu.ar/tesis/te.955/te.955.pdf
Villaverde J (2016) Perigosas pedaladas: Os bastidores da crise que abalou o Brasil e levou ao fim do governo Dilma Rousseff. Geração, São Paulo
Waldmann P (1978) Caudillismo als Konstante der Politischen Kultur Latin Amerikas? Jahrbuch für Geschichte Lateinamerikas 15(1):191–208
Watson C (1991) Political violence in Colombia: another Argentina? Third World Q 12(3/4):25–39
Weyland K (1993) The rise and fall of President Collor and its impact on Brazilian democracy. Journal of Interamerican Studies and World Affairs 35(1):1
Weyland K (2000) La paradoja del éxito: Los determinantes del apoyo político al presidente Fujimori. Debates en Sociología 01:25–26
Weyland K (2006) The rise and decline of Fujimori's Neopopulist leadership. In: Carrión J (ed) The Fujimori legacy: the rise of electoral authoritarianism in Peru. Pennsylvania State University Press, University Park, pp 13–38
Zuanazzi PT, Moraes GI, Stella MA, Cabral PHV (2015) Avaliação e Evolução do Programa de Aceleração do Crescimento (PAC 1 e PAC 2). Sindicato das Empresas de Serviços Contábeis do Rio Grande do Sul, Relatório, p 14

Chapter 4
Legal Aspects of Impeachment in Comparison

4.1 On the Juridical Nature of Impeachments

Legal scholars and practitioners often raise questions regarding the legal or juridical 'nature' or 'character' of a certain institute. What they are truly asking is what kind of relations such institute aims to regulate or what function it performs inside the whole of the legal system—in other words, what its essence is. This is not a trivial or an inconsequential question. The conclusion suggests that the legal relations regulated by certain institute ought to conform to the general rules of its nature.

The institute of marriage, for example, if it is said to have the nature of being of 'family law', then all sorts of legal relations that fit the category of 'marriage' must obey the specific set of rules stablished by family law. These set of rules stablish the 'logic' of the system and their guiding principles. If a contract is deemed to be a prenuptial agreement (a common family law contract), for example, a legal practitioner will expect that the property rights derived from such contract will follow the logic of family law specifically and not the general logic of civil law. Family law is known to have, among other things, special protections to minors or give special rights and duties peculiar to a certain party given their role in the family structure, which would otherwise not be present (or even legally possible) were the contract purely civil in nature and, thus, should lead to different and arguably more appropriate outcomes for that legal relation. Moreover, the consequences of these discussions can also be extended into matters of state organization. If, for example, the Constitution ascribes or detracts competence for legislating on matters of criminal law to an organ, it is important to have a clear idea of what constitutes criminal law so that such competence may be exerted within its constitutional limits and to its constitutional potential.

The same sort of considerations must be extended to impeachments. To ask about the 'nature' of impeachments is to ask about what kind of relations it aims to regulate, how to interpret them, how to respond to them, who may most appropriately dispose upon them, etc. Do presidential impeachments aim to punish and

G. Palamone, *Presidential Impeachment in Latin America*,
https://doi.org/10.1007/978-3-031-44188-2_4

prevent crimes committed by the President? Do they aim to regulate the balance of power between Branches? Do they aim to protect the private property of citizens or to seek compensation for mismanagement? Do they aim to bring conciliation and pacification to society and political elites? Whatever the nature of impeachments, it should be able reflect the answers to these questions.[1] If the verdict is for criminal law, then it could mean that the special prerogatives of the defendant in a criminal lawsuit apply to impeachment procedures. If the verdict for the remaining hypotheses is true, on the other hand, then the defendant would be more vulnerable to negative outcomes. As such, this can be an important question with high stakes for the involved actors.

There are at least two ways of going about the answer to this question, which here will be referred to as (i.) ontological arguments, and (ii.) phenomenological arguments. The first line of argumentation identifies the (i.) *'essential or character defining features' of impeachment*, that is, the most basic set of characteristics that make impeachment itself and not something else. Is it the special procedure? Is it the content of the actions object of the procedure? Is it the person or persons involved in the procedure? Is it the consequences of the procedure? Is it the goal of the procedure? Is it a sum or a combination of these factors? If the political sphere of law can better accommodate these features than, say, the criminal sphere, then probably the best way of dealing with the legal relations encompassed by impeachment is through the set of rules and tools offered by the political sphere.

A second way of going about it would be to identify and observe the (ii.) how impeachments are experienced as phenomena (hence phenomenological arguments), its praxis. Regardless of the 'essential features' of impeachments, under what historical circumstances did they first appear? What motivated the creators to design such a creature? The jurists who made sense of it and applied impeachments in practice, how or why did they do it? How was the general perception of the procedures by those who observed it from outside?

Regarding American-style presidential impeachments, the answer seems to be nowadays very clear: the 'nature' of impeachments is political, meaning that they should subject themselves to the rules and sphere of politics, which are defined by the written rules of the Constitution, specific laws of impeachments, and the political traditions of the Nation. Senator Charles Sumner answered the question in its both ontological and phenomenological forms when he, during President Johnson's impeachment, delivered the following speech:

---

[1] This should not be confused with the question debated in Sect. 2.3. In that instance, the discussion aimed to describe how jurists and laymen associate and use the words 'legal' or 'political' to describe impeachments. There, the conclusion was that calling impeachments political was value-laden description of the procedure, claiming a certain impeachment had gone beyond its constitutionally or morally allotted authority. Here, on the other hand, the discussion purports to answer what set of rules within a constitutional system ought to be applied of impeachments. This sort of judgment strives to be descriptive, albeit it must be admitted that, whenever talking about 'aims of impeachment', some normative judgment unavoidably infiltrates the analysis.

> As we discern the true character of impeachment under our Constitution we shall be constrained to confess that it is a political proceeding, before a political body, with political purposes; that it is founded on political offenses proper for the consideration of a political body and subject to a political judgement only. Even in case of treason and bribery the judgement is political and nothing more.[2]

Ontologically, Sumner notes the essential features of impeachment under the interpretation of constitutional rules: its unique environment, purpose, actors, and object, all of which he classifies as political. Phenomenologically, Sumner performed his understanding, thus, he materialized the political nature of impeachments into its practice, as he voted for Johnson's conviction on what many considered at the time to be purely political infractions.[3]

While Sumner's response is arguably more than enough to settle this (already settled) debate[4] and is entirely corroborated by the observations made in Chaps. 2 and 3, there are a few things about this topic that are generally taken for granted and thus deserve a more detailed discussion.

4.1.1 *Man* Versus *(Juridical) Nature: A Cautionary Note*

An interesting aspect of the literature discussed in this section is that it initiates the debates around the impeachment's nature without ever justifying its basic assumptions. The authors take for granted that the reader will know what it means to attribute one sort of nature over another to impeachments. It is as if the distinctions between the scope of politics, criminal law, administrative law, etc., are clear and uncontroversial, or as if other distinctions, such as those between political punishments and criminal punishments, for example, are also self-evident. This leads to confusing exchanges, as authors seemingly talk past each other, drawing inspiration to answer the question of 'nature' from what seems like arbitrarily selected aspects of the procedure.

One author may say 'impeachments are political institutions because the offenses they address concern society as a whole',[5] while another may say 'impeachments are

---

[2] Supplement to the US Senate (1868), p. 464 (40th Congress, 2nd Session, Trial of Andrew Johnson).

[3] Labovitz (1978), p. 58 ff. Though Johnson's impeachment charges were 'translated' into legally grounded articles of impeachment by the House Judiciary Committee, they were first discussed under broader labels. Representative James Ashley first introduced them as 'the corrupt use of appointment power', 'corrupt use of pardoning power', 'corrupt use of veto power', etc. See also Congressional Research Service (1998), pp. 4–7.

[4] There are a few contrarian but minoritarian opinions, however, as will be pointed out in the next sections.

[5] As expressed by Hamilton et al. (2001), p. 338: "The subjects of its jurisdiction are those offences which proceed from the misconduct of public men, or, in other words, from the abuse or violation of public trust. They are of a nature which may with peculiar propriety be denominated POLITICAL, as they relate chiefly to injuries done to society itself" (emphasis in original).

criminal because an impeachment can only be warranted if an offense is grievous enough to be at least considered a crime'.[6] The first answer suggests that the quality of legal interests or goods define the nature of impeachments, while the second answer suggests it is the seriousness of the infraction. How may one assess the best answer without having a framework as reference? In these specific cases, for example, would it really be true that the commission of a crime 'does not concern the society as a whole', or that grievous offenses necessarily need to be criminal?

Although the reasons for avoiding a complete analysis of these questions are not totally clear, it is an understandable outcome. On one hand, an appeal to common sense is arguably enough to win over most readers. On the other, stablishing an objective framework of comparison can be truly a difficult endeavour and, perhaps, the appeal to common sense is the best that can be realistically offered anyways. Stablishing, for example, the outlines of political responsibility means achieving some degree of consensus on highly contentious topics, which a legal scholar may not feel comfortable or authorized to speak about, particularly because many of these outlines go beyond what is provided by constitutional and statutory law (*e.g.*, a responsibility to be responsive to a responsibility popular demands, to remain loyal to electoral, partisan and ideological commitments, to represent the country and group interests in dignifying manner, to pacify and not escalate internal or external tensions).

Given the complexity of the task in question, therefore, establishing such a framework in any sort of authoritative fashion escapes the scope of this book, which deserves its own study. In a way, this section will repeat the pitfalls of its predecessors, but perhaps more systematically and in full conscience of its limitations. There are nonetheless some concepts which are frequently contrasted with those of political nature and are less controversial. Though they will not outright clarify what 'political nature' is, they might point out to what it is not, thus, giving more rational grounding to the discussion.

4.1.2 *Impeachment* Versus *Criminal Law and Criminal Punishments*

While a detailed and encompassing theory of political responsibilities is still amiss, one may recall neighbouring theories of responsibility, which are already vastly theorized and should, thus, be capable of providing the general outlines of the missing puzzle piece in question. A good place to start is with theories of criminal responsibility, since a criminal nature has been often attributed to impeachments in the past. Why is there a criminal system? What gives the state the right of

[6] Samuel Chase's defence attorney stated that the Senate does not sit "to scan and punish paltry errors and indiscretions too insignificant to have a name in the penal code, too paltry for the notice of a court of Quarter sessions". Labovitz (1978), pp. 38–41.

prosecuting crimes (*jus puniendi*)? What makes a particular act legally relevant and amenable to the rules of criminal law?

The answer to these questions, when talking about modern, secular societies, is perhaps best given by Cesare Beccaria, one of the most influential philosophers of criminal law. According to Beccaria, criminal law is at the heart of the State, among its foremost reasons for existence. Building on Thomas Hobbes' political philosophy,[7] Beccaria argues that the State is a product of a social agreement among its citizens, who, exhausted by the predatory competition presupposed from a state of nature, come together to stablish conditions for cooperation and limit the use of violence among individuals. The State, by virtue of such pact, centralizes the use of violence on itself and commits to applying it only in the case of one of its citizens violating the pact's rules. Through such arrangement, violence is minimized, and individual freedoms are maximized/upheld, as the State will discourage/prevent individuals from predating upon each other through the rational application of punishments. This amenability to the State is part of the freedom individuals must waver to maximize and secure their remaining freedoms. The punishment, on the other hand, is only warranted to the extent that it is needed to uphold the social pact, and any excess may be considered tyranny.[8]

In principle, the law that regulates such punishments is the law of punishments, namely penal or criminal law. Beccaria's definition of crime is formidably broad, however, as he defines it as anything that falls in between "the highest grade [of wrong actions] consist in those which spell the immediate destruction of society, and the lowest those which involve the smallest possible injustice".[9] Confusingly, he suggests the qualifying characteristic of a crime (as opposed to non-criminal legal offenses) would be violation of a public good, but later claims that even private infractions are ultimately also offensive against society.[10]

Indeed, these last assessments by Beccaria are accurate: criminal law concerns itself with big infractions, such as murder, but also small ones, such as public intoxication; it is also not concerned only with legal goods of public interest, such

[7] See Hobbes and Warrender (1983), Chapter V; and Hobbes (2014), Chapter XIV ff. Modern state theory has moved past Hobbes' fiction of social contracts for explaining state formation, but the conclusions argued by Beccaria remain sound. Cooperation to overcome (mutual) predation, as proposed by Tilly (1985), p. 172 ff., for example, is still the most common explanation of state formation, but the essentialism and the dimensions of 'consent' and 'general will' presumed by contractualism are now seen much more critically.

[8] Beccaria and Bellamy (1995), pp. 9–20. There are other justifications for punishment which will not be discussed here since they are more based on conceptions of justice, rationalizations of moral principles (e.g., punishment as retribution for harm), or criminal policymaking (e.g., punishment as deterrent) rather than on institutional functions of the criminal system. For the purposes of this section, they do not provide as much explanatory power. For a detailed account on these other justifications, see Honderich (2006), or Roxin (2006), pp. 69–96.

[9] Beccaria and Bellamy (1995), p. 20.

[10] Beccaria and Bellamy (1995), p. 25.

as life, but also of private interest, such as personal honour.[11] Modern criminalists, however, would contend the idea that these latter characteristics (small and/or private offenses) define the character of criminal law, which, in their reasoning, *should* be reserved as the last resort to dealing with legal infractions (*ultima ratio* principle), since criminal law has in its arsenal the most invasive and severe means of coercion available to any field of law.[12] Criminal law would be, therefore, *subsidiary to all other fields of law*, which, on their turn, are presumed to have milder and more adequate responses to the lesser legal infractions.[13]

Such suggestion implies that there are significant differences between sanctions imposed by criminal law and other fields of law. The accuracy of such assertion, it should be noted, can be highly contingent on the historical moment.[14] Generally speaking, however, contemporary criminal punishments are associated with deprivation of liberty,[15] even though criminal law contemplates (and currently promotes) many alternative punishments, while other fields of law also occasionally back their primary sanctions with incarceration.[16]

With these considerations, it should already be possible to have a more grounded debate around impeachment's nature, at least in what concerns to its relation to criminal law. If impeachment were to fall within the sphere of criminal law, it should, according to the considerations above, (a) aim to preserve the development of the individual and the cohesion of society's most basic rules; (b) it should be subsidiary to other forms of conflict resolution permitted by law; (c) it should provide a criminal sanction, most likely in the form of deprivation of liberty. As it

[11] The theory of legal goods (*Rechtsgüter*) or legally protected interests has its obvious flaws, as one may observe from the not totally clear reason for why life should be a public good and honour not, or vice-versa, as both have private and public dimensions. Jareborg (2004), pp. 524–525, fn. 6, claims it caused more confusion than clarity. Nonetheless, it is still a theory widely employed in civil law systems (*i.e.,* all of Latin America). For critical appraisals, see Paeffgen (2013), or Roxin (2006), pp. 14–18. In the common law systems, the harm principle is more current. Its focus is on the harmfulness of the behaviour rather than the legal goods. See Dubber (2006).

[12] Jareborg (2004), p. 524 ff. Some authors may treat the *ultima ratio* principle under different names or argue for its logical equivalence for other principles, such as the "prospect proportionality principle" or the "subsidiarity principle". See Ibid., pp. 532–533, including footnotes. Roxin (2006), pp. 31–32.

[13] Jareborg (2004), p. 525; Roxin (2006), pp. 32, 45–52.

[14] Rusche et al. (2003), p. 14 ff., trace a parallel between criminal sanctions, predominant modes of production, and certain features of social organization. In their account, fines were applied nearly indistinctly as primary punishments, giving place to corporal punishments only when the subjects were unable to pay fines. The brutality of punishments correlated with the need for deterrence, which, on its turn, was largely determined by a particular population's degree of pauperization.

[15] Foucault (2012), p. 231 ff.; Rusche et al. (2003), p. 24 ff; Roxin (2006), pp. 57–59.

[16] Despite often being described as a barbaric offshoot from distant times, imprisonment for debt is present in many countries. Debtor's prisons and the legally prescribed periods of incarceration ('detention'), however, are substantially less punishing than their criminal counterparts—currently, of course. It bears reminding that debt in Roman law could be 'compensated' as brutally as criminal punishments, including subjecting debtors to execution, slavery, or abduction of their flesh. Patterson (2008), Ford (1926).

is going to be demonstrated, however, the authors who argue in favour of the criminal aspect tend to overlook such considerations.

Charles Black Jr., for example, argues that:

> The president is impeachable for 'Treason, Bribery, and other high Crimes and Misdemeanors'. Treason is a crime. Bribery is a crime. It would seem that a 'high Crime' must in some sense be a crime. What about a 'misdemeanor' or 'high misdemeanor'? It seems unlikely that such a phrase, in such a string, abruptly changes the subject.[17]

Despite ultimately dismissing the question as inconsequential to how impeachments are conducted, he goes on to argue that the punishments of impeachment are severe as "removal by conviction on impeachment is a stunning penalty, the ruin of a life", while acknowledging that "even more important, it unseats the person the people have deliberately chosen for the office". Black Jr. does not give much further attention to what seems to be a peculiar aspect of impeachments, but only affirms that such considerations should impact the standards of proof of the given procedure, and that, consequently, he wishes that such standard would fall somewhere in between civil and criminal standards, as to be neither too lax to allow for sloppy decisions, nor too strict to frustrate accountability.[18]

Another example of the similar logic can be found in perhaps one the most influential accounts on impeachments of all time, Raoul Berger's "Impeachment: The Constitutional Problems". Berger argues that "our impeachment provisions may seem to point out in the direction of criminality because they employ criminal terminology" and then cites articles on trial by jury and presidential pardons, both which exclude impeachment from their effects, whilst describing criminal contexts.[19] Berger, however, does not equate the consequences of impeachment to criminal punishment, for not affecting "life or property"[20] and confirms the political nature of the procedures, albeit still considering the constitutional redaction on presidential pardon to be incongruent with impeachment's nature.[21]

---

[17] Black and Bobbitt (2018), p. 15. A similar argument exists in Brazilian scholarship, as impeachable offenses are named "crimes of responsibility". See Brossard de Souza Pinto (1965), p. 78, quotes on Aureliano Leal.

[18] Black and Bobbitt (2018), pp. 15–19.

[19] Berger (1974), pp. 78–85.

[20] This is done without discussing a material concept of crime or of criminal punishment. At other points, he cites English scholarship using the criteria of "life and limb" instead. Berger (1974), p. 81.

[21] Berger (1974), pp. 84–85. A few authors disagree with this last part. They agree the procedure is political but insist that any form of punishment introduces a criminal aspect. To them, therefore, it would be a mixed-nature procedure, in which the procedures are political, but the consequences are criminal. *E.g.*: Juan García Cotarelo 1995, p. 570, *El regimen politico de los Estados Unidos*, *apud* Roldán (2017), p. 13; or Brossard de Souza Pinto (1965), p. 78 ff., quotes on Pedro Lessa.

4.1.3 *Impeachment* Versus *Administrative Law and Disciplinary Punishments*

Second only to criminal law, administrative law makes frequent appearances in discussions on impeachment's nature. There seems to be an even greater overlap between goals, objects, and consequences between both fields: Like in impeachments, administrative law also "canonically" contemplates the removal and disqualification for office as its most serious sanctions. The President, like the public officer, also works in the public administration. Ultimately, moreover, sanctions from both fields aim at upkeeping society's trust in government and protecting society from malfeasance and abuse.[22]

There are, however, at least three very fundamental differences between the relationships dealt with by impeachments and by administrative law. The first (i.) pertains to the verticality and inequality of power relations. Administrative law deals with the subjection of citizens and its own officers to public machinery, whereas impeachments deal with the confrontation of two (potentially three) of the highest branches of power, in which both are autonomous from each other and have leverages to engage in bargaining and persuasion.[23] The second difference is perhaps the most important and pertains (ii.) the nature of the activities exercised by the officers. The administration concerns itself with managerial acts, with limited degree of discretion and which thus require no direct democratic legitimacy (*i.e.*, they are unelected). The authorities involved in presidential impeachments, on the other hand, are elected and receive a democratic mandate to act politically.[24]

These characteristics create the implication that, in the event of litigation, (a.) an administrative procedure will be deciding the fate of an officer the administrative branch had selected by itself, whereas in an impeachment, one branch will be deciding the fate of an officer of another branch, who was selected by yet a third actor, the people. It means, consequently, also that (b.) the sanctioning of the President has much broader political implications than any administrative procedure can have, precisely due to the political mandate the presidency entails. Holding a President accountable potentially frustrates a popular will absent from of lower offices and poses a greater challenge to the political autonomy of the Executive branch. There is a crucial degree of publicity, transparency, and popular participation that impeachments require, and which disciplinary proceedings cannot match.

---

[22] Roxin (2006), p. 60.

[23] Jellinek (1929), p. 2.

[24] Jellinek (1929), pp. 3–4. A third possible difference is that disciplinary (administrative) infractions tend to be duty-oriented, whereas impeachments are action-oriented. A lower officer generally suffers sanctions when he or she fails to comply with certain expectations, whereas a President is punished when he performs an act typified as impeachable. See Roxin (2006), p. 61. As will be comment in the Sect. 4.2, however, there a few countries in which both orientations coexist.

The authors who argue for an administrative nature for impeachments typically do so due to the scope of their studies.[25] They consider impeachment in general and not presidential impeachment specifically. It is more understandable that the accountability of justices, ministers and a few higher officers can be made effective with strict rules of administrative law, as the aspects of democratic legitimacy and horizontality of power relations are much less pronounced. Ministers, for example, have some democratic legitimacy indirectly attributed to them by virtue of the presidential nomination, but they are not in position to make the same sort of claims to legitimacy or apply the same sort of pressures a President would in a confrontation with Parliament. There is an argument to be made in favour of these cases as a sort of *sui generis,* heteroclite, or mixed-nature administrative procedure, but it would be hardly extensible to the procedures involving Presidents.

4.1.4 Political Nature by Essence: Catalogue of Ontological Arguments

In philosophy, ontology is primarily understood as the study of what there is. It is to ask, in other words: "If it looks like a duck, and quacks like a duck, we have at least to consider the possibility that we have a small aquatic bird of the family anatidae on our hands".[26] Though philosophers are generally not as interested in ducks as Douglas Adams' fictional characters, they may discuss whether some entity exists in physical reality (*e.g.,* God, numbers), whether the presence of certain features constitutes a certain being (*e.g.,* humans vs. featherless bipeds), and how the interaction/relation between different entities may alter their being (*e.g.,* person eating cookie), as these can have significant implications for science and morality.[27] This section will concern itself with the second and third discussions in what they may be applicable to the 'political being' of impeachments, and will present a systematized catalogue of arguments found in the literature. The features and relations pointed by the literature are as follows:[28]

Offense Certain features of the impeachable offenses may be indicative of their predisposition to generate a political procedure or, if anything, of their impropriety of being understood the same way most common legal standards are. One way one

---

[25] *E.g.,* Franz von Liszt, *apud* Brossard de Souza Pinto (1965), p. 76; Hidalgo (2005).

[26] Douglas Adams (1987), Dirk Gently's Holistic Detective Agency, Chapter 30.

[27] Two other discussions could be considered part of ontology, namely the discussion of how to approach these ontological questions (ontological commitment) and the discussion of what asking such questions really mean (meta-ontology). Both were already discreetly addressed in the previous introductory sections.

[28] A cautionary note to avoid the misrepresentation/misunderstanding of the literature: despite this section's division between individual features, the authors mentioned mostly argue for (or against) a *set of features,* which will hold a 'net positive' in favour of impeachment's political nature.

may come to this conclusion is through the observation of the unusual degree of discretion allowed by the text of impeachable offenses. As commonly repeated after Alexander Hamilton, impeachments cannot be tied down by such strict rules of criminal or administrative law, and, thus, their offenses need to be defined broadly to warrant accountability of public men.[29] As Edmund Burke, serving as accusation manager in the impeachment against Warren Hastings, once expressed it with perhaps more sincerity than most modern jurists would allow themselves:

> God forbid – that those who cannot defend themselves upon their merits and their actions may defend themselves behind those fences and entrenchments that are made to secure the liberty of the people; that power and the abuse of power should cover themselves by those things which were made to secure liberty.[30]

Tyranny should not be enabled by the means which were created to contain it. This understanding, which is shared by many influential accounts on impeachment theory,[31] seems to be contingent on a particular understanding of impeachment's purpose as a measure of prevention of infringements upon the public trust, public safety, and society as whole. Such legal goods are said to be so fundamental to the political system that failing to defend them on technicalities would be intolerable. Having, thus, this pronounced concern with legitimacy inbuilt into the offenses would give impeachment an inherent political nature which is arguably better addressed by the toolbox of politics rather than strict legal rules.

Some authors and authorities choose not to speculate on or posit goals for impeachments, and instead simply acknowledge that such unclarity of legal standards for impeachable offenses ultimately makes the procedure political. Although fuzzy concepts are not foreign to jurists, impeachments, due to their extraordinary and sporadic nature, do not offer a system capable of producing precedent and limited concepts which bind their interpretation in a traditional legal sense. The US Supreme Court, for example, has specifically denied jurisdiction over impeachments, arguing they would be "political questions" due to the lack of justiciable standards.[32] It is to say, like some jurists put it, that impeachable offenses ultimately are "whatever House and Senate jointly consider it to be".[33]

Some countries which have striven to build highly limited or clear-cut impeachable offenses such as Brazil or Peru may find these arguments less convincing. Despite this, scholars and authorities in these countries have also concluded for a political nature of impeachments by observing the fact that the offenses of the President, whatever they may be, will necessarily have an overt political dimension,

[29] Hamilton et al. (2001), p. 338.

[30] US Senate (1868), p. 464 (Senator Charles Sumner).

[31] US Senate (1868), p. 464 ff. (Charles Sumner); Labovitz (1978), p. 188 (Joseph Story); Tocqueville et al. (2002), Chapter 7.

[32] Gerhardt (2019), pp. 120–121.

[33] Berger (1974), p. 86, quoting Congressman Gerald R. Ford.

as they are committed in the way political power is conducted.[34] The impact of the offense on the dignity of the office, on the national identity and on the trust in the political institutions, for example, are things often mentioned in impeachment procedures because of the special status and investiture of the President.[35]

Defendant Beyond the fact that the actions of the President end up having clear political connotations as mentioned above, there are other aspects of the office which make procedures against its holder political. The first and most obvious is the fact that the President is democratically elected and, thus, challenge to the office implicates by transference also a challenge to and potential frustration of the will of the people.[36] Any decision on the President's future should, therefore, be sensible to the people's perception of the procedures, as to be perceived as fair. As such, certain well stablished strict legal standards may come off as cynical if applied to political procedures in case they are used to override the popular consensus on the matter. Legal truths operate on a different level than historical truths. A case in point was perhaps commented in Fernando Collor's case study. Collor's impeachment conviction conflicted much with his later criminal acquittal before the Supreme Court. In the absolutory sentence, Supreme Court Justice Sepúlveda Pertence lamented:

> (...) when one sees that big companies, like some of the referred – "suddenly, and no more than suddenly" – since 1990 or the election of Fernando Collor, convinced themselves that the destiny of their entrepreneurial planning depended on the 'services' of an obscure company in Maceió of property of [Collor's campaign manager], it is evident that a lot had to be discovered about the true cause of those payments. We cannot, however, escape the documental evidence brought to these procedures, the declaration of businessmen and the proof of tax collection, which could not completely destroy this montage of apparent service provision.[37]

Arguably, the members of Congress involved in impeachment procedures could not allow themselves the same luxury, both for reasons of self-preservation and preservation of the political system. This issue cannot be simply resolved by lowering standards of proof and require, indeed, a different set of rules, which may deviate significantly from those of civil, criminal, or administrative law in terms of, for example, admissible evidence *(e.g.,* illegally leaked admission of crime) and admissible offenses.

A further aspect of the defendant that should be considered is his or her reach into people's lives and into institutions. Unlike regular court cases where the parties and the adjudicator are unknown to each other, in impeachments all the involved know

[34] Luís María Diez Pícazo (1996), La criminalidad de los gobernantes, p. 69 *apud* Roldán (2017), p. 10 (Peru).

[35] *E.g.,* Collor's behaviour was often contrasted with the dignity expected of a President. Fujimori's removal was presented as the rehabilitation of Peru's democracy and international respectability.

[36] Lozano Villegas (2009), pp. 243–244 (Colombia).

[37] Author's translation of Supreme Court decision AP 307-3/DF, pp. 2785–2786 *(voto sobre Art. 299, CP – Paulo César Farias).*

the President and his agenda.[38] The involved may, moreover, have even voted for or against the President in the elections, may hold strong emotions towards his or her achievements, or even hold some sort of affiliation to him/her in some way. While a compromised court of law or judge may delegate their jurisdiction to someone else to prevent biased decision-making, a Court of Impeachments cannot be substituted by any other collegiate. As such, a different sort of understanding is necessary to accommodate impeachments and such understanding is not satisfactorily supplied by the traditional fields and conceptions of law.

Adjudicator The same logic can be extended to the adjudicating organ, which is equally elected to defend certain policies and political ideas and, by virtue of such mandate, cannot maintain the same pretence of impartiality presupposed of a common court of law.[39] The adjudicator is pressured and influenced by the circumstances and the electorate, their affiliations and oppositional stances are widely known, and ulterior motives in their opinions can always be suggested. Congress, therefore, cannot really act as a judicial organ in a traditional legal sense,[40] and impeachment, like its other activities, has to be a procedure of political nature, governed in some sense by the rules of politics.[41] It is important to remember, moreover, that the choice for Parliament as the Court of Impeachments was strongly motivated by the concern of having an organ with similar democratic legitimacy to that of the President. It is imagined that in the eyes of the people only an organ with such strong legitimation can have actual authority to confront and decide the fate of the President.[42]

Accusation and Investigation Still deeply intertwined with the points made about the adjudicator is the political nature of the accusation and investigation organs. Since both activities are also largely led by parts of Congress, usually through its members, associates, and Commissions of Inquiry, the same limitations to the rule of law are present. The neutrality, independence, and impartiality of the investigators and accusation managers is not comparable to that of a Prosecutor working on a common crime.

What is often overlooked about the investigation and accusation in impeachments, however, is its historical symbology, which is denoted by the usual

[38] Hamilton et al. (2001), p. 338, noted that "The prosecution of [impeachable offenses] (. . .) will seldom fail to agitate the passions of the whole community, and to divide it into parties, more or less friendly, or inimical, to the accused."

[39] Berger (1974), p. 95 ff.

[40] Some authors are content in positing that, by the mere fact that the trial is led by a political organ and not a judicial organ, impeachments should have political nature. They do not go the extra step of arguing how exactly the adjudicator may imprint its political character onto the procedure. *E.g.*, Acuña (2012), p. 21 (Paraguay); Sabsay (2004), p. 506 (Argentina), US Senate (1868), p. 464 (Charles Sumner).

[41] Impartiality, neutrality, and independence are important aspects of the procedure, but they manifest differently. See Sect. 4.7.2 for a detailed discussion.

[42] Hamilton et al. (2001), pp. 339, 344.

description of impeachments as a "method of NATIONAL INQUEST into the conduct of public men".[43] Such expression is inherited from the English tradition[44] and signifies the aspect of popular self-determination implied by the practice impeachments in their historical struggle against irresponsible government and in the mandate of the Lower House, which is theorized as the closest representative of the people.[45] This sort of accountability can be better described as political/constitutional than criminal, civil or administrative. A sort of procedure that in a typical legal context would, for example, be accused of being a "fishing expedition" could, in the context of impeachments, be well warranted politically, as it may have the potential of pacifying growing suspicions behind presidential conduct. In a sense, these inquiries, even when used to dispel ungrounded rumours, have the potential to reinforce the public trust in the presidency and restate the legitimacy of its mandate.

Discretion and Opportunity "The awful discretion which a court of impeachments must necessarily have"[46] goes beyond the already commented power of broadly defining impeachable offenses and a few other rules, which need to be created in short-term to address unforeseen procedural needs. It also encompasses the discretion of choosing the adequate opportunity for carrying out an impeachment. Such spontaneity and subjection to the will of Congress is often understood as characteristic to the political nature of the procedure.[47] Presidential transgressions do not automatically trigger parliamentary investigations and a respective impeachment procedure. They must, instead, be individually received and appreciated by the Lower House, who is reserved the right to reject them on any grounds. Given that an impeachment is by design an encumbering and stressful activity, Congress may choose to dismiss it if it does not seem urgent or relevant, as carrying it out indiscriminately could mean aggravating or causing a crisis between branches. Such expedience, therefore, is given by events which are best described as political, such as intense popular demand, imminence of democratic rupture, or persistent deadlocks, which would be irrelevant in any other strictly legal environment.

Consequence In the making of this section, it became clear that both in the literature, as well as in conversation with other scholars, the first impulse of jurists when confronted with the question of nature is to talk about consequences. If a procedure produces criminal consequences, then the criminal nature should take precedence in defining its character. Those who deny the criminal nature of impeachments commonly choose two paths, namely they argue that (i.) the punishment

[43] Emphasis in the original. Hamilton et al. (2001), p. 338.

[44] Tite (1974), p. 158 ff.; Hoffer and Hull (1984), p. 10.

[45] The Higher House, by contrast, was seen as a council of sages, guardians of legality and tradition. In more modern accounts, the Higher House enhances other forms of representation (*e.g.*, regional, institutional), introducing a counter-majoritarian aspect to Congress.

[46] Hamilton et al. (2001), p. 339.

[47] Manuel Aragón (1995), p. 82, 92, *apud* Roldán (2017), p. 11 (Peru); Perkins (2003).

brought by impeachments is not criminal in any sense,[48] or (ii.) that the sanction does not even configure a punishment.[49] Arguably, however, upon closer inspection these arguments can be less convincing than expected.

If one has the framework proposed by the previous section in mind, the idea of impeachment punishments not being criminal is uncontroversial. Deprivation of liberty is not in the realm of possible outcomes of an impeachment trial, and, therefore, the application of the rules of criminal law are unnecessary and perhaps even detrimental. If one, however, considers the reality of criminal law in Latin America, this argument may become a lot less convincing, as some countries (*e.g.*, Costa Rica, Colombia) do have removal and disqualification from office in their criminal code, specifically for crimes that may only be committed by public officers.[50] In such countries, an argument from consequence could be less appealing.[51]

The second argument can be more difficult to find common ground, as classifying a sanction as punitive can be debatable and highly subjective at times.[52] It is not rare, for example, to find authors who conflate *nearly any sort of punishment* with a sort of criminal nature,[53] not realizing perhaps that legal sanctions, also when they impact individual rights, are to be found in any field of law. Ultimately, it seems that this argument is based on how painful its proponents perceive the consequences of impeachment or how they choose to frame them, as a sort of condemnation to personal ruin. Raoul Berger offers an interesting answer with an analogy comparing impeachment and deportation. Deportation, he argues, is a painful consequence, which, however, is merely indirect result of an alien not having complied with the conditions laid down for his residence.[54] Removal and disqualification from office, therefore, could be equally seen as the unfulfillment of conditions for staying or re-entering office, namely the investment of public trust from the people and institutions. It would be, before all else, a measure of public salvation and

[48] Hamilton et al. (2001), p. 338; Sunstein (2017), p. 154; Acuña (2012), p. 4 (Paraguay).

[49] According to Supreme Court Justice Joseph Story and Senator Charles Sumner. US Senate (1868), p. 463; Acuña (2012), p. 4, affirms punishment may only be applied by the Judiciary.

[50] The rule still seems to be a separation between liberty deprivation in criminal law and the penalty of removal and disqualification from office in administrative law. Also in Latin America, generally, if a criminal conviction leads to removal or disqualification, it is usually indirectly, through different (non-criminal) procedures.

[51] Zaffaroni and Risso (2008), pp. 725–729 (Argentina), for example, argue that disqualification is a criminal consequence meant to inflict pains upon one's honour, and that Congress does not have competence to impose criminal sanctions. The authors ultimately argue that such portion of impeachment dispositions constitute an unconstitutional constitutional rule.

[52] Joseph Story, for example, does not consider disqualification a personal punishment, others do. Berger (1974), p. 79.

[53] Berger (1974), pp. 75–81, cites authors who consider any sanction against "life or property" or "life and limb" a criminal punishment.

[54] Berger (1974), p. 81.

preservation of power from those who abuse it, and not particularly the ostracism of a reprehensible person.[55]

Finally, there is a third, less common line of argumentation which claims impeachments undeniably have political nature because its consequences may influence future elections (*e.g.*, through disqualification of a potential candidate) or even realize policy change, as its mere threat may coerce a sitting President into political agreements, such as cabinet reshuffles and pet project financing with Congress.[56]

Aims and Purposes The aims and purposes of impeachment can be interpreted to be incongruent with the traditional legal fields. Impeachment, it is argued, is not a mechanism meant to preserve personal securities or the very basic societal values, but instead one which means to preserve society and state in a much broader and perhaps also higher sense,[57] thus having overt political motivation. It would be a mechanism of realizing goals of government by upkeeping public trust and preserving the republican form of government, which should not allow the entrenchment of private persons or their interests in the public thing.[58]

Systemic Considerations Some arguments in favour of impeachment's nature as political do so on considerations about its place within the legal and constitutional system. Since the rules on impeachment tend to relegate criminal and civil responsibilities to adjudication in autonomous and posterior procedures to that of impeachment, impeachment would have its own distinct place within the system, which is neither civil, administrative, or criminal.[59] Arguing against that, moreover, could possibly mean the incidence of double jeopardy (*bis in idem*), as the person of the President would face double prosecution for a single fact.[60]

Purely by itself, however, this argument may not be entirely convincing, as a single fact can be framed in different ways as to highlight different offenses, different subjects, and different legal interests.[61] Given the peculiar democratic legitimacy of

---

[55] Tocqueville et al. (2002), Chapter 7; Also in this sense, a Framer of the first republican Constitution of Brazil, Senator José Higino. See Brossard de Souza Pinto (1965), p. 75.

[56] Future electoral process argument: Luís María Diez Pícazo (1996), *La criminalidad de los gobernantes* (Spain), p. 70, *apud* Roldán (2017), p. 10 (Peru); Political concessions argument: Lozano Villegas (2009), p. 242 (Colombia).

[57] Hamilton et al. (2001), p. 338.

[58] US Senate (1868), p. 464; Brossard de Souza Pinto (1965), p. 75, quoting Senator José Higino; Tocqueville et al. (2002), Chapter 7.

[59] Hamilton et al. (2001), p. 338; Sunstein (2017), p. 154. Berger (1974), p. 62, notices for the impeachment in the US, moreover, that "high crimes and misdemeanors" have no parallel in criminal law.

[60] Brossard de Souza Pinto (1965), p. 74, quoting Senator José Higino (Brazilian Senate, Session of October 19th, 1891). Berger (1974), p. 80, citing James Wilson; Tocqueville et al. (2002), Chapter 7.

[61] One could perhaps analogously consider how this happens even in other 'strictly legal' contexts such as inheritance disputes. While the fact of someone's death is the starting point of such disputes,

the President, it is not unreasonable to imagine Congress being responsible for one part of his sanctions in one procedure, while the rest is taken to a regular court of law, even in the hypothetical case the legal community would have agreed impeachment had any other nature than political.

To be sure, some of those who argue against the political nature of impeachments may also come from a place of systemic considerations. Samuel Chase's lawyer famously argued that, if impeachable offenses had anything else other than criminal nature, Congress would be violating the separation of powers and being destructive of the US system of government by removing the high officers of other branches of power on its pleasure.[62]

One more potential systemic consideration is applicable to the so called mixed or semi-presidential systems, which, in Latin America, could correspond only to Peru or Venezuela (per self-ascription in the 1999 Constitution). In such cases, some jurists tend to deny any sort of political accountability of the President, since, in their judgement, the political accountability should remain with the presidential cabinet, which would be held accountable by Congress via votes of confidence and censure.[63] Particularly for Peru this argument does not sound very convincing, as the President still retains considerable political powers[64] and, thus, a commitment to responsible government would evoke some sort of political accountability from the presidency as well, while it may be true that the catalogue of impeachable offenses is indeed fairly limited.[65]

Contextual Considerations Finally, one could talk about a series of features of impeachment procedures which are not immediately evident from a reading of the legal text by itself, but which are nonetheless implied by it. As mentioned before, impeachments are encumbering, traumatic, and extraordinary procedures and, thus, their use will generally be left as an instrument of last resort, usable only when a large fraction of the Parliament becomes convinced that further dialogue with the

---

the actual court proceedings and legal interests that originate from it may be enormous, spanning in all fields of law.

[62] Labovitz (1978), pp. 91–98. This case dealt with the impeachment of a Supreme Court Justice, but the logic is sound also when applied to the President and has since made reappearances in presidential impeachments. In the Framer's logic, separation of powers was a central point in the choice for the match between impeachments and presidentialism. This reasoning was later also restated by the US Supreme Court in the attempted judicial review of Nixon's case. See Gerhardt (2019), pp. 120–121. Guimarães Natal (Brazil) also claimed non-criminal offenses would be incompatible with the presidential system of government. Brossard de Souza Pinto (1965), p. 80. See also Berger (1974), pp. 78–85.

[63] Cesar Delgado Gembes 2012, p. 423, *apud* Roldán (2017), pp. 10–11. Roldán rather call it "diffuse political responsibility" to differentiate from other forms of political control he considers more genuine and are enforceable against the presidential cabinet ("institutional political responsibility" in his words). Roldán (2017), p. 11.

[64] Shugart and Carey (1992), p. 74; Samuels and Shugart (2010), p. 22.

[65] A *sitting* President may be impeached for curtailment of elections, treason, hampering of the functions of other constitutional organs and the illegal dissolution of Congress (Art. 117 of the 1993 Peruvian Constitution).

President is no longer possible or acceptable. Impeachment, therefore, necessitates *a context of intense institutional confrontation* and a departure from the everyday practice of politics.[66] The environment in which impeachments develop will likely be strongly charged, both on the parliamentary floors and on the streets, due to how much may be at stake.[67] The President may lose his/her mandate and doom his/her political career to ruin; the Parliament will likely be severing its chances at collaboration with government, while, at the same, being under intense scrutiny of the media and the public. The people, moreover, will have high and mixed expectations, either hoping at accountability or the preservation of their democratic will.

Arguably, such sort of environment would unavoidably contaminate the procedures with political considerations which should never be mixed with criminal, civil, or administrative matters, and which may take precedence over them. The sort of judiciousness expected from a common court of law simply cannot be replicated in impeachment procedures and, therefore, the rules applicable to them should expect and address this special context.

The importance of context has been argued in impeachment proceedings, where actors perceived a lack of proportionality between infraction and punishment, such as that generated by unforeseen cuts to the accusation, or by the impracticality of dealing with complex offenses with quasi-judicial rigor. In Rousseff's impeachment, for example, a few Senators argued that one had to look at 'the big picture' (*conjunto da obra*), pointing that the few articles of impeachment integrated a larger pattern of persistent recalcitrance and mismanagement.[68] Charles Sumner argued similarly against Andrew Johnson, whom he perceived as an embodiment of a tyrannical strive towards continued segregation and slavery:

> The formal accusation is founded on certain recent transgressions, enumerated in articles of impeachment, but it is wrong to suppose that this is the whole case. It is very wrong to try this impeachment merely on these articles. It is unpardonable to higgle over words and phrases when for more than two years the tyrannical pretensions of this offender, now in evidence before the Senate, as I shall show, have been manifest in their terrible, heart-rending consequences.[69]

[66] Jorge Carpizo (1986), El presidencialismo mexicano, p. 212, *apud* Lozano Villegas (2009), p. 243 (Mexico). The original argument combines the element of political confrontation with that of radical discretion by Parliament. Although political branches confront each other with some frequency, this is one of the few instances in which one of the parties holds practically unrestrained power to decide about the fate of the other, which would, in Carpizo's understanding, give the procedure a particular political characteristic.

[67] Alexander Hamilton in The Federalist n. 65, Labovitz (1978), pp. 28–29.

[68] *Diário do Senado Federal* n. 141/2016, p. 8 ff.

[69] Supplement to the US Senate (1868), p. 463.

4.1.5 Political Nature by Appearance: Catalogue of Phenomenological Arguments

In a rough simplification, phenomenology is the realization that human reasoning has its limitations, and that reality will not necessarily conform to the rules and caprices of such reasoning.[70] The most objective way of acquiring knowledge would be, therefore, not to project one's rationalization onto the world, but, instead, to observe phenomena and attempt to 'reverse engineer' such observations into understanding, may they subvert one's rational expectations or not. Conversely, to the context of the current discussion, a phenomenological account would favour observations about impeachments over the original plan some jurists might have had for them. It would attempt, in other words, to highlight the gap between the expectations and intentions of legislators, scholars, and politicians had for impeachments, on one side, and the actual practice and results of impeachments, on the other. Some ideas of how these arguments could go are as follows:

Behaviour The nature of a thing may be defined through the observation of its behaviour. A procedure may have the features of one thing but behave like another. The constitutional, criminal, administrative features could be merely 'window dressing' hiding a deeper reality. This sort of claim could be leveraged against the late-Stuart era impeachments of England, for example, where procedures were initiated without a chance of success in reaching a criminal conviction, though they continued being effective ways of communicating discontent about policy and materializing political change in the royal Ministries nonetheless.[71]

Regarding presidential impeachments, this claim is frequent and generally comes from a cynical or sceptical account of impeachments' praxis. In William Perkins' study, he reveals how partisan impeachment votes have been in the United States' history, and how often serious constitutional and legal offenses were consciously left unchecked by Congress. From such observations, Perkins concluded that impeachment had little to do with holding the President accountable in any legal sense, but rather played a role in the political power play between parties who have become fed up the Executive's policies.[72]

This account is also common in journalistic accounts of single case impeachments, as commented back in Chap. 2. As explained in that opportunity, the claim of 'being political' is associated with a challenge to impeachment's authority as a control mechanism, since politics and law are popularly comprehended in an antithetical relation. Such accounts tend to carry an impoverished and arguably misguided understandings of both fields, and do not contribute much to the question

[70] In Husserl's own words: "Only phenomena are genuinely given to the knowing subject, and the knowing subject never gets beyond the interconnections of its own experiences". Husserl and Hardy (1999), p. 17.

[71] See Chap. 2 or Roberts (1966) for details.

[72] Perkins (2003), in particular p. 44.

being asked in this section, which, again, concerns itself with the discussion on impeachment's nature in ideal or technical language. It is nonetheless completely plausible that legal means be instrumentalized or subverted to serve as a political weapon, as has been the case more clearly in relation declarations of vacancy than it has been the case with impeachments, as the latter was directly designed as a political tool.

Ascription To ascribe means to attribute something to something else. Defining impeachment's nature through ascription would mean, therefore, to attribute it to a certain sphere of law, regardless of any features it may possess or any sort of deeper logical/historical reason. It is to say, 'impeachment is (for example) political, because I say it is so'. It may sound like an underwhelming explanation to the question posed by this section, but realistically it is one of the most honest accounts one may ultimately give. Acknowledging an implicit or explicit agreement on the matter is a valid answer to the question, although it may ultimately be pointed out as arbitrary, unappealing, or unreasonable.

There is no need, for example, for a grand narrative to justify 'murder as being matter of criminal law', nor must there be a relation of logical necessity between a system and its outcomes. It suffices jurists are taught or mandated by an authoritative source to treat the matter in a certain way.[73] One just needs to understand the rules and 'play the game', so to say. That is probably how most practitioners of law learn to operate it. Tradition, that is, the transmission of practices through generations, does not need to be and often is not entirely rational. Perhaps something can be said about impeachments in this same regard.

One way this argument may appear is as a declaration of self-evidence: "[the political trial] is an institution of clear political nature, which is carried out by an organ eminently of the same type, such as the Parliament or Congress".[74] This seems to be more common in the countries of Latin America who chose to translate impeachments officially[75] under the title of *juicio politico* (lit. trans., political trial), namely Argentina, Colombia, Ecuador, Honduras, Mexico, Paraguay, Peru and Paraguay,[76] and the political dimension is just too openly acknowledged to be glossed over or argued against.[77] The Honduran law of impeachments (Decree n. 51-2013), for example, openly posits in its art. 8 that the nature of impeachments

[73] *E.g.*, Alexis de Tocqueville takes for granted that impeachments are political, even in their English and European forms which allowed for criminal punishments. See Tocqueville et al. (2002), Chapter 7.

[74] Author's translation of Nieves Ruiz (2017), p. 59 (Peru).

[75] Other countries may use the terminology unofficially, likely due to the influence of comparative legal works and common translations of literature on English and North American impeachments.

[76] Articles in the respective, current constitutions: Argentina, art. 53, 59; Colombia, art. 174, 175; Ecuador, art. 129, 145; Honduras, art. 234; Mexico, art. 110, 111; Paraguay, art. 225; Peru, art. 99, 117 (and parliamentary by-laws, art. 89); Uruguay, art. 93, 102.

[77] This is common strategy used by Courts, *e.g.*, Peru, 2010, TC 00013-2009-AI, or Brazil, 1937, HC 26.544. There are also those who claim a sort of mixed political-criminal nature, as if to be

is political and that, therefore, what is decided in the scope of its procedure bears no sort of relationship or subjection to the spheres of legal responsibility.

Attitude Finally, a last imaginable account would be through the observation of the attitudes of those who conduct an impeachment. A procedure could have all the right legal features and be conducted with all the proper legal 'etiquette', and yet mask the true intention of those who instrumentalize it. This could arguably be pointed out through the observation of the prevailing arguments in favour or against an impeachment, and perhaps also a conjectural analysis, which may indicate that those involved had other things in mind that came before the legal accountability of a President.

This claim could arguably be used, for example, in the description of the Venezuelan system, after the precedent set by the impeachment of President Carlos Andrés Pérez, who after narrowly surviving two coup attempts and refusing to resign in the context of constant and intense popular and parliamentary pressure, was removed by cooperative efforts of the Parliament and the Supreme Court due to offenses many would describe as mere clerical errors of his administration.[78] All leads to the conclusion that, despite its legal merits, CAP's removal was foremostly motivated by an intent in preserving Venezuela's then vulnerable democracy and stabilizing internal political tensions. Such were goals which could not be fitted squarely under Venezuela's paradigms of constitutional law, but which could be accommodated under a broader understanding of politics and political responsibility.

4.1.6 Nature of Non-Parliamentary Impeachments and Pretrials

Should the form of an impeachment have any impact on its nature? As discussed in the previous sections, the character defining features of these procedures go well beyond their mere form or adjudicating organ, although these are admittedly contributing factors. It can be said with some confidence that the aspects that dictate such nature point overwhelmingly towards a political character and, thus, also towards the need of political rules and interpretative framework. When dealing with impeachment surrogates, however, there will be a stronger tendency to a dual nature, given that surrogates, as the name suggests, are not created to serve as means of presidential accountability, but may end up doing so, given the appropriate circumstances and the creativity of the actors involved. In this section, a tentative classification of these alternatives will be offered. It should be noted, once more, that many of these instruments escape the scope of this book but are included for

found, for example, in Juan García Cotarelo 1995, p. 570, *El regimen politico de los Estados Unidos*, *apud* Roldán (2017), p. 13.

[78] See the respective case study for details.

contrastive purposes. Specialized studies on each of these forms are necessary so that a definitive answer on their nature may be offered.

Predominantly Judicial Impeachments

The judicial impeachments carry over all aspects of the parliamentary impeachments (American-style impeachments), with exception to the adjudicating organ, the Court of Impeachments. Congress still needs to initiate and/or approve impeachment proceedings and, by doing so, will introduce an element of opportunity to the judicial impeachment. As such, these impeachments still overwhelmingly retain the politicizing features observed in the parliamentary counterpart. They do often, however, tend to have a more limited scope in terms of impeachable offenses. The Brazilian and Colombian variants of the judicial impeachment, for example, are only applicable to common crimes.[79] In these cases, as the conviction may generate criminal consequences on top of the removal and disqualification from office, criminal rules will necessarily apply, even if in somewhat limited fashion. These cases will have a mixed criminal-political nature, applying, thus, in part rules of criminal law and rules of politics. This is certainly problematic from both the perspective of legal and democratic theory, as the Court will likely deliver unsatisfying results both fronts. On one hand, the Court will see itself sacrificing too many judicial safeguards to properly accommodate an ideal of rule of law, and, on the other, will see itself lacking the democratic legitimation and representativeness to decide the political fate of the President.

The countries with judicial impeachments that accept a broader scope of impeachable offenses, such as, arguably, Venezuela, Costa Rica, or Bolivia, on the other hand, are less problematic in this sense, and *can* eventually retain a pure political nature to their procedures, despite the legalistic pretension implied by high Courts.

The *Sui Generis* Case of Bolivia After the 2010 Law of Impeachment

In Bolivia, the President may be removed through a judicial impeachment (*juicio de responsabilidades*) or through a criminal suit.[80] In short, the Chamber of Deputies and the Senate must deliberate upon a request coming from the General Prosecutor on whether the President has committed an offense (*delito*) in the exercise of his or her functions. The Supreme Court then acts as the Court of Impeachments, trialling the matter in every legal sense, be it political, criminal, and civil. It may impose removal, disqualification, criminal penalties, and demand civil reparations for whatever damages created by the presidential conduct. The impeachable offenses defined in the art. 12 of the law of impeachment (Law n. 44 of 2010), however, offer an array of conducts that may have political, criminal, and civil nature. As such, the nature of the procedure itself may vary from case to case, according to the charges put forward by the authorities. Naturally, a political nature may be prevalent in most cases for the reasons mentioned in the previous sections, but a mixed or *sui generis* situation may

[79] Brazil: art. 86 of the 1988 Constitution; Colombia: art. 175, 3 and 235, 2 of the 1991 Constitution.

[80] Arts. 161, 7 and 184, 4; and art. 170, respectively, of the 2009 Constitution. There are no mentions to presidential immunities in the Constitution.

be eventually created, particularly in the case of impeachments against former Presidents.[81] There is currently little practical evidence for making a grounded assessment.

Surrogate: Political Pretrial (*Antejuicio politico*) or Immunity Removal (*Desafuero*)

The political pretrial is an incomplete procedure when compared to the others contemplated in this book. It serves the removal the President's protection from judicial persecution (though *criminal suits* are most common) and may, in some cases, cause temporary suspension from office.[82] By itself it is arguably a predominantly political procedure where members of Congress have significant discretion to assess the political opportunity for removing the presidential immunity, while also considering the criminal pertinence of the supposed accusations (*i.e.,* proportionality, robustness of evidence, imputability, etc.)[83] as would happen in the presentment of a criminal case. From the evidence gathered in the writing of this book,[84] it remains unclear how capable legislators are to appropriately gauge these latter elements, which require some acquaintance with and commitment to theory of criminal law. Intuitively, it should fall short of the expectations of the legal community for reasons already discussed and should result in a procedure strongly political in nature.[85] The consequence of suspension from office, moreover, can bring about numerous considerations about of political order, as, in practice, such suspensions are likely to be as good as a terminal removal, since criminal suits may last longer than the remaining time of the presidential mandate.

Guatemala's Particular Commitment to Apolitical Pretrials

Guatemala is one of the few countries where the term pretrial (*antejuicio*) does not come qualified by the adjective "political". In fact, its pretrial legislation (Decree n. 85 of 2002) goes further and suggests that the National Congress should reject criminal charges, if they seem to be motivated by "spurious, political or illegitimate reasons" (art. 17, g). Ontologically, this feature may give the Guatemalan pretrial a pure criminal nature. The fact that the removal of immunity *does not* cause

---

[81] Former Presidents lack most of the institutional power, legitimacy, and relevance that makes the presidency impact the nature of impeachments as politicized procedures, making the mixed-nature thesis defensible.

[82] Countries with automatic suspension upon immunity removal: El Salvador (art. 236, 237; lasts duration of trial); Costa Rica (art. 121, 10; duration contingent on provisional arrest for common crimes only), Mexico (art. 111; lasts duration of trial); Venezuela 1961 (art. 150, 8; lasts duration of the trial). The Constitutions of Ecuador (2008), Peru and Guatemala do not stablish suspension.

[83] In Spanish and Portuguese this is called respectively *formación de causa/condiciones de procesabilidad*; and *formação de causa/condição de procebilidade.*

[84] In the parliamentary records of pretrials against Pérez Molina (Guatemala, 2015), or Jimmy Morales (Guatemala, 2016–2020), for example, there is very little to work with in terms of legal argumentation. Dedicated comparative studies on this impeachment surrogate are needed for a better assessment, however.

[85] All reasons given in the previous sections may also apply here. Particularly impactful is the distance between *ethos* and *habitus* of the legal community vis-à-vis the Parliament.

suspension from office, which is undeniably a significant political consequence of most *antejuicios*, would corroborate that conclusion.[86] Phenomenologically, however, these features may also lead to two other outcomes. On one hand, it could still be used politically, despite all its commitments to a strict legalism. On the other, its commitments could be taken so seriously as to effectively frustrate any form of presidential accountability whatsoever, given that, for reasons already sufficiently discussed, a political motive for the removal of the President may always, and convincingly so, be argued.

Recent history gives a somewhat unsatisfactory answer to this question, or at least a two-phase sort of answer. The first and only President to ever be stripped of immunity was Otto Pérez Molina (2015), and since then other three frustrated attempts were directed against his immediate successor, Jimmy Morales (2016–2020).[87] The first failed pretrial against Pérez Molina displayed perfect partisanship, with every party but the President's voting in favour of the immunity removal. This, however, turned into a unanimous vote two weeks later deciding for the immunity removal, and led Pérez Molina to resign immediately.[88] Such an unanimity suggests that the preponderance of factors beyond partisan politics, as Pérez Molina's party, the *Partido Patriota* (PP), did have control over the veto threshold but chose in large part not to shield the President. As a result, a case could be made for criminal nature for the procedures.

After the experience with Jimmy Morales, however, this argument became less persuasive. The records display short debates and consist mostly of roll calls of vote, giving no insight into the motives and understandings of the Deputies regarding the legal issues at hand. The few who manifest themselves argue either for the abstract idea that a pretrial is salutary to the reinforcement of public trust democracy and should succeed, or that the accusations are politically motivated and should therefore be rejected, although similarly in abstract manner.[89] The focus on political expedience over legal substance could suggest a political nature, although a case could be made for an irresponsible presidency as well (that is, pretrial would be mere dead letter). This last conclusion could be corroborated by the fact that the officers

[86]The issuing of an arrest warrant would nonetheless cause removal from office under such conditions.

[87]Pretrials against Pérez Molina: *Antejuicio* n. 197-2015 and n. 401-2015; Pretrials against Jimmy Morales: *Antejuicio* n. 246-2017 (voted twice), and n. 815-2018. Other charges against both Presidents have offered since these pretrials but were blocked by either the Constitutional or the Supreme Court.

[88]Prensa Libre, August 13th, 2015: "*Congreso salva a Pérez Molina y busca cambios en el MP*"; Prensa Libre, September 1st, 2015: "*Pérez Molina queda sin inmunidad*".

[89]*Diario de Sesiones del Congreso de la República de Guatemala* n. 61, September 11th, 2017, pp. 31–47. For a breakdown of partisanship, see Prensa Libre, September 22nd, 2017: "*Jimmy Morales: Así votaron los diputados para frenar de nuevo el antejuicio contra el presidente*".

responsible for the accusations were since expelled from the country, while the high Courts, who act as the gatekeeper of pretrial, were packed with loyalists.[90]

Peru's Pretrial of Former Presidents
In the 1993 Constitution, the hypotheses for impeaching a *sitting* President are limited to four specific categories (*i.e.,* treason, irregular dissolution of Congress, embarrassing elections, or electoral organs; art. 117). Accountability for any other offense, be it constitutional or criminal in nature, must wait for the end of the presidential mandate (arts. 99 and 100). If in the pretrial Congress convicts for a criminal offense, the former President must be indicted before the Supreme Court, who will trial the case as a criminal suit. If unsuccessful, the Court's acquittal will overturn the pretrial conviction and its consequences. If the pretrial conviction does not entail a criminal offense, however, but just a constitutional one, then there is no trial in the Supreme Court. This creates two different situations for the pretrial, arguably demanding two different natures.

As commented before, former Presidents lose most aspects of their political influence after leaving office, making the arguments of the previous sections weaker. It becomes more defensible, therefore, to argue for a pure criminal or mixed political nature in the case of the pretrial, particularly when referring to accusations grounded on criminal offenses. With less at stake, it is at least plausible to imagine instances in which Congress could make a strictly legal-technical decision about whether the presidential immunity should be stripped. Phenomenologically, however, there often are lingering political issues that need resolution in these procedures, as well as persistent political disputes due to partisan affiliation that inevitably weigh in the considerations. Pretrials against Fujimori or Vizcarra are testament to this, despite being centred on formalistic legal disputes.[91] As such, realistically, such pretrials should have at least a mixed political-criminal nature, if not pure political.

4.2 Objective Element: *Actus reus* of Impeachable Offenses

Impeachable offense is an umbrella term that encompasses any sort of behaviour amenable to impeachment procedures. Such behaviour may encompass common crimes or crimes committed only in the exercise of office (*propter officium;* also known as proper crimes), but also other forms of non-criminal conduct that endangers or harms the political system, society itself, or the national honour, such as

[90] El Faro, July 20th, 2021: "*Un poder a la sombra se ensaña contra la resistencia en Guatemala*"; BBC News, January 10th, 2019: "*Expulsión de la CICIG de Guatemala: Supremo tramita desafuero de jueces de la Corte de Constitucionalidad en medio del pulso de poderes*".

[91] Fujimori was impeached for violating a statute that required parliamentary approval for presidential travel, while Vizcarra was impeached for skipping queue for taking the COVID vaccine. Admittedly, the latter was framed as abuse of office for personal gain. See *Informe Final Denuncias Constitucionales 423 y 427.*

abuses of power, hampering the relations between branches, undermining electoral processes, among other things.

Although Latin America took inspiration from the impeachment in the US Constitution, the Latin American Framers tailored the institute to fit their ideals of justice, of democracy, of republicanism, of rule of law, and of separation of powers. Countries that valued a strict separation of power, for example, may have chosen to reduce either their impeachable offenses purely to 'common crimes' or to a limited list of infractions. Those that valued responsible government above all, selected a vast list of infractions or open-ended formulations, giving their Parliaments ample discretion to check the Executive. Table 4.1 shows how these visions manifested themselves in the Latin American adaptations of impeachment:

This section will discuss the general outlines of how impeachable offenses are organized in Latin America and what peculiarities these choices may impart on the overall design of impeachments. It will indicate that presidential accountability is more often exerted through (1.) open-ended formulas, although mentions to (2.) common and proper crimes rank high in impeachment provisions. The offense of (3.) treason, which can fit either of the previous categories, will be discussed separately due to its ambiguity and special historic charge. For contrastive purposes, some commentary will also be directed at (4.) alternative forms of presidential removal, which have been employed before as surrogates for impeachment procedures. These are removals grounded on the onset of (a.) vacancy of the presidency, usually due to prolonged absence, or physical, mental, or moral incapacity, (b.) crises and popular commotion, and (c.) electoral illegitimacy. An overview of impeachable offenses in Latin American history can be found in Table 4.3 at the end of this section.

4.2.1 Constitutional Violations

During the 1787 Convention, the Framers of the US Constitution had to deal with two apparently irresoluble tensions. On one side, they wanted a strong Executive branch, who would be able to react energetically and diligently to needs of government, without getting necessarily bogged down by encumbering parliamentary deliberation and scrutiny.[92] They also, however, abhorred the idea of reproducing the tyrannical system of government they fought so dearly to overcome, that is, a form of monarchy capable of oppressing its people without consequence.[93] It was, therefore, their goal to accomplish the difficult balancing act of creating a powerful, yet tame and just government. The key to achieving such balance depended on,

[92] Wood (2006), p. 48 ff.

[93] Examples of (outward) repulsion to the monarchy are plentiful throughout the Convention (e.g., Farrand 1911b, p. 33 ff.). There has always been ambiguity regarding the monarchy, however. See Wood (2006), p. 48 ff.

Table 4.1 Description of impeachable offenses in Latin America and the United States

Country (Constitution)	Impeachable offenses
Argentina (1994)	**Art. 53:** Poor performance or crimes committed in the exercise of the presidential functions, and common crimes.
Bolivia (1967)	**Art. 68, 12 and 127, 6**: Infractions (*delitos*) committed in the exercise of the presidential mandate
Bolivia (2009)	**Art. 184:** Infractions (*delitos*) committed in the exercise of the presidential mandate; **Art. 2 IL**: Infractions (*delitos*) committed in the exercise of the presidential mandate; **Art. 4 IL:** Violations of basic rights and constitutional guarantees; **Art. 12 IL:** 1. Treason and subjection, total or in part, of the Nation to foreign domination; 2. Violation of individual rights; 3. Influence peddling; 4. Engaging in negotiations incompatible with office; 5. Resolutions against the Constitution; 6. Anticipation or extension of functions; 7. Racketeering (*concusión; exacciones*); 8. Genocide; 9. Bribery (*soborno y cohecho*); 10. Any other official infractions committed during the exercise of presidential functions.
Brazil (1988)	**Art. 85:** Menace 1. the existence of the Union; 2. the free functioning of constitutional organs and federative units; 3. the exercise of political, individual or social rights; 4. the internal security of the country; 5. the probity of the administration; 6. the budget law; 7. the enforcement of laws and judicial decisions. Each of these items are further defined in 67 articles of the IL. **Art. 86, §4**: Proper crimes committed during the current mandate.
Chile (1980)	**Art. 52, 2, a:** Acts of the presidential administration that may have gravely compromised the honour or safety of the Nation or may have openly violated the Constitution or the laws.
Colombia (1991)	**Art. 178:** Constitutional grounds; **Art. 329 PBL**: Crimes committed in the exercise of one's functions, indignity, poor conduct, or common crimes.
Costa Rica (1949)	**Art. 149:** 1. Compromise in any way the liberty, political independence or the territorial integrity of the Republic; 2. Hinder or embarrass, directly or indirectly, popular elections; menace the principles of presidential alternation or succession, as well as the freedom, order and purity of suffrage; 3. Hinder or embarrass the functions of the Legislative Assembly, or curtail its freedom and independence; 4. Deny publishing or enforcing the law or other legislative acts; 5. Hinder or embarrass the functions proper to the Judiciary Power, curtail Courts from the liberty necessary to dispense justice; Embarrass in any way the function of electoral organs or of Municipalities; 6. All other cases of action or omission that violate written law.
Cuba (2019)	–
Dominican Rep. (2010)	**Art. 83**: Severe foul play (*faltas graves*) in the conduct of one's functions.
El Salvador (1983)	–
Ecuador (1979)	**Art. 59, f:** Infractions (*infracciones*) committed in the exercise of one's official functions.
Ecuador (*reform 1996*)	**Art. 82, g:** Treason, bribery (*cohecho*), or any other infraction that gravely harms the national honour.
Ecuador (1998)	**Art. 130, 9:** Offenses against the security of the State, crimes (*delitos*) of racketeering (*concusión*), bribery (*cohecho*), embezzlement (*peculado*), or illicit enrichment.

(continued)

Table 4.1 (continued)

Country (Constitution)	Impeachable offenses
Ecuador (2008)	**Art. 129:** 1. Offenses against the security of the State; 2. Crimes of racketeering (*concusión*), bribery (*cohecho*), embezzlement (*peculado*), or illicit enrichment; 3. Crimes of genocide, torture, forceful disappearing of persons, kidnapping or murder, for reasons of political or conscientious nature.
Guatemala (1985)	–
Honduras (1982)	–
Honduras *(reform 2013)*	**Art. 234:** Serious charges for conduct in office, actions against the Constitution or the national interest, signs of clear negligence, incapacity or incompetence for the performance of office; **Art. 5 IL:** 1. partake in illegal activities, receive benefits incompatible with the office, seek personal benefit not conceded by law; 2. Actions or omissions in clear contrariety with the functions, duties or attributions stablished by the Constitution or to the National Interest; 3. Negligence, incapacity or incompetency for performing duties of office; Malice, clear lack of proficiency or illness that limits the diligent performance of the duties of office and that may cause harm to the public interest.
Mexico (1917)	**Art. 108:** Treason and serious common crimes.
Mexico *(reform 2021)*	**Art. 108:** Treason, corruption, electoral crimes, and common crimes.
Nicaragua (1987)	–
Panama (1972)	**Art. 160:** Harming the free functioning of Public Power or violating the Constitution or the laws; **Art. 191:** 1. Transgression of constitutional functions; 2. Acts of violence or coercion in electoral procedures; hindering of meetings of the National Assembly; hindering the functions of other constitutional organs or public authorities; 3. Crimes against the international personality of the State or against the Public Administration.
Paraguay (1992)	**Art. 225:** Poor performance, infractions committed in office or common crimes.
Peru (1993)	**Art. 117:** *(sitting Presidents)* Treason, hindering presidential, parliamentary, regional, or municipal elections, dissolving Congress for grounds not stated in art. 134, and hindering meetings or the function of electoral organs; **Art. 99**: *(former Presidents)* Any constitutional or legal violation occurred during or in 5 years after leaving office.
United States (1789)	**Art. 2, Sec. 4:** Treason, Bribery, or other high Crimes and Misdemeanours.
Uruguay (1967)	**Art. 93:** Constitutional violations or other serious infractions (*delito*).
Venezuela (1961)	**Art. 150, 8 and 215**: Any justiciable act.
Venezuela (1999)	**Art. 266:** Any justiciable act.

Source: Own elaboration and translation. Some formulations were simplified and summarized. IL refers to the impeachment laws of the respective country. These would be for Bolivia Law n. 44 of 2010, for Brazil Law n. 1079 of 1950, and for Honduras Decree n. 51 of 2013. PBL refers to parliamentary bylaws. This would be, for Colombia, Law n. 5 of 1992. Words such as delito, infracción and crime are not necessarily employed in a technical sense by the law maker. Countries without offenses listed only have the pretrial (antejuicio) as a form of accountability or have irresponsible presidencies

among a few other things,[94] having a very clear definition of what lines the Executive ought not to cross. Limiting government incursion in matters illegitimate, while maximizing its reach in those that are legitimate, was the key to this project.

The Framers, therefore, first rejected overly broad definitions of impeachable offenses, as they feared such level of parliamentary discretion had the potential to subvert their project entirely.[95] If the President were accountable for any act, the whole Executive Branch could be held hostage at the Parliament's whims and become its creature. Despite having reached an apparent consensus on this conclusion, the Framers came back to a formula of impeachable offenses which nonetheless revealed itself to be considerably broad: "Treason, Bribery, or other high Crimes and Misdemeanours" (art. 2, sec. 4) before the Convention was over.[96] The reason why that is, however, has not been entirely documented by James Madison, who transcribed most of the debates of that Convention. The only tip Madison gives the reader is that George Mason, inspired by the impeachment of Warren Hastings, Governor-General of India, suggested treason, and bribery were insufficient grounds to protect the Constitution, and later proposed the addition of "high crimes and misdemeanours".[97]

The first real clarification for this design choice is revealed later, through Alexander Hamilton's defence of impeachment in the Federalist Papers, which were published the following year in New York as pamphlets meant to convince sceptical member states to adopt the proposed Federal Constitution.[98] There, Hamilton, while discussing the choice for the Senate as the Court of Impeachments, states:

> The necessity of a numerous court for the trial of impeachments, is equally dictated by the nature of the proceeding. This can never be tied down by such strict rules, either in the delineation of the offence by the prosecutors, or in the construction of it by judges, as in common cases serve to limit the discretion of courts in favour of personal security.[99]

In other words, so that a procedure like impeachment may achieve its goal of protecting society,[100] it must make a few sacrifices to the main protector of personal securities, namely the rule of law in its commitments to the certainty of legal norms or to impartial adjudication in its commonsensical understanding. This idea, for those who followed the Hastings impeachment trial closely, should not come as a surprise. Edmund Burke, lawyer who acted as accusation manager in the case, argued:

[94] For further discussions on other aspects relevant to such balance, see Hamilton's comparison of Presidents and Monarchs in The Federalist n. 69.

[95] Mason's proposal of impeachable "maladministration" was rejected on such grounds. Farrand (1911a), p. 550.

[96] Farrand (1911b), pp. 63–78; Farrand (1911a), p. 550.

[97] Farrand (1911a), p. 550. Madison's notes become scarcer by the end of the Convention, this instance being a particularly notorious case.

[98] Hamilton et al. (2001), pp. xli ff. and 337 ff.

[99] Hamilton et al. (2001), p. 339.

[100] Hamilton et al. (2001), p. 338.

> God forbid – that those who cannot defend themselves upon their merits and their actions may defend themselves behind those fences and entrenchments that are made to secure the liberty of the people; that power and the abuse of power should cover themselves by those things which were made to secure liberty.[101]

It is to say that tyranny should not be enabled or legitimized by the securities which were created prevent it. Although one cannot know exactly to what extent, it is a sensible to imagine that the Hastings trial held a special place in the minds of the Framers. It represented, ultimately, the clash between two visions of empire: one in which the colonizer had the right to conquest anything it could subdue, and another in which the colonized had fundamental rights to be respected.[102] Burke's indictment of Hastings' abuses in the Governorship of India was an endorsement of the latter view, and this was one that presumably resonated with the Framers, given that they also had just recently gone through similar experiences. In some ways, the 1789 Constitution was bound to enshrine these principles.

While it is true that the Hastings trial ultimately perished in the judgment of the House of Lords, who were thought to act as the 'guardians of legality',[103] and that its defeat represented "a transatlantic instance of incompetency" of a procedure that was "tedious and uncertain at best", as some put it,[104] it gave important lessons about the workings of legalized tyranny and about how their vision of impeachment should go beyond certain limitations of its English predecessor. The American impeachment was to be revolutionary on its own right, and open-ended concepts introduced by the definitions of impeachable offenses were integral to that fate, as they indirectly extended the people's right to decide more of their own political fate. Given the particular context of the presidential impeachment, the justness and legitimacy of an impeachment conviction was to be derived not from the technically perfect legal subsumption of air-tight definitions of impeachable offenses, but rather from the general and representative consensus achieved in Congress on the necessity of removing a President who no longer acted in the best interest of the Nation.

4.2.1.1 High Crimes and Misdemeanours: The English and American Precedents

The first appearance of the terminology "high crimes and misdemeanours" is, according to the most careful accounts, on February 12th of 1642, in England.[105]

---

[101] As quoted (and endorsed) by Senator Charles Sumner in Andrew Johnson's impeachment: Supplement to the US Senate (1868), p. 464.

[102] Mukherjee (2005), pp. 589–590.

[103] Tite (1974), p. 170 ff.

[104] As described by John Vinning of Delaware. Labovitz (1978), pp. 23–24.

[105] Roberts (1975), p. 1431. In the cited article, Clayton Roberts corrects many imprecisions regarding this terminology and associated assumptions, which somehow keep being repeated even in recent studies on the American impeachment. An eventual clash between what is said here and major works on impeachment may be due to their oversight of Roberts' contributions.

Its use was mostly careless and confused, and its meaning in the understanding of the high Court of the Lords did not stray from that of common courts. The word ‘high’ was used for emphasis, and the word ‘misdemeanours’ merely indicated offenses that were not serious enough to configure ‘felony’.[106] This was, however, a time in which the Commons were already making use of impeachment without intent of going to trial. Many officers were being impeached for behaviour that, for the standards of the time, were mere ‘acts of folly’, that is, reprehensible but not illegal behaviour; misjudgements perhaps, but not of the punishable kind.[107] Buckingham’s impeachment was a clear example of this, as the Commons energetically condemned his mismanagement of the military and pernicious influence on King James I.[108] Although officers were impeached for such acts, the Lords consistently rejected any creation of a new category of non-criminal offenses, and the Commons, being aware of such resolution, abandoned most impeachments after approving them, lest they were compounded with robust charges of bribery, treason or the like.[109] As commented back in Chap. 2, the mere signalling of dissatisfaction by the Commons through impeachments eventually became nearly the goal itself, as it at times sufficed to produce the ministry change sought after.[110]

The American tradition of “high crimes and misdemeanours” was arguably inspired in the Commons’ use of the expression, albeit such use condemned most impeachment trials of its time to failure. The endorsement of non-criminal offenses is visible in George Mason’s and Alexander Hamilton’s arguments commented above, but also in discussion of the ratifying conventions,[111] all of which denoted an implicit recognition of the President’s duty of conducting the public thing responsibly. The President would incur in high crimes and misdemeanours in case he would “deviate from his duty”,[112] “abuse powers vested in him by the people”;[113] it would be “the misconduct of public men, (. . .) the abuse or violation of some public trust”.[114] For being potentially so unpredictable, it has been argued that these offenses would be “so utterly incapable of being defined, or classified, that the task of positive legislation would be impracticable (. . .)” and that, therefore, “no previous statue is necessary to authorize an impeachment for any official misconduct”.[115]

This design choice naturally suffered pushback, particularly under the watch of defence attorneys who correctly identified how much more difficult a defence against a malleable impeachment charge can become. A few of their arguments

[106] Roberts (1975), p. 1432 ff.

[107] Roberts (1975), pp. 1432–1433.

[108] Roberts (1975), p. 1433 ff. See Chap. 2 for details on the Buckingham impeachment and context.

[109] Roberts (1975), pp. 1436–1439.

[110] Roberts (1975), p. 221 ff.

[111] Gerhardt (2019), p. 107 ff.

[112] A. MacLaine of South Carolina, Elliot (1836c), p. 47.

[113] S. Stillman of Massachusetts, Elliot (1836b), pp. 168–169.

[114] Hamilton et al. (2001), p. 338.

[115] Gerhardt (2019), pp. 107–108, quoting Justice Joseph Story.

have been presented in the past Chapters: How can a certain conduct be called "high crime", if the legislator did not even bother including it in its criminal statutes? How can law serve its goal of informing behaviour, if the legal subject cannot know beforehand what conduct is illegal? How can a punishment for a certain conduct be fair, if the subject has no opportunity to reach a rational agreement with the pact that enacted such punishment? How can the principle of separation of powers be taken seriously, if the supposed adjudicating organ is allowed to fundamentally also "make" the rules after the fact? Not only would this choice concentrate legislative and judicative powers into one actor, but it would also arguably undermine the independence of the Executive branch, who has to submit to its overseer's will.[116] These are all valid critiques which bear a deep connection with theory and history of law, but which, in the specific case of presidential impeachments, may seem high-minded in a retrospective look at how the terminology "high crimes and misdemeanours" was applied in the American practice of impeachments.

Andrew Johnson was impeached essentially for obstructing Congress' efforts at reconstruction and for obstructing the enforcement of laws he opposed, all of which were exacerbated by his crude behaviour, racist statements, and contemptuous relation with some members of Congress.[117] Richard Nixon faced an impeachment resolution for using his office to obstruct congressional investigations, conceal the existence of crimes, encroach congressional competencies, violate of individual rights, among other things.[118] Bill Clinton was impeached for perjury and obstruction of justice.[119] Donald Trump was impeached twice, once for abuse of power and obstruction of Congress, and later for inciting insurrection, whereby endangering the lives of members of other political branches and democracy itself.[120]

While one may disagree with the merits or the framing of certain charges in this list, it is difficult to seriously argue that the charges, abstractly considered, fatally harm the rule of law or the separation of powers. It does not seem to follow that such ample discretion provided by the term "high crimes and misdemeanours" results in the sort of radical legal indeterminacy that renders the individual or the Executive branch supine to their overseers. Most offenses that were not criminal, were at least illegal; those that were not illegal, seemed to fundamentally subvert presidential powers and other arrangements of the political system, arguably breaking them if left unchecked. To name a few examples: Johnson could have predicted that his indiscriminate vetoing of bills or non enforcing of approved policies had potential to nullify one branch of power, corrupting the constitutional dispositions; Nixon could

[116] These arguments are inspired in those presented by the defence counsel of Supreme Court Justice Samuel Chase. For details and a much more eloquent exposition of such arguments, see Labovitz (1978), pp. 38–47. For other related considerations, see the section on rule of law in this Chapter.

[117] van Tassel and Finkelman (1999), pp. 221–224.

[118] van Tassel and Finkelman (1999), pp. 261–266.

[119] van Tassel and Finkelman (1999), pp. 267–287.

[120] House Resolutions n. 755, of December 18th, 2019, and n. 24, of January 25th, 2021, respectively.

have predicted that using the State's apparatus to spy on his opposition without any legal justification and subsequently stonewalling any effort in the investigation of the facts would draw the ire of Congress and subvert the equilibrium of democracy; Trump could have predicted that directing an angry mob at Congress would endanger officers located there and hamper its functioning. Note how one could even perhaps say that these impeachments and impeachment attempts, contrary to the set expectations, did more to reinforce separation of powers and the authority of law than to truly undermine them.

4.2.1.2 Broad or Open-Ended Constitutional Violations

The adaptations of impeachment in Latin American constitutions largely followed the same formula, although with less cryptic language, given that the concept of "high crimes and misdemeanours" did not belong to the Iberic, Roman-German legal traditions. Instead, what can be observed is the stipulation of impeachable offenses in more modern language, broadly defined as 'constitutional violations' or 'serious infractions' of any kind. Both arguably provide the functionality created by 'high crimes and misdemeanours', as the abstractness of constitutional regulations give a lot of leeway for interpretation of possible trespasses to the Court of Impeachments, encompassing a large array of non-criminal or legal but abusive presidential behaviour in need of correction. In case there is broad consensus, therefore, around presidential misbehaviour that, for example, undermines the separation of powers, menaces the democratic order, and so on, the Court of Impeachments would not be held down by potential legal technicalities or imperfections that would allow an overbearing President to continue inflicting harm. Multiple Framers of Latin American constitutions and legal scholars recognize this shared genealogy and role model of responsible government.[121]

Naturally, as mentioned before, this large degree of discretion can invoke a lot of suspicion from lawyers who have a traditional, individual-oriented understanding of the rule of law. Under this understanding, such broad concepts make the President's individual rights themselves vulnerable to the tyranny of Congress, or whoever else is in charge of the Court of Impeachments, and are ultimately incapable of providing a just and, therefore, also legitimate outcome. It would be akin to solving tyranny with more tyranny, which would bear no significant gain for society or, at most, a corrupt one. It could also be akin to sacrificing some constitutional goods, typically that of separation of powers and the people's sovereignty, for the sake of another, though arguably marked by an unjustifiable degree of arbitrariness.

[121] *E.g.*, Brossard de Souza Pinto (1965), p. 13 ff.; Eguiguren Praeli (2008), p. 111 ff.; Zaffaroni and Risso (2008), p. 717 ff. Many authors (*e.g.*, Eguiguren Praeli 2008, p. 113) indicate the trial of residence as a possible precursor to impeachment in Latin America. For a discussion of that hypothesis, see Sect. 2.1.9.

4.2.1.3 Limited Constitutional Violations and Other Serious Infractions

A 'middle-of-the-road' solution to this kind of challenge would be to still provide space for constitutional infractions, albeit through a limited list, which would thus provide the sort of legal certainty and security the rule of law in its traditional understanding demands. Such was the solution of choice of a few countries, which seem to be more committed to this stricter conception of rule of law. Peru stablishes something of the sort when it reduces impeachable offenses only to the hindering of elections or to the irregular dissolution of Congress, for example. Brazil goes to much further extents to define some of its impeachable offenses. Its first impeachable offense, for example, 'offenses against the existence of the Union', is developed into eleven subcategories within the law of impeachments (Law n. 1079/50, art. 5) that range from aiding foreign powers in war against the Nation (art. 5, I), to allowing foreign troops to stay or transit in the domestic territory without justification or congressional approval (art. 5, VIII). Whether these strategies really work in limiting the scope of impeachable offenses to the point of rehabilitating a strict conception of rule of law, however, is debatable. As will be pointed out, some of the popular limited subcategories of constitutional violations can nonetheless permit enormous discretion.

It must be noted, moreover, that broad and limited categories may very well coexist (see Table 4.2). In such cases, it makes more sense to interpret the limited categories not as a form of limiting discretion or as accidental redundancy, but as centres of special interest of the political system. Some countries may, for example, have a painful past marked by corruption, human rights violations, and authoritarian encroachments, and by describing these offenses in closer detail they may be denoting special concern regarding these types of violations.

Compromising the Security, Safety, and Interests of the Nation/State

The most common subcategory of constitutional violations found in Latin America pertains the compromise of the Nation's security, safety, or interests by the President, being overtly present in 7 out of 23 constitutions analysed (Brazil, Chile, Costa Rica, Ecuador 1998, Ecuador 2008, and Honduras 2013). This should not come as a surprise, as the defence of security and safety of society as whole is described as the main goal of impeachments in what was certainly the most influential piece of literature on impeachments.[122] As such, it stands to reason that, if constitutional violations need to be restricted to better limit congressional overreach, then it should be done in such a fashion as to still preserve the core of what impeachment was arguably created for. Moreover, selecting this particular constitutional violation underscores the sort of fail-safe function that is so central to presidential impeachments.

[122] Hamilton et al. (2001), p. 338.

Table 4.2 Distribution of impeachable offenses in the American Constitutions

	Constitutional Violations							Legal Violations						Ambiguous
	Broad	*Limited*						*Broad*	*Limited*					
Country (Const.)	Any	National Security or Interest	National Honor and Indignity for Office	Performance and Duties of Office	Separation of Powers	Basic Rights	Elections	Any	Common Crimes	Proper Crimes	Corruption	Genocide	Electoral Crimes	Treason
Argentina (1994)				x				y	x	x	y	y		
Bolivia (1967)										x	y	y		
Bolivia (2009)	x				y	x	y			x	x	x		
Brazil (1988)		x	x		x	x	y			x	y	y		
Chile (1980)	x	x	x		y	y	y					y		
Colombia (1991)	x		x	x	y	y	y	y	x	x	y	y		
Costa Rica (1949)		x			x		x	x	y	y	y	y		
Cuba (2019)														
Dominican Rep. (2010)	x				y	y	y					y		
El Salvador (1983)														
Ecuador (1979)										x	y			
Ecuador (*reform 1996*)			x								x			x
Ecuador (1998)		x									x			
Ecuador (2008)		x									x	x		
Guatemala (1985)														
Honduras (1982)														
Honduras (reform 2013)	x	x		x	y	y	y	x	y	y	x	y		
Mexico (1917)									x*	y	y	y		x
Mexico (reform 2021)									x	y	x		x	x
Nicaragua (1987)														
Panama (1972)	x				x	y	x			x	y	y		
Paraguay (1992)				x				y	x	x	y	y		
Peru (1993) former Pres.	x				y	y	y	x	y	y	y	y		
Peru (1993) sitting Pres.					x*		x							x
United States (1789)	x				y	y	y	x	y	y	x	y		x
Uruguay (1967)	x				y	y	y	x	y	y	y	y		
Venezuela (1961)	x				y	y	y	x	y	y	y	y		
Venezuela (1999)	x				y	y	y	x	y	y	y	y		

Source: Own elaboration. Constitutions are followed by their date of enactment or reform in parenthesis. Key: X: Expressed in the Constitution; Y: Presumable from broader categories; (*): The category brings special qualifications

Table 4.3 Overview of presidential offenses and crises in Latin America since 1990

Name	Year	Country	Instrument	Charge	Detail
Fernando Collor	1992	Brazil	Impeachment	Presidential indignity	Deliberate oversight of crimes committed by the presidential inner circle, lies in public announcements
Jorge Serrano	1993	Guatemala	Resignation	–	Outrage at failed self-coup attempt prompted resignation
Carlos Andrés Pérez	1993	Venezuela	Impeachment and Vacancy	Malfeasance in office	Falsely accounted funds applied in international missions as being invested in domestic affairs; Vacancy for abandonment of office applied after 3-month suspension
Joaquín Balaguer	1996	Dominican Republic	Resignation	Electoral fraud	Tampered with ballot boxes removing 200.000 voters
Ernesto Samper	1996	Colombia	Impeachment	Presidential indignity	Illegal campaign funding, violation of autonomy of the Judiciary and auxiliary organs, obstruction of justice
Abdalá Bucaram	1997	Ecuador	Vacancy	Mental incapacity	Economic mismanagement, undignified behaviour, deliberate oversight of crimes, betrayal of campaign promises
Rosalia Arteaga	1997	Ecuador	Resignation	–	Congressional and military pressure
Raúl Cubas Grau	1999	Paraguay	Impeachment and Resignation	Poor performance	Mismanagement and inciting of civil wars through the misuse of presidential

(continued)

Table 4.3 (continued)

Name	Year	Country	Instrument	Charge	Detail
					pardon prompted resignation
Alberto Fujimori	2000	Peru	Impeachment and Vacancy	Abandonment of office, and noncompliance of duties	Abandoned official diplomatic mission without congressional approval; declared morally unfit
Fernando de la Rúa	2001	Argentina	Resignation	–	Public outrage induced by economic mismanagement
Adolfo Rodrígues Saá	2001	Argentina	Resignation	–	Public outrage induced by (continued) economic mismanagement
Jamil Mahuad	2002	Ecuador	Military Coup and Vacancy	Abandonment of office	Unwillingness to resign after invasion of the presidential palace and military threat prompted vacancy vote
Luis Ángel González Macchi	2002, 2003	Paraguay	Impeachment	Poor performance, corruption	Economic mismanagement, handling illegal goods, embezzlement
Gonzalo Sánchez de Lozada	2004	Bolivia	Impeachment and Resignation	Human rights violations	Extrajudicial killings committed during the 'Gas War' (October Massacre)
Hugo Chávez	2004	Venezuela	Presidential Recall	–	–
Carlos Mesa	2005	Bolivia	Resignation	–	Public outrage and political isolation induced by policy failure
Lucio Gutiérrez	2005	Ecuador	Vacancy	Abandonment of office	Illegal dissolution of the Supreme Court under state of emergency was interpreted as overreach and reason for vacancy
Manuel Zelaya	2009	Honduras	Military Coup and	Treason, abuse of authority,	Ordered referendum on a

(continued)

Table 4.3 (continued)

Name	Year	Country	Instrument	Charge	Detail
			Anomalous Criminal Suit	competence encroachment, crimes against the form of government	Constituent Assembly without authority to do so, repeatedly disobeyed court orders to stop the referendum
Fernando Lugo	2012	Paraguay	Impeachment	Poor performance	Aggravation of internal insecurity, unsatisfactory handling of land-less movements and other land conflicts
Otto Pérez Molina	2015	Guatemala	Pretrial and Resignation	Corruption	Customs fraud, bribery, and association with mobsters (*La Linea* affairs)
Dilma Rousseff	2016	Brazil	Impeachment	Offenses against public finances	Delayed payments to manipulate public accounts, issued supplementary credit without congressional approval
Nicolás Maduro	2016	Venezuela	Impeachment	Corruption	Embezzlement, bribery, criminal association
Michel Temer	2017 (2)	Brazil	Impeachment	Corruption	Bribery, obstruction of justice
Jimmy Morales	2017, 2018	Guatemala	Pretrial	Campaign financing fraud	Did not report campaign costs/ donations to electoral authorities
Pedro P. Kuczynski	2017, 2018	Peru	Vacancy	Moral incapacity	Involvement in corruption and influence peddling
Mario Abdo Benítez	2019	Paraguay	Impeachment	Poor performance	Signing an unfavourable treaty regarding the Itaipú powerplant
Evo Morales	2019	Bolivia	Military Coup	Electoral fraud	Controverse third term re-election, irregularities indicated by OAS electoral audit

(continued)

Table 4.3 (continued)

Name	Year	Country	Instrument	Charge	Detail
Sebastián Piñera	2019	Chile	Impeachment	Offense against national honour, violation of laws and constitution	Consented with recurring human rights violations committed by security forces in the repression of popular protests (*estallido social*)
Martín Vizcarra	2020	Peru	Vacancy	Moral incapacity	Oversight of crimes committed by presidential inner circle
Manuel Merino	2020	Peru	Resignation	–	Public outrage induced by policy switching and violent popular repression
Mario Abdo Benítez	2021	Paraguay	Impeachment	Poor performance	Mismanagement of the COVID-19 crisis
Janine Áñez	2021	Bolivia	Impeachment	Offenses against public finances, human rights violations	Taking loans without agreement or disclosure of conditions, violations of freedom of expression, captivity of migrant populations
Martín Vizcarra	2021	Peru	Impeachment	Influence peddling, collusion	Jumping queue for COVID vaccine
Sebastián Piñera	2021	Chile	Impeachment	Offense against national honour, violation of laws and constitution	Not disclosing assets and transactions found in tax havens (*Pandora Papers*), suggesting influence peddling in favour of mining companies; Failure to honour treaty of Escazú
Pedro Castillo	2022 (2)	Peru	Vacancy	Moral incapacity	Contested nominations, personal rule, reprehensible public announcements, influence peddling.

(continued)

Table 4.3 (continued)

Name	Year	Country	Instrument	Charge	Detail
					Improvised addition: Attempted self-coup.
Guillermo Lasso	2022	Ecuador	Mutual dissolution	Serious internal crisis	Weeks of protests and violent confrontation due to deteriorating social circumstances
Dina Boluarte	2023 (2)	Peru	Vacancy	Moral incapacity	Human rights violations in repression of protestors; Campaign financing violations
Guillermo Lasso	2023	Ecuador	Impeachment	Embezzlement	Involvement in a corruption network

Source: Own elaboration based primarily on official records. Note: "Year" refers to the year impeachment or comparable procedures were initiated. "Charge" refers to the offense category accusations fit. "Detail" describes underlying facts that the charges were subsumed from or the circumstances which may have led to a resignation

As an open-ended formula, albeit a limited one, the threatening of national security and safety by the President can be argued in a wide range of different ways. Of all countries that openly stablish this constitutional violation as an impeachment offense, only Brazilian legislation offers what could be considered a somewhat fleshed-out definition of its constituent parts (arts. 5 and 8 of Law n. 1079/50).[123] Even so, however, a total of at least 19 impeachable offenses can be fit under the umbrella of 'compromising the Nation's security'. A few examples would be: (i.) aiding enemies in wars against the Republic or provoking other foreign powers, causing them to become hostile towards the Republic; (ii.) declaring war without congressional approval; (iii.) inciting the secession of member States or territories from the Union; (iv.) revealing state and military secrets; (v.) not taking necessary measures to defend against enemies; (vi.) attempting to change the form of government or the Constitution in general by force; (vii.) declaring state of emergency in the absence of the legal conditions for doing so; (viii.) leaving the country without congressional approval; among others.

[123] Other countries offer criminal standards that could be used analogously, but these are arguably not binding. Regarding the constitutions of Ecuador, this conclusion, however, depends on how one interprets the word '*delitos*'. In a strong or textualist interpretation, it would refer exclusively to criminal offenses, in which case the arts. 336 to 364 of the criminal code would establish binding standards. In a broader interpretation, it could refer generically to the constitutional violation described here. See Pacheco Pinos (2019), p. 43 ff.

A Court of Impeachments looking to make use of this constitutional violation as an impeachable offense may meet two central difficulties: (1.) the unpredictable ways national security may be endangered; and (2.) the urgency the circumstances may impose on the procedure. The first problem (1.) is more applicable to Brazil, who, despite its long list of impeachable offenses, still leaves a lot of vulnerable spaces for the endangerment of national security. The case studies had a few cases in which the argument of national security was claimed, but which would have remained unaddressed by Brazil's impeachment law due to its strive to specificity. The week-long hunger riots caused by Carlos Andrés Pérez economic policies and the disastrous response of the Venezuelan security forces, for example, caused significant instability, two coup attempts and nearly a civil war, and yet, the situation would remain unaddressed by Brazil's 19 impeachable offenses on national security. A similar case could be made about Jamil Mahuad's defiance and taunting of domestic military forces.

In practice, a Parliament in the situation above will look for an alternative impeachable offense to be used as a proxy for the larger goal of protecting national security. Such strategy, however, has the downside of sacrificing the legitimacy of the procedures, as the smaller impeachment article offered in its place will likely be perceived as being of minor importance, and, thus, make the consequence of impeachment look disproportionate to the offense committed. In the examples discussed, Pérez ended up being removed for violating bureaucratic rules of internal resource allocation, and Mahuad for a questionable charge of 'abandonment of office', both of which severely misrepresented and underplayed the gravity of the situation the procedures against them addressed.

Secondly (2.), it should be noted that the situations in which national security is at risk tend to be of such urgency that the slow and cumbersome nature of the impeachment procedures can end up being at odds with the accomplishment of its very core goal. In the situations commented above, impeachment surrogates were applied in *lieu* of or in conjunction with proper impeachments, presumably in the attempt of ending the situation of instability and insecurity as quickly as possible.[124]

Harm to National Honour and Presidential Indignity

Much less frequent than the previous limited constitutional violation (4 out of 23 constitutions), offenses to national honour rank as the second most common among Latin American constitutions, tied with offenses against the separation of powers and against the duties of office. To some degree, however, national honour and national security seem to bear some association. Both the Chilean and Brazilian impeachment provisions associate both categories, suggesting that harm to national honour could have the comparable existential implications to the Nation as risking

[124] Such was arguably the case in the oustings of Carlos Andrés Pérez, Abdalá Bucaram, Alberto Fujimori, Jamil Mahuad, Lucio Gutiérrez, and Pedro Castillo.

its safety would have. Brazil, for example, among its other impeachable offenses referring to presidential indignity, assigns the offense of 'celebrating treaties and conventions that compromise the Nation's dignity' (art. 5, (6) of the Law n. 1079/50) as a 'crime against the existence of the Union'. Ecuador, in its transition from the 1978 to the 1998 and 2008 Constitutions, exchanged the impeachable offense of 'infraction that gravely harms the national honour' for 'offenses against the security of State', also suggesting some degree of relatability between both categories, albeit to a lesser degree than implied by the Brazilian or Chilean impeachment dispositions.[125]

This existential link between honour and safety of the State/Nation may seem a bit tenuous from a modern perspective, but it was an issue that occupied the minds of statesmen of the past, particularly those born on times in which national states could not be taken for granted and state capacity had yet to reach today's robustness. In the Federalist n. 17, for example, Alexander Hamilton does hint on the existential implications honour and esteem may have on the State, whose lack may be seen as an invitation to anarchy:

> [Belonging to the province of state government] is the most powerful, most universal, and most attractive source of popular obedience and attachment. It is this, which, being the immediate and visible guardian of life and property; having its benefits and its terrors in constant activity before the public eye; regulating all those personal interests, and familiar concerns, to which the sensibility of individuals is more immediately awake; contributes, more than any other circumstance, to impress upon the minds of the people affection, esteem, and reverence towards the government. This great cement of society (. . .) would ensure them so decided an empire over their respective citizens (. . .).[126]

When commenting specifically about national governments, however, Hamilton suggests such moral binding to the state entity to be much weaker or fragile, as the acts of a higher level of government would be much less visible and, thus, less likely to inspire appreciation and consequently also command authority over the citizens.[127] The concentration of power on the Executive made possible by the presidential system, particularly at national level, addressed this vulnerability commented by Hamilton, who identified the demise of feudal governments as being largely founded on their incapacity of inspiring such moral bonds.[128] Such concentration would make the national government more visible and, thus, more appreciated and, consequently, also more stable and free from internal commotions.

[125]Notice that Colombia also establishes indignity as an impeachable offense, but not as a particularity of presidential misbehaviour. Peru may be included in the list of countries with this "impeachable offense" if the surrogate of declaration of vacancy on grounds of moral incapacity is given equivalency with impeachment.

[126]Hamilton et al. (2001), p. 82. The existential aspect of honour was arguably also something close to the Framers at a personal level. Hamilton himself, after all, died from a lethal wound inflicted by his rival Aaron Burr in a duel for his honour in 1804.

[127]Hamilton et al. (2001), pp. 82–83.

[128]Hamilton et al. (2001), pp. 82–83.

Considering that the presidential system's tendency for breeding personalism,[129] with the President often being thought as the embodiment of the Nation itself,[130] it makes sense for the Latin American Framers to raise equivalencies between national indignity/dishonour and presidential indignity/dishonour. Arguably, having a President uncapable of commanding authority or who generates strong repulsion in his/her own people would also have the potential to put the Nation's security and interests at risk.[131]

In two cases studied based on charges of presidential indignity (Fernando Collor and Ernesto Samper), however, such existential fears were not ventilated. The charge of presidential indignity was arguably used in a more strategic form. It was used in such a way to make the accusation encompassing of all the sorts of misbehaviour these Presidents committed while in office, which could not be squarely fitted in other categories offered by the list of impeachable offenses. Fernando Collor was involved in many shady dealings, acts of gross misadministration and other abusive behaviour that either pended judicial confirmation or that, despite the undeniable outrage they caused, fitted other impeachable offenses too awkwardly. In similar measure, Ernesto Samper's core infraction was of electoral nature, followed by a series of abuses determined in covering it up, none of which could be made to fit the available impeachable offenses other than indignity for office.[132]

The use of this impeachable offense is often accompanied with definitional difficulties. The accusation piece against Collor was indicative of this, as, in search of some legal substance to build upon, it reached back as far as to definitions offered by Cicero and those used in Roman law, both which associate a special kind of honour to the exercise of a public office.[133] Despite such efforts, however, the parliamentary debates revealed that Deputies and Senators still clung to their personal understandings of honour and dignity. Arguably, this makes defence more difficult, as the defence lawyer cannot possibly identify beforehand all interpretations of honour or dignity being used to formulate a cohesive and encompassing response. The 'goal posts' of accusation are multiple and in constant shift, so to say. From the perspective of impeachment theory, this is immaterial, as what matters is that the final decision is representative of a general consensus on the unfitness of the President for office; from the perspective of someone with strict commitment to the

[129] Linz (1990), p. 52 ff.

[130] More than just being acknowledged as a representative of the State, some Constitutions further state that the President truly embodies, in part or in whole, the Nation. This can be seen, for example, in the art. 188 of the 1991 Constitution of Colombia, which states that "the President symbolizes the national unity (. . .)" or art. 110 of the 1993 Peruvian Constitution, stating that "the President of the Republic is the head of State and personifies the Nation". Author's translations.

[131] Hamilton did not directly argue that the person of the President could spark such unrest, but in his understanding the presidency would logically only be filled by someone who is "in an eminent degree endowed with the requisite qualifications" and such possessed such talents that "establish him in the esteem and confidence of the whole union". Hamilton et al. (2001), p. 354.

[132] See respective case studies for details.

[133] *Diário do Congresso Nacional* n. 1/1992 (Diversos n. 12), pp. 7–27.

rule of law, however, this can be seen as a fatal flaw of the procedure, which curtails the right of defence.

Maladministration, Poor Performance, and Duties of Office

Of all limited open-ended formulas, poor or corrupt presidential performance received most consideration from the Framers of the US Constitution. The expressions "malpractice", "neglect of duty", "maladministration", "misconduct in office", "malversation" and "corrupt administration" were all considered by the delegates,[134] before being dropped as some considered "so vague a term will be equivalent to a tenure during pleasure of the Senate",[135] which was considered an unacceptable compromise to the strict separation of powers.

Indeed, with exception of the offense of 'neglect of duty', these offenses generally lack a legal framework stablishing a sort of administrative standard Presidents should strive towards. The standards stablished for the public administration in general may offer inspiration for analogous application, but there is no real safeguard against an impeachment motivated uniquely by outstanding policy differences between Parliament and presidency, other than those common to all impeachments (high thresholds, representative body).[136]

The case study on Fernando Lugo shows how tenuous these charges can be. The accusation piece narrated 5 facts that were attributed to the President: (1.) a socialist youth meeting under the auspices of the Armed Forces, authorized by Lugo, which was characterized as political use of the state machinery; (2.) the meetings of Lugo with leaders of landless movements and the non-engagement of security forces to protect landowners from these movements; (3.) the growth of insecurity in the country, despite Congress making funds available for dealing with the issue; (4.) the signing of the Protocol of Ushuaia II, a treaty part of the MERCOSUR which deepened the member states' commitment to democracy, which was but interpreted as an unacceptable sacrifice the country's sovereignty; (5.) the massacre of Curuguaty, which somehow was thought to be imputable to the President's negligence.[137]

As argued before, this case was filled with many fatal flaws, and, therefore, whatever it produced is probably better not understood as a reliable source of information on the rules of Paraguayan presidential impeachments, much less impeachments in general. Nonetheless, one could at least speculate that the choice

---

[134] Farrand (1911a), pp. 61–69, 116, 337.

[135] Farrand (1911a), p. 550.

[136] Commentaries to the relevant constitutions (*i.e.,* Argentina, Colombia, Honduras, and Paraguay) typically admit this condition and only indicate standards applicable to other higher officers such as judges and ministers. See for example Gelli (2004), p. 457 ff. on Argentina, Londoño Ulloa (2020), pp. 43–39, on Colombia, or Balbuena Pérez (2013), pp. 359 ff. and 371 on Paraguay.

[137] *Libelo acusatorio* presented to the National Congress in response to Resolution n. 1431 of 2012, of the Chamber of Deputies, pp. 1–7.

of facts and narratives the case provides, as well as their development in arguments and debates, are symptomatic of the basic vulnerabilities and difficulties of this type of offense. For instance, most claims made were not backed by any sort of empirical analysis or even a suggestion of applicable standards.[138] Regarding accusation n. 3, for example, what would be an unacceptable growth of insecurity? How does the President's behaviour relate to such growth exactly? How could such growth be objectively measured? No answers are offered for these questions, and, thus, the Senators are left to their own intuitions about what was opportune or just for the case. It became quite clear that Lugo's fatal flaw as a President was more closely related to his political or ideological distance from Congress than proper misbehaviour *per se*.[139]

Finally, regarding the offense of neglect of duties of office (see Table 4.4), it could be said that it does a lot less to limit discretion than one may predict. In effect, this 'limited' open-ended formula can at times create discretion that rivals the larger categories. The lists of presidential duties are usually lengthy and very likely include the duty of enforcing and upholding the constitution and the laws. In theory, therefore, a President could be impeached for breaching any aspect of the constitution just as much as it would be possible in the larger categories. Encroaching competencies from other branches of power, or undermining democratic elections, for example, all could figure as a breach of the duties of office. In practice, however, accountability for neglect of duty (or any other omissive offense) has been sharply criticized by representatives and legal communities, given that the tension between constitutional norms requires Presidents to prefer the enforcement of one norm over the other, thus always leaving an open flank to accusations of neglect.[140]

Compromising the Separation of Powers

Despite not having open recognition in most of the Latin American constitutions (exceptions being Brazil, Costa Rica, Panama, and Peru), violations to the separation of powers constitute the most prevalent source or collaborating circumstance of impeachment related conflict. The textbook case of an overbearing President certainly would be one telling the tale of an officer who surreptitiously or by force

[138] The evidence and demonstration were simply declared as of common knowledge by the accusation.

[139] Because of this, the Paraguayan impeachment has been accused of being a *de facto* motion of censure or a vote of no-confidence. See València i Montes (2015) or Llanos et al. (2012).

[140] See Labovitz (1978), pp. 104–107; and the Sebastián Piñera case study. As argued during Nixon's impeachment: "'No President who attempts to make full use of the lawful powers of his office is likely to complete his term without having committed, even in good faith, a constitutional violation' (...). His duties and responsibilities 'frequently expose him to conflicting constitutional demands,' when he must choose whether to act, knowing that his action may prove to violate the Constitution, or to refrain from acting, knowing that inaction while technically not a violation of his oath of office may be the worst policy of all". Labovitz (1978), pp. 106–107.

Table 4.4 Presidential duties, responsibilities, and powers in the Americas

Country (Constitution)	Enforce law and constitution	Oversight of ministerial activity	Conserve internal integrity/peace	Commander in chief	Declaration of war	Declaration of state of emergency	Pardon	Dissolve Congress	Reference articles
Argentina (1994)	Limited	Limited	–	Yes	Limited	Limited	Limited*	No	Art. 99
Bolivia (2009)	Yes	Yes	Yes	No	No	Yes	Limited	No	Art. 172
Brazil (1988)	Yes	Yes	Yes	Yes	Limited	Yes	Limited	No	Art. 84, 85
Chile (1980)	Yes	No	Limited	Limited	Limited	Yes	Limited*	No	Art. 24, 32
Colombia (1991)	Yes	Limited	Yes	Yes	Limited	Yes	No	No	Art. 188, 189, 198, 212, 213
Costa Rica (1949)	Yes	Yes	Yes	Yes	No	No	No	No	Art. 139, 140
Cuba (2019)	Yes	Yes	Limited	Yes	Limited	Yes	Yes	No	Art. 128
Dominican Rep. (2010)	Yes	No	Limited	Yes	No	Limited	Yes	No	Art. 127, 128
Ecuador (2008)	Yes	No	Yes	No	No	Yes	Yes	Limited	Art. 171, 180
El Salvador (1983)	Yes	No	Yes	Yes	No	Limited	Limited	No	Art. 157, 159, 168
Guatemala (1985)	Yes	No	Yes	Yes	No	No	No	No	Art. 182, 183, 195
Honduras (1982)	Yes	No	Yes	Yes	Limited	No	Yes	No	Art. 245

(continued)

Table 4.4 (continued)

Country (Constitution)	Enforce law and constitution	Oversight of ministerial activity	Conserve internal integrity/peace	Commander in chief	Declaration of war	Declaration of state of emergency	Pardon	Dissolve Congress	Reference articles
Mexico (1917)	Yes	No	Yes	No	Limited	No	Limited	No	Art. 89
Nicaragua (1987)	Yes	No	No	Yes	No	No	Limited	No	Art. 150, 138
Panama (1972)	-	No	Yes	No	No	No	Limited	No	Art. 183, 184
Paraguay (1992)	Yes	No	No	Yes	No	Limited	Yes	No	Art. 238, 288
Peru (1993)	Yes	No	Yes	Yes	Limited	Limited	Yes	Limited	Art. 118, 134, 137, 167
United States (1789)	Yes	–	No	Yes	No	–	Limited*	No	Art. 1, s.10; 2
Uruguay (1967)	Yes	No	Yes	Yes	No	–	No	Limited	Art. 159, 168
Venezuela (1999)	Yes	No	Yes	Yes	Yes	Yes	Yes	Limited	Art. 232, 236

Source: Own elaboration. Key: "Yes" means the duty/power is given without explicit caveats; "No" means it is not listed among presidential duties or other reference articles; "Limited" means the act depends on confirmation of other organs or has other significant constraints; "–" means the situation is unclear; *prohibited against impeached officers

attempts to encroach on competencies of other Branches, potentially concentrating enough power to subvert the whole political system. Such subversion could, for example, be used to nullify democratic decision making and power sharing, resulting in a quasi-authoritarian, irresponsible governments.

The examples seen were plentiful: the abuse of presidential veto power (*e.g.*, Andrew Johnson), the selective enforcement of laws (*e.g.*, Andrew Johnson), both used to delay or block the policy decisions made by Congress; the abuse of rule-by-decree (*e.g.*, Fernando Collor) and other emergency powers (*e.g.*, Alberto Fujimori) to circumvent negotiation and compromise with Congress; the undermining of judicial autonomy to evade accountability (*e.g.*, Richard Nixon, Ernesto Samper) or to gain advantages in upcoming elections (*e.g.*, Alberto Fujimori); the illegal dissolution of Congress (*e.g.*, Alberto Fujimori); the encroachment of the power of purse (*e.g.*, Alberto Fujimori, Dilma Rousseff), and so on.

Unlike the previous limited categories, the violations to the separation of powers tend to be well defined, Panama being an exception. Peru, for example, stablishes that sitting Presidents may only be impeached for illegally dissolving Congress or for interfering in elections or organs of electoral justice (art. 117, of the 1993 Constitution). Similarly, Brazil stablishes as offenses against the separation of powers: (1.) attempts to dissolve Congress; (2.) violating prerogatives of legislators; (3.) allowing foreign forces to stay or transit in the national territory against the Congress' will; (4.) hindering acts and decisions of the Judiciary; (5.) to threaten or use violence against judges and jury; (6.) intervene in the municipal or state-level business, neglecting constitutional norms (art. 6, of the Law n. 1079/50). Costa Rica also stablishes as offenses (1.) hindering or embarrassing functions proper to the Legislative Assembly; (2.) denying the enactment or enforcement of laws; (3.) hindering or embarrassing functions proper to the Judiciary (art. 149 of the 1949 Constitution of Costa Rica).

Compromising Basic Constitutional Rights

One of the least frequent limited violations, openly recognized only by Brazil and Bolivia, relates to violations of constitutional rights of the individual, that is, fundamental, human, civil and political rights. The focus on violations of basic rights is a bit counter-intuitive considering that impeachment theory tends to point at the larger picture, that is the protection of the society rather than the individual. Naturally, however, if the violations of constitutional rights are widespread enough, the societal element impeachments seek to protect reappears and gains the kind of systemic relevance that would justify the activation of the procedures. Much like impeachment, constitutional rights also originate and serve as guarantees against institutional tyranny and arbitrariness.[141] Their widespread violation can be indicative, therefore, of the endangerment of democracy in its liberal component.

[141] Sajó and Uitz (2019), p. 41 ff.

Despite being a common occurrence in constitutional crises related with impeachments, violations to basic rights do not commonly integrate the accusation pieces of impeachment. As commented before, even someone as Alberto Fujimori was not impeached for violations of basic rights, despite being associated with a long list of scandals that included the use of death squads, bombings, censorship, and mass sterilization of indigenous peoples, among other things.[142] Arguably, the avoidance of such sorts of accusations may be more strategic in nature, despite their potential for kicking impeachments into high gear. The investigation and trial of systemic violations of constitutional rights can be complex and demanding of extensive hearings, two things are at odds with the quick resolution of a constitutional crisis and perhaps also the congressional setting of impeachments. As a result, the urgency of impeachment seems to point accusation managers towards simpler, straight-forward charges that create less room for delays and quarrels. Accountability for such violations is more likely to be sought through criminal suits after the President is out of office.[143]

Compromising the Realization of Elections

Finally, the last limited category of constitutional violation is related to the free and fair realization of elections, a category overtly present in the Constitutions of Costa Rica, Panama, and Peru. These are not violations of electoral rules by the President as a candidate, but his or her interferences as one potential actor in the organization of elections. Examples would be the undue interference on organs of electoral justice and administration, tampering of ballots, disenfranchisement of voters, persecution of political candidates, and so on.

4.2.2 *Legal Infractions*

The logical next step in reduction of congressional discretion would be to circumscribe offenses only to the realm of legal violations, as law tends to deal with smaller topics and to much higher detail than constitutions. Some constitutions apply the broad term "legal infractions", "violation of the law" or "justiciable offense", which may apply to any legal field, though the most common approach is to restrict it only to certain categories of criminal offenses, or specific crimes that are deemed of

---

[142] See Sect. 3.2.1.5 for details.

[143] The two impeachments for human rights violations were directed against ex-Presidents, namely against Gonzalo Sanchéz de Lozada (2004) and Janine Áñez (2021). Alberto Fujimori had multiple impeachment resolutions against him for such violations, but he was impeached and convicted for 'abandonment of office' before these were brought to trial (2001), making them superfluous. He was criminally convicted in 2010.

special magnitude or significance for that community, such as corruption, treason, and/or genocide.

These categories are the least troublesome in terms of the actual challenges they pose to the rule of law, but they also tend to be misunderstood by the public and the legal community nonetheless, particularly when their treatment in impeachment procedures does not live up to expectations. The reality of it is that despite being legal offenses that presuppose certain administrative, civil, or criminal standards, they are ultimately measured up to political standards, since that is the purpose of a presidential impeachment: stablishing accountability in the political sphere. A conviction in an impeachment procedure, therefore, is representative of the fact that the presidential behaviour has cast sufficient doubt on the President's fitness for office and not necessarily of his or her personal culpability in a specific crime. The impeachment procedure seeks to protect society from a potential harmful actor, someone who has lost the confidence of the nation, and not to impose criminal punishment. This, however, is a distinction that is frequently lost on observers of such procedures or that is purposely obscured by the defence team or the impeachment opposition to raise the standards in their favour or to delegitimize the impeachment claims. To be sure, this does not mean that the Parliament's decision is entirely up for grabs because "it is political". The legal and criminal categories impose real constraints, but it simply does not follow that they communicate all aspects of their spheres of accountability to the impeachment procedures.

Common and Proper Crimes

Common crimes (*crímenes comunes; crimes comuns; Allgemeindelikte*) are crimes which can be committed by anyone, whereas proper crimes (*crimes próprios; Sonderdelikte*) are those which can only be committed by someone who possesses a certain set of attributes, such as holding an office (*e.g.*, officer accepting bribes), having a degree of kinship with the victim (*e.g.*, domestic and spousal violence), or performing a function of special relevance (*e.g.*, witness providing false testimony).[144] Naturally, in the context of impeachments, the relevant kind of proper crimes are those that are committed by someone holding an office (*delitos oficiales, delitos cometidos en el ejercício de funciones*), such as malfeasance in office, graft and certain forms of embezzlement and bribery.[145]

Making the President amenable to impeachment for all crimes is an efficient way of communicating that 'no one is above' the law, but less than half of constitutions

[144] Roxin (2006), pp. 339–340. The Constitutions written in Spanish do not refer to proper crimes in general, but rather to a specific category of *delitos oficiales*.

[145] Roxin (2006), p. 340. The literature also differentiates between genuine and non-genuine proper crimes (*echte/unechte Sonderdelikte*). Genuine are those that may only be committed by the power given by the office; non-genuine are crimes that may be committed by anyone, but because they are committed in office, they are qualified as different crimes altogether. A common example of the latter for Latin America would be the difference between embezzlement (*abuzo de confianza, apropriação indébta*) and peculate (*peculado, peculato*), which describe the exact same criminal activity, but in the latter is committed by an officer over public property.

do so (11 out of 23; Argentina, Colombia, Costa Rica, Mexico*, Honduras*, Paraguay, Peru*, United States*, Uruguay and Venezuela*).[146] A few other Constitutions choose to restrict accountability for crimes committed in office (5 out of 24; Bolivia 1967 and 2009, Brazil, Ecuador 1979, Panama), as these are understood to better reflect the President's unfitness for office and, thus, serve as more legitimate grounds for impeachment. The most common formula, however, is a mix and match of both, with highlights to the crimes (usually corruption related) deemed especially symbolic or reprehensible,[147] following what is arguably the role model of the American Constitution. These are better visualized in Table 4.2 or Table 4.1.

Electoral Crimes and Infractions

While removing a President who was unfairly elected seems to be in line with the purposes and motives of impeachment, electoral crimes, and infractions (*e.g.*, voter fraud, illicit campaign financing, and other forms of disloyal competition) are not typically included among impeachment provisions, the notable exception being that of Mexico (art. 108, of the 1917 Constitution, after the reform of 2021). The reason for that is arguably one of system design, as Latin American countries have specialized ways of dealing with such abuses through the organs of electoral justice.[148] Every now and then, however, presidential elections receive their certification from the competent organs, only to be later put into question as evidence of electoral crimes comes to light, as seen, for example, in 1994 with Joaquin Balaguer (Dominican Republic), in 1996 with Ernesto Samper (Colombia), in 2015–2017 with Dilma Rousseff and Michel Temer (Brazil), and in 2019 both with Jair Bolsonaro (Brazil), or with Evo Morales (Bolivia),[149] to name a few. The presidential crises that originate in such situations are awkward to resolve, either because the electoral organ, usually highly technocratic and lowly democratic in nature making any decision it makes suspected. Mexico is the only nation whose impeachment does not have a blind spot on this regard, although other countries can theoretically use

[146] (*) Venezuela is accounted for twice. Before being amended, the Mexican Constitution considered only "serious common crimes" and the Honduran Constitution had an irresponsible presidency. Peru only deals with common crimes of *former* Presidents. Accountability for crimes may also be sought through the pretrial modality in the case of Peru, Bolivia (1967), Guatemala, and El Salvador. The inclusion of the United States is debatable for reasons discussed in Sect. 2.1.11. Arguably, the Clinton trial decided that crimes committed in the private life of the President are not impeachable offenses, but that may be subject to change.

[147] Ecuador's impeachable offenses, for example, are also the crimes which have no prescriptive period according to its criminal *codex* (art. 75).

[148] Orozco-Henriquez et al. (2010), p. 37 ff., especially p. 47.

[149] See Los Angeles Times, May 17th, 1994: "*Dominicans Vote; Signs of Fraud Emerge*"; The Washington Post, January 3rd, 1996: "*Colombian president took drug funds, aide says*"; BBC News, March 28th, 2017: "*Ação que pode cassar chapa Dilma-Temer entra na reta final: e agora?"*; Tribunal Superior Eleitoral, June 30th, 2020: "*TSE retoma julgamento de ações que apontam abuso eleitoral pela chapa Bolsonaro-Mourão"*; BBC News, December 6th, 2019: "*Evo Morales: Overwhelming evidence of election fraud in Bolivia, monitors say*".

proxies or broad impeachment categories to make up for this vulnerability.[150] The impeachment's slowness, however, can predictably introduce its own flavour of awkwardness, as the longer someone is in office, the more naturalized they become in that position to be removed for a selection error.

4.2.3 *Treason*

Despite the blueprint offered by the Constitution of the United States, currently only two Latin American Constitutions openly maintain 'treason' as an impeachable offense (Mexico and Peru; historically, also the 1979 Ecuadorian Constitution, after the reform of 1996). Arguably, however, most countries have the crime of treason in their criminal statutes dispersed as multiple categories of common and proper crimes, and should, thus, extend (with considerable limitations) the applicability of such offense to nearly all studied polities. While it is not clear why the Latin American Framers avoided such design choice, treason is known to be a notoriously problematic concept in law and its avoidance is not particularly surprising.

A lot of the pushback stems from the repeated and questionable use of treason throughout history. The particular sort of value judgement the category presupposes may easily lend itself to authoritarian incursions of the state, which, associated with severe punishment, made the crime of treason into an effective tool of suppression of opposition and critique of the regime, arguably often when those were broadly legitimate.[151] This is a fact that was well known to the Framers of the US Constitution, who discussed the topic in length during and after the Conventions.[152] In their judgment, however, having a highly specified and limited conception of treason within the Constitution itself (Art. 3, sec. 3) would likely serve as a better guarantee against its abusive application by overbearing actors and would prevent the creation of an ever-expanding criminal type, akin to that of "constructive treason", which existed in England.[153] The negative charge associated with the category and its

[150]The Samper case (see Sect. 3.2.1.3) addressed with the proxy use. Illegal campaign financing could not be used as a charge in the impeachment accusation, but the attempts at cover up could.

[151]Thomas Jefferson famously wrote: "Treason (. . .) when real, merits the highest punishment. But most codes extended their definition of treason to acts not really against their country. They do not distinguish between acts against the government and acts against oppressions of the government; the latter are virtues; yet they have furnished more victims to the executioner than the former; real treasons are rare; oppressions frequent. The unsuccessful strugglers against tyranny have been the chief martyrs of treason laws in all countries." Letter to Carmichael and Short, April 24th, 1792.

[152]For discussions on treason, see: Federal Convention: Farrand (1911a), p. 345 ff.; Ratifying Conventions: Elliot (1836a), v1: pp. 382–383 (Luther Martin's letter); v2: pp. 469, 487–488 (Pennsylvania debates); v3: pp. 168, 493–494 (Virginia debates); v4: p. 209 (North Carolina debates). See also James Wilson's lectures on article 3 ("Of Crimes Immediately against the Community"), and James Madison's considerations in The Federalist n. 43.

[153]Leek (1951), p. 605 ff. The US Constitution is one of the few in the world to include the definition of treason among its dispositions. Honduras also defines treason in the Constitution (art. 2). For details on "constructive treason", see Roberts (1975), p. 1420 ff.

severe punishment also make it likely for its application in practice to be frowned upon or highly suspected, if not avoided altogether.[154]

The second issue, incidentally mentioned above, is one of definition. The line separating treason from genuine critique or resistance can be awfully thin, making the severe punishments of treason come off as particularly unwarranted and tyrannical. The categories, whose connection with a "breach of allegiance" of any sort can be extremely tenuous, may end up serving to punish attitudes rather than actual harmful conduct. As commented in Chap. 2, the English conception of treason varied wildly and tended to reduce any sort of overstepping of regal competencies to a major offense against the existence of the Monarchy.[155] This could leave the accused entirely at the mercy of the authority, whose choice for punishing or not such trespasses were to be ultimately dispensed according to affect or political expedience.

These issues are naturally a lot more serious in the scope of criminal liability than that of political liability, due to the severity of consequences to the person of the accused and the challenges the category imposes to the rule of law. It seems, however, that Latin America's aversion to including treason to its lists of impeachable offenses is nonetheless well placed. The only instance of an accusation of treason being used in the ousting of a President is that against Manuel Zelaya, which is incidentally one of the most unanimously condemned oustings of recent history. The prosecutor who accused Zelaya claimed, among many other things, that, by insisting in conducting a referendum consulting the population about a new constitution, he was trying to "supplant People's sovereignty and usurp the constituted powers", as it had the potential to change sensible aspects of the political system, including the democratic form of government.[156] Although the use of instruments of direct democracy for the purpose of installing an authoritarian regime is definitively not unheard of,[157] the fact that the referendum did not even take place and that the accusation presupposed the worst possible intent without any material indication whatsoever makes treason work as an entirely attitudinal offense, against which arguably no defence is possible. That being the case, it seems that modern day application of the category of treason still carries over the vices of its historical counterparts and its avoidance, even in the overtly political contexts of impeachment, may be for the best.

[154] Fletcher (2004). Fletcher suggests, moreover, that the current ambivalence about treason is founded on the category's anachronism, as it no longer fits certain of its feudal assumptions.

[155] Roberts (1966), p. 95 ff.

[156] *Requerimiento fiscal contra el Presidente de la Republica José Manuel Zelaya Rosales*, June 25th, 2009, p. 8. It bears reminding that Zelaya was not removed by an impeachment procedure, but by a secret and summary criminal procedure.

[157] The 1929 Referendum of the Republic of Weimar rejecting the Treaty of Versailles, which is often associated with the rise of Adolph Hitler, or the 1996 Belarusian Referendum, which enabled Alexander Lukashenko's entrenchment in power, are arguably strong examples of this practice.

4.3 Subjective Element: *Mens rea* of Impeachable Offenses

A crime is a conduct that violates criminal law.[158] The question, however, of whether the person who commits the crime shall be held accountable for it (and to what degree), is a different one. For such purposes, *modern* criminal law will *generally* require one more element,[159] namely that the crime be committed with ill-intent or with the deliberate aim of breaking the law. This intention or state-of-mind that underlies the harmful act categorized as crime is known as *mens rea* ('guilty mind') or the subjective element of the crime.[160] The logic behind this requirement is that a punishment can only be just, if it is dispensed in a way capable of reforming transgressive behaviour. A person who breaks the law unintentionally arguably does not need to have his or her behaviour reformed, and, thus, a punishment would be superfluous/excessive and would not contribute in any meaningful way to the maintenance of the social contract (*nulla poena sine culpa* principle).[161] To be sure, there are plenty of exceptions and qualifications to this conclusion, which will be commented shortly, but by and large so is the general rule.

Knowing this, one is compelled to ask a few questions when transposing the same debate to the context of this book: Do impeachable offenses also require a subjective element? Does or should the impeachment conviction depend on whether the President intended to perpetrate the harmful act or not? Would the sanctions dispensed through impeachments be superfluous or excessive in face of a lack of intentionality? How can one know if there is such a requirement?

4.3.1 *Subjective Element and Impeachment Theory*

The first step in answering this question is acknowledging that the sphere of political accountability is much different than that of criminal accountability, as both fields seek to accomplish distinct goals. The fact that jurists often resort to principles of criminal law to find clarity and inspiration in questions of accountability in general should not be confused with the idea that these questions, by transference, also possess some degree of criminal nature. This is a conclusion that should be self-

[158] Roxin (2006), p. 205 ff.; Perkins (1939), p. 905.

[159] In the past, a *mens rea* was immaterial to criminal convictions. Often, however, pardons were conceded, for example, to those who "committed homicide by misadventure, in self-defence, or while of unsound mind", eventually being incorporated by criminal law. Maitland and Pollock (2010), pp. 494–505 [470–480].

[160] Roxin (2006), p. 207; Perkins (1939), p. 905; Wasserstrom (1959), p. 734.

[161] This is assuming Beccaria's justification of criminal law or prevention theory of criminal law, which is the mainstream position in Latin America. See Beccaria and Bellamy (1995), p. 10 ff. or Roxin (2006), pp. 205–211, 64 ff. If punishment for the sake of punishment is considered acceptable or criminal law is understood to serve no functional goal, this argument falls apart. For a broader debate, see Roxin (2006), pp. 211–220.

evident, but the practice of impeachments often shows that it really is not so. Impeachments are often confused with criminal procedures that just happen to be oddly structured, making discussions on the political responsibility of the President surreptitiously derail into discussions on his or her criminal responsibility.

That said, one should test if the principle of justice mentioned above also fits the context of impeachments. Do impeachment *sanctions* really serve to reform the transgressive behaviour of Presidents? Based on the theory and practice discussed in the previous sections, the answer seems to be negative. Presidents who were convicted in impeachment procedures were removed from the presidency not in hopes that their behaviour might be reformed in the future, but in the hopes that their harmful influence on the political system and national affairs ceased immediately. In all honesty, convicted Presidents are presumably unlikely to return to power, given how much societal consensus on their rejection needs to be realized for a successful conviction. A convicted felon, by contrast, eventually returns to society and thus to a position where their unreformed behaviour could generate new risks. Reformation is meaningful in this latter case, but not so much against Presidents.

Impeachment sanctions, therefore, must act under a different principle of justice or, more specifically, a principle of political justice. It is probably impossible to give a general answer as to how such principle should look like across all political systems, but perhaps an attempt at conceptualization may be given as a 'conversation starter'. Arguably, for a political system said to be democratic and republican, it would be reasonable to say that a political sanction is fair if it is imposed with the intent of protecting the People's best interests and political desires. The political sanction of removing the President, therefore, would be fair inasmuch it is able the harms and risks being inflicting upon society, and inasmuch the decision is imposed by the general will. These are secured through the systems of representation within a democracy, channels of dialogue and deliberation between society and political elites, as well as the appropriate conduction of the impeachment procedures, which need to produce a just decision informed by a wide societal consensus.

In this proposed framework, *mens rea* has only secondary importance, if any at all. The focus is on detecting harm to society and appropriately identifying the popular desires on the issue. The President's intentions would be important only inasmuch they qualify the harm/risks created, that is, only when the requisite for the consequences brought by the presidential behaviour is that they are ill-motivated in some sense. Such hypothesis can be clearly observed, for example, in the Ecuadorian Constitution of 2008, when it stablishes in art. 129, 3 that "homicide *for reasons of political or conscientious nature*" may be object of impeachment. Presumably from this text the involvement of the presidency in homicides only becomes impeachment-justifiable, or in other words, an actual risk to society at large, if they are committed with the mental state that objectivates political or conscientious gain. A President, for example, who employs the army in the combat of drug cartels, but produces civilian casualties in the process, may arguably not make himself subjectable to impeachment, while another who employs it to kill opposition leaders or dissident journalists may be committing an impeachable offense.

4.3.2 *Subjective Element in the Gradation of Impeachment Sanctions*

Though the subjective element is not a key component of impeachable offenses, its mention in impeachment procedures is frequent. When contending the objective element is impossible, Presidents try to justify the harm or risk they created by attributing or qualifying a subjective element of their offense, claiming that the offense was committed in pursuance of honourable goals (justification) or while lacking awareness of its harms or risks (excuse). Examples of these strategies were seen in the case studies of Rousseff, Piñera, or Samper. Rousseff claimed her budget violations were excusable because they were committed with the noble motivation of enabling the federal government to honour its welfare programs and benefits. She also claimed to have enacted supplementary credit without knowing it violated rules of financial law. It would be, in other words, no more than an honest mistake. Similarly, Samper claimed to have no idea that his electoral campaign had been generously financed by drug cartels. Piñera, on the other hand, had to acknowledge that he knew of the human rights abuses perpetrated by the armed forces against rioters, but argued he had done everything within his grasp to avoid them. His defence also tried to stablish that some violations were to be expected in exceptional circumstances imposed by the rioters, and that the instances of state repression were proportionate to the violent acts encountered.

Such strategies draw heavily from theory of criminal law, which posits, among other things,[162] that the severity of consequences should correlate positively with the increasing presence of the subjective element. The act of violating the law by mistake, for example, should be less reprehensible than the act of violating the law with the unambiguous ill-intention of causing harm, and thus the punishment must reflect such. On the example criminal law, it is said that violations committed with *dolus directus* (consciously acting in manner to cause harm) are more reprehensible than *dolus indirectus* or *dolus in the second degree* (consciously acting in manner to cause harm, but part of the harm caused is undesired by the agent), which are more reprehensible than *dolus eventualis* (consciously acting in manner that may foreseeably cause harm, but such harm is undesired by the agent; recklessness), which are more reprehensible than *culpa* (acting in manner that may cause harm, but such harm undesired and is either unforeseen or believed to be avoidable by the agent; carelessness).[163] There are, moreover, exceptional situations which cannot be graded in comparable terms of severity, because the subjective element is entirely irrelevant to them. Such cases stablish what is known as strict criminal liability,

[162] The subjective element as constitutive part of the offense itself will be discussed in the next section.

[163] Roxin (2006), p. 436 ff.

under which an agent may be criminally sanctioned regardless of any conscious design or awareness of the harms or risks created.[164]

The impact of such gradation on impeachments procedures, however, cannot be as direct as it would be in criminal law, where sanctions are flexible enough to measure up to the crime they seek to address. The President is either removed or not. The constitutions that stablish the concurrent sanction of disqualification from office usually offer no more leeway: the Court of Impeachments is generally obliged in applying the disqualification as part of the conviction, and its duration is pre-established and non-negotiable.[165]

In other words, impeachments do not meet half-way in their treatment of political accountability. A very *blameworthy* President who is convicted (or acquitted) will face the same severity of legal consequences a less *blameworthy* President would. This all-or-nothing arrangement arguably makes impeachments less predictable in terms of outcomes even when considering completely counterfactual examples. Criminalists perhaps disagree on how much time in prison a murderer should spend when they commit their crime under effect of emotional disturbance or as a hate crime, but they will agree on the principled conviction of such persons. Politicians, by contrast, will surely disagree greatly on the impeachment conviction of Presidents found in the same situation. Contextual factors (*e.g.*, presence of crisis, popular outrage, etc.) held constant, the impossibility of grading blameworthiness will make them choose between radically different alternatives.

[164] This form is relevant for 'impersonal crimes', that is, crimes committed not by individuals, but by corporations. A parent company, for example, may be held criminally liable for the harms created by its subsidiaries. They are also relevant for situations in which the agent has a positive duty of protecting special juridical goods. *E.g.*, bankers may be prohibited in taking large loans from their own institutions; parents may be obliged in providing education to their children; car drivers may be obliged to keep safe distance from bikers—in all these cases, agents could be held criminally accountable whatever their mental state may be. See Wasserstrom (1959).

[165] Only Peru (art. 100, Const. 1993) and Bolivia (art. 4, Law n. 44 of 2010) allow for grading of the sanction of disqualification. Ecuador, (art. 129, Const. 2008), Paraguay (art. 225, Const. 1992), Uruguay (art. 102, Const. 1967), and Venezuela (art. 233, Const. 1999), allow only the sanction of removal. The Constitutions of Argentina, Brazil*, Chile, Colombia, Dominican Republic, Mexico, and Panama indicate removal and disqualification for fixed durations as automatic consequence of conviction. As seen in the case studies, the procedure against Rousseff (Brazil) had the consequences of conviction voted separately, creating the possibility of removal without disqualification. The 1949 Const. of Costa Rica (art. 121, 9) is unclear about consequences for constitutional violations, but criminal violations can cause disqualification for a gradable period (art. 57, Penal Code).

4.3.3 Subjective Element as Constitutive Part of Impeachable Offenses

It must be noted, however, that the mentioned arguments presented by Rousseff, Samper, or Piñera most likely aimed at challenging the *blameworthiness* of the impeachment charges only at a secondary level. Primarily, they arguably sought to challenge the *wrongfulness* of the alleged offenses, still drawing strongly from the moral foundations given by the *nulla poena sine culpa* principle of criminal law. Rousseff would have sought to protect the welfare of her citizens and Piñera would have sought to re-establish Chile's internal security. Perhaps they would be to blame for the violations, but such violations were committed in pursuance of noble goals and thus justifiable or not warranting of legal sanctions.

As mentioned before, by extension of the *nulla poena sine culpa* principle, some harmful outcomes are only punishable or understood as criminal if they are bound to some specific mental state of the agent. Such rule is usually enshrined in the criminal code of the respective legal system, stating that the therein specified categories are only "punishable" or "criminally relevant" when committed with intention, but exceptionally when otherwise stated also without intention (*e.g.*, in the respective penal codes of Germany, § 15; Brazil, art. 18; Colombia, art. 21; Chile, art. 2 and 4; Ecuador, art. 27; etc.).

The same general rule is not enshrined anywhere in constitutions regarding impeachable offenses, making the extension of this rule to impeachments questionable. Dispositions on impeachable offenses are remarkably vague in their descriptions and, as history seems to suggest, consciously so. If one accepts the framework argued by this book, there is no reason to suppose the absence of such rule to be a mere relapse on the side of legislators across the American Continent. If anything, there is reason to believe that the general rule *is* the absence of the requirement of *mens rea*, which is only necessary in exceptional cases.

Not only there lacks a rule for the subjective element, the impeachable offenses which bring some mention to a mental state with expressions typically found in criminal law such as "knowingly", "against better judgment", "intent to destroy a group", "intent to hide another crime", "with the intention of inducing another person to (. . .)", "intent to cause loss to another", "motivated by bad-faith/self-interest", etc.,[166] are few and far between.[167]

---

[166] Roxin (2006), pp. 309–319.

[167] Ecuador has one mention to "homicide for political or conscientious reasons" (art. 129, 3, Const. 2008); Brazil has "use of violence or threat to coerce judges" (art. 6, VI, IL), "use of subordinate authorities to practice abuse of power or tolerate the abuse of power of subordinate authorities" (art. 7, V, IL), "intentionally delay the enactment of laws" (art. 9, I, IL), "use violence or threat against public officer to coerce him to commit illegal acts" (art. 9, VI, IL); Honduras has "[impose illegal orders] over others, to satisfy personal objectives outside of the scope of law" (art. 5, I, IL), "manifest (. . .) malice (. . .) that causes harm to the public interest" (art. 5, III, IL). Note: Brazil's impeachment law (IL) is Law n. 1.079 of 1950; and Honduras' is Decree n. 51 of 2013.

Not only that, but among impeachable offenses there is a category of violations which is entirely incompatible with modern criminal law and its necessitation of mental states. Criminal law, as is well-established, ought to punish persons for their undesirable *conduct* against society, and not persons for their undesirable *traits* or other *subjective qualities*.[168] Impeachable offenses such as those of "presidential indignity" or "poor performance", for example, which are not exactly objectively founded on the conduct of the President itself, but on the general public's perception of the President's morale as a leader and administrator would fit the latter category. In such offenses, whether the President arrived at such status out of malice, negligence, or even despite most virtuous efforts, is arguably immaterial to the public's lack of confidence in his or her abilities and leadership.

The only impeachment charges that would consistently require the consideration of the subjective element are those that are concretely based on the criminal code. Such offenses are irreparably bound to the general rules of criminal law, which, on their turn, do frequently necessitate mental states for the constitution of culpable and wrongful conduct.

4.3.4 Subjective Element and Causal Link in Chains of Command

The question of indirect, vicarious, or derivative liability (*i.e.*, accountability for the acts of others) is more complex than the previous questions. It brings within itself not only a question of mental states, but also questions regarding offensive causality, that is, the link between the perpetrators, their accomplices' conducts, and the illegal outcome. Authorship, intellectual or factual, and participation, concurrent or accessorial ('aiding and abetting'), are all forms of contributing to an illegal outcome that may nonetheless presuppose very distinct conducts, levels of awareness, and perhaps even designs by those involved. In face of such variety of forms and degrees of involvement, many questions may arise about when to hold the involved accountable, to what degree, for what offenses, and so on. Is, for example, enabling or facilitating the commission of an offense an offense itself? Does it matter if the conduct of the enabler is illegal or not? What about connivance? Is it acceptable to know about the existence of an offense and put no effort towards its prevention or the deterrence of the offender? What about neglect? Maybe the involved does not know about the activities of the offender, but does it play a role if he was legally obliged to oversee and contain these sorts of offenses? What if there is no legal obligation, but the offense was foreseeable by anyone in the same position? When should one be held accountable for contributing to an illegal outcome, if their conduct does not

[168] The criminalization of status offenses such as loitering, vagrancy, or drug-addiction persists occasionally in criminal law, but there is a clear trend in the gradual exclusion of such categories. Kieschnick (2018), p. 1578 ff., and Roxin (2006), pp. 178–185.

contribute in anything essential to its creation? What about moral complicity? Should it be legal for a person to protect the offender from accountability? Should it be legal for a person to profit from offenses of others?

The complexity of real-world scenarios makes it difficult to formulate overarching principles capable of providing fair and balanced solutions for all these questions all the time. As from the example of criminal, such solutions seem to offer trade-offs between being fair in most situations but being overly lenient in some of the more critical ones or addressing all situations but being too punishing in some of them. One could perhaps argue that the theory of the dominion of the act (*Tatherrschaftslehre*) is an example of the former, while the unitarian system of perpetration (*Einheitstätersystem*) is an example of the latter. As the name dominion of the act implies, the involved would only, *grosso modo*, be imputable those offenses towards which he contributed decisively (*i.e.,* he could have averted the outcome if he wished so), while the unitarian system would hold all involved accountable for all offenses committed, thus not differentiating between perpetrator, accomplice, and accessory (the grading of the punishment may still vary).[169] While the first arguably produces the fairer results for most ordinary crimes, it does have a tendency of being lenient on crimes committed by corporations, joint criminal enterprises, white collar crimes (in which proving intent is particularly difficult), and omissive crimes, which, in turn, are better addressed by the unitarian system. In practice, these theories may find a sort of patchwork application, being employed for the situations in which they are perceived to be more adequate or being modified/rationalized to better suit real-world cases.[170]

Such sort of refinement is something that is possible to criminal law due to its intense practice, which allows the detailed consideration of every single aspect, application, and implications of such theories. When it comes to presidential impeachments, however, theories of accountability are a lot less "battle-tested" and thus much more speculative and experimental. They tend also to be more influenced by the political passions of those who advocate them, given that the opportunities for debate are most of the time dominated by people who have stakes in the outcomes of impeachment, that is, the President's lawyers, his or her accusers, and the parties in Parliament, who may have something to gain in either the preservation or change of the presidency.

In the Rousseff impeachment, for example, accusation at times proposed something in the lines of *command* or *superior liability*, that is, a variant of unitary perpetration in which the persons in command must answer for all misdoings of their subordinates. In the Piñera impeachment, by contrast, the defence proposed the near exact opposite, a theory of liability in which the President should only answer for the offenses he or she directly and voluntarily perpetrated, thus excluding of omissive offenses and most offenses with indirect (mediate) perpetration—something which

[169] Roxin (2003), § 25, 27; and Ambos (2005), p. 173. For a detailed overview of these and other theories, see Roxin (2022).

[170] Stewart (2016).

in criminal law would be akin to what was known as *objective-formal liability*. The Nixon impeachment presented a sort of middle-of-the-road solution comparable to the dominion of the act theory, which was, however, then referred to as James Madison's *superintendency theory*. In this reading, the President would make himself liable for the acts of his subordinates whenever he or she is the sole responsible for checking their misconduct and he or she had knowledge of their involvement in offenses – in other words, the President would be liable for others whenever his mental state can have decisive influence on the course of offenses committed by them.[171]

One could perhaps try to describe all possible perpetration theories ever observed or conceived and advocate for a 'best one'. Such endeavour, however, would be simultaneously pyrrhic and sisyphean given to how little constitutions offer on the matter to work with[172] and how impossible it actually is to tiedown Representatives to strict rules of this kind – one would know how hard enough it already is to hold proper experts strictly bound to theories of perpetration they themselves propose or advocate.[173] There is only so much complexity that may be successfully implemented in a system that, unlike the Judiciary, is not operationalized by trained experts, nor consistently and systematically seeks to wash out extravagant and conflictive rule application.

In almost all official records examined during the Chapter of case studies the Representative's disregard for suggested frameworks for a subjective element in offense perpetration was palpable.[174] Few Representatives ever considered the subjective element as proposed by the accusation or defence, and instead, just presumed the offenses to be voluntarily sought by the President or to be completely unreasonable to impute them to him or her. Some Representatives do end up adopting interpretations by the accusation or defence, but the frameworks themselves serve more as rhetorical devices that justify the sense of *wrongfulness* or *blameworthiness* of the acts of the President to the personal sensibilities of a said Representative than as binding guidelines for conviction. In the end of the day, no vote by a single Representative can be reviewed or disqualified for being 'conceptually' unsound. Factually, what remains as safeguard against unlawful convictions is the individual consciences of the Representatives, who presumably must have some degree of responsibility to not pin an offense on someone who is unrelated to their perpetration. Such consideration is, furthermore, compounded by the high thresholds typical of impeachments, which require a strong consensus of among a

[171] Labovitz (1978), p. 106.

[172] Some lawyers suggest that the criminal standards should be applied where impeachment law is silent. This has some truth in it, as some impeachment laws do indeed elect the rules of criminal procedure to have subsidiary application where they leave gaps (*e.g.*, Brazil, Colombia). This consideration cannot be extended to the rules on the subjective element, however, because such rules are of substantive and not procedural law.

[173] Stewart (2016).

[174] This contrasts much with the objective element, which receives more attention and critical consideration.

large and broadly representative body of people. In such arrangement, a generalized breach of societies' sense of equity should not be an expected outcome.

There are, however, some rules that are simple to follow and are suggested by some constitutions that may more meaningfully impact accountability in chains of command. As discussed in Chap. 2, presidentialism does seek to insulate the Executive Branch, particularly Presidents, from outside influence, and thus create a strict separation of powers. Some constitutions go to greater lengths to achieve such goal and strictly cut the "causality chain", so to say, between the President and his subordinates under certain circumstances. Some constitutions with authoritarian and/or hyper-presidential ambitions seem to seek such interruption of liability more intently.

Pinochet's Constitution of 1980 (Chile), for example, stablishes in art. 36 that "The Ministers will be *individually* responsible for the acts they subscribe (. . .)".[175] Considering that almost every presidential act must be subscribed by a Minister, one can already guess what kind of liability this arrangement produces. Fujimori's Constitution of 1993 (Peru) achieves a similar outcome, but by stablishing impeachment in only four very limited situations, most of which cannot be performed autonomously by subordinates of the President.[176] Colombia's 1991 Constitution is not nearly as insulating, but still protects the President in the occasions he chooses to delegate functions.[177]

On the other side of the spectrum, Costa Rica's 1949 Constitution is crystal clear about demanding a proactive stance from the President for the behaviour of some of his subordinates, namely his or her Ministers, when it states:

> Art. 149. The President of the Republic and the Minister of Government who participated in acts as described next will be jointly held accountable:
>
> (1) When they compromise in any way the liberty, the political independence, or the territorial integrity of the Republic.
> (2) When they hinder or embarrass popular elections (. . .).
> (3) When they hinder or embarrass functions proper to the Legislative Assembly (. . .).
> (4) When they deny publishing or enforcing laws (. . .).
> (5) When they hinder or embarrass functions proper to the Judicial Branch (. . .).
> (6) Any other case in which, by act or omission, they violate express legal order.[178]

El Salvador's 1983 Constitution also openly acknowledges a shared responsibility among the President and his immediate subordinates:

---

[175] Author's translation. Curiously, however, Chile's impeachable offenses give mixed signals when they mention the "presidential administration" and not the only the President as their potential perpetrator.

[176] See Eguiguren (2007), p. 197 ff.

[177] "Art. 221. The delegation [of presidential duties] exempts the delegating party of any accountability, which will correspond exclusively to the delegated party, whose acts or resolutions may at any moment be reformed or revoked by the former, resuming the ensuing accountability". Author's translation. Art. 198 does, however, acknowledge the President's responsibility for his omissive acts, which may expand his liability for the acts of others.

[178] Author's translation.

> Art. 171 – The President, the Vice-President, the Ministers, and Vice-Ministers of State are jointly responsible for the acts they authorize. Ministers are responsible for resolutions taken up by the Council of Ministers, unless they have been defeated in their vote, or handed their resignations immediately thereafter.[179]

A similar argument could be perhaps made about Brazil's 1988 or Bolivia's 2009 Constitutions, as they stablish an abstract duty of the President in overseeing the Ministers/Secretaries of State (see Table 4.4). The true scope and reach of these duties have not been revealed by impeachment practice or constitutional provisions, but at least in Brazil's case there is such offense as "tolerating [abuses of power] committed by [immediately subordinate] authorities without reprimand" (art. 7, V, Law n. 1079 of 1950), which arguably creates the possibility of liability for the acts of others, so long the President has some knowledge of the offenses (implied by the verb "tolerate"). Somewhat comparable is the case of Honduras, which, though it does not stablish the duty of oversight, stablishes among its offenses the sort of negligent behaviour which causes harm to the public interest (art. 5, Decree n. 51 of 2013). Presumably, the failure to check the harm or risks caused by subordinates could be described as such negligent behaviour.

4.4 Limitations: Impeachable and Prescriptive Periods

Not every conduct that abstractly fits the definition of an impeachable offense can be politically punished through impeachment. There may be temporal aspects that proscribe either that (1.) the conduct may at all be considered an impeachable offense, or that (2.) the matter be appreciated by a Court of Impeachments. Most Latin American Constitutions, as well as the US role model stablish, for example, that the *only* sort of relevant misbehaviour is the one that is committed *while* the President is in office, which, to be punished through impeachment, *needs* to be taken to the Court of Impeachments *while* the President is still in office as well. Despite that being the general rule, there are meaningful ways in which these provisions may vary, bringing interesting trade-offs and supporting arguments.

4.4.1 Impeachable Period

Regarding item (1.), what will be called *impeachable period* for the lack of a better term, impeachable offenses may be (a.) only those committed while in office; (b.) also those committed before office; and (c.) also those that are committed after office.

The argument for the first case (a.) is that, if impeachment is to protect society from an abusive officer, then the only impeachment-relevant behaviour is that that

[179] Author's translation.

occurs while in office. An officer may have erred before, but if he or she is nonetheless elected, it may mean that he or she still merits the confidence of the People and is deserving of exercising the duties of office undisturbed by the past. Only an actual misbehaviour in office is indicative of unfitness for office. The argument for the second case (b.) is one that would qualify these last claims. It would argue that past misbehaviour is sufficiently symptomatic that the person of the President is not to be trusted with an office and that they too should be impeachable. As such, if previous misbehaviour comes to light while the President is in office, impeachment may still be useful in preventing future abuse. Finally, there is the third case (c.), which can also follow the same line of thought as the last one ('those who misbehave are not to be trusted in office') but may also serve another goal. In this latter hypothesis impeachment would act as an extra layer of political protection from legal action, requiring that first the President be impeached, only then to make him or her amenable to criminal or administrative suits.[180] In this last case impeachment will not result in removal from office, but may still generate disqualification.

It should be noted that in relation to certain legal systems, the discussion on impeachable period can be fairly dry. Some systems stablish impeachable conduct which can only be committed while in office, as the indicated acts presuppose the powers of the presidency. In such a constellation, there is little to be discussed on the issue, as never an issue that precedes or succeeds the presidency will pose legally or morally relevant questions. Other systems that stablish impeachability for common crimes or other misconduct in public offices, however, may occasionally challenge the dominating paradigm of impeachability circumscribed only to the period during which the person of the President is in office. The Samper and the Rousseff impeachments gave interesting insights into this question. Neither Samper, who might have committed electoral campaign financing fraud, nor Rousseff, who was accused of having grossly mismanaged public contracts (estimated US$ 2 billion of damages) while working as Minister of Energy for a previous administration, could be impeached on such grounds, as the acts preceded their entry in the presidency.[181] While neither is really representative of an abuse of the power of the presidential office, thus, straying from the main purpose of impeachment, they nonetheless imply certain moral risks and challenges to the presidential legitimacy, which designers of future constitutions and impeachment legislation may want to take into consideration.

[180]This is a particularity of the system of impeachments created by the 1993 Constitution of Peru. This creates a conflation between pretrial and impeachment procedures in the special case of former Presidents.

[181]See respective case studies. The contractual mismanagement of Rousseff was the leading impeachment charge in the accusation piece, which was later scrapped by the President of the Chamber of Deputies for violating the rule of impeachable period. Similarly, Samper had to be charged for his acts which attempted to cover up the campaign financing fraud, as the fraud itself was not amenable to impeachment (both for material and temporal reasons).

4.4.2 Prescriptive Period

The prescriptive period pertains to when an impeachment claim may be filed and taken to trial. This aspect also has three main formats: (a.) Impeachments can only be filed and taken to trial during the presidential mandate; (b.) Impeachments can be filed and taken to trial only after the President has left office; and (c.) Impeachments may be filed in both situations (Table 4.5).

Table 4.5 Impeachable and prescriptive periods in the American Constitutions

Country (Constitution)	Impeachable Period (when the offense is committed)	Prescriptive Period (when the claim is filed and trialled)	Reference article or case
Argentina (1994)	During	During	Art. 53
Bolivia (2009)	During	During, after (variable)*	Art. 111, 112, 184
Brazil (1988)	During	During*	Art. 86, §4/ Collor
Chile (1980)	During	During, after (6 months)	Art. 52, n. 2
Colombia (1991)	During	During	Art. 329 PBL
Costa Rica (1949)	During	During, after (4 years)	Art. 150
Cuba (2019)	–	–	–
Dominican Rep. (2010)	During	During	Art. 83, n. 1
Ecuador (2008)	Undefined	During	Art. 129
El Salvador (1983)	–	–	–
Guatemala (1985)	–	–	–
Honduras (1982)	During	During	Art. 234
Mexico (1917)	During	During, after (1 year)	Art. 108, 114
Nicaragua (1987)	–	–	–
Panama (1972)	During	During	Art. 160
Paraguay (1992)	Undefined	During	Art. 225
Peru (1993) *sitting Pres.*	During	During	Art. 117
Peru (1993) *former Pres.*	During, after (5 years)	After (5 years)	Art. 99
United States (1789)	During	During*	Art. 2, sec. 4/Trump
Uruguay (1967)	Undefined	During, after (6 months)	Art. 93, 102, 172
Venezuela (1999)	Undefined	During	Art. 266

Source: Own elaboration. Note: The frame of reference is either during or after the President is/was in office. When time is declared as 'undefined', it may also stretch to offenses before entering office. This chart reflects only the sphere of political accountability. If a conduct also configures criminal, civil, or administrative infraction, and there is intention to trial it as such, it will be subjected to the specific rules of those spheres of accountability. Articles indicated are from the respective Constitution, unless indicated otherwise. PBL indicates parliamentary bylaws of the respective country (Colombia: Law n. 5 of 1992). Key: (*) the issue is controversial; (–) impeachment not applicable

The reasons for making the President accountable during the mandate (a.) have already been discussed extensively in this book. In short, the electoral system may filter among candidates who enjoy esteem and confidence of the Nation, but that is not by itself sufficient safeguard against abuse of the presidential powers, as voters may mistake themselves in the judgment of a candidate's character and abilities, as well as about his or her capacity of not falling into the temptations of power. The possibility of removal in case of abuse of power and corruption before the end of the mandate, therefore, guarantees that the concentration of power in the person of the President does not become too great of a liability to the democratic and republican form of government.

Less explored, however, are the reasons to extend impeachment also for the period after the presidential mandate (c.). Impeaching Presidents after they have left office may guarantee that they are actually made politically accountable for misbehaviour committed near the end of the mandate, such as seen with the Rousseff and Trump cases. In the Trump case, the second attempt at impeachment had to be arguably rushed to be finalized before the end of his term, as the impeachable offense occurred in the last month of office. The situation produces an outcome that is good for neither party. The defendant runs the risk of having his defence and due process rights steamrolled by Congress, who is eagerly looking for a timely conclusion of affairs, and the managers of accusation have little time piece a robust and coherent case that adequately represents the grievances in play. The People may be left without a sense of closure, as the procedure will likely be riddled with flaws, and accountability will lack the proper thoroughness to satisfy a sense of justice. Regarding Rousseff, the issue was even more serious. Rousseff's offenses occurred mostly in the first mandate, but accountability was sought only in the second one. All offenses committed in the first mandate were scrapped by Congress and only feeble charges that arguably lacked depth remained. The situation not only instituted a sense of leniency but also made the impeachment charges look disproportionate to the consequences of removal and disqualification from office, damaging the legitimacy of the procedures.

Holding the President politically accountable after the end of the mandate avoids issues such as these. Naturally, however, the consequence of removal from office is not applicable in a case like Trump's, but the disqualification for office may still take place. The consequence of disqualification is one that should not be taken lightly. It may prevent an overbearing candidate from reaching power once again, as the electoral process, as mentioned above, is not infallible in selecting only those of high esteem and probe character. Former Presidents remain influential, and many voters may be willing to overlook their flaws in exchange for simple solutions, as was commented in the case study of Alberto Fujimori.

After-term procedures can have adverse effects, however. They can, for example, remove an incentive for an overbearing President to resign when threatened by impeachment. If resignation no longer serves as a guarantee against disqualification, a President may feel inclined to see the procedure through, even when conviction seems certain, thus delaying the resolution of a crisis.

Finally, there is also a case to be made in favour of accountability that takes place only after the President leaves office (b.). Certain countries which have a very strict commitment to separation of powers, such as Mexico,[182] Peru, or some of the Central American nations, may find the idea of the Parliament checking the Executive intolerable and destructive of their political system, but may desire to commit themselves to the republican ideal to some degree. In such circumstances, restricting accountability only to after the mandate may allow the presidency to remain entirely autonomous, while keeping a sense of accountability down the line. This, as has been argued many times in this book, is a problematic approach, as it produces a system with no outlet for mounting political tensions, that is thus prone to producing violent and/or alternative solutions of questionable constitutionality. Peru has 'repurposed' the declaration of vacancy on moral grounds to patch the insufficiency of its impeachment system, and Mexico recently debated how to make its impeachment workable due to popular pressure.[183]

4.5 Formal Aspects of Impeachment

4.5.1 Procedural Variations and Constitutional Design of Impeachments

Reflecting upon the different ways impeachment had been adapted in the state constitutions, the Framers of the US Constitution acknowledged that stablishing an adequate framework for impeachments was among some of the greatest challenges they faced.[184] There is arguably no unflawed, unquestionable way of holding the chief magistrate accountable. There is no structure that comes without its trade-offs, and which may, thus, place any given arrangement above critique or suspicion.[185] That is an unfortunate realization which every presidential democracy must come to terms whenever confronted by the need, imagined or actual, of having their central political actor removed. Overturning the results of a popular election, even when the President is clearly overbearing, comes with high costs for those involved. Expectations are broken, new ones are created. The legitimacy of a government comes into check and its change does not guarantee the renewal of the People's trust. This being the case,

[182] Despite the impeachment dispositions of the 1917 Constitution, many Mexican jurists to reject the possibility of presidential impeachment due to the separation of powers. See Martínez Robledos (2008), pp. 170–172.

[183] The discussion led to a referendum which took place in August 2021. The Guardian, September 15th, 2020: *"Mexico's Amlo proposes referendum on prosecuting country's ex-presidents"*.

[184] James Madison (October 1788), commenting Jefferson's draft of the Constitution of Virginia. Accessible here: https://founders.archives.gov/documents/Jefferson/01-06-02-0255-0005.

[185] Such trade-offs may be immanent to the design or may appear only when interacting with other institutions or environmental conditions. For a general discussion on possible factors that influence institutional 'success', change and stability, see North (1990), p. 73 ff.

Table 4.6 Overview of the instruments for presidential removal in Latin America

Country (Constitution)	Houses	Parliamentary Impeachment	Judicial Impeachment	Pretrial	Declaration of Vacancy
Argentina (1994)	2	Art. 53, 59, 60; Art. 194 PBL	No	No	Art. 88
Bolivia (1967)	2	No	Art. 118, 5; Art. 68, 11	No	Art. 93, 95
Bolivia (2009)	2	No	Art. 161, 7; 184, 4; 4 ff. IL	No	Art. 169, 170, 173; Art. 105 PBL
Brazil (1988)	2	Art. 86; Art. 14 ff. IL; Art. 218, §2 PBL	Art. 86; Art. 14 ff. IL; Art. 217 PBL	No	Art. 83; (Art. 8, 6 IL)
Chile (1980)	2	Art. 52, 2a; 53, 1	No	No	Art. 28, 29; 53, 7; Art. 7 PBL
Colombia (1991)	2	Art. 174, 175; 178, 3; Art. 341 PBL	Art. 175, 3; 178, 4; 235, 2; Art. 341, 347 PBL	No	Art. 194, 196, 202; Art. 118; 313, 3; 323, 326 PBL
Costa Rica (1949)	1	No	Art. 121, 9 & 10; 149, 150; Art. 27, 7; 156; 215 ff. PBL	Art. 151; 121, 9; Art. 391 CCP	Art. 121, 8; 135; 138,5
Dominican Rep. (2010)	2	Art. 80, 1; 83, 1	No	No	Art. 129, 2; 131
El Salvador (1983)	1	No	No	Art. 236 ff.; Art. 120 ff. PBL	Art. 131, 20; 155
Ecuador (1978)	1	Art. 82, g	No	No	Art. 100, d
Ecuador (1998)	1	Art. 167, 5; 130, 9	No	Art. 130, 10	Art. 167, 4 and 6;
Ecuador (2008)	1	Art. 145, 3; 129; Art. 86 ff. PBL	No	Art. 120, 10; 195	Art. 145, 4 and 5; 146
Guatemala (1985)	1	No	No	Art. 165, h; D.n. 85/2002	Art. 165, i; 189
Honduras (1982)	1	No	No	Art. 205, 15	–
**After 2003 reform*	1	No	No	No	–
** After 2012 reform*	1	Art. 234; Art. 4, 10, 11 IL	No	No	Art. 205, 12 & 13; 242 (Art. 5, 3 IL)
Mexico (1917)	2	Art. 108, 110 x 111	No	Art. 108, 111	Art. 84; Art. 9, 10, 125 PBL

(continued)

Table 4.6 (continued)

Country (Constitution)	Houses	Parliamentary Impeachment	Judicial Impeachment	Pretrial	Declaration of Vacancy
Nicaragua (1987)	1	No	No	Art. 131 x 148	–
* *After 2000 reform*	1	No	No	Art. 130; L.n. 83/1990	Art. 149
Panama (1972)	1	Art. 152, 160; Art. 467 ff CCP	No	No	Art. 187, 188, 189
Paraguay (1992)	2	Art. 225	No	No	Art. 227, 233, (190)
Peru (1993)	1	Art. 117, 99; 89 PBL; L.n. 27379	Art. 100; Art. 89 PBL	(†)	Art. 113, 115; 89-A PBL
Uruguay (1967)	2	Art. 93, 102, 172	No	No	Art. 150, 170
Venezuela (1961)	2	No	Art. 150, 8; 215, 1	(†)	Art. 186-188
Venezuela (1999)	1	No	Art. 187, 3; 222, 233, 266	No	Art. 233, 234, 235

Source: Own elaboration based on indicated constitutions and legal texts. Key: (No) indicates the absence of legal instrument, (–) indicates legal undefinition, (Houses) indicates number of chambers in Congress. Articles refer to respective constitution, unless indicated otherwise. (PBL) Parliamentary bylaws, (IL) Impeachment law, (CCP) Code of criminal procedure; (L.n. or D.n.) Law or decree number; (x) Antinomy between indicated articles; (†) Classification as pretrial controversial

having an objectionable procedure to channel all these transformations can be arguably dangerous for the survival of democracy both in the short or the long run.

Out of such need for cautiousness, Latin America produced a wide array of procedural variants for holding their chief magistrates accountable (see Table 4.6 for a partial overview), much like the British colonies had before it. The two main variants are known as the (i.) predominantly parliamentary impeachment and the (ii.) predominantly judicial impeachment, predominance being defined by the institution responsible for serving as the court of impeachments.[186] A third and less common variant was also developed by unicameral systems in the last two decades, which may be called (iii.) trial-less impeachments, that is, impeachment procedures in which there is no Court of Impeachments, thus conducting no impeachment trial.

Beyond these systems of impeachment, there are also other *non-impeachment alternatives or surrogates to presidential ousting* that have been present at the region and which are often object of confusion in the media and scholarly works. These are: (iv.) the declaration of vacancy on grounds of incapacity or absence, (v.) the pretrial (*antejuicio*) or immunity revocation procedures (*privación de inmunidad, desafuero*), (vi.) the presidential recall or presidential mandate revocation

[186] As originally proposed by Kada (2002) apud Pérez-Liñán (2007).

procedures (*revocatoria de mandato*), (vii.) the procedure of mutual dissolution (*muerte cruzada*) between Executive and Legislature, and (viii.) the suits of electoral slate cassation (*ação de investigação judicial eleitoral: ação de impugnação de mandato eletivo*). These do not necessarily serve to hold the President accountable in the same sense as the impeachment but may serve as the 'next best thing' when impeachment is unavailable or unpracticable. Although they do not constitute impeachment *per se*, contemplating them and contrasting them with impeachments may provide important insights into the boundaries of impeachment itself.

This section will discuss the constitutive features of all these procedures, clarifying their realm of use, their purpose, and their potential trade-offs as tools of constitutional design. For the sake of thoroughness, a short *excursus* on the (ix.) vote of no confidence will be offered to piece together many points made throughout this book.

4.5.1.1 Parliamentary Impeachment *Versus* Judicial Impeachment

Features The impeachment is a procedure for conducting national inquest into misconduct of high officers. In its adaption to presidential systems, the impeachment focuses mostly on misconduct of the President. Its use against Ministers and Justices is possible in many places in Latin America, but much like in the United States, its introduction was mostly an afterthought in the constitutional design. As a result, the procedure is likely ill-suited or entirely obsolete for holding any other officer accountable than the President.[187] Key features of the impeachment are that it may be conducted entirely autonomously from (and entirely against) the will of the Executive branch and that an aspect of national representation is always present. These features make the procedure embody a few major developments of constitutionalism' history, such as the supremacy of the Parliament, the right to people's self-determination, and the commitment to responsible and balanced government.

In the Americas, any form of impeachment necessarily has the participation of Parliament at one point or another of the procedure. What may fundamentally vary is the degree to which it can determine its outcome. The so-called (i.) predominantly parliamentary impeachments have the largest part, if not the totality, of the procedure conducted within the Parliament (Table 4.8). The judiciary may be invoked to make interlocutory decisions (*e.g.,* deciding some of the basic rules and interpretations, allowing certain kinds of evidence to be produced) or conduct/collaborate in part of the procedures (*e.g.,* investigation, presentment), but the merit of the impeachment will remain within the Parliament's sovereign grasp. In other words, the distinctive feature that separates one form of impeachment from the other is *who acts as the Court of Impeachments*, that is, who will trial the articles of impeachment offered against the President and, thus, decide for his or her acquittal or conviction.

[187] See, for example, the account offered in Gerhardt (2019), pp. 33–65, on the impeachment of judges.

Table 4.7 Countries with predominantly judicial impeachments

Country (Constitution)	Gatekeeper	Referral threshold	Commission veto power	Impeachment threshold	Suspension	Conviction threshold	Disqualification	Duration	Reference articles
Bolivia (2009)	General Prosecutor	–	No	2/3 LH+HH	No	1/2 SC	Cond.	0.5 to 10 years	Art. 161, 7; 184, 4; 4 ff. IL
Brazil (1988) ↳*Criminal offenses*	Supreme Court	–	No	2/3 LH	Yes	1/2 SC	Yes	8 years	Art. 86; Art. 14 ff. IL; Art. 217 PBL
Colombia (1991) ↳*Common crimes*	Permanent Commission	–	No	1/2 LH	Yes	1/2 SC	Yes	0 to permanent	Art. 175, 3; 178, 4; 235, 2; Art. 341, 347 PBL
Costa Rica (1949)	President H	1/2 H (appeal)	No	2/3 H	Cond.	1/2 SC	Cond.	0.5 to 12 years	Art. 121, 9 & 10; 149, 150; Art. 57 ff. CC; art. 27, 7; 156; 215 ff. PBL
Peru (1993) ↳*Criminal offenses*	Sponsor or Permanent Commission	35% H	Yes	1/2 H	–	1/2 SC	2/3 H	<10 years	Art. 100; Art. 89 PBL
Venezuela (1999)	Supreme Court	–	–	(-) H	–	1/2 SC	–	–	Art. 187, 3; 222, 233, 266

Source: Own elaboration. Key: (-) legally undefined or inapplicable; (LH) Lower House; (HH) Higher House; (H) Single House; (SC) Supreme Court; (IL) Impeachment law; (PBL) Parliamentary bylaws; (CC) Criminal code; (Cond.) Outcome dependant on special conditions (e.g., nature of offense). (Impeachment rules for Venezuela are incomplete in the 1999 Constitution or relevant bylaws. The Constitution self-identifies itself as "semi-presidential or semi-parliamentarian", and consciously focuses on ministerial accountability (*i.e.*, censure, interpellation) or plebiscitarian removal mechanisms (*i.e.*, recall). In practice, however, the system behaves arguably as hyper-presidential as none of such mechanisms is practicable)

Table 4.8 Countries with predominantly parliamentary impeachments

Country (Constitution)	Gatekeeper	Referral threshold	Commission veto	Impeachment threshold	Suspension	Conviction threshold	Disqualification	Duration	Reference
Argentina (1994)	Sponsor	1/2 LH	No	2/3 LH	No	2/3 HH	Yes	Permanent	Art. 53, 59, 60; Art. 194 PBL; Art. 9 IL
Brazil (1988) ↳Const. offenses	President LH	–	No	2/3 LH, 1/2 HH	Yes	2/3 HH	Yes	8 years	Art. 86, Art. 14 ff. IL; Art. 218, §2 PBL
Chile (1980)	10–20 Sponsors	–	No	1/2, 1/2 LH	No	2/3 HH	Yes	5 years	Art. 52, 2a; 53, 1
Colombia (1991) ↳Const./ proper crimes	Permanent Commission	–	No	1/2 LH	Yes	2/3 HH	Yes	0 to permanent	Art. 174, 175; 178, 3; Art. 341 PBL
Dominican Rep. (2010)	Sponsor	1/2 LH	Unclear	3/4 LH	Yes	2/3 HH	Yes	10 years	Art. 80, 1; 83, 1
Mexico (1917)	–	–	–	(1/2 LH)	(Yes)	(2/3 HH)	(Yes)	–	Art. 108, 110 x 111
Panama (1972)	Permanent Commission	–	Yes	1/2 Perm. Comm.	No	2/3 H	Yes	Mandate	Art. 152, 160; Art. 467 ff CCP
Paraguay (1992)	Sponsor	1/2 LH	No	2/3 LH	No	2/3 HH	No	–	Art. 225
United States (1789)	Sponsor	1/2 LH	Yes	1/2 LH	No	2/3 HH	Yes	Permanent	Art. 1, sec. 1, 2; 2, sec. 4
Uruguay (1967)	Sponsor	–	–	1/2 LH	Cond.	2/3 HH	No	–	Art. 93, 102, 172

Source: Own elaboration. For parliamentary proceedings in Ecuador, Honduras, or Peru, see next section. Information on Mexico is hypothetical (On February 19th of 2021, the Mexican Constitution was amended in ways that make it unclear whether the President is amenable to impeachment/pretrial. Art. 111 indicates the President ought to be tried according to Art. 110, which delineates rules for impeachment. Art. 110, however, does not include the President in its *numerus clausus* list of impeachable officers, generating an antinomy. In the literature, the issue remains controversial.). Key: (-) legally undefined or inapplicable; (LH) Lower House; (HH) Higher House; (H) Single House; (IL) Impeachment law; (PBL) Parliamentary bylaws; (CCP) Code of criminal procedure; (Cond.) Outcome dependant on special conditions (Uruguay: impeachment vote passed with 2/3 supermajority)

By contrast, the (ii.) predominantly judicial impeachment (Table 4.7),[188] therefore, will involve some of the country's highest courts in the trial of the merit of impeachment and is a much larger deviation from the role model offered by the US Constitution. This adaptation comes with trade-offs that will be discussed below, but also with the interesting innovation that attempts to patch some of the most criticized legal loopholes/inconsistencies introduced by the system of impeachments. The Venezuelan and Bolivian models of impeachment, for example, introduce a kind of two-step initiation procedure involving both the Supreme Court and Parliament. In this arrangement, the Supreme Court is able to filter legally unsound attacks against the President, while Parliament filters the politically inopportune or illegitimate attacks in a second step. By doing this, both systems tackled a potential risk of a 'hostile takeover' by an overbearing Parliament, although arguably introducing a risk of creating a presidency impervious to scrutiny if such Court ever gets captured by the Executive power.

Realm of Use Predominantly judicial impeachments tend to be reserved to the trialling of impeachable offenses one would call 'strictly legal', such as the trialling of common crimes or certain civil, administrative, or electoral misbehaviour. This characteristic arguably denounces the reason behind the design choice, namely the idea of having legalistic issues resolved by an authority properly specialized and experienced with the dispensing of justice. This specialization allows, moreover, the Court of Impeachments to apply sanctions which are more than just political in nature, such as the removal and disqualification from office are typically seen. By virtue of being a specialized organ of justice, such courts may also have competence to apply criminal, civil, and administrative sanctions of all sorts, and will most likely do so in case of conviction.

The prototypical use of judicial impeachments is perhaps for the trialling of common crimes, such as seen in the Brazilian and Colombian Constitutions. These constitutions have both forms of impeachment, but if the President is impeached on articles from the criminal code rather than on impeachable offenses in the strict sense, they will require the Supreme Court to act as the Court of Impeachments.

Predominantly parliamentary impeachments, on the other hand, tend to have a broader scope of action. They are generally focused on legal offenses with ample political implications but may also occasionally contemplate strictly technical legal offenses with little political spill over. They must, however, restrict themselves to political sanctions as the Parliament likely lacks the competence for adjudicating matters of any other field of law.

[188] Most US-American authors use the term judicial impeachment to refer to the impeachment procedure against Judges and Justices, and parliamentary impeachments to refer to procedures against members of Congress. In this book or part of the Latin-American literature, however, the terms judicial/parliamentary are not referring to the persons subjected to impeachment, but to the form of impeachment.

Purpose The purpose of impeachment has been discussed thoroughly in Sect. 4.1 and it should not be altered simply by a preponderance of the judicial or parliamentary setting, although the choice admittedly implies a different focus or a different set of values by those who designed the impeachment system. The judicial impeachment arguably values of the strict commitment to the rule of law over other values such as political stability and accountability, at least in comparison to the parliamentary impeachment. It carries within itself the lawyerly mindset that, any legal question, even when permeated by and embedded in relations of power, ought to be as divorced from politics as it possibly can. One could argue, therefore, that the judicial impeachment acts in the forefront as an instrument of legal accountability of the President in the strict sense, while the parliamentary impeachment shifts such balance towards political accountability. This is so only in theory and in a high-minded sense, of course, as has been vastly argued in this book. Such strict separation is impossible, and the political nature of the accountability sought through impeachment, whatever its form, will predominate in any real-world scenario.

Nomenclature Impeachments are known in Latin America under a variety of epithets other than the English word *impeachment* itself. The most common and widespread translations of the Spanish-speaking realm are, in first place, political trial (*juicio politico*), followed by constitutional suit (*acción constitucional*) or constitutional accusation (*accusación/denuncia constitucional*). Bolivia and Brazil are unique in calling it a liability or responsibility procedure (Span.: *juício de responsabilidades*; Pt.: *processo de responsabilidade*), where impeachable offenses are known as liability or responsibility crimes (Span.: *crimenes de responsabilidad;* Pt.: *crimes de responsabilidade*). Brazilian jurists most commonly use the direct translation of impeachment procedures (*processo de impedimento*) into Portuguese.[189]

Trade-Offs

- *Judicial independence*: The two forms allow for different degrees of independence in their decision-making process, which may shield them from certain biases or fear of personal repercussions.

  The parliamentary form has its strength in numbers, as well as in political experience and authority. The Parliament is not easily intimidated or awed by the President, and the repercussions of its decisions are dispersed among a large body of politicians, who are used to dealing with the public opinion and are more resistant to military pressure. Its weaknesses lie on the need it otherwise has for cooperation with the Executive and in the partisan affiliations of its members. Fear of severing channels to power and patronage if they support a failed

[189] *Impedimento* means 'impediment', 'hinderance' or 'embarrassment'. These are original primary meanings for the cognate 'impeachment', which, although no longer current in modern English, remain so in both Spanish and Portuguese. See Oxford Dictionary for etymology and use. In current use, the verb 'to impeach' is more commonly employed with the meanings of 'to challenge', 'to call into question', or 'to bring accusation against'.

impeachment, as well as fear from disciplinary punishments from their party may undermine their autonomy.

The judicial form has its strengths in its isolation from government and in its dominance of the legal methodology. Since the Justices generally have nothing to gain from the presidency, there is little it can *legally* offer or threat to sway their judgment. The Justices, moreover, are arguably better suited to form their own legal opinion on the subject uninfluenced by mainstream opinions, as they likely are experts in these legal issues themselves. The weaknesses of the judicial form come in the small number of justices and their nomination procedure. The small size of the courts makes Justices easier to be singled-out for their opinions and, thus, easy to intimidate and to awe by *extra-legal* means (*e.g.*, popular pressure). The military intimidation of Justices raises fewer red flags than that of the Parliament, as one is generally a non-elected, contra-majoritarian institution, and the other is elected and democratic. Finally, the selection of Justices likely has the President as a key stakeholder, possibly biasing their selection in favour of leniency towards him or her.

- *Specialization*: From its infrastructure to the practice of its core activities, the Judiciary is better equipped to dispense justice and decide technical legal aspects of impeachment. The small size of the organ is more adequate to the creation of an environment conducive to serious and judicious decision-making. On the other hand, however, inasmuch Justices may possess the technical prowess to make a reasoned and well-informed decision, their work may isolate them in a certain societal bubble and deprive them from the sort of political acuity an impeachment decision may require. Congress is less afflicted by this, as part of its work requires it to comprehensively screen, channel, and embody public demands. Some members of Congress, however, may lack the proper understanding of the legal issues debated in impeachments and may at times make impertinent considerations and decisions.
- *Division of labour*: The judicial form allows for greater or clearer division between the functions of those who conduct impeachment, which may improve efficiency and legitimacy of the procedures, as well as reduce the likelihood of a biased decision. A member of Parliament who, for example, acts in the investigation is arguably more prone to convict the investigated out of a confirmation bias. The situation of creating a single organ who is "judge, jury, and executioner" may undermine the legitimacy of the procedures. The division of labour between houses of Parliament may diminish these negative effects, but such is not an option available to unicameral Parliaments, who may profit from the cooperation with the Judiciary.
- *Sanctions*: The judicial form of impeachment may be legally empowered to decide the merit involving presidential misbehaviour in multiple fields of law simultaneously, presumably guaranteeing a cohesive decision on the issue of presidential accountability across the board. The parliamentary form cannot offer the same sort of cohesion. Parliament is not constitutionally endowed to adjudicate ordinary fields of law and must, thus, restrain itself to the scope of political accountability. This creates the possibility of having dissonant decisions between

Parliament and High Court in different fields of law, raising doubts about the soundness of either decision.

- *Legitimation*: The judicial form of impeachment may command more authority regarding the legal validity of an impeachment, but as a decision made by a small and unelected organ, it lacks democratic legitimation to be widely accepted as a decision "of the People". The parliamentary form is less likely to be seen as a work of cabal and more as a true representation of societal consensus. The partisan affiliation of the members of Parliament, however, may suggest that the decision was to some degree motivated by self-interestedness and other legally unfitting considerations, thus undermining the authority impeachment seeks to draw from legal rationality.
- *Slowness and cumbersomeness:* Although any form of impeachment tends to consume a considerable amount of time, the parliamentary form is likely quicker than its judicial counterpart. The cautiousness and procedural safeguards proper to judicial procedures make them prone to drowning into legal quarrels that may extend beyond the duration of the presidential term, possibly undermining a timely solution to a crisis. The parliamentary form cannot be halted as much but may take up attention and time from the members of Parliament, who compose a much larger body than that of the high Court. The parliamentary form can, thus, become the more costly procedure, and possibly a nuisance to the resolution of other pressing matters.

4.5.1.2 Traditional Impeachments *Versus* Trial-Less Impeachments

Features Trial-less impeachments (Table 4.9) are parliamentary proceedings which share all characteristics of the forms of impeachment commented above, apart from their trial phase. Since they do not have a court of impeachments, they also do not fit the suggested dichotomy of predominantly parliamentary/predominantly judicial impeachments. They can be at times referred to as a motion of censure (Ecuador, Art. 95, Parliamentary bylaws).

Realm of Use Although nothing holds back on trial-less impeachments from being implemented anywhere in Latin America, they currently only exist in a limited number of unicameral Parliaments (Honduras after 2013, Ecuador after 2008, and Peru in procedures against *sitting* Presidents, or constitutional violations of *former* Presidents). Its use comes with clear caveats vis-à-vis the traditional impeachment. The Honduran variation can tackle an enormous scope of impeachable offenses but requires particularly high thresholds to even be taken into consideration and cannot result in disqualification for office. The Ecuadorian and Peruvian variations, on the other hand, are strongly limited in terms of applicable offenses, tackling only acts established as particularly pernicious. The Peruvian variant increases significantly in scope after the President leaves office. All variants have expedited procedures, programmed to last just a few days, and so give quick resolution to a crisis.

Table 4.9 Countries with trial-less impeachments

Country (Constitution)	Gatekeeper	Referral threshold	Commission veto	Impeachment threshold	Suspension	Conviction threshold	Disqualification	Duration	Reference
Ecuador (2008)	Permanent Commission and Const. Court	1/3 H	Yes	2/3 H	–	–	No	–	Art. 145, 3; 129; Art. 86 ff. PBL
Honduras (1982) ↳*After 2012 reform*	Sponsor	2/3 H	No	3/4 H	Yes (at referral)	–	No	–	Art. 234; Art. 4, 10, 11 IL
Peru (1993) ↳Const. offenses	Permanent Commission or General Prosecutor	–	Yes	2/3 H	–	–	2/3 H	<10 years	Art. 117, 99; 89 PBL; L.n. 27379

Source: Own elaboration. Key: (-) legally undefined or inapplicable; (H) Single House; (SC) Supreme Court; (IL) Impeachment law; (PBL) Parliamentary bylaws; (L.n.) Law number

Purpose As an institution, the trial-less impeachment serves the same purposes as any impeachment, as already discussed in previous sections. It is clear deviation of the tradition of impeachments that attempts to fix its slowness and/or cumbersomeness, while preserving some of the rationality of their rituals. It may also fix a problem of representativity typical for these procedures under a unicameral environment. It avoids an arbitrary division of the House into accusers and judges, allowing it to perform one function cohesively.

Trade-Offs

- *Quickness:* Removing the trial means removing the procedural step that may potentially take the longest. Such design may thus substantially improve the impeachment's capacity of offering a timely response to a constitutional crisis caused by the presidency, but results in a sacrifice of cautiousness.
- *Transparency and rationality:* The trial is an important part of the procedure for expanding the public discussion into presidential misconduct, as well as confronting it with competing understandings of the law and the facts offered by accusation and defence. As such, the trial may confer much needed clarity and rationality to a problem that meets in the intersection of law and politics, and which cannot be merely reduced to one or the other. In absence of a trial, therefore, the procedure may fail to suitably communicate to the public the grounds and soundness of accusation against the President. Its rationality may, thus, be more readily dominated by impertinent considerations or factional disputes.
- *Legitimation:* The legal rationality introduced by the trial may further strengthen the legitimation of a decision removing the President, given that the law, in some sense, also represents a field of neutrality or non-partisanship. Having strong legal arguments and a well-developed procedure, with ample space for defence, thus, may arguably dispel suspicions and narratives of a 'hostile takeover' by Parliament. With a trial phase absent, the legal side of impeachment may lack the opportunity to reach full maturity, weakening the legitimation of the procedures.

4.5.1.3 Impeachment *Versus* Declaration of Vacancy

Features The (iii.) declaration of vacancy is a quasi-notarial procedure of the Parliament used to declare the office of the presidency vacant and, thus, operationalize the ensuing legal consequences foreseen in law, such as temporary or permanent (also called absolute or definitive) presidential succession, or the calling of new presidential elections. In Latin America, the causes of vacancy are foreseen in a limited list within the respective constitution or the parliamentary bylaws, being generally related to the physical or mental incapacitation of the President (see Table 4.10). For this reason, the declaration of vacancy is also popularly referred to as "declaration of incapacity". The most common 'forms of incapacitation' or 'grounds for vacancy' are death, prolonged absence from office,

Table 4.10 Declaration of vacancy in Latin America and the United States

Country (Constitution)	Approval Threshold	Physical	Mental	Certification	Absence	Tolerance	Consequence	Reference articles
Argentina (1994)	(2/3)	Yes	Yes	–	Yes	–	Succession	Art. 88, (66)
Bolivia (2009)	1/2 LH	Yes	Yes	–	Yes	10/90 days	Succession	Art. 169, 170, 173; Art. 105 PBL
Brazil (1988)	–	–	–	–	Impeach.	15 days	Succession	Art. 83; (Art. 8, 6 IL)
Chile (1980)	1/2 LH	Yes	Yes	Constitutional Court	Yes	–	Elections	Art. 28, 29; 53, 7; Art. 7 PBL
Colombia (1991)	1/2 HH	Yes	–	Expert Committee	Yes	–	Succession	Art. 194, 196, 202; Art. 118; 313, 3; 323, 326 PBL
Costa Rica (1949)	1/2 H	Yes	Yes	–	–	–	Succession	Art. 121, 8; 135; 138,5
Dominican Rep. (2010)	–	–	–	–	–	15 days	Succession	Art. 129, 2; 131
El Salvador (1983)	2/3 H	Yes	Yes	Expert Committee	–	6 months	Succession	Art. 131, 20; 155
Ecuador (2008)	2/3 H	Yes	Yes	Expert Committee or Const. Court	Yes	3 months	Succession	Art. 145, 4 and 5; 146
Guatemala (1985)	2/3 H	Yes	Yes	Expert Committee	–	–	Succession	Art. 165, i; 189
Honduras (1982) **After 2012 reform*	–	Impeach.	Impeach.	–	Yes	15 days	Ind. Election	Art. 205, 12 & 13; 242 (Art. 5, 3 IL)
Mexico (1917)	1/2 LH +HH	–	–	–	–	30 days	Elections	Art. 84; Art. 9, 10, 125 PBL
Nicaragua (1987) **After 2000 reform*	2/3 H	Yes	Yes	–	Yes	15/90 days	Ind. Elections	Art. 149
Panama (1972)	1/2 H	–	–	–	Yes	10/90 days	Succession	Art. 187, 188, 189
Paraguay (1992)	(1/2)	Yes	Yes	(Supreme Court)	Yes	10 days	Succession	Art. 227, 233, (190)
Peru (1993)	20%, 40%, 2/3 H	Yes	Yes	–	Yes	–	Succession	Art. 113, 115; 89-A PBL

Uruguay (1967)	1/2 LH +HH	–	–	–	Yes	48 hours	Succession	Art. 150, 170
United States (1789)	1/2 LH +HH	Yes	Yes	–	–	–	Succession	25th Amendment
Venezuela (1999)	1/2 H	Yes	Yes	Expert Committee	Yes	5/90 days	Elections or succession	Art. 233, 234, 235

Source: Own elaboration. Key: (-) legally undefined. Articles indicated are from the respective Constitutions unless indicated otherwise: (PBL) Parliamentary bylaws; (IL) Impeachment law; (LH) Lower house; (HH) Higher house; (H) Single house (unicameral system). Inputs between parenthesis are based the hypothetical use of other legally defined vacancy provisions by analogy. (Argentina: Congressional vacancy (art. 66) suggests a threshold of 2/3, by analogy. On general rules for passing resolutions, however, such threshold falls to 1/2. There is in the literature an argument in favour of vacancy only being applicable through impeachment procedures, which, in turn, would raise the threshold to 1/2, 2/3 LH, and 2/3 HH. In such case, vacancies would be fit under the offense of "poor performance". See Zaffaroni and Risso (2008), p. 724. Paraguay: Congressional vacancy (Art. 190) suggests, by analogy, a 1/2 threshold and certification by the Supreme Court in case of mental or physical incapacity.) Note: Criteria for indicated tolerance periods may vary (e.g., maximum period of suspension from office; maximum absence from country). The periods may also be extended upon request to or spontaneous concession of Parliament and incapacitating medical conditions. Vacancy may be declared temporarily, if the return of the President to office is expected within the duration of the mandate or other legally stipulated period, or may be declared permanent, if the President is not expected to return under neither of those conditions.

Beyond the grounds for vacancy, most constitutions and parliamentary bylaws do not stablish many procedural rules. This is presumably indicative of the fact that the procedure was not envisioned to act as a surrogate to impeachment, but rather merely as an ordinary parliamentary task, requiring no special procedure or caution. The countries with extensive regulation, such as Ecuador or Peru, are the ones with a history of abuse of such procedures.

Realm of Use The declaration of vacancy is *not* a quasi-judicial procedure like the presidential impeachment. This means that no trial or complex normative adjudication is supposed to take place. It *declares a situation of fact* and *does not decide a situation of law*. The only evidence that is produced or acknowledged in these procedures are medical certificates attesting to the incapacitating nature of an illness or to the circumstances of the President's death, as well as documents proving or certificating the presidential absence.

The declaration of vacancy is not a national inquest into presidential misbehaviour. Although an incapacitating mental deficit of the President has been deduced from misconduct and irresponsible behaviour in the past,[190] the incapacitation is subsumed from medical criteria, certified by an accredited medical team. Parliamentary involvement in the merit is restricted to the nomination of a team of experts and the adoption of its final report.

Some legal systems allow for the object of a declaration of vacancy to be 'adjudicated' as the object of an impeachment. Honduras stablishes incapacitation as a ground for impeachment. Some impeachable offenses can include causes of vacancy. The impeachable offense of 'presidential indignity' present in some systems, for example, can be arguably subsumed from etheromaniac behaviour, which may also be an incapacitating physical or mental condition. Unique to Peru: Since the Fujimori ouster was confirmed by the Constitutional Court, the declaration of vacancy on grounds of 'moral incapacity' has enabled what would be otherwise a matter of impeachment to be simply deliberated upon as vacancy.[191]

Purpose The declaration of vacancy serves a sort of notarial purpose, that is, it turns a situation of fact into a legally recognized situation that may, thus, generate other

[190] See the Bucaram case study. Despite being removed for mental incapacity, the parliamentary records reveal that no representative actually doubted of or argued against Bucaram's mental fitness for office.

[191] In October 2021, the Castillo administration submitted a bill to Congress (*Oficio* n. 603-2021) proposing a reform to the vacancy provisions. If approved, vacancy on grounds of moral incapacity will be substituted for vacancy on grounds of *mental* incapacity. As such, the legal basis commented here may soon become outdated. La Ley, October 19th, 2021: "*Ejecutivo propone eliminar la vacancia por incapacidad moral*".

legal consequences. When used as a surrogate to impeachment, it is used to quickly defuse a constitutional crisis Congress believes to be caused or complicated by the President's permanence in office. In this latter capacity, it can serve as an instrument of balance of power and democratic preservation. Unlike in impeachment, presidential accountability is not the subject of vacancy procedures, although it may at times be also taken into consideration.

Nomenclature Vacancy proceedings are referred to directly or indirectly by Constitutions under a variety of epithets. The procedure itself may go as declaration/motion of vacancy, declaration of incapacity, or declaration of absence. The first form being the more encompassing, and the latter two being more specific to certain forms of vacancy. Grounds for vacancy are commonly referred to as *incapacidad* (incapacity or unfitness), *inhabilitación* (disqualification or inability), *impedimento* (impediment or hindering), *faltas* (fault or absence), or *en defecto* (in absence). The kind of vacancy that results in ouster can be qualified by the terms permanent, definitive, or absolute, all of which indicate the same thing, namely the impossibility of the President's return to office within the duration of his or her mandate. The multiplicity of ways to communicate the same thing can generate some confusion, as many of these terms can shift meaning significantly in different contexts. Particularly problematic is perhaps the term *inhabilitación*, as it can both mean disqualification for office (no longer being eligible to take public office) and stripping of office (removal). Though the ambiguity can be avoided by qualifying it as "*inhabilitación para ejercício cargos públicos/empleo en la nación*" (disqualification for the exercise public office/jobs in the nation) and "*inhabilitación para ejercício de sus funciones*" (disqualification for the exercise of one's functions), such wordy qualifiers are generally ditched for the sake of intelligibility but with sacrifice to clarity. The same can be said about *falta*, as it may mean absence, violation, or offense. The latter two tend to be qualified by the adjective *grave* (serious, grievous), while the first is qualified by adjectives such as absolute, definitive, or permanent.

Trade-Offs (When Used as a Surrogate to Impeachment)

- *Legitimation:* The most obvious drawback of the surrogate use of declaration of vacancy is its doubtful constitutionality and legitimation. Even in the event the declaration of vacancy may successfully pacify society by ousting a President that is inciting riots and coups, the decision will attract criticism from the legal and international communities and will likely generate its own set of negative and destabilizing consequences. Congress may be interpreted as a usurper of power and the decision for the ouster as unjust and undue.
- *Ease of use:* Comparatively to impeachment, the vacancy is much easier to use as it is deliberated upon similarly to a bill, and not like an adjudicative procedure. The lower technical requirements make it the more accessible and intelligible procedure, but also inadequate for screening and assessing presidential misbehaviour.
- *Quickness:* The procedure is quicker than impeachment and may thus be able to minimize the damage a crisis would otherwise inflict. Quickness, however, may generate unreasoned and precipitated decisions that may be harmful in their own

ways. It may, moreover, allow for the exploitation of short moments of presidential unpopularity.

- *Sanctions*: The only 'sanction' (it is more of an effect) of a declaration of vacancy is the removal of the President from office. It cannot disqualify a misbehaving actor from re-entering politics and thus prevent future damage.

4.5.1.4 Impeachment *Versus* Pretrial/Immunity Revocation Procedures

Features The pretrial (*antejuicio*) or immunity revocation procedure (*privación de inmunidad; desafuero*) is a parliamentary procedure through which the President loses immunity to judicial suits of potentially any field of law. By its design, the object of discussion in a pretrial *ought* to remain constrained to the question of whether the facts imputed to the President are serious in character and likely to be true, both sufficiently so to justify initiation of court proceedings.[192] The procedure does not generally entail the creation of special commissions for additional investigation, neither does it foresee the application of sanctions. In some jurisdictions, however, a successful pretrial may cause suspension from office during the time of the trial or other stipulated period (Table 4.11).

The pretrial is not, therefore, a procedure that serves as a 'grand inquest of the nation' into presidential behaviour, nor a procedure that creates a special range of political offenses (and thus a political realm of accountability), but one that works more as a prerogative meant to isolate the presidency from legal harassment. The consequence of suspension from office may nonetheless bring about direct change on government and policy and, thus, imbues the procedure with an explicit political dimension. In face of such constellation, the reasoning behind pretrials may in practice go well beyond the analysis of requisites of legal admissibility and may also consider elements of political opportunity.

In Latin America, the system of pretrial often coexists with the system of impeachment. A few countries, however, reject the system of impeachments altogether and accept only pretrial as an instrument of presidential accountability. Such arrangement may arguably result in a stricter separation between powers.

Realm of Use Although the pretrial can be initiated to vulnerate the President to judicial suits of any nature, typically only criminal suits will be serious enough to cause the revocation of presidential immunity, especially if suspension from office is foreseen as a legal consequence of the revocation. Most current provisions on the issue openly restrict the pretrial to the preliminary consideration of criminal matters. As such, the pretrial generally cannot serve as a direct channel to the political accountability of the President, as political-constitutional misbehaviour

---

[192] García Chávarri (2008), p. 17.

Table 4.11 Countries with pretrial provisions

Country (Constitution)	Referral	Gatekeeper	Approval	Suspension	Scope	Coexists with impeachment	Pretrial
Costa Rica (1949)	–	Supreme Court	2/3 H	Yes	Criminal	Yes	Art. 151; 121, 9; Art. 215 ff. PBL; Art. 391 CCP
El Salvador (1983)	–	Permanent Commission	1/2 H	Yes	Criminal	No	Art. 236 ff.; Art. 120 ff. PBL
Ecuador (2008)	–	General Prosecutor	2/3 H	–	Criminal	Yes	Art. 120, 10; 195
Guatemala (1985)	Any Court	Judge Inquisitor	2/3 H	Cond	Criminal (apolitical)	No	Art. 165, h; D.n. 85/2002
Nicaragua (1987) *After 2000 reform	–	–	2/3 H	–	Any	No	Art. 130; L.n. 83/1990

Source: Own elaboration. Indicated articles belong to respective constitution, unless indicated otherwise. Key: (PBL) Parliamentary bylaws; (CCP) Code of criminal procedure; (D.n.) Decree number; (L.n.) Law number; (H) House (unicameral system); (Cond.) Suspension from office is conditioned to the issuance of a provisional arrest warrant. Note: the judge inquisitor (juez pesquisidor) is a judge nominated by the Supreme Court to investigate criminal accusations and to report whether they are substantiated enough to justify a criminal procedure does not fall within its scope unless it is simultaneously constitutive of a criminal offense.[193]

Purpose The pretrial serves to protect the presidency from legal harassment. It allows the *person* of the President to focus on its duties, performing them without fear of immediate consequences, of financial ruin from expenditures with legal fees, or of persecution from political enemies. The pretrial does not exclude or delay State liability for damages caused by the President, but only protects him or her from *personal* legal consequences.

Contrast with Judicial Impeachment At a first glance, the pretrial can look much alike the judicial impeachment. In both cases, Parliament will conduct a procedure that acts as a preliminary step to a Court proceeding and, in both cases, the object of analysis is *likely* to be a criminal offense. As indicated above, however, the pretrial does not necessarily imply parliamentary investigation into the accusations of presidential misdoing, nor can such misdoings potentially have a predominant political nature or be punished with political sanctions.[194] Moreover, the procedures may have different symbolic charges, despite relating to accountability in one way or another. While the impeachment embodies and develops the right of the people of self-determination and good government, allowing the public to discover the truth about those who rule them and remove rulers who endanger the general interest, the pretrial is *arguably* more akin to a corporatist prerogative designed *in part* to legitimize the insulation of and/or leniency towards the ruling political class.[195]

Trade-Offs (as an Exclusive Alternative to Impeachment)

- *Executive autonomy:* Reducing the scope of presidential accountability to merely justiciable causes may potentially increase the President's autonomy vis-à-vis the Parliament. It does, however, come with the drawback of making him or her less responsible for political offenses.
- *Improper outlet for political tension build-up:* If political offenses cannot be scrutinized and sanctioned by the Parliament, political tensions may build-up unalleviated by any release mechanism. In such context, the Parliament will need to first wait for a legal, or even more specifically in some cases, a criminal offense to take place for only then to a resolution to be attempted or leveraged against the presidential misbehaviour. If such offenses, moreover, are of minimal significance or unrelated to the crisis at hand, the actions of the Parliament may become suspected, and their legitimacy may be undermined.

---

193 García Chávarri (2008), p. 15. Guatemala may be an exception to this caveat, as its rules on pretrial openly refuse criminal accusations that may potentially be motivated by "spurious, political, or illegitimate" interests (art. 17, g, Decree n. 85/2002). Presumably, such provision originally meant to raise standards of what could be investigated and thus deny jurisdiction to unsubstantiated, persecutory claims. It might, however, currently be applied in a much broader, stronger sense, as suggested by its use against Jimmy Morales (2017–2018).

194 García Chávarri (2008), p. 4.

195 While historically the impeachment was created to introduce ministerial accountability in England, the pretrial is said to have been originally introduced in France as an attempt at limiting that same accountability and creating a sort of official privilege. Roldán (2013), p. 130 ff.

- *Weak democratic legitimation*: The removal of the President based off on a decision by a small and unelected organ lacks the sort of democratic legitimation necessary to rival that of the President. The decision may look like a work of cabal and a perversion of the will of the people. This is perhaps even more evident than in the judicial impeachment, where cooperation and exchange between Judiciary and Legislature is more constant and transparent.
- *Other trade-offs of the judicial form of impeachment:* As the removal of the President is ultimately decided in a judicial proceeding, the pretrial (broadly considered as instrument of removal)[196] shares many of the same advantages and disadvantages of the judicial impeachment. See the considerations above (item 1) on specialization, division of labour, sanctions, legitimation, and slowness/cumbersomeness.
- *Dependence on Executive-nominated authorities:* Criminal accusations against the President likely depend to some degree of involvement coming from the General Prosecutor or the Supreme Court, which are likely nominated by the President and thus also likely loyal to him or her in some degree. That may translate in delayed responses or lenient attitudes to accusations of presidential misconduct, possibly amounting to executive irresponsibility.

4.5.1.5 Impeachment *Versus* Recall/Mandate Revocation Procedures

Features The presidential recall or presidential mandate revocation (*revocatoria de mandato*) procedure is a plebiscitary (*i.e.*, direct democratic) instrument of presidential removal. It consists in a referendum carried out at national level, asking the population whether the President should remain in power. The procedures do not depend on presidential misdoing to be initiated, neither do they demand the scrutiny of suspected acts of the President. The only formal requirements are a certain threshold of popular support for the recall referendum, measured by the number of signatures collected, and the endorsement of the demand by members of Parliament (Table 4.12).[197] The procedures are quick and relatively uncomplicated in comparison to impeachment, but are nonetheless costly, as they require the preparation, coordination, and oversight of the electoral apparatus at national level. The direct-democratic nature of the procedures does not necessarily translate into a representative, responsible and strongly legitimated decision for presidential removal/survival. The quality of the procedures depends on the active and conscientious popular engagement.[198] As such, it may suffer from most of the common

---

[196] The court proceeding that follows the pretrial does not integrate the pretrial proceeding itself. There is effectively no analogous sort of 'Court of Impeachments' in pretrial proceedings. The considerations of this item are meant in a holistic sense.

[197] Eberhardt (2017), p. 110 ff.

[198] Welp and Milanese (2018), p. 1380 ff.

Table 4.12 Countries with presidential recall

Country (Constitution)	Signatures required	Turnout presidential elections	Available after	Window of use	Mandate duration	Consequence	Reference articles
Bolivia (2009)	15% Electorate (1.1 mi - 2020)	88.4% (2020)	Half-mandate	Year 3 and 4	5 years	Elections	Art. 240, 170
Ecuador (2008)	15% Electorate (1.95 mi - 2021)	81% (2021)	First year	Year 2 and 3	4 years	Succession	Art. 61, 6; 105, 106; 145, 6
Venezuela (1999)	20% Electorate (4 mi - 2018)	46% (2018)	Half-mandate	Year 3	6 years	Elections	Art. 76 ff.

Source: Own Elaboration. Indicated articles refer to respective Constitutions. Voter turnout and size of electorate is based on official statistics published during presidential elections that took place in the years indicated between parentheses

shortcomings of electoral procedures, such as, for example, highly polarized and antagonistic interactions, muddy discourse, and the spread of misinformation, as well as low turnout and attempts at fraud and voter disenfranchisement.

Realm of Use The presidential recall is applicable to situations in which there is widespread popular dissatisfaction with the President. Misdoing or the violation of electoral promises are not prerequisites to recalls at national level,[199] but they are expected to take place in such immediate context.[200] Recalls may be used in situations in which Parliament does not, for whatever reason, want to personally champion the cause of presidential accountability. Realistically, however, political parties may still play a key role in organizing civil society to collect the minimum signatures necessary to start these procedures. Its use may, moreover, be limited by arbitrary limitations that undermine the interests of the people.[201]

Purpose The foremost purpose of the presidential recall is to keep the presidency (electorally, politically, morally) accountable to the People throughout the duration of the mandate.[202] It is meant to inhibit demagogues from the tendency of making many popularly demanded promises to secure electoral support, only to subsequently abandon them once in office (*e.g.*, the 1990s 'neoliberalism by surprise' as described by Susan Stokes).[203] Even when the recall fails, it may nonetheless serve as a reaffirmation of the public's confidence in the presidency, thus, defusing political tensions to some degree.[204]

Trade-Offs (When Used as a Surrogate to Impeachment)

- *Independence from Parliament:* The recall does not depend as much from the participation of the Parliament, allowing presidential accountability to take place even when the parliamentary majority is colluding with the presidency.[205]
- *Dependence on the Executive:* The execution of the recall depends on the organization and oversight of the Executive power itself. Such control over the procedures may be exploited by a President looking to stay in power by, for example, refusing to conduct the referendum, as well as undermining its free and fair execution.[206]

---

[199] Eberhardt (2017), p. 114 ff. For details into subnational recalls, see Welp and Milanese (2018).

[200] Welp and Milanese (2018), p. 1383.

[201] The Venezuelan variant (art. 71 ff. of the 1999 Constitution), for example, is usable only once in the middle of the presidential mandate (3rd year of a 6-year mandate). Popular dissatisfaction must take place early and remain sustained for long or be well-timed to fit the window of use the presidential recall may have.

[202] Eberhardt (2017), p. 107.

[203] Stokes (2001).

[204] Eberhardt (2017), p. 127.

[205] Although it may be conducted by initiative of the Parliament, collecting signatures is also a legal way of propelling a presidential recall. Eberhardt (2017), pp. 116–117.

[206] Eberhardt (2017), p. 121. See, for example, the many suspicions raised against the recall carried out against Hugo Chávez in 2004, or the arbitrary difficulties imposed to the collection of signatures

- *Quickness:* The recall may be able to defuse a crisis involving the person of the President quickly. The quickness, however, also means that the procedure may be instrumentalized to exploit the momentaneous unpopularity of the President.
- *Legitimation:* As a plebiscitary instrument, the recall has potential to be more strongly legitimated than the impeachment. Prerequisite for such situation, however, is strong and active popular participation, as well as enabling conditions for the free and fair execution of the recall referendum. If such conditions are not achieved, there is arguably a risk of the referendum being much less representative or legitimated than the impeachment alternative. A small fraction of the population may impose their political will over the rest, if this rest too apathetic to participate in the recall. A minority in Parliament may be able to exploit such vulnerability for immediate gain.

4.5.1.6 Impeachment *Versus* Mutual Dissolution (Ecuador)

Features The mutual dissolution (*muerte cruzada*) is a *sui generis* sort of procedure that terminates constitutional crises by dissolving the Legislature and the Presidency in quick succession. It was first introduced in Latin America by the 2008 Constitution of Ecuador. It may be requested by the President (art. 148) or by the Parliament (art. 130) themselves when cooperation for solving an ongoing crisis seems to be out of question. The conditions and procedural steps for its requisition vary according to the nature of the crisis at hand.

Parliament may invoke the mutual dissolution whenever there is (i.) encroachment of competences by the President, or (ii.) intense political crisis or internal commotion. The first case requires participation of the Constitutional Court, who must certify that usurpation of competencies did indeed take place. The dissolution must be approved by the 2/3 of the Parliament within 72 hours of its offering. If successful, the Vice-President takes over the presidency until the realization of new presidential and parliamentary elections.

The President, on the other hand, may also unilaterally invoke a mutual dissolution whenever there is (i.) encroachment of competences by the Parliament, (ii.) the Parliament 'unjustifiably and recurrently' obstructs the national plan of development (*Plan Nacional de Desarrollo*), or (iii.) there is an intense political crisis or internal commotion. The first case requires the certification of the Constitution Court about the existence of an encroachment of competences. If invoked, the mutual dissolution does not drive out the President from power immediately, who rules by decree until a new Parliament is constituted. This may last up to six months, considering the

for a recall against Nicolás Maduro in 2022. CNN, January 21st, 2022: *"Recolección de firmas para posible referendo revocatorio de Maduro será el 26 de enero, dice el CNE"*. El País, March 2nd, 2004: *"El Consejo Electoral anula un millón de firmas necesarias para convocar la consulta contra Chávez"*.

average duration of electoral proceedings at national level. Such rule-by-decree remains under the oversight of the Constitutional Court.

Realm of Use The mutual dissolution is applicable to situations in which the impeachment is either too slow or too limited to appropriately address the cause of a crisis that involves the presidency. It can be even more of an 'instrument of last resort' than the impeachment, as it requires from Parliament its mutual sacrifice, which is something many representatives may understandably be reluctant to do, due to the costs and risks posed by new elections.

Purpose As a constitutional instrument, the mutual dissolution serves as a quick solution for crises for which both branches of power likely hold some degree of co-responsibility. As a design choice, the mutual dissolution covers a gap left by Ecuador's impeachment, which could no longer be sustainably covered by the surrogate use of the declaration of vacancy. Due to its highly restricted scope, the Ecuadorian impeachment has been long unable of defusing crises involving the presidency, as suggested by the events regarding Presidents Bucaram, Mahuad, and Gutiérrez. The declaration of vacancy, moreover, was a poor alternative that brought negative repercussions to Ecuador due to its questionable constitutionality.

In other words, the mutual dissolution is an attempt at introducing a 'middle of the road' solution to Ecuador's commitment to responsible and balanced government. It greatly expands the grounds for removal from power, making up for the limitations of impeachment's design. It also theoretically imposes the conscientious use of removal procedures by making all involved parties simultaneously co-responsible, which, as seen in the case studies, seems to have been a major issue in Ecuador's history.

At any rate, the procedures seem like a presidential adaptation of the so-called '*simul-simul* provision' first described by Maurice Duverger in his study of semi-parliamentary systems, that is, the sort of provision stablishing that the vote of no confidence generates the simultaneous dissolution of government and Parliament.[207]

Trade-Offs (as an Alternative and Complement to Impeachment)

- *Hyper-presidential tendencies:* When invoked unilaterally by the President, the mutual dissolution can impose too much of a threat to Parliament, making it submit into cooperation. If nonetheless Parliament is dissolved, moreover, the President may rule by decree for a period of up to six months afterwards. A President threatened by impeachment or other parliamentary inquiry may be able use the dissolution to frustrate accountability and undermine the commitment to responsible government.[208]

[207] *Simul-simul* refers to the Latin adage "*aut simul stabunt aut simul cadent*" (transl.: together they stand or together they fall). For details, see Ganghof (2018); Praino (2017), p. 11.

[208] This was observed in recent exchanges between President Guillermo Lasso and the National Assembly. In the context of widespread prison riots, Lasso demanded unwavering support for bills he deemed fundamental to the situation, while claiming that any parliamentary resistance would be met with mutual dissolution. El Comercio, October 15th, 2021: "*Guillermo Lasso dice que si la*

- *Quickness*: Once initiated, the mutual dissolution must be resolved in 72 hours, making it a speedy solution for pressing crises. The drawbacks of quickness are those already mentioned, namely potential rushed and unreasoned decisions that may exploit brief moments of unpopularity and may, as a result, inflict more harm than good.
- *De-personification of crisis resolution:* The procedures break away with the tendency of scapegoating one single or a few actors for a comprehensive crisis. As such it may offer more mature resolutions to crises that have multiple and complex causes and may allow for debates that focus on the systemic issues that really are to blame.
- *Reduced erosion of institutional trust:* As the procedures may minimize the clashes between branches, public trust in institutions will be presumably less affected than it would be in a context of constant blame-shifting and smearing campaigns.

4.5.1.7 Impeachment *Versus* Electoral Slate Cassation Suits (Brazil)

Features The electoral slate cassation procedures are judicial procedures of the electoral branch of Justice, meant to either remove (*ação de impugnação de mandato eletivo*) or disqualify (*ação de investigação judicial eleitoral*) elected political candidates (and their slate, if applicable) involved in electoral fraud (art. 14, §10, of the 1988 Brazilian Constitution; art. 22 of complimentary law n. 64 of 1990). The procedures are meant to be resolved either before or in the very first days an elected officer comes to power. As judicial procedures may drag due to a multitude of legal quarrels, however, these procedures remain a threat throughout the duration of the presidential mandate, being unearthed or restarted once new evidence or new political interest is discovered in past electoral practices. The protagonists of these suits tend to be political parties, as they tend to oversee electoral practices most intently. Presidential elections are conducted through electoral slates, meaning that, if fraud is discovered, accountability is extended to all participants. As such, both the President and Vice-President will suffer the consequences of a conviction.

Realm of Use The scope of these procedures is quite different from that of impeachment, as the latter typically concerns itself only with misbehaviour while in office, and not before it (exception: Mexico). It is applicable to any sort of dishonest and illegal practices that undermine free and fair elections. Increased interest on this form of removal seems to be associated with the recurrent failure of impeachment to hold the President accountable for misbehaviour in office, as seen recently against Presidents Michel Temer and Jair Bolsonaro.

Asamblea bloquea sus leyes irá a la muerte cruzada". On May 17th, 2023, Lasso dissolved the Assembly, interrupting an impeachment against himself. Lasso characterized the impeachment as malicious and intent on generating commotion. See Decree n. 741 of 2023.

Purpose The procedures are meant to safeguard the integrity of Brazil's electoral system and, consequently, its democracy. Their practice reveals, however, that the procedures can be instrumentalized to achieve other immediate political-partisan goals.

Trade-Offs (When Used as a Surrogate to Impeachment)

- *Weak legitimation:* The procedures suffer from the same drawbacks as any other judicial form of removal, but to a higher degree. These procedures have no participation of Congress whatsoever, leaving an analysis of political opportunity for presidential removal entirely out of the frame and failing to borrow some of Congress' authority and democratic legitimation. The longer the procedures drag, moreover, the more awkward a removal becomes, as the passage of time naturalizes the person in the presidency as a legitimate occupier of that position. Practice shows that the Justices can become intimidated by the prospect of unilaterally removing the President so late into the term. The decision is also not taken by the highest Court, but the highest electoral authority, making it look even more like a work of cabal than otherwise.
- *Breach of legislative shield*: In circumstances in which the presidential grasp over Parliament is too strong, this procedure can bypass it entirely.
- *Inappropriateness as means of political accountability*: As Congress is not involved in any part of the procedure, it is questionable how much it may serve as a broadly representative solution for a crisis. It does not contribute directly to good government, nor does it provide public clarification of presidential misbehaviour. Removals through these means, therefore, are more likely to be perceived as formalistic and opportunistic rather than a 'necessary evil' as many other surrogates are seen.
- *Accountability for 'original sins'*: One glaring gap in the scope of impeachments is its ignorance of electoral fraud. Impeachments remove presidents who have become illegitimate while in office but offer no transparent solution for those who are illegitimate from the get-go. The cassation suits may cover this loophole.

4.5.1.8 *Excursus:* Impeachment *Versus* Vote of No Confidence

Features The vote or motion of no confidence is a parliamentary procedure used to dissolve government whenever cooperation between Executive and Legislative branches becomes troubled or unlikely. Unlike impeachment, the procedure *generally* has no key conditions or requirements that need to be fulfilled for it to be initiated and ends up being boiled down to whether the majority in Parliament wills it or not. No other consequences affect those targeted by the vote, other than the removal from the Executive office they were occupying.[209] Some ousted members

[209] Lento and Hazan (2022), pp. 4–6.

may be reconducted to office once a new government is formed. The vote of no-confidence is a key ingredient of parliamentary systems, giving it the distinctive feature to set parliamentarism decisively apart from presidentialism. The vote of no-confidence may and often does co-exist with impeachment, but it likely makes the latter almost totally obsolete. In case of misbehaviour of the Head of Government, it is easier to seek accountability through the vote of no-confidence, followed by the appropriate judicial suits, than through impeachment directly. Misbehaviour of the Head of State is unlikely to trigger impeachment, as the role has few abusable powers within the scope of impeachment.

As a procedure typical of parliamentary systems, the vote of no confidence is not found in Latin America as defined in this book. Peru, as a semi-presidential or presidential-parliamentary system, has a comparable procedure, known as vote of confidence (*cuestión de confianza*, art. 130 and 133 of the 1993 Constitution). It is used in similar situations as the vote of no-confidence, but it is initiated by the President, either directly or through his or her Ministers, and has different consequences. When the President asks for a vote of confidence, the Parliament is asked to participate in the reformulation of the presidential cabinet (*Consejo de Ministros*). The President (who largely shares government competences with the Prime Minister) is not ousted, but the rest of government is. By the end of the procedure, it is hoped that the newly constituted government can work harmoniously alongside the Parliament. If not, a new vote of confidence may be asked. In case it fails once again, the President is allowed to dissolve the Parliament and call for new legislative elections, which, it is hoped, may constitute a new Parliament that is better aligned with the presidency.

Realm of Use The vote of no-confidence has a much broader scope of use than the impeachment, albeit both may often share contextual similarities in practice, namely that crisis, coalition breaks, and Executive misbehaviour commonly provide impulse to them. Crises and coalition breaks (also known as cabinet crises, when critically affecting government) cannot trigger impeachment by themselves, but Parliaments may opt to resolve these issues quickly and transparently with a vote of no confidence. As such, the procedures can have a variety of uses that may be totally disconnected from Executive accountability.

Purpose The vote of no-confidence is the historical successor of the impeachment, serving thus similar purposes, but to an arguably more radical degree. It allows the Parliament to hold a much tighter grip on the Executive, as it has significantly more freedom to subject the Executive to the majority consensus in the Parliament. Impeachment, by contrast, can realistically impose such realignment only under critical circumstances (*i.e.*, requires impeachable offense) and to limited extent (*i.e.*, requires agreement of legal successor).

Trade-Offs (as an Alternative to Impeachment)

- *Impersonality*: The focus of no confidence being away from a single person in the Executive reduces the likelihood of scapegoating and allows for the creation of an unmuddied channel for discussion of larger systemic issues that need to be addressed. It is also a normal and expected part of the parliamentarian landscape, bringing most likely no personal detriment to those who propose or support it.

- *Transparency*: While in presidentialism crises often must be rationalized through the lens of impeachable offenses and presidential accountability, the vote of no confidence allows for political disagreements to be openly addressed. Society profits from the clarity in public discourse, and the branches of power are spared of erosion of public trust stemming from the general perception of a potential dishonest infighting.
- *Ease of use:* The vote of no confidence does not depend on a full blown investigative and judicial apparatus to be made operable, decreasing barriers of use. If there is too much external pressure, for example, the vote of no confidence will likely offer a solution to crisis that is more legally palatable than a rushed impeachment. It also does not depend on supermajorities for approval, making it a more predictable alternative.
- *Quickness:* Such ease of use correlates with a quicker procedure, which is more likely to provide timely remedies to conflict. Quick resolution, however, comes with the drawbacks discussed in the previous sections.[210]
- *Flexibility:* The broad scope of use makes the vote of no confidence an effective and flexible tool for many situations. Such feature, however, may be positive or detrimental, depending on the political context. Flexibility allows for quick adaptation to changes in the environment, thus reducing frictions caused by the process of accommodation. If the environment is too polarized and in constant change, too much flexibility can mean too much instability, hindering a breakthrough out of crisis.
- *Executive dependence on Parliament:* The introduction of a vote of no confidence in a constitutional system vulnerates the strict separation of powers severely, as the existence of the Executive power is entirely predicated on it staying within the Parliament's good will. The Executive becomes, in turn, less autonomous and independent, being practically unable of confronting the Parliament, when needed. At the same time, however, this strong connection between powers can be conducive to more cooperative and power-sharing behaviour.
- *Co-responsibility*: Considering the context of parliamentarism, the vote of no confidence is less likely to produce situations in which blame is constantly shifted between branches. As the Legislature constitutes government, it cannot deny its own share of responsibility for the shortcomings of the said government.
- *High and undisputed legitimation*: Still considering the same context, as government and Parliament share the same democratic origins, one can hardly claim to be "more democratically legitimated than the other". In an impeachment procedure, the President can always claim to be '(morally) above the majority in

[210]There may be a minimum duration requirement between the introduction and the vote of a motion of no-confidence (*e.g.,* Poland requires 7 days between one and the other). This fixed timeframe may reduce the incidence of the indicated drawback of 'exploitable moments of unpopularity', but not in ways comparable to what is expected from impeachments, which take much longer and result in wider public engagement. See Lento and Hazan (2022), p. 6.

Parliament', as he or she was directly elected by the majority of the People (*ergo* being more representative of their will) and may thus always make use of the 'hostile parliamentary takeover' narrative to delegitimize the procedures. That same thing cannot be as convincingly argued within the context of a no confidence vote.

4.5.2 *Phases of Impeachment*

Impeachments vary considerably in their general outlines, but the way they are processed seems to follow clear patterns. As often commented in this book, impeachment is not a mere parliamentary instrument for the ousting of a President who has become suspected, unpopular and/or uncooperative. It is much more than that: it is also an instrument of accountability and balance of power, and, as such, it has many other goals to achieve before considering whether to kick the highest Magistrate out or not. Such intermediary moments are arguably as important as the final outcome.

The impeachment channels and sifts through public demands and grievances related to the conduct of the presidency. It provides clarity and unearths the truth behind suspected activity that may erode trust in democracy. It provides a public display of commitment from the Branches of Power to the integral handling of the public thing and engages society as a whole in a discourse about power and citizenship. It rationalizes and provides outlets for the resolution of mounting tensions within society and within power itself. The structure of the presidential impeachment, as will be argued next, reflects all that in most cases, even though its performance in practice may be lacklustre at times.

In this section, each phase will be discussed as to point out some of their main features, practical challenges, and critical design choices.

4.5.2.1 Initiation

Features A complaint lodged against presidential misconduct bears no consequence until it is officially accepted or sponsored by the competent authority. The phase in which such acceptance is externalized is what will be referred to in this book as the phase of initiation. When the Parliament is the competent authority, the initiation will depend on its acceptance by a key stakeholder (*e.g.*, the president of the Lower House, a commission of constitutional affairs) or, in some cases, on the sponsoring of the complaint by a fraction of the House. If accepted or approved, the impeachment procedure will be materialized through a legislative resolution, which may, moreover, define basic rules of impeachment and timelines. Following the resolution, the matters will be submitted to an impeachment commission, which needs to be formed, if a permanent commission for such affairs does not already exist.

In some circumstances (*e.g.,* conduct involves the practice of common crimes, or some forms of predominantly judicial impeachment), the General Prosecutor and/or the Supreme/Constitutional Court will take over the responsibility of initiating the procedures. In this case, however, an independent investigation by these authorities will precede the creation of an impeachment commission in the Parliament.

The complaints offered to the authorities responsible for initiating impeachment may vary considerably in quality and detail. They may be very informally written, abstract and unsubstantiated, but they may also be as thoroughly documented and argued as a criminal case would be. Since these are often authored by persons with no special access to information or other resources of investigation, it is common that interested citizens with legal knowledge will make a case using investigative work presented originally by the media, which can be nonetheless fairly thorough. Political parties also will commonly employ jurists and investigators to put together a case against a President turned overbearing. The author(s) of the complaint can be an important piece of the 'equation' about whether the complaint will be picked up by the competent authority, as they may be especially significant or influential in the particular context/society (*e.g.*, BAR association, oversight agencies, respected historical figures).

Challenges The greatest challenge of the initiation procedures is producing an arrangement that offers balance between the need of isolating the presidency from constant existence-threatening attacks, and the need of providing a reliable and representative outlet for grievances against the presidential conduct. A system that with too easy access to impeachment initiatives can cause instability, allowing (and forcing) the Parliament to constantly delve into business of the Executive. It may become very costly and inefficient for both branches of power to constantly disrupt their core activities to confront each other and engage in negotiation. On the other hand, if access become nearly impossible, an effectively irresponsible presidency may be constituted, making impeachment obsolete and subverting the commitment to the republican form of government.

Standard of Proof The initiation phase is one that needs to answer the following question: Are the acts of the President *suspicious* to the point of *justifying* further official scrutiny? The standard, therefore, is one of possibility and plausibility. The accusation piece will have to credibly demonstrate that there has been (a.) the *potential* commitment of an impeachable offense, (b.) which holds a *potential* link with the presidency, and (c.) which is not excluded by potential limitations to accountability (*e.g.,* accountability is not precluded by timeframes foreseen in law). Given the examples from impeachment practice, a fourth element may be needed to constitute the justifying need of further scrutiny: (d.) the indication of political opportunity for the investigation of presidential acts (*e.g.,* typically constituted in popular demand for accountability, or a widespread sense of the President's harmful influence on the state or democracy).

Design Choices

- *Gatekeeper:* The initiation of an impeachment procedure may depend entirely on a single or few actors, who may arbitrarily choose to acknowledge or not complaints lodged in the Parliament, the General Prosecutor's office, or other organ responsible for such oversight. Control of initiatives becomes considerably easier under such conditions, as Presidents may focus their effort on building allegiances with one easily identifiable and predictable stakeholder rather than many. Automatic initiation (*e.g.*, complaint must be analysed 1 session after being offered) is arguably a more transparent and comprehensive alternative, but it may be disruptive of the work of the Parliament, as multiple and frequent impeachment commissions will likely have to be formed.
- *Overruling provisions:* To avoid complete control of the initiation phase by gatekeepers, some provisions may exist to bypass their negligence or collusion with the presidency. Such may entail setting deadlines for the complaints to be analysed, creating the right of the plenum to appeal and overrule their decision of shelving complaints, creating concurrent competences for initiation, and so on.
- *Initiation alternatives*: A few constitutions have alternative pathways to impeachment initiation, which, however, may come associated with some limitations to the moment of impeachment (*e.g.*, before or after office) or the nature of the impeachable offense (*e.g.*, common crimes or political offenses). At any rate, such alternatives may lower the risks imposed by one gatekeeper who may be unresponsive.
- *Expiration dates:* Complaints lodged may have expiration dates, which can help pressuring the gatekeeper into taking a stance on their merit. Recurrent expiration of complaints can be indicative of negligence and, thus, be used as an argument for change in gatekeeping.
- *Admissibility analysis*: Any gatekeeper who picks up a complaint will necessarily have to consider whether it meets the basic requirements to be contemplated as an impeachment procedure (*e.g.*, the charges must be related to presidential conduct, the statute of limitations should not be applicable, the complaint should be offered by the competent person, etc.). This is generally implied by the function of gatekeeping, but the law may as well design a specific opportunity, a list of requirements and a specific quorum for such analysis.

4.5.2.2 Impeachment Commission

Features The parliamentary commission of impeachment is the organ responsible for verifying the charges and evidence levelled against the President, expanding, diminishing, or reformulating their scope as it best sees fit. The final product of the commission is a report containing the narrative and evaluation of the supposed presidential misbehaviour, as well as their categorization into *articles of impeach-*

ment.[211] Once the report neatly fits such basic requirements, it may be taken to vote by the plenum of the respective House, entering, thus, the next phase of the procedure.

There are essentially two ways through which such commissions are formed: they are either permanent organs of Parliament responsible for the investigation of these kinds of matters (*e.g.*, the House Judiciary Committee in the United States, the *Comisión de Investigación y Acusaciones* in Colombia) or they are formed on the spot (*ad hoc*; for the situation), immediately after the impeachment is introduced (*e.g.*, *Comissão Especial de Impeachment* in Brazil). The formation, thus, tends to reflect an aspect of proportional representation of the diverse fractions within the Parliament. Due to its small size, however, the commission's representativity may at times be considerably distorted by the exclusion of small parties, or overrepresentation certain interest groups.

Even in the event the impeachment charges are already well argued and grounded on evidence at the time of their introduction, as for example may happen when other inquiry commissions discover presidential misbehaviour in originally unrelated investigations, or in the occasion the General Prosecutor/Highest Court have done their investigations pre-emptively, the creation of these impeachment commissions may nonetheless be required. Such evidence and arguments may still need to be 'translated into the language of impeachment', that is, they need to be representative of more than just a robust case against the President, but a case that subsumes discovered misbehaviour into the appropriate categories of impeachable offenses and which satisfies every other impeachment-relevant legal requirement. These reports often contain political considerations (*e.g.*, popular demand for impeachment, context of constitutional crisis, etc.) which technical organs may feel uneasy or unauthorized to make.

The members who participate in the impeachment commission may be required to stay out of the impeachment and trial votes carried out by the plenum of the Parliament, as to provide a separation between the function of judge, investigator, and accusation manager. This is more so the case in unicameral Parliaments because the same House is required to act in all the phases by itself.

The commission will likely have a few of its members participating in three key functions, namely the presidency, the rapporteur, and the principal investigator(s). The president is the person responsible for guiding the investigations and moderating the discussion of the commission, ensuring the execution of its goals in orderly and responsible fashion. The rapporteur is the person responsible for keeping record and writing a final report that is representative of the commission's opinions. In case

[211] In the United States, this final report would be referred to as the 'impeachment resolution'. It should not be confused with the type of resolution that introduces accusations against the President to the plenum of the House of Representatives, asking for referral of the accusations to the House Judiciary Committee. This other type of resolution has no legal name but is at times colloquially referred to as an impeachment *probe* resolution. For details, see Congressional Research Service (2019), p. 11.

there are strong disagreements with the final report, be it in part or in totality, a minoritarian or individual reports opposing it are sometimes allowed and presented together to the plenum of the House responsible for impeachment. Finally, the principal investigators are members who are delegated some investigating powers to deal with specific focus points of the impeachment charges. They may preside their own taskforces or subcommittees.

Challenges Historically, impeachment committees' greatest challenge has been to function without disruption and with sufficient tools to fulfil its goals. The Executive branch can be very uncooperative with investigations into its activities, seeking to, for example, hamper the committee's access to information from its officers and official records. For such situation to be prevented, it is necessary that the commission formed is sufficiently autonomous from the Executive (and the government coalition), that it has the necessary powers to perform its investigation, and that such powers are respected by the respective authorities. Full transparency of the procedures, in association with close public and media scrutiny, may help the committee build leverages in face of a recalcitrant Executive. It may also compel the committee members to faithfully defend the public's best interests.

Design Choices

- *Investigative power and Executive autonomy:* Parliamentary commissions may have limited power in relation to what they may legally investigate within the Executive power, as to protect crucial information and to isolate it from harassment. If such limitations are too great or if the Executive is allowed to disrespect orders without consequence, the commission may end up being crippled and unable to fulfil its duties.
- *Decisive power:* The impeachment commission may have power to decide certain things for the plenum of the Parliament. It may choose, for example, to single-handedly remove a few charges originally offered, giving the plenum no opportunity to discuss whether they were pertinent or not. It may even end the procedures before they reach the plenum. Some other impeachment commissions, on the other hand, may have no such power, and would have to produce a report merely recommending the rejection of the impeachment charges to the plenum.
- *Bindingness of the full report:* The plenum may be required to either approve the whole report as proposed by the commission or vote for each proposed article of impeachment at a time. Having a full report may favour the cohesion of accusation, making a case that offers a strong and encompassing narrative of impeachment. If the report has a few fatal flaws, however, they may undermine the entirety of the report and doom the impeachment to failure. Voting article by article avoids this last problem, as only the portions of the report that satisfy the representatives are approved. It may, however, end up offering a set of accusations too small or too weak to justify impeachment and/or conviction, introducing problems of proportionality.
- *Publicity:* The work of the commission may be public or secret. The public format allows for popular and media scrutiny, keeping the members of the commission accountable for their efforts. It may, however, expose members to be singled-out

and pressured to act against their conscience. The secret format reduces accountability but may make it easier to work accusations involving national security and other sensible information. At any rate, commissions may choose to do their work partially in secret, when there is real and notorious need to do so.

- *Vote publicity:* Votes may be equally public or secret. Secrecy reduces accountability but may theoretically allow members of Parliament to vote according to their conscience and autonomously from partisan lines. In practice, however, votes are generally known beforehand due to the engagement of the commission members in the investigative and deliberative efforts. There is only so much that secrecy can achieve. Publicity, on the other hand, promotes accountability and stablishes clearer and more honest channels of communication with society at large.
- *Composition:* Commissions may have different sizes and different composition criteria. Larger groups may be more difficult to organize and coordinate but may allow for better division of labour in subgroups, which facilitate the investigation of complex or multiple issues. If participation in the commission causes exclusion from the rest of the procedures, the larger size may be detrimental to the representativity of posterior decisions. Composition criteria can be a major issue in the success of investigations. If done uncritically, it may bias the outcome and be unrepresentative of the interests of the Parliament. Generally, proportional criteria are used, but this may end up excluding small parties from the commission, if no effort is put into safeguarding some of their representativity.
- *Presidency:* The presidency of the commission has the potential to make or break the investigations. If the decisions of the presidency cannot be overturned by the rest of the members, the president may be legally empowered to dominate the commission's work entirely, blocking the consideration of crucial evidence, silencing dissenting opinions and biasing the conclusions of the final report.
- *Duration:* The duration of the commission may be fixed or flexible. A fixed duration will ensure that the procedure can follow its course in foreseeable time but may harm the investigation's outcome if the accusations are complex. A flexible duration may avoid this risk, but may result in drawn out procedures, which compounds with the general slow character of the impeachment procedures.
- *Permanent vs. ad hoc:* Permanent commissions are formed in the beginning of the legislative period and, thus, tend to collect valuable experience over time. Since its members are known beforehand, however, the presidency may attempt to stablish a solid clientelistic network with them, ensuring favourable decisions and leniency. Ad hoc commissions can be unpredictable, as their composition must be elected for the specific situation. If the impeachment accusations involve members of the Parliament in consort with the presidency, moreover, it is easier to exclude potentially compromised actors from the commission on abstract suspicions.
- *Minority rights:* Some commissions may have more democratic structure than others, giving a stronger voice to those in the minority. That may be translated in rules that give equal time for manifestation as the majority, rules that require less

than 1/2 in agreement to take decisions on what kind of evidence ought to be produced, or simply in the *ethos* of respecting the minority wishes. It may also materialize in the creation of an opportunity for the minority to make its own independent report challenging the evidence and conclusions of the final report. At any rate, having some minority rights may strengthen the legitimacy of the procedures, as it denotes a commitment to truthfulness and openness. It weakens, thus, the suspicions of 'hostile takeover' and parliamentary self-interestedness that can always be levelled against impeachment initiatives.
- *Defence rights:* The defence may be allowed to participate in the investigations of the impeachment commission, suggesting (or demanding) the production of evidence and questioning other evidence presented. Alternatively, such opportunity can be left to the trial phase. If impeachment in strict sense comes with the consequence of suspension from office, however, the earlier introduction of opportunities for defence may prevent hasty decisions with dire consequences.
- *Exclusion of participating members from rest of the procedures:* Members of the commission may be required to stay out of votes for the rest of the procedures, ensuring a strict division between accusation and adjudication. Such exclusion, however, may distort the representativity of the plenum, particularly in relation to smaller Parliaments. This may compound with the high thresholds required for impeachment or conviction, which likely pass or fail on tight margins. Disproportionate representation of the government coalition in the commission, for example, may undermine its efforts of resisting impeachment.

4.5.2.3 Impeachment (*Stricto Sensu*)

Features The impeachment in the strict sense is the key phase of the impeachment procedure, where the demeanour of the President is officially put into question. After considerable discussions and deliberation, it may confirm that the evidence collected, and the accusations brought forward are sufficiently robust and damning to warrant a full trial. The impeachment phase will often restrain (but not expand) the scope of the accusation that will be taken to trial. A successful impeachment may, moreover, cause suspension from office during the time of the trial, arguably hindering the President from using the office to influence the trial or cause more harm.

The decision to impeach is one that only Parliament can take, even in predominantly judicial impeachments. In bicameral systems, the decision is made by the Lower House, which is the one thought to better represent the People's will. The approval thresholds vary between 1/2, 2/3, or 3/4, reflecting in part the party system at hand (highly fragmented systems necessitating higher thresholds), the wish of isolating the presidency from parliamentary incursion (thus stablishing a stricter separation of powers), the severity of the immediate consequences of impeachment, and the country's history with ousting procedures. Following the tradition stablished by the English impeachment after the 1701 Act of Settlement, a few constitutions determine that, once the President is impeached, the conduct imputed to him or her may no longer be subject to pardon of any kind.

Challenges Creating the proper environment for judicious examination of the impeachment charges, as well as achieving balance between considerations of legal and political order in the decision for impeachment, are among the hardest tasks of the impeachment phase. The large size of the Lower House and the polarized context of impeachment can make it difficult to tame the Representatives, when spirits get heated. Debate between them can easily stray from the object of debate, and turn into uncharitable and impertinent exchanges, harming public perception of the procedures and the quality of its outcome. Moreover, there can be great variation among what representatives consider 'impeachment relevant'. Some may be hyper-focused on legal issues, some on political issues, while others may be more interested in using the spotlight for themselves or to the promotion of other aspects of their political agenda. If tight discipline is not kept, the procedures can descend into unseemly exchanges, unsatisfactorily commanding the authority necessary to hold the President accountable.

Standard of Proof The impeachment vote will answer the question of whether the President *ought to be taken to trial.* It is, therefore, *not a judgement on certainty* about the case made by the accusation, *but on its high likelihood.* By this point, the impeachment commission may have investigated enough to stablish that (a.) an impeachable offense is indeed very likely to have been committed (materiality), (b.) in such a way to implicate the presidency (imputability). Beyond these matters, impeachment praxis indicates that the trial may nonetheless be dismissed if the evolution of circumstances suggests that furthering the procedures seem superfluous or harmful (*e.g.,* offenses are revealed to be milder than originally proposed, public opinion changed its course, alternative forms for resolving the conflict or legal violations became preferred, the presidency is no longer generating threats to democracy or the state). Standards for impeachment may be higher if temporary suspension from office is among its consequences or the procedures are in the trial-less modality.

Design Choices

- *Publicity:* The impeachment phase needs to be public, due to the sort of decisions and clarifications that take place in its scope. What may vary is the degree of publicity, which recently has ramped up significantly. More than just keeping detailed public records and keeping the Parliament's doors open to the media and interested visitors, most recent presidential impeachments are being widely televised, increasing citizen engagement and the accountability of the participants.
- *Vote publicity:* Votes may be public or secret. Secret votes relieve external pressure from representatives but may make them unaccountable to the public and their parties. It may make them more easily corruptible, as some of their suspicious patterns of behaviour cannot be confirmed. Public votes increase

accountability and assure better coherence between what is argued within the procedures and their outcomes.

- *Opportunity for debate and manifestation:* After the impeachment commission and the defence present their cases, the floor is open for reactions of the representatives. Given the size of some Parliaments, however, space for such activities often needs to be limited, otherwise the whole procedure may become unwieldly. Manifestations may be held very briefly, to limited number of participations, done through few party/parliamentary bloc leaders or speakers, and/or spaced throughout many days.
- *Pardon preclusion:* One consequence of impeachment may be that the facts imputed to the President can no longer be object of pardon. This covers a potential loophole allowing the convicted President to avoid accountability by being pardoned, for example, by the Vice-President. It increases the leverages Parliament has vis-à-vis the President, incentivizing a resignation before the conclusion of the impeachment.
- *Suspension from office:* The suspension prevents a suspected President to continue causing harm during the period of the trial or other defined period. It may, moreover, critically reduce his or her power to direct the Parliament's decision via patronage or intimidation. It may, however, create a lame-duck President, who becomes vulnerable to the designs of a coveting Vice or interim President. Such substitutes could use the power of office to influence Parliament through patronage or intimidation, and so seek to consolidate themselves in the presidency.

4.5.2.4 Trial

Features The final and potentially longest phase of the impeachment procedures is the trial. It is the phase responsible for examining and determining the guilt of the accused President. In the predominantly parliamentary form, it largely consists in reperforming key steps taken by the impeachment commission, but before the plenum of the Higher House, such as hearing witnesses, depositions, and so on. The trial gives considerably more space for the defence and accusation to make their case and critically confront the narratives and evidence presented. The procedures are generally presided by a member of the judiciary (*e.g.*, the president of the Supreme Court), who is, thus, well acquainted with the conduction of judicial proceedings and may competently suggest solutions to legal questions the Representatives may raise. The final product of the trial, after the votes are taken, is generally a report and/or a legislative resolution resembling a judicial sentence.

In the predominantly judicial form, the impeachment accusation is trialled as ordinary legal matter, with all steps expected from a judicial trial. The resulting sentence, however, generally needs to be submitted back to the Parliament, who will put into effect the political consequences of an impeachment conviction (*i.e.*, removal, disqualification, presidential succession, new elections) or acquittal (*i.e.*, reconduction to office, in case the President had been suspended).

Challenges The challenges faced in the trial are essentially the same as those of the impeachment in strict sense: creating a judicious environment and keeping the adjudicators objectively on track and attuned to the intersectional nature of impeachments. The solemnities and symbolism of the trial, however, impose on the Higher House a much greater duty of embodying the legal rationality that in part also legitimizes impeachment and its consequences. In predominantly judicial impeachments, moreover, there may be the additional challenge of sufficiently isolating the Justices from outside influence and thus guarantee a just and representative outcome.

Standard of Proof The trial seeks to consolidate the legal truth of the impeachment narrative. It must, thus, bring an outcome supported by *an even higher degree of confidence than in the impeachment vote*. The trial must be able to confidently stablish (*in addition to what was pointed out for impeachment votes*) that (a.) the President is indeed culpable for the impeachable offense (*culpability*), and (b.) ought to be sanctioned for the violations (*'punishability'*). *These are issues which are not purely empirical in nature* and demand a good deal of normative considerations. The trial is gives space for deliberation and persuasion on both fronts, as common ground would ideally be found regarding the framework, guiding principles, and subsumption of culpability and punishability in the practical case.

Design Choices

- *Accusation management:* Before the trial starts, someone needs to be nominated to manage the accusation case. In some systems, this is done by a group of members of the Parliament (generally, from the Lower House) or by an outside group of lawyers, possibly those who authored the accusation piece(s) that initiated the impeachment procedure (if the case). The former choice is often referred to as the more problematic option, as, though there often are many jurists of talent working in the Parliament, they are likely long disconnected from the practice of law and may have other concerns on their minds. It is feared that the case made by the group of representatives will be comparatively lacklustre to that of the full-time lawyers, even though it may receive legal support from the Parliament's staff or outside counsel.
- *Trial commission:* Some systems may create another commission to conduct the bulk of the trial and produce a suggested sentence. In that case, only few witnesses, the President's cross-examination and the closing arguments are presented to the plenum. This frees the rest of Parliament to engage in its other core activities, although it must be noted that the theme 'impeachment' has a nagging tendency of infiltrating those as well during the period of the trial. This design choice can be redundant and may not necessarily optimize the time and cost efficiency of the Higher House.
- *Workload reduction:* The Higher House may temporarily reduce the scope of its typical activities to focus on the impeachment trial (*e.g.*, hinder the work of

parliamentary commissions during the period of the trial). This may improve the quality and quickness of the trial but is possibly disruptive of other affairs.

- *Duration:* Longer duration for trials arguably allow for more thorough examinations and discussions, producing, thus, a more just outcome. It may, however, last too long and fail to give a timely resolution to the tensions building up in society and between branches of power. Delayed justice may also mean injustice. Shorter durations may give timely, but possibly also hasty resolutions. The duration is mainly determined by the minimum number of sessions that are to be dedicated to the trial, their length and the spacing between them. Spacing is a major factor as it influences the preparations of arguments, witnesses and how much the representatives may be able to reflect on the themes presented.
- *Conflict of interest:* Some systems allow for the defence or accusation to demand the exclusion of representatives thought to be in conflict of interest (*e.g.*, relatives of the President, declared enemies). In the partisan setting of the Parliament, this may be a difficult task to fulfil objectively. While this faculty may theoretically improve the neutrality of the House, the right may be used to disproportionally affect representativity of certain groups and thus distort the outcome of the trial.
- *Presidency:* The presidency of the impeachment trial may be exercised by different actors, such as the Chief Justice, the Vice-President, the President of the Senate and so on. The first option is generally preferred as the more neutral between the alternatives, and the one probably most capable of recreating the seriousness of a judicial setting. The legal experience, knowledge and authority of the Chief Justice may be particularly useful for resolving legal questions representatives raise throughout the trial. Having a member of the Parliament in the presidency of the procedures may mean having to exclude him or her from votes taken during the trial.
- *Separate votes:* The articles of impeachment may be voted together or separately. Voting them together results in a stronger, more coherent sentence, but may undermine the vote in general, as the adjudicators may feel uneasy with giving a blanket confirmation/rejection when some of the charges contain critical flaws. Separate votes mitigate this problem but may generate incoherent and/or weak sentences. Rejecting only part of the charges may generate a problem of proportionality between punishment and offense, and thus undermine the legitimacy of the procedure. The sanctions of impeachment may be voted separately as well, if the procedure in question offers more than just removal (or just disqualification, for impeachments against former Presidents). The separate vote for sanctions may be used to mitigate problems of proportionality.
- *Consequences*: Some systems of impeachment may result only in removal from office, others may also bring disqualification from office. Having only removal as a consequence helps to depersonalize and simplify the impeachment a bit, as the removal is decidedly less personal of a punishment than disqualification. Adding disqualification to the consequences, however, may add an important leverage to the Parliament that may compel suspected Presidents to resign, as to not risk being entirely ostracized from politics. Disqualification may perform an important preventive function, as even after impeachment former Presidents remain

nationally influential figures who may with some ease reach other offices, potentially using them to cause more harm or evade other spheres of accountability. If the trial is conducted in the judicial form, the court of law may be competent to apply sanctions of ordinary justice. New elections can be called whenever the President lacks a proper legal successor and is removed relatively early into the mandate. New elections as a consequence can reduce the risk of a legitimacy crisis caused by having unpopular and unelected officers occupying the presidency, but at the same time may stimulate narrowly defeated presidential candidates to see in the impeachment an avenue for electoral rematches.[212]

4.6 Judicial Review

General Considerations Under the paradigm of the rule of law, judicial review plays a significant role. It guarantees a degree of certainty and responsibility in the application of law by requiring courts to interpret law in similar ways. If a court decides in a way considered arbitrary or unreasonable by the legal community, odds are that such decision will be reformed by other courts, when asked on a 'second opinion'. Such arrangement generates a system that is stable, and conducive to the homogenous and predictable application of law, as the isolated and unorthodox decisions will be ironed out by the system in the long run.

As much as paradigm shifts in law may be desirable every now and then, this sort of security through stability and predictability can be of value to society due to its capacity of revealing irrational, reckless, or persecutory use of authority. Judges (or any other public agents) who are tempted in applying the law in a novel way must ultimately consider that they may attract criticism by doing so, whenever their decisions are reformed by their peers or superiors. They must accept that such insistence in innovating is likely to be both futile (the decision is likely to be reformed anyway) and detrimental to their career (it may put their competence and honesty in question), and that, therefore, they are better off respecting the expectations of their class and the legal community, rather than challenging them.

Challenges and Limitations of Judicial Review in Impeachments Such is admittedly an ingenious arrangement, but it is also one that requires certain conditions to be in place for its implementation to be successful. It is difficult to talk about

[212] Ginsburg et al. (2021) argue in favour of new elections as the golden standard for impeachment design, as it would reduce the likelihood of its abuse. They argue impeachments perceived as unfair would likely bring an electoral backlash to those usurping this power and thus be of unclear strategic advantage. While this is possible, it is important to remember that impeachments take place in moments of special presidential vulnerability and unpopularity, even when used uncharitably. Trespasses are often rationalized under such circumstances, and may be potentialized by presidentialism's personalistic tendencies, which allow political personalities to act as entities dissociated from their parties.

homogenous and predictable application of law, for example, if only one or two decisions have ever been made on a particular subject. So that one can talk about stablished expectations, one needs to first, of course, stablish expectations. There can be no indicator of regularity if there is no framework against which those suspected of being irregular can be compared. Such framework is one that should stablish itself over time, through recurrent application of law in clearly identifiable patterns, which then inform the rationality of the precedent.

This system also presumes that the reviewing organ has similar or superior authority *vis-à-vis* whoever made the original decision. It is only reasonable that such revision is done by an organ who also shares the competence to make such decisions and that has perhaps even more authority to do so, as it may likely override the authority of the original actor. Ideally, therefore, vertical (hierarchical) relations lend themselves best to those ends, but other arrangements can also achieve such legitimacy, such as having the decision reviewed by a collegiate of the original actor's peers or other organs of comparable importance.

There are perhaps other 'conditions of (successful) implementation' that could be mentioned here, but for the purposes of this book these two arguably present *the* defining challenges of implementing judicial review in the scope of presidential impeachments. Notice how both elements, that is, (i.) the stablished or 'stablishable' framework of expectations, and (ii.) reviewing organ with comparable competence and authority, are difficult to reproduce in the system of presidential impeachments. The first is difficult because presidential impeachments are remarkably extraordinary procedures, meaning that a revision of an impeachment decision is likely to bring no major qualitative improvement over the original decision. Such situation could be boiled down, in other words, to the favouring of the decision of one organ over the other for the mere sake of 'reviewing' and not for the sake of upholding stablished standards, as these are not produced by the system of impeachments.[213] Regarding the second issue, it is unfeasible to have another organ with greater authority than the Court of Impeachments to review its decisions. Such is the case, because the Court of Impeachments, be it the Parliament or the Supreme/Constitutional Court, is already the highest authority in the issue to begin with. Having its decisions reviewed will likely only reduce the authority commanded by

[213] As discussed in Sect. 2.3.3. In short, the key problems of the system of impeachments are that, among other things, (i.) the system is not bound to an unifying *habitus* and *ethos* as the legal community would be; (ii.) its decisions are sparse, meaning that the patterns they stablish, if at all existent, have limited informational value; (iii.) impeachment decisions are strongly context sensitive and carry at least two layers of considerations (legal and political), meaning that a conviction or acquittal is not necessarily a step towards crystallizing legal standards; (iv.) impeachment decisions, final or interlocutory, may often be made on tight margins of agreement, which also limit the predictability of the system over time; (v.) the preponderant reasoning behind the decisions is not always clear, as the adjudicators often list a multitude of reasons for their votes, which are weighed differently and which may or may not be mutually inclusive of the reasons presented by their peers.

the impeachment decision, not to mention other problems such arrangement could introduce relative to matters of separation of powers and of democratic legitimation.

Theoretical Realm of Use Not all decisions made in the scope of a presidential impeachment, however, are made by the highest authority itself. Interlocutory decisions, for example, may be made by a single actor or by a small fraction of the adjudicating organ. Such decisions could be revised by other organs of higher status or by a larger collegiate of their peers in ways that would positively impact the fairness of the procedures and would, thus, serve as a meaningful implementation of the judicial review in the context of presidential impeachments. The review by a larger organ can prevent that nefarious or incompetent actors undermine the procedure at large, ensuring that the decisions, especially the more controversial ones, are representative of a larger, presumably more reliable consensus. The sort of decisions being considered here are, for example, decisions that stablish the concrete course of the procedure (*e.g.*, opportunity and duration for defence, debate, deadlines), aspects of evidence production (*e.g.*, list of acceptable evidence and witnesses, opportunity for hearing experts and independent studies), and other significant details (*e.g.*, form of voting, criteria, and proportion for participation in the impeachment commission). These are all formal aspects of the presidential impeachment, which may make or break the procedure and which, therefore, can potentially profit of a system that reduces arbitrariness and the risk of domination by single actors or small and unrepresentative groups.

Judicial Review in the Practice of Presidential Impeachment
Indeed, such seems to incidentally be the pattern followed by Latin American countries in the past few decades.[214] As a general rule, the final decisions on the merit[215] of impeachment may not be reviewed under any circumstance,[216] and, at least in part, the interlocutory decisions may be reviewed, although the form of doing so varies along the lines indicated above, that is, reviewed either through a collegiate

[214]Disclaimer: Some of the conclusions here are based on decisions concerning impeachments of judges. Even though these same decisions often also consider their own implications on the presidential impeachment, it is remains unclear whether the standards stablished in them will be reproduced when the stakes of a presidential impeachment are at play. Moreover, not all countries in the region have judicial decisions on impeachments that reveal relevant pieces of information. At any rate, this is a tentative analysis of a very plural and diverse region and, thus, these conclusions should be taken with a grain of salt.

[215]For the purposes of this section, merit decisions (as opposed to interlocutory decisions) are those that import the adjudication of the object under analysis. Three merit decisions are generally made in impeachment procedures, which will answer the following questions: (1.) should presidential misbehaviour be scrutinized (referral resolution), (2.) should the President be brought to trial (impeachment resolution), and (3.) should the President be convicted (sentence). Whether all three steps should be considered merit may vary (*e.g.*, in Chile the referral is automatic and requires no involvement of gatekeepers in adjudication).

[216]In Honduras, for example, decisions made during impeachment procedures are expressly declared to be political and, therefore, not subject to any form of review (Decree n. 51 of 2013, art. 8).

of peers of the same organ,[217] or through a different organ of higher status.[218] Since rules on the issue of judicial review are notoriously absent in rules on impeachment,[219] the justification for that consolidated arrangement cannot come from a place of system design as suggested above, but from the perspective of system insiders. Whoever wants to challenge a decision made in the course of the procedures cannot simply suggest that a certain arrangement is the best and that, therefore, it should be used, but must instead use the limited tools offered by the system to find a way to enforce it. Naturally, the way of doing so varies according to the available tools and to the prevalent understandings of how and when they can be used. Such insider perspectives will be explored next:

- **Are decisions in impeachments at all reviewable? If so, by what means?**

The first and most obvious thing one may argue is that, if the rules on presidential impeachment do not provide any means for decisions made in the course of the procedures to be reviewed, then there are no legal means of challenging such acts.[220] That securely is not the case, as any modern Latin American state enshrines the right to remedies such as *habeas corpus*, *habeas data*, writ of *mandamus* (Spanish America: *mandado de amparo*; Brazil: *mandado de segurança*), and so on.[221] If the decisions are formalized in the form of a legislative resolution or a law, suits dedicated to constitutionality control may be applicable.[222] In exceptional cases, judicial review in the more traditional sense has been accepted.[223]

---

[217] In Colombia, for example, monocratic decisions that restrict the rights of defence may be reviewed by the plenum of the Impeachment Commission (Law n. 05 of 1992, art. 338). Brazil, by contrast, has no impeachment-dedicated rules on review, but the bylaws of the Chamber stablish general rules that allow Deputies to bring any monocratic decision to the plenum's review (Resolution n. 17/1989, art. 100, § 1 and 226, I).

[218] In Bolivia, for example, decisions made during the proceedings may be reviewed by the Penal Chamber of the Supreme Court. The decisions of the Penal Chamber may be reviewed once by the other Chambers of the same Court (Law n. 044 of 2010, art. 15).

[219] The only mentions to judicial review (or lack thereof) in legal documents are to be found in Bolivia (Law n. 044 of 2010, art. 15), Colombia (Law n. 05 of 1992, art. 338), and Honduras (Decree n. 51 of 2013, art. 8).

[220] As observed, for example, in 1992 regarding the impeachment of judge Walter Nixon, in the United States (Nixon v. United States, 506 U.S. 224): "(...) there is no separate constitutional provision which could be defeated by allowing the Senate final authority to determine the meaning of the word "try" in Art. I, § 3, cl. 6. While courts possess power to review legislative action that transgresses identifiable textual limits, the word "try" does not provide such a limit on the authority committed to the Senate". This standard is mentioned by multiple Latin American courts.

[221] For an overview of the constitutional jurisdiction in the region, see Pérez Tremps (2003).

[222] Such was, for example, the path chosen to challenge Lugo's impeachment conviction (AI n. 1533).

[223] Argentina, for example, presents a peculiarity in its understanding of the Court of Impeachments. In 1993 the Supreme Court (decision 316:2940) established that the Court of Impeachments was equivalent to a court of justice, and that, therefore, its decisions could be reviewed with a *recurso extraordinario* (*i.e.*, a sort of appeal against aspects of judicial decisions that violate due process).

In short, the idea is that an illegal act made by an authority (*e.g.*, because it violates its scope of competence, a constitutional right, or the procedural rules of impeachment themselves) should, therefore, be subjectable to review by a court of law, even if no dedicated institutional means for challenging such act is explicitly foreseen by law. Besides this possibility, moreover, there are at times forms of review stablished in the bylaws of Parliaments or Courts responsible for impeachment. The general rules that would be applicable to the review of acts of the president of investigative commissions, for example, could also find applicability in impeachment commissions.

Such conclusions, however, were not self-evident or broadly accepted in the past, particularly in relation to the review function carried out by the Judicial branch. Courts in Latin America have been reluctant of reviewing any decisions made during impeachment procedures, arguing under their own conceptions of judicial self-restraint that any decisions made during impeachments were outside of their scope of competence.[224] Regardless of whether the decision had been made only by a small fraction of the Parliament, or if it touched or not upon the merit of impeachment, or even if it was blatantly illegal, Courts did for a long time consider it unreasonable for them to interfere and, thus, arguably violate the separation of powers or appear to engage in political activity.[225] As part of the exclusive core activity of the Parliament, such decisions were said underlie its absolute discretion.

Coinciding with the re-democratization of the region,[226] however, a shift occurred regarding this understanding. Realms of absolute power became less palatable, and with it, also such blanket refusal to review legal violations.[227] Courts started recognizing that even in exercise of their core activities the branches of power remained bound to the forms and means stablished in the law and the

Such decision, however, was directed at the impeachment of a judge (Alberto Nicosia) and it is, therefore, unclear whether the same standard would find application in presidential impeachments.

[224] Peru, 2010, TC 00013-2009-AI: "(. . .) the political-punitive function is not [a prerogative of the Judicial branch]. Neither could it be, as the principle of separation of powers requires the absence of any political judgement [*valoración*] in the decisions of the Judicial Branch"; Argentina, CSJN decisions in 1922, 136:147 and in 1980, 302:186; Brazil, 1937, HC 26.544 *apud* Brossard de Souza Pinto (1965), p. 161; see also, from 2019, MS 34970 AgR/DF.

[225] As argued, for example, by Justice Paulo Brossard in light of the hitherto dominating opinion (Brazil, 1990, MS 20.941-1/DF, author's translation): "In matters of impeachment, all takes place, from beginning to the end, in the Legislature, (. . .) being [thus of its] exclusive and unreviewable [competence]" (vote was defeated); Peru, 2014, TC 04968-2014-HC, acknowledged the same historically overcome thesis: "This Court should not be interpreted to subscribe to the orthodox thesis of *interna corporis acta*, according to which the acts of Congress have no external incidence, that is to say, they would be exhausted within the Parliament's own sphere and not susceptible to review".

[226] The 1980s were, moreover, a period of great expansion in the constitutional jurisdiction of Latin American courts. See Feoli Villalobos (2010).

[227] For a discussion of this phenomenon as a world-wide occurrence and its implications, see Hirschl (2007), p. 169 ff.

Constitution.[228] Truly absolute remained only the aspects of such decisions that were not bound by legal commands and whose review resulted in courts encroaching functions of Parliament.[229] The merit or the material aspects of the impeachment procedures remained, therefore, non-reviewable by the Judicative.

- **Non-reviewability of merit decisions**

In addition to the thesis of judicial self-restraint, the non-reviewability of merit has been argued in association with at least three other concerns. One concern was the fear of undermining the constitutional provisions on impeachment indirectly by reallocating a *de facto* power on the Judiciary to be the actual decider of impeachments.[230] Another concern posits the impeachment jurisdiction to be entirely and strictly separated from ordinary justice, as a sort of purely political jurisdiction governed by its own and exclusive logic.[231] Another concern regarded the nature of the political fallout that could ensue from a judicial decision reviewing the outcome of an impeachment. The mere possibility of review could cause political

---

[228] Brazil, 1990, MS 20.941-1/DF: "(. . .) Although it may be certain that the impeachment is a predominantly political measure, acts relative to the investigation of impeachable offenses cannot be excluded from the scrutiny of the Judiciary, as they may be bound to strictly constitutional or legal norms of procedural nature (. . .)"; Peru, 2010, TC 00013-2009-AI: "(. . .) the Constitutional Court may review the constitutionality of measures adopted [by Congress] on request of the [affected] party (. . .) for any arbitrary act would be null according to (. . .) the Constitution". Decisions with similar content: Colombia, 1996, C-222-96 (*arguably*); Argentina, 1993, CSJN 316:2940 ('Nicosia'); 2004, CSJN 327:1914, and *arguably* also, 1986, CSJN 308:961 ('Graffigna Latino Carlos').

[229] Argentina, 1993, CSJN 316:2940 ('Nicosia' decision): "To this Court, from the [conclusion of] non-reviewability of the merit of impeachment does not follow that the safeties imposed to the exercise of [impeachment] by the fundamental law are [also] subjected to [non-reviewability] (. . .)". Brazil, 2011, MS 30.672/DF: "IV – Matters involving convenience or merit do not compete to the Judiciary, under risk of [usurpation] of the Legislature's eminently political [adjudication] of such matters". Paraguay, 2012, AI n. 1323: "'Poor performance' constitutes grounds that are to be outlined by the free discretion of Congress".

[230] Brazil, 2016, MS 34.441/DF: "To accept the possibility of judicial review of the merit of the Legislature's decisions would mean to turn the [rules of impeachment in the] Constitution into dead letter (. . .)". Similar decisions: Argentina, 1993, CSJN 316:2940 ('Nicosia' decision); Peru, 2010, TC 00013-2009-AI.

[231] Brazil, 1937, HC 26.544 (*apud* Brossard de Souza Pinto 1965, p. 161): "The [Court of Impeachments] is a court of political nature, [thus] bearing no connection or subjection to the Judiciary whatsoever". Paraguay, 2012, AI n. 1323: "(. . .) The National Congress is sovereign (. . .) to conduct impeachment, as it constitutes a fundamental instrument to democratic preservation and the principle of separation of powers (. . .). [Impeachment] is not an ordinary trial of jurisdictional nature (. . .)". Colombia, by contrast, dealt with a similar proposition (C-198-94), but rejected such narrow understanding of 'political', and characterized impeachment as a special kind of 'constitutional jurisdiction' (C-222-96), which on its turn is subjected to some real legal and constitutional constraints. As such, although not (yet) overtly assumed, the Constitutional Court may have implicitly suggested it is within its jurisdiction to review violations committed in the course of impeachment.

instability due to the prolonged uncertainty regarding the situation of the President.[232]

The more traditionally minded jurists have been sceptical of the Courts' avoidance of merit decisions, however. In their understanding, legal subsumption, whether done by Courts or by the Legislature, is necessarily subjected to the real constraints imposed by the law and the Constitution. If the subsumption of the abstract impeachable offense onto the acts practiced by the President is generally understood to be incorrect, so should, logically, such decisions be subjectable to review.[233] Similarly, the conviction with less than the necessary threshold (usually 2/3) should also uncontrovertibly warrant review of merit.[234] These jurists, however, offer no answer to the second question posed above, about whether the universalization of this understanding will lead to a net negative of political consequences. That is an understandable outcome, as in the traditional understanding of law, in which law and politics are sharply separated, concerns of institutional design are not within the scope of legal practice and are rather to be left to politicians. Whether law causes inconveniences or embarrassments to citizens or politics would be immaterial to their technical assessment. As it currently stands, however, Courts, also as the technical institutions they can possibly be, are still refusing to interfere in merit decisions, even if they blatantly violate the legal community's hegemonic perception of law.[235]

[232]Brazil, 1992, MS 20.941-DF, argument for the denial of review of a decision of initiating impeachment procedures: "(...) [impeachment] is a procedure of great gravity, which the mere filing (*simples abertura*) by itself may mean [the installation of] a crisis". In the US the argument has been presented as an evidence of non-justiciability (Nixon v. United States, 506 U.S. 224): "Justiciability is also refuted by (1) the lack of finality inherent in exposing the country's political life particularly if the President were impeached—to months, or perhaps years, of chaos during judicial review of Senate impeachment proceedings, or during any retrial that a differently constituted Senate might conduct if its first judgment of conviction were invalidated (...)".

[233]Bahia et al. (2017); Camargo and Vieira (2019); Jardim (2016); Lobo (2017).

[234]This hypothesis was acknowledged by the Argentinian Supreme Court in 1993 (316,2940): "If any of the impeachable officers claimed, *verbi gratia*, to have been removed by a majority inferior to the two thirds required (...), it would not be doubtful that, if taken to court, these Justices would be empowered to disqualify the result, as this fraction of the Senate would lack the attributions to resolve in such a fashion". It is, however, *the only situation* in which merit could theoretically be affected, as the Court recognized it cannot analyse the merit of impeachment itself: "(...) grounds for impeachment (...) are of exclusive and definitive discretion of the Senate, not being judicially reviewable".

[235]The only exception being that of Argentina in the specific circumstance mentioned in the footnote above. It is nonetheless unclear whether such standard would ever find applicability in the practice of presidential impeachments. Decisions in Peru (*e.g.*, TC 03760-2004-AA, which discusses the penalty of disqualification applied to Fujimori) claim that the application of law by Congress should be subjected to review regarding their *reasonableness* and *proportionality*. As it currently stands, the consideration of these two elements has been restricted to what has been described here as non-merit decisions. Given the wording of these decisions, however, it is imaginable that a merit decision with extreme disregard to such elements could prompt an intervention in the future.

- **Reviewability of *some* interlocutory decisions**

This leaves the conclusion that at least interlocutory decisions could be reviewed, as such decisions do not necessarily shape the merit of the procedures. Verifying what sort of interlocutory decisions were successfully reviewed in practice, however, one will find that there are aspects of form which Courts nonetheless refuse to reform. If a decision on the formalities of impeachment would generate outcomes that embarrass the procedures too much or, even more conspicuously, outcomes that may potentially nullify a merit decision, then the refusal to review persists.[236] Even when revision only affects the decision negatively (*i.e.,* it cancels a certain outcome, but does not lock in any particular adjudicative stance), the incidental infringement upon merit has shown to be sufficient to ward off any potential judicial intervention in impeachment procedures.

- **Is review the only way of preventing violations to the rule of law?**

Violations against the rule of law can, moreover, be prevented in less conflictive ways than just by judicial review. The highest Courts have been called pre-emptively to give their opinion on the legality and correct interpretation of certain rules of impeachment.[237] Such pre-emptive interference may be achieved by requesting the collaboration of courts in their advisory function[238] or in the pre-emptive use of the constitutional jurisdiction, that is, through the already-mentioned *habeas corpus, habeas data,* writ of *mandamus,* unconstitutionality suits, etc., before actual violations take place. Resolving potentially controverted issues before they have a chance to undermine the process may avoid the conundrum of nullifying or re-enacting important steps within it, and all the ensuing negative consequences these acts may bring.

4.7 *Excursus*: Rule of Law and Impeachments

The inflexion of law and politics observed in impeachment procedures is prone to being received with scepticism by the general public, especially when expressions of political reasoning seem too present in a procedure that presents itself as legalistic, solemn and quasi-judicial. The discussion offered in Chap. 2 sought to reveal and

[236] Brazil, 2016, MS 34193 MC/DF and MS 34441 MC/DF; or Paraguay, 2012, AI n. 1533. These decisions acknowledge certain procedural wrongs, but only engage with those that do not existentially interfere with the course of the procedures. In one of them (MS 34441 MC/DF), the justice rapporteur stablishes very clearly that: "(. . .) only when the indispensable need to prevent serious grievous harm to institutions or democracy is demonstrated (. . .) is that an intervention of the kind asked may be justified (. . .)".

[237] *E.g.,* in Brazil: *Estadão*, December 21st, 2015: "*Cunha e líderes partidários discutirão impeachment com presidente do STF*"; or in Peru: 0006-2003-AI/TC.

[238] For a general discussion of the judicial advisory function, see Rogers and Vanberg (2002).

explain the discursive function claims that "impeachment is political" may have, how they impact its legitimacy as a procedure, and what kind of conflictive theoretical underpinnings such claims presuppose.

The thrust of the argument presented there was that legality, albeit being commonly understood and posited as a sort of neutral and impartial institution, does carry within itself a range of political commitments which coexist in permanent tension. Such political side of law can successfully conceal itself within the ordinary legal system, due to the sort of legal relations it deals with and due to the sort of "ecosystem" such system generates. When transposed to the setting of impeachments, however, the same *façade* becomes much harder to hold together. The adjudicators of an impeachment cannot pose as neutral towards the person of the President, the politically charged context of the procedures cannot be ignored or dealt away with, and the safeguards that ensure a degree of certainty in legal issues (*e.g.*, judicial review, precedent) simply cannot be reproduced at that high level of government. As a result, the political side of law comes clearly into evidence and, with it, doubts about law really being 'reason free from passion', as Aristotle once suggested.[239]

This section will deal directly with this issue, analysing how the difference in context (*i.e.*, regular citizenry, in ordinary law *versus* the President, in inter-branch disputes) informs the rule of law in all its dimensions. It will answer the criticism levelled against impeachments as being notorious violators of the rule of law, more than just from the perspective of the legal communities finding them broadly legitimate, but also in the technical sense.

The section will ultimately argue that, though the rule of law is also part of impeachments, it manifests itself differently than it does in ordinary legal contexts and is thus deserving of an understanding that reflects and accommodates such differences.

4.7.1 General Considerations on the Rule of Law

The rule of law is considered an integral part of any modern constitutional state.[240] In general outlines, the rule of law stablishes that men shall be 'governed by law, and not by men'.[241] What is meant by such a maxim is that humanity is more justly commanded by the sort of procedurally generated rules known as laws, and not by

[239] Paraphrasing his book *Politics*, Book III, Chapter 16. See Aristotle 1998 trans. CDC Reeve, p. 97.

[240] Pierson (2011), p. 20. As famously remarked by Max Weber, perhaps the distinguishing feature of the modern state in comparison to those that are not deserving of the same title, is that its rule is not based on grace, favour, or any other sort subjective and arbitrary will of particular men, but on a "system of order claims binding authority", extensible to anyone, without exceptions, under its jurisdiction. Weber (1978), p. 56.

[241] Paraphrasing of John Adams (1776), *Thoughts on Government*. See Bernstein (1990), p. 131.

the arbitrariness of whoever finds itself in power in a particular moment. That is a conclusion that can be arrived at from different approaches, such as from philosophical reasoning or historical experience.[242] The latter tends to be particularly more compelling and is incidentally one that has been described in this book. The use of impeachments to make ministers accountable for their illegal acts in Stuart England, for example, was a direct attempt at binding rulers to the laws and not leaving them to do as they will, in the hopes that justness would spontaneously manifest in their actions. At that point in history, it was already clear that many rulers were more than willing to receive the emoluments and powers of office, but not as much willing to own up to their failures and abuses, resulting in arguably disastrous and self-serving governments. As it seems to be not only England's case but the general experience, power, when unrestrained, tends to concentrate and recursively reproduce itself, as well as turn arbitrary.[243] The strict and generalized bindingness of law diminished such risks and thus consolidated itself as a cornerstone of modern states.

Bindingness to law by itself, however, does not guarantee that a political system becomes free from arbitrariness. For that goal to be achieved in any meaningful capacity, such bindingness must be actual, that is, it must not allow for those in power to circumvent it or to render it inconsequential. It is to say, in other words, that it is not sufficient that law exists, if it is not also capable of meaningfully and significantly limiting the scope of human action, and thus effectively direct and inform conduct. Man is not free to interpret law as he wants, or to apply it only when he wants or only to whom he wants.

From that foundational idea, a whole spectrum of consequences may be drawn, which, however, vary according to legal tradition (*e.g.*, common *versus* civil law, English *versus* US-American, rule of law *versus Rechtsstaat*) and particular national history.[244] To make this discussion as cross-cultural as a work on comparative constitutional law must be, this section adopts the framework offered by Danilo Zolo.[245] Zolo composes a coherent and unitary framework of rule of law that encapsulates, as much as possible, the variety of consequences and focus points different cultures give to the rule of law.

As Zolo argues, the consequences of the rule of law generally unfold based on two fundamental principles. The first is the "principle of distribution of power", which seeks distribute rights among individuals within a political community, allowing them to lay legitimate claims against state interference. Such claims may entail, for example, the right to be treated equally to other legal subjects. The second

[242] Zolo (2007), pp. 7–48.

[243] Zolo (2007), p. 21.

[244] Zolo (2007), pp. 7–18. The following explanations will not entail how one may get to the conclusions posited by Zolo. The explanations, both historical and philosophical, are too lengthy for the scope of this study. For the sake of brevity, they will be taken at face value and the focus will instead be dedicated to their relationship with impeachments. For those interested, complete explanations from different perspectives and traditions may be found at the same volume from which the referenced framework is taken from.

[245] Zolo (2007).

fundamental principle is the "principle of differentiation of power", which, on its turn, seeks to compartmentalize and differentiate multiple spheres of power, avoiding thus their excessive concentration and encouraging self-restraint. Such differentiation may be found in the distinction made between powers (*e.g.*, Executive *versus* Legislative *versus* Judicative; law-making *versus* law-enforcing), between subsystems of power (*e.g.*, politics *versus* religion *versus* economics), and so on.[246]

4.7.2 Rule of Law as Distribution of Power

The rule of law as a principle of "distribution of power" may concretely translate into the following sub-principles: (i.) the unity of law, that is, the law is applicable to all legal subjects; (ii.) the isonomy of law, that is, the law is to be applied in the same measure to everyone; (iii.) the certainty of the law, or namely that the content of law must be understandable and foreseeable to effectively guide human agency; and, finally, (iv.) the law must recognize basic individual rights, and thus stablish concrete safeguards against arbitrary intrusion.

4.7.2.1 Unity: No One Is Above (or Beside) the Law

Definition Under the rule of law, all individuals are subjects of law. They are, therefore, granted equal capacity of being holders of rights and of performing acts bearing legal consequences.[247] Law is applied as a unity to all individuals, not allowing for parallel systems of legality being applicable to different orders of individuals (*e.g.*, nobility *versus* peasantry, free men *versus* slaves, episcopates *versus* laymen, one race/religion/ethnicity *versus* another, colonizers *versus* colonized).

Challenges Posed by the System of Presidential Impeachment One objection that may posed against presidential impeachments is that they create a parallel system of legality that unduly privileges the person of the President (and other officials subjected to the same rules). As indicated throughout this book, many claims levelled against the President may only be sought judicially after the end of the mandate or after a successful impeachment. Such arrangement would raise the President to a different order within the legal system, above all other individuals.

Compromises and Justifications This objection, it must be noted, is not directed at the impeachment itself, but at the set of rules that usually accompany it. There is no logical impediment to having an ordinary system of legal accountability set up

[246] Zolo (2007), pp. 19–29.

[247] Zolo (2007), p. 23.

parallel to the system of impeachments. The choice, however, is usually made out of democratic and theoretical concerns. It is imagined that, if anyone may sue the President, he or she may be exposed to judicial persecution from opposing interests[248]—a concern that seems valid, given how often a President is likely to step on some toes, even in cases the policies sought by him or her are widely demanded by society. It is also imagined that unelected authorities such as judges and prosecutors lack the sort of broad democratic legitimacy necessary to challenge the presidency and, consequently, also lack the legitimacy to wield the power of single-handedly overturning the results of a popular election.[249] At any rate, such exploitable vulnerability would harm the autonomy and effectiveness of the Executive branch, as well as maximize the risk of hostile takeovers of the government by illegitimate groups, and of regime instability (both due to uncompromising competition among political forces and due to popular unrest caused by democratically illegitimate decisions). Moreover, one could argue that such arrangement does not abolish ordinary accountability, but, out of practical concerns, just delays it for after the President leaves office. It would be a necessary inconvenience and, thus, not constitute an aggression to the unity of law in an absolute sense.

Against the justifications for the compromises pointed above, one could point out that most of these expectations are entirely theoretical. It could well be the case that, if tested empirically, such enunciated fears would not materialize or would not generate the predicted outcomes. Many jurists have already suggested that the system of impeachments should not preclude or delay presidential accountability before ordinary justice.[250] Such accounts are particularly prominent in the US, where the political system seems to be strongly conducive to the failure of impeachments.[251] The empirical argument disproving the need of the compromises pointed out, however, still remains to be seem. Even with all recent constitutional innovations in Latin America, no constitutional Framers seem to have trusted themselves to abolish the immunities introduced alongside impeachments. Even the latest

---

[248] *E.g.*, in the justification for a 'special jurisdiction' for holding high officers accountable, the Colombian Constitutional Court stated: "(. . .) it is sought to avoid that, through the abuse of the right to access to jurisdiction, one may be able to illegitimately paralyze state activity (. . .)" (C-222-96).

[249] That is, presuming the hypothesis of a criminal conviction causing removal from office, for example.

[250] Finkelstein and Painter (2022).

[251] As is known, the US has a bipartisan system with alternating hegemony, in which parties tend to vote strictly within partisan lines. As a result, a President will predictably never be convicted within such a system, as the 2/3 threshold is effectively unreachable in such highly polarizing events such as impeachments. Impeachment, thus, offers only an illusion of potential accountability, creating effectively what could be called a violation to the unity of law. The situation can be quite different in Latin America, however, where (fragmented) multiparty systems and low party discipline are the rule.

Bolivian[252] and Honduran[253] Constitutions which abolish all forms of official immunities, still keep the exception for the impeachment system for Presidents.

4.7.2.2 Isonomy: All Are Equals Before the Law

Definition Under the rule of law, equivalent actions generate equivalent legal consequences.[254] This is not to be confused 'substantial equality', that is, the idea that all should share the same effective enjoyment of rights they formally have (*e.g.*, equalizing property possession among all citizens). Such would be a goal of policymakers and not an intrinsic goal of law itself. It means that, under same circumstances, law is applied in the same measure to all legal subjects, with no unreasonable discriminatory practices.

Challenges Posed by the System of Presidential Impeachment Isonomy may not be achieved, if impeachment really creates a separate legal subsystem for the President. It is to say, in other words, that legal consequences do not operate on the President the same way or in the same measure they would operate against other legal subjects. If the President, for example, commits a crime, he likely will not be subjected to a criminal procedure, unless a successful impeachment creates the opportunity for such. Such differentiation would be an unacceptable departure from the isonomy of law.

Compromises and Justifications The difference in legal consequences relative to the President is arguably very reasonable. As mentioned before, there is a drastic difference between the actual impact caused on the whole political system by the act of, for example, arresting the President and that of arresting an ordinary citizen. The former may mean a change in government, a shift in the balance of power between political actors, the cancellation of the results of a popular election, the creation of societal unrest and of regime instability, and so on. All these consequences may largely outweigh the harmfulness of a criminal act committed by the President and, thus, 'making justice' could just cause even more injustice through indirect means. There is a degree of responsibility which is particular to decisions that affect the presidency and that, therefore, should be reflected in the legal system, by treating different circumstances in different ways. Isonomy does not mean absolute equality or the blindly indiscriminate application of law. If ordinary legal subjects had the same degree of democratic legitimation or the same kind of direct impact on society and government, then maybe their accountability would also require the interference of the Parliament and the consideration of aspects of political opportunity. But as

[252] Art. 112, 152, 161 and 184, 4 of the 2009 Constitution.

[253] Art. 205, 15 stablished immunities and was revoked in October 2003. Impeachment was introduced in 2013.

[254] Zolo (2007), p. 23.

that is not the case, the distinct treatment between President and other legal subjects is justifiable and necessary.

4.7.2.3 Certainty: Law Is Knowable and Intelligible

Definition Under the rule of law, legal subjects (can) know and understand the law enough to inform their actions before they perform them.[255] This means, for example, that any individual may have access to the word of law, that the text is reasonably understandable, and that its consequences are predictable without excessive extraneous effort. Naturally, part of this presupposes that the content of law already exists before the legal subjects perform their acts, as it is unreasonable to expect from anyone to have precise foresight of legislative or judicative practices. Such aspect may also be called the principle of anteriority and has its own set of consequences in the different fields of law (*e.g.*, *nullum crimen sine lege* of criminal law).

Challenges Posed by the System of Presidential Impeachment Impeachments challenge this aspect of rule of law in two ways. First, (i.) impeachable offenses can be arguably too broad in their definitions, not serving as effective guides to behaviour, nor allowing for an informed defence, in case they are used in accusation. It would be unreasonable to expect that Presidents should avoid violating laws (or defend themselves from the said violations) which they cannot know the limits until the Court of Impeachments tells them what they are. Second, (ii.) much of impeachment legislation (mostly of procedural nature) is not known until a legislative resolution that defines it is introduced in the initial phases of impeachment. This may generate multiple problems, such as making a defence more difficult to plan (risk to individual basic rights), giving distinct treatment among multiple Presidents (risk to isonomy), or even turning the procedure prone to manipulation (risk of arbitrariness).

Compromises and Justifications The (i.) relative sense of uncertainty caused by the broad definitions of impeachable offenses is something with which the legal community must come to terms. Impeachable offenses are, as in Alexander Hamilton's words, incapable of being 'tied down by such strict rules', either in their positive delineation or in constructive effort by judges.[256] That is due to the unpredictable nature of the abuses of power impeachment seeks to inhibit, as well as from the extraordinary and sporadic nature of the impeachment system, which is not subjected to the same *habitus* and *ethos* which gives lawyers a sense of certainty of law they sense in the ordinary legal system.[257] What guarantees that impeachable

[255] Zolo (2007), p. 24.

[256] Hamilton et al. (2001), p. 339.

[257] Bourdieu (1987). Alternatively, see also Chap. 2 of this book, item on specific problems of legal interpretation, for a detailed explanation of what is meant by *habitus* and *ethos* in this context.

offenses are not applied in arbitrary ways is the larger threshold required for conviction (2/3 or 3/4) and the fact that a large organ of democratic representation is involved in the decision making process. A sense of societal consensus should be implied by the combination of both characteristics, and an arbitrary decision should consequently not be derived from such procedure. In other words, this is perhaps truly an exception to the certainty of the rule of law, but one that is made up for through other safeguards particular to impeachment procedures.

The (ii.) relative improvisational nature of impeachment legislation, on the other hand, is decidedly more problematic. Such rules are not subjected to the same thresholds or democratic processes that reduce potential arbitrariness, and thus are more vulnerable to being moulded *ad hoc* in favour or disfavour of a particular President. Ideally, such gaps for discretion should be closed or underlie tighter oversight, which is a direction that has become more common in the past decades.[258] As seen in a few case studies, oversight committees (*e.g.*, *Comisión Ciudadana de Seguimiento* in Colombia) have been created and Supreme/Constitutional courts have interfered to ensure fair and consistent creation and enforcement of such improvised norms. Nonetheless, there are a few systems in which Courts cannot review interlocutory decisions of the Parliament (*e.g.*, Paraguay) and in which no alternative safeguard is offered. In such circumstances, a violation of the rule of law in the sense argued may well take place.

4.7.2.4 Individual Basic Rights: Law Enforces Substantive Protections

Definition Under the rule of law, legal subjects are given basic rights, which may be claimed judicially, even against the state.[259] It is not sufficient that law exists, is knowable and faithfully applicable to everyone equally, if it does not also guarantee substantive safeguards against arbitrariness.[260] If a law's content is intrinsically arbitrary, there is no rule of application that will devoid it from manifesting its arbitrariness. As such, the safeguards are needed to secure that such laws, if they are to be enforced at all, are enforced in consonance with a basic level of existential or civilizational freedoms. Such minimum is typically embodied in rights such as the right to *habeas corpus*, right to due process, freedom of speech and thought, inviolability of personal communication and so on.

Challenges Posed by the System of Presidential Impeachment While impeachments create an extraordinary procedure to hold the President accountable, they also extinguish or limit access to resources present in ordinary procedures. One may

[258] A few countries created or reformed their own impeachment legislation to make it decidedly more definite (*e.g.*, Bolivia, Colombia, Chile, Ecuador, Peru, and Honduras).

[259] Zolo (2007), p. 25.

[260] The classic examples would be that of laws instituting slavery, apartheid, and concentration camps.

argue, therefore, that the system of impeachments removes too many individual rights from the President, such as the right to appeal from unjust decisions, the right to a full defence, the right to an impartial judge, and so on. As a result, the President may be left unreasonably vulnerable to the arbitrariness of the Court of Impeachments.

Compromises and Justifications The impeachment really is a procedure that cannot generate the same kinds of conditions for defence existent in the ordinary legal system. The access to an impartial judge is something that can only be fictively offered, as certainly any member of a country has to some degree an opinion about the conduct of the President. The right of appeal cannot be reproduced, as there is no organ hierarchically above the Court of Impeachments. The compromise offered to such practical limitations, however, is that the scope of accountability in impeachments is limited to the sphere of politics. Further safeguards are, again, the involvement of the Parliament in the process of decision-making and the high thresholds for conviction, which should ensure decisions to be rational and representative of a wide social consensus and, consequently, not an expression of arbitrariness. Inspired by Tocqueville, one could argue that the President may nonetheless be victimized by the 'tyranny of the (super)majority', but that is a trade-off that must be assumed. History tends to show that it is better to risk the tyranny of the Legislature than that of the Executive, in virtue of the tendency of the former of producing more moderate outcomes, due to its mixed and representative composition, as well as its deliberative procedures. Shifting the balance of power in impeachments in favour of the presidency is arguably the more dangerous choice.

4.7.3 *Rule of Law as Differentiation of Power*

As a principle of "differentiation of power", the rule of law may generate the following sub-principles: (i.) Law serves as a delimitation of political power; (ii.) Law stablishes a clear-cut division between administrative and legislative functions; (iii.) Law embodies the supremacy of legislative act above administrative acts; (iv.) Law is created respecting existing individual rights; (v.) Law is applied by an organ with judicial autonomy. Apart from item (iv.) which is not relevant to the scope of this book, the other sub-principles are applicable to impeachments as will be described next.

4.7.3.1 Law as Delimitation of Political Power

Definition Under the rule of law, the law stablishes the scope of legitimate political power, thus conceding it with a degree of objectivity and reducing *undue* interference from other social subsystems (ethics, religion, economics).[261] The rule of law, therefore, should stablish a clear line between what are public and private matters, between legally relevant and legally irrelevant facts. This is not to say that ethics, religion, economics and so on offer no rationality to law—such a claim would be absurd. It means, however, that they must be incorporated into law before they may generate legal effects, otherwise they are likely to be arbitrarily and unevenly enforced by authorities.

Challenges Posed by the System of Presidential Impeachment There are a few ways impeachments may violate this aspect of the rule of law. As discussed in this book, the matters of "political opportunity" are invariably discussed in impeachment procedures. There are, however, no legal standards for what constitutes an opportune impeachment.[262] There are no lists of legally relevant criteria from which the "political opportunity" of an impeachment may be subsumed. The judges of impeachment are left with near total freedom to say that an impeachment is merited, common place being claims that the impeachment will bring an improvement in economic conditions, the end of a constitutional crisis, the moralization of the public machinery and so on. Even less noble (and arguably even less legally pertinent) interests are also often externalized, such as those who claim an impeachment to be merited merely out of partisan or ideological differences, personal animosity, or clientelistic relations. As such, a case can be made against impeachments in the sense that they open too much space for undue influence of social subsystems that have no legal legitimation in deciding the fate of a President.

Compromises and Justifications Unlike ordinary courts, the decisions of the Courts of Impeachment need to find a balance between justice and democratic legitimacy. The decisions of the Court of Impeachment produce consequences that extend vastly beyond the confines of the procedure itself, potentially producing outcomes that are in of themselves more harmful than the impeachable offenses which they purport to scrutinize. As such, it would be unreasonable or even detrimental to require the Court of Impeachments to expurgate the elements of political opportunity, as they can be as materially relevant, if not more, to the impeachment than the presidential offense itself. The vulnerability to the rule of law that such special discretion creates is unavoidable, but, like in the other points of contention, is something that is reduced by requiring the participation of a numerous organ of representation and the high thresholds for conviction.

The infiltration of impertinent subsystems into law can potentially be reduced by legally entrenching those fractions of such subsystems which can be considered legitimate aspects of political opportunity—such is a path already being explored by the Ecuadorian Constitution of 2008, when it requires that the Constitutional Court needs to attest to the existence of a constitutional crisis for the mechanism of mutual

[261] Zolo (2007), pp. 27–28.

[262] See the final Chapter, however, for a suggested framework, as well as a list of empirical indicators that may be (and often are) used to inform the judgment of political opportunity.

dissolution to be invoked.[263] If the law in similar ways, for example, posits that concerns with the preservation of democracy, of the public's trust in institutions, of the material well-being of the Nation, etc. are necessary elements of an impeachment, then perhaps the legal community would consider the element of political opportunity more reasonable and less of a liability to the rule of law, as then at least a basic framework/standard for debate will be made clear. Whether such entrenchment would ultimately impact the impeachment procedures meaningfully, however, remains to be tested.

Regarding the challenge posed by conduct such as bribery, intimidation, pork-barrelling, and other unsavoury practices related to the influencing of impeachment adjudicators, there is no real panacea that can be offered, as such are problems that may exist even in ordinary courts of law. The main safeguards offered in impeachments against these practices are: (i.) public accountability of adjudicators, and (ii.) large adjudicating organs. Public accountability is created with broad transparency of all parts of the procedures, including things such as open (nominal) votes, public hearings in investigative commissions, and tight media scrutiny of the procedural practices, ensuring that the adjudicators keep their behaviour at tuned to the general interest. Regarding the second element, it is theorized that the larger the adjudicating organ is, the less likely such practices are to be effective and the more likely it is that the corrupted or intimidated opinions are ideally to be washed out by an overwhelming rest of genuine votes.[264] The question of whether the legitimacy of the procedures are to be questioned is one that will depend on the perceived level of pervasiveness of such practices, as realistically it is impossible to make large bodies as these entirely impervious to undue influence. If the theoretical expectations are correct, however, then the number of corrupted adjudicators should be nonetheless insufficient to undermine the procedure as whole.

4.7.3.2 Law Separating Legislative and Administrative Functions

Definition Under the rule of law there is a tangible separation between the activity of enacting general and abstract norms (laws) and the activity of issuing specific and concrete norms (executive acts and judgements).[265] As mentioned in Chap. 2, there is a certain subtlety in separating between the former and the latter, as they certainly exist within a spectrum of discretion conceded to authorities in defining 'normative meaning'. Nonetheless, most of the time there are some qualitative differences that can be noted, allowing power to be successfully and uncontrovertibly separated into

[263] Art. 130.

[264] Hamilton et al. (2001), pp. 339, 346–347. There are a few other practices mentioned in the case studies, such as getting courts to exclude compromised adjudicators from the procedure.

[265] Zolo (2007), p. 28.

functions and, thus, guarantee that it does not become dangerously concentrated into one single branch.[266]

Challenges Posed by the System of Presidential Impeachment A criticism that may be levelled at impeachment is at the amount of discretion conceded onto the Court of Impeachments by the description of impeachable offenses. One could argue, for example, that a certain impeachable offense is so broadly defined that applying it amounts to legislating on the theme it suggests. The separation between adjudication and law-making would be a nominal one, meaning that the Court of Impeachments would be dangerously amalgamating functions of two branches of power into one whenever it decides the merit of impeachment. Such concentration of power would be dangerous and, thus, a violation of the rule of law.

Another criticism may be directed exclusively at trial-less impeachments or those impeachments with such flawed implementation, that no effective trial phase takes place (*e.g.*, the Lugo impeachment). In such cases, the act of convicting the President may dangerously resemble the act of passing a bill. One could make the case that such an act, despite the name, is more akin to a bill of attainder than to an impeachment, which is perhaps one of the most notorious violators of the rule of law in historical perspective. Such constellation of impeachments would make the adjudicative and legislative acts nearly, if not entirely phenomenologically indistinguishable.

Compromises and Justifications Regarding the first challenge, one may argue that the exception created by the system of impeachments to be too constrained to a specific circumstance to effectively undermine the separation between administrative, legislative, and judicative functions. The fact that the Parliament may be performing a legislative function on a circumstance where it should be exclusively performing a judicative function is not pervasive enough to undermine the general character of such separation of functions. To be sure, it is important to notice that the separation of powers is a meaningful constitutional ideal, but it is also one that often entails exceptions in its practices. For such reason, many theorists rather use the term 'checks and balances' *in lieu* of 'separation of power (or of functions)', as it is a more accurate, albeit less didactical, expression for addressing this sort of interlocking mechanism that mitigates concentration of power.[267] At any rate, one may bypass these considerations altogether, and argue that solving such adjudicative indeterminacy in practice does not actually amount to the act of legislating and, therefore, there is no real confusion of functions at play. Such indeterminacy is a feature commonly found in other fields of law in terminology such as 'reasonable', 'appropriate', 'proportional', etc., which nonetheless are entirely compatible with the rule

[266] As famously argued by Montesquieu, The Spirit of Laws (1777), 11.6. The division of functions, moreover, allows for specialization and increased efficiency. Increased efficiency, on its turn, likely positively impacts the legitimacy of power. Weber (1978), p. 959.

[267] Finer et al. (1995), p. 57.

of law.[268] It is, moreover, necessary for such indeterminacy to exist in a list of presidential abuses of power, given the difficulty in predicting and squarely defining all potential offenses at such level of government.[269]

Regarding the second contention, it must be noted that trial-less impeachments are the strongest breach in impeachment tradition. Like the original presidential impeachment, they serve as a national inquest into presidential misbehaviour, but are divorced from its legalistic ambitions in doing so. As such, it is questionable whether trial-less impeachments should be measured by the same standards, as they are decidedly and assumedly a more politically inclined adaptation of the impeachment. In that context, it seems justifiable that the rule of law is applicable to lower standards. Such consideration naturally does not extend itself to flawed implementations of the traditional impeachment, as these are still committed to the original legalistic ambitions and, so, must honour the higher standards of the rule of law implied by such.[270] The comparison to the bill of attainder is unwarranted, however, as the consequences of the trial-less impeachment are strictly bound to the political sphere, and the procedure still possesses some crucial differences implied by the work of the impeachment commission and the subsumption of articles of impeachment, albeit in more superficial nature than would be the case with the traditional form of impeachment.

4.7.3.3 Law as a Legislative Act Has Primacy Over Administrative Acts

Definition Under the rule of law, legislative acts (general norms) have primacy over administrative acts (executive acts and judgments). It is to say that it is not enough that both functions distinguish themselves in practice, but it is also necessary that administrative functions subordinate themselves to the legislative ones, otherwise the legislative function will not create effective restraints on administration.[271]

Challenges Posed by the System of Presidential Impeachment The challenges posed by this feature are the same as those posed by the feature above, but framed on a slightly different perspective, at least in relation to the discussion proposed by this book. Confusing legislative, administrative and adjudicative acts may also lead to the consequence of abolishing the primacy of legislative acts above the rest. Equally,

[268] See Lanius (2019), p. 169 ff. for a comprehensive list of explanations to the need or unavoidability of indeterminacy.

[269] For more details on this argument, see the section on the objective element of impeachable offenses.

[270] A similar sentiment is expressed by the Argentinian Supreme Court (316:2940) when it stated: "The National Constitution has given the impeachment a nature that does not necessarily have to hold itself strictly in line with the forms that stablish the procedure or the decision of controversies before the Judicial Power. It needs, however, to equally comply with the basic requisites that make the essence and validity of every trial (. . .)".

[271] Zolo (2007), p. 28.

too much discretion allowed by rules of impeachment could have the effect of transferring the primacy of legislation over to the organ of adjudication. To avoid repetition, this item will not be further developed.

4.7.3.4 Law Requires Judicial Autonomy

Definition Under the rule of law, all judges are only subject to the law. Their decisions must genuinely reflect their understanding about a matter of law, without distortion coming from hierarchical relations, intimidation, or any other legally impertinent interests.[272]

Challenges Posed by the System of Presidential Impeachment The infiltration (and domination) of legally impertinent influence in impeachment procedures may arguably spoil all legal rationality behind an impeachment decision. Presidents may use their influence to corrupt or intimidate the adjudicators, parties may impose disciplinary punishment on party members who deviate from partisan lines, societal and military forces may pressure or encourage adjudicators to vote in ways that are not consonant with the legal merits of the case. At any rate, if the law is not its guiding factor, an impeachment may arguably boil down to a pure expression of arbitrariness and fatally violate the rule of law. If the adjudicators are members of the Parliament, moreover, they will all have some degree of alignment and proximity to the presidency that arguably undermines their neutrality and impartiality as adjudicators. The same may be said to some degree in relation to the members of the Highest Court, as Presidents (or their parties) are often involved in the selection of its members. Some degree of selection bias could be expected in the adjudicators, if not outright partisan fidelity.

Compromises and Justifications Making an organ of adjudication that is entirely autonomous from the *de facto* or *de jure* influence of the President or other powerful actors is a major difficulty. The best that may be offered to mitigate the problems above is the creation of a system of impeachments that is thoroughly transparent, and which is conducted by an organ that is relatively difficult to bribe, manipulate, intimidate, or awe. Such conditions are best created by the Parliament, despite all its potential flaws. The alternative to such arguably unsatisfactory arrangement would be to have an unaccountable presidency or the conduction of the procedure by other even more flawed (or weakly legitimized) institutions. Neither solution offers a more adequate accommodation of the rule of law, not being, therefore, reasonable alternatives. There are some additional safeguards that may be created (*e.g.*, verification of legal soundness of impeachment charges by a technical organ), but none is able to entirely expurgate the problem of interfering powers in the procedures.

[272] Zolo (2007), p. 29.

References

Acuña LMJ (2012) El juicio político como mecanismo de control constitucional. Revista Paraguay desde la Ciencias Sociales 1:1–24

Ambos K (2005) Joint criminal enterprise and command responsibility. J Int Crim Just 5(1): 159–183

Bahia A, Oliveira MAC, Vecchiati R (2017) Supremo Tribunal Federal deve barrar ou nulificar impeachment sem crime de responsabilidade. Empório do Direito

Balbuena Pérez D (2013) El juicio político en la Constitución Paraguaya y la destitución del presidente Fernando Lugo. Revista de Derecho Político 87:355–398

Beccaria C, Bellamy R (1995) On crimes and punishments and other writings. Cambridge University Press, Cambridge

Berger R (1974) Impeachment: the constitutional problems, 2nd edn. Harvard University Press

Bernstein RB (1990) John Adam's thoughts on Government, 1776. In: Schechter SL, Bernstein RB, Lutz DS (eds) Roots of the Republic: American founding documents interpreted. Madison House, Madison, pp 118–137

Black CL, Bobbitt P (2018) Impeachment: a handbook. Yale University Press, New Haven

Bourdieu P (1987) The force of law: toward a sociology of the juridical field. Hast Law J 38:814

Brossard de Souza Pinto P (1965) O impeachment: Aspectos da responsabilidade política do Presidente da República. Saraiva, Sao Paulo

Camargo ML, Vieira JR (2019) O impeachment e o seu desenho constitucional conflitivo. Direito Público 16

Congressional Research Service (1998) Congressional resolutions on presidential impeachment: a historical overview. The Library of Congress

Congressional Research Service (2019) The Impeachment Process in the House of Representatives. R45769

Dubber M (2006) Rechtsgut and Harm Principle. Am J Comp Law 53:679

Eberhardt ML (2017) La revocatoria presidencial en América Latina: Ventajas y limitaciones. Los casos de Venezuela, Bolivia y Ecuador. Colombia Internacional 92:105–133

Eguiguren F (2007) La responsabilidad del presidente: Razones para una reforma constitucional. Pontificia Universidad Católica del Perú, Lima, Perú

Eguiguren Praeli FJ (2008) Antejuicio y Juicio Político en el Perú. Pensamiento Constituticional 13(13):111–162

Elliot J (1836a) The Debates in the Several State Conventions on the Adoption of the Federal Constitution as Recommend by the General Convention at Philadelphia: Volume 1, 2nd edn. Washington

Elliot J (1836b) The Debates in the Several State Conventions on the Adoption of the Federal Constitution as Recommend by the General Convention at Philadelphia: Volume 2, 2nd edn. Washington

Elliot J (1836c) The Debates in the Several State Conventions on the Adoption of the Federal Constitution as Recommend by the General Convention at Philadelphia: Volume 4, 2nd edn. Washington

Farrand M (1911a) The Records of the Federal Convention of 1787: July 14 to September 17, 1787. Yale University Press, New Haven

Farrand M (1911b) The Records of the Federal Convention of 1787: May 14 to July 13, 1787. Yale University Press, New Haven

Feoli Villalobos M (2010) De la justicia constitucional o las justicias constitucionales: La contribución de América Latina (los casos de Colombia y Costa Rica). XIV Encuentro de Latinoamericanistas:2094–2112

Finer SE, Bogdanor V, Rudden B (1995) Comparing constitutions. Clarendon, Oxford

Finkelstein C, Painter R (2022) Presidential accountability and the rule of law: can the president claim immunity if he shoots someone on fifth avenue? Univ Pennsylvania J Const Law 24(1): 93–210

Fletcher G (2004) Ambivalence about treason. North Carolina Law Rev 82:1611–1628

Ford R (1926) Imprisonment for debt. Mich Law Rev 25(1):24

Foucault M (2012) Discipline and punish: the birth of the prison. Random House US, New York

Ganghof S (2018) A new political system model: semi-parliamentary government. Eur J Polit Res 57(2):261–281

García Chávarri MA (2008) Acusación constitucional, juicio político y antejuicio: Desarrollo teórico y tratamiento jurisprudencial. Pontificia Universidad Católica del Perú, Departamento Académico de Derecho, Lima

Gelli MA (2004) Constitución de la Nación Argentina: Comentada y concordada, 2. ed., ampliada y actualizada. La Ley, Buenos Aires

Gerhardt MJ (2019) The federal impeachment process: a constitutional and historical analysis, 3rd edn. The University of Chicago Press, Chicago

Ginsburg T, Huq AZ, Landau D (2021) The comparative constitutional law of presidential impeachment. Univ Chicago Law Rev 88(1):81–164

Hamilton A, Jay J, Madison J, Carey GW, McClellan J (2001) The federalist: a collection. Liberty Fund, Indianapolis, Indiana

Hidalgo E (2005) Juicio Político: Glossary of the Argentine Chamber of Deputies. https://www.hcdn.gob.ar/secparl/dgral_info_parlamentaria/dip/glosario/J/juicio_politico.html

Hirschl R (2007) Towards juristocracy: the origins and consequences of the new constitutionalism, First Harvard University Press Paperback edn. Harvard University Press, Cambridge

Hobbes T (2014) Leviathan. Touchstone, New York

Hobbes T, Warrender H (1983) De cive: The English version entitled in the first edition philosophical rudiments concerning government and society. Clarendon, Oxford

Hoffer PC, Hull N (1984) Impeachment in America, 1635-1805. Yale University Press, New Haven

Honderich T (2006) Punishment: the supposed justifications revisited, Rev edn. Pluto Press, London

Husserl E, Hardy L (1999) The idea of phenomenology. Kluwer Academic Publishers; Kluwer Academic, Dordrecht

Jardim AS (2016) O significado técnico da expressão "julgamento jurídico e político do impeachment" do presidente da república."

Jareborg N (2004) Criminalization as Last Resort (Ultima Ratio). Ohio State J Crim Law 2:521–534

Jellinek W (1929) Verwaltungsrecht. Springer, Berlin

Kada N (2002) The politics of impeachment. Dissertation. San Diego

Kieschnick H (2018) A cruel and unusual way to regulate the homeless: extending the status crimes doctrine to anti-homeless ordinances. Stanf Law Rev 70:1569–1621

Labovitz JR (1978) Presidential impeachment. Yale University Press, New Haven

Lanius D (2019) Strategic indeterminacy in the law. Oxford University Press, New York

Leek JH (1951) Treason and the constitution. J Polit 13(4):604–622

Lento T, Hazan RY (2022) The vote of no confidence: towards a framework for analysis. West Eur Polit 45(3):502–527

Linz J (1990) The perils of presidentialism. J Democr 1(1):51–69

Llanos M, Nolte D, Tibi Weber C (2012) Paraguay: Staatsstreich oder "Misstrauensvotum"? GIGA Focus Lateinamerika, no. 8

Lobo E (2017) O (des)controle judicial do impeachment. Universitas Jus 27(3):7–16

Londoño Ulloa JE (2020) Los juicios politicos en América Latina: El caso colombiano. Teoria & Derecho 25:33–50

Lozano Villegas G (2009) Control político y responsabilidad política en Colombia. Revista Derecho del Estado 22:231–244

Maitland FW, Pollock F (2010) The history of English law before the time of Edward I: Volume 2. Liberty Fund

Martínez Robledos M (2008) El juicio político en México. Eorrúa, México

Mukherjee M (2005) Justice, War, and the Imperium: India and Britain in Edmund Burke's prosecutorial speeches in the impeachment trial of warren hastings. Law Hist Rev 23(3): 589–630

Nieves Ruiz PdP (2017) Precisiones conceptuales entre antejuicio politico, juicio politico y acusacion constitucional en la responsabilidad de los altos funcionarios del Estado

North DC (1990) Institutions, institutional change and economic performance. Cambridge University Press, Cambridge

Orozco-Henriquez J, Ayoub A, Ellis A, Aman A (2010) Electoral justice: the international IDEA handbook. International IDEA, Stockholm

Pacheco Pinos AI 2019. La institución del Juicio Político en la Constitución de la República del 2008: Análisis de caso. Dissertation. Cuenca, Ecuador

Paeffgen H-U (2013) Das "Rechtsgut": ein obsoleter Begriff? In: Zöller MA, Wolter J (eds) Gesamte Strafrechtswissenschaft in internationaler Dimension: Festschrift für Jürgen Wolter zum 70. Geburtstag am 7. September 2013. Duncker & Humblot, Berlin, pp 125–165

Patterson E (2008) Civil contempt and the indigent child support obligor: the silent return of Debtor's prison. Cornell J Law Public Policy 18(1):95–141

Pérez Tremps P (2003) La justicia constitucional en la actualidad. Especial referencia a América Latina. Revista del Foro Constitucional Iberoamericano 2:66–81

Pérez-Liñán A (2007) Presidential impeachment and the new political instability in Latin America. Cambridge University Press, Leiden

Perkins R (1939) Rationale of Mens Rea. Harv Law Rev 52:905–928

Perkins W (2003) The political nature of presidential impeachment in the United States. In: Baumgartner JC, Kada N (eds) Checking executive power: presidential impeachment in comparative perspective. Praeger, Westport, pp 21–44

Pierson C (2011) The modern state, 3rd edn. Routledge, London

Praino D (2017) A new system of government? Defining the confidence relationship of the EU model. J Eur Integr 39(3):319–332

Roberts C (1966) The growth of responsible government in Stuart England. Cambridge University Press, Cambridge

Roberts C (1975) The law of impeachment in Stuart England: a reply to Raoul Berger. Yale Law J 84(7):1419–1439

Rogers JR, Vanberg G (2002) Judicial advisory opinions and legislative outcomes in comparative perspective. Am J Polit Sci 46(2):379

Roldán O (2013) El juicio político en la Constitución peruana. Pensamiento Constituticional 18: 121–143

Roldán O (2017) La responsabilidad jurídica del presidente de la República en el Perú. Pensamiento Constituticional 22:9–20

Roxin C (2003) Strafrecht Allgemeiner Teil: Besondere Erscheinungsformen der Staftat. Beck, München

Roxin C (2006) Strafrecht Allgemeiner Teil: Grundlagen. Der Aufbau der Verbrechenslehre, 4. vollständig neu bearbeitete Auflage. Beck, Munchen

Roxin C (2022) Täterschaft und Tatherrschaft, 11th edn. De Gruyter, Boston

Rusche G, Kirchheimer O, Melossi D (2003) Punishment and social structure. Transaction Publishers, New Brunswick, NJ

Sabsay DA (2004) El Juicio Político a la Corte Suprema en la República Argentina. Anuario Iberoamericano de Justicia Constitucional 8:493–519

Sajó A, Uitz R (2019) The constitution of freedom: an introduction to legal constitutionalism. Oxford University Press, Oxford

Samuels D, Shugart MS (2010) Presidents, parties, and prime ministers: how the separation of powers affects party organization and behavior. Cambridge University Press, Cambridge

Shugart MS, Carey JM (1992) Presidents and assemblies: constitutional design and electoral dynamics. Cambridge Univ. Press, Cambridge

Stewart J (2016) The strangely familiar history of the unitary theory of perpetration. In: Ackerman B, Ambos K, Sikiri H (eds) Visions of Justice: Liber Amicorum Mirjan Damaška. Duncker und Humblot Verlag, Berlin

Stokes SC (2001) Mandates and democracy: neoliberalism by surprise in Latin America. Cambridge University Press

Sunstein CR (2017) Impeachment: a citizen's guide. Harvard University Press, Cambridge

Tilly C (1985) War making and state making as organized crime. In: Evans PB, Rueschemeyer D, Skocpol T (eds) Bringing the state back in. Cambridge University Press, Cambridge, pp 169–191

Tite C (1974) Impeachment and parliamentary judicature in early Stuart England. Athlone Press, London

Tocqueville A, Mansfield HC, Winthrop D (2002) Democracy in America. University of Chicago Press, Chicago

US Senate (1868) Congressional Globe, 40th Congress, 2nd Session, Trial of Andrew Johnson. Congressional records

València i Montes LX (2015) El juicio político por mal desempeño de funciones como moción de censura: La destitución de Lugo. XI Jornadas de Sociología

van Tassel E, Finkelman P (1999) Impeachable offenses: a documentary history from 1787 to the present. Congressional Quarterly, Washington

Wasserstrom R (1959) Strict liability in the criminal law. Stanford Law Rev 12:731–745

Weber M (1978) Economy and society, [Nachdr.]. California University of California Press, Berkeley

Welp Y, Milanese JP (2018) Playing by the rules of the game: Partisan use of recall referendums in Colombia. Democratization 25(8):1379–1396

Wood GS (2006) Revolutionary characters: what made the founders different. Penguin Press, New York

Zaffaroni ER, Risso G (2008) Inhabilitación y juicio político en Argentina. In: Eduardo Ferrer Mac-Gregor, and Arturo Zaldívar Lelo de Larrea (eds) La ciencia del derecho procesal constitucional: Estudios en homenaje a Héctor Fix-Zamudio en sus cincuenta años como investigador del derecho. Universidad Nacional Autónoma de México; Instituto Mexicano de Derecho Procesal Constitucional; Marcial Pons, México, pp 717–729

Zolo D (2007) The rule of law: a critical reappraisal. In: Costa P, Zolo D, Santoro E (eds) The rule of law: history, theory and criticism. Springer, Dordrecht, pp 3–72

Chapter 5
Conclusion

5.1 Legal and Political Accountability: A Meaningful Distinction?

In many places throughout this book, it has been claimed that law and politics are indissociable and complementary to each other. That may be because law is no more than a delegation of power onto a legitimated authority, thus transferring some degree of discretion over the respective political realm and necessarily making the said authority an actor of politics. The actor may be unaware of his political role or of the political commitments that underpin his activity or may even consider the role itself to be too inconsequential to be politically relevant, but that does not change the fact that he has power to make decisions and consequently also power to shape his political community in accordance his choices. Taking this understanding to its last consequences, one should conclude that every time law is applied, so is political power being enforced; every time someone is held accountable to the law, so is he being held politically accountable.

Policemen, for example, have some degree of discretion on how to enforce laws. Whenever they consider intervening on a legal violation, they will go through many legal calculations regarding the interpretation of the facts before them, the harm caused by the observed violation, the opportunity costs and risks generated by the intervention, and so on. All these considerations are informed by legal principles: is the violation serious enough to warrant intervention (principle of insignificance, and harm principle)? Is an intervention capable of addressing the observed violation (reserve of the possible)? Do the consequences of intervention justify it (principle of proportionality)? There will be, therefore, policemen who will, for example, seek exemplar punishment of every drug-policy violation they lay eyes on – from the drug lord to the recreational and medicinal user-, regardless of what such hard-line stance may mean to their political community in terms of human, monetary, and opportunity costs. They may justify such stances by claiming "the law is the law" and that it ought to be enforced regardless of circumstances, or that drugs do indeed pose such a

G. Palamone, *Presidential Impeachment in Latin America*,
https://doi.org/10.1007/978-3-031-44188-2_5

harm that is never socially insignificant and thus ought to be confronted in every opportunity. Different policemen may choose to only go after those drug crimes which truly impact their community, cutting some slack on the small-scale occasional user or dealer of desperate circumstances. To them, the latter cases would be too insignificant and harmless to justify the stigmatizing consequences the undiscerning criminalization may have on the community.

Both stances mentioned can coexist within a single legal system/community and may have clear political underpinnings. Such discretion is something that is afforded by the law: both are justifiable by interpretations of the principle of proportionality, which, however, are informed by the political beliefs of the involved actors. The only thing capable of shielding each of these groups from accusations of "usurping the law for furthering their political agenda" is the skill of their actors in convincingly framing them as legitimate interpretations of the law. That will require, of course, some grasp on legal principles, as well as some rhetoric and hermeneutic capabilities in the interpretation of the law's many broad concepts such as "reasonable", "significant", "appropriate", and so on.

Such discretion is what makes the law just, it is what makes it go from written abstract ideals into rules that fit real-world cases and are capable of pacifying disputes between individuals in a community. Justice, therefore, is a political activity, even though law may try to limit the discretion involved in its achievement by contriving elaborate formulas for social conduct.

To part of the readers of this book, this will be enough of an answer: The type of accountability sought by impeachments is both legal and political, as it is the case in any other kind of legal relations. Not only that, the complementary nature of law and politics is even more evident and undeniable in impeachments, given their grounding in constitutional law. As constitutional rules tend to be remarkably open-ended, the discretion given to the judges of impeachment is immense. The way such discretion is exerted in impeachments, moreover, is much more disagreeable and controverse then elsewhere in law, given how evident the political underpinnings of any such decision are. Sizeable social groups will predictably take issue with the impeachment decision, regardless of the supposed soundness and eloquence of the legal arguments that justify it. Modern claims accusing impeachment of being purely political are thus explained such by aspects of decision-making, though they should be ultimately dismissed as subjective, arguably unreflected disagreements in judgement.

Other readers will not be satisfied by such an answer, however. One may claim that it does not provide meaningful insights and, in fact, misunderstands that very question it seeks to address. The contention political scientists, jurists, journalists, and citizens in general typically pose against impeachments is not that their judges have discretion within legal limits, but that in the past few decades they have been exceeding such limits. The issue is that the supposed "legal" accountability is being enforced with such ample discretion that it has become literally undistinguishable from expressions of pure arbitrariness—a degree of arbitrariness thought to belong only to politicians and not judges. The "political" being questioned does not pertain to the expression of general plurality of interests and ideologies within the polity, but only to the specific and cynical self-interests of political parties.

It is difficult to give an objective answer to this other perspective. One must either subscribe to an understanding of law where certain spheres of legality are by definition "apolitical" (*e.g.*, jus-naturalism, where certain laws are discovered by investigating "human nature", the word of God, etc., thus preceding the state and politics itself), which thus allow for clear separation between law and politics, or one must make many compromises to make the separation workable under specific circumstances. As this book rejects the former as a possibility, the latter is the option that will be explored next.

5.2 Legal and Political Accountability: The Workable Distinctions

One of the strategies used in this book to separate the legal sphere of accountability from that of the political consisted in attributing the most basic spheres of legality to the former. If impeachment predominantly displayed characteristics that associated it with the criminal, administrative, or civil spheres of accountability, then it would be a matter of legal accountability. If impeachment, on the other hand, displayed characteristics predominantly associated with open-ended formulas/broadly defined legal matters (*e.g.*, constitutional principles, such as democracy, republic, or separation of powers) or legally undefined matters (*e.g.*, policy preferences, partisan relations, popular outrage, etc.), then it would be attributed to the political realm of accountability.

That seems to be the strategy implied by many political science manuals when they establish the difference between parliamentarism and presidentialism. One of the key differences argued tends to be that the chief of government in a parliamentary government is politically accountable to the Parliament, whereas his counterpart in a presidential government may only be held accountable by the Parliament for legal or criminal transgressions. The distinction, therefore, presupposes a gap between legal and political spheres to the extent that they may meaningfully contrast to one another.

By doing so, this study may hopefully give a minimally objective and palatable answer to those who see law and politics as separable entities. As mentioned in the introduction, however, there is no single answer to this question that can fit all perspectives the readers may have (*e.g.*, what function the impeachment was designed to serve? What did its historical implementation achieve? Did these results repeat in recent cases as well? How did its actors perceive it? What factors may make one function predominate over the other?)

5.3 The Historical Role of Impeachment

When the historian Clayton Roberts, perhaps the one of the greatest authorities on English impeachments, dealt with this same question in relation to his field of study, he concluded that English impeachments duly served as mechanisms of legal accountability. To support this conclusion, he argued that although the Commons attempted to turn it in a political weapon by impeaching the King's disliked ministers with unsubstantiated accusations, the Lords had always rigorously rejected any such impeachments and thus effectively served the role of "guardians of legality". He also recalled that the Commons were fully aware of the shaky legal grounds upon which they based their accusations, often using impeachment only to harass ministers and having no actual intention of following through with a trial.

While Roberts makes such an argument, however, he also concedes that the unbased accusations often were enough to realize change in the Ministries, as many Monarchs sought a friendly relation with their Parliaments, upon whom they depended for supplies. As such, ministers would often resign or be removed by the King, and through tortuous ways, a political goal would nonetheless be achieved.

Intrinsic vs. Extrinsic Perspectives Arguably, therefore, one could answer the question from two different perspectives, coming to contradicting conclusions. If the frame of reference is that of what can be intrinsically achieved with the English impeachment, then Roberts is right: he who impeaches a minister for political trespasses, expecting that the Lords will concede to their political interests, will invariably be frustrated. If the frame of reference, however, also takes into consideration what can be achieved indirectly, by factors that are extrinsic to the impeachment procedure, then Roberts is wrong: Regardless of the will of the Lords, impeachment did really serve to oust overbearing ministers in the judgment of the Commons, and thus *de facto* served the goal of political accountability.

Holistic Perspective There is also a third perspective that Roberts did not consider, but one could presume to be the case based on his and Colin Tite's detailed accounts on the English impeachments. Under this third perspective, one could conclude that these impeachments were mostly both things at once, both political and legal. One thing that neither author considers in much detail is the selection criteria behind these impeachments, though they often describe a recognizable pattern of targeting public men or private men of stature, who likely defied the parliamentary animus and interests. One could say, therefore, that yes, it served legal accountability, but targeted mostly those who were seen as special threats to certain interests and who had some influence. It was, in fact, a legal instrument that infringed upon the political constitution of the English community, or, in other words, a legal instrument that served as proxy for political demands of the English Parliament. Now, this may have been a coincidence, or perhaps the descriptions given by the authors may not reflect the totality of the animus of the members of Parliament—only a true expert who knows these procedures in detail and knows what cases the Commons chose to not impeach can answer -, but it seems to be the case that the power of impeachment was not used as a general prosecutorial power, seeking to enforce criminal law indiscriminately for the sake of legality. This being the case, one could convincingly argue that such impeachments were predominantly characterized by the simultaneous presence of both spheres of accountability.

Longitudinal Perspective Finally, there is the perspective in which one gets to consider the totality of English history and speculate about what all these impeachments, if taken together, were truly about. Roberts, Tite, Maude Clarke, and many other great legal historians made the case that these impeachments were truly revolutionary for their time. Challenging the King's choices for ministers, meant ultimately challenging his very authority and his legitimation principle, which, as a being so closely associated to God, was not supposed to be fallible. Impeachments nonetheless proved over and over that Kings could in fact do some wrong, slowly but surely eroding their claim to divinity and strengthening the Parliament to set itself as the actual authority in government. By targeting the ministers and making them answer to the law as any other man, the impeachment made the King more accountable and sensible to the political demands of his community. It was an integral part of the English struggle for self-determination and the creation of a national sentiment.

Designer's Perspective. Presidential Impeachment The same sort of considerations can be made in relation to the presidential impeachment originated in the Constitution of the United States, with the addition of yet another perspective. One could ask what purpose impeachment ought to fulfil, though there may be a gap between such an ideal and the reality that ensued. Regarding the English impeachment, this question arguably does not make much sense, because such impeachment was not created with any specific intent in mind, but just happened to be adopted or adapted by the Parliament due to pressures of the circumstances. There was no ideal such impeachment purposefully strived to achieve, though it did organically and half-consciously become a beacon for specific political demands. The presidential impeachment, by contrast, was from its inception a product of conscious and rational debate and was thus introduced in the political system to serve specific purposes or to address specific concerns the Framers of the constitution might have had.

The key concern of the Framers at the time was in creating a state that would be strong and cohesive. That goal, however, had to be achieved in ways that would not reconstitute a monarchy—a regime they had fought so hard to free themselves from. The idea, therefore, was to create an Executive branch that concentrated enough powers to act diligently and energetically, while remaining accountable to and respectful of the People. This accountability was meant both in a legal sense and in a political sense. The President had to be accountable to the law, as no man was to be above it anymore, but also accountable to society, whom he was expected to genuinely serve. This latter portion was one the Framers struggled to implement, often fearing that giving Congress too much discretion to hold the President accountable for injuries against society would hamper his or her independence and encumber its decision-making. They ultimately opted for a wording of impeachable offenses that drew much from the authority and language of criminal law, but ultimately still left ample discretion to the Parliament. The most detailed explanation available on the topic from a Framer was offered by Alexander Hamilton, where he bluntly and literally stated that impeachable offenses were indeed political offenses. Presumably he meant political in the sense of constitutional violations, given that impeachment accusations need to be grounded on past misconduct (*i.e.,* therefore not founded on ideological or factional disagreements).

Intrinsic, Extrinsic, and Holistic Perspectives in Presidential Impeachments The fact that impeachment was to target political offenses did not automatically exclude the goal of legal accountability. Many lawyers argued and continue arguing that both must be simultaneously present—the defence lawyers more specifically really insisted in a criminal nature, often interpreting the language of impeachable offenses literally or presupposing direct and integral transference from the English tradition to the American tradition of impeachments.

If one reads the records of most presidential impeachments in the United States, one will see how legalistically presidential offenses tend to be argued, though the narratives they are embedded in have clear political/constitutional features: Andrew Johnson used the office to effectively nullify Congress by vetoing legislation indiscriminately, and Richard Nixon used state infrastructure and resources to gain undue advantages on his political opponents and evade accountability, as Donald Trump would similarly do in the recent years. The case against Bill Clinton had also clear political attributes, but in a different sense. His case was about the defilement of the presidential office, which is the type of conduct that poses less of a constitutional threat, but that nonetheless instigates moral outrage that can be capitalized by political opponents.

From the intrinsic perspective, one will therefore see Presidents being held accountable for violations of the statutes such as the Act of Tenure, for refusing to comply with orders from Congress, for committing perjury and so on, and may conclude that indeed the presidential impeachment is truly about legal accountability. The Trump impeachments may be a bit different in that they openly mention abuse of power and may indicate a shift towards political impeachments even in the intrinsic perspective. From the holistic perspective, however, the political aspect is undeniable, as indicated by the narratives described in the previous paragraph. The accusation of perjury against Clinton, for example, being a legalistic proxy for the formally unannounced political misconducts, that of defilement of office and damage to the national honour/image.

One could also try to read the situation with the same sort of outcome-oriented approach as Roberts did for England, measuring the gap between the nature of the charges and the nature of the results. As far as I am aware, there is no clear consensus of the legal community regarding the merits of these cases, except for Richard Nixon's, which, however, never got to trial stage. The only way left to do it somewhat objectively, therefore, is the way done by William Perkins, where he compared the vote distribution in impeachment proceedings with the partisan distribution of the Houses of Congress. He concluded for a sharp alignment between both, suggesting that parties vote exclusively in line with their immediate partisan interests and not necessarily the law. It is possible, but arguably unlikely that partisan affiliation may influence one's interpretation of the law, though not to such an extent as indicated in his study. As such, one could also make an argument for impeachments being intrinsically political, in the non-constitutional sense.

Finally, in the extrinsic perspective, there is still much open to debate, which is arguably better left to those who are more knowledgeable in American politics. Only one President was ever truly in risk of an impeachment conviction, while most other attempts were known by the public from the start to be destined to fail. Some Presidents chose to double-down on overbearing conduct after being impeached, putting into question whether impeachment may even have a deterrence value both for political and legal offences. On a surface level, therefore, one could say that the American impeachment has been better at ousting governmental aides than Presidents, given how much more often whistle-blowers and investigators are the ones to face the consequences of (cooperating with) impeachment. The American impeachment seems to be following the footsteps that led its English predecessor into obsolescence, being nullified as an instrument of accountability purely due to the Presidents'/Kings' will to disrupt the flow of information onto their conduct. Apparently, moreover, the United States (but arguably also every other country) has made a tradition of being lenient with Presidents even after leaving office, as rarely one is held accountable for as little as traffic violations, though many of them are known for much more serious conduct.[1] One could make the case for criminal/administrative law being "political", but that is perhaps topic for a different book.

5.4 Latin American Cases and the Role of Impeachment

Longitudinal Perspective The proliferation of impeachments in Latin America has given many Latin Americans mixed feelings regarding what it achieves. To many, as the records of parliamentary debates often reveal, impeachment was the vessel through which the republic was rediscovered and through which a commitment to democracy was for the first time ever genuinely implemented. The birth of impeachment as part of Latin American politics in the 1990s represented the final death of '*El Señor Presidente*', this sort of democratically elected deity that once in power did whatever it felt was the case, likely in complete disregard of the commands of the law, much less of the demands of the People.

To many others, however, impeachment is no more than a new and marginally improved modality of coup, whose value consists merely in being more palatable to the established elites and to external powers. It continued to be a cynical game of power grabbing, less bloody but equally inimical to the true interests of the People or

[1] Ross (1988).

of democracy as a form of government. As proof, it is often pointed out to the many instances in which impeachment has failed, with ideological comparisons made among the Presidents who survive and those who are ousted. It is also pointed out to the times impeachments failed to live up to the judicial ideal they aspire to achieve and try to draw authority from. The examples of Representatives being purposefully obtuse and partisan, as well as showing utter disregard for objectivity and decorum, during such procedures are plentiful.

One thing is certain, however, both sides could agree that there definitively is room for improvement when it comes to presidential impeachments. What both sides may not see, on the other hand, is that the quality of impeachments, as the quality of any other instrument of democracy for that matter, is contingent on the quality of the democracy it is embedded in. An impeachment will produce fair and genuine results inasmuch its actors—most of which tend to be democratically elected—are willing to equally be genuine and fair. There is only so much institutional design can achieve and, at the end of the day, the letter of the law will only command as much authority as such actors are willing to concede. The failure of impeachment, before being a failure of the institution itself, may be symptom of more deeply rooted failures, failures of democracy.

It makes more sense to admit that impeachment is the symptom of problems in democracy, not a cause of problems *per se*. If it takes place, it is because all other democratic alternatives have failed. If impeachment is recurrent, then it is probably a sign that the democratic system is lacking a certain balance or the mechanisms to relieve tensions before they reach a critical stage that necessitates traumatic resolution. Impeachment is the amputation solution for when all other prophylactic care of the *corpus politicum* reaches its limit. Though impeachment is bound to esteemed values such the preservation of democracy and republican principles, its use offers an unpleasant sight, similarly to how amputation is ideally bound to the preservation of life.

Neither the ugly facets of impeachment, nor its idealistic shine should be taken as representative of the whole. It is an ambiguous instrument, with imperfect outcomes. Arguably, however, the presidential impeachment in Latin America achieved more to preserve democracy than to harm it. Most impeachment results were aligned with societal expectations/demands for impeachment, suggesting to some degree that the consensus on presidential involvement in misconduct to have been accurately confirmed by the Assemblies of the respective countries. The times in which impeachment succeeded, there was some palpable risk to democracy or the republic that had been identified by the involved actors, generally in the form of persistent riots, threats of civil war, or rumours of imminent coups, but also in clear signs of co-optation of the state machinery for the furthering corrupt goals. The use of impeachment, therefore, was mostly used to achieve political goals in the constitutional sense, although there were some cases studied in which partisan-political interests clearly aligned with or took precedence over those constitutional concerns.

As means of legal accountability, the Latin American experience is like that of the United States, in that legalism played a limited and strategical rather than substantial role. Many Presidents were accused of basic, clean-cut legal violations, which were served as proxy for deeper issues. Fujimori's case is perhaps the clearest and most radical example, for being impeached for violating laws regulating presidential leave, though a much more disturbing list of offenses awaited to be addressed by the authorities, such as genocide, state terrorism, and racketeering, to name a few. The opposition, moreover, was adamant about its goals with Fujimori's impeachment: block him from the next presidential bid, so that history would not get a chance to repeat itself and Peru would get a real chance at consolidating itself as a democracy. Although any trained lawyer could quickly note that there is some clear 'legal' problem with this impeachment, in that the legal transgression is perhaps too minute to justify ostracizing someone perpetually from politics, it is doubtful anyone (other than Fujimori's cronies) would ever seriously argue such, completely overlooking the political context mentioned.

Intrinsic, Extrinsic, and Holistic Perspectives In any way the question is sliced, when it comes to Latin America, impeachments serve foremostly political goals, with law as valuable rhetorical devices. Observing the procedures from inside, one will see Representatives questioning the President's policies, their impact on the economy, his or her capacity of articulating/establishing a functioning coalition, of addressing popular demands, and so on. Broken laws and constitutional commitments are debated often with similar intensity, but not exactly to legal standards of evidence. Evidence seems to be significant inasmuch it serves to tell a compelling story about how much the President is to be trusted with the powers of office, rather than about stablishing his or her perpetratorship beyond reasonable doubt. Naturally, the same standards also seem to adapt to the interests of whoever is arguing or to the general sense of contextual urgency. Impeachment supporters propose lower legal standards or encompassing interpretations of impeachable offenses, and opposers demand "strict" adhesion to the letter of the law, in its most limiting interpretation. Similarly, if the country is doing well, it is very difficult for Parliament to break its inertia and 'go out of its way' to enforce ideals of presidential accountability. Both strict legalism and a more laidback approach to law can be useful for justifying such inertia, depending on the sort of accusation brought against the President. In countries with multiple impeachments, it is often interesting to observe a same Representative adapt his or her legal interpretation and attitudes towards the law according to the situation at hand.

Such considerations compound with the fact that Latin America tends to be candid about the political side of impeachments, starting from the names for the procedure (*e.g.*, political trial, constitutional accusation) to the selection of charges, which beside the usual legally clear-cut charge, come accompanied by allusions to other unapologetically broad dispositions that necessitate political judgements on the presidential conduct (*e.g.*, offense of poor performance, injury to national honour, indignity for office). All these features arguably inform to some degree the attitudes of the actors involved, making them more accepting of the idea that the political aspects of the impeachment game are legitimate and constitutive parts, despite any judicial and solemn aspirations these procedures entail.

Most presidents in the cases studied have shown to be reactive in the political arena when impeachment accusations against them became more than empty threats. Cabinet reshuffles, PR campaigns, mobilization of the supporter base, distribution of patronage, and even radical, 180-degree-policy-shifts were tactics often adopted by a cornered President looking to survive an impeachment. These tactics did not always work, as the complexity of the situation is not always totally understood or controllable by the involved actors as the procedures develop, but they showed that Presidents truly understood what was at stake in the procedures: the public opinion and the confidence of the Parliament. Extrinsically, therefore, these procedures have unambiguously served political accountability, though less obviously in the higher, constitutional sense.

Given the predominance of elements of political accountability in both intrinsic and extrinsic perspectives, there is little more that can be said about the holistic perspective other than to equally conclude for the predominance of a political nature of accountability. The question then shifts towards speculating around what kind of political nature impeachments have, that it, if they predominantly serve general constitutional purposes or partisan interests. This is a question whose answer certainly will reflect one's personal outlook for the region. Those who have more pessimistic outlooks and are sceptical of the ruling elites will probably come to the more cynical conclusion, while those who are more optimistic will conclude for the less cynical one. The perspective offered by this book is one that acknowledges the many flaws impeachment may have, as well as the times its ideals and purposes were subverted by a few actors, circumstance, or poor design. All-in-all, however, the book was optimistic, recognizing that, when impeachment succeeded, it more frequently was an event that contributed to the deepening of democracy and the upholding of other constitutional commitments than to their demise.

Implications of Impeachment's Absence or Unavailability Corroborating this conclusion, one can point out the cases in which surrogates had to be used to patch up gaps left by unworkable or non-existing impeachment provisions (*e.g.*, Bucaram, Gutierrez, Mahuad, Zelaya, Kuczynski, Vizcarra). The lack of impeachment to solve latent political tensions and crises made these cases more conflictive than they needed to be, putting democracy at risk with great uncertainties, or generating suspicion in society given the questionable constitutionality of these other solutions. While these solutions may have most of the time ultimately halted more democratic backsliding, they show that there is some wisdom underpinning the impeachment's rituals, solemnities, and rationality that make it an integral part of a functioning presidential government. The risks attributed to impeachment's encumbering, overly cautious nature often espoused by the classic literature on the theme seem to be overstated, at least when compared to the quicker alternatives found by politicians in recent history.

5.5 Latin American Constitutions and the Role of Impeachments

Designer's Perspective Though the idea of presidentialism was adopted by every Latin American country studied, their commitment to its cornerstone tenet of separation of powers was implemented to clearly distinguishable degrees, having direct implications on design of impeachment procedures. There were those who sought maximal separation between Executive and Legislative and arguably created a nearly unaccountable presidency, to which no removal mechanism other than term limits was available, except perhaps to the underwhelming alternative of the pretrial (*antejuicio*). Others sought to restrict impeachment only to criminal offenses, or to an even more limited pool of legal or constitutional infractions. Finally, there were those who embraced broader categories of offenses that gave the Parliament ample degree of discretion, though still circumscribed by high thresholds of approval or other procedural limitations.

Also holding a strong correlation with the list of offenses is the choice for the Judiciary or the Parliament as the Court of Impeachment. The choice for one over the other may be telling of this separation, as the former is usually understood as the more impartial and technically oriented (thus less likely to use its powers for partisan goals) of both, though comparatively lacking much in democratic legitimation. It is, therefore, no coincidence that the more legalistic charges tend to be designed for a judgement before the Judiciary, while the more politically charged dispositions are left to the control of the Parliament.

These choices reflect not only the perception of the respective constitutional Framers on the historical moment—constitutions born in authoritarian contexts unsurprisingly seem to be overly trusting of their strongman leaders and to display antipolitical attitudes –, but also tell a story about the prevailing values and ideas of separation of law and politics in the minds of the respective legal community. Strictly from the design perspective, therefore, one could make a case for presidential accountability having legal nature when materialized through strictly defined lists of offenses, with bonus points in case the Supreme or Constitutional Court takes the role of Court of Impeachments; and for a political nature, when broad charges are in play, in the eminently political playing field of the Parliament.

Reception by the Legal Communities Regardless of what these legal texts may seem to be communicating, Latin American jurists have initially pushed back against any form of political control of the presidency. Being mostly traditionally minded about a clear-cut separation between law and politics, jurists were long in denial of rules that seemed to impart too much discretion on the Parliament or that recognized a political nature to the type of accountability sought in impeachments, often conflating the idea of politically motivated decisions with expressions of pure arbitrariness. Impeachments, for being defined in law and having adjudicative qualities to their procedures, were expected to entail strict legal subsumption, produce robust legal standards, and be insulated from legally impertinent influences similarly to how a court of law would. The fact that the trial was against the President did not make the procedure more political—on the contrary, such characteristic confronted the Judges of Impeachment with the fierce demand of submitting themselves to the will of the law, given the deep democratic implications of removing the chief magistrate, which could entail the subversion of the results of popular elections.

In line with these preconceptions and understandings, Latin America produced many curious rationalizations that sought to fit impeachment in the legal system as extensions from civil, criminal, or administrative law. Most common was the criminal interpretation, which focused on the impeachment sanctions as forms of punishment, as well as on the language of offenses and procedural steps, which criminal law inspired terminology. To these purely theoretical and idealistic perspectives, impeachment had to serve legal accountability.

Legal Communities Confront New Realities The literature spawned after the 1990s gradually changed its perspectives, as it finally could observe how the previously posited expectations translated into reality. Generally, jurists have become more accepting of a political nature to presidential accountability achieved in impeachments but continued seeking some degree of reliable anchoring in legality. One way of achieving such anchoring while acknowledging the inevitability of political influences was by distinguishing among phases and among outcomes, creating the possibility of mixed-nature impeachments. One could argue, for example, that the impeachment phase was political, but the trial phase had to be legal: the lower house was to represent public demands as they came, while the higher house had to sift through such demands and only acknowledge those legally compelling, acting as true guardian of legality. Another plausible argument based on mixed nature stated that the decision for acquittal could be politically motivated, but the decision for conviction could only prosper if strictly legally grounded, given the consequences of impeachment and the idea of separation of powers.

The Pervasiveness of the Political This study presented arguments against all these conceptions, acknowledging the political nature of impeachments to be just too pervasive to be expurgated or compartmentalized in any capacity. The whole system of impeachments lacks key characteristics present in the Justice system that grant it with the sort of legal certainty and intelligibility that jurists expect from judicial decisions. Among the many differences, some of the most relevant are that Judges of Impeachment are not conditioned to decide in certain ways by a system designed to wash out extravagant decisions, and that they are not lawyers for the most part and are thus lacking the *habitus* and *ethos* that unify and define the rationality of the legal community. Moreover, paraphrasing Charles Sumner yet again, one cannot expect that a decision about the most prominent political actor, for alleged political misconducts, trialled in a political forum, with deep political consequences be anything else than a decision predominantly determined by political considerations.

5.6 Closing Remarks

The Possibility of Arbitrariness Behind every genuine worry about the political use of law there is some suspicion about arbitrariness and the co-optation of law's authority for tyrannical or corrupt purposes. Such concern denotes a strive towards objectivity and fairness that is commendable and necessary, but that is at the same time elusive. Simplistic or reductionistic outlooks run the risk of overlooking actual tyranny or misclassifying legitimate democratic decisions as tyrannical, neither of which is a desirable outcome. A fair and democratic society should not tolerate or legitimize tyrannical acts, nor suppress democratic ones.

Separating wheat from chaff is a difficult task, however, especially in the context of impeachments, which are likely to be highly complex, ambiguous, and imperfect endeavours. Just and unjust, if not already easy to mix up by virtue of such characteristics, may be further distorted by one's own passions and prejudices. It is important, therefore, to be very cautious in the analysis of impeachments to avoid misjudgement.

Such cautiousness is built through the achievement of a comprehensive and balanced understanding of the facts and context at hand. This entails stablishing a clear picture of the popular sentiments regarding the national government, the main competing narratives, the main characteristics of the political system, and having a detailed overview of the course and main topics of the impeachment proceeding (see next section for concrete suggestions). Only then one can start discerning what is/has been effectively relevant for an impeachment. Starting the search for such answers from a 'hunch', without any rational method or aspiration to capturing the big picture, has the tendency of producing analyses that hyperfocus on secondary issues and consequently measure the merits of impeachment to inadequate standards and with inadequate tools.

In doing so, one must also have sensibilities towards what the political activity entails. Political decisions should not be conflated with arbitrariness, nor be presumed to lack in justice, though these things may happen. These decisions are often informed by different principles of justice intertwined with principles of government, which may be disagreeable from one's own perspective, but may nonetheless be representative of the understandings of significant sectors of society, if not the general will. In the words of Otto Kirchheimer, "[Political justice] is necessary and beneficial because without the intercession of the legal instrument the fight for power would continue to be unrelenting, but much more disorderly".[2]

Political competition will always exist in society and, therefore, means and rules for releasing unresolved tensions and frustrations must exist to accommodate such competition in orderly and rational fashion. Impeachment may be unwieldly and uncomfortable, but it is still preferable to resolutions achieved in violence and/or normlessness. Democracy, as Samuel Huntington reminds us, "*does not mean that*

[2] Author's translation of Kirchheimer (1981), pp. 472–473.

problems will be solved; it does mean that rulers can be removed (. . .). Democracies become consolidated when people learn that democracy is a solution to the problem of tyranny, but not necessarily to anything else."[3]

Windows of Opportunity Even if despite all cautiousness and sensibility an impeachment turns out to be a failure in a particular case, something good may still come out of it. The perception of failure is likely a manifestation of the underlying democratic deficits in the decision of impeachment itself. The unrepresentativeness of the general will of a decision is likely to be deeply rooted in the party, electoral, and congressional systems, or perhaps of a point of vulnerability of the procedure of impeachment itself, some of which were discussed in this book (*e.g.*, overbearing influence of key stakeholders or commissions to disrupt the flow of information, reduce transparency, curtail defence or discussion, silence opposition, etc.). What an impeachment can achieve can only go so far as what democracy enables it to achieve. The failure of the former should not be presented as an indictment of the procedure itself, but of the many surviving vicissitudes of the political system. The symptoms should not be confused with the causes, and impeachments, when truly understood, offer valuable insights into how to treat the latter.

5.7 *Excursus:* A Framework of Analysis

A lot goes into the making of an impeachment. Upon trying to understand the kind of political crisis that situate such procedures, it is easy to end up dealing with years and perhaps even generations of power disputes that eventually escalate to the point of an attempt at removing the President. It is, therefore, often difficult to see a clear narrative regarding the events leading to an impeachment due to the amount of noise they tend to be tangled up with. Some policy disagreements may be misidentified, some may over-blown, others may go under the radar completely. Same goes for the assessment of popular demands, partisan relations, economic frustrations, and so on. To avoid being overwhelmed by information and thus also avoid the temptation of defaulting to the most comforting explanation,[4] one should try to stablish objective baseline of contextual information about the case.

[3] Huntington (1993), pp. 262–263.

[4] Perhaps due to status quo bias and the pressure to conform to in media/peer group established narratives, it is not uncommon to find studies on impeachments that (half-)consciously endorse hypotheses in which (1.) part of the facts is erased or dismissed without justification, (2.) offer an interpretation that ought to be taken as true regardless of evidence that suggest competing explanations, or (3.) offer rationalizations that cannot be universalized for other cases.

The strategy used by this study to create such baseline was, at first, to survey every aspect typically associated with presidential or executive instability.[5] This includes both those aspects that are related only to the specific administration at hand (see below, item A), as well as those that are more structural in nature and may thus influence any past or future administration alike (item C). Further, it is then necessary to produce an analysis of the procedures themselves (item B), with an eye for the pesky details generally overlooked or undervalued in mainstream reporting of the facts. Such work entails establishing a clear timeline of the procedures and following the debates in each step with attention to context. Debates often present opportunities to verify mainstream narratives, if they do not offer entirely new ones, which may be worth investigating. In more concrete terms, the framework of analysis used in the case studies looked the following way:

Suggested Framework of Analysis for Presidential Impeachments

(A) Extra-procedural elements

a. Democratic demand

i. Low approval/high rejection rate of the administration
ii. High support for impeachment
iii. Frequent or/and massive protests
iv. Generalized mediatic criticism of the presidency

b. Circumstantial urgency

i. Negative economic indicators (*e.g.*, high inflation, unemployment, steep increase in debt-to-GDP ratio, low or negative GDP growth,[6] recurrent budget deficits, depletion of foreign reserves, decrease in per capita income, decrease in social spending, increase of households in extreme poverty, increase of workforce in informal economy etc.)
ii. Gross signs of mismanagement
iii. Incapability of redressing pressing issues
iv. Loss of trust in democratic institutions

[5] The literature on this topic is vast, and much of it was considered to some degree. The main influences have been, however, Baumgartner and Kada (2003), pp. 7–19, Mainwaring (2018), pp. 17–101, and Pérez-Liñán (2007), pp. 176–202. The framework suggested in this section is an aggregate of elements identified in these (or other therein cited) studies, as well as elements identified throughout the cases studies in Chap. 3.

[6] GDP by itself can be an unreliable indicator, as at times its sways may over- or understate the social frictions and benefits caused by its variation. As the anthropologist Jason Hickel explains: "If you enclose a forest and sell it for timber, GDP goes up. If you burn subsistence farms and turn the land into cotton plantations, GDP goes up. But this accounting tells us nothing of what local communities lose in terms of their use of that forest or their access to food. The cost to their livelihoods and wellbeing is swept under the statistical rug." New Internationalist, August 7th, 2019: "*Progress and its discontents*".

   v. Administration associated with recurrent scandals uncovered by the media or investigative organs

c. Political vulnerability

   i. Unstable coalition/over-reliance on *ad hoc* alliances
   ii. Outburst of factionalism within President's party (special relevance in lowly fragmented party systems)
   iii. Inefficacy of parliamentary management techniques (*e.g.*, cabinet reshuffles, pork-barrel, etc.)
   iv. Loss of control over veto thresholds
   v. Lack of allegiance or increasing antagonism from political power brokers (*e.g.*, vice-president, presidents of lower and higher houses)
   vi. Gridlock or lasting governability struggle (hostile Congress)
   vii. President resorts to rule-by-decree

(B) Procedural elements

a. Procedural soundness

   i. Rules deliberated and stablished beforehand
   ii. Sufficient time, space and conditions provided for defence in all relevant steps of the procedure
   iii. Observation of defence/accusation rights within the limits of what is possible in a procedure of this nature
   iv. The procedures are sufficiently insulated from external forces (*e.g.*, military, lobbyists, organized crime, international powers)

b. Substantive plausibility

   i. Charges tightly fit description of impeachable offenses
   ii. Presidential acts are meaningfully connected with impeachment charges
   iii. (Ideally) Each charge is enough to justify removal from office
   iv. Posterior modifications in the scope of accusation do not disfigure the original charges
   v. Conclusion follows from produced evidence and legal arguments
   vi. Legal arguments recognized by substantial part of the legal community

c. Institutional legitimacy

   i. The organ that decides is competent to do so
   ii. The organ that decides has comparable legitimacy to the President
   iii. The organ provides a court-like environment where debate is feasible and respectable
   iv. Debate is transparent and mediated by a capable and respectable authority
   v. Voting according to one's conscience is viable and likely

(C) Constitutional context/structure

a. Party system

  i. Institutionalization (*e.g.*, rootedness, discipline, volatility)
  ii. Fragmentation
  iii. Trust (*e.g.*, trends in consolidation/erosion)
  iv. Presidential party/coalition profile (*e.g.*, rootedness, behaviour, ideological alignment, rhetoric)

b. Electoral system

  i. Competition profile (*e.g.*, centripetal vs. centrifugal, fair vs. uncompromising, artificial vs. genuine)
  ii. Financing (*e.g.*, private vs. public, high vs. low cost)
  iii. Turnout
  iv. Fairness
  v. Presidential profile (*e.g.*, votes, supporter base, promises, legitimation)

c. Congressional system

  i. Balance of power (*e.g.*, Executive vs. Legislative dominance, distribution of leverages, opportunities for cooperation)
  ii. Behaviour profile (*e.g.*, confrontative vs. cooperative, ad hoc vs. long-term, principled vs. pragmatic)
  iii. Presidential profile (*e.g.*, share of seats, alignment with stakeholders)

d. Democracy

  i. Institutionalization (*e.g.*, rootedness, trust)
  ii. Transition (*e.g.*, complete vs. incomplete, factual vs. de jure, authoritarian entrenchment, top-down vs. bottom-up concession, unresolved conflicts)
  iii. Attitudes towards democracy

This framework, moreover, can be a useful resource in assessing the legitimacy of an impeachment, as items A and B may reveal with some clarity where the procedures may have failed. Item A will perhaps indicate where Congress' decision is representative of a popular demand or is motivated by actual political urgency, while item B will assure the procedure was conducted fairly within what is feasible in impeachments. For details on the justification of this framework, see Sect. 2.3.4.2.

References

Baumgartner JC, Kada N (eds) (2003) Checking executive power: presidential impeachment in comparative perspective. Praeger, Westport

Huntington SP (1993) The third wave: democratization in the late twentieth century. University of Oklahoma Press, Norman

Kirchheimer O (1981) Politische Justiz: Verwendung juristischer Verfahrensmöglichkeiten zu politischen Zwecken. Europäische Verlagsanstalt, Frankfurt am Main

Mainwaring S (ed) (2018) Party systems in Latin America: institutionalization, decay, and collapse. Cambridge University Press, Cambridge

Pérez-Liñán A (2007) Presidential impeachment and the new political instability in Latin America. Cambridge University Press, Leiden

Ross S (1988) Fall from grace: sex, scandal and corruption in American politics from 1702 to the present. Ballantine Books, New York

MIX
Papier aus verantwortungsvollen Quellen
Paper from responsible sources
FSC® C105338

If you have any concerns about our products,
you can contact us on
ProductSafety@springernature.com

In case Publisher is established outside the EU,
the EU authorized representative is:
Springer Nature Customer Service Center GmbH
Europaplatz 3, 69115 Heidelberg, Germany

Printed by Libri Plureos GmbH
in Hamburg, Germany